KERUX COMMENTARIES

ZEPHANIAH—MALACHI

ZEPHANIAH–MALACHI

A Commentary for Biblical Preaching and Teaching

GARY V. SMITH
TIMOTHY D. SPRANKLE

Herbert W. Bateman IV

EDITOR

KREGEL
MINISTRY

Zephaniah–Malachi: A Commentary for Biblical Preaching and Teaching

© 2020 by Gary V. Smith and Timothy D. Sprankle

Published by Kregel Ministry, an imprint of Kregel Publications, 2450 Oak Industrial Dr. NE, Grand Rapids, MI 49505-6020.

Unless otherwise indicated, the translation of the Scripture portions used throughout the commentary is the authors' own English rendering of the original biblical languages.

All Scripture quotations, unless otherwise indicated, are from the New American Standard Bible® (NASB), Copyright © 1960, 1962, 1963, 1968, 1971, 1972, 1973, 1975, 1977, 1995 by The Lockman Foundation. Used by permission. www.Lockman.org

Italics in Scripture quotations indicate emphasis added by the authors.

The Hebrew font, NewJerusalemU, and the Greek font, GraecaU, are available from www.linguistsoftware.com/lgku.htm, +1-425-775-1130.

All photos are under Creative Commons licensing, and contributors are indicated in the captions of the photos.

Herbert W. Bateman IV, creator of the chart "General Chronology of the Prophets" that first appeared in *Isaiah: How to Read, Interpret and Understand the Prophet* (Leesburg, IN: Cyber-Center for Biblical Studies, 2016), grants Kregel Publications permission to use its adapted form in the Kerux volume *Zephaniah, Haggai, Zechariah, Malachi* by Gary V. Smith and Timothy D. Sprankle.

Herbert W. Bateman IV, author of the "History" section adapted from *History of the Second Temple Period: An Examination of Judaism During the Second Temple Period*, rev. ed. (Winona Lake, IN: n.p., 2004), 24–34, grants Kregel Publications permission to use its adapted form in Kerux volume *Zephaniah, Haggai, Zechariah, Malachi* by Gary V. Smith and Timothy D. Sprankle.

Photos on pages 36, 45, 47, 78, 79, 109, 116, 126, 150, 191, 248, 310, and 356 are under Creative Commons licensing and contributors are indicated in the captions of the photos.

Illustration on page 162 is under Creative Commons licensing and contributed by Internet Archive Book Images / Flickr (public domain).

Illustration on page 167 is by Hannah Vander Lugt. Used by permission.

Map on page 39 is under Creative Commons licensing and contributed by Nigyou (public domain).

Maps on pages 60, 77, 125, 205, and 286 are from the Kregel Bible Atlas by Tim Dowley, copyright © 2003 Angus Hudson Ltd./Tim Dowley & Peter Wyatt trading as Three's Company. Used by permission.

ISBN 978-0-8254-2573-8

Printed in the United States of America
20 21 22 23 24 / 5 4 3 2 1

Contents

MALACHI

EDITOR'S PREFACE TO THE SERIES

The Kerux Commentary series, unlike other commentaries written for preachers, joins experts in biblical exegesis with experienced communicators of biblical truth. Together they bring a heightened refinement in the handling of the Bible. Every volume emphasizes text-based truths that bridge from the context of the original hearers and readers to the twenty-first-century world. The name, *kerux* (KAY-rüxs) captures the aim of the series. Just as a *kerux* was one who proclaimed the official announcement of the king, so the forty-five volumes in this series will enable the preacher or teacher to accurately and authoritatively communicate the message of our divine King.

Every volume presents preaching units that offer *exegetical*, *theological*, and *homiletical* material to guide preachers and teachers to accurately interpret the Bible and ultimately engage today's world.

EXEGETICAL ANALYSIS	➡	THEOLOGICAL FOCUS	➡	PREACHING/ TEACHING STRATEGY

Solid *exegetical analysis* of the biblical text reveals the literary-theological movement of every biblical passage. The exegetical authors (trained experts in interpretation) engage the biblical text by interacting with original languages that shed light on interpretation (e.g., syntax, grammar, structure), hermeneutical issues relevant to a given passage (e.g., genre analysis), and pertinent secondary literature. From the exegetical analysis is derived a theological focus. The gnomic truths of a passage—those truths that transcend time and culture—emphasize the *theological focus* of each preaching unit. Following the careful exegetical analysis and insightful theological synthesis, homiletical authors (trained experts in preaching) offer suggestions for communicating the text. Based on the popular "big idea" preaching model, every preaching unit offers *preaching strategies*, contemporary connections, suggestions for creative presentation, illustrations, and more. These tools help the preacher and teacher effectively proclaim Scripture.

Kerux commentaries are written for trained pastors and teachers who speak regularly, who have some knowledge of Greek and Hebrew, and who spend a significant time preparing to preach and teach God's Word. As a result, each volume offers:

- a detailed introduction and outline.
- a summary of all preaching sections with their primary exegetical, theological, and preaching ideas.
- preaching pointers that join the original historical context with the contemporary one.
- insights from the Hebrew and Greek text.
- a thorough exposition of the text.
- sidebars of pertinent information and historical background.
- appropriate charts and photographs.
- a theological focus to passages.

- a contemporary big idea for every preaching unit.
- present-day meaning, validity, and application of a main idea.
- creative presentations for each primary idea.
- key questions about the text for study groups.
- lists of books and articles for further reading.

Many thanks to Jim Weaver, Kregel's former acquisition editor, who conceived of this commentary series and further developed it with the team of Jeffrey D. Arthurs, Robert B. Chisholm, David M. Howard Jr., Darrell L. Bock, Roy E. Ciampa, and Michael J. Wilkins. Much appreciation is extended to Dennis and Paul Hillman, whose thirteen-year tenacious commitment to the series contributed to Kerux becoming a reality. Finally, gratitude is extended to the two authors for each Kerux volume; the outside reviewers, editors, and proofreaders; and Kregel staff who suggested numerous improvements.

—Herbert W. Bateman IV

EXEGETICAL AUTHOR'S PREFACE

This book is dedicated to Janson Chan,
the director of Timothy Training International,
a missions organization dedicate to the education of Chinese pastors.
He provided me the opportunity to share with them the message of the Minor Prophets.

Understanding what God said through his prophets hundreds of years ago, in a culture very different from ours, requires the Spirit's guidance, careful attention to the meaning of words, the analysis of difficult sentences, knowledge of ancient Near Eastern history and literature, and a great deal of patience. Thankfully, God has directed many earlier authors to ponder over these prophetic messages, which makes it possible for us today to weigh alternative interpretations and at times humbly suggest new ways of interpreting what the prophets said. But the goal of this commentary is not just for the reader to gain knowledge about what a prophet said; it is to guide all those who read and study God's words (and especially the pastor who preaches it) to understand the heart of the theological message that can shape the preaching of the truth in a way that will be persuasive, biblically based, and relevant to the people we interact with today.

In order for this to happen, God had to guide the leaders and publishing staff at Kregel to design the format in such a unique way that the reader will approach each passage with certain questions that will naturally produce insights that might otherwise be missed. So I am thankful for those who designed the format of this commentary, and for our editors (particularly Dr. Herb Bateman) who repeatedly pushed us to stick with the format, who corrected our grammar, and who challenged us to rethink or defend an interpretation.

Of course, in a joint effort where two writers (Pastor Tim Sprankle and myself) are working together, it is essential for each of us to do our part to assist the other author in his task. So I am thankful for Pastor Tim's ability to think and apply the ancient truth in new ways that are faithful to the principles the prophets were communicating. Each person reading Tim's material would be wise to learn from his suggestions, to dare to illustrate a point in unusual ways, to address issues in a way that speaks to the people of the next generation who will soon be leading the church.

Through faith we believe that God is able to do abundantly more than we can ask or think (Eph. 3:17–20), if our ministries are rooted and grounded in love and if we are faithful in sharing the truth in ways that people understand.

—Gary V. Smith

PREACHING AUTHOR'S PREFACE

This book is dedicated to my wife and kids,
who endured many hours of my disappearing into my basement study
to wrestle with words, both mine and the prophets'—and to
D. Brent Sandy, who first tuned my ear to hear the prophets preach.

The last time I spoke at a nursing home chapel service, I opened my copy of the Bible to the book of Haggai. Looking out over a group of senior saints, I told them I simply wanted to read them some encouraging words. In their lifetime, they had heard more than enough sermons, homilies, and devotional talks. And I, a thirtysomething pastor, assumed I had little wisdom to offer them. Instead, I opted for some encouraging words from God's Word. They consented.

Then I gripped the edges of the pulpit, leaned into the microphone, and began to recite Haggai. The ancient words (ever true) resounded. The ancient words (ever true) related. The ancient words encouraged me and my present company.

The words of the minor prophets were meant to encourage, correct, inform, and inspire. They spoke of past failures, present challenges, and future realities. Most importantly, they spoke of God and for God. And God still speaks through them today.

Writing a commentary for the Minor Prophets is no small task. Neither is preaching the Minor Prophets. We read and study, draft and edit notes, deliver and apply a sermon, and then move on to the next section. Somewhere along the way we can get lost in the technicality of it all. Fortunately, prophets demand to be heard.

Zephaniah, Haggai, Zechariah, and Malachi shout. They shout *of* God—his goodness and power, mercy and judgment, and demand for purity and faithfulness to his promises—and they shout *for* God. They've been shouting to me as I've written. I pray they shout to you as you read.

—Timothy D. Sprankle

OVERVIEW OF ALL PREACHING PASSAGES

Zephaniah 1:1–2:3

EXEGETICAL IDEA
Zephaniah supported Josiah's reform movement by warning that God would thoroughly judge all forms of false worship in Jerusalem on the approaching day of the Lord (1:1–15), so the only hope was for people to turn away from their sinful ways, humble themselves, and intercede for God's mercy before the beginning of the day of the Lord (2:1–3).

THEOLOGICAL FOCUS
Since one cannot hide from God's judgment, the prophet tries to motivate people to humble themselves and seek God before he executes his wrath on them.

PREACHING IDEA
Quit playing hide-and-seek with God.

PREACHING POINTS
Zephaniah did not bear good news for the people of Judah. Although his audience had several reasons for happy feelings—Assyria's decline, Israel's independence, and Josiah's initial reforms—their circumstances had not sparked widespread revival. God's covenant people continued to act, dress, and praise like their pagan neighbors. Using stark images of God's coming, doing battle, and bringing destruction, Zephaniah shattered their status quo. He sounded the trumpet of judgment, mercifully offering his people a final call to come clean and seek God.

Today, God's people could benefit from a similar wake-up call. The spiritual climate in the West is lukewarm, as believers have pressed the snooze button on alarming spiritual realities: the decline of biblical literacy, rise of sexual impurity, and pursuit of selfish gain. Furthermore, faith no longer claims a place of privilege or influence in society. Religious leaders are responsible for spiritual drift. Everyday believers are complicit. In an age of indifference and idolatry, the prophetic voice of the past offers an antidote. This passage serves as a plea to quit playing hide-and-seek with God.

Zephaniah 2:4–3:8

EXEGETICAL IDEA
The Lord would judge the nations for their pride (2:4–10) and people in Jerusalem for not trusting God or accepting correction (3:1–8), but he would bless a remnant of Judah (2:7a, 9b) and many from the nations who honor God (2:11).

THEOLOGICAL FOCUS

God will punish those who refuse to accept correction, as well as those who have oppressed God's people, so that people will repent and worship God.

PREACHING IDEA

When people all around you fall, check your path for pitfalls.

PREACHING POINTS

Zephaniah circled the compass to point out neighbors on every side of Judah who would face God's judgment. If the original audience in Jerusalem heard these oracles in a spirit of self-righteousness or indifference, the prophet disturbed their peace by pointing the finger at guilty Jerusalem. She was not immune to God's discipline; her record of wrongs had not gone unnoticed. The message was a warning to God's people to check their path for pitfalls after watching their neighbors stumble.

God's people today continue to wrestle with a sense of immunity to his discipline. Diagnosing God's judgment is slippery business, but it does not take a sage to see that others fall. All around us people's lives come crashing down: their marriages crumble, their businesses tank, their nations implode with civil war, their social circles shrink to a point, or their bodies bend to the will of cancer. Some falls may be bad luck or happenstance in a fallen world. But many falls are propelled by foolish choices and arrogance. This section urges us to check our path for pitfalls when people all around us fall.

Zephaniah 3:9–20

EXEGETICAL IDEA

People from around the world who have pure hearts and lips would enter the joy of living with God their King without fear of any enemies.

THEOLOGICAL FOCUS

People who seek God will be transformed and dwell in God's presence.

PREACHING IDEA

Look forward to a fearless and festive future with God.

PREACHING POINTS

Zephaniah turned a corner in the final section to address another motivation for seeking God. The prophet shifted from words of woe to images of hope, replete with singing, dancing, and international peace. At the center of the festivities stood Israel's God and King, Yahweh. For the original audience, such promises of fearless and festive living would have revived their hope. However, the question remained as to whether this hope would renew their character.

Today, God's people could use a fresh word of hope. Constant news cycles broadcast local and global suffering. Social media posts have perfected the art of cynicism and shame. Even the typical list of prayer requests is filled with illnesses, financial woes, and family problems. In other words, life has a way of causing stress and choking out joy. A look beyond this life—not as a mere escape to a place in the clouds but finding our home as renewed people with God—lifts us up and gives everyone great hope. This closing passage teaches us to look beyond our present sufferings and anticipate a fearless and festive future with God.

Haggai 1:1–15

EXEGETICAL IDEA
Haggai confronted the excuses people used to explain why they were delaying work on the temple and challenged them to glorify God by changing their priorities and building the temple.

THEOLOGICAL FOCUS
God is pleased with people who set aside their excuses for delaying his work and give priority to honoring him by immediately doing what he expects them to do.

PREACHING IDEA
Put an immediate end to "eventual" obedience.

PREACHING POINTS
Haggai shared a timely message with God's people. Eighteen years after a remnant had returned to Jerusalem to rebuild the temple, the project remained incomplete. The inhabitants made excuses, sought to further their own comfort, and ignored signs of God's displeasure. The prophet assumed that Persian politics had fed Israel's procrastination. Haggai implored his original audience—Zerubbabel the governor, Joshua the high priest, and the Jerusalem populace—to gather wood and resume working. They responded immediately and ended their delayed obedience.

In today's age of instant gratification, high-speed information, and one-click activation, God's people have developed an ironic habit of putting off spiritual commitments. We hedge, weigh options, and wait for better opportunities. We make excuses and procrastinate, rather than make his will our priority. Why pray now, when I can pray later? Why share my faith now, when another opportunity will arise? Why give a portion of this paycheck to global missions, when I can make up for it next month? This passage redresses our tendency to put other priorities before God, exhorting us to put an immediate end to "eventual" obedience.

Haggai 2:1–9

EXEGETICAL IDEA
Although many were discouraged because this temple did not match the splendor of Solomon's temple of bygone years, they should persevere because God promised that his Spirit would be with them. He would supply all their material needs to build the temple, and this temple would have more glory than Solomon's temple.

THEOLOGICAL FOCUS

God's people are to persevere in carrying out God's expectations, to move beyond the past ways of doing things, and to trust in God's ability to supply all their needs.

PREACHING IDEA

Beat the "good old days" blues by trusting God today.

PREACHING POINTERS

One month after the temple building project resumed, Haggai relayed his second message. Despite their recent activity, spirits remained low among Israel's leaders and the general populace. Not even a week's worth of celebrating the Feast of Tabernacles sustained optimism among them. Instead, nostalgia for Solomon's more glorious temple reigned in the minds of many. But God would not have his people sulk. He rallied them with imperatives: "fear not" and "look forward." Haggai's promise of God's presence, provision, and peace were meant to instill trust in his people for better days to come.

Getting stuck in nostalgia is an old problem. As forward-thinking and progress-oriented as the Western world seems to be, we continue to hear voices in the church pine for the "good old days." We lament the technological invasion, sexual perversion, moral corruption, political division, social tolerance, and secular convictions ruling our day. We recall better times when public schools mandated student prayer, marriages lasted a lifetime, and mothers stayed home to keep house. We think a return to "former glory" would revive national trust in God. Sadly, not only does nostalgia gloss over past sins, it also fosters a sense of defeat. But we must not be discouraged; God is not stuck in the past. This passage compels us to beat the "good old days" blues by trusting him today.

Haggai 2:10–19

EXEGETICAL IDEA

Applying the Levitical principle that God-honoring living could not be gained by touching something holy like the temple caused many people to realize they were already defiled and needed to repent, so that when they did God could bless them as he promised.

THEOLOGICAL FOCUS

God-honoring holy living is not achieved through works, service, or sacrifices but through the removal of defilement inside so that God can provide his blessings.

PREACHING IDEA

A clean start with God starts within.

PREACHING POINTERS

Three months into the temple renovation project, Haggai brought the people a bad diagnosis. They were unclean. Their defilement was like a transferrable disease. Their material blessings were lacking. The original audience would have recognized Haggai's appeal to the covenant curses. Fortunately, their revived effort to rebuild the temple showed God their desire for a clean start and future blessings.

The need for a clean start with God continues today. Fortunately, he welcomes a change of heart and grants fresh starts. Like a passionate father, he watches for prodigal sons and daughters in the distance and races to embrace them upon their return. Sadly, we wait too long to recognize our compromised motives and calloused consciences. We excuse our inner corruption as a personality quirk, pathology, or work in progress. Conversely, we deem ourselves holy, in varying degrees, due to religious activity, church attendance, and proximity to "spiritual giants." Outside-in holiness breeds legalism, activism, and nagging guilt. This passage exposes our need for a clean start with God starts within.

Haggai 2:20–23

EXEGETICAL IDEA
Since God controlled the political rise and fall of every nation, Zerubbabel should lead Israel with confidence, knowing that he was God's chosen servant, empowered by God to lead the nation.

THEOLOGICAL FOCUS
God's leaders are to find their confidence in God's plans for the future and in God's ability to carry out these plans through them.

PREACHING IDEA
Circumstances don't shake those with deep trust in God.

PREACHING POINTERS
Haggai's final message had an immediate audience of one: Zerubbabel. The first three oracles addressed governor Zerubbabel, high priest Joshua, and the remnant in Jerusalem. In the last speech, the prophet singled out Zerubbabel. God identified his need for a climatic word of assurance. Despite undesirable appearances—lack of material blessings, a sluggish rebuilding project, and Persian rule—God remained in control. Moreover, he had chosen Zerubbabel to lead his people forward. Haggai's message pointed to Zerubbabel as God's chosen servant, signet ring, Davidic successor, and unshakeable leader for the days ahead.

God continues to advance his kingdom efforts today through leaders with deep conviction. He provides gifted men and women to lead faith-based organizations, churches, businesses, nongovernmental organizations, sports teams, and healthy homes. Their unshakeable trust, remarkable courage, and consistent virtue shines in a world opposed to God. Not only has the religious climate in the West turned cold toward biblical values, it has become hostile. Coaches and teachers are fired for sharing their faith. Christian business owners are picketed for making their convictions public. Pastors are dismissed for their "outdated and intolerant" views. Amidst the torrents of cultural change and faith decline, God's firm control of the world buoys these leaders. This passage reminds us that circumstances don't shake those with deep trust in God.

Zechariah 1:1–6

EXEGETICAL IDEA
God was angry with former generations because they did not repent, so he judged them; but if the present generation would learn from these mistakes and turn to God, he would turn to them.

THEOLOGICAL FOCUS
Sinful people who repent can restore their relationship with God.

PREACHING IDEA
Redirect your heart toward God to receive his heartfelt welcome.

PREACHING POINTERS
Zechariah's opening words were a summons. He beckoned his people to redirect their hearts to God. For nearly two decades, the original audience had dwelled within the borders of Judea after returning from Babylon. However, they had stopped work on the temple rebuilding project. The prophet Haggai's gave them an initial burst of motivation, but construction stopped soon after it started because God's people let sin, doubt, and despair come between them and God. Political and religious leaders failed to stir revival. To inspire genuine repentance, Zechariah promised a warm reception from God.

Today's church would benefit from an invitation for its people to redirect their hearts toward God. Externally, God's people may appear close to him: always smiling, morally upstanding, and active in their churches. But externals do not tell the whole story. Church gatherings may play host to hollow religious performance. Strong doctrinal positions may disguise ongoing moral compromises. Sin, doubt, and despair affect today's church as much as they hurt ancient Israel. This passage urges us to redirect our hearts toward God to receive his heartfelt welcome.

Zechariah 1:7–17

EXEGETICAL IDEA
God knew what was happening in every nation, so he announced his anger with some nations, his compassion toward his own people, the building of the temple, and the filling of Jerusalem with joyful people.

THEOLOGICAL FOCUS
God's anger with sinful people does not overshadow his compassion for those who follow him.

PREACHING IDEA
God's not blind to our trials but brings healing on his timeline.

PREACHING POINTERS
Three months after sharing his first message, Zechariah recorded his first of eight visions. He saw a patrolling horseman and angelic messengers. To the original audience, the imagery

would have brought assurance of God's watchfulness and power. While the specific details of the vision—different colored horses, myrtle trees, ravines, and various speakers—remain in question, the overall message is clear: God's plan to intervene on behalf of his people was a foregone conclusion. He would manifest his sovereign control in compassion for Jerusalem and rage against the nations.

The view of God in today's church must be challenged. For many believers, God appears as a distant despot or indifferent deity. God does not oversee our lives, answer our prayers, or heal our wounds. And on rare occasions of divine intervention, God's timing does not align with our wishes. We easily dismiss such a distant and indifferent God. Of course, God remains emotionally engaged with his people, working a plan for restoration in his timing. He maintains absolute control, shows tender compassion, and expresses justified fury. This passage rebuffs modern misunderstandings of God, offering assurance that he's not blind to our trials but brings healing in his timeline.

Zechariah 1:18–2:13

EXEGETICAL IDEA
God's zeal for Jerusalem would result in stronger nations defeating the nations that scattered his people, but God's presence in Zion signaled the restoration of his people, and this would draw many Gentiles to worship him.

THEOLOGICAL FOCUS
God will judge the sinful people of this world and protect those who follow and worship him.

PREACHING IDEA
Old losses are fertile ground for new beginnings.

PREACHING POINTERS
God showed Zechariah two more visions meant to instill his hearers with hope. First, God would bring judgment (i.e., "four artisans/craftsmen") on the nations (i.e., "four horns") that scattered God's people from their land. Then he would set in motions a plan to expand Jerusalem and dwell within the city. This news would result in joyful songs and awed silence. While the visions lack specific names and set timelines, the imagery would have uplifted the original audience. God's loving affection and good intentions for his people overshadowed their painful losses in exile.

God's people suffer many losses today. In many countries around the world, following God leads to the loss of political freedom, job security, personal comfort, and one's own life. In the West, evangelicals are losing their majority voice in the public realm while the religiously nonaffiliated (e.g., Nones) and antagonistic (e.g., New Atheists) camps continue making gains. Political battles favoring secular values (e.g., same-sex marriage, transgender bathrooms, recreational drug use) over biblical values make God's people feel like they have lost their influence on the nation's conscience. Fortunately, losses in popularity, political persuasion, and personal comfort do not spell the end of Christian faith in the

West or anywhere else. In fact, these losses often catalyze greater efforts to trust God and live according to his purposes. This passage challenges us to rethink old losses as fertile ground for God's new beginnings.

Zechariah 3:1–4:14

EXEGETICAL IDEA
After God's Adversary accused God's religious servant the high priest Joshua of sinfulness, God cleansed Joshua and restored him to serve in the temple; then God encouraged the political leader Zerubbabel with the promise that God's Spirit would enable them to complete the restoration of the temple.

THEOLOGICAL FOCUS
God's servant leaders should not be discouraged because of difficult circumstances, for God forgives sins and will empower them to do the work he has called them to do.

PREACHING IDEA
God can powerfully use imperfect leaders.

PREACHING POINTERS
The fourth and fifth visions narrow from a national to personal focus. Zechariah received heavenly insight concerning Jerusalem's earthly leaders: Joshua the high priest and Zerubbabel the governor. The original audience likely had a low view of its leaders. Persian rule, lackluster harvests, regional tensions, and a stuttering temple project had done little to impress anyone. But God assured Zechariah that these two leaders had his vote of confidence; they were called, cleansed, and empowered to undertake their tasks.

Leaders in today's church and parachurch organizations face tremendous pressure. Leadership books create an expectation for them to master time management, vision casting, self-analysis, motivation, delegation, innovation, and countless other abilities. Leaders live under a microscope: every accomplishment is analyzed; every failure, exposed. If they do not change their organizational culture or build the bottom line fast enough, they are questioned or replaced. We prefer effective leaders over faithful elders, dynamic speakers over dutiful shepherds. This section suggests that God's approval of a leader matters more than man's opinion. Indeed, God can powerfully use imperfect leaders.

Zechariah 5:1–11

EXEGETICAL IDEA
God's curse would fall on all sinners (those who steal and swear falsely), then God would remove the wickedness of idolatry from the land.

THEOLOGICAL FOCUS
Before there can be spiritual restoration with God, all forms of evil must end.

PREACHING IDEA
Evil has a divine expiration date.

PREACHING POINTERS
Zechariah observed God's intention to put an end to evil in two visions. First, the prophet saw a flying scroll whereby God cursed upon the people for theft and misuse of his name, and he called out their transgressions. Next, there appeared a covered basket containing a woman who symbolized idolatry; God would rid the land of her wickedness. For both visions an angel provided the prophet with an interpretation. The original audience would have understood the need for God to stamp evil with its expiration date. In fact, they would have welcomed it, knowing that the blessings of the covenant cannot coexist with human rebellion.

Evil lingers yet today. Endless news cycles harp on the misdeeds of sinful men and women, corrupt nations and institutions: child trafficking and sexual harassment, bullying and mass shootings, insider trading and corporate deceit, racial and sexual inequality. Much of the evil that plagues us today is the product of misguided human efforts. Our attempts to eradicate evil through education, politics, activism, finances, and religion may be well-intentioned but are often as unrealistic as Hollywood's endless line of superhero films. Until God puts an end to evil, we will experience its effects. Fortunately, this passage assures us that evil has a divine expiration date.

Zechariah 6:1–8

EXEGETICAL IDEA
God's angelic forces were everywhere, doing his will and appeasing his wrath.

THEOLOGICAL FOCUS
God's sovereign presence everywhere enables him to carry out his desires everywhere.

PREACHING IDEA
God has every square inch of the earth under his watch.

PREACHING POINTERS
Despite the ever-expanding borders of the Persian Empire, secured by the efforts of King Darius, God's rule remained a reality. This is the meaning of Zechariah's eighth and final vision: horses marching in every direction, sent by God on patrol. Although the original audience lived under the umbrella of Persian rule, marked by instability and uncertainty, Zechariah assured them that they lived under God's watch. He was in control. He would prevail over the nations. The picture of patrolling chariots and horses assured them that the divine reign has no borders.

Today God's people doubt his control of local and global events. We doubt his power when our prayers remain answered. We doubt his sovereignty when tragedy strikes or suffering persists. The complex of global problems proves especially troublesome to our faith: the advance of Islam and secular humanism; widespread malnutrition and inequality for females; terrorism and mass shootings; drug abuse and overdose fatalities; kidnappings and human trafficking. People can cherry-pick evidence from across the planet that God is capricious or impotent. This passage curbs such fallacious thinking, affirming that God has every square inch of the earth under his watch.

Zechariah 6:9–15

EXEGETICAL IDEA
The placing of a crown on the head of Joshua the high priest elevated his status, encouraged people to return to Jerusalem, and was a sign that in the future God would raise up a messianic Branch/Sprout who would serve as both priest and king.

THEOLOGICAL FOCUS
God's promise of a future Davidic King reinforces and underscores God's plans for his people now and in the future.

PREACHING IDEA
Only God can give an absolute guarantee.

PREACHING POINTERS
God returned his focus to the restoration of the temple and role of the high priest. In a previous vision, Joshua received God's vote of confidence; now Joshua received an ornate crown. Fashioned from the offerings of three men returning from exile, the decorative headpiece signaled God's favor. More importantly, God bestowed on Joshua a symbolic name: Branch. The crown and title assured the original audience of God's current support of the temple restoration and his future installment of a royal-priestly leader. Such assurance intended to inspire their faithful work.

In an age of uncertainty, people crave guarantees. We look for guarantees as we face a major surgery, purchase a new car, or invest for retirement. We want guarantees that our marriage will last, ministry programs will impact lives, and medication will relieve chronic pain. Sadly, many guarantees cannot hold weight, leading us to disappointment, doubt, and cynicism. We can project this on God. It is not enough that he has promised to remain present in our lives; we want constant reassurance that his word proves true. We want writing on the wall, lucid dreams, prophetic words, or symbols in our soup to reaffirm his promises. This passage reminds us that only God can give an absolute guarantee.

Zechariah 7:1–14

EXEGETICAL IDEA
Some people wondered if they still needed to keep the fasts that commemorated the defeat of Jerusalem, but Zechariah exhorted the audience to focus on what God wanted them to do (execute justice, show kindness, and show compassion) and to remember God's eschatological promises, for in the future they would feast and not fast over their past failures.

THEOLOGICAL FOCUS
God does not accept worship from insincere people who refuse to follow his ethical standards.

PREACHING IDEA
Real remorse provokes positive change.

PREACHING POINTERS
Two years had passed since Zechariah's first vision, but the people remained reluctant to declare God's victory. A group of folks living outside Jerusalem came to the priests to inquire about the need to continue their memorial fasts. Rather than answer their questions, God raised a few of his own through Zechariah to expose their false remorse and insincere worship. Then he stressed the need for acts of love—justice, mercy, and compassion—rather than acts of penance. For the original audience this was not a new message but an echo of Moses and other prophets. The encounter reiterated their need to dispense with their solemn rituals and return to showing justice.

It's embarrassing when God's people today prefer showing a gloomy face to doing good deeds. Evangelicals lament their loss of political influence, legal protections, and opportunities to speak freely about their faith in public. We bemoan today's loose sexual ethic, consumer impulse, and vulgarity. We groan about diminishing loyalties to church activities and flighty tendencies of younger generations. Sadly, our remorse neither accepts personal responsibility nor motivates positive change. Inauthentic remorse looks inward and acts pathetic. Real remorse looks outward and acts positive. This passage reminds us that real remorse provokes positive change.

Zechariah 8:1–23

EXEGETICAL IDEA
God's great zeal for his covenant people would result in God saving them, returning them to their land, giving them peace, and blessing them, so God's people should practice justice in all their relationships and turn their fasting days into days of feasting and rejoicing.

THEOLOGICAL FOCUS
In the future, God's people will be restored and transformed, so they will celebrate rather than mourn.

PREACHING IDEA
"Save the date" for an upcoming party with God.

PREACHING POINTERS
God had something great in store for his people. He had planned a series of feasts with his restored people and their neighbors. Zechariah shared this news in his answer to the question of fasting raised in the previous chapter. The exile had ended. Rebuilding had begun. Renewal was on the horizon. To the original audience, this news was meant to breathe fresh hope into their labors and curb any defeatist (or nationalistic) leanings. The Lord of Hosts had scheduled a feast (several, actually) and invited all who obey him to indulge.

The church today could benefit from a second glance at God's festive side. The Lord Almighty has infused his creation with wonders galore: teeming animals, rushing waters, succulent greenery, savory flavors, and glorious image-bearers. Too many people settle for a gloomy God bent on enforcing rules and inflicting punishments. While we cannot whitewash his jealousy, anger, and wrath, neither should we minimize his joy. The present abounds with a million little gifts from the Father of lights. The future will abound with parties and peoples beyond counting. This passage instructs us to "Save the date" for an upcoming party with God.

Zechariah 9:1–17

EXEGETICAL IDEA
After God had consumed the nations on the northern (Syria and Phoenicia) and western (Philistia) borders, he would raise up a righteous and humble messianic Savior-King who would restore a time of peace, joy, and freedom from foreign domination.

THEOLOGICAL FOCUS
God will restore his people by eliminating his enemies, installing a humble King, and defending his people.

PREACHING IDEA
God has a grand plan for lasting peace.

PREACHING POINTERS
While the first eight chapters of Zechariah centered around visions, the closing five chapters recounted God's words verbalized (i.e., oracles) by the prophet. Each oracle cycled through key themes of God's protection, justice, mercy, and Messiah. They looked beyond immediate circumstances to far-off realities. The first of these speeches predicted an era of peace, following the defeat of local and distant opponents. Zechariah spoke of deliverance and peace coming through a divinely appointed King to inspire his original audience to maintain their trust in God.

We do not live in peaceful times. Unrest defines Western politics, the global arms race, civil rights, economic inequality, climate change, gun violence, and the spread of disease. Two minutes of nightly news and social media may quicken our pulse and cloud our willingness to think critically. Our growing anxiety has led to myriad attempts to foster inner peace. Yoga, meditation, mindfulness, massage, daily affirmations, salt caves, and kombucha teas head the list. As effective as these interventions might feel in the short term, they cannot secure long-term peace. Global and spiritual unrest require divine intervention. This passage teaches us that God has a grand plan for lasting peace.

Zechariah 10:1–11:3

EXEGETICAL IDEA
Although problems abound all around, God's people must depend on him (not false gods or godless leaders), follow God's leader, and believe God's promises to restore his people and defeat their enemies.

THEOLOGICAL FOCUS
Trust God in difficult times, for he will strengthen his people as he has promised.

PREACHING IDEA
It's best to bank on God in bad circumstances.

PREACHING POINTERS
Circumstances did not look promising in Zechariah's day. Lack of rain led to poor vegetation. Lack of leadership led to religious confusion, vulnerability to enemies, and geographical displacement. But in this passage, God helped Zechariah look beyond bad circumstances. The prophet spoke of God—mighty and compassionate, jealous and angry—gathering his people and empowering them against their enemies. Neither dead idols nor empty rituals could guarantee them victory; God would win their battles. This message was meant to restore the joy and confidence of Zechariah's original audience.

Bad circumstances plague God's people today. Messages about global poverty, political strife, untreatable diseases, unhealthy foods, economic disparity, and racial tensions abound. Personal struggles with mental illness, high blood pressure, career disappointment, theological confusion, and family dysfunction disrupt our lives. And churches are hindered by untrustworthy leaders, biblical illiteracy, laws affecting religious freedom, and rising tides of disaffecting believers. Rather than trusting God to remedy bad circumstances, we have learned to bank on common sense, slick marketing, church programs, technical savvy, political strategy, social networks, and personal abilities. In other words, we trust our flawed systems and limited resources to turn our bad circumstances into bright outcomes. This passage reminds us that it's best to bank on God in bad circumstances.

Zechariah 11:4–17

EXEGETICAL IDEA
Evil shepherds would be removed and a good shepherd would restore God's covenant between Judah and Israel, but the people would reject this good shepherd, so unity and delight would be lost and a foolish shepherd would come and destroy the flock.

THEOLOGICAL FOCUS
The rejection of the good leaders will lead to destruction, for many will follow worthless leaders.

PREACHING IDEA
Let's cut loose from bad leaders.

PREACHING POINTERS
God gave Zechariah a new role in this section of the text. The prophet was to act *like* a shepherd to God's people. As the narrative unfolds, Zechariah gripped a staff in each hand and sent uncaring leaders packing. Sadly, the people showed preference for their godless figureheads,

resulting in a series of prophetic signs—two broken staffs, thirty shekels tossed aside—capped off by an oracle of woe. Shepherding imagery struck a familiar note with Zechariah's original audience, for they had known both God and Israel's kings as their shepherds. The intense language and evocative gestures intended to fill his hearers with dread if they remained in the shadow of uncaring shepherds.

Bad leaders in any context threaten the well-being of people under their care. This is true today. An arrogant pastor can belittle his congregation. A stubborn coach can sabotage his team's chance of victory. Distant parents can undermine the security of their children. An ambitious CEO can create a culture of restlessness and fear in the workplace. Leaders set the tone and standard in which their followers rise and fall. Unfortunately, we allow careless leaders to remain in their post because we are more comfortable with the status quo. Instead, as the passage suggests, we should cut loose from bad leaders.

Zechariah 12:1–9

EXEGETICAL IDEA
In the future, the nations would gather together against Jerusalem, but God would watch over his people, save the people of Jerusalem, and pour out his grace on them.

THEOLOGICAL FOCUS
God's people know that God will watch over and rescue them from their enemies.

PREACHING IDEA
God's strength is our secret weapon.

PREACHING POINTERS
Zechariah's preaching remained focused on what would happen in days ahead. He delivered another speech from God predicting future battles and firm victory for his people. The Lord would come to Jerusalem's defense. He would empower his people to fight, transforming the weakest of men into warriors. Vivid imagery—a colossal stone and fiery pot—and allusions to Israel's past—exodus, covenant, David and Goliath—grab the listener's ear. For the original audience, "that day" Zechariah spoke of could not come too soon. While they may not have looked forward to facing enemies, they certainly longed to see God's strength at full force.

God's people need to remember the greatness of his strength yet today. The Western world has trained us to be radically self-reliant. We have learned to harness science and technology, consult data and research, amass wealth and weapons, and practice medicine and mindfulness techniques to increase human potency. At our fingertips, we have more power than any people before us. Our glowing screens are a "portkey" to global knowledge and networks. Who needs God's wisdom when Google gives us our information? Who needs a community of faith when Facebook provides us unlimited social connectivity? But no amount of human progress can rival God's power. This passage reminds us that God's strength is our secret weapon.

Zechariah 12:10–13:9

EXEGETICAL IDEA
In the distant future when God's grace and compassion would be poured out on the families of Israel, they would weep bitterly for the one they had pierced, be cleansed of their sins, reject false teachings, and renew their covenant with God.

THEOLOGICAL FOCUS
God's grace brings mourning for past sins, purification from sin, an end to false prophecy, and the restoration of the covenant with God.

PREACHING IDEA
Fresh starts often leave deep scars.

PREACHING POINTERS
Renewal for God's people came at a cost. Starting fresh, like many of life's battles, required some casualties. In Zechariah's day, God issued a death sentence for idols, false prophets, his Messiah, and many of God's people. While reminders of God's grace were intended to encourage the original audience, the prophet also exposed their grievous sin. Grace was costly. Zechariah's message evoked a longing for a fresh start, even if the path appeared painful.

Those desperate for a fresh start in our day must beware of quick, pain-free fixes. Changing our thinking, actions, and relationships requires both human intention and divine intervention to habituate. A perfectly clean slate will not happen this side of heaven. Sadly, the world peddles self-improvement as a cheap imposter to starting fresh. We're compelled to improve everything—from our sleeping habits and sex life to our reading speed and waistline—in a few simple steps. Take a nap. Swallow a pill. Scan first sentences. Avoid carbs. Meanwhile, new rules for self-improvement will replace old ones, and we remain in a state of spiritual decay. This passage offers a helpful corrective, assuring us that fresh starts often leave deep scars.

Zechariah 14:1–21

EXEGETICAL IDEA
At the climax of history, the nations would attack Jerusalem, but God would deliver the city, bring major changes in nature, and reign as king; then all nations would pay homage to him.

THEOLOGICAL FOCUS
In the distant future, God will rescue his people, reign as King, and restore his kingdom.

PREACHING IDEA
Get in God's corner: he's the undisputed, everlasting King of the world.

PREACHING POINTERS
Talk of end times continued as Zechariah painted a conclusive picture of days ahead. God would defeat his enemies and renew creation. Jerusalem would become an international

hub of praise. Holiness would spread to all peoples. While Zechariah's original audience realized these climatic events may not occur soon, the message still intended to lift their spirits. None of their enemies—from Egypt to Babylon to unforeseen opponents—would prevail. God's justice, nearness, and holiness would win out. The assurance of his reign instilled trust and inspired celebration.

God's reign often goes unnoticed in our day. We bow our hearts to cheaper versions of ascendency: sports trophies, academic honors, business achievements, and celebrity awards. Moreover, the rise of social media has expanded the spotlight, giving the illusion that anyone can achieve fifteen minutes of fame with enough followers, likes, retweets, and activity from a given post. Gluttons for attention abound in our modern age. People build their platforms and careers like personal empires. Our tiny kingdoms and temporary fame will not endure. This passage redirects our focus; we celebrate because God's the undisputed, everlasting King of the world.

Malachi 1:1–5

EXEGETICAL IDEA
God demonstrated through his action that he chose to love the Israelites, the children of Jacob, rather than the Edomites, the children of Esau.

THEOLOGICAL FOCUS
God loves his people despite the way his people feel about it.

PREACHING IDEA
God's deep love should stir our dull senses.

PREACHING POINTERS
Malachi opened with a bold declaration of God's love to Israel. Sadly, the Jewish audience disputed the claim and asked for proof of God's commitment. Recent history had caused them to question God's affection: the destruction of the temple, exile, foreign rule, and their return to a ruined country. Malachi countered their argument with evidence of God's covenant fidelity, namely, the selection and preservation of Jacob (i.e., Israel) rather than Esau (i.e., Edom). The dispute caused his original audience to give God's deep love a second look.

Even today, to question God's love is human. During life's tragedies, unanswered prayer, or lonely moments, we doubt the quality of God's love. We equate love with feelings; we conflate it with warm affections, giddy emotions, happy thoughts, and perpetual smiles. By contrast, the love of God centers on his choice, commitment, acts of sacrifice, and selfless care. His love is an undeniable, historical fact. The passage affirms that God's deep love should stir our dull senses.

Malachi 1:6–2:9

EXEGETICAL IDEA
Israel's priests did not honor God when they conducted sacrificial worship at the temple (1:6–10), did not keep the Levitical covenant with God (2:8), and did not instruct the people

faithfully (2:6–8). God would disqualify these priests from temple service and send a curse on them (2:1–3:9), but God would be honored among the nations (1:11, 14).

THEOLOGICAL FOCUS
All worship leaders and worshippers need to fear God, faithfully teach the Torah, and honor God in their worship.

PREACHING IDEA
Shortcuts in worship can come back to bite us.

PREACHING POINTERS
Although sacrificial worship had resumed in Jerusalem after the exile, a necessary sense of reverence was missing. This provoked God's second dispute with his people, which Malachi voiced to his original audience. God, through his prophet, called out the priests for cutting corners and cheating the sacrificial system. Their acts would fool neither parent nor local politician; they certainly could not fool their divine King. Malachi exposed how their errant thinking devolved into egregious worship. Fortunately, the original audience heard God's rebuke and took steps to improve their relationship with him.

Our furious pace of life today spurs a similar temptation for taking shortcuts. We prefer SparkNotes to unabridged literature. We listen to audio books at an accelerated pace. We watch YouTube channels for video game hints and tricks to amass extra lives and resources to win more quickly. Skimping on taxes, rolling through stop signs, and taking credit for others' work is epidemic. When so many areas of life tolerate cheating, it's no surprise to catch God's people cutting corners as we honor him. We lowball our tithes and offerings, give better energy to sports and business than weekly church gatherings, and treat evangelism as an add-on to life rather than an essential component. Malachi's message reminds us that shortcuts in worship come back to bite us.

Malachi 2:10–16

EXEGETICAL IDEA
Israel was a nation that worshipped one God, so people should not be unfaithful to that God or unfaithful to one another in marriage.

THEOLOGICAL FOCUS
Unfaithful treachery toward God and a marriage partner does not please God.

PREACHING IDEA
Let's cherish marriage and make it great again.

PREACHING POINTERS
God's case against Israel continued in a third dispute. Malachi addressed the people's infidelity to God and the miserable state of marriage in the land of Judah. The original audience was living in a time when both Ezra and Nehemiah encouraged men to divorce their pagan wives to maintain the spiritual purity of the nation. Sadly, many turned this exception for divorcing

a foreign bride into a general rule that permitted them to divorce any wife. The twisted result of this process led some to think that it was permissible even to divorce a Jewish wife and then marry a foreign bride. The ugly situation resulted in a polluted temple, rejected worship, unhappy marriages, and future progeny imperiled by these unholy mixed marriages—a far cry from God's intended design and deviation from the divorce imperative in Ezra and Nehemiah. Thus, Malachi begged his original audience to resurrect God's design for marriage.

In today's world, marriage does not always reflect God's ideal. Politicians have redefined marriage as a social contract, not a spiritual covenant. No-fault divorce laws have softened the sting of marital dissolution. The oft-cited fifty-percent statistic reveals that half of marriages end in divorce; Christian marriages are not immune. Moreover, cohabitation, polyamory, pornography, and domestic partnerships continue to gain mainstream approval. The solution is not for God's people to campaign just for a return to old-fashioned values, but to resurrect God's ideal. A good marriage is a gift and social good. This passage exhorts us to cherish marriage and make it great again.

Malachi 2:17–3:5

EXEGETICAL IDEA
Although some questioned God's justice, a messenger would prepare the way for God's coming to his temple, and then the Messenger of the Covenant would refine the wicked and present the righteous to God.

THEOLOGICAL FOCUS
God is just, and the Messenger of the Covenant will establish justice through refinement.

PREACHING IDEA
Someday God will scrub out the stains of social injustice.

PREACHING POINTERS
God voiced his fourth dispute against the people of Israel over their persistent moaning about injustice. They had accused God of being slow and soft in his treatment of wrongdoing. He responded by giving a preview of his future arrival, his plans to establish justice at that time, and the special message bearer leading the charge. God's coming would refine the world, judging obstinate people for breaking the covenant and purifying priests for holy service. Malachi's message exposed his original audience's doubt, intending to replace it with trust in God's justice.

The existence of evil, suffering, and social injustice serve as obstacles to belief for many people today. They cannot imagine a good and powerful God allowing injustice to persist. The fast-paced, nonstop, one-click ethos of the Internet Age has generated an inability to wait. We are conditioned for speed not slowness, efficiency not patience. The hurried nature of life affects our view of God. He does not act quickly enough to stop terror, eradicate disease, and end inequality. His justice lags, while we grow restless with social injustice. We fuss. We complain. We may even take matters into our own hands. This passage calls us to pause, take a breath, and remember: someday God will scrub out the stains of social injustice.

Malachi 3:6–12

EXEGETICAL IDEA
God was faithful and didn't change his character, so if people repented of their sins, turned to God, and showed their trust by tithing, then he would remove the curse on their crops and provide his blessings.

THEOLOGICAL FOCUS
If people change and quit robbing God, then he will prosper his people with all their physical needs.

PREACHING IDEA
Ante up and give God his due.

PREACHING POINTERS
The reality of judgment in the fifth dispute resulted in a call to return to living God's way. The Lord brought a new charge against his people: they had skimped on their tithing. The Law demanded a percentage of produce and livestock set aside for God to support the priesthood. The people's failure to give God his due had resulted in lackluster harvests—a covenant curse. In this dispute, the prophet Malachi drew attention to his original audience's self-deception, which only hurt them. God's words were a reality check. He had better in store for the whole nation than the storehouses currently contained. He wanted Israel to return to him and receive his blessings.

People struggle to give God his due today. The Western world promotes greed and consumption rather than generosity and stewardship. We are taught to pay ourselves first so we can retire in style. We learn to spend in advance—credit cards, college loans, and financing options—accruing debt and adding interest. Greed says to buy more than we need, often on a whim. This lack of financial restraint often leads to thin margins, spotty giving, and general anxiety. And when we do give, it may be to assuage guilt as much as aid others in need. Failure to view our financial resources from God's perspective results in our robbing God. This passage implores us to rethink our relationship to money: to ante up and give God his due.

Malachi 3:13–4:3

EXEGETICAL IDEA
Although some questioned if it paid to serve God, when God would come to judge the world he would distinguish between the righteous and the wicked, between those who feared and served God (his "prized possessions") and those who refused to fear and serve him.

THEOLOGICAL FOCUS
God will spare those who fear and serve him but destroy the arrogant who refuse to honor him.

PREACHING IDEA
God is inclined to stick a pin in our pride.

PREACHING POINTERS

The prophet Malachi spoke on God's behalf in a sixth and final dispute with his people. He redressed his original audience's cynicism about serving God, which to them apparently paid less than self-service. The argument echoed an earlier complaint that God's justice was lacking. In the current section, the prophet reassured them that God remembered and rewarded the righteous, humble, and God-fearing, but he despised the arrogant. Those who revered the Almighty would help God as he uprooted those who refused to honor him in a climatic, coming day. This glimpse into the future aimed to inspire Malachi's original audience towards humble service.

Pride is prime currency in our age. We tend to exalt big-headed athletes, celebrities, and CEOs for their bravado and bold accomplishments. We often ignore the elderly, disabled, less educated, or ethnic outsider. We teach young people to prize self-esteem above integrity. Even the church is seduced by self-importance, as evident in the numerous church campuses that look like shopping malls, leadership conferences that promise to catalyze growth, and programming that claims to be the best hour of the week. When excellent performance becomes the measuring stick for a worship service, arrogance overtakes God as the focus. Such religious pomp will not last. This passage reminds us how God's inclined to stick a pin in our pride.

Malachi 4:4–6

EXEGETICAL IDEA

The people should read and obey the Mosaic laws and remember that God would send another Elijah before the day of the Lord to bring restoration to many.

THEOLOGICAL FOCUS

People who read and heed the Bible can expect a revival before the coming of God's glorious kingdom.

PREACHING IDEA

Until God finishes his work, we must rely on the Bible.

PREACHING POINTERS

The final few verses of Malachi rehearsed earlier themes: obedience to God's law, future judgment, and an invitation to change. Moses represented a voice from Israel's past; Elijah represented a forthcoming word from God. In this closing utterance, the original audience heard one last plea to observe God's word in order to escape judgment and experience a better future.

The Bible remains relevant for following God today. It is his primary communication tool. Sadly, biblical literacy is plummeting despite mass printing, distribution, and digitation of Bible translations. Furthermore, some people consider the Good Book old-fashioned, outdated, and oppressive. Secular scholars have deconstructed the Bible. Pragmatic preachers have reduced the text into a self-help manual. Religious hypocrites have turned the Scriptures into soapboxes. The authority and life-shaping power of God's Word is long-forgotten on many. Malachi's epilogue teaches us that until God finishes his work, we must rely on the Bible.

ABBREVIATIONS

GENERAL ABBREVIATIONS

A.D.	in the year of our Lord (*anno Domini*)
ANE	ancient Near East
B.C.	before Christ
B.C.E.	before the Common Era
DSS	Dead Sea Scrolls
Eng.	English
LXX	Septuagint
NT	New Testament
OT	Old Testament

TECHNICAL ABBREVIATIONS

ca.	circa
cf.	compare (*confer*)
ch(s).	chapter(s)
col(s).	column(s)
ed(s).	editor(s)
e.g.	for example
etc.	and so forth, and the rest (*et cetera*)
et al.	and others (*et alii*)
i.e.	that is (*id est*)
lit.	literally
p(p).	page(s)
r.	reigned
repr.	reprinted
rev.	revised
§ (*pl.* §§)	section(s)
v(v).	verse(s)
vs.	versus
vol(s).	volume(s)

BIBLICAL

Old Testament

Gen.	Genesis		Exod.	Exodus
			Lev.	Leviticus

Old Testament (continued)

Num.	Numbers
Deut.	Deuteronomy
Josh.	Joshua
Judg.	Judges
Ruth	Ruth
1 Sam.	1 Samuel
2 Sam.	2 Samuel
1 Kings	1 Kings
2 Kings	2 Kings
1 Chron.	1 Chronicles
2 Chron.	2 Chronicles
Ezra	Ezra
Neh.	Nehemiah
Esther	Esther
Job	Job
Ps./Pss.	Psalm(s)
Prov.	Proverbs
Eccl.	Ecclesiastes
Song	Song of Songs
Isa.	Isaiah
Jer.	Jeremiah
Lam.	Lamentations
Ezek.	Ezekiel
Dan.	Daniel
Hos.	Hosea
Joel	Joel
Amos	Amos
Obad.	Obadiah
Jonah	Jonah
Mic.	Micah
Nah.	Nahum
Hab.	Habakkuk
Zeph.	Zephaniah
Hag.	Haggai
Zech.	Zechariah
Mal.	Malachi

New Testament

Matt.	Matthew
Mark	Mark
Luke	Luke
John	John
Acts	Acts
Rom.	Romans
1 Cor.	1 Corinthians
2 Cor.	2 Corinthians
Gal.	Galatians
Eph.	Ephesians
Phil.	Philippians
Col.	Colossians
1 Thess.	1 Thessalonians
2 Thess.	2 Thessalonians
1 Tim.	1 Timothy
2 Tim.	2 Timothy
Titus	Titus
Philem.	Philemon
Heb.	Hebrews
James	James
1 Peter	1 Peter
2 Peter	2 Peter
1 John	1 John
2 John	2 John
3 John	3 John
Jude	Jude
Rev.	Revelation

EXTRABIBLICAL SOURCES

Old Testament Apocrypha

1 Macc	1 Maccabees

Classification of the Dead Sea Scrolls

[a], [b], [c], etc.	manuscript identifiers
1Q	Cave 1, Qumran
4Q	Cave 4, Qumran
Q	Qumran

Dead Sea Scrolls

Number	Abbreviation	Name
CD	Damascus Document	Cairo Genizah copy of the Damascus Document
IQIsa	IQIsa^a	The Great Isaiah Scroll
1Q28	1QS	Rule of the Community
1Q28a	1QSa	Rule of the Congregation
4Q161	4QpIsa^a	Isaiah Pesher^a
4Q174	4QFlor	Florilegium
4Q252	4QCommGen A	Commentary on Genesis A
4Q285	4QSM	Sefer ha-Milḥamah

Classical Greek and Jewish Historians

Arrian — Greek Historian A.D. ca. 86–ca. 160
- *Anab.* — *Anabasis*

Diodorus — Greek Historian ca. 90–ca. 30 B.C.
- *Bib hist* — *Bibliotheca historica*

Xenophon — Greek philosopher, historian, and soldier; ca. 430–ca. 354 B.C.
- *Anab.* — *Upcountry March (Anabasis)*

Herodotus — Greek historian of the Greco-Persian Wars; ca. 484–ca. 430–420 B.C.
- *Hist.* — *Histories (Historiae)*

Josephus — Romano-Jewish historian; A.D. 37–100
- *A.J.* — *Jewish Antiquities (Antiquitates judaicae)*

Periodicals

AJSL	*American Journal of Semitic Languages and Literature*
BSac	*Biblica*
BibOr	Biblica et Orientalia
BT	*The Bible Translator*
CBQ	*Catholic Biblical Quarterly*
CT	*Christianity Today*
CTJ	*Calvin Theological Journal*
CTR	*Criswell Theological Review*
GTJ	*Grace Theological Journal*
IEJ	*Israel Exploration Journal*
JBL	*Journal of Biblical Literature*
JSOT	*Journal for the Study of the Old Testament*
JTS	*Journal of Theological Studies*
OTS	*Old Testament Studies*
TJ	*Trinity Journal*
TynBul	*Tyndale Bulletin*
VT	*Vetus Testamentum*
ZAW	*Zeitschrift für die alttestamentliche Wissenschaft*

Series

AB — Anchor Bible

CBC	Cornerstone Biblical Commentary
CC	Communicator's Commentary
HSCOT	Historical Commentary of the Old Testament
ICC	International Critical Commentary
JSOTSup	Journal for the Study of the Old Testament Supplement Series
LCL	Loeb Classical Library
NAC	New American Commentary
NICOT	New International Commentary on the Old Testament
NIVAC	New International Version Application Commentary
OTL	Old Testament Library

Reference

ANET	*Ancient Near Eastern Texts Relating to the Old Testament.* 1969. Edited by J. B. Pritchard. 3rd ed. Princeton, NJ: Princeton University Press
ABD	*Anchor Bible Dictionary.* 1992. Edited by D. N. Freedman. 6 vols. New York: Doubleday
BDB	Brown, F., S. R. Driver, and C. A. Briggs. 1906. *A Hebrew and English Lexicon of the Old Testament.* Oxford: Clarendon Press. Repr. with corrections, 1966
IBD	*International Bible Dictionary.* 1912. Edited by F. N. Peloubet. Philadelphia: Winston. Repr., Plainfield, NJ: Logos International, 1977
ISBE	*International Standard Bible Encyclopedia.* 1979–1988. Edited by G. W. Bromiley. 4 vols. Grand Rapids: Eerdmans
NIDOTTE	*New International Dictionary of Old Testament Theology.* 1997. Edited by W. A. VanGemeren. 5 vols. Grand Rapids: Zondervan
TDOT	*Theological Dictionary of the Old Testament.* 1974–2006. Edited by G. J. Botterweck, H. Ringgren, and H.-J. Fabry. Trans. J. T. Willis et al. 8 vols. Grand Rapids: Eerdmans

Bible Translations

ASV	American Standard Version
CEB	Common English Bible
CEV	Contemporary English Version
CSB	Christian Standard Bible
ESV	English Standard Version
HCSB	Holman Christian Standard Bible
LXX	Septuagint
NASB[95]	New American Standard Bible
NEB	New English Bible
NIV	New International Version
NKJV	New King James Version
NLT[SE]	New Living Translation
NRSV	New Revised Standard Version
RSV	Revised Standard Version

INTRODUCTION TO ZEPHANIAH

OVERVIEW OF INTRODUCTORY ISSUES

Author: Zephaniah

Place: Jerusalem

Date: around 625 B.C.

Readers: Judeans

Historical Setting: Shortly after the Assyrian king Ashurbanipal died, Josiah declared political independence and some religious reforms.

Occasion for Writing: Judah is free from Assyria, so Zephaniah is supporting Josiah's reforms to return to worship YHWH (Yahweh) to escape his wrath.

Genre: Prophecy

Theological Emphasis: The day of the Lord is near, so seek God and experience his blessing.

AUTHORSHIP OF ZEPHANIAH

The superscription (1:1) claims that this collection of prophecies was a record of what God spoke to the prophet Zephaniah in the days of Josiah (2 Kings 18–20; 2 Chron. 29–32). The accounts about Josiah in Chronicles or the book of Kings provide no information about Zephaniah's ministry, but the genealogy of Zephaniah (Zeph. 1:1) indicates that one of his ancestors was Hezekiah, most likely the righteous King Hezekiah (Robertson, 1990, 34; Motyer, 1998b, 898). If this was the case, then Zephaniah was part of the extended royal family and a member of the upper class in Jerusalem. This status would suggest that he likely advised King Josiah and encouraged him to remove all pagan worship (Zeph. 1:3–6). This close association with the royal court may explain Zephaniah's observations about the king's sons wearing foreign clothing (1:8; probably Assyrian clothes), his criticism of the violent behavior of the princes and judges in Jerusalem (3:3), and his knowledge of international affairs in neighboring and distant nations (2:4–15). Zephaniah's call for the people to be humble and seek the Lord (2:1–3) indicates that Zephaniah was a strong supporter of Josiah's reforms.

If the prophet was born in the dark era of Manasseh (2 Chron. 33), then his public ministry coincided with the early years of King Josiah before the young king removed all pagan worship in his major reform in 621 B.C. (2 Chron.

34:1–33; Zeph. 1:4). This record claims that these are Zephaniah's prophecies, so he was the source or author of these messages.

PLACE OF WRITING

Zephaniah spoke the words of God in the city of Jerusalem (1:4, 12; 3:1), but Zephaniah left no record about where he was when he wrote down these messages. Since the written message was for the people in Jerusalem and addressed issues that pertained to problems in Jerusalem in the time of Josiah, one would assume that these sermons were written in Jerusalem to warn additional people who did not hear Zephaniah preach these messages. This would enable many more people to respond to his message.

DATE OF WRITING

Zephaniah spoke these prophetic messages during the reign of King Josiah (1:1; 640–609 B.C.) before his great revival. There is no evidence that the major revival of 621 B.C. had happened by the time his sermons were put in writing, so a date before this event is most likely. Zephaniah wrote this scroll at a time when evil practices were still prevalent in Jerusalem (3:1–5), although Zephaniah 1:4 refers to only a "remnant of Baal religion" being left during his ministry. This would suggest that Zephaniah was preaching around 625 B.C. and put his prophecy in writing sometime after Josiah's initial reforms to remove Baalism in his twelfth year (628 B.C.; 2 Chron. 34:3–7) but before his major reform in his eighteenth year when they found the Mosaic law book in the temple (621 B.C.; 2 Chron. 34:8–33).

Bronze statue of the god Baal (the Canaanite god of rain and fertility), dated from the fourteenth to twelfth century B.C., found in the tell of Ras Shamra, the ancient Mediterranean port city of Ugarit. Courtesy of Daderot.

during the dry season. Hosea 1–2 indicate that the northern nation of Israel was heavily involved with Baal worship, and Athaliah (2 Chron. 22), Ahaz (2 Chron. 28:1–4), and Manasseh (2 Chron. 33:1–9) promoted Baalism in Judah.

Although some date Zephaniah's ministry and his writing of his prophecy right after Josiah found the law book and instituted major reform (621 B.C.) based on the presence of several phrases in Zephaniah that are parallel to phrases in Deuteronomy (Robertson, 1990, 254–56; DeRouchie, 2018, 563), this argument is weakened by the presence of most of these phrases in other prophetic books before Zephaniah.

The Baal Religion

The Baal religion was a fertility religion celebrating Baal's (the god of fertility) ability to bring rain to make the crops grow, cause animals to be fertile, and bring prosperity to all. The Baal myth involved a conflict between Baal, who ruled the world during the fertile, rainy season, and the god Mot ("death"), who ruled the world

GENERAL CHRONOLOGY OF THE PROPHETS				
Prophet	Estimated Ministry	Period	Audience	
Amos	767–753	Pre-exile	Northern Israel	A S S Y R I A 900 B.C. to 612 B.C.
Hosea	755–715	Pre-exile	Northern Israel	
Micah	735–701	Israel in exile Pre-exile Judah	Judah	
Isaiah	739–685	Pre-exile	Judah	
Nahum	663–612	Israel in exile Pre-exile Judah	Nineveh / Assyria	
Zephaniah	**632–628**	**Israel in exile Pre-exile Judah**	**Judah**	B A B Y L O N 612 B.C. to 539 B.C.
Habakkuk	626–609	Israel in exile Pre-exile Judah	Judah	
Jeremiah	605–586	Israel in exile Pre-exile Judah	Judah	
Daniel	605–535	Judah in exile	Judah	
Ezekiel	597–571	Judah in exile	Judah	
Obadiah	After 586	Judah in exile	Edom	
Jonah	??	Judah in exile	(about) Nineveh	
Haggai	520–520	Post-exile	Returned Jews	P E R S I A
Zechariah	520–480	Post-exile	Returned Jews	
Joel	515	Post-exile	Judah	
Malachi	450	Post-exile	Returned Jews	
Chart created by Herbert W. Bateman IV, *Isaiah: How to Read, Interpret and Understand the Prophet* (Leesburg, IN: Cyber-Center for Biblical Studies, 2016). Reprinted by permission of Herbert W. Bateman IV.				

Zephaniah, however, was not the only prophet encouraging the godly King Josiah, for just a few years earlier (around 630 B.C.) the prophet Nahum assured Josiah that God would free him from the power of Assyria (Nah. 1:9–14; 2:3–13; 3:1–19), and Jeremiah's messages reported similar sins in Judah (Jer. 1:16; 2:8, 23; 3:9) and a similar call for sinners to repent (Jer. 3:6–4:4).

HISTORICAL SETTING AND OCCASION FOR WRITING

The religious situation in Judah before the reign of Josiah was filled with pagan worship promoted by Manasseh and Amon. For many years Manasseh supported Baal worship and even put pagan idols and altars to Baal and the host of heaven in the Jerusalem temple complex (2 Chron. 33:2–5). He allowed witchcraft, divination, sorcery, mediums, and spiritists to flourish, and near the end of his reign he began to remove pagan worship (33:10–17). Although the religious and political situation in Judah improved because the good King Josiah was able to declare political independence from Assyria and was beginning to remove false gods from Judah (Zeph. 1:4), Zephaniah's preaching addressed what still needed to be done. Instead of congratulating the king for this positive turn of events, Zephaniah focused on the sad fact that many people were still worshipping pagan gods (1:4–5) and a national revival had not yet caught fire in 625 B.C. Zephaniah, who was supportive of Josiah's reforms, warned that if God did not see a much broader movement of people back to the worship of God, disaster would fall on Judah. He wrote to persuade the people who questioned God's power to control their future (1:12), who did not trust God (3:2) to seek God before it was too late. He taught them that God expected them to fear him and listen to his instruction, but that was not happening (3:2, 7).

The political situation in Judah was difficult before Josiah's reign because Assyria was the dominant power in the ancient Near East. Their political influence on the southern nation of Judah became significant when the Assyrian rulers Esarhaddon (681–669 B.C.) and Ashurbanipal (669–627 B.C.) established Assyrian control over Judah during Manasseh's reign. At one point Manasseh was imprisoned in Assyria (2 Chron. 33:11), possibly for supporting the rebellion by Shamesh-shum-ukin in Babylon (652 B.C.; Robertson, 1990, 6). While in prison, Manasseh humbled himself and confessed his sins, so God returned him to power to carry out religious reforms in Judah (33:10–17). After Manasseh died, his evil son Amon ruled for two years (33:21–24). Then, the eight-year-old boy Josiah was installed as king (640 B.C.).

The Assyrian Empire

About ten years later (around 630 B.C.) the Assyria political situation deteriorated, and in Josiah's twelfth year (628–627 B.C.) King Ashurbanipal died. The political conflicts that Zephaniah reported between Judah and other nations (Philistia in Zeph. 2:4–7; Moab and Ammon in 2:8–11; Egypt in 2:12; and Assyria in 2:13–15) reflected a time of political unrest between nations because Assyria was losing control of her empire. In the midst of this confusion, Josiah declared political independence from Assyria and extended his influence to parts of the northern tribes (2 Chron. 34:3–7). Now that the nation was independent, they had the opportunity to choose a new path unhindered by foreigners, so Zephaniah's sermons supported Josiah's reforms, and his written prophecies were a challenge to reorient the nation's commitments to God so that his judgment would not fall on them.

The socioeconomic situation improved greatly at this time when Judah became independent of Assyria's iron rule and heavy taxation, but instead of supporting a just economic and social environment for all, some powerful people in Jerusalem took advantage of the situation and got their way through violence (Zeph. 1:9) and became quite wealthy (1:18). Other leaders and judges used their power unjustly (3:3, 5c). Zephaniah's writings were a warning that Judah may lose her independence soon on the day of the Lord if the people do not seek righteousness, humility, and the fear of God (2:3; 3:7a).

ORIGINAL READERS

Zephaniah's prophecies were written to influence the policies of the righteous King Josiah, his government, and the people of Judah who were in the midst of a reform movement. He also wanted to impact the choices and beliefs of those who were worshipping foreign gods (1:4–6), the younger political leaders of the nation (the king's sons in 1:8), and the wealthy who had a sense of false security (1:13, 18). He wanted them to know that God's judgment was coming if the people did not change their ways. He wrote to anyone who was willing to seek God (2:3), even the humble person who might intercede for the rest of the nation (3:3). In addition to these warnings of judgment, Zephaniah wrote words of comfort to the righteous remnant (2:7, 9b) and he reminded these people that all who would call on the name of the Lord would one day rejoice and have no fear because God their King will dwell among them (3:14–17).

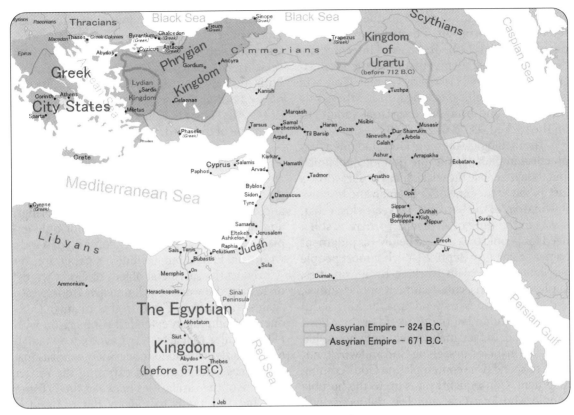

The Assyrian Empire. Courtesy of Ningyou.

THEOLOGICAL EMPHASIS OF ZEPHANIAH

The major theological theme in Zephaniah is that of God's judgment. The prophet Zephaniah developed his message of judgment around the phrase "the day of the LORD" by emphasizing both the negative impact of God's wrath on the wicked (Zeph. 1:2–18; 3:1–8) as well as the positive impact of God's gathering of the righteous remnant into his kingdom to dwell with him (3:9–20). Knowing that the terrible day of the Lord was so near (the defeat of Jerusalem was the intermediate day of the Lord in Zephaniah), Josiah began to reverse the sinful patterns that flourished during the reign of Manasseh. These warnings were designed to motivate the sinners in Zephaniah's audience to stop what they were doing, repent, and ask for God's mercy (2:1–3)

and for the humble and righteous people in Judah to intercede for God's mercy on Judah. If they would do this, the practical results would be that these people will enjoy the final day of the Lord with God in his glorious kingdom (3:9–20). That will be a time of great rejoicing, and God himself will rejoice over all who gather there (3:17). God will pour out his love and bountiful blessing on his people and restore them as a glorious witness to all who see them (3:20). Plainly put, the status quo was unacceptable; action must be taken or the terror of God's wrath would soon fall on Jerusalem (1:14–18)

Earlier the prophets Amos addressing Israel (Amos 5:18–20) and Isaiah addressing Babylon (Isa. 13) warned about God's plan to destroy these nations on the day of the Lord. Zephaniah viewed the day of the Lord as a time when God would intervene in the history of the world and bring great destruction on sinful people (Zeph. 1:2–3). These were intermediate days of the Lord as precursors to the final eschatological day of the Lord when God will inaugurate his glorious kingdom for the godly (Isa. 2:1–5) and bring his disastrous judgment on the wicked (Isa. 2:6–22; 34; 63:1–6).

The theological theme of God's judgment has practical implications in the time of Zephaniah and today because the wickedness in our world is just as bad as the time of Zephaniah and because the final day of the Lord is 2,500 years closer than it was in the time of Zephaniah. There is still a need for people to seek God before his judgment comes again (as in Zeph. 2:1–3), but most people are far too busy with working responsibilities, family obligations, entertainment opportunities, and other activities to spend time thinking about God's final judgment of this world or their need to seek God. In fact, many would not know what would be involved in seeking God and would not want to spend time contemplating God's coming judgment. Consequently, it is up to the humble people who love God and live righteous lives (as in 2:3) to intercede for every nation and in each era of history before that day of judgment arrives and it is too late. These prayers of intercession should include acknowledging our sinfulness, confessing these sins, and then turning from these sinful ways. Reform involves trusting God and accepting any correction he may bring

(cf. 3:2). Having humbly interceded for God's grace, the righteous need to follow in the footsteps of Zephaniah and spend time talking with their friends and neighbors in order to explain both the judgment that will happen on the day of the Lord as well as the great kingdom hope (3:14–20) that awaits all the humble who call on the name of the Lord (3:9–13).

Some such as DeRouchie (2018, 566–68) search for a more direct connection to the NT and the life of Christ because they believe "all the prophets" (not just Isaiah, Ezekiel, Daniel, and Micah) foretold of the life, the sufferings, and the glory of Christ. Thus, he not only explains the texts about the coming of God's wrath on Judah, but includes a paragraph on "Christ as the sacrificial object of God's wrath" or "Christ the warrior will unleash God's wrath against his enemies," and in this manner DeRouchie produces an extended comparison with NT teaching that goes far beyond Zephaniah or his audience understood. Such expositional essays have the benefit of exposing the reader to some of the similarities between the OT and NT, but this tends to quickly draw attention away from Zephaniah's message to his audience and replace it with something that was totally unknown to the prophet.

OUTLINE OF ZEPHANIAH

The messages of Zephaniah are structured into three parts and can be preached in three

The Day of the Lord

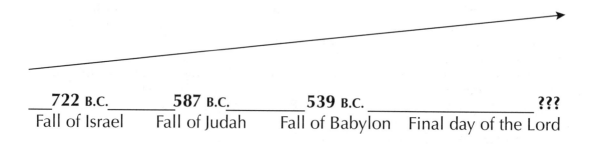

722 B.C.	587 B.C.	539 B.C.	???
Fall of Israel	Fall of Judah	Fall of Babylon	Final day of the Lord

sermons. They are organized around the theme of the approaching day of the Lord. They contrast what will happen to the wicked and the righteous.

- Seek God before His Judgment Comes (1:1–2:3).

- Reasons Why the Remnant Should Have Hope (2:4–3:8).

- Seeking God Will Bring Transformation and Joy in God's Presence (3:9–20).

FOR FURTHER READING

Motyer, J. A. 1998b. "Zephaniah." In *Zephaniah, Haggai, Zechariah, and Malachi*, 897–962. Vol. 3 of *The Minor Prophets: An Exegetical and Expositional Commentary*, edited by T. E. McComiskey. Grand Rapids: Baker.

Ragozin, Z. 2017. *The Rise and Fall of the Assyrian Empire.* n.p., Jovian Press.

Vlaardingerbroek, J. 1999. *Zephaniah.* Historical Commentary on the Old Testament. Leuvan: Peeters.

Zephaniah 1:1–2:3

EXEGETICAL IDEA

Zephaniah supported Josiah's reform movement by warning that God would thoroughly judge all forms of false worship in Jerusalem on the approaching day of the Lord (1:1–15), so the only hope was for people to turn away from their sinful ways, humble themselves, and intercede for God's mercy before the beginning of the day of the Lord (2:1–3).

THEOLOGICAL FOCUS

Since one cannot hide from God's judgment, the prophet tries to motivate people to humble themselves and seek God before he executes his wrath on them.

PREACHING IDEA

Quit playing hide-and-seek with God.

PREACHING POINTS

Zephaniah did not bear good news for the people of Judah. Although his audience had several reasons for happy feelings—Assyria's decline, Israel's independence, and Josiah's initial reforms—their circumstances had not sparked widespread revival. God's covenant people continued to act, dress, and praise like their pagan neighbors. Using stark images of God's coming, doing battle, and bringing destruction, Zephaniah shattered their status quo. He sounded the trumpet of judgment, mercifully offering his people a final call to come clean and seek God.

Today, God's people could benefit from a similar wake-up call. The spiritual climate in the West is lukewarm, as believers have pressed the snooze button on alarming spiritual realities: the decline of biblical literacy, rise of sexual impurity, and pursuit of selfish gain. Furthermore, faith no longer claims a place of privilege or influence in society. Religious leaders are responsible for spiritual drift. Everyday believers are complicit. In an age of indifference and idolatry, the prophetic voice of the past offers an antidote. This passage serves as a plea to quit playing hide-and-seek with God.

SEEK GOD BEFORE HIS JUDGMENT COMES (1:1–2:3)

LITERARY STRUCTURE AND THEMES (1:1–2:3)

The first literary unit begins with news of God's impending plans to cut off life on the earth on the day of the Lord, including the pagan worshippers in Jerusalem (1:1–6), to search and destroy sinners from every corner of Jerusalem (1:7–13), and to pour out wrath so powerfully that no one can escape (1:14–18). Therefore, people should humble themselves and seek God's grace (2:1–3).

The main themes are that God's judgment of sinners would happen on the day of the Lord, so people needed to seek God before the day of the Lord.

- *God's Sweeping Judgment (1:1–6)*
- *God's Judgment of Jerusalem (1:7–13)*
- *The Great Terror of the Lord (1:14–18)*
- *Seek God before the Day of the Lord (2:1–3)*

EXPOSITION (1:1–2:3)

When the time was right, namely, when the Assyrian military power was weak because of Ashurbanipal's death and while Josiah was conducting a religious reform, Zephaniah confronted the people of Judah with a warning about God's coming judgment on everyone, including Judah's political and religious leaders (1:7–9). He claimed that no one, not even the rich, will be able to hide from God wrath (1:12–13). Because of the severity of God's judgment, Zephaniah called for the people to humble themselves and seek God before the commencement of that approaching day of severe judgment (2:1–3).

God's Sweeping Judgment (1:1–6)

Zephaniah proclaimed to the people of Judah (1:1) that God's powerful judgment would impact all life on earth, including life in Judah, for they would experience his punishment for their sinfulness (1:2–6).

1:1. This introductory superscription identifies the historical event when God spoke to the prophet Zephaniah during the reign of Josiah (around 625 B.C.). This introduction claims that what Zephaniah wrote on this scroll was a divine revelation, making it similar to the inspired writings of Moses and other prophets. If this is true, then the people listening to the prophet Zephaniah should accept these words as authoritative because they provide insight into God's thinking and his plans for the future.

Nothing much is known about the prophet Zephaniah except what can be gleaned from the unusually long genealogy in 1:1. Although one might be tempted to conclude that Zephaniah's father, Cushi, or his grandmother (Bruckner, 2004, 283) was an African from Ethiopia, the name Cush does not always point in that direction (Sweeney, 2003, 48–49), for at times this name appears to be an Israelite name (Jer. 36:14; Ps. 7:1). Many conclude that the ancestor four generations back was King Hezekiah (Motyer, 1998b, 898; Barker and Bailey, 1998, 408), but not all accept this conclusion because this person was not explicitly identified as a king (Achtemeier, 1986, 61). Nevertheless, it seems likely that this person was the righteous King Hezekiah, and if so, this means that Zephaniah was part of the extended royal family and probably had direct access in the royal court to give advice to King Josiah.

Josiah began to reign at age eight because his father, Amon, was murdered (2 Chron. 33:21–25; 640 B.C.) after a short two-year reign. In the eighth year of Josiah's reign (at age sixteen; 632 B.C.), he began to seek God, and then in his twelfth year (at age twenty; 628–627 B.C.), he began to remove Baalism from Judah and declared independence from Assyria after their king died (2 Chron. 34:1–7). Zephaniah's prophetic words probably came shortly after this (around 625 B.C.) and before the major reforms in Josiah's eighteenth year (Roberts, 1991, 166) when the Torah scroll was found in the temple (at age twenty-seven; 621 B.C.).

1:2. One way for the prophet to motivate his audience in Jerusalem to turn from their sinful ways and seek God was to communicate the dire consequences of not turning to God. Thus Zephaniah's initial announcement of God's complete and utter destruction of the earth was emphasized by combining "I will bring an end" (אָסֵף from סוּף) with "by gathering" (the infinitive absolute from אָסַף) everything on "the land" (הָאֲדָמָה) for judgment. The land he was referring to was the tillable, civilized world of the Fertile Crescent, which included the land of Judah and her neighbors. This "gathering" theme was consistent with the prophet's exhortation for anyone who wanted to avoid God's judgment to "gather" (2:1) and repent before God's destructive decree goes forth, as well as God's later statements that he would "gather" the nations for judgment in 3:8.

1:3. The massive extent of God's gathering was emphasized by picturing God cutting off everything living on earth, including humankind, beast, birds, and even the fish. This would be a disaster bigger than Noah's devastating flood (Gen. 6:7; 7:4, 21–23; 8:8). This would remove the wicked and their idolatrous

"stumbling-blocks" (וְהַמַּכְשֵׁלוֹת, the images, altars, and pagan gods, 1:4–6). Although this massive destruction may sound like the final day of the Lord at the end of history, the focus of this destruction in 1:4–13 was primarily on Judah and Jerusalem. Zephaniah's language is a hyperbolic way (Barker and Bailey, 1998, 411; Patterson, 2008, 455) of stressing the terrible destruction that would happen when God sent an enemy nation to bring destruction on Jerusalem and the surrounding nations (605–587 B.C.). This kind of rhetoric would catch the audience's attention and motivate them to do something to avoid God's terrible wrath.

1:4. People in Jerusalem would easily accept Zephaniah's concept of divine judgment on the wicked, so many probably assumed that Zephaniah was talking about God's punishment of other nations, not Judah. Zephaniah removed this misconception by claiming that God had a specific concern for what was happening in Judah and especially in Jerusalem. The people in Jerusalem needed to seek God (2:1–3) before God "reached out, stretched out" (from נָטָה) his mighty hand in judgment against them. This kind of action could signal God's powerful movement to (a) stretch out his hand to judge a nation, like the destruction of Egypt by the plagues (Exod. 7:5; Deut. 7: 19), his punishment on his own people in the time of Isaiah (Isa. 5:25; 9:12), or God's unstoppable plan to destroy the nations (Isa. 14:26–27). In addition, this action can signal God plans to (b) stretch out his hand to deliver his people from danger (e.g., from Egyptian slavery in Deut. 5:15; 9:29; 26:8). Zephaniah predicted that God's powerful hand would reach out against the people in Judah because of their sin. God decisively declared, "I will cut off" (1:4b; הִכְרַתִּי) five different activities, especially the activities of people involved in various types of pagan worship (the "stumbling-blocks" in 1:3; 2 Chron. 28:23). These things were especially offensive to God because they were at "this place" (הַמָּקוֹם־הַזֶּה), meaning in the courtyard of the temple in Jerusalem. The first thing God would cut off would be the remaining Baal idols and altars as well as the remnant of people who still worshipped the fertility god Baal. Josiah began to remove Baal worship in his twelfth year (628–27 B.C.), but he had not eliminated all of it by 625 B.C. Second, God would remove even the recollection of the names of the "cultic officials" (הַכְּמָרִים) who served pagan gods along with any Israelite priests at these pagan places of worship (1:4). The term "cultic officials" (הַכְּמָרִים) is rare, but elsewhere it refers to non-Levitical priests serving at the golden calf at Bethel (Hos. 10:5) or the pagan priests who offered incense to Baal, the moon god, or other deities represented by stars and planets (2 Kings 23:5).

WORD ANALYSIS: The word הַמָּקוֹם refers to "the place" where God was worshipped. God directed Abraham to offer his son Isaac at a "place" (Gen. 22:9, 14) on Mount Moriah, and later God said that he would choose a "place" (Deut. 12:5, 11, 14) for his name to dwell so people could worship him there. God revealed this place to David when he offered a sacrifice after he sinned by numbering his people (1 Chron. 22:1), and Solomon built the temple on the "place" (2 Chron. 3:1) on Mount Moriah. This was the "place" (2 Chron. 6:20, 21, 26) where God would dwell among his people, where people could pray to God for the forgiveness of sins.

1:5–6. Third, God was against the common Israelites who worshipped the sun, moon, and stars at private shrines constructed on the roofs of homes (1:5a), activities outlawed in Deuteronomy 4:19; 17:3–7. This worship was common in the time of Manasseh and Amon (2 Kings 21:3–5, 21; 2 Chron. 33:3–5) and was condemned by the prophet Jeremiah (Jer. 7:18; 8:2; 19:13; 44:19). Fourth, God's wrath would fall on the people who syncretisticly

honored other gods such as "Milcom" (RSV, NEB, NASB[95], HCSB, an Ammonite god; 2 Kings 23:13) or "Molech" (NIV, a Canaanite god; 2 Kings 21:6; 23:10) and at the same time swore loyalty to Yahweh, the God of Judah (Zeph. 1:5b; cf. Josh. 2:12; 9:19). These signs of hypocrisy were unacceptable to God. Finally, the fifth group of people (Zeph. 1:6) were those who acted unfaithfully by completely ignoring God, turning away from the things of God, and not even bothering to "seek" (בָּקַשׁ) after God or "inquire" (דָּרַשׁ) of God in prayer. These people purposely rejected the idea of following God's instructions, rejected God's wisdom, and had no interest in developing a personal relationship with God.

Standing Stones representing two gods at the Arad Temple in southern Judah. Two incense altars stand at the entrance to this holy of holies. Courtesy of Acer11 / CC BY-SA (https://creativecommons.org/licenses/by-sa/3.0).

God's Judgment in Jerusalem (1:7–13)

In order to prepare the people of Judah for God's coming judgment, Zephaniah explained how God's wrath would impact Jerusalem's political and religious leaders (vv. 7–9), causing everyone in Jerusalem to grieve (vv. 10–11), for no one could hide from God (vv. 12–13).

1:7. The prophet called for silence to bring attention to the seriousness of the moment, the awesomeness of God's glory that will appear in a theophany, and the gravity of God's actions (1:7a). Earlier the prophet Amos called for silence (Amos 6:10; 8:3) in the midst of many dead bodies caused by God's terrifying, destructive presence in Israel. Later, the prophets Habakkuk and Zechariah (Hab. 2:20; Zech. 2:13 [2:17]) would call for silence as they stand in the presence of God. This command for silence involved respect, submission, fear, and humility before Almighty God. If the people would follow this approach, it would prepare them to humble themselves and seek God (Zeph. 2:1–3). The prophet's audience needed to hush immediately because God's glorious appearance in frightening judgment was very near. They did not have years to waste or lots of time to debate what they should do. God was about to enter into their world in devastating ways.

The day of the Lord was a time when God powerfully intervened in the affairs of all people, and its origin may go back to holy war experiences when God's power decisively defeated his enemies.[1] This day seemed to be a well-known concept in Israel at the time of Amos (760 B.C.) and in Judah at the time of Isaiah (750–690 B.C.). This was a day when God would dramatically show his power, sometimes in a theophany by defeating Judah's enemies (the Egyptian army at the Red Sea in Exod. 14–15), so Amos's audience in Israel probably thought that this would be a positive day for them because God would defeat their enemies

(as in Amos 5:18–20). Amos shocked his audience by announcing that the sinful people of Israel were among God's enemies, so they would see only darkness and gloom on that day. In a similar manner, Zephaniah emphasized the negative characteristics of the day of the Lord for the people in Judah (Zeph. 1:4–13), so he probably surprised many by the idea that Judah would soon (the day is "near" קָרוֹב, not in the distant future) experience God's wrath.

Equally confusing to some would be Zephaniah's announcement that God had prepared a sacrifice (Zeph. 1:7) and had consecrated "his guests" (קְרֻאָיו "his called ones") who were "consecrated, set apart" (הִקְדִּישׁ). The irony here is that the "consecrated called ones" would be the ones God would sacrifice. Probably some in Jerusalem thought that they would be God's guests who would enjoy this feast (cf. Exod. 24:9–11; Isa. 25:6–10), but that possibility is removed in the following verses. Since God does not sin, he did not need to bring a sacrificial offering, so the use of the sacrificial metaphor here must be for the purpose of providing a sacrificial banquet (Patterson, 1991, 311–12). This was the case in Isaiah 34:1–7 when God announced that he would sacrifice Edom (a symbol of the nations) on the final day of the Lord, in Ezekiel 39:17–20 when Gog and Magog would be defeated and sacrificed, and in Revelation 19:17–21 where the King of kings would destroy the beast and his armies in preparation for the feast of God (Motyer, 1998b, 918).

1:8. This verse gives a fuller description of some of the specifics concerning what would happen on the day of the Lord. First, Zephaniah clarified that on the day when God sacrifices, he would punish various political leaders, the king's sons, and all who wear foreign clothes (like the clothes worn by the royal officials in Assyria in the relief below). None of these individuals were

---

1   Gerhard von Rad, *Old Testament Theology*, trans. D. M. G. Stalker (New York: Harper & Row, 1965), 2:119–25.

named, but they must have been officials in the royal court in Jerusalem (Sweeney, 2003, 84) as well as the children of the past kings (Manasseh and Amon—Josiah was still quite young) who ran various parts of the government, plus Judean and Assyrian officials who wore Assyrian clothing. The prophet's description did not refer to strange clothes worn by the pagan priests (Baker, 1988, 95; Robertson, 1990, 276); rather, this was an example of how strongly Assyrian culture had influenced the leadership in Jerusalem. Some political leaders in Judah no longer dressed in their traditional Judean garb but for political purposes identified with their foreign rulers. Notice though that there is no condemnation of the king himself, for Josiah was still a young man who was seeking God and attempting to remove the influence of Baalism and other pagan religious practices (2 Chron. 34:1–7). Maybe God would remove these political leaders because they did not support Josiah reforms. There was a political movement away from Assyria, which began in 628–627 B.C. (a couple years before Zephaniah's prophecy) when Josiah declared independence from Assyria, but Zephaniah foresaw a future time when the lingering influence of Assyria would be totally removed.

1:9. There is a fair bit of ambiguity surrounding the interpretation of Zephaniah 1:9. Contextually, one might think this verse should refer to the sins of the political leaders in 1:8, especially the reference to violence and deceit in 1:9b. But many (Bruckner, 2004, 288; Patterson, 2008, 457; Vlaardingerbroek, 1999, 87–89) believe "leaping over the threshold" refers to religious syncretism by priests in Judah who were adopting the superstitious religious practices of the Philistines (1 Sam. 5:4–5). Since the Philistine idol Dagan fell on the threshold of the temple of Dagan and broke apart, the Philistine priests did not step on the thresholds of that temple. It is not clear who committed the violence in 1:9b. It could refer to violence in the house (the palace) of their lord the king or to the priests filling the temple of their gods with the results of violence and deceit (Walker, 1985, 547). In either case, the religious officials displeased God and ignored God's condemnation of such acts. Once the moral foundation of the nation was eroded, violence and deceit became the means of accomplishing their goals. Jeremiah condemned the people of Judah in the early years of Josiah for stealing, murdering, adultery, and perjury (Jer. 7:1–9), accusations that fit with the observations of Zephaniah.

Clothes worn at Ashurbanipal's Garden Feast, seventh century B.C. Courtesy of Daderot.

1:10. The need for the people to seek God and humble themselves is heightened by (a) the severity of God's destructive visitation on his people, (b) the number of people affected by God's judgment, and (c) the strength of the peoples' emotional response to his action. On this near and approaching day of the Lord, people would wail when they see what the destructive hand of God would do to the people of Jerusalem and the walls of the city. God would visit many parts of Jerusalem, especially the commercial districts. This would include the area around the Fish Gate on the north side of Jerusalem (cf. 2 Chron. 33:14; Neh. 3:3; 12:39; 13:16) where people bought and sold fish (Zeph. 1:10). It is possible this was another name for the Ephraim Gate (2 Kings 14:13; 2 Chron. 25:23), which was on the northern wall (Sweeney, 2003, 89). Another place where people would suffer under God's judgment would be the Second District ("the New Quarter," Zeph. 1:10 NIV), the area west of the city of David and the temple. Hezekiah put walls around this area because a large expansion of the population settled around Jerusalem. In addition, Zephaniah mentioned that a loud sound would come from the hills around Jerusalem, a sound that would come from the destruction of walls as they crashed to the ground.

1:11. Another area God would visit would be a low, hollowed-out location in Jerusalem that may have originally been a quarry (1:11; the "Mortar" NASB[95], NRSV; "market district" NIV, NLT[SE]; the "Hollows" HCSB; Lower Hollows" CEV), possibly a commercial area where the merchants (or the Canaanites) bought and sold goods in the Tyropoeon Valley. These people would wail at first, but then the horror of the situation would bring silence to the area because all these wealthy people would die (נִכְרְתוּ, lit., "they will be cut off"). This would mean that the beauty, vibrancy, culture, and riches of Jerusalem would come to an end on the day of the Lord.

1:12. At that time (the day of the Lord), God would thoroughly search (אֲחַפֵּשׂ, "I will search") Jerusalem. The intensity of the search was described by picturing God checking the darkest hiding places with a lamp. This implies that no one would be able to hide from God's eyes or escape his punishment (cf. Amos 9:2–4). God would punish the people who are "thickened upon their lees" (הַקֹּפְאִים עַל־שִׁמְרֵיהֶם). This metaphor comes from the process of making wine. The lees are the sediments of the grapes that give the wine color, body, and flavor. Over time they gradually settle to the bottom of the container holding the wine, but at an appropriate time the good wine must be poured off into another container because eventually the lees (sediments) will turn into a thick, congealed, syrupy mixture that can mold and spoil the good wine. One can view this metaphor as referring to people who are drunk from drinking this syrupy mixture, but it probably refers more directly to the difficult, thick, confused, and complacent way of thinking these people have. These people were having difficulty thinking about the place God played in their lives (Zeph. 1:12b). They discounted God as a determining force in their past as well as their future. This way of thinking was connected to the fact that these people were self-sufficient and wealthy members of high society (1:13) who had achieved status and power on their own. They felt that God had nothing to do with their great accomplishments (cf. James 4:13–17). This was similar to the attitude of the people in Zephaniah 1:6, for in both cases people ignored God and did not give him credit for blessing them. In their minds God was irrelevant, but in Zephaniah's day it was rare to find people like this who were "irreligious."

This was uncommon in the ancient Near East, for most people in every culture (Egypt, Mesopotamia, Canaan, etc.) believed that the gods determined what would happen in their lives. People who did not believe the gods were in control of the world were rare, so it is doubly surprising to find that there were people in Judah when Zephaniah prophesied who did not believe that God was the power behind what happened in their lives. Isaiah 5:18–24 refers to a similar group of people who thought God did not control what happened in this world.

TRANSLATION ANALYSIS: הַקֹּפְאִים עַל־שִׁמְרֵיהֶם
"thickened upon their lees"

NASB[95]	"who are stagnant in spirit"
NIV	"who are complacent"
NRSV	"who rest complacently"
NKJV	"who settle in complacently"
HCSB	"who settle down comfortably"

1:13. This way of thinking would soon change, for on the day of the Lord, God would be very involved with their lives. He would demonstrate his sovereignty by allowing others to take away their money and plunder their valuable possessions. They would learn that God's covenant curses were real and that their future would be totally dependent on what God would decide to do with them. God would control the future; he would not reward these wealthy sinners, and they would not enjoy the fruits of their labor. Instead, God would take away their homes and decimate their farms and vineyards (1:13; cf. Amos 5:11; Deut. 28:30–34)[2] if they did not seek God (Zeph. 2:1–3).

The Great Terror of the Lord (1:14–18)

Just before Zephaniah's dramatic call for people

to humble themselves and seek God (2:1–3), the prophet added a couple additional reasons why the audience in Jerusalem should think clearly, act wisely, and humble themselves before God gives the decree that would start the day of the Lord (i.e., the day of Judah's destruction).

1:14. The repeated use of the word "day" (יוֹם) with a variety of terrifying modifiers described the impact of a theophany appearance of God (Robertson, 1990, 282) to execute a holy war (Achtemeier, 1986, 71) against his enemies. Zephaniah began by reminding his audience again (as in 1:7) that this great day of the Lord was in the very near future. In fact, it was approaching "quickly" (מְהֵר); there was no time to waste. In order to stir people to action and to provide proof of this great calamity, the prophet described what would happen. They would soon hear the "screams, desperate cries" (צְרַח) of the defeated warriors of Judah (1:14b).

1:15–16. This day would be horrific almost beyond description. The prophet piled up several negative adjectives in order to emphasize

---

2 Delbert Hillers notes the similarity between political treaty curses that promise a life of futility without rewards for your work and prophetic curses in which God states that a person would not be able to enjoy what they have worked to build (cf. Hos. 4:10; Hag. 1:6). Delbert R. Hillers, *Treaty-Curses and the Old Testament Prophets*, BibOr 16 (Rome: Pontifical Biblical Institute, 1964), 28–29.

the emotional and physical terror of that day. It would be a day when the full power of God's wrath (cf. Isa. 13:9; Ezek. 7:19) would cause great distress and psychological "stress" (Sweeney, 2003, 99). This destruction would make cities desolate, dark (due to burning), and full of gloom (cf. Joel 2:2). One could associate the clouds and thick darkness with an eclipse, the theophany appearance of God (Exod. 19:18; 20:18; Berlin, 1994, 90; Motyer, 1998b, 923), or the effects of God's wrath on the burning city. The day of the Lord would involve a military battle (Zeph. 1:16), including the trumpet call to fight and the shrieking screams of enemy troops as they charged into hand-to-hand combat against Judah's major fortified cities (including Jerusalem) in order to topple their defenses. This may be a prophecy about the Babylonian army that would devastate Jerusalem in the coming years (2 Kings 25; Jer. 39; 52), but it was clearly an act of God.

1:17. If there was still any doubt about why these people needed to seek God and repent, Zephaniah offered some additional reasons. The unambiguous rationale for God's severe affliction of the human population of Jerusalem was their sin against God. This reinforced the direct link between the unfaithful acts of rejecting God and worshipping pagan gods (1:4–6) with the destructive action of God on the day of the Lord. Although one might connect this verse to an eschatological destruction of all humankind (cf. 1:2–3), the context of 1:4–13 points to the sinfulness of the people in Judah and the human suffering that would happen when a foreign army would defeat Jerusalem in the near future. The savagery of this war would result in the sight of dead bodies surrounded by blood with their bowels pouring out of rotting carcasses. In the midst of this unimaginable nightmare the people, would become disoriented, confused, and filled with panic, so they would stumble around like blind people (1:17; cf. Isa. 59:10).

1:18. Although some of the wealthy among the upper class might have thought that they could buy their way out of trouble by bribing soldiers for special favors, this would be futile (cf. Ezek. 7:19). Escape from God's wrath would be impossible, and any attempt to gain deliverance from the Babylonian army would not work. The reason this judgment would be so severe was because God was extremely zealous about his love for his people and their love for him (Zeph. 1:18b). Thus he would not allow his covenant people to be unfaithful and worship other gods (cf. 1:4–6). The nation's sinfulness would cause God to zealously punish them if they did not choose to change their ways and seek God.

Contrasting Destinies on the Day of the Lord

God's curse on his enemies
1:2–3	Massive destruction of life
1:4–6	Removal of false religions
1:14–16	War, distress, destruction, darkness
1:17–18	Confusion and blood everywhere
1:18	No escape from God's wrath

God's blessing on the righteous
3:9	Restoration of those who serve God
3:12	No one would be ashamed
3:13–16	No need to fear
3:17	God would rejoice over and love his people
3:18–20	God would gather and make them famous

Seek God before the Day of the Lord (2:1–3)
In spite of the coming judgment, there was hope for those who humble themselves and seek the Lord.

2:1–2. The climactic call to action at the end of this first message contains two calls (2:1; 2:3) for two different audiences to take immediate action in order to influence God's response through their prayers. The first instruction was addressed to the "nation" (גּוֹי), a term that usually was applied to the pagan nations. In this context Judah was not addressed as "my people"; instead, they were described as a "nation" (גּוֹי), "not desired" (לֹא נִכְסָף). They were called to action with an emphatic (the verb is used twice) imperative call to "gather together" (קֹשֵּׁשׁ), "gather" (קֹשֵּׁשׁ) before the time when God would give the decree for the day of the Lord to begin. In 2:2 the prophet repeated his encouragement for quick action "before" (used three times in this verse) the day of God's decree (it could happen quickly), for then God's anger would fall on them. Although this group should respond positively to the prophet's challenge, their past undesirable status as a "pagan nation" (גּוֹי) and their past sinfulness (1:4–6) raised doubts about this. About this same time, the prophet Jeremiah reported that "no one repents of his sin" (Jer. 8:6) and that they claimed, "I am innocent, surely his anger will turn away from me" (Jer. 2:35).

WORD ANALYSIS: This root כָּסַף is used only five times in the OT. In four contexts, it refers to a "longing for, being eager, desiring" (Gen. 31:30; Job 14:15; Ps. 17:12) as in Psalm 84:2, "My soul longs for, even yearns for the courts of the LORD." The Bible translations render the usage of this term in Zephaniah 2:1 in two different ways: either (a) "undesirable" (HCSB, NKJV) or (b) "shameless" (RSV, NRSV), "shameful" (NIV), or "without shame" (NASB[95]). This latter option is based on the Akkadian meaning "be pale, ashamed," but either meaning can make sense in this context.

2:3. Consequently, the prophet challenged the humble people in Judah who followed the law of God to act on behalf of the nation. Some (Robertson, 1990, 294) connect the "humble, meek" (עָנָו) with the people of the land who put Josiah on the throne (2 Kings 21:23–24; 2 Chron. 33:24–25), but this reads

too much into this designation. The humble people were those at the bottom of the social order, not the king makers. They were the people who had broken and contrite hearts before God (Ps. 34:18), who recognized their sinfulness, repented (Ps. 51:17), and trembled at what God said (Isa. 66:2). Those who sought the Lord were those who rejected wickedness and turned to the Lord because he was a God of compassion (Isa. 55:6–7). The humble were dependent on God and can be contrasted with the proud who were self-sufficient. God's desired for them to do three things: "seek the LORD . . . seek righteousness, seek humility" (Zeph. 2:3). As intercessors for their nation these humble people needed to seek God's mercy by crying out to him in prayer (Ps. 10:17), by pleading with God to graciously intervene on their behalf (cf. Jer. 14:17–22), and by submitting themselves to the will of God.

> **Judah's Political Hierarchy**
> - **Kings**: often based on firstborn son in a royal family
> - **Royal Family**: close family ties led to favors
> - **Nobles**: wealth and power gave influence
> - **High Priest**: controlled temple wealth and anointed kings
> - **Merchants**: loaned money and owned property/goods
> - **Farmers, herders**: no control over weather or prices for goods
> - **Orphans, widows, aliens**: no power, often abused

The prophet did not promise that this intercession would cause God to reverse his decision and not bring the frightful day of the Lord on Judah. He was fully convinced that a terrible judgment would fall on the nation in the coming days. He believed that the humble prayers of the righteous can influence God's action, but he offered only a "perhaps" (אוּלַי) God would have mercy and some might be hidden from his wrath.

This perspective "safeguards God's sovereign freedom . . . [but] God's forgiveness should not be misused as 'cheap grace'" (Baker, 1988, 104).

THEOLOGICAL FOCUS

The exegetical idea (Zephaniah supported Josiah's reform by warning that God would judge all forms of false worship in Jerusalem on the approaching day of the Lord [1:1–15], so the only hope was for people to turn away from their sinful ways, humble themselves, and intercede for God's mercy before the beginning of the day of the Lord [2:1–3]) leads to this theological focus: Since one cannot hide from God's judgment, the prophet tries to motivate people to humble themselves and seek God before he executes his wrath on them. God's eventual judgment of anyone who does not honor him is a motivating factor for people to be humble and seek God before God executes his judgment.

Two theological themes are emphasized in this section: (1) divine judgment and (2) the necessity for God's people to seek God and repent. First, the basis for God's judgment was (a) God's holiness and complete separation from anyone or anything that was sinful and (b) his all-powerful sovereign control of this world (Zeph. 1:2–3). This control involved both the pouring out of his terrible wrath on the wicked on the day of the Lord (1:14–16) and the gift of his great blessings on the righteous who humble themselves and seek God (3:9–20). His covenant with Israel at Mount Sinai indicated that God would send blessings on those who love him, fear him, worship him, and obey him (Deut. 6:5; 12:10; 28:1–14), but he would pour out the wrath of his curses on those who refuse to honor him as their God (Deut. 27:15–26; 28:15–68). For years the Israelites worshipped pagan gods, especially during the years of Manasseh and Amon (2 Chron. 33). Now it was time to face the wrath of God's curses that would come on the day of the Lord. The city of Jerusalem would soon suffer defeat because the people worshipped other gods (Zeph. 1:4–6).

Second, the necessity for people to repent appears in Zephaniah's call for national repentance (Zeph. 2:1–3) in support of Josiah's reforms. Specifically, the prophet challenged the humble believers in Judah to intercede for God's forgiveness. God did not want any to perish (cf. Ezek. 18:23), so people needed to confess their sins and appeal to him for mercy. The rationale behind this call for repentance was supported not just by the desire to avoid God's wrath, but later in Zephaniah 3:9–20 by a deep desire to participate in the glorious kingdom of God where God would reign as king over the people he loves.

PREACHING AND TEACHING STRATEGIES

Exegetical and Theological Synthesis

Zephaniah 1:1–2:3 stresses the reality of God's judgment: its immanence, intensity, and inclusivity. The exegetical section spells out both the intended audience of God's judgment—Judah and her leaders—and its effects—grief, darkness, desolation, and exile. The prophet employs dramatic imagery, reminiscent of Noah's flood (Gen. 6–8) and Sinai's curses (Deut. 28), to describe God's wrath and the coming "day of the LORD."

Modern readers may chafe against the idea of a day of reckoning, but most people are not without a desire for justice. The proliferation of TV dramas, bestselling novels, and superhero films betray the universal hunger for law and order. However, people often fail to see themselves in the cosmic drama, where God acts as eternal judge and divine prosecutor. People often fail to see their culpability in God's case against sinful people. Modern idols are less evident than the handcrafted gods of Israel's day (Isa. 44:9–20), but modern people take an endless number of substitutes for God as their primary escape, first joy in life, or ultimate source of meaning. For example, sex, health, power, success, family, entertainment, or alcohol may all be modern-day idols.

Moreover, the rest of our rap sheet bears a striking resemblance to the criminal record for people in Zephaniah's day. The prophet indicts Israel for the sins of syncretism (Zeph. 1:4–5), self-sufficiency (v. 6), and stagnant faith (v. 12). Syncretism blends pop culture and folk religion with biblical values. The church often apes its culture in worship expressions, media usage, and sexual ethic. Self-sufficiency puts personal resources before God. We rely more on finances and health, innate talent and learned skills, accrued wisdom and experience than patiently seeking God's direction. Finally, stagnant faith emerges where religious privilege formerly reigned. In this context, people do not pursue God but assume he waits in the background of their lives ready to help when crises arise. The blend of syncretism, self-sufficiency, and stagnant faith exposes the pressing need for revival.

Preaching Idea
Quit playing hide-and-seek with God.

Contemporary Connections

What does it mean?
What does it mean to play hide-and-seek with God? What makes it hard to quit this childish game? People are accustomed to hiding their sins from God. Adam set a precedent in the garden of Eden, ducking behind a tree after breaking his Creator's command (Gen. 3:8). Achan buried gold under his tent that God had declared "under the ban" (Josh. 7:21). King David stayed silent about his adulterous affair with Bathsheba (2 Sam. 12:12). Jonah holed up in a boat heading in the opposite direction of Nineveh where God called him to preach (Jonah 1:5). In each case, God summoned his people from hiding so they could own their misdeeds.

While we knowingly conceal socially unacceptable sins (e.g., pornography, drug usage, abuse), other offenses remain hidden even from ourselves. Spiritual indifference and idolatry often hide in plain sight. The rise of pluralism, campaign for tolerance, privatization of religion, and erosion of truth have fed spiritual indifference. We feel powerless against the current of culture. Over time our defensive posture turns indifferent, and we slowly adopt secular values of health, wealth, and personal happiness as biblical rights. Once enshrined, these cultural values become idols, albeit hidden from us. And only when our lives come crashing down do idolatry and indifference rise to the surface. A pastor may not admit his indifference until his church attendance plummets. A woman may not realize her marriage is an idol until it teeters on the edge of dissolution. A young man may not notice his body image is an idol until he faces a major medical crisis.

Rather than hiding in the shadows of indifference and idolatry, God's people should heed Zephaniah's call to come out of hiding through confession (Zeph. 2:3). The OT narrative is dotted with dramatic confessions. The personal laments of David (Pss. 32, 51) and corporate cry of Nehemiah (Neh. 9) are profound examples of admitting guilt and seeking forgiveness. After Solomon dedicated the temple, God promised to hear, forgive, and heal his people when they come out of hiding (2 Chron. 7:14). Confession restores our relationship with God and brings our sin into the light of his forgiveness (Ps. 103; cf. 1 John 1:9).

Is it true?
Do we play hide-and-seek with God? Do we conceal our spiritual indifference and idolatry from him? Indeed, we do. Spiritual indifference and idolatry are a problem for God's people today. According to sociologist Christian Smith (2009), many self-proclaimed, twenty-something Christians reflect something less

than a hearty devotion to God.[3] He coined the term "moralistic therapeutic deism" to describe a shallow belief in a god who makes us feel good when we do good. Such theology is thoroughly secular, bearing the fingerprints of pop psychology and pragmatism. Moralistic therapeutic deism has crafted an idol.

But we cannot blame secular influences alone for producing spiritual foment. The status quo may also lead to indifference and idolatry. The wilderness generation became indifferent to God's daily, miraculous supply of manna (Num. 11). Spiritual indifference marked the generation that succeeded Joshua and settled in the Promised Land (Judg. 2:10–23). Israel's subsequent protests for a king betrayed the nation's indifference to God's reign (1 Sam. 8:1–9). Sadly, most of the kings in Israel's history rated poorly for their allowance of high places and tolerance of idols (e.g., 1 Kings 17:7–17).

Thus, the prophetic refrain—to seek God, come out of hiding, and confess our sins—promises spiritual renewal. If indifference is a fog, then coming clean is a blue sky. The prophet Isaiah considered confession a reasonable act, necessary for securing God's forgiveness (Isa. 1:16–18). Confession should be humble and earnest, not a formality. God sees our hearts (Ps. 139:23–24). Simply going through the motions does not guarantee his grace but likely reinforces our indifference.

Now what?

What are appropriate ways to bring our spiritual indifference and idolatry into the light? Does God's plea to come out of hiding require believers to practice unfiltered, public confession? These are important questions in the digital age. Too many people use social media as an emotional dumping ground, airing out their loneliness or broadcasting their rage. The Internet is a poor confession booth. God should be our primary audience for self-disclosure.

When we come to God, we should show personal awareness, humility, and knowledge of him. Since spiritual indifference conceals itself, some form of self-evaluation might prove helpful. Certain passages of Scripture or accountability questions can prompt spiritual introspection.

Self-evaluation Scriptures and Reflection Questions

Pray Psalm 139:23–34 (NASB[95]): "Search me, O God, and know my heart; try me and know my anxious thoughts; and see if there be any hurtful way in me, and lead me in the everlasting way."

Use these Scriptures to direct self-evaluation (Pss. 15:1–5; 19:13; 24:3–6; Prov. 4:23–27; 6:16–19)

Ask the following questions:
1. How hot or cold has my love toward God and others been recently?
2. What idols have crept into my heart and taken hold of it?
3. How honest have I been with my spouse, friends, and coworkers?
4. Where have I shown haste rather than restraint?
5. Where have I shown self-reliance rather than dependence on God?
6. In what areas does my life reflect holiness? Where is holiness lacking?

---

3   While millennials may be prone to moralistic therapeutic deism, Christian Smith notes that they learned it from their elders. In fact, older generations often get stuck in spiritual routines and traditions, and are more likely to issue complaints than initiate changes. Their "good-old-days" god would not condone tattoos but might tolerate sexism. Christian Smith, with Patricia Snell, *Souls in Transition: The Religious and Spiritual Lives of Emerging Adults* (London: Oxford University Press, 2009), 115, see also Ch. 8.

Self-evaluation may be bolstered by honest feedback from trustworthy friends. Having one or two accountability partners—people who regularly speak into our lives with candor—exposes blind spots. Granting access to others to challenge, admonish, and rebuke us requires humility. But such humility keeps us from living hidden in the shadows.

Finally, true knowledge of God makes coming out of hiding and seeking forgiveness more urgent. Too many believers settle for simplistic portraits of God, ignoring justice and wrath as central to his holy character. They conceive of a god who is indifferent to their moral lapses and many idols; they become like the god they worship (Beale, 2008). God forgives, but not without a cost. He blesses, but not free of charge. Seeking God's forgiveness means doing robust theology.

Creativity in Presentation

Most people can relate to the children's game Hide-and-Seek. Consider soliciting a few volunteers and staging a game in the worship center. Identify a seeker who will close his eyes and count to twenty, giving the volunteers a chance to conceal themselves. Take no more than two minutes for the illustration. After finding one or two participants, give the "Come out, come out, wherever you are" cry, followed by "All ye, all ye, in come free." Ask one of the hidden people to describe what it felt like to have someone draw close to their hiding spot and eventually find them. Ask another to share her relief at getting the "Come in free" call.

Setting Up a Hide-and-Seek Game

1. Designate boundaries in the church building where people can hide. Don't let them get too far from the worship center, since you have a limited amount of time.
2. Preselect four to five volunteers to hide.
3. Identify one volunteer as the Seeker, who will close his eyes and count to twenty.
4. The other three to four volunteers are Hiders, who will find a place to conceal themselves during game.
5. Set a 90-second timer once the Seeker begins to hunt for Hiders.
6. Play background music.
7. After timer sounds, stop music and invite the congregation to shout with you the following: "Come out, come out, wherever you are." And: "All ye, all ye, in come free."
8. Ask 1 Hider: "How did it feel to get found?"
9. Ask 1 Hider: "How did it feel to hear the 'in come free' all?"

Edgar Allen Poe's story "A Telltale Heart" or Dostoyevsky's ([1866] 2008) novel, *Crime and Punishment*, both capture the havoc that hidden sin wreaks over the course of time. In the adapted-for-film courtroom drama *A Few Good Men* (directed by Rob Reiner, 1992), Lieutenant Daniel Kaffee (played by Tom Cruise) presses Colonel Nathan Jessup (played by Jack Nicholson) to confess his cover-up in a murder case. "I want the truth!" Kaffee demands. Indignantly, Jessup offers his classic retort: "You can't handle the truth!" Within minutes Jessup comes of out hiding and gives a full confession of the events. Each of these examples illustrates the challenge of coming clean, as well as the self-destructive effects (perhaps a natural means of God's punishment) of keeping one's crimes hidden.

Of course, modern examples of business professionals exposed for embezzling (e.g., Enron, 2001), athletes outed for performance-enhancing drugs (e.g., Olympic medalist Marion Jones, 2007), entertainers criminalized for sexual abuse (e.g., Bill Cosby, 2017), or politicians caught in scandal (e.g., Nixon, 1974) abound. These are cautionary tales you may recall of men and women whose hidden sins came back to haunt them.

As effective as biblical, literary, and historical examples may be, the preacher should guard against presenting spiritual indifference and idolatry as a problem for "others." According to Zephaniah, indifference and idolatry infect every human heart. To encourage self-examination, consider setting up several large mirrors around the worship area. Keep a mirror on the stage to reference throughout the message. At some point, stand before it and ask the self-evaluation questions aloud (see sidebar above), modeling their power in surfacing spiritual indifference.

Ultimately, the message should depict God's judgment of everyone who does not honor him as a motivating factor for people to humble themselves and seek God before he executes wrath on them. Hence, we should quit playing hide-and-seek with God.

- God doesn't hide his coming judgment (1:1–6).

- God calls us out of hiding (1:7–13).

- God sends his sweeping judgment (1:14–18).

- Seeking God may spare us (2:1–3).

DISCUSSION QUESTIONS

1. In what ways does the prophecy of Zephaniah help you understand the severity of God's wrath as well as the goodness of the Lord?

2. What would you consider to be the most common idols of our day?

3. What are the signs of spiritual complacency and how serious a problem is it?

4. What sort of spiritual self-analysis keeps you from becoming indifferent or idolatrous? Who else speaks into your spiritual life to keep you honest?

5. What are the benefits to confession? What are potential ramifications if you choose not to confess your sins?

Zephaniah 2:4–3:8

EXEGETICAL IDEA

The Lord would judge the nations for their pride (2:4–10) and people in Jerusalem for not trusting God or accepting correction (3:1–8), but he would bless a remnant of Judah (2:7a, 9b) and many from the nations who honor God (2:11).

THEOLOGICAL FOCUS

God will punish those who refuse to accept correction, as well as those who have oppressed God's people, so that people will repent and worship God.

PREACHING IDEA

When people all around you fall, check your path for pitfalls.

PREACHING POINTS

Zephaniah circled the compass to point out neighbors on every side of Judah who would face God's judgment. If the original audience in Jerusalem heard these oracles in a spirit of self-righteousness or indifference, the prophet disturbed their peace by pointing the finger at guilty Jerusalem. She was not immune to God's discipline; her record of wrongs had not gone unnoticed. The message was a warning to God's people to check their path for pitfalls after watching their neighbors stumble.

God's people today continue to wrestle with a sense of immunity to his discipline. Diagnosing God's judgment is slippery business, but it does not take a sage to see that others fall. All around us people's lives come crashing down: their marriages crumble, their businesses tank, their nations implode with civil war, their social circles shrink to a point, or their bodies bend to the will of cancer. Some falls may be bad luck or happenstance in a fallen world. But many falls are propelled by foolish choices and arrogance. This section urges us to check our path for pitfalls when people all around us fall.

REASONS WHY THE REMNANT SHOULD HAVE HOPE (2:4–3:8)

LITERARY STRUCTURE AND THEMES (2:4–3:8)

Zephaniah motivated the people in Judah to seek God by contrasting what God would do for the righteous remnant of Judah and God's judgment of two groups: (a) the proud and sinful nations (2:4–15) and (b) those in Judah who refused to trust God, would not accept correction, and oppressed others (3:1–8).

The themes emphasized here explain why God would judge the nations and Judah (including taunting God's people, pride, refusing to listen to God, refusing to trust God, violence, and profaning God's temple), and the result of this great devastation of this earth would be that people would worship God (2:11) and some would be restored back to Judah (2:7, 9b).

- *Woe Philistia: The Remnant Will Inherit Your Land (2:4–7)*
- *God Will Judge Moab's and Ammon's Arrogance, but Some Will Honor God (2:8–11)*
- *Pride Brings Destruction to Cush and Assyria (2:12–15)*
- *Jerusalem's Judgment (3:1–5)*
- *Learn and Wait in Hope (3:6–8)*

EXPOSITION (2:4–3:8)

The problems on earth were not limited just to the failures of those living in Judah. People in the nations around Judah would also experience God's wrath for their violence, worship of idols, and their arrogance as well as for their mistreatment of God's people. The political demise of the Neo-Assyrian Empire meant that the strong hand of Assyrian control was not as tight, so nations thought they could misbehave and get away with it. But God saw what they were doing and noticed how they mistreated weaker neighbors such as Judah, so he would hold them accountable, just like Judah would be held accountable.

Woe Philistia: The Remnant Will Inherit Your Land (2:4–7)

God would give Philistia's desolate land to the remnant of Judah.

2:4–6. Zephaniah used God's plans for Philistia (with a woe oracle in 2:5) to warn his audience in Judah (with a woe oracle in 3:1) about the seriousness of God's destructive threats and to encourage the remnant in Judah to be humble and seek God (as 2:1–3 instructed them) so they would not have to go through what Philistia would endure. Many in Jerusalem would find it easy to accept the idea that God would judge the Philistines, a perennial enemy on Judah's western border, but would find it more difficult to accept the idea that Jerusalem would suffer a similar punishment.

> **Woe Oracles**
>
> A woe oracle came out of the experience of lamenting a person's death or the news that someone was about to die. Zephaniah was announcing that the Philistines would soon be crying out in laments of woe because of the destruction that God would bring on them. In these cultures, men and women would loudly show their emotional grief and lament for days. They were not emotionally reserved and stoical like many people in our culture.

At first the prophet warned that God would destroy the four major cities of Philistia (Gaza, Ashkelon, Ashdod, and Ekron)[1] in southwest Canaan and depopulate them (2:4). The fifth city of Gath was not mentioned (also omitted in Jer. 25:20) because at this time Gath was under Judah's control (2 Chron. 26:6). In this woe oracle (Zeph. 2:5), Zephaniah lamented the terrible fate of the Philistines (called Cherethites from Caphtor or Crete; Deut. 2:23). Because the word of God was against these cities by the Mediterranean Sea (Zeph. 2:5), their "portion of land by the sea/coastal territory" (חֶבֶל הַיָּם) would be decimated and unoccupied, and the destroyed Philistine cities would serve as a place for shepherds to seek shelter ("make encampments" [כְּרֹתִים]) for their sheep among the abandoned buildings in the evening.

2:7. This prophecy against Philistia, however, ended with a positive promise to the remnant of Judah (2:7), which provided additional motivation for the people of Judah to seek God (2:2–3). The remnant refers to the righteous people who would be left after the judgment of Judah in 3:1–5. This concept gave hope to the righteous, but it implied that only a few from Judah would survive (Baker, 1988, 105). Zephaniah linked these changes to the time when Yahweh their God would "visit" (פָּקַד) the humble and righteous remnant of Judah and would restore their covenant blessing. Such promises of hope should have convinced some hearers and readers of these prophecies to humble themselves and seek God so that they might enjoy his blessings.

God Will Judge Moab's and Ammon's Arrogance, but Some Will Honor God (2:8–11)

God heard the taunts and boasting of Judah's neighbors, Moab and Ammon, so God would turn their land into a wasteland and give it to the remnant of Judah.

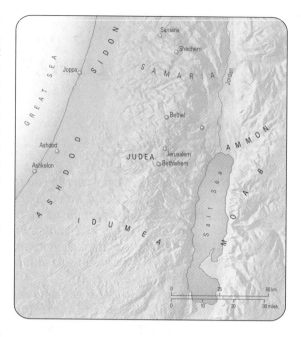

The Nations God Would Judge

Moab and Ammon: These nations were located to the east across the Jordan River, with Moab south of Ammon. The Israelites were related to the people in Moab and Ammon because these two nations were the descendants of Lot (Gen. 12:4–5; 19:30–38), but over the years there were many conflicts between them (Amos 1:13–2:3; Jer. 48; Ezek. 25). Balak, the king of Moab, hired Balaam to curse Israel (Num. 22–24), and Eglon the king of Moab oppressed Israel for eighteen years in the time of the judges (Judg. 3:12–15). The "reviling of, insults of" (גִּדּוּפֵי) the Ammonites may refer to how the Ammonite king threatened to humiliate the Israelite people of Jabesh-gilead by gouging out their right eyes (1 Sam. 11). In addition, Amos said the Ammonites viciously abused the pregnant women of Israel while living in Gilead (Amos 1:13) in order to enlarge their borders.

2:8. Throughout Scripture God heard both cries for help (the Israelite groaning in Egypt in Exod. 2:24; 6:5) and the sinful words people say (for example Sennacherib's words in Isa. 37:4). God heard the "reproaches, insults" (חֶרְפַּת) that the Moabites spoke against the Israelites, but in this passage Zephaniah did not connect

---

1   For example, Ashdod fell to the Egyptian army in 611 B.C. about fourteen years later.

what they said to any specific historical event. Zephaniah accused these nations of "making great" (גָּדַל), which some (Robertson, 1990, 301) explain as the Ammonites making "arrogant, great" speeches about expanding their borders, or making "threats" (Barker and Bailey, 1998, 459). Others (Baker, 1988, 106; Sweeney, 2003, 133) believe this refers to "making great, enlarging" their borders by taking land.

2:9a. "Therefore" (לָכֵן) introduces God's logical response to the sinful ways of the Moabites and Ammonites. The phrase "as I live" was typically part of a divine oath in which God absolutely committed himself to doing something (Num. 14:21, 28; Deut. 32:40; Isa. 49:18; Ezek. 5:11). This meant that as long as the Lord of the hosts of heaven and God of Israel was alive, he swore to unconditionally fulfill his words. When God swore an oath, it was absolutely certain.

TRANSLATION ANALYSIS: גָּדַל
NASB[95]	"become arrogant"
NKJV	"made arrogant threats"
NIV	"made threats"
HCSB	"threatened"
NRSV	"made boasts"
ESV	"made boasts"

God's plan was to make Moab and Ammon like Sodom and Gomorrah (cf. Gen. 18–19). Since Moab and Ammon were situated on the east banks of the Dead Sea, they could witness in the valley below the devastation that obliterated Sodom and Gomorrah. Consequently, there was no confusion about what God was planning to do. Like Sodom and Gomorrah, parts of their land would be completely useless for agriculture because of desert weeds and salt pits.

2:9b–10. The prophet ended this small paragraph with a word of assurance (as in 2:7b) that the remnant of God's people would receive the benefit of God's actions against the proud Moabites and Ammonites. Moab's pride was

well known to Isaiah (Isa. 16:6) and Jeremiah (Jer. 48:29), and God's hatred of pride was evident in many situations (Isa. 2:9, 11–12, 17; 5:15; 13:11; 10:5–15; 14:12–15; 37:10, 17–29). In this context, the righteous remnant of Judah ("remnant of my people") would plunder these nations so they could inherit their territory. Such news should motivate some to humble themselves and seek God so they could enjoy God's promised blessing.

2:11. The Lord would reveal his "fearsome, awesome power" (נוֹרָא), presumably through a dramatic defeat of these enemies, though the exact way this would happen was not explained. Through this marvelous demonstration of power, God would "minimize, make thin" (רָזָה) the power of the idol gods. They would be proven to be powerless to defend the people who worshipped them. Then people from the furthest parts of the world would bow down and worship Yahweh, the God of Israel, on the day of the Lord. Isaiah 2:3 refers to the nations streaming to Jerusalem to worship and hear God teach, even "all humankind" (cf. Isa. 60:1–16; 66:18–23). In this verse, many would worship God in the far-flung corners of the world, not just in Jerusalem.

WORD ANALYSIS: The verb רָזָה is used twice (Isa. 17:4; Zeph. 2:11) and it is parallel to "lean" (the opposite of fatness). In Numbers 13:20, the adjective means the opposite of a fertile land, in Isaiah 10:16 it describes a person who is wasting away, in Psalm 106:15 it refers to a wasting disease, in Ezekiel 34:20 it describes the thin sheep as opposed to the fat ones, and in Micah 6:10 it refers to a reduced, minimized ephah that was used by merchants to cheat customers. Thus Zephaniah refers to gods who metaphorically are "thin, diminished, minimized" in their power and significance. Proof of their insignificance would be evident when the people bowed before Israel's God and ignored the powerless gods of the nations.

Pride Brings Destruction to Cush and Assyria (2:12–15)

Major distant nations (Cush and Assyria) would suffer desolation when God judges them.

2:12. The prophet Zephaniah only took a few words to announce the "piercing of" (חַלְלֵי) the Cushites by God's sword in a military battle (2:12). The territory of Cush was located in southern Egypt and Sudan, but since no verb was put in this sentence, it is hard to know if this refers to God's past defeat of the Cushite Pharaoh in the twenty-fifth Dynasty by the Assyrians in 663 B.C. (Sweeney, 2003, 146) or to the future battle against Cush when Cambyses the Persian ruler would defeat Egypt in 525 B.C. (Baker, 1988, 108) or to an eschatological battle (Motyer, 1998b, 936).

2:13–14. In what appears to be a climactic message, God revealed that he would also defeat the great northern power of Assyria (2:12–15), the empire that tried to control Judah for most of the last hundred years (from Ahaz to Josiah). Like the main cities of Philistia in 2:4–6, Nineveh the great capital of Assyria would be destroyed and become a place for flocks and wild animals to live (2:13–14).

> **Other Prophets**
>
> Around 790 B.C., the prophet Jonah warned the people of Nineveh of God's coming punishment, but they repented and were spared. Isaiah predicted the defeat of Assyria (Isa. 10:5–34; 14:24–27; 30:27–33; 31:8–9; 37:21–29), and their army was defeated by the angel of God at Jerusalem in 701 B.C. (Isa. 37:36). Around 630 B.C., the prophet Nahum assured king Josiah that God would defeat Nineveh (Nah. 1:8–11; 2:3–13; 3:1–19), so Zephaniah was saying something similar to what God had communicated through other prophets.

2:15. Finally, the prophet quoted the optimistic claims of the proud and secure city of Nineveh that thought of itself as a god by claiming "I am and there is no other." This was similar to the blasphemous claim made by Babylon (Isa. 47:8, 10) and its king (Isa. 14:13–15). But this was a claim only Yahweh, the God of Israel, could make (cf. Isa. 45:5, 21–22; 46:9). When Nineveh would be destroyed people would mock, whistle, and shake their hands in defiance of this powerless giant. This news gave Josiah and the remnant of Judah hope and a reason to seek for God to intervene on their behalf.

Jerusalem's Judgment (3:1–5)

People should lament the coming judgment of the rebellious, prideful, and violent people of Jerusalem.

3:1–2. The audience probably agreed with the preceding messages against the foreign nations (cf. Amos 1:3–2:16), but now the prophet would lament in a woe oracle[2] (as in 2:4) over the city of Jerusalem because it rebelled against God, was defiled with pagan cults, and economically oppressed the weak (3:1, 3). Conditions were deplorable, for they broke their covenant relationship with God (they did not listen to him, respond to his "correction" [מוּסָר], trust him, or seek him; 3:2).

3:3–4. Jerusalem's political leaders (the princes and judges) acted like vicious wild animals and did not protect the people, while the city's religious leaders (prophets and priests in 3:4) deceived and misled people, did not protect the holiness of the temple, and perverted God's instructions. In many ways, Jerusalem was worse than the surrounding nations in 2:4–15, for its people

---

2 Woe oracles were common in prophetic literature (Isa. 5:8, 11, 18, 20, 21, 22; 10:1; 28:1; 29:1; 30:1; 31:1; 33:1; Hab. 2:6, 9, 12, 15, 19). They begin with an announcement of "woe" that describes God's judgment and usually include some statement that explains why God was punishing them (see 3:1b–4).

had received God's revelation through the prophets, had the holy temple of God in their midst, and knew what they should and should not do based on God's instructions in the law through Moses and the preaching of many prophets.

3:5. Meanwhile, Judah's holy and just God was dwelling in the temple among a people who were unjust and unholy. The character, instructions, and consistent acts of God were just the opposite of the people, but his daily ("each morning") attempts to instill his righteousness into the lives of his people were rebuffed by a hardened people whose conscience did not sense any shame when they sinned.

Contrasting Comparisons	
The God of Jerusalem	**The city of Jerusalem**
Spoke (3:5)	Did not listen/obey (3:2a)
Brought justice each morning (3:5)	Did not accept discipline (3:2)
Was holy and just (3:5)	Was unjust and unholy (3:3–4)
Was in her midst (3:5)	Did not seek God (3:2b)

Learn and Wait in Hope (3:6–8)
In spite of seeing God's severe punishment of other nations, Judah did not learn to fear God; therefore, the righteous must wait in hope while God poured out his wrath on the wicked.

3:6–7. This literary unit ends with a summary of God's actions. Viewing the prophecies in 2:4–15 as if they had already happened, God reminded the people of Judah that he oversaw the destruction of the military defenses and the residential areas in several foreign cities, making them an uninhabitable mess. God thought that when the people of Judah saw this, they would fear God, worship him, and respond positively to God's "discipline/correction" (מוּסָר) so that he

would not need to destroy Jerusalem. However, this did not happen; instead, the people of Jerusalem became more corrupt.

3:8. Consequently, God instructed the righteous remnant "to wait, endure, hope" (from חָכָה), expecting God to act, for he would pour out his wrath on the gathered nations, including Judah (3:8; cf. 1:2–3). This prophecy repeated the warning of 1:18 that God's wrath would bring great destruction on many nations throughout the earth. Such dire warning provided a rationale for the audience to seek God before this happened (2:1–3).

THEOLOGICAL FOCUS
The exegetical idea (The Lord would judge the nations for their pride [2:4–10] and people in Jerusalem for not trusting God or accepting correction [3:1–8], but he would bless a remnant of Judah [2:7a, 9b] and many from the nations who honor God [2:11]) leads to this theological focus: God will punish those who refuse to accept correction as well as those who have oppressed God's people so that people will repent and worship God.

Four key theological themes are emphasized in this section that should motivate people to humble themselves and seek God. First, God punished people for their arrogant taunts and pride (2:8, 10, 15), their ungodly character, and unwillingness to accept correction (3:1–5). Second, God rewarded and blessed the righteous remnant (2:7, 9b). Third, many Gentiles would repent and worship the true God (2:11). If the people of Judah followed a similar path, and accept correction, they also could enjoy God's favor and be among the remnant of Judah. Finally, the remnant must patiently wait with expectations, for God would fulfill his promises when he would gather many nations for judgment (3:8). They could be certain that his zeal for justice would accomplish all that he had promised.

PREACHING AND TEACHING STRATEGIES

Exegetical and Theological Synthesis

Zephaniah 2:4–3:8 reveals God as an equal opportunist in the realm of judgment. He announced the verdicts of six nations. While the details of each sentence differ (e.g., Zephaniah goes city by city through Philistia and does a flyby for Cush), the certainty and intensity of God's judgment was clear. Of the nations mentioned, Judah received final and fullest treatment. God expected more of his people. Their obstinance, violence, and mistrust of God contrasted with his righteousness, justice, and fidelity. In effect, the prophet screamed, "Correction or condemnation? Your choice."

To circle the globe in handing out judgments is a common prophetic ploy. Amos enumerated sins of Israel's neighbors before accusing his kin in the northern kingdom (Amos 1:3–2:16). Isaiah prophesied against Egypt, Damascus, Cush, and Babylon before taking a shot at Jerusalem (Isa. 17–22). Jeremiah reversed the order, dealing out judgment for Jerusalem (Jer. 7) before listing the injustices of Egypt, Philistia, Moab, Babylon, and others (Jer. 46–50).

The pitfalls of God's people were numerous, dividing neatly into two categories: breeches of their vertical relationship to God and abuses of their horizontal relationships to neighbors. Toward God the people were disobedient, defiled, distant, distrusting, and indignant (Zeph. 3:1–2). Toward the surrounding nations the people were violent, arrogant, and unholy. Thus, God pronounced "woe"—a word spelling divine disappointment and coming disaster that God's people would wish only upon their opponents. Sadly, Israel had heard the word "woe" far too often (e.g., Isa. 5:8–30). Fortunately, "woe" was not God's last word; rather he promised a fresh start in the land to the faithful remnant who patiently waited for him to fulfill his promises (Zeph. 2:9).

Preaching Idea

When people all around you fall, check your path for pitfalls.

Contemporary Connections

What does it mean?

What does it mean that people all around you fall? What pitfalls should you check for? The imagery of falling may indicated clumsiness or accidents. In this context, however, fall connotes something graver: the natural consequence of neglect, selfishness, or unwise decisions. Since Adam and Eve's rebellion in Eden (Gen. 3), the world has remained in a free fall. Every generation is responsible for an endless list of evils: murder, adultery, deception, idolatry, prejudice, ingratitude, greed, and abuse. Corruption taints every human heart (2 Chron. 6:36; Jer. 17:9). Unless we diligently guard our hearts, we are prone to fall into numerous pits (Ps. 119:9; Prov. 3:6; 4:23–27).

Pitfalls come in many forms. First, we may doubt God when facing the crippling effects of physical, emotional, or relational adversity. Life will knock us down with bad diagnoses, vocational stress, family strain, and unfair blows to our reputation. In these cases, Scripture encourages us to steel our faith and steady our feet. Second, we may drift from God's path when chasing pleasure, prioritizing hobbies, or giving little attention to God's Word. Drifting from the path, whether deliberately or unintentionally, makes us vulnerable to selfish and unwise decisions. Finally, we may directly disobey God. Dramatic falls often follow a pattern of violent, proud, and indulgent living. To employ an image from wisdom literature: sinners are often caught in their own snares (Prov. 1:18). Modern examples include the pornography addict destroying his marriage, the deceptive child losing phone privileges and her parents' trust, and the controlling boss getting pegged with a harassment suit. Additionally, falls are not limited to individuals, but also include corporations and countries. The greed of mortgage brokers and collapse of the housing market (late 2007 and 2008) remind us not to overreach. Instances of doubt, drifting, and disobedience should constantly urge us to examine our path.

Is it true?

Is it true that people all around us will fall? Yes, falls are inevitable. What causes these falls is a more complex question. God causes some falls, others he has built into the fabric of this fallen world. Sometimes he intervenes immediately, causing crowds to literally fall into cracks in the earth (Num. 16:31–34). Other times he delays punishment, as evident in the slow decline of Jerusalem or longing for justice in lament psalms (Jer. 13:22–27; Ps. 22). And some falls come on the heels of choosing an immoral path fraught with pitfalls, like the unraveling of David's family after his sin against Uriah (2 Sam. 11–18).

What we must guard against is naively pronouncing divine judgment where we cannot be sure God has directly acted. For example, declaring AIDS to be God's punishment for homosexuality is a bald claim lacking biblical authority. People who say this speak from their bias not the Bible. While Scripture records a limited number of divine judgments, it does not tell us if massive forest fires, destructive hurricanes, civil warfare, deadly parasites, plane crashes, or painful miscarriages are acts of God. We do not have access to God's thoughts in these circumstances (Isa. 55:8–9).

> **Old Testament Examples of God's Judgment:**
> God destroyed Sodom and Gomorrah, turned Lot's wife into a pillar of salt (Gen. 19), sent ten plagues on Egypt (Exod. 7–11), consumed Nadab and Abihu with fire (Lev. 10), gave Miriam leprosy (Num. 15), had Achan executed (Josh. 7), struck Uzzah dead (2 Sam. 6), and allowed the Babylonian exile (Jer. 25).

In addition to admitting our incomplete understanding of God's judgment, we should also strive to avoid pitfalls. Each of us is merely one misstep away from stumbling. We should learn from our mistakes and others' errors, asking ourselves, "Where am I prone to fall?" We may be prone to anger, having watched our parents' emotional tirades. We may be prone to workaholism, having drilled into our heads the need for productivity. We may be prone to self-harm, having accepted a degrading view of self or desperate need for control. Walking toward pitfalls unawares increases the threat of falling. Humble people walk attentively in this fallen world.

Now what?

Should the prevalence of pitfalls dishearten us? Should it discourage us from pursing God? Certainly not! No one walks with God without facing pitfalls and problems. We all struggle and stumble. And yet, the righteous person rises again and again (Prov. 24:16).

Pitfalls are nothing new to God's people. In fact, God expects us to learn from past failures, our own or others' (1 Cor. 10:1–12). He wants us to avoid those who take us down paths of folly (Ps. 1:1–2) and journey with those who will lift us when we fall (Eccl. 4:10). In addition to learning from the past and walking with others, we may dodge pitfalls through ruthless self-examination. Knowing our emotional triggers, judgmental tendencies, negative self-talk, and misrepresentations of God can spare us from pitfalls. All along the way, we can ask God to direct our path and guard us from the pitfalls we're prone to step in.

Finally, we acknowledge that God's desire goes beyond simply helping us avoid falls. He wants rich relationships, integrity, and ministry impact for his people. A fall does not preclude us from flourishing. Star athletes, exceptional students, and successful businesspeople maintain a balanced outlook on their falls. They embrace failure and disappointment as a possibility. They learn from it when it happens but refuse to let pitfalls define them. They focus more on moving forward, winning, and staying out of pits. The win for a person of faith is the resolve to stay on God's path of loving him and others.

Creativity in Presentation

Consider using hiking to illustrate the danger of pitfalls. I (Tim) have endured many laborious hiking trips, from a descent into the Grand Canyon to reaching the peak in the Rocky Mountains. These trips required sturdy shoes, skilled footwork, steady pacing, and constant attention to loose gravel and steep cliffs. I have pictures to prove it. A misstep or straying from the path could be deadly. Discuss how seasoned hikers plan their route, heed signs, dress appropriately, pack rations, stay hydrated, and, of course, watch where they're going. Showing pictures from a personal trek or wearing hiking gear could reinforce the importance of checking your path.

News media provide an ever-growing list of politicians, athletes, businesspeople, celebrities, and religious leaders who have fallen from grace. Their dirty laundry may serve as a what-not-to-do illustration. Consider President Clinton's affair (1995–97); Pastor Mark Driscoll's deceptive book sales (2014); the NFLs crackdown on domestic violence (2014–15); or one of many #MeToo sexual harassment claims (more than forty indicated) in 2017 to discuss moral pitfalls.

However, if sharing a famous person's fall from public grace won't connect with your congregation, consider describing something more personal you learned from the fall of a parent, coworker, friend, or former mentor. Harry Chapin's mournful tune, "Cat's in the Cradle" (released 1974), provides a harrowing account of a son repeating the pitfall of his emotionally distant father. Of course, we must be careful when using another person's fall as an illustration not to vilify the person. After one of my former mentors was let go from a ministry position for an affair, several friends and I talked about setting healthy boundaries in our marriages, while fighting the urge to slander the accused. Lest we think ourselves immune to stumbling, at the end of the illustration we should ask: "Have you ever taken a shortcut, told a lie, mistreated someone of the opposite sex, or said something you wouldn't want publicized?"

In the 1990s, the television show *Survivor* popularized a game called "Minefield" where select teammates were blindfolded and directed through a perilous path by listening to their partner's voice. If they did not heed their teammate's constant correction and touch a "mine," they died. Consider setting up a Minefield (search Pinterest for design ideas) or filming your journey through one. Neither the design nor symbolic mines matter as much as the blindfolded person's ability to take correction and make it through the path without stumbling. Describe the mines as violence, pride, idolatry, and other pitfalls akin to Zephaniah's day. Having a volunteer brave the minefield is sure to engage your people.

Regardless of which creative approach you choose, the sermon should teach that God will punish those who refuse to accept correction as well as those who have oppressed God's people so that people will repent and worship God. Therefore, when people all around us fall, we should check our path for pitfalls.

- People all around Jerusalem fall (2:4–15).

- People in Jerusalem fall (3:1–5).

- Check your path for pitfalls (3:6–8).

DISCUSSION QUESTIONS

1. Do you believe that the Lord still uses nations to bring disciplinary judgment on people for sins?

2. What are the dangers of pronouncing natural disasters or personal suffering as God's judgment? What is a healthy perspective on God's judgment?

3. Who are prominent leaders or people you respect who have fallen? What caused their fall? What could have prevented it?

4. What pitfalls often present themselves to you? To your congregation? How do you avoid them?

Zephaniah 3:9–20

EXEGETICAL IDEA
People from around the world who have pure hearts and lips would enter the joy of living with God their King without fear of any enemies.

THEOLOGICAL FOCUS
People who seek God will be transformed and dwell in God's presence.

PREACHING IDEA
Look forward to a fearless and festive future with God.

PREACHING POINTS
Zephaniah turned a corner in the final section to address another motivation for seeking God.[1] The prophet shifted from words of woe to images of hope, replete with singing, dancing, and international peace. At the center of the festivities stood Israel's God and King, Yahweh. For the original audience, such promises of fearless and festive living would have revived their hope. However, the question remained as to whether this hope would renew their character.

Today, God's people could use a fresh word of hope. Constant news cycles broadcast local and global suffering. Social media posts have perfected the art of cynicism and shame. Even the typical list of prayer requests is filled with illnesses, financial woes, and family problems. In other words, life has a way of causing stress and choking out joy. A look beyond this life—not as a mere escape to a place in the clouds but finding our home as renewed people with God—lifts us up and gives everyone great hope. This closing passage teaches us to look beyond our present sufferings and anticipate a fearless and festive future with God.

---

1   Jason DeRouchie makes the diverse content of 2:1–3:20 fit into one long segment and entitles it with the unusual title "The Substance of the Savior's Summons to Satisfaction: Charges to Pursue the Lord Patiently Together." Jason S. DeRouchie, "Zephaniah," in *ESV Expository Commentary*, eds. Iain M. Duguid, James M. Hamilton Jr., and Jay Sklar, 12 vols. (Wheaton, IL: Crossway, 2018), 7:570.

SEEKING GOD WILL BRING TRANSFORMATION AND JOY IN GOD'S PRESENCE (3:9–20)

LITERARY STRUCTURE AND THEMES (3:9–20)

Zephaniah's final hopeful message to the remnant of Judah is divided into paragraphs describing the spiritual transformation of the remnant from Judah and the nations (3:9–13) and the joy of the remnant living in the presence of God their King (3:14–20).

The themes emphasized here include the characteristic of the remnant (from all nations, no shame, no pride, pure lips, humble, no lies, no fears) and the nature of God's future kingdom (joyful, no fear of enemies, God their king would exult over them, transform lives, and give them new blessings).

- *Transforming the Remnant (3:9–13)*
- *Joy for the Righteous Remnant (3:14–20)*

EXPOSITION (3:9–20)

After completing his warning to avoid God's judgment, Zephaniah provided positive arguments to encourage his audience to seek God. If they would do this, one day he would transform their lives, remove sinfulness (3:9–12), and dwell among them as their King in a time of joy, peace, and restoration (3:14–20).

Transforming the Remnant (3:9–13)

Purity, humbleness, unity, trust, and truthfulness would characterize the remnant from many nations who worship God.

3:9–10. This paragraph starts with the conjunction "for then, after that" (כִּי־אָז), which connects it to the time of the day of the Lord. It introduces a time when God "will change, transform" (הָפַךְ) people so that they would be ready to enter God's eschatological kingdom (3:14–20). First, God would transform the evil speech of the past (cf. 2:8) and purify peoples' lips (cf. Pss. 15:2–3; 24:4; Isa. 6:5–7) so that they would worship, call on the name of the Lord, and serve God (similar to the transformation of the worshippers in Josiah's reforms) as one unified group (lit., "with one shoulder"). This unity would exist in spite of the fact that the remnant would be made up of many different nations (cf. Isa. 60:1–11; 66:18–23). It appears that some would come from Cush in Africa (Zeph. 3:10; cf. Isa. 19:18–25), though this might function as a metaphor for "the farthest ends of the earth" (cf. Zeph. 2:11). Other dispersed people from areas around the world would also be part of God's people (cf. Isa. 2:3–4; 11:11–12; 66:18–23), but all would come to seek God through "prayer' (עָתָר) and to honor God with their "offerings, gifts" (מִנְחָה).

3:11. Second, God would transform the "shame" (בּוֹשׁ) of Judah (3:11; cf. 3:5b) and the nations, due to their rebellious deeds (cf. 1:4–5; 3:1–5) by removing everyone who is proud (cf. 3:8, 10, 15) from the holy city of Jerusalem where God would dwell among his people. Thus, the people left would be humble people who found their security in "trusting, taking refuge" (חָסָה) in God, not in other gods or their military.

3:12–13. Third, God would transform the things this remnant would do and say (3:13). Because their hearts, the true source of all thoughts and speech (cf. Matt. 12:34), would be changed, their actions and speech would be transformed.

People would become humble, trust in God, tell the truth, and not lie to one another. Deceitful words would not characterize these people as it did in the past (cf. Jer. 4:10; 8:5; 14:14; 23:26; 29:8; 49:16). This new world would be one of prosperity and peace (cf. Ps. 23:2; Mic. 4:4) with nothing to make people fearful, for evil would not exist in the new heavens and the new earth.

Joy for the Righteous Remnant (3:14–20)

Living in the kingdom of God with our King would be a joyous time for us and for God.

3:14–15. The preaching of Zephaniah ended by giving one more reason why the audience in Jerusalem should immediately humble themselves and seek God. This rationale should help the people who were willing to accept correction (3:7), trust God (3:8), and be transformed (3:9) by God's power to make up their minds. Although these people would include both Judeans and non-Judeans, Zephaniah's focus was on motivating his Judean audience ("the Daughter of Zion; Zion; Daughter of Jerusalem in 3:14) by picturing what it would be like to live in God's ideal kingdom in the future. This would be a time of singing, rejoicing, and exulting because God would take away their judgment and remove all their enemies (not just the Assyrians). People would rejoice because God himself, the King of the nation,[2] would dwell in their midst in Jerusalem; consequently, there would be no need to fear because the enemies of God (including sin) would be defeated.

3:16–17. Since this glorious future was available to the righteous remnant, God's people did not need to fear or feel powerless on the approaching day of the Lord. God, the Divine Warrior, would save his people just as he did when he defeated the Egyptians at the exodus (Exod. 14–15), 185,000 Assyrian troops around Jerusalem in the days of Hezekiah (Isa. 36–37), and all sinful nations on the final day of the Lord. Instead, he would show his love for his people by exulting and rejoicing over them with shouts of great joy (Zeph. 3:17).

3:18. This salvation oracle ends with promises of how God would care for his people on the day of the Lord. The text of 3:18 is difficult to understand, but it appears that God was referring to those who would "suffer/be grieved" (נוּגֵי, which is a *niphal* form from יָגָה) at the "appointed time" (presumably the appointed time of the day of the Lord) when God would gather the people together for punishment (1:2–3; 3:8), when a great burden and reproach would fall on Jerusalem.

3:19–20. Those who would go through this terrible time could be assured that God would deal justly with their oppressors and that with great care he would gather all of his people to himself, for everyone (even the lame and outcasts) are important to God. When God would do this, he would transform what seemed like a time of great shame into a time of great honor and renown in the eyes of people throughout the earth. This idea is expanded in 3:20, for this verse repeats the promise to gather all the remnant together, and it repeats the promise that God would give the people great honor in the eyes of people from other nations (cf. Deut. 26:19; Isa. 14:1–2; 52:10; 60:4–9)

---

2   The covenant relationship established a theocracy in which God was the divine King who sovereignly controlled the destiny of his people. Like human kings, God gave laws, judged the sinful, protected the weak, was the commander in chief of the armies of heaven, and ruled his land as well as the world around his people. For more on the similarities and differences between the concept of God in Israel and the surrounding nations, see Gary V. Smith, "The Concept of God / The Gods as King in the Ancient Near East and the Bible," *Trinity Journal* 3 (1982): 18–38.

THEOLOGICAL FOCUS

The exegetical idea (People from around the world who have pure hearts and lips would enter the joy of living with God their King without fear of any enemies) leads to this theological focus: People who seek God will be transformed and dwell in God's presence.

This prophecy makes it clear that people who humble themselves, turn from their sinful ways, and seek God will be able to live in the presence of God their King. The prospects of joy, peace, no fear, restoration, and great renown among the nations are appealing, but the enjoyment of these promises will be possible only to those who are transformed.

PREACHING AND TEACHING STRATEGIES

Exegetical and Theological Synthesis

Zephaniah 3:9–20 describes a glorious future for God's people, but it would not arrive without a few provisional steps. Prior to the ingathering of nations and celebration of peace, God would do some purging. He would purify lips, remove the proud, exalt the humble, and expunge his enemies. As Israel's true King and faithful warrior, his guarantee is inviolable.

However, what is most striking in Zephaniah's theology is neither God's might nor mercy, but his merrymaking. The God of Israel would dance and sing over his people. He would throw a lavish banquet and swing the doors wide for crippled people and foreign nations to enter. Not only would his guests enjoy his presence, they would share in his honor.

Other prophets echoed this picture of God's extravagant welcome. Zechariah envisioned a future Feast of Booths open to faithful foreigners (Zech. 14). Isaiah spoke of a future banquet shared by many; an outpouring of God's spirit would spell freedom for the poor, imprisoned, and brokenhearted, giving them cause to join the Jubilee celebration (Isa. 25; 61). In fact, the annual schedule of festivals demonstrated God's

joyous welcome (Lev. 23; Deut. 16). Likewise, the dazzling elements of corporate praise—song, dance, instrumentation—reflected God's bright invitation to enjoy him (cf. Pss. 145–50).

Preaching Idea

Look forward to a fearless and festive future with God.

Contemporary Connections

What does it mean?

What does it mean that we should look forward to a fearless and festive future with God? How central is God to our vision of the future? Sadly, we tend to paint our pictures of eternity with selfish ornamentation. We describe the afterlife as a large family reunion, ethereal playground, and pain-free existence where our new bodies have glorious capacities (e.g., perfect pitch and zero gravity). These may be real features of the new heavens and new earth, but they are not its essence. God's glorious presence is central to our future, not an afterthought.

Since Eden, God has sought to restore his presence among his people. Whether in one form or another—the wilderness tabernacle (Exod. 25:10), angelic witness (Josh. 1:9), prophetic reminder (Isa. 41:10; 43:2), outpouring of his Spirit (Joel 2:28–29), or arrival of his Son (Isa. 7:14, cf. Matt. 1:23)—God reveals his desire to dwell among people. To be clear, God's people have not always responded well to his presence. Often awareness of his presence petrifies them, resulting in the divine refrain: "Do not be afraid" (Gen. 15:1; Josh. 1:9; Isa. 41:10; Hag. 2:5). Scripture proves he is a deeply personal God, who sings and dances, hosts parties and brings healing, shows mercy and spreads joy. Too many of us adhere to the sterile theology of a remote God whose ire is constant and happiness occasional. This probably explains our self-centered view of heaven where we choose to orbit around God rather than interact with him.

Is it true?

Can we really look forward to a fearless and festive future in God's presence? How fearless can we be in the presence of a holy God? It is true that most encounters with God in Scripture result in people cowering. Moses hid in the cleft of the rock (Exod. 34:8), Isaiah pronounced his own woe (Isa. 6:5), and Abraham and Joshua bowed when the angel of the Lord appeared (Gen. 18:1–2; Josh. 5:14). Someday, in fact, every person will kneel in God's presence, confessing his Sovereignty (Ps. 2; Isa. 45:23)

But other images of eternity with God emphasize jubilee. Isaiah 65:17–25 envisions a new creation unburdened by the curse of sin. The banquet pictures people from diverse nations enjoying the fruits of peaceful relations and abundant harvest (Isa. 25; cf. Rev. 19). Trumpet blasts and corporate songs convey God's great victory (Pss. 18; 68; 145–150). Of course, we need not wait for ultimate restoration to enjoy God's company. God's people may now experience "fullness of joy in [his] presence" (Ps. 16:11), even if life circumstances remain difficult.

Now what?

How do we look forward to a fearless and festive future in God's presence? Are we to deny present troubles and responsibilities? Anticipation of a festive future with God should energize, not immobilize us. God wants our lives to foreshadow the coming future. He has created a partnership with his people. He saves, cleanses, and empowers us; we confess, strive for, and serve him. We practice pure speech, humility, and social justice as a dress rehearsal for eternity. Looking forward to eternity with him should inform how we reflect him now.

But we also acknowledge the present is wrought with problems that cause fear and dampen festive feelings. Our current challenges may include degenerative disease, creeping debt, work stress, rebellious children, or malicious neighbors. We must be honest about these present sufferings without obsessing over them.

They do not define us; God does. Even in our darkest hours, God remains with us (Ps. 23:4). He remained with Israel through fire and flood (Isa. 43:1–3). He stood beside Daniel in the lion's den (Dan. 6:19–22). He abided with Job in his loss and with Joseph through many rises and falls, maintaining their resolve to hope. In hardships, God's presence not only affirms us, but also foreshadows glory to come.

Finally, we may nurture hope through a few disciplines. Meditating on Zephaniah's festive imagery may increase our longing for God's presence. Keeping a list of joys encountered each day—things that make us smile, laugh, dance, and sing—may increase awareness of God's generosity. Silence and solitude may help us identify driving fears and submit them to God's care. Singing upbeat praise songs stirs our affections for God. These practices remind us that we need not wait until the new heavens and new earth to taste and see God's goodness (Ps. 34:5).

Creativity in Presentation

This passage calls for a party. More specifically, it calls for a dance party. Consider making a few modifications to your worship area to inspire some festivities for this sermon. Hang a disco ball from the ceiling, dim the lights, and hand out glow sticks. Play upbeat music, live or recorded (e.g., Chris Tomlin's "God's Great Dance Floor" or David Crowder Band's "Oh Happiness"). Preselect a few people to share some choreographed dance moves or invite some brave participants (especially children) on the stage to wiggle and shake while music pumps through the speakers. Encourage the congregation to join the throng. The key is to make the experience merry, not awkward and contrived; you're providing a foretaste of heavenly festivities free from self-conscious inhibition. For many church people, this is a stretch!

Various ceremonies provide a wonderful picture of celebration. Wedding receptions, family reunions, and graduation/birthday/retirement parties give people reason for singing, dancing, and celebrating after seasons of transition or closure. After twenty-five years of working at his orthopedic company, my (Tim's) father-in-law held a retirement party filled with personal stories, tasty food, and humorous decorations. During my wedding reception, my cheeks burned from constant smiling. We did not dance, but my wife and I made up for this for at our ten-year anniversary party, where we invited a DJ and turned our two-car garage into a dance floor. I have plenty of pictures to recall the event. Consider using pictures, props, and personal stories from a party you attended as a window into the heavenly reception we will all enjoy in God's presence.

Plan a church picnic, potluck, or love feast to follow the service. Ask everyone on the congregation to bring their favorite dish to share. Make sure there are plenty of desserts! Appoint a hospitality team to decorate tables and set them with real silverware and ceramic plates. Commence the meal by toasting God; provide sparkling grape juice and stemmed glasses for people to raise. Have music playing in the background; set up lawn games to enjoy. Let people know the feast and festivities foreshadow our glorious future in God's presence.

Throughout the message be sure to communicate this truth: People who seek God will be transformed and dwell in God's presence. Thus, we should look forward to our fearless and festive future in his presence.

- A fearless future in God's presence (3:9–13).

- A festive future in God's presence (3:14–20).

DISCUSSION QUESTIONS

1. How do you understand Zephaniah 3:17? How does it fit with your typical portrait of God?

2. Do you think the Lord rejoices and exults over his people now, or is this reserved just for a day of future restoration?

3. What evidence from Scripture and your life helps you view God as a "merrymaker"?

4. What festivities have you enjoyed in life without feeling self-conscious or fearful?

5. How do you nurture a healthy sense of hope for the future? What role do praise, worship, and thanksgiving play in sustaining hope in God?

6. What are ways to "practice the presence" of God today?

FOR FURTHER READING

Beale, G. K. 2008. *We Become What We Worship: A Biblical Theology of Idolatry.* Downers Grove, IL: IVP Academic.

Bruckner, J. 2004. *Jonah, Nahum, Habakkuk, Zephaniah.* NIV Application Commentary. Grand Rapids: Zondervan.

Motyer, J. A. 1998b. "Zephaniah." In *Zephaniah, Haggai, Zechariah, and Malachi,* 897–962. Vol. 3 of *The Minor Prophets: An Exegetical and Expositional Commentary,* edited by T. E. McComiskey. Grand Rapids: Baker.

Robertson, O. P. 1990. *The Books of Nahum, Habakkuk, and Zephaniah.* New International Commentary on the Old Testament. Grand Rapids: Eerdmans.

Smith, C., with P. Snell. 2009. *Soul Searching: The Religious and Spiritual Lives of Emerging Adults.* Oxford: Oxford University Press.

INTRODUCTION TO HAGGAI

OVERVIEW OF INTRODUCTORY ISSUES

Author: Haggai

Place: Jerusalem

Date: 520 B.C.

Readers: Judeans in Jerusalem

Historical Setting: Darius the Great assumed control of Medo-Persia's throne and reissued Cyrus's degree for some of the exiles from Judah to rebuild the temple in Jerusalem.

Occasion for Writing: The people living in Jerusalem at this time found many excuses for not giving priority to rebuilding the temple in Jerusalem, so Haggai challenged them to prioritize honoring God, living holy lives, and serving God.

Genre: Prophecy

Theological Emphasis: Glorifying God must be a person's highest priority.

AUTHORSHIP OF HAGGAI

Haggai is a book of four sermons preached by the prophet Haggai. According to the records in Ezra 4:24–5:2, Haggai (along with the prophet Zechariah) spoke to the Jewish people living in Jerusalem in the second year of the Persian king Darius (520 B.C.). The introductions to all four sermons claim that Haggai was the speaker who gave a message from God, so he is identified as a prophet (Hag. 1:3, 12; 2:1, 10) and a messenger of the Lord (1:13). These prophetic messages refer to Haggai in the third person and have God, the original author of these statements, speaking in the first person (1:8–9, 11, 13; 2:4–9, 14, 17, 19, 21–23), a common practice in prophetic books. Although some suggest that this book may not be an exact record of the oral speeches of Haggai (Verhoef, 1987, 10), the careful dating of each message suggests that someone (the prophet or one of his disciples) conscientiously recorded the date and the essence of each message shortly after it was delivered.

PLACE OF WRITING

Haggai's oral presentations and the written record of these messages addressed Zerubbabel, the governor of the people, Joshua the High Priest, and the common people living in Jerusalem about the issue of building the temple in Jerusalem. These issues were directly applicable to only one group of people at this time, so they only make sense in a Jerusalem setting.

GENERAL CHRONOLOGY OF THE PROPHETS				
Prophet	Estimated Ministry	Period	Audience	
Amos	767–753	Pre-exile	Northern Israel	A S S Y R I A 900 B.C. to 612 B.C.
Hosea	755–715	Pre-exile	Northern Israel	
Micah	735–701	Israel in exile Pre-exile Judah	Judah	
Isaiah	739–685	Pre-exile	Judah	
Nahum	663–612	Israel in exile Pre-exile Judah	Nineveh / Assyria	
Zephaniah	632–628	Israel in exile Pre-exile Judah	Judah	B A B Y L O N 612 B.C. to 539 B.C.
Habakkuk	626–609	Israel in exile Pre-exile Judah	Judah	
Jeremiah	605–586	Israel in exile Pre-exile Judah	Judah	
Daniel	605–535	Judah in exile	Judah	
Ezekiel	597–571	Judah in exile	Judah	
Obadiah	After 586	Judah in exile	Edom	
Jonah	??	Judah in exile	(about) Nineveh	
Haggai	520–520	Post-exile	Returned Jews	P E R S I A
Zechariah	520–480	Post-exile	Returned Jews	
Joel	515	Post-exile	Judah	
Malachi	450	Post-exile	Returned Jews	

Chart created by Herbert W. Bateman IV, *Isaiah: How to Read, Interpret and Understand the Prophet* (Leesburg, IN: Cyber-Center for Biblical Studies, 2016). Reprinted by permission of Herbert W. Bateman IV.

DATE OF WRITING

All four (1:1; 2:1, 10, 20) of the messages of Haggai were connected to specific days, months, and a year (the second year of the Persian king Darius, 520 B.C.), and this agrees with the dating of Haggai's ministry in Ezra 4:24–5:2. This also places these sermons eighteen years after Cyrus's original decree (in 538 B.C.) that allowed the Jewish people in the Babylonian exile to return to Judah and rebuild their temple (Ezra 1:1–4; cf. *ANET*, 315–16). No date was provided for the writing down of these messages on a scroll or for when these messages were collected together to form this book, but the precise dating of each message argues for an early recording of Haggai's words by the prophet or one of his disciples (Koole,

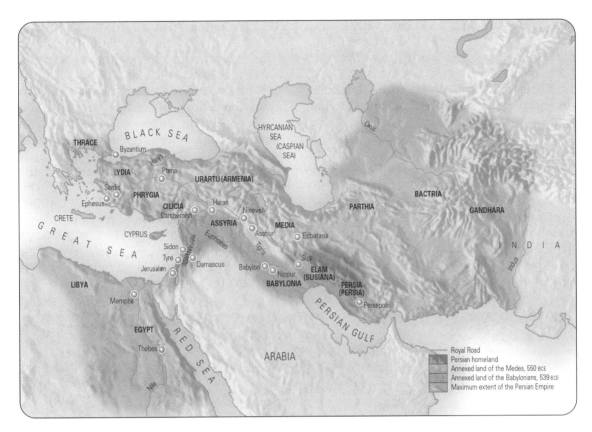

1967, 5–10). Some suggest that someone wrote this book one or two centuries after the time of Haggai,[1] but there is no hard evidence for this hypothesis, and it would seem to be impossible for someone to precisely date each of these messages so many years after they happened.

HISTORICAL SETTING[2]

After Persian princ named Cyrus usurped and established the Medo-Persian kingdom (549 B.C.), he expanded his kingdom westward by defeating Assyria, Mesopotamia, Syria, Armenia, Cilicia, and Cappadocia. In May 547 B.C., Cyrus marched to the land of Lydia, took its booty, and placed his own garrison in there (Nabonidus's Chronicle 2.16–18). On October 12, 539 B.C., Cyrus turned his attention on Babylon (Herodotus, *Hist.* 1.178–87). Once Cyrus's army entered the city of Babylon, the current king of Babylon, Belshazzar, was immediately killed (Dan. 8:1–4, 20), but Nabonidus was spared and may have died in exile (Herodotus, *Hist.* 1.190–92).

Cyrus personally entered the city of Babylon on October 29, 539 B.C. After these conquests, he said of himself, "I am Cyrus, king of

1 Rex A. Mason, "The Purpose of the 'Editorial Framework' of the Book of Haggai," *Vetus Testamentum* 27 (1977): 413–21.

2 This "Historical Setting" section is taken and adapted from Herbert W. Bateman IV, *History of the Second Temple Period: An Examination of Judaism During the Second Temple Period*, rev. ed. (Winona Lake, IN: Publisher, 2004), 24–34. Reprinted by permission of Herbert W. Bateman IV.

the world, great king, legitimate king, king of Babylon, king of Sumer and Akkad, king of the four rims (of the earth)" (*ANET*, 316 [Oppenheim]).

Cyrus died in 530 B.C. while defending the northeastern frontier of his kingdom leaving his vast kingdom to his son, Cambyses. Unfortunately, Cambyses was not well liked. In fact, Herodotus says that he "was completely out of his mind" (*Hist.* 3.38 [Godley]). It is said that he was subject to fits of rage. In one instance, he kicked his pregnant wife to death. He was not, however, aggressive against Greece, but he did consider the Ionian Greek City states (Ephesus, Sardis, etc.) his slaves. His efforts were directed against Egypt, which he subjugated in 525 B.C. (Herodotus, *Hist.* 2.1; 3.61–67, 89) and was invested with the designation "offspring of Re," emphasizing his legitimacy as ruler over Egypt (Yamauchi, 1990, 108).

While Cambyses was campaigning in Egypt, a coup arose in Persia. Gaumata seized the Medo-Persian throne in July 522 B.C. in the name of Cambyses's dead brother, Smerdis. On his return to Babylon, Cambyses received word of Pseudo-Smerdis's usurpation of the throne. While returning home from Egypt, Cambyses may have died near Mount Carmel, Israel, perhaps by suicide, perhaps murdered by Darius (Whitcomb, *ISBE* 1:582–83). In September 522 B.C., Darius overthrew Gaumata. Darius was a great military technician, but he was a greater politician and

The Cyrus Cylinder. Photograph by Mike Peel (www.mikepeel.net).
Modifications by یفانم / CC BY-SA (https://creativecommons.org/licenses/by-sa/4.0).

administrator. He divided the empire into twenty large satrapies, each run by a satrap appointed by the crown (Dan. 6:1–3). Local ordinances of each province remained in effect, administered by native judges and officials.

List of Persian Kings
Cyrus (539–530 B.C.)
Cambyses (530–522 B.C.)
Pseudo-Smerdis (522 B.C.)
Darius I (522–486 B.C.)

These historical events had an impact on the Jewish people, particularly those who had been taken captive under Nebuchadnezzar's rule (Jer. 25:8–12). Cyrus adopted a conciliatory policy toward all the nations the Babylonians defeated and their exiles in Babylon. This meant that he granted official authority for Jews living in Babylon to return to Jerusalem and rebuild the temple (2 Chron. 36:22–23; Isa. 44:24; 44:28–45:7). Cyrus declared that all exiled peoples could return to their homelands and rebuild their temples, according to Cyrus's clay barrel inscription. Although the rebuilding of the temple did not happen immediately, when the Persian King Darius heard about this, he reaffirmed Cyrus's directives and financially supported the completion of the temple reconstruction (Ezra 6:8).

OCCASION FOR WRITING

After Cyrus issued his decree, Ezra described the preparations for the Jewish exiles' journey back to Jerusalem (Ezra 1:5–11), listed the number of people who returned to Judah (about fifty thousand in 2:64–65), described the rebuilding of an altar to worship God (3:1–6), but reported that the neighboring people living around Samaria intimidated the Jews and hired lawyers to persuade

Behistun inscription reliefs. Courtesy of Hara1603 (public domain).

the Persians to stop construction on the temple (4:4–5). This led to sixteen years of frustration, for no progress was made on rebuilding the temple until Haggai and Zechariah challenged the people to rebuild the temple in the second year of Darius (4:24–5:2).

The international political situation was somewhat chaotic at the beginning of Darius's reign. The Behistun Inscription, which was written during the reign of Darius (r. 522–486 B.C.), tells how Darius became king, recounts his significant accomplishments, and celebrates his great military victories. Included in this account was a record of the problems Darius faced in securing the throne at the beginning of his reign. Clearly Darius was one of the great Persian kings, but when Darius first became king there was great political unrest because Gaumata the magician claimed to be the royal heir, Smerdis, because he wanted to take his place on the throne. This meant that Darius, the real heir to the throne, had to battle many enemies, defeat Gaumata, and put down several rebellions in the first two years of his reign. It was not until 520 B.C. that Darius was able to restore law and order to the nation. God's timing for sending Haggai to encourage the Jews to build the temple was perfect, for if the Israelites had started building the temple earlier than 520 B.C., the Persians might have considered their action to be part of the rebellion against Darius. God did not send Haggai to prod the leaders in Jerusalem to begin the temple reconstruction until the rebellion ended in 520 B.C.

The political situation in Judah itself was problematic, for the governor Zerubbabel was a weak leader (Hag. 2:20–23; Zech. 4:6–10) and controlled by the Persians. Persian kings retained and maintained the royal residences in Ecbatana, Sardis, Bactra, Babylon, Susa, Saïs, and Memphis, which served as the empire's seats of power. "From the inception of the Empire," according to Briant (2002, 352), "it was this dominant socioethnic class that held power from the Indus to the Mediterranean and intended to keep it." As a result, Zerubbabel had no army to carry out his decrees and could not resolve the conflict with the neighboring people around Samaria.

The socioeconomic setting was difficult because God sent a drought and a poor harvest (Hag. 1:9–11). The religious leader, Joshua the High Priest, was without a temple, so he seemed rather powerless, and there were some questions about his worthiness for this role (Zech. 3:1–5). All this led to an overwhelming sense of hopelessness about getting the temple rebuilt. Yet all of this changed when God sent Haggai to challenge the people to rebuild the temple. A short time after Haggai started speaking God's message, God inspired the prophet Zechariah to share eight visions that supported and supplemented the words of Haggai.

CHRONOLOGY OF PERSIAN KINGS AND INFLUENCES ON JEWISH PEOPLE

Cyrus (559–530 B.C.)	Cambyses (530–522 B.C.)	Darius (522–486 B.C.)	Xerxes (486–465 B.C.)	Artaxerxes (465–424 B.C.)
Started building Zerubbabel/Joshua	no building	temple completed Haggai/Zechariah	Haman's threats Esther/Mordecai	Reform/Wall rebuilt Ezra/Nehemiah/Malachi

ORIGINAL READERS

The prophet Haggai's written record of God's messages addressed the governor of Yehud (Judah), Zerubbabel (Hag. 2:21), the High Priest Joshua (1:1), and the rest of the people (2:2, 14). Haggai's messages indicated that a big part of the problem was with the leaders (Zerubbabel and Joshua). They were not challenging the people's misplaced priorities and not confronting the people when they were discouraged (2:3) or not living like God's holy people (2:14).

THEOLOGICAL EMPHASIS OF HAGGAI

On the one hand, there are the theological concerns Haggai addressed. Haggai confronted the people's theological belief that it was impossible to build a temple where they could worship God. Haggai challenged the people in Jerusalem to change their thinking in order to make glorifying God their top priority. They needed to give priority to honoring him by building the temple and not spend all their time and energy on selfish goals (Hag. 1:8). They must persevere, believe in God's promises, be strong and resolute, and not give up on the task of building the temple (2:4–5). As they build the temple, they must live holy lives and not assume that they were holy just because they were working on rebuilding the temple (2:10–14). Plus, those in leadership must not be discouraged by their limited power and inability to resolve every problem. Leaders must be faithful servants, knowing that God has chosen them and that he will support them (2:23).

On the other hand, the practical issue in these prophetic messages is centered around several questions: What should be the most important thing in the life of God's people?

What guiding theological principle should govern all of a person's choices? What was the purpose for the existence of God's people in Jerusalem? The answer to these questions is that the people of God should center their lives around activities that please and glorify God. So in this situation, this meant that God's people should build a place to worship God (e.g., the temple).

Once the people began to build the temple, it was important for them to persevere in building the it, even if the new temple was not quite as glorious as Solomon's temple. God was not requiring or expecting a spectacular temple, just a place for him to dwell and for the people to gather for worship. Once they accepted this challenging task, it was important for the people not to give up, to trust God to provide for them, to be strong, and to depend on God. In addition, believers must regularly confess their sins and repent if they want God to bless them. They cannot assume that religious activities (like building the temple) will automatically make them acceptable in the eyes of God.

OUTLINE OF HAGGAI

Haggai divides into four preaching units.

- Giving Priority to God Brings Him Honor (1:1–15).

- Maintaining God's Priorities Brings God Glory (2:1–9).

- Giving Priority to Holiness Brings God's Blessings (2:10–19).

- God's Priorities for a Discouraged Leader (2:20–23).

FOR FURTHER READING

Clines, D. J. A. 1979. "Cyrus." *The International Standard Bible Encyclopedia*, edited by G. W. Bromiley, 1:867–68. Grand Rapids: Eerdmans.

Clines, D. J. A. 1979. "Darius." *The International Standard Bible Encyclopedia*, edited by G. W. Bromiley, 1:847–49. Grand Rapids: Eerdmans.

Moyter, J. A. 1998. "Haggai." In *Zephaniah, Haggai, Zechariah, and Malachi*, 963–1002. Vol. 3 of *The Minor Prophets: An Exegetical and Expositional Commentary*, edited by T. E. McComiskey. Grand Rapids: Baker.

Yamauchi, E. M. 1990. *Persia and the Bible*. Grand Rapids: Baker.

Haggai 1:1–15

EXEGETICAL IDEA
Haggai confronted the excuses people used to explain why they were delaying work on the temple and challenged them to glorify God by changing their priorities and building the temple.

THEOLOGICAL FOCUS
God is pleased with people who set aside their excuses for delaying his work and give priority to honoring him by immediately doing what he expects them to do.

PREACHING IDEA
Put an immediate end to "eventual" obedience.

PREACHING POINTS
Haggai shared a timely message with God's people. Eighteen years after a remnant had returned to Jerusalem to rebuild the temple, the project remained incomplete. The inhabitants made excuses, sought to further their own comfort, and ignored signs of God's displeasure. The prophet assumed that Persian politics had fed Israel's procrastination. Haggai implored his original audience—Zerubbabel the governor, Joshua the high priest, and the Jerusalem populace—to gather wood and resume working. They responded immediately and ended their delayed obedience.

In today's age of instant gratification, high-speed information, and one-click activation, God's people have developed an ironic habit of putting off spiritual commitments. We hedge, weigh options, and wait for better opportunities. We make excuses and procrastinate, rather than make his will our priority. Why pray now, when I can pray later? Why share my faith now, when another opportunity will arise? Why give a portion of this paycheck to global missions, when I can make up for it next month? This passage redresses our tendency to put other priorities before God, exhorting us to put an immediate end to "eventual" obedience.

GIVING PRIORITY TO GOD BRINGS HIM HONOR
(1:1–15)

LITERARY STRUCTURE AND THEMES
(1:1–15)

In his first sermon, Haggai opened his work with an introduction that directed the leaders of Jerusalem (1:1). He then provided a review of the people's excuses for not building the temple (1:2–6) and recorded his encouragement for the audience to build the temple in order to glorify God (1:7–11). Haggai closed with how the Spirit moved the people to honor God by rebuilding the temple (1:12–15).

This literary unit is centered around the theme of rebuilding the temple. The decision to build or not build was centered around what priorities were important. Those who wanted to honor God started to build his temple.

- *A Well-Timed Message (1:1)*
- *Misplaced Priorities (1:2–11)*
- *People Who Honor God Obey (1:12–15)*

EXPOSITION (1:1–15)

Ezra 5:1–5 describes how the people of the land (the people living around Samaria) persuaded the Persians to stop reconstruction of the temple in Jerusalem around 536 B.C. This moratorium on building continued on and on for sixteen years until God sent the prophets Haggai and Zechariah (Ezra 5:1–2) to encourage the people to get to work on restoring the temple. Times had changed and now that the Persians were led by a new king (Darius), and the uprising caused by the usurper Gaumata was over, it would be expected that the new government would be open to new policies and initiatives that would further the

political stabilization of distant provinces. Now there were no good political excuses, such as it is not the right time for rebuilding the temple (Hag. 1:2).

Yet, religious and political problems were occurring in Jerusalem (Hag. 1:1). Haggai addressed the issue of misplaced priorities and the need for the people in Jerusalem to put God first by rebuilding the temple (vv. 2–11). In response, the people had a change of heart, accepted the challenge, and started rebuilding God's temple (vv. 12–15).

A Well-Timed Message (1:1)

The word of God came at a specific time in the postexilic era to the leaders of Jerusalem to confront them with their need to listen to God's message.

1:1. This introduction to the messages of Haggai identifies the historical setting as the time when the Persian Empire (539–332 B.C.) controlled much of the civilized world and about eighteen years after Cyrus originally declared (in 538 B.C.; Ezra 1:1–4; cf. *ANET*, 315–16) that all exiled people in Babylon could return to their homeland and rebuild their temples, a declaration that appears on the Cyrus Cylinder. Towards the end of the Cyrus Cylinder the king said, "I returned to (these) sacred cities on the other side of the Tigris, the sanctuaries of which have been ruins for a long time, the images which (used) to live therein and established for them permanent sanctuaries. I (also) gathered all their (former) inhabitants and returned (to them) their habitations" (*ANET*, 316 [Oppenheim]).

So after the Jewish exiles returned from Babylon to Jerusalem, they built an altar to restore sacrificial worship and laid the foundation for the temple (Ezra 3). But rebuilding the temple was halted for the rest of the reigns of Cyrus and Cambyses (for sixteen years) because of threats and legal opposition by people north of Jerusalem in Samaria (4:1–5).

These people were led by Zerubbabel the governor of Judah (in Aramaic Yehud) and Joshua the High Priest, the son of the High Priest Jehozadak and grandson of the High Priest Seraiah who served when the temple was destroyed by the Babylonians (2 Kings 25:18). God's message was directed to the leaders Zerubbabel and Joshua, but the accusations and encouragements in Haggai 1:12, 14; and 2:4 applied God's words to everyone living around Jerusalem.

> WORD ANALYSIS: The name of the High Priest is "Joshua" יְהוֹשֻׁעַ in Haggai 1:1, 12, 14; 2:2, 4; Zechariah 3:1, 3, 6, 8, 9; 6:11, but his name is spelled slightly different as "Jeshua" (יֵשׁוּעַ) in Ezra 2:2; 3:8, 8, 9; 4:3; 5:2.

Misplaced Priorities (1:2–11)

Although human excuses led to wrong priorities and delays in their obedience (1:2–6), God called his people to think seriously about accepting the priority of honoring God (1:7–11).

The LORD of Hosts

The dominant clauses that introduce God's messages are "Thus says the LORD of hosts" (Hag. 1:2a, 5a, 7a), "the word of the LORD came through Haggai the prophet" (1:3), "declares the LORD of hosts" (1:9), and "declares the LORD" (1:13). God's words are contrasted with what "this people said" (1:2) and what "you" (1:4, 6, 9) have done. God explained why the people were having such a difficult time in Jerusalem and offered a theological solution to them. The first paragraph (1:2–6) exposes the people's wrong priorities while the second (1:7–11) challenges them to set new priorities. Thus, human excuses and delayed obedience led to wrong priorities and hard times.

1:2. God was aware that "this people/these people" in Jerusalem thought that this was not a good time to work on rebuilding the temple. Some probably thought they did not have enough time to run their farms and build the temple at the same time (Baldwin, 1972, 39). Others may have thought they did not have the financial resources to complete the expensive task of building a temple covered in gold (Meyers and Meyers, 1987, 21). In light of the political rebellion by Gaumata (522–520 B.C.), the Persians might have thought rebuilding the temple was an act of rebellion (Taylor and Clendenen, 2004, 119). Thus, rebuilding could not begin until seventy years after the temple was destroyed in 587 B.C. (Boda, 2004, 89), or it would not hurt to delay it a few years until conditions were more favorable. But since the temple was the place where God's presence dwelt among his people, these excuses showed a lack of concern for the restoration of God's glorious presence among them (Motyer, 1998a, 974). This raised the practical question, would there ever be a right time to give priority to the temple and the spiritual things that happen at the temple?

1:3–4. Haggai's second word from God reminded the audience that God was not pleased with their choices. The prophet's rhetorical approach expressed God's concern in a comparative question that unmasked their priorities. The probing question was: Why was it appropriate for people to live in houses with nice wood "paneling" (סְפוּנִים),[1] while "this house" (God's temple) was still a pile of rubble? The

---

1   Joyce Baldwin prefers "roofed in, ceiled" rather than referring to "paneled" walls. Joyce G. Baldwin, *Haggai, Zechariah, Malachi*, TOTC (Downers Grove, IL: InterVarsity Press, 1972), 40.

Babylonians destroyed the temple (2 Kings 25:8–10; Jer. 39:9; 52:12–14) and left a mound of desolate "ruins" (חָרֵב; cf. Jer. 22:5; 33:10–112; Ezek. 36:35, 38). This area probably looked like an abandoned farmstead, overgrown with weeds, briars, and trees. Haggai contrasted the beautiful homes with the ruins of the temple in order to unveil the hypocrisy of those who thought they did not have enough money or time to rebuild the temple.

WORD ANALYSIS: Some translations describe the houses of the wealthy as having "paneling" סְפוּנִים; but the NEB has "roofed" and the RSV has "ceiled") with wood on the inside. These wood walls would cover the rough stone walls and provide a luxurious decorating touch to the rooms. The word was used to describe the expensive walls inside Solomon's temple (1 Kings 6:9, 15; 7:3, 7) and the richly decorated paneled walls in a later palace (Jer. 22:14). Having this paneling implies that their houses were finished (Meyer and Meyer, 1987, 23), yet they were not working on God's house.

1:5. Haggai challenged the people to "reflect on what you are doing." When people "set their hearts" on something or reflect on it they usually recall what they have done, evaluate their actions, and consider the advisability of changing their approach. If these people would reflect on their past policy of giving priority to building their own homes instead of God's house, they should realize that something was wrong with their spiritual commitments.

Literal Hebrew	"Set your heart on your ways"
NIV	"Give careful thought to your ways"
HCSB	"Think carefully about your ways"
NRSV	"Consider how you have fared"
NKJV/NASB[95]	"Consider your ways

1:6. Haggai wanted his audience to reflect on the reasons why they were facing disappointing circumstances. Was it just coincidental? The pastoral heart of the prophet probed deeper in order to identify the cause of God's action. Were they innocent of all sins or did these difficulties come on them because they had sinned? Why did the farmers sow "much" (הַרְבֵּה) (many bushels of grain) but get very "little" (מְעָט) grain at harvest time? Why were people eating but never satisfied, or drinking but never drunk? Why were people putting clothes on but never staying warm? Why did the money of the workers seem to evaporate from their wallet/purse?[2] This final point could be metaphorically pointing to a problem with high inflation or taxation (Mason, 1977, 16)

Normal Activity	Expected Results	Actual Results
Sow seed	Great harvest of grain	Little grain
Eat	Fully satisfied	Not satisfied; not full
Drink	Thirst quenched; drunk	Not drunk
Put on clothes	Warm	Not warm
Earn money	Have lots of money	No money

---

2 The word "wallet/purse" (BDB, s.v. "צְרוֹר" p. 865) refers to a small bag or pouch that could be used to carry "silver, money" (Gen. 42:35; Prov. 7:20).

that severely limited the purchasing power of the wage earner (Taylor and Clendenen, 2004, 128). If just one of these things happened, it might not be considered unusual, but when everything seems cursed by God (Motyer, 1998a, 977), there must be some reason. Was there not some way to stop this pattern?

1:7. The second part of this message in 1:7–11 is closely connected to the preceding paragraph, for 1:7–11 repeats many aspects brought up in 1:2–6. The right priority was to glorify God by building the temple. Repetition creates emphasis on what is important, so the prophet repeated his call for the people to hear what God was saying and to reflect on their attitudes and actions (1:7). Haggai 1:8 conveyed the central theme of this prophetic message (Verhoef, 1987, 64) and God's solution to their problems. God instructed the people to do three things. They must stop delaying action and go up to the mountain, bring down wood, and build the temple. Timber was needed for the scaffolding, the walls, and the roof because this wood had been destroyed when the Babylonians burned the temple (2 Kings 25:9). The large wood beams of cedar for the roof and the wood placed between every third layer of stones on the walls (cf. Ezra 6:4) would need to be brought from further away in Lebanon (cf. 2 Chron. 2:3–8, 16; Ezra 3:7), but local timber (the sycamore tree) could be used for scaffolding.

1:8. The rationale for responding positively was that this would please and glorify God (1:8b).

God "will be pleased, accept, act with favor, take pleasure" (רָצָה) with people who offer a sacrifice (Lev. 1:3, 4; 7:18; 19:5; 2 Sam. 24:23; Ps. 51:19), who fear him (Ps. 147:11), and who do his will (Prov. 12:2; 16:7). Building God's temple would demonstrate that the people desire to please God, and this building will enable God "to be glorified" (כָּבֵד) when people praise him. Certainly, a God who has a grand temple will receive more honor and praise than gods who have no temple.

1:9. The prophet now explained why the people had so many difficulties (cf. 1:6). They planted their crops expecting to harvest "much" (הַרְבֵּה), but the harvest amounted to "little" (מְעָט). As if this was not disappointing enough, once the small harvest was brought safely into their own homes for storage, God blew it away. Although God could "blow" life into dry bones (Ezek. 37:9), in this case God figuratively would "blow" judgment on those who did not honor him (cf. Isa. 40:7; Jer. 20:26; Ezek. 22:21). Probably the grain spoiled with mildew or mold; thus, it became unusable (cf. Hag. 2:17).

Why did this happen? God did this "because" (יַעַן) the temple was still in "ruins" (חָרֵב as in 1:4) and everyone was busy working on their own homes. This contrasted a total inattention to "my house" (the temple) and a great deal of attention to every person for "his house." God's explanation helped the people realize their misplaced priorities. Their priority was not to seek first the kingdom of God (Matt. 6:33).

ISRAEL'S AGRICULTURE AND RAIN CALENDAR

March–April	May–August	September–February
Latter rains	No rain	Early rains
Barley harvest	Fig, grape harvest	Ploughing and planting

1:10–11. Haggai spelled out the consequences (עַל־כֵּן, "therefore, on account of this") of their wrong priorities in 1:9b and the consequences listed in 1:10–11. The course of nature was disrupted and the sky withheld the dew that normally fell on the vegetation during the dry summer months. Consequently, it was predictable that if there was no dew, the nutrient in the land would not be able to produce good crops.

Now several things get clarified. To begin with, God was responsible for bringing the drought on the land. Furthermore, God sent this drought on both the fertile fields in the lowlands as well as the orchards on the hill sides. God designed the drought to affect the production of all crops (grain, grapes, olives, and everything else). Finally, God intended that this drought would have an impact on what the animals and what people could eat and manufacture. The work of the farmers would come to nothing because of God's curse.

People Who Honor God Obey (1:12–15)

When God touched a person's heart, the proper responses was to act according to his instructions and trust him.

1:12. When some prophets spoke, people refused to listen or repent of their sinful ways (2 Kings 17:14; Ezek. 3:4–7; Amos 7:1–16; Mic. 2:6), but this message hit a soft spot in the hearts of the people. They responded with determination to work on rebuilding the temple even though they knew there might be opposition (Ezra 5:1–17).

The governor Zerubbabel and the High Priest Joshua seemed to lead this change of heart (Hag. 1:12), but the rest/remnant of the people followed their example and made a commitment of their hearts to "fear/honor" (יָרֵא) God and a commitment of their hands to "listen/obey" (שָׁמַע) God by rebuilding the temple. Their acceptance of this challenge changed their attitude toward God (they feared him) and changed their action (they got

to work). The "remnant" of the people referred to all the people living around Jerusalem (Taylor and Clendenen, 2004, 139).

1:13. Once the people made this decision, all their problems did not suddenly disappear. The drought was still there, the Persians did not immediately approve the rebuilding of the temple, the people in Samaria were still opposed to any rebuilding, and the people still had limited financial resources to spend on this expensive project. So, God's messenger Haggai delivered a message of hope, proclaiming that God's presence was with them. The simple statement that "I am with you" was a strong word of assurance that came to God's people from time to time (Jacob in Gen. 28:15; Moses in Exod. 3:12; 33:14; and Jeremiah in Jer. 1:8). God's promise of his presence offered support, protection, guidance, and providential care that should alleviate their anxiety.

1:14–15. Some might get the impression that the changes in the perspective of the leaders and the people was the result of the good rhetorical persuasiveness of the prophet Haggai, the airtight logic of his argumentation, or his ability to shame the people into making a change in their priorities. Although these factors may have assisted in the persuasion process, Haggai 1:14 clarifies that it was God who "stirred up" (עוּר) the spirit of the leaders and all the rest of people. The result of God's powerful stirring was that they began to work on the rebuilding of the temple on the twenty-fourth day of the month. One might interpret the time (three weeks) between Haggai's initial prophecy and the beginning of construction in more than one way. First, maybe it was necessary for the prophet to preach his message in several locations over a couple weeks before there was a dramatic movement of God's Spirit to bring about this change of priorities. A second possibility is that the people responded fairly quickly, but it took time to schedule the workforce, assign duties, draw up plans, and go to the mountains to cut and transport the needed lumber to the temple area. Thus, the delay in building was a matter of having adequate preparations before the construction work could begin.

THEOLOGICAL FOCUS

The exegetical idea (Haggai confronted the excuses people used to explain why they were delaying work on the temple and challenged them to glorify God by changing their priorities and building the temple) leads to this theological focus: God is pleased with people who set aside their excuses for delaying his work and give priority to honoring him by immediately doing what he expects them to do.

Two theological themes are emphasized in this first sermon of Haggai's prophecy. First, God wants people to give him priority. The central point Haggai emphasized was that God should have priority in the lives of his people (1:8). He wanted them to worship him, honor him, love him, and the serve him alone (Deut. 10:12). But this was not easy for the postexilic community in Jerusalem, for it did not have much political or economic power, life was hard, and food was not plentiful because of a drought (Hag. 1:6, 10–11). Religious life was depressing because the Samarians and Persians stopped the rebuilding of the temple (Ezra 4:4–5). It probably seemed like God was not giving much priority to helping his people, but why was he not intervening on their behalf? The answer was not that difficult to comprehend. God brought hard times on the nation to drive the people back to himself. The key to their future was to prioritize the things of God (Hag. 1:8).

Second, God expects obedience without delay, for doing what God says pleases him and brings him glory. In this situation, the people listened to what God said and responded positively by honoring God (1:12) and changing their priorities. Their obedience was based on several factors; their desire to put God first (v. 8), their fear of God (v. 12), God's promise

to be with them (v. 13), and God's act of stirring up the spirit of the leaders as well as the common people. All these factors contributed to a change of heart and a willingness to get to work on rebuilding the temple.

PREACHING AND TEACHING STRATEGIES

Exegetical and Theological Synthesis

Haggai 1:1–15 exposes a grave problem: Israel had tuned out God for too long. Almost eighteen years had passed since Jewish exiles had returned to Jerusalem with King Cyrus's blessing to rebuild their temple, but they had long since abandoned the project. The political reasons might explain Israel's reluctance to build—Samaria's opposition to rebuilding the temple (Ezra 4:1–5) and Guatama's fight for the Persian throne—but Haggai did not excuse them. The Lord of Hosts (Hag. 1:2, 5, 7) was not happy with their indolence, evident in his detached reference to Israel as "this people" (1:2 cf. 2:14).

God used diverse means to confront his people, including hard questions (1:4, 9), direct commands (v. 7), and covenant curses (vv. 9–11 cf. Deut. 28). In addition to speaking (Hag. 1:1, 3, 13), God sent adversity to his people in order to gain their attention. He might limit local harvests or allow foreign powers temporary reign, in either case, underscoring his total sovereignty (Isa. 45:1; Amos 4:6–10; 9:13–15; Hab. 1:6).

Fortunately, God's disappointment and discipline did not erase his mercy. He clearly leaned into them when they showed a change of heart (Hag. 1:12). He stirred their spirits and affirmed his presence (vv. 13–14). Ultimately, their getting back to work required God's intervention. Scripture maintains this balance between God's initiative and human responsibility. The wilderness tabernacle provides a model: God initiated the project and the people responded with monetary gifts and skilled labor (Exod. 20:8; 35:4–35). We rarely work heartily without his help.

Preaching Idea

Put an immediate end to "eventual" obedience.

Contemporary Connections

What does it mean?

What is "eventual" obedience? How immediate must our obedient response be? These are fair questions worthy of clarification. Scripture consistently conveys God's call to obedience. He asks his people to love, serve, sacrifice, praise, forgive, speak truth, give witness, destroy idols, and, summarily, be holy. Generally, God expects the same character and behavior from his people across generations. Loving God and loving others represent the cornerstones to his moral law (Lev. 19:18; Deut. 6:4–5; cf. Matt. 22:34–40; Gal. 5:14); we need not hesitate to embody these commands. Thus, we need not wait until Sunday to praise God; we can speak well of him immediately. We need not consult our weekly calendar before providing a word of comfort to a friend in crisis; we can encourage her immediately.

Other times God might ask specific people to obey personalized instructions. He asked Noah to build an ark (Gen. 6:14). He told Abram to leave his homeland (12:1). He ordered Samuel to anoint David (1 Sam. 16:1). He urged Isaiah to walk naked around Israel for three years (Isa. 21:2). In each case, the person charged did not delay but obeyed immediately. Unlike these men, Jonah serves as a common example of "eventual" obedience. It took him two tries and three nights in the belly of a fish to heed God's call to preach in Nineveh.

When no moral command or clear personal calling from God is in view, it is permissible to take our time making decisions. God's specific will can be murky. As individuals, we regularly choose between several good options (e.g., restaurants) or the lesser of two evils (e.g., political candidates). We must discern before we decide. Taking time to weigh pros and cons on such matters does not disappoint God. He commands wisdom, which opposes haste.

Is it true?

Should obedience really be immediate? In most cases, delayed obedience is not ideal. God, however, gives a grace period for discernment. His calls to Moses (Exod. 3–4) and Gideon (Judg. 6) showed his willingness to field their questions and condescend to a few signs. Sadly, one question or sign is rarely enough for our feeble hearts, and God must rebuke our reluctance and thrust us into action. "Go. Fight. Sacrifice. Lead. *Now!*" he says. Consequently, we often prove our trust in God by getting to work.

Beneath the surface of our delayed obedience, doubts and fears fester. Moses likely delayed because past failure told him he wasn't up to the task. Gideon delayed because the Midianites terrified him. These hidden motives wave like a white flag before God. This is equally true for lesser motives for delayed obedience: lack of compassion, love of comfort, selfishness, and cynicism. Jesus encountered a succession of would-be followers who sought exemption from "immediate" obedience, and the Lord rebuffed them all (Matt. 8:18–22). Over time our self-justified delays calcify into spiritual complacency. Haggai's audience suffered this pattern—their brief pause during Cyrus's reign turned into a perpetual vacation by Darius's day.

Fortunately, Israel had a few bright spots of people whose obedience stands out. As mentioned above, Noah, Moses, Samuel, and Isaiah made the list. The lesser known Boaz was heralded for his commitment to do what needs done "in the day" to redeem Ruth (Ruth 3:18). Daily obedience is the drumbeat of Deuteronomy: it secures life and blessing, whereas eventual obedience breeds death (Deut. 30:15–20). The present moment is the perfect time to live God's way, whether heeding a specific calling, repaying a debt, observing Sabbath, helping a neighbor, rejecting an idol, or praising God.

Now what?

So how do we put an end to "eventual" obedience? Is this simply a matter of rising from our seats and setting off into action? Probably not. Eventual obedience usually takes time to develop and will take time to overcome. The will is a difficult muscle to motivate, especially when our comfort is tested. Admitting our delay is merely a start. We must also admit that we often enjoy delayed obedience, preferring it to immediate action. Thus, the first step to end eventual obedience requires us to confess our procrastinating ways as sins.

Second, we should identify areas of our lives where we have grown spiritually indifferent. We may even ask our family members or close friends to gently identify such areas. Once we have developed a short list of growth areas (and calling them "growth" areas takes away some guilt), we should devise a plan for how we will mark our growth. Plans imply priority. Without a plan for feedback and accountability, old habits of indifference and delay are certain to overcome our will and return us to a state of eventual obedience.

Finally, we should remember that God is not a cruel taskmaster but a benevolent Lord. He desires to secure our good. Haggai cited the covenant blessings and curses of Deuteronomy 28. God sent a poor harvest in Jerusalem to seize the attention of his people. Had they obeyed, Haggai implied, their crops would have flourished. Of course, God's people today are no longer under those covenant regulations. But obedience to God's law and response to his calling results in flourishing (Pss. 1:2–3; 19:7–11; 119). Truth-telling, sabbath-keeping, marital fidelity, sexual purity, wise spending, and holiness have built-in rewards. Delaying obedience in these areas hurts us, pushing back God's blessing for another day.

Creativity in Presentation

In his book *War of Art: Break Through the Blocks and Win Your Inner Creative Battle*, Steven Pressfield (2012) makes a compelling case for abandoning the word "procrastination"

for the idea of "Resistance." The former term encultures a sense of defeat; the latter presses us to overcoming obstacles. Nevertheless, many people have an unhealthy tendency to procrastinate. Consider taking an informal "Procrastinator's Poll" to surface this problem. Then challenge them to become people who no longer procrastinate but overcome resistance for God!

Procrastinator's Poll

All questions are a simple yes or no response (raised hands or online polling site)

"I finish my taxes the second week of April."

"I pay most of my bills *on* or *past* their due date."

"I return library books *on* or *past* their due date."

"I'm still buying Christmas presents the week of Christmas."

"I even buy presents on Christmas eve."

"I usually cram for my tests."

"I usually finish my papers or work projects last minute."

"I have unfinished house projects, car projects, and hobbies."

"I leave unwashed dishes in the sink."

A humorous skit (live or recorded) called "Eventual Joe" could illustrate how often we plan to "get around to it" in life. Cast a male to play the part of "Eventual Joe" who will repeat the tagline "I'll get around to it." (Alternatively, you may cast a female to play the part of "Eventual Jo" and adjust the script accordingly.) The following scenarios serve as a good starting point:

PARENT: Joe, dinner's ready. Come and eat.
JOE: I'll get around to it.
DRIVE-THRU VOICE: Order when you're ready.
JOE: I'll get around to it.
TEACHER: Joe, it's your turn to share a book report.
JOE: I'll get around to it.
BOSS: Joe, go plunge the toilet in the men's room.

JOE: I'll get around to it.
GIRLFRIEND: Are you going to propose to me?
JOE: I'll get around to it.
GOD: Joe, give me your heart.
JOE: I'll get around to it.

A wealth of books on productivity have circulated since the start of the twenty-first century. Each proposes a creative system, sustainable habits, and customized methods for maximizing efficiency in personal and business matters. Chief among the productivity writers is David Allen (2001, 12), whose *Getting Things Done: The Art of Stress-Free Productivity* calls any unfinished business (as trivial as returning a text or crucial as solving global hunger) an "open loop." The key to closing loops, he argues, is collecting the clutter, prioritizing, and clarifying the "next steps" (18–19). Giving people an opportunity in the sermon to list their spiritual "open loops" (i.e., collect the clutter), prioritize, and clarify the next step (e.g., "gather wood"; Hag. 1:6) could prove powerful. Provide an example:

Collect the Clutter
My spiritual "open loops" include the need to share my faith, give a tithe, pray more, read the Bible, etc.

Prioritize the Loops
Caring for my body is my most immediate need. Visiting the knitting club is the least immediate.

Clarify Next Steps for "Caring for My Body"
Step 1: Write out what a "healthy me" looks like.
Step 2: Evaluate three core health areas: sleep, diet, and exercise.
Step 3: Note ways I can increase the quality of my sleep: bedtime routines, essential oils, etc.

Step 4: Note ways I can improve my diet: portion sizes, intake of sweets, water consumption, etc.
Step 5: Note ways I can increase my exercise: time, place, and type of exercise; partner, etc.
Step 6: Set specific, measurable goals related to output rather than outcome.
Step 7: Start working goals for a few days; be consistent, not letting a slipup stop progress.
Step 8: Log output in a journal or app for a month and share your success with someone.
Step 9: Reevaluate after a month, tweaking goals as necessary to continue progress.

However, if business self-help principles may not resonate with your congregation, consider Arnold Lobel's (1979) delightful story entitled "Tomorrow" from his children's classic *Days with Frog and Toad*. This children's story shows how Toad overcomes the anguish of delaying his domestic work until tomorrow. Instead, he rises from bed, gets to work, and finds himself better for it.

Whatever creative approach you adopt or adapt, be sure to emphasize this focus: God is pleased with people who set aside their personal excuses and give priority to living out God's expectations. We should put an immediate end to "eventual" obedience.

- A time for rebuke (1:1).

- God rebukes "eventual" obedience (1:2–11).

- God inspires immediate obedience (1:12–14).

- A time for obedience (1:15).

DISCUSSION QUESTIONS

1. What motivated people in Haggai's day to delay their temple rebuilding project? How do you see similar motives affecting today's church?

2. Where are you most likely to procrastinate and what motivates it?

3. What are specific means God has used to get your attention about an area in your life in need of change?

4. What can God's people learn from the glut of productivity books as it relates to "eventual" obedience?

Haggai 2:1–9

EXEGETICAL IDEA
Although many were discouraged because this temple did not match the splendor of Solomon's temple of bygone years, they should persevere because God promised that his Spirit would be with them, he would supply all their material needs to build the temple, and this temple would have more glory than Solomon's temple.

THEOLOGICAL FOCUS
God's people are to persevere in carrying out God's expectations, to move beyond the past ways of doing things, and to trust in God's ability to supply all their needs.

PREACHING IDEA
Beat the "good old days" blues by trusting God today.

PREACHING POINTERS
One month after the temple building project resumed, Haggai relayed his second message. Despite their recent activity, spirits remained low among Israel's leaders and the general populace. Not even a week's worth of celebrating the Feast of Tabernacles sustained optimism among them. Instead, nostalgia for Solomon's more glorious temple reigned in the minds of many. But God would not have his people sulk. He rallied them with imperatives: "fear not" and "look forward." Haggai's promise of God's presence, provision, and peace were meant to instill trust in his people for better days to come.

Getting stuck in nostalgia is an old problem. As forward-thinking and progress-oriented as the Western world seems to be, we continue to hear voices in the church pine for the "good old days." We lament the technological invasion, sexual perversion, moral corruption, political division, social tolerance, and secular convictions ruling our day. We recall better times when public schools mandated student prayer, marriages lasted a lifetime, and mothers stayed home to keep house. We think a return to "former glory" would revive national trust in God. Sadly, not only does nostalgia gloss over past sins, it also fosters a sense of defeat. But we must not be discouraged; God is not stuck in the past. This passage compels us to beat the "good old days" blues by trusting him today.

MAINTAINING GOD'S PRIORITIES BRINGS GOD GLORY (2:1–9)

LITERARY STRUCTURE AND THEMES (2:1–9)

Haggai introduced this second sermon by identifying the time when God spoke to him (2:1–2) about the discouragement induced by an unimpressive temple (2:3). Through this message, Haggai encouraged the people to be strong because God was with them and would provide the gold to make the temple glorious (2:4–9).

The key themes in this message are that discouragement came from looking at things from the human perspective rather than God's point of view. Since God's presence and power could shake the foundation of this world, God's plans would happen and would bring him great glory.

- *A Needed Message (2:1–2)*
- *Comparisons Bring Discouragement (2:3)*
- *The Basis for Encouragement (2:4–9)*

EXPOSITION (2:1–9)

Historically, the Feast of Sukkot (סֻכּוֹת) was a major festival celebrated on the fifteenth of the seventh month of Tishri. During Sukkot (or the Feast of Booths/Shelters) Israelites were expected to remember how their ancestors lived in booths for forty years in the Sinai wilderness. They were also expected to celebrate God's blessings of a good harvest. There was a special sacred assembly of all the people on the last day of this feast (Lev. 23:33–43).

During the Feast of Sukkot, Haggai spoke to a large group of people gathered for this very special day of celebration (Hag. 2:1–2) in order to confront the discouragement caused by comparing this temple with the glory of Solomon's temple (2:3). Haggai encouraged these people with God's promise that this temple would have great glory (2:4–9).

Jewish Calendar					
Month number (biblical)	Hebrew Month	Length	Gregorian Month	Jewish Holiday	References
1	Nisan	30 days	Mar.–Apr.	Passover (Pesach)	Exod. 13:4; 23:25; 34:18; Deut. 16:1
2	Iyar	29 days	Apr.–May		1 Kings 6:1; 6:37
3	Sivan	30 days	May–June	Shavuot (Feast of Weeks / Pentecost)	
4	Tammuz	29 days	June–July		
5	Av	30 days	July–Aug.		
6	Elul	29 days	Aug.–Sept.		
7	Tishri	30 days	Sept.–Oct.	Rosh Hashanah Yom Kippur Sukkot	1 Kings 8:2

Jewish Calendar					
Month number (biblical)	Hebrew Month	Length	Gregorian Month	Jewish Holiday	References
8	Cheshvan	29/30	Oct.–Nov.		1 Kings 6:38
9	Kislev	30/29	Nov.–Dec.	Hanukkah (Feast of Dedication)	1 Macc 4:41–61 John 10:22 Josephus, A. J. 12.7.6 §325
10	Tevet	29	Dec.–Jan.		
11	Shevat	30	Jan.–Feb.		
12	Adar	29	Feb.–Mar.	Purim	

A Needed Message (2:1–2)
God's words spoke to the need of his people and were appropriately timed.

2:1–2. God's new message to Haggai came on the twenty-fourth day of the seventh month, almost two months after his first message (1:1) and about a month after the people began to work on the temple (v. 15). Haggai made sure that the leaders of Judah (the High Priest Joshua and the governor Zerubbabel) as well as the people of Judah heard what God said.

The twenty-first day of the seventh month was a last day of the seven-day Feast of Sukkot (the Feast of Booths/Shelters) At this feast the Israelites were to remember how their ancestors lived in booths for forty years in the Sinai wilderness and to celebrate God's blessings of a good harvest. There was a special sacred assembly of all the people on the last day of this feast (Lev. 23:33–43). Haggai spoke the words of 2:3–9 on that day. This was an advantageous opportunity to address the issue of rebuilding the temple because a large crowd was there. During this feast, people had time to observe the slow progress made on the temple. The people could see the glory of this temple was not that impressive.

Comparisons Bring Discouragement (2:3)
Comparing the glory of the first temple with what was now being rebuilt made people feel discouraged because this temple had little splendor.

2:3. Haggai did not avoid the problem people were talking about at the feast but addressed it head on. A few older people remembered seeing Solomon's temple before it was destroyed about sixty-seven years earlier, and they were discouraged about the unimpressive

TIMELINE OF EVENTS

1:1	First day	sixth month	August 29, 520 B.C.	Haggai spoke
1:15	Twenty-fourth day	sixth month	September 21, 520 B.C.	Started building the temple
	Tenth day	seventh month	October 7, 520 B.C.	Day of Atonement
	Fifteenth day	seventh month	October 11, 530 B.C.	Sukkot festival started
2:1	Twenty-first day	seventh month	October 17, 520 B.C.	Sukkot ended / Haggai spoke
2:10	Twenty-fourth day	ninth month	December 18, 530 B.C.	Haggai spoke

glory of this new temple.[1] Haggai asked these older people if this rebuilt section of the temple seemed like nothing in comparison to the glory of Solomon's temple. Apparently some were voicing this negative opinion about this rebuilding project. Comparing the glory of the first temple with what was now being rebuilt made people feel discouraged because this temple had little splendor.

Although Haggai did not condemn this comparison, it was based on an unfair comparison between two very different eras of Israelite history. The Solomonic era was a time of unprecedented strength, whereas the time of Haggai was characterized as a time of great political weakness. Consequently, one would expect that the two construction projects would be quite different. It would be quite unrealistic to expect the rebuilt temple in these postexilic times to have anything close to the glory of Solomon's temple. Those who made these comparisons were discouraged by the poverty of the postexilic setting and their limited ability to rebuild a temple that would match the splendor of Solomon's temple.

The Basis for Encouragement (2:4–9)
Encouragement was based on God's great strength, his powerful Spirit, and his sovereign control of all nations.

2:4. At this point, the prophet did not criticize the people for their past memories of Solomon's temple in those past "good old days," refute their biased comparisons of these two temples, or call for a new fundraising push. Instead, Haggai offered several positive words of encouragement and an amazing prophecy about the future glory of the rebuilt temple.

In contrast ("but now, nevertheless"; עַתָּה) to the people's present negative thinking, Haggai offered three identical words of

encouragement from God. "Be strong" (חֲזַק) was God's specific message to the governor Zerubbabel, "be strong" (חֲזַק) was God's separate word of encouragement to the High Priest Joshua, and "be strong" (חֲזַק) was God's challenge to the people in the land (Taylor and Clendenen, 2004, 153). This parallels God's threefold encouragement to another Joshua when he became the leader of the children of Israel (Josh. 1:6–9), and it was similar to David's words to Solomon when Solomon was faced with the huge responsibility of building the first temple (1 Chron. 28:20). Being strong required a radical change from their present disillusioned attitude, for strength implied being determined or resolute in purpose.

But why should these people think that it was possible for them to be strong? The drought was still there, the Persians still ruled the world, and the people in Samaria had not reversed their opposition to this project. The community still did not have the financial resources to make a glorious temple. Thus, Haggai needed to provide some solid reasons for optimism and some motivation for maintaining their priority of glorifying God by rebuilding this temple.

The first reason Haggai gave for maintaining this priority was the simple yet powerful divine covenant promise (Hill, 2008a, 508) that "I am with you." This repeated the promise in Haggai 1:13 and reminded the audience of God's promise to be with Moses (Exod. 3:12) as he led the people out of Egyptian bondage and God's promise to dwell among his people in the tabernacle (Exod. 29:42–46) as well as God's promise to be with Joshua during the conquest of the Canaanites (Josh. 1:5).

2:5. God promised that his Spirit would be "continual standing, be persistently present" (עֹמֶדֶת) among his people, and he compared this to the Spirit's long-standing presence with

---

1   This dissatisfaction should not be confused with the weeping of the older men when the temple foundation was dedicated in Ezra 3:10–14, for that event took place at least sixteen years earlier.

the Israelites when they came out of Egypt and wandered in the wilderness.[2] That same Spirit was still present to guide, protect, and empower his people in the postexilic era.

2:6. The second reason for hope was that God would shake the heavens and the earth to bring about some significant changes in the present state of affairs (2:6). The breadth of God's action seems to cover all international affairs on earth. Thus, God was claiming his sovereignty over what would happen in the future. In addition, God's plan was to accomplish his will by timing his action at the appropriate time ("in a little while").

2:7. God's shaking of all nations will result in a "desirable thing/desirable one" (חֶמְדַּה) coming from the nations to Jerusalem. Although some interpret this as the "Desired One," giving it messianic significance (Kaiser, 1992, 268), the solution to the people's problem in this context was that the people in Jerusalem needed silver and gold to beautify the temple.

2:8. Thus, God assured the Israelites that he controlled all the silver and gold on earth. God was able to cause these "desirable things" (great riches) to come from other nations to Jerusalem in order to make this rebuilt temple glorious. This was exactly what happened a short time later when God caused the Persian king Darius to order Tattenai, the governor of the province beyond the river to pay the full cost of reconstructing the temple out of the royal treasury of that region (Ezra 6:6–8). There is an irony here, for this decree required that some of the taxes from the people of Samaria (they opposed the building of the temple in Ezra 4:1–5) would end

up being used to pay for the construction of this Jewish temple. What a marvelous fulfillment!

2:9. Commentators have interpreted the idea that God would fill this house with glory (2:7, 9) in different ways. First, based on the lack of glory in 2:3, some believe the glory in 2:7, 9 referred to the physical splendor of the temple. But since this temple was not really as big as Solomon's temple, Baldwin (1972, 48) thinks this prophecy refers to the latter expansion of the temple mount and lavish improvement in the temple building by Herod the Great (Mark 13:1). Another interpretation (Boda, 2004, 125; Meyers and Meyers, 1987, 54) connects this glory to the splendor of God's glorious presence above the ark of the covenant in the Holy of Holies (cf. Exod. 40:34–35; 2 Chron. 5:14; 7:1–2), but there is no reference to the ark being present in this rebuilt temple. Although Haggai was pointing to an external physical glory, his prophecy is broad enough to include the prophetic idea that the glorious Son of God would be in this temple (Matt. 12:1).[3]

The final word from God in Haggai 2:9 was that God would grant his people "peace" (שָׁלוֹם). It is unclear if this refers to peace from war, spiritual peace when people came to "this place" (the temple) to confess their sins, or an eschatological peace that would come to the whole world (Verhoef, 1987, 107). Unfortunately, this prophecy ends with no record of how the people responded to Haggai's challenging words.

THEOLOGICAL FOCUS
The exegetical idea (Although many were discouraged because this temple did not match the splendor of Solomon's temple of bygone

---

2 Although the exodus narrative does not mention the Spirit abiding in the midst of those exiting Egypt, later texts (Neh. 9:20, 30; Isa. 63:10–14) connect the Spirit with the pillar of fire, the cloud that protected the tribes at the Red Sea (Exod. 14:19–20, 24), and the angel of God (Baldwin, *Haggai, Zechariah, Malachi*, 47; Verhoef, *Books of Haggai and Malachi*, 100–101) in later narratives (Exod. 33:2).

3 In John 2:13–22, Jesus even referred to himself as the temple.

years, they should persevere because God promised that his Spirit would be with them, he would supply all their material needs to build the temple, and this temple would have more glory than Solomon's temple) leads to this theological focus: God's people are to persevere in carrying out God's expectations, to move beyond the past ways of doing things, and to trust in God's ability to supply all their needs.

Two theological themes are emphasized in this second sermon of Haggai's prophecy: (1) persevere in doing God's work; and (2) trust God to supply for your needs. First, this message from God argued that these people should persevere (2:4) and resist the temptation to give up on their priorities because the temple was not as impressive as they hoped (v. 3). Reality differed significantly from what was expected and this caused some to question the value of rebuilding the temple. But a failure to maintain God's priorities raised a serious problem that needed to be addressed with a series of encouraging statements that lifted the spirit of the workers. Impediments to accomplishing any spiritual goal would be experienced from time to time, but people should not give up just because things do not pan out according to expectations. These people needed to stop complaining about the appearance of the building and focus their attention on the spiritual gain of rebuilding the temple. They needed to persevere.

Second, there is the promise that God was able to supply the spiritual and physical support that was needed to complete the tasks he assigned to his people. God's solution to every problem would not be an unlimited supply of silver and gold from foreigners (2:7–8), but he would provide for his people's needs, and his powerful Spirit would always be present with them. At times the answer might come quickly or be years off, so in every situation God's people must follow his leading, trust in his promises, be strong and resolute (vv. 4–8), and wait for the fulfillment of his promises.

PREACHING AND TEACHING STRATEGIES

Exegetical and Theological Synthesis

Haggai 2:1–9 clearly addresses a disheartened people. It was not the first time God had encountered lack of courage or distrust in Israel. The "fear not" refrain echoes throughout Scripture, from Abraham (Gen. 15:1) to Moses (Num. 21:34) to Joshua (Josh. 8:1) to Solomon (1 Chron. 28:20) to Nehemiah's workers (Neh. 4:1). God desires people to look beyond their circumstances—bad weather, big armies, towering responsibilities—and see his power and provision. Only God deserves our fear, and this is the beginning of wisdom (Prov. 1:7).

Upon closer inspection, Haggai provided persuasive evidence to fear God, approaching him reverently. Five times in this brief section the passage reaffirms God's sovereignty, referring to him as "Lord of all." God recited old promises (his presence and deliverance) and made new ones (shaking the heavens and all nations). The exegesis explores his providential (and ironic) use of Samaritan monies to rebuild the temple. Moreover, it points toward later developments for the temple, including Herod's expansion and Jesus's ministry.

God's presence and provision did not discount the importance of human effort. Just as he previously "stirred" Zerubbabel and company to get to work (Hag. 1:14), God maintained a sense of urgency. He prefaced the "fear not" challenge with a thrice-repeated cheer to "take heart." God both catalyzed and completed the work he started in his people (Phil. 1:6; 2:12). For example, after pronouncing Joshua cleansed, the Lord commanded the high priest to live and work according to his holy requirements (Zech. 3:4–7). Meaningful work is often a partnership between God (who gives the mission) and people (who apply their muscles).

Preaching Idea

Beat the "good old days" blues by trusting God today.

Contemporary Connections

What does it mean?

What are the "good old days" blues? Are they really something to beat? First, we must distinguish between healthy memory and unhealthy nostalgia. The former recounts God powerful deeds and sweeping forgiveness to provoke worship (Pss. 103, 104, 136). The latter uses selective events from the past to justify discontentment in the present. Healthy memory shapes ethics (Exod. 20:1–3; Deut. 5:12–15); unhealthy nostalgia leads to "good old days" grumbling.

Haggai's audience is not alone in waxing nostalgic about former days. Weeks after their exodus, the Israelites expressed their longing for food from Pharaoh's pantry (Exod. 16:3). The wilderness generation made a similar complaint (Num. 11:5). Chronicles reminisces about King David's glorious age, skipping the more scandalous details of his spotted history (e.g., Bathsheba, Absalom). No, King David remains the golden standard of the "good old days." Today people overlook the racism and sexism of past decades, when they pine for the "good old days" and family values of the 1950s.

Not only does unhealthy nostalgia cause grumbling and taint memory, it forestalls moving forward by fixating on what lies behind. The TV, automobile, personal computer, and mobile phone came into existence because inventors were not willing to cling to past technologies, even if the horse-and-buggy days sounded romantic. We may miss an old house, former job, or deceased parent, but it does us little good to obsess about our losses. God wants his people to fix their eyes forward: a day will come when he will make all things new (Rev. 21:5).

Is it true?

Can we really trust God today? Indeed! God has a history of providing for daily needs. During the exodus from Egypt, God supplied his people with food and water while they wandered in the wilderness (Exod. 16:1–17:7). God secured victory for the nation of Israel as they entered the Promised Land or engage enemy forces (Josh. 6; Judg. 7:15–23). God made food miraculously appear and multiply for Elijah and his hosts (1 Kings 17:1–16). Finally, God's daily provision foreshadows the abounding provision he will lavish upon the new heavens and new earth (Isa. 65:17–25).

Authors who wrote about trusting God's daily provision were no strangers to suffering; they experienced exile, imprisonment, and public scorn. Apostles underwent similar trials, as did an ever-expanding list of martyrs throughout the church's history. In other words, God's daily supply does not exempt anyone from daily struggles. People still experience cancer, car crashes, financial woes, hormonal imbalances, peer pressure, and countless obstacles. However, many can testify how they have felt the nearness of God and comfort of his people most acutely in pain (Ps. 23:4; cf. 2 Cor. 1:3–11).

Therefore, we are wise to trust God without adopting naive optimism. Just as we can twist healthy memory into unhealthy nostalgia, we can also substitute biblically informed hope with blissfully ignorant positivity. Trusting in God's daily provision does not guarantee us gourmet meals and perfect weather. God remains trustworthy even if the sun does not shine this week.

Now what?

What are practical ways to beat the "good old days blues"? How does this build trust in God for today? First, we should realize our trust in God today is conditioned by our awareness of his faithful activity in the past. History records many wonders God has worked for his people. We should remember that God created the heavens, blessed Abraham, empowered Moses, delivered judges, protected Elijah, honored Ruth, and spoke through the prophets. On a more personal note, we should gratefully recall his activity in our lives: providing a good job, rebuilding a tough marriage, overseeing a quick recovery from surgery, ensuring three healthy childbirths, preventing injury in a car accident, and providing a trusted friend. Gratitude does not gloss over challenges in the past—we all have them—but chooses to focus on the good that God worked to bring from them.

After reviewing God's past faithfulness, we recall his future promises. He does not promise health and wealth for individual believers, but he does guarantee to put an end to evil and remain present with his people. Someday God will eradicate global poverty, abuses of power, terrorism, pollution, abortion, racism, and other social ills. Someday he will dethrone demonic forces and remedy environmental hazards. Someday God will dwell with humanity in a new and just world; creation and nations will experience shalom. This eschatological vision pairs wonderfully with God's faithful past. When we take time to meditate on God's faithful past and promised future, it builds assurance for today.

Lest we swing from nostalgia to eschatological fervor, we must remember that God never intended prophecy to inspire escapism. His vision of better days ahead should motivate us to work today toward a "preferred future." As we long for ultimate restoration, God expects us to practice it in the moment by welcoming strangers, showing kindness, and extending mercy.

Creativity in Presentation

Haggai serves as a model motivator. His threefold "take heart" exhortation conjures up motivational memes and images commonly posted in workplaces, schools, gyms, or locker rooms. Type "motivational posters" in a search engine for numerous examples. Consider compiling a series of these posters—some serious, some humorous—and tell the congregation you intend to get them motivated to do God's work today. If you opt to use more humorous samples, be sure to address the underlying blocks to motivation—fear of failure, lack of progress, internal resistance, external opposition, unclear direction, and plain old laziness.

"Motivational" Mock-Ups!

Haggai simply used redemptive reminders to inspire action. Modern-day motivators may resort to showmanship, emotional appeals, and parlor tricks. Some hilarious examples include:

- Chris Farley's character, Matt Foley, who lives "in a van down by the river," originally featured on *Saturday Night Live*
- Also from *SNL* are Hans and Franz (played by Dana Carvey and Kevin Nealon, respectively), who want to "pump you up"
- Greg Kinnear who plays Richard Hoover, a struggling author and hapless motivator in the film *Little Miss Sunshine* (2006), pathetically peddling his multistep self-help book
- Actor Shai LaBeouf's "Just Do It" motivational speech, which went viral on YouTube for his excessive call to action

---

To surface the "good old days" blues in your congregation, you might select people from different generations to share reflections from their childhood. Ask them pointed questions to help reveal their feelings about former days: How much violence was in your schools? How often did you have family dinners? How many of your friends came from divorced families? Could you ride without a seatbelt on long road trips? How bad was the pornography problem? How many genders were there? How many gay couples on TV? How invasive was technology? Adapt questions to suit your congregation, but be sure to close by asking if they think our culture has progressed or regressed morally since their childhood. It's safe to bet most evangelicals in the West will chose "regress," at which point you ask, "Do you want to go back?" (A less risky version of this exercise is to invite the entire congregation to silently reflect on the questions. It will produce a similar bias for the "good old days.")

Since healthy memory is such a powerful motivator for God's people, it might be worth weaving personal testimonies of God's faithfulness into the message. Ask individuals to recall a time where God's presence or provision—themes from Haggai—felt palpable. Video testimonies will allow you better control of timing and content but likely require a skilled editor. (Live testimonies always run the risk of rambling.) Alternatively, to engage more of the audience, you might distribute sticky notes and designate a Wall of Testimony for people to post two-sentence stories of God's faithfulness—presence and provision—in their life. (Example: God provided clarity and peace when I faced a major career decision. His answers to prayer in the past assure me he will hear me in days to come.)

The central truth to communicate is this: God's people are to persevere in carrying out God's expectations while depending on and trusting in his ability to supply all their needs. Thus, we should beat the "good old days" blues by trusting God today.

- God acknowledges the "good old days" blues (2:1–3).

- God inspires working today for a better tomorrow (2:4–5).

- God describes better days ahead (2:6–9).

DISCUSSION QUESTIONS

1. How did Haggai address his audience's disheartened state? What is the interplay between our view of God and our fears?

2. What is the difference between healthy memory and unhealthy nostalgia? (Provide examples of each.) What makes nostalgia unhealthy?

3. What are the marks of someone who trusts God? What are areas where daily trust is essential?

4. How has God demonstrated his faithfulness in your life and those in your church?

Haggai 2:10–19

EXEGETICAL IDEA
Applying the Levitical principle that God-honoring living could not be gained by touching something holy like the temple caused many people to realize they were already defiled and needed to repent, so that when they did God could bless them as he promised.

THEOLOGICAL FOCUS
God-honoring holy living is not achieved through works, service, or sacrifices but through the removal of defilement inside so that God can provide his blessings.

PREACHING IDEA
A clean start with God starts within.

PREACHING POINTERS
Three months into the temple renovation project, Haggai brought the people a bad diagnosis. They were unclean. Their defilement was like a transferrable disease. Their material blessings were lacking. The original audience would have recognized Haggai's appeal to the covenant curses. Fortunately, their revived effort to rebuild the temple showed God their desire for a clean start and future blessings.

The need for a clean start with God continues today. Fortunately, he welcomes a change of heart and grants fresh starts. Like a passionate father, he watches for prodigal sons and daughters in the distance and races to embrace them upon their return. Sadly, we wait too long to recognize our compromised motives and calloused consciences. We excuse our inner corruption as a personality quirk, pathology, or work in progress. Conversely, we deem ourselves holy, in varying degrees, due to religious activity, church attendance, and proximity to "spiritual giants." Outside-in holiness breeds legalism, activism, and nagging guilt. This passage exposes our need for a clean start with God starts within.

GIVING PRIORITY TO HOLINESS BRINGS GOD'S BLESSINGS (2:10–19)

LITERARY STRUCTURE AND THEMES (2:10–19)

Haggai's third sermon opened with an introduction to a new prophecy (2:10) that offered illustrations about holiness and defilement (2:11–14). Haggai then uttered a prophetic announcement that God would turn past droughts into future agricultural blessings (2:15–19).

Haggai's theme was holiness. His message raised the question, What was the source of defilement and holiness? He concluded that the removal of defilement would make it possible for God to send his blessing.

- *A Vital Message (2:10)*
- *A Lesson about Defilement (2:11–14)*
- *God's Discipline Will Turn into a Blessing (2:15–19)*

EXPOSITION (2:10–19)

When the term "holy" (קָדוֹשׁ) appears in Scripture, it typically implies that someone or something is set apart from evil or sin. Here in Haggai, the temple was holy because no sinful person could enter it, for it was set apart from normal human use and was the place where God dwelt among people. The furniture in the temple was holy because it was set apart for use by God in the holy temple. A priest was holy when he had made atonement for his sins and consecrated himself to God's service in the temple.

The people were unholy not because they were working on the temple. They needed to repent of their inner sinfulness that defiled them so that God could bless them. Applying the Levitical principle that God-honoring living could not be gained by touching something holy like the temple caused many people to realize they were already defiled and needed to repent so that when they did, God could bless them as he promised.

A Vital Message (2:10)

At key junctures in life, God confronted his people with new challenges concerning a God-honoring life of holy living.

2:10. The next word from God came to Haggai approximately two months (December 18, 520 B.C.) after the message in 2:1–9 and three months after work began on the temple in 1:15 (September 18, 520 B.C.). Three facts are important to understand this message. First, when Haggai spoke, the winter crops were now planted and it was time for the autumn rains to fall. People were hoping for an end to the drought and an abundant harvest. Thus, the promise in 2:19 referred to a large harvest of the seeds they had recently sown as well as the coming harvest from vines and trees. Second, about a month before this message, Zechariah spoke in the eighth month (Zech. 1:1–6) about the need for people to turn from their evil ways and turn back to God. This resulted in some people repenting (Zech. 1:6b). Although Zechariah did not pinpoint one particular sin, it is clear from Haggai 2:1–9 and Zechariah 1:1–6 that a spiritual revitalization of the hearts of the people in Jerusalem was needed in the seventh month (Hag. 2:1–6), the eighth month (Zech. 1:1–6), and in the ninth month (Hag. 2:10, 17b). The third factor is that this day marked the time when the foundation of the temple was completed and probably dedicated (as in other ancient Near Eastern cultures;

cf. Boda, 2004, 111; Petersen, 1984, 89) similar to the dedication of the foundation sixteen years earlier described in Ezra 3:10–13. Many priests were there, musicians praised God, and a large gathering of Israelites gave thanks to God. This would mark the completion of a major step in the building process, for now it was possible to raise the walls of the temple.

A Lesson about Defilement (2:11–14)
Real, God-honoring holy living required more than just a close association with holy things.

2:11–12. The Lord spoke again to Haggai three months after work began on temple reconstruction in 1:15. If this message was given in the temple area, there would be many priests available to give a basic "Torah ruling" (תּוֹרָה) concerning the transfer of purity or impurity (2:12). Since sacrificial animals were skinned and cut up off to one side of the altar, it was necessary for a priest to carry the parts of the prepared sacrifice from that area to the altar in the fold of his robe. The first test case asked "if" (הֵן) it was possible for there to be a transfer of holiness from the holy sacrifice to the priest's robe and then to something else (bread, stew, wine, oil) that the priest might touch. The priests answered that it was not possible for a sacred temple object that was set apart to God to transfer its sacred holy status to a third object just by touching it (however, in Exodus 29:37; 30:29; and Leviticus 6:18, it was possible to pass this sacred holy status by direct contact to a second object).

The motive for asking this question was not given, but one can imagine that some people felt that attending the festivals, bringing their sacrifices to an altar, or working on the temple construction enabled them to establish a sacred holy relationship to God because they were working on the temple, a building set apart to God. But real holiness involved the heart, not just touching something holy (the temple).

TRANSLATION ANALYSIS: תּוֹרָה
NASB[95] "Ask now the priests for a *ruling*"
NIV "Ask the priests what the *law* says"
HCSB "Ask the priests for a *ruling*"
NRSV "Ask the priests for a *ruling*"
NKJV "Now ask the priests concerning the *law*"

2:13. The second test case inquired if uncleanness can be passed from an "unclean soul, corpse" (מְמֵא־נֶפֶשׁ) to a person who might touch the unclean dead body and then on to a third object (2:13–14). In this case the answer was yes.

2:14. The application of these rulings was applied to Haggai's audience with the shocking announcement that "this people and this nation," the things they have touched (their agricultural efforts; Verhoef, 1987, 120), and their offerings were defiled. As in Haggai 1:3, the use of "this people" is a derogatory term quite different from the endearing covenantal term "my people." The exact nature of this defilement was not explained, but the seriousness of defilement was evident, for it impacted the people, their work, and their sacrifices.

God's Discipline Will Turn into a Blessing (2:15–19)
Past failures brought God's curse, but his blessing would be available to those who do his will.

2:15. Haggai moved the conversation (וְעַתָּה, "and now") from the problems of defilement in 2:10–14 to the call for reflection on God's lack of blessing in 2:15–17. Mirroring the call for people to "consider, reflect" (lit., "set it upon your heart") in Haggai 1:5, 7, the prophet called for his audience to think about their situation. The contrast to consider was between the past judgment of God (2:15–17) and his future blessing (vv. 18–19). But the prophet's primary aim was for them to think about the future, "from this day onward" (1:15, 18, 19). In order to see a change from "this day and onward," they had to look at what happened before this day.

The importance of "this day" was explained as the day when the laying the foundation blocks (2:15) of the "temple" (הֵיכַל) was completed (2:18). This day may have included a dedication ceremony as in Ezra 3:10–13 (Petersen, 1984, 89–90; Boda, 2004, 147), but Haggai said nothing about that ceremony.

2:16–17. Instead of offering further comment, Haggai moved immediately to raise the question concerning how things were "before" (מִטֶּרֶם) that day. From the earlier account in 1:6, 9–11, it was clear that God sent drought, poor crops, and a spoiling of some of the harvest. In this context, the prophet explained how this divine curse impacted what was left for them to eat and drink. The prophet indicated that the farmer only ended up with half the grain that was expected (from twenty down to ten units) and even less wine from the vineyard (from fifty down to twenty units). The reason for this decrease in produce was not some freak accident. No, this was purposely brought by God ("I struck" הִכֵּיתִי) who caused a curse (Lev. 26:24) to fall on all agricultural land. Haggai described God's judgment as a plague of blight, mildew, and hail (cf. Amos 4:9). A good size ball of hail would have had a disastrous on their crops of grain as well as the fruit on the vine. But the people responded just like they did in the time of Amos: they did not immediately turn to God in repentance (Hag. 2:17) and humble themselves.

Ancient winepress, south of Hebron mountain. On the right, the treading pit; in the middle, the precipitation pit; the vat on the left. Courtesy of זמרפ וחיא [CC BY 3.0 (https://creativecommons.org/licenses/by/3.0)].

2:18. In sharp contrast to what happened in the past (2:15–17), the prophet Haggai now offered hope for the future. He called for reflection on finding a resolution that would bring future blessings in 2:18–19. Twice he asked the people (as in 1:5, 7; 2:15) to "reflect" (lit., "set it on your heart") on what would happen in the future. From this crucial day forward (picking up this idea from 2:15) things would change dramatically. The importance of this day (December 18, 520 B.C.) was either the time when the community would finish laying the foundation blocks for the temple building or the community would start repairing the temple. Since there is no information on the status of the stone foundation or walls at this time, it is impossible to determine the exact situation. The important thing is that in both interpretations the people were working on restoring the temple and that seemed to be the reason why God promised to pour out his blessing on the people in the coming months.

2:19. This verse begins with a question that inquired about the amount of grain still left in farmer's storage bins. The implied answer is that there was only a little grain left. This was due to a combination of factors: the drought, the need to use some grain to make bread, and the need to reserve some grain for the next planting. In contrast to the little grain in their barns now, Haggai predicted that there would be a great harvest in the future. Though the vine, fig, pomegranate, olive tree, and other crops had not produced their fruit in the past, there was now hope. This hope was based on the promise of God's blessing on their harvest. This was God's response to the people's change of behavior, for they were now giving priority to building God's house.

THEOLOGICAL FOCUS

The exegetical idea (Applying the Levitical principle that God-honoring living could not be gained by touching something holy like the temple caused many people to realize they were already defiled and needed to repent so that when they did, God could bless them as he promised) leads to this theological focus: God-honoring holy living is not achieved through works, service, or sacrifices but through the removal of defilement inside so that God can provide his blessings.

Two important theological themes are emphasized in this third sermon of Haggai's prophecy: (a) the basis of holiness and (b) God's blessing on his holy people. Living a holy life in a way that is pleasing to God was absolutely essential. It was not enough to give some money as an offering to God or to present a sacrifice at the altar. God was not satisfied until the whole heart had turned in repentance and the will had submitted to the priority of following God's instructions. The heart, the will, and the hands must be free from sin and dedicated to serving and honoring God. Holiness was not attained by simply touching something or doing something good (e.g., working on the temple) and ignoring another things God expects (2:12–13). How could God bless those who did not prioritize holy living? On the other hand, holy living would make it possible for God to pour out his blessings (2:19).

The second theme deals with the idea that God would bless his people with abundant crops and reverse the curse on the crops described in Haggai 1:10–11 when they stand before him as holy people. When this happens God would provide rain for the seeds they had sown in the fields, moisture to produce grapes on the vines, olives on the trees, and a good amount of grass for their cattle.

PREACHING AND TEACHING STRATEGIES

Exegetical and Theological Synthesis
The exegetical section highlights the role of priests in interpreting the Torah for the people. The temple reconstruction project revitalized the priestly ministry, which administered sacrifices, officiated at festivals, and declared people "clean" or "unclean." The return of the cult or practice of these beliefs and rituals also likely stirred a spirit of promise among God's people. But the hypothetical rulings in 2:11–14 gave a warning: uncleanness transfers more readily than holiness.

If the reminder alarmed the Israelites, the prophet made another reference to the covenant curses of Leviticus 26 (cf. Deut. 28). The dearth of material blessings stemmed from the disobedience of God's people. God "struck" the land with blight, mildew, and hail, greatly reducing their crop yields. God did not discipline his people arbitrarily or capriciously but caused ruinous circumstances to grab their hearts. He desired repentance, disciplining those whom he loves (Hos. 11; Prov. 3:12; cf. Heb. 12:6).

Finally, the resounding note of Haggai's message was not judgment but hope. God had better things in store for his people (Hag. 2:19; cf. 2 Peter 3:13; Heb. 12:25–29). The Lord promised fuller harvests, spiritual fruit, new bodies, and eternal peace in his presence in the new heavens and new earth (Isa. 65:17–25; cf. Rev. 21–22). Although for some, eschatology leads to escapism, its true purpose is to inspire holiness in the present (Zech. 14:20–21). Indeed, our pursuit of holiness—an inside-out job—is the pathway to beholding God (Heb. 12:14).

Preaching Idea
A clean start with God starts within.

Contemporary Connections

What does it mean?
What does it mean that a clean start with God starts within? What is a clean start? While no one can claim to be sinless (2 Chron. 6:36; Eccl. 7:20), God's people can receive a clean start in the form of forgiveness (Pss. 32:1; 103; Lam.

3:22–23). In the OT, the Lord made provisions for a clean start through the sacrificial system (Lev. 4–5). The Day of Atonement served as an annual cleansing for his people (Lev. 16). Penitential psalms showed God's willingness to cleanse the hearts of remorseful people (Ps. 51). Prophetic calls to return to God betrayed his desire to offer Israel a fresh start (Isa. 1:18).

A clean start is more than going through the motions of confessing sin. That can be external, outside-in behavior management. God sees through such posturing, knowing the difference between lip service and a pure heart (Isa. 29:13). A changed heart cannot be faked or formed by religious activity. God knows within the human heart stirs idolatry, greed, bitterness, lust, selfishness, pride, and complacency. Fortunately, he promises to aid inside-out change through the impartation of his Spirit (Jer. 31:31–34). God grants a clean start; we do not earn it.

Without a clean start, God's people may feel distant from him, their prayers rejected, his blessings withheld. David's corrupt heart resulted in inner turmoil (Ps. 51). An addict or adulterer may feel similar guilt. Any lie, lust, or breech of love toward another strains the relationship. Change within begins by acknowledging our unclean motives, admitting our unclean deeds, and asking God to forgive us as we resolve to obey him.

Is it true?
Is it true that a clean start with God starts within? Yes. External acts clearly do not bring internal cleansing (Isa. 64:6). Rather, inward change starts with the heart, the volitional core of the human person. The heart is something to be guarded, as it sets the course for one's actions (Prov. 4:23–27). Otherwise, the heart might become callously hardened or selfishly stubborn, leading to all sorts of wickedness (Gen. 6:5; Exod. 7:3). Thus, Moses commanded people to orient their hearts toward loving God (Deut. 6:4). And David called for pure hearts in approaching God for corporate praise (Ps.

24:3–4). In fact, David habitually presented his inner life to God, asking him to search his heart for anything displeasing (Pss. 17:3; 26:2; 139:23–24).

As mentioned above, a clean heart cannot be earned but is granted by God. No amount of good behavior can appease God or curb our hearts from their sinful bent (Jer. 7:24; 11:18; 16:12; 17:9). Attending a candlelight vigil or serving food to the homeless does not earn us a clean start with God. Teaching a children's Bible study or giving money to purchase mosquito nets in Africa does not earn us a clean start with. God must intervene and declare us clean (Zech. 3:3–5).

Confessing our sin to God activates his mercy and initiates a clean start. We should admit our selfish acts, gross attitudes, reckless anger, anxious plotting, or loveless behavior without making excuses. Psalms 32 and 51 are exceptional prayers of confession. David noted his remorse, owned his mistake, begged God for a clean start, resolving to trust God moving forward. These psalms model humility and authenticity—marks of inside-out change.

Now what?
How do we assure a clean start with God? How do we work from within? The starting point to these questions differs depending on our relationship with God. If we have never dragged our sorry and soiled self to God, begging him for cleansing, then our clean start begins with an initial act of repentance—turning away from life as we know it to life as God designed it. Our self-effort is a filthy rag that will never satisfy God's holy standard (Isa. 64:6). Fortunately, he shows abundant mercy (Exod. 34:6; Pss. 25:6–7; 41:4; Lam. 3:22–23).

For those who have walked with God for years but continue with calloused hearts and bloodied hands, inside-out change requires the spadework of spiritual formation. Not to be confused with a new legalism, spiritual formation uses ancient practices—prayer and fasting,

Scripture reading and meditation, silence and solitude, giving and service, simplicity and corporate worship—as ways of posturing ourselves before God. The distinction is important: spiritual disciplines set a heart posture that says to God, "Here I am, make me whole." The disciplines themselves, which are external acts, do not change our heart, but they open our hearts to learn from God, receive his mercy, and resolve to change.

Finally, we can take advantage of natural turning points and transitions in life to ask God for a clean start. Every new day, every new week, every new month, every new year, every birthday, every paycheck, every Sunday worship service signals renewal. Haggai's specificity with dates inspires greater sensitivity to the calendar when marking fresh starts with God. Perhaps a daily prayer asking God for a clean start is in order: "Father, renew my heart on this new day."

Creativity in Presentation

One of the parenting techniques my wife and I (Tim) have adopted is called the "re-do" or "do-over" (Purvis, Cross, and Sunshine, 2007, 97). Delightfully simple, the re-do allows disobedient children a fresh start. Typically, kids seize the opportunity for a re-do. For example, if a child slams the front door, the parent replies, "Oops. That's not the way we shut the door. We shut it gently. Do you want a re-do?" When the child agrees (and if he doesn't, you playfully let him know he will take a re-do because you're "the boss"!), you praise his efforts the second time around. Why? Every shamed kid wants a clean start. Consider asking the congregation, "How many of you if God asked for a 're-do' would take it?" Don't be afraid to be specific: How many need a re-do with your spending habits? How many need a re-do with their attitude toward their spouse? How many need a re-do with time wasted online, looking at things that make you jealous, angry, or sexually tempted? Remind them that we will continue to need re-do's until we change within.

I live next to an abandoned house. The previous owners struggled to keep their lawn mowed and porch clear of clutter. It was symptomatic of a larger problem: they were hoarders. Stuff filled every square inch of their home. They recently rented two, twenty-foot dumpsters to clear out their stuff. Now they live across town in a new residence, enjoying a fresh start. Anyone who plans to move into their old, abandoned home will likely have to gut the place and remodel starting from the bare joists and studs. Clean starts often require purging and deconstructing from within, whether it's an old home, car engine, computer tower, knee replacement, or ministry program. Describe a clean start story in vivid detail for your congregation.

Victor Hugo's classic story, *Les Misérables*, powerfully captures the idea of a clean start when former convict, Jean Valjean is caught stealing from a priest. Instead of turning him over to the self-righteous Inspector Javert, the priest vouches for Valjean, and he is released. In the theatrical version of *Les Misérables* (directed by Tom Hooper, 2012), Valjean (played by Hugh Jackman) stands amazed at his clean slate. His song "Valjean's Soliloquy" expresses the agony of inside-out change.

Any historical research on a plague will surface the power of contamination. Whether the Justinian (sixth century A.D.) or Bubonic plague (fourteenth century A.D.), Spanish flu or COVID-19 (1917 to 2020 A.D.), these events spread from one person to the next upon touch or close contact. You might use the following illustration to visualize the spiritual defilement Haggai's audience suffered from. First, warn the congregation an epidemic is immanent. *You have the plague.* Then walk to the front row and tap the shoulder of someone sitting. *He has the plague.* Ask that person to tap the shoulder of someone else—who will have the plague—as you find another lucky contestant. Each person tapped must stand and tap another. After a minute have everyone take note of the number of "plagued" people standing. Summarize:

112

"Disease spreads externally. It spreads rapidly. It spreads naturally. Cures work internally, often slowly, and sometimes only supernaturally."

As you integrate various, creative elements, be sure to emphasize that temple activity (various external works, service, or sacrifices) will not automatically make one holy, for sin can defile a person; so it is necessary to remove inner defilement so God can pour out his blessings. A clean slate with God starts within.

- Externals don't make us clean (2:10–12).

- Uncleanliness is contagious (2:13–14).

- A blessed state is coming (2:15–19).

DISCUSSION QUESTIONS

1. What did the answer returned by the priests in 2:12–14 imply about Haggai's audience?

2. How did ancient Israel seek out and receive forgiveness? How do God's people apprehend it today?

3. What role does the "heart" play in getting a "clean start" with God? What makes external acts ("outside-in" holiness) such an attractive substitute?

4. Where does the church need a "re-do"? Where do you need one?

Haggai 2:20–23

EXEGETICAL IDEA
Since God controlled the political rise and fall of every nation, Zerubbabel should lead Israel with confidence, knowing that he was God's chosen servant, empowered by God to lead the nation.

THEOLOGICAL FOCUS
God's leaders are to find their confidence in God's plans for the future and in God's ability to carry out these plans through them.

PREACHING IDEA
Circumstances don't shake those with deep trust in God.

PREACHING POINTERS
Haggai's final message had an immediate audience of one: Zerubbabel. The first three oracles addressed governor Zerubbabel, high priest Joshua, and the remnant in Jerusalem. In the last speech, the prophet singled out Zerubbabel. God identified his need for a climatic word of assurance. Despite undesirable appearances—lack of material blessings, a sluggish rebuilding project, and Persian rule—God remained in control. Moreover, he had chosen Zerubbabel to lead his people forward. Haggai's message pointed to Zerubbabel as God's chosen servant, signet ring, Davidic successor, and unshakeable leader for the days ahead.

God continues to advance his kingdom efforts today through leaders with deep conviction. He provides gifted men and women to lead faith-based organizations, churches, businesses, nongovernmental organizations, sports teams, and healthy homes. Their unshakeable trust, remarkable courage, and consistent virtue shines in a world opposed to God. Not only has the religious climate in the West turned cold toward biblical values, it has become hostile. Coaches and teachers are fired for sharing their faith. Christian business owners are picketed for making their convictions public. Pastors are dismissed for their "outdated and intolerant" views. Amidst the torrents of cultural change and faith decline, God's firm control of the world buoys these leaders. This passage reminds us that circumstances don't shake those with deep trust in God.

GOD'S PRIORITIES FOR A FAITHFUL LEADER
(2:20–23)

LITERARY STRUCTURE AND THEMES
(2:20–23)

Haggai's final sermon opened with a dated introduction (2:20) before engaging in the divine judgment of foreign nations (2:21–22). The message, however, ended with a reassurance of God's choice of his Davidic servant Zerubbabel (2:23). Haggai's theme was simply this: God is in control.

- *A Promising Message (2:20)*
- *Be Reassured, God Controls the Nations (2:21–22)*
- *God Reassures Zerubbabel (2:23)*

EXPOSITION (2:20–23)

Zerubbabel, governor of Jerusalem, was a weak leader (Hag. 2:20–23: Zech. 4:6–10) who was controlled by the Persians. Persian kings retained and maintained their royal power structure in seven residences: Ecbatana, Sardis, Bactra, Babylon, Susa, Saïs, and Memphis. These localities served as the empire's seats of power. "From the inception of the Empire," according to Briant (2002, 352), "it was this dominant socioethnic class that held power from the Indus to the Mediterranean and intended to keep it." As a result, Zerubbabel had no army to carry out his decrees and could not resolve the conflict with the neighboring people around Samaria. Nevertheless, Haggai made it clear that Zerubbabel should not be discouraged, for God would accomplish his will through him.

So, when the time was right, God's provided words of encouragement (Hag. 1:20) that highlighted the need for Zerubbabel to trust God's power over secular leaders (1:21–22)

and provided reassurance that Zerubbabel was God's chosen leader (1:23). Since God controlled the political rise and fall of every nation, Zerubbabel should lead Israel with confidence, knowing that he was God's chosen servant, empowered by God to lead the nation.

A Promising Message (2:20)

God's word came at the right time when Zerubbabel needed encouragement.

2:20. The date of this message was December 18, 520 B.C., the same day Haggai received the message in Haggai 2:10–19. Although Zerubbabel was the governor of Judah, the slow progress on rebuilding the temple would suggest that Zerubbabel was not a great leader and that he needed reassurance that he was the one God wanted to lead the people. Zerubbabel's leadership was weak because he had no Jewish army to enforce his decrees, Jerusalem's walls and gates were still in disrepair, and he was a pawn in the hands of much stronger nations around him. These conditions led to a feeling of powerlessness.

Be Reassured, God Controls the Nations (2:21–22)

Godly leaders could trust in God's power over the political powers in this world.

2:21–22. God promised Zerubbabel that he would shake the heavens and the earth, as in 2:6. This shaking was God's plan to "overthrow" (הָפַךְ) the political rulers of foreign nations (2:22). God can undermine the military strength of any nation by defeating their armies (their horses and chariots) causing their demise

(Verhoef, 1987, 143). Thus, Zerubbabel should not be discouraged by the little power he has, for he would not determine the political future of Judah, God would.

God Reassures Zerubbabel (2:23)
Zerubbabel should be hopeful, for he was God's chosen servant.

2:23. This prophecy ended with three separate declarations that should encourage Zerubbabel, the governor of Judah. These reassurances indicated that Zerubbabel would play a key role in God's future dealings with the people in Judah. Some believe that the introductory temporal marker, "on that day" (בַּיּוֹם הַהוּא) and the imagery of shaking the heavens and the earth marks this prophecy as an eschatological prediction (Taylor and Clendenen, 2004, 196), but it is better to understand this imagery to refer to the revolutionary action God would take in the life of Zerubbabel.

WORD ANALYSIS: The meaning of the phrase "on that day" can be determined by context. For example, (a) Isaiah 3:1–6 refers to an attack on Jerusalem and the loss of leaders, so "on that day" in Isaiah 3:7 refers to that time; (b) "on that day" in Isaiah 4:1 refers to the time when many solders would die (3:25); but (c) "on that day" in Isaiah 4:2 is eschatological in meaning based on the context of 4:2–6.

First, God assured Zerubbabel that God "will take" (לָקַח) him and use him for his unique purposes. God's plan was for Zerubbabel to be "my servant" (עַבְדִּי), a term of endearment that God would give to one who did his will. Thus, Zerubbabel was to function as a leader who would dedicate his life to doing the will of God like his forefather David. Second, Zerubbabel should understand his role as governor as something God "chose" (בָּחַר) for him to do. In some small way this was the start of the restoration of the Davidic royal line to a leadership role over

God's people, so it was a sign that God was beginning to fulfill his Davidic promises (2 Sam. 7:1–14). Finally, God compared Zerubbabel to be as a "signet ring" (חוֹתָם) that a king might wear.

Signet Ring

Ancient kings throughout the ancient Near East used signet rings to identify their authority behind a decree, to communicate to the reader of a document their high political status, or to claim ownership over something. Each king would have his metal workers design a signet ring with a unique design or image, plus his name. Official scrolls from the king were usually rolled up, tied with two or three strings and them wax was put on the string and stamped with the king's signet ring to seal it. The king's seal certified that the document was genuine. Some kings would allow their most trusted advisor or prime minister to use the signet ring because they trusted them and knew that they would do exactly as the king would do. God was expressing his confidence in Zerubbabel by in effect making him his signet ring.

Signet ring that bears the throne name of the Egyptian pharaoh Akhenaten (1351–1334 B.C.). Courtesy of Walters Art Museum (public domain).

When the Persian king Xerxes gave his signet ring to the evil prime minister Haman (Esther 3:10–12), this gave Haman the power to enact laws and exert the power of the king. When God viewed Zerubbabel as having God's signet ring, God was expressing his confidence in Zerubbabel as a genuine Davidic ruler with the power to enact God's rule over this land. This was a reversal of God's act of taking away his authority (removing the signet ring) from the evil king Jehoiachin (Jer. 22:24). God did shake up the Persian policy toward Judah (Ezra 6:1–9), caused the Persian king Darius to pay the full cost of reconstructing the temple, and enabled Zerubbabel to accomplish an important spiritual goal for the people in the sixth year of Darius (Ezra 6:15).

THEOLOGICAL FOCUS

The exegetical idea (Since God controlled the political rise and fall of every nation, Zerubbabel should lead Israel with confidence, knowing that he was God's chosen servant, empowered by God to lead the nation) leads to this theological focus: God's leaders are to find their confidence in God's plans for the future and in God's ability to carry out these plans through them.

Two important theological themes are emphasized in this fourth sermon of Haggai's prophecy. First, it is God who choses someone to be his chosen leader. Although the leadership role might be small and not a prestigious role, leaders should have confidence serving in the role God has chosen for them. If leaders understand who appointed them and who supports them, then that leader will have courage and confidence in the role God assigns them.

Second, the fundamental responsibility of God's chosen leaders is to serve God by promoting the will of God among his followers and depending of God. Once leaders are chosen and installed, they need to lead wisely realizing that they are responsible to do the will of God and provide as it were his stamp of approval (like a signet ring) on his plans. Having confidence

in one's leadership skills and a strong sense in God's providential control of the future enables good leaders to make wise decisions consistent with God's direction (Hag. 2:21). But when leaders are confused with the events unfolding all around them, seem helpless to change or influence the course of history, and have uncertainty about God's plans, things can turn hopeless and a leader can become discouraged.

Leaders need to have a clear understanding of who is sovereign over the events in this world and who is in charge of the future (2:21), know what God's priorities are, and understand their role as God's servant. If God be for us, who can stand against us?

PREACHING AND TEACHING STRATEGIES

Exegetical and Theological Synthesis

Haggai 2:20–23 spells out several reasons why Zerubbabel needed targeted encouragement. Residents of Jerusalem were not impressed with his title as governor. Instead, they were focused on their circumstances. They were subject to a foreign king, the army was nonexistent, construction on the temple was progressing slowly, and agricultural produce in Jerusalem was lacking. Haggai's message to the governor reassured him of God's appointment despite undesirable circumstances and a doubting constituency.

More important than dispelling Zerubbabel's doubts, Haggai's message emphasized God's authority. These few verses paint the Lord of Hosts as a God who speaks, remembers his covenant, predicts the future, controls international politics, relates to individuals, and choses leaders. The theological portrait aims to reassure Zerubbabel of God's character.

Finally, a note about God's use of prophecy is in order. The exegesis explains the importance of context clues for interpreting the phrase "on that day." Additional historical details (Ezra 6:1–9, 15) suggest God means a "shake up" in the near future, not the far-off end of days. This does not, however, rule out eschatological fulfillment when the Messiah comes (Mark 10:45; Heb. 12:25–29). Prophecy often has both an immediate and far-off fulfillment.

Preaching Idea

Circumstances don't shake those with deep trust in God.

Contemporary Connections

What does it mean?

What does it mean that circumstances don't shake those with deep trust in God? What is deep trust? Haggai directed his final message to Zerubbabel, the political figurehead in Jerusalem. His confidence in God set the tone for the people. God often appointed individual leaders to motivate people and move them forward. In the OT, Moses, Joshua, David, and Josiah stand out as leaders who relied on God to deliver, guide, and protect his people despite difficult circumstances, including enemy threats, idolatrous practices, and personal failure. While trust in God can be taught by strong leaders, it is the responsibility of each person to develop their own unshakeable confidence that inspires other people.

Trusting deeply is not the same as being unaffected by the difficulties of life. Physical ailments, personal tragedies, bad weather, relational challenges, and financial crises will occur. They will often cause stress, pain, and frustration. They may cause us to question God, but they do not knock us down into a state of doubt or despair. The shaken person considers walking away from God in adversity. Those with deep trust cling to God no matter what happens.

God's word to Zerubbabel reminded him to look past the slow progress of the temple rebuilding project and fixate on the larger reality of God's trustworthiness. He walks with his people in valley of the shadow of death, through the fire and flame, securing them new mercies day by day (Ps. 23:4; Isa. 43:2–3; Lam. 3:23).

Is it true?

Is it true that circumstances don't shake those with deep trust in God? Yes, but trust takes time to cultivate. Trust requires us to look beyond immediate realities to enduring theological truths. Trust demands that we affirm the goodness of God when our feelings are hurt, our joy depleted, our career struggling, and our body aching. Trust sees our personal stories as part of the larger redemption story, so that even when our circumstances seem awful, we can recall the faithfulness of God to his people (Deut. 1–4; Josh. 24; Pss. 105; 136; Neh. 9).

Deep trust does not rule out the occasional doubt. But it does not allow doubt a lasting foothold. It brings our uncertainty into the light of Scripture, prayer, and relationship with God, so doubt doesn't get the final word. Sometimes a psalm of trust (e.g., Pss. 16, 63) will reassure us that God is our refuge. Sometimes a spiritual friend will remind us that God isn't finished with us yet. Sometimes, in our prayers, the Spirit will reiterate our unshakeable status as God's beloved (Isa. 41:10; 49:15–16; 54:5, 10; 62:2–5). Thus, deep trust is more than a passing feeling but an unshakeable conviction in our unbreakable relationship with our God who upholds us.

Now what?

How do we develop deep trust in God? As stated above, building trust takes time and requires theological memory. The starting point is a robust, biblical understanding of God as faithful and good. Not only do the psalms reiterate these themes (e.g., Pss. 136, 145), but also famous narratives in the OT: Abraham's unlikely child (Gen. 20), Joseph's rise to power (Gen. 41), Moses's triumph over Pharaoh (Exod. 5–12), Ruth's redemptive marriage (Ruth 3–4), and Hezekiah's protection from Assyria (Isa. 37–39). Such stories inform the "Hall of Faith" (Heb. 11) given to inspire God's people to develop deep trust.

In addition to biblical examples, we should recall personal experiences that nurtured deep trust in God. The more we mentally replay stories of God's provision, peace, courage, joy, love, and comfort in undesirable circumstances, the more unshakeable we become. Perhaps he intervened during a surgery, spared us from injury in a car accident, provided a financial gift to cover an expensive bill, or opened the door for a dream job. Memory of God's past faithfulness helps us trust deeply in present hardships.

Finally, trust grows out of obedient risk. At certain times, God may nudge us to make a major decision: to change jobs, sell a home, propose marriage, or adopt a child. God does not draft these plans in ink and send them to our home address. He moves in our spirit, circumstances, and close relationships to point in a direction. Trust means taking a step toward an uncertain future with certainty that God will not leave us. At other times, the obedient risk is not situational but moral, where God asks us to speak truth, even if it costs us a promotion, or stop a sinful behavior, even if it means losing a friend.

Creativity in Presentation

Good theology and memory set a firm foundation for our confident, unshakeable trust. One way to illustrate this principle is to gather ten to twenty cinder blocks. Set them on the stage with various attributes of God written on them in bold marker. These could include such words as *powerful, loving, good, faithful, kind, merciful, present, just, able, near,* and *mine.* Be sure to select terms expressed in Haggai to highlight Zerubbabel's theology. Other blocks might include biblical names of characters who modeled a confident unshakeable faith (e.g., Noah, Abraham, Moses, Rahab, Ruth, David, Jeremiah, Jesus, Paul). Even contemporary models (e.g., Grandma Sallie, my dad) could help broaden the foundation as well as blocks indicating personal stories (e.g., remission, baptism). Contrast the firm foundation with a shaky one made of cardboard boxes. Inscribe on the face of the boxes, words like *feelings, self-image, bank account, circumstances, health,* and *social network.* Try standing on the boxes and show how

they crumble under your weight. Then stand on the cinder blocks to illustrate their ability to support your weight.

Another way to visualize the steadiness of trust is to use a collection of helium balloons tied together. Loosen them one by one and either tie each one to a heavy weight or paperclip it to a sheet of paper. The weights represent God's character; the paper represents something circumstantial.

Great leaders will face terrible odds with unshakable courage. Their stories, like Zerubbabel's, prove motivating. I (Tim) recently heard former Heisman-winner Tim Tebow share his spiritual journey, choosing a college, winning a championship, playing professional sports, addressing Philippine missionaries, and launching a national "Night to Remember" prom for teens with special needs. Along the way he faced various forms of opposition but remained unshaken because God stayed with him. In *Shaken: Discovering Your True Identity in the Midst of Life's Storms,* Tebow's (2018) book and video curriculum capture the many ways God stood behind him.

I've witnessed similar deep trust in individuals facing a cancer diagnosis, preparing for international mission work, providing foster care to a child with special needs, or sharing their faith with unbelieving coworkers, classmates, and family members. My deep trust in God has kept me grounded while facing my mother-in-law's death, our five-year adoption process, and a failed church plant. A personal testimony or two (live or video) from someone within the congregation will have the desired effect of shaping memory and building trust in God.

Ultimately, the message must stress the following: God's chosen servants should have confidence in God's plans for the future. Circumstances don't shake those with a deep trust in God.

- God knows what's before us (2:20–22).

- God stands behind us (2:23).

DISCUSSION QUESTIONS

1. How did Haggai's final speech differ from the previous three?

2. What fears, doubts, or concerns did Zerubbabel face? What fears, doubts, or concerns do you face?

3. How can personal difficulties either strengthen or subvert trust in God?

4. What is deep trust in God and how do God's people develop it?

FOR FURTHER READING

Boda, M. J. 2004. *Haggai, Zechariah.* NIV Application Commentary. Grand Rapids: Zondervan.

DeYoung, K. 2012. *A Hole in Our Holiness: Filling the Gap between Gospel Passion and the Pursuit of Godliness.* Wheaton, IL: Crossway.

Heath C., and D. Heath. 2011. *Switch: How to Change When Change Is Hard.* New York: Random House.

Merrill, E. H. 1994. *Haggai, Zechariah and Malachi: An Exegetical Commentary.* Chicago: Moody.

Pressfield, S. 2012. *War of Art: Break Through the Blocks and Win Your Inner Creative Battle.* New York: Black Irish Entertainment.

Verhoef, P. A. 1987. *The Books of Haggai and Malachi.* New International Commentary on the Old Testament. Grand Rapids: Eerdmans.

INTRODUCTION TO ZECHARIAH

OVERVIEW OF INTRODUCTORY ISSUES

Author: Zechariah

Place: Jerusalem

Date: 520–515 B.C.

Readers: Judeans in Jerusalem

Historical Setting: Darius the Great assumed control of Medo-Persia's throne and reissued Cyrus's degree for some of the exiles from Judah to rebuild the temple in Jerusalem.

Occasion for Writing: The visions in Zechariah 1–6 were spoken in the second year of Darius's reign after the people had worked for two months at rebuilding the temple, so the leaders needed encouragement (Zech. 3–4), some needed to repent of their sins (1:1–6), and everyone needed to trust God to accomplish what he promised (1:7–21). Zechariah 7–8 happened in the fourth year of the reign of Darius when people were discouraged about all the fasting and mourning they were observing, and the messages in Zechariah 9–14 were spoken at some undefined later date when the people needed to see the hand of God defeating their enemies

Genre: Prophecy

Theological Emphasis: Zechariah assured his readers that God was sovereignly in control of their future, for he would defeat their enemies and restore Zion. His sovereignty would extend into the future when he would reveal his Messianic Branch who would be pierced, but in the end he would defend Zion and reign as King forever.

AUTHORSHIP OF ZECHARIAH

The prophet Zechariah (along with Haggai) gave words of prophetic encouragement to the Hebrew people about building the temple (Ezra 4:24–5:2). Three passages in the writings of Zechariah (1:1, 7; 7:1) directly connect the name of the prophet Zechariah to this book, but in many other passages the first person pronouns "I, me"[1] refer to what the prophet said or did; yet there are no references to Zechariah in chapters 9–14.

Little is known about Zechariah, but according to the genealogical information in Zechariah 1:1 and 1:7, he came from a priestly background. The man named Iddo (found in the phrase "Zechariah son of Iddo" in Ezra 5:1; 6:14) was listed among the priestly leaders

---

1   For example, Zechariah 1:8, 9, 14, 15, 18, 19, 20, 21; or 5:1, 2, 3, 5, 6, 9, 10, 11.

in the postexilic era when Joiakim the son of Joshua was the high priest (Neh. 12:4, 12, 16; VanderKam, 2004, 1–42, 491). Apparently, Iddo was Zechariah's grandfather who came to Jerusalem from Babylon with Zerubbabel (Neh. 12:4), while Berechiah was Zechariah's actual father (Baldwin, 1972, 88–89). This would suggest that Zechariah was probably a younger man when he prophesied in 520 B.C. (Boda, 2004, 33).

The date and nature of Zechariah's call to the prophetic role are not included in his writings, but the term "prophet" (נָבִיא) is used to describe him (Ezra 5:1; Zech. 1:1, 7), and on many occasions Zechariah claimed that he transmitted the "word of the LORD" that came to him (Zech. 1:1, 7; 6:9; 7:1, 4, 8; 8:1, 18), spoke what God said to him,[2] and reported what he saw in visions God gave him (Zech. 1:8, 18; 2:1; 3:1; 5:1, 5; 6:1). There is little information about his personal life because his writings focus on what God told him to do or say. In his messages, Zechariah encouraged the nation to rebuild the temple in Jerusalem (1:8–17; 4:1–14), challenged the priests to live holy lives and serve the people in the temple (3:1–10), and called the people to turn from sin (1:2–6; 5:1–11; 7:4–14).

Some critical scholars[3] suggest that the prophet Zechariah wrote Zechariah 1–8, sometime after 520 B.C., and a later anonymous prophetic author wrote Zechariah 9–14 (some place these chapters as late as the Maccabean period). Others find a strong level of unity within the book because they believe that Zechariah 9–11 is a reinterpretation of Zechariah 1–8, and Zechariah 12–14 is a reinterpretation of the messages in 9–11. In addition, some maintain that parts of "Zechariah 1–8 attained their final form through a long history of transmission, during which the text may have undergone several revisions" (Tollington, 1993, 11) Most evangelicals reject this approach and hold to the position that Zechariah was the author of all the messages in this book, though it is possible that Zechariah wrote 9–14 many years later than Zechariah 1–8 (Hill, 2008b, 523; McComiskey, 1998, 1014–18; Wolters, 2014, 3, 16–23).[4]

PLACE OF WRITING

Zechariah's visions gave assurances to the people of Jerusalem that God would again choose Jerusalem (1:17; 2:12), was zealous for Jerusalem (1:14), and promised that his temple in Jerusalem would be built (1:16). He promised joy for the daughter of Zion and Judah, and a future time when he would dwell in their midst (2:10–11). God promised to remove the sins of Joshua the high priest at the Jerusalem temple (3:1–7) and to enable Zerubbabel to complete the construction of the temple in Jerusalem (4:7–10). The envoy from Bethel came to Jerusalem to ask Zechariah about fasting (7:10), and God promised to return to Jerusalem and dwell in their midst (8:2–3). Although Jerusalem is mentioned frequently in Zechariah 9–14 (9:9–10; 12:2–3, 8; 13:1; 14:2, 4, 8, 10, 16, 21), these chapters about the future are more broadly presented as a message to all the people of Judah (9:7, 13, 16; 10:6; 12:5–7), to God's flock or people (10:3; 11:4–17; 12:12–14; 13:9; 14:11, 14).

---

2   Zechariah 1:3, 4, 14, 17; 2:5, 8; 3:2, 7, 10; 4:6; 7:9, 13; 8:2–23; 11:4, 6, 13, 15; 12;1, 4; 13:8.

3   Paul Redditt argues that "it would seem best to date the final edition of Zechariah 1–8 . . . between November of 518 and April of 516 B.C.," that is, before the completion of the reconstruction of the temple in 516 B.C. Paul L. Redditt, *Haggai, Zechariah, Malachi*, New Century Bible Commentary (Grand Rapids: Eerdmans, 1995), 80.

4   R. K. Harrison discusses the various arguments for and against the unity of Zechariah. R. K. Harrison, *Introduction to the Old Testament: With Comprehensive Review of Old Testament Studies and Special Supplement on the Apocrypha* (Grand Rapids: Eerdmans, 1969), 950–56.

GENERAL CHRONOLOGY OF THE PROPHETS				
Prophet	Estimated Ministry	Period	Audience	
Amos	767–753	Pre-exile	Northern Israel	A S S Y R I A
Hosea	755–715	Pre-exile	Northern Israel	
Micah	735–701	Israel in exile Pre-exile Judah	Judah	
Isaiah	739–685	Pre-exile	Judah	
Nahum	663–612	Israel in exile Pre-exile Judah	Nineveh / Assyria	900 B.C. to 612 B.C.
Zephaniah	632–628	Israel in exile Pre-exile Judah	Judah	B A B Y L O N
Habakkuk	626–609	Israel in exile Pre-exile Judah	Judah	
Jeremiah	605–586	Israel in exile Pre-exile Judah	Judah	
Daniel	605–535	Judah in exile	Judah	612 B.C. to 539 B.C.
Ezekiel	597–571	Judah in exile	Judah	
Obadiah	After 586	Judah in exile	Edom	
Jonah	??	Judah in exile	(about) Nineveh	
Haggai	520–520	Post-exile	Returned Jews	P E R S I A
Zechariah	**520–480**	**Post-exile**	**Returned Jews**	
Joel	515	Post-exile	Judah	
Malachi	450	Post-exile	Returned Jews	

Chart created by Herbert W. Bateman IV, *Isaiah: How to Read, Interpret and Understand the Prophet* (Leesburg, IN: Cyber-Center for Biblical Studies, 2016). Reprinted by permission of Herbert W. Bateman IV.

DATE OF WRITING

Twice (1:1, 7) the messages of Zechariah were connected to the second year (520 B.C.) of the Persian king Darius (522–486 B.C.), and this would agree with the dating of the ministry of Zechariah and Haggai in Ezra 4:24–5:2. In one text (Zech. 7:1), Zechariah's interaction with the people was connected to the fourth year of Darius (518 B.C.), but Zechariah 9–14 has no date formulas and often describes future events, so it is difficult to propose a date for these prophecies. Thus, the historical setting for Zechariah 1–8 can be defined, but there can be no certainty about the historical setting in the lifetime of Zechariah for the prophecies in 9–14 and no clear references to the time when these prophecies were actually written down on a scroll.

A key ancient Near Eastern document about this Persian period is the Cyrus Cylinder (see photograph in "Introduction to Haggai"), which recorded the Persian occupation of Babylon and Cyrus's plan to let all exiled people return to their original homeland and rebuild their temples. Ezra 1:1–11 views Cyrus's decree in 538 B.C. as an act of God's sovereign intervention; then it describes the preparations for the journey back to Jerusalem. Once the people arrived in Jerusalem, they built an altar to worship God, but the neighboring people living north of Jerusalem around Samaria intimidated the Jews with various threats and hired lawyers to persuade the Persians to stop all construction on the temple in Jerusalem (Ezra 4:4–5). This led to sixteen years of no progress until Haggai and Zechariah challenged the Jewish people living in Jerusalem to rebuild the temple in the second year of Darius (520 B.C.; Ezra 4:24–5:2; Hag. 1:1; Zech. 1:1; cf. VanderKam, 2004, 1–42). It would seem that the writing of the prophecies in Zechariah 1–8 happened shortly after they were orally shared with the people in Jerusalem so that more people would hear and respond positively to Zechariah's promises, for several of these prophecies were fulfilled with the completion of the temple in 516 B.C. Zechariah 9–14 was likely added to chapters 1–8 some months or possibly a few years later.

HISTORICAL SETTING[5]

After a Persian prince named Cyrus usurped the throne and established the Medo-Persian kingdom (549 B.C.), he expanded his kingdom westward by defeating Assyria, Mesopotamia, Syria, Armenia, Cilicia, and Cappadocia. In May 547 B.C., Cyrus marched to the land of Lydia, took its booty, and placed his own garrison in there (Nabonidus's Chronicle 2.16–18). On October 12, 539 B.C., Cyrus turned his attention on Babylon (Herodotus, *Hist.* 1.178–87). Once Cyrus's army entered the city of Babylon, the current king of Babylon, Belshazzar, was immediately killed (Dan. 8:1–4, 20), but Nabonidus was spared and may have died in exile (Herodotus, *Hist.* 1.190–92). Cyrus personally

entered the city of Babylon on October 29, 539 B.C. After these conquests, he said of himself, "I am Cyrus, king of the world, great king, legitimate king, king of Babylon, king of Sumer and Akkad, king of the four rims (of the earth)" (*ANET*, 316 [Oppenheim]).

Cyrus died in 530 B.C. while defending the northeastern frontier of his kingdom leaving his vast kingdom to his son, Cambyses. Unfortunately, Cambyses was not well liked. In fact, Herodotus says that he "was completely out of his mind" (*Hist.* 3.38 [Godley]). It is said that he was subject to fits of rage. In one instance, he kicked his pregnant wife to death. He was not, however, aggressive against Greece, but he did consider the Ionian Greek City states (Ephesus, Sardis, etc.) his slaves. His efforts were directed against Egypt, which he subjugated in 525 B.C. (Herodotus, *Hist.* 2.1; 3.61–67, 89) and was invested with the designation "offspring of Re," emphasizing his legitimacy as ruler over Egypt (Yamauchi, 1990, 108).

While Cambyses was campaigning in Egypt, a coup arose in Persia. Gaumata seized the Medo-Persian throne in July 522 B.C. in the name of Cambyses's dead brother, Smerdis. On his return to Babylon, Cambyses received word of Pseudo-Smerdis's usurpation of the throne. While returning home from Egypt, Cambyses may have died near Mount Carmel, Israel, perhaps by suicide, perhaps murdered by Darius (Whitcomb, *ISBE* 1:582–83). In September 522 B.C., Darius overthrew Gaumata. Darius was a great military technician, but he was a greater politician and administrator. He divided the empire into twenty large satrapies, each run by a satrap appointed by the crown (Dan. 6:1–3). Local ordinances of each province remained in effect, administered by native judges and officials.

---

5   This "Historical Setting" section is taken and adapted from Herbert W. Bateman IV, *History of the Second Temple Period: An Examination of Judaism During the Second Temple Period*, rev. ed. (Winona Lake, IN: n.p., 2004), 24–34. Reprinted by permission of Herbert W. Bateman IV.

List of Persian Kings
Cyrus (539–530 B.C.)
Cambyses (530–522 B.C.)
Pseudo-Smerdis (522 B.C.)
Darius I (522–486 B.C.)

These historical events had an impact on the Jewish people, particularly those who had been taken captive under Nebuchadnezzar's rule (Jer. 25:8–12). Cyrus adopted a conciliatory policy toward all the nations the Babylonians defeated and their exiles in Babylon. This meant that he granted official authority for Jews living in Babylon to return to Jerusalem and rebuild the temple (2 Chron. 36:22–23; Isa. 44:24; 44:28–45:7). Cyrus declared that all exiled peoples could return to their homelands and rebuild their temples, according to Cyrus's clay barrel inscription. Although the rebuilding of the temple did not happen immediately, when the Persian King Darius heard about this, he reaffirmed Cyrus's directives and financially supported the completion of the temple reconstruction (Ezra 6:8).[6]

OCCASION FOR WRITING

The political situation in Judah was problematic during the years of the governor Zerubbabel, for the Jewish governor was a weak leader who needed a lot of encouragement (Hag. 2:20–23; Zech. 4:1–10). He was largely controlled by the provincial Persian authorities above him, he had no army to carry out his decrees, and he could not resolve the conflict with the neighboring people living around Samaria. In addition, there were political revolts in Babylon around 522 B.C. and in Egypt around 519 B.C., so the Persians were somewhat suspicious of

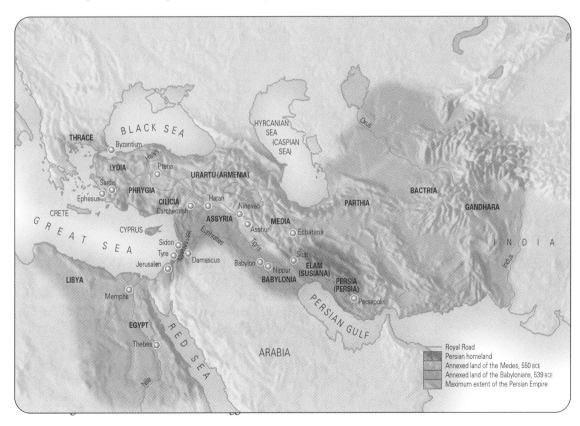

any nationalistic activity in the surrounding nations. Although Darius was credited with numerous significant accomplishments, these all came later than his second year. His first two years were primarily a time of defeating internal enemies (like the imposter Gaumata), putting down rebellious provincial leaders, and consolidating his power and authority.

The socioeconomic setting was difficult for this agricultural community because God sent a drought that resulted in very poor harvests (Hag. 1:9–11). Thus, it was hard for the small Jewish population in Judah to survive and nearly impossible for them to be able to pay for the building of an expensive new temple. The religious leader, Joshua the high priest, was without a temple, so he seemed rather powerless, and there were some questions about his worthiness for this spiritual role (Zech. 3:1–5). All this led to an overwhelming sense of hopelessness about the possibility of rebuilding the temple. But this discouraging situation changed when God sent Haggai and Zechariah to challenge the people to rebuild the temple. When Zechariah spoke in the eighth month (Zech. 1:1, 7), the people had already started rebuilding the temple in response to the preaching of Haggai in the sixth month (Hag. 1:1–15; Ezra 5:1–2).

A few months earlier, Haggai (2:10–19) confronted the people with the challenge to live holy lives, and Zechariah (2:1–6; 5:1–4; 7:1–14) expressed the need for some people to repent, turn from their sins, and be just in their dealing with others. Zechariah (1:8–17) also assured the people in Jerusalem that God was angry with the surrounding nations[7] and promised the Jews that Jerusalem would be rebuilt. The events in Zechariah 7–8 happened in Darius's fourth year (518 B.C.), and many assume that the prophet spoke or wrote Zechariah 9–14 at a later date after the temple was completed in Darius's sixth year (Ezra 6:15; 516 B.C.) because the prophet did not focus his attention on the issue of rebuilding the temple in these chapters. One might expect that these messages were gathered together and written on a scroll by Zechariah or one of his followers as early as 520–500 B.C. (Hill, 2008b, 523).

ORIGINAL READERS

Those who originally heard or read the later recorded prophecies of Zechariah were the Jews in Jerusalem who needed encouraging news about God's care for his people and his

Darius the Great. Courtesy of Leen van Dorp / CC0.

---

7   Mark Boda argues that the nation God was angry with in Zechariah was Babylon, a nation that was rebellious in the time of Darius when Nidintu-Bel revolted in 522 B.C., but God seemed to be angry with more than just one nation. Mark J. Boda, "Terrifying the Horns: Persia and Babylon in Zechariah 1:7–6:15," *Catholic Biblical Quarterly* 67, no. 1 (2005): 22–41.

promises to fulfill the prophecies found in earlier prophetic books and in the visions of Zechariah's messages. It is possible that some were wondering when the bright hopeful prophecies in Ezekiel 40–48, some of the glorious predictions in Isaiah 40–55, and Zechariah's prophecies would be fulfilled. Zechariah indicated that some promises would be fulfilled soon and that others would have an eschatological fulfillment.

THEOLOGICAL EMPHASIS OF ZECHARIAH

The theological issues that the prophet Zechariah addresses were as follows: First, God's defense of Zion would lead to the restoration of God's people, a restoration of the worship of God at the rebuilt temple, and God dwelling in their midst (2:10–12; 8:3; 14:9, 16–17). Second, God's defense of Zion would bring his anger against the nations (1:15), destroying some (1:21; 2:8–9; 9:1–8, 13–16; 12:2–9; 14:1–3) and causing others to become part of his people (2:11; 9:7b; 14:16–21). Third, one day God would send the Branch of the Lord who will rule (6:12–13) as a humble King (9:9–10), the good Shepherd who would be rejected at first (11:4–14), then pierced (12:10), and later mourned (13:10). Fourth, in the end God the King would defeat his enemies, rule over the whole earth, and receive holy worship from many nations (14:1–21).

Zechariah spoke about many practical issues that would impact the lives of God's people in the coming years as well as in the distant future. God planned to restore his relationship with his people and with people from many nations because he is a compassionate and forgiving God (1:13–14, 17; 3:1–4, 9). But the actual practical fulfillment of this plan would be dependent on the repentance of people and the nations (1:2–6; 12:10; 13:9). This earthly restoration would include many people being involved in the restoration of worship and in the defeat God's enemies. This would be possible if people believed God's

promises about the rebuilding of the temple, trusted him, and got to work (1:16; 4:6–10; 8:9). If the people would follow God's instructions about how they should treat others (8:8–13), and if the priests faithfully would fulfill their duties (3:6–9), God would use his sovereign control over all the earth to take care of the rest of their needs and political concerns (6:1–8). The eschatological prophecies about the coming of the Branch of the Lord (3:8; 6:12), God dwelling in the midst of his people (2:10–13), and God's miraculous plan to rescue many of his people in the final battle for Jerusalem (14:1–11) were a strong encouragement to the readers. They gave the people confidence in God's plan for the future and a desire to be part of his plans.

OUTLINE OF ZECHARIAH

The book of Zechariah can be outlined as follows according to its structure. Zechariah 1–6 has eight visions, Zechariah 7–8 records God's response to a question about fasting, and Zechariah 9–14 has prophecies about God's plans for the future. The following outline identifies four major sections and fifteen corresponding preaching units.

GOD'S RESTORATION OF HIS PEOPLE AND HIS TEMPLE (1:1–6:15)

- Restoration through Repentance (1:1–6)
- God's Compassion Brings Restoration (1:7–17)
- God's Judgment of His Enemies and Restoration of Worship (1:18–2:13)
- Restoration of God's Servants (3:1–4:14)
- Restoration Requires the Removal of Evil (5:1–11)
- Restoration of God's Sovereign Rule of the Earth (6:1–8)
- God's Restoration of the Branch/ Sprout and the Temple (6:9–15)

GOD'S RESTORATION OF JUSTICE AND BLESSINGS, NOT FASTING (7:1–8:23)

- Questions about Worship and Fasting (7:1–14)
- God Plans to Bless His People, So Feast Instead of Fast (8:1–23)

GOD WILL DEFEAT JUDAH'S ENEMIES AND RESTORE THE NATION, BUT THE PEOPLE WILL REJECT THEIR SHEPHERD (9:1–11:17)

- God Will Remove Judah's Enemies and Install a Messianic King (9:1–17)
- Trust God for Strong Leaders, Restoration, and the Defeat of Your Enemies (10:1–11:3)
- The Shepherds and the Sheep (11:4–17)

FUTURE RESTORATION OF GOD'S PEOPLE AND THEIR SHEPHERD (12:1–14:21)

- God's Strength Will Defeat the Nations That Attack Judah (12:1–9)
- God's Grace and Cleansing Will Transform All Israel and Judah (12:10–13:9)
- After Defeating His Enemies, God Will Reign as King (14:1–21)

FOR FURTHER READING

Clines, D. J. A. 1979. "Darius." *The International Standard Bible Encyclopedia*, edited by G. W. Bromiley, 1:847–49. Grand Rapids: Eerdmans.

Johnston, G. H. 2012. "Part 3: Promises of a King." In *Jesus the Messiah: Tracing the Promises, Expectations, and Coming of Israel's King*, by H. W. Bateman IV, D. L. Bock, and G. H. Johnston, 37–209. Grand Rapids: Kregel. See esp. chap. 7, "Messianic Trajectories in Zechariah."

VanderKam, J. C. 2004. "The Beginnings." In *From Joshua to Caiaphas: High Priests After the Exile*, 1–42, 491. Minneapolis: Fortress.

Yamauchi, E. M. 1990. *Persia and the Bible*. Grand Rapids: Baker.

GOD'S RESTORATION OF HIS PEOPLE AND HIS TEMPLE (1:1–6:15)

God wanted his people to turn from their sinful ways (1:1–6), to follow his instructions, to trust him to guide and protect them, to worship him, and to tell others about his plans for the future. The prophet Zechariah informed the people in Jerusalem about each one of these issues in order to get them to turn from their sins (1:1–6) and trust in God's forgiveness and faithfully serve him (3:4–5), to convince them that God will defeat their enemies (1:15, 18–21) and deal compassionately with them (1:13–14) because he is sovereignly in control of the whole world (6:1–8), and to assure them that he would enable them to complete the rebuilding of the temple in the near future. Zechariah told his audience that God's present ways of dealing with people were consistent with his future promised actions, so they could rest secure that he would defeat their future enemies, strengthen his people, and send his shepherd King, who would temporarily be rejected (11:4–14) but later would reign as King over the whole earth.

Zechariah 1:1–6:15 can be divided into seven preaching units: (1) Restoration through Repentance (1:1–6), (2) God's Compassion Brings Restoration (1:7–17), (3) God's Judgment of His Enemies and Restoration of Worship (1:18–2:13), (4) Restoration of God's Servants (3:1–4:14), (5) Restoration Requires the Removal of Evil (5:1–11), (6) Restoration of God's Sovereign Rule of the Earth (6:1–8), and (7) God's Restoration of the Branch/Sprout and the Temple (6:9–15). At the very end of this section is a list of books and articles for further reading that may helpful in understanding these preaching units.

Zechariah 1:1–6

EXEGETICAL IDEA

God was angry with former generations because they did not repent, so he judged them; but if the present generation would learn from these mistakes and turn to God, he would turn to them.

THEOLOGICAL FOCUS

Sinful people who repent can restore their relationship with God.

PREACHING IDEA

Redirect your heart toward God to receive his heartfelt welcome.

PREACHING POINTERS

Zechariah's opening words were a summons. He beckoned his people to redirect their hearts to God. For nearly two decades, the original audience had dwelled within the borders of Judea after returning from Babylon. However, they had stopped work on the temple rebuilding project. The prophet Haggai's gave them an initial burst of motivation, but construction stopped soon after it started because God's people let sin, doubt, and despair come between them and God. Political and religious leaders failed to stir revival. To inspire genuine repentance, Zechariah promised a warm reception from God.

Today's church would benefit from an invitation for its people to redirect their hearts toward God. Externally, God's people may appear close to him: always smiling, morally upstanding, and active in their churches. But externals do not tell the whole story. Church gatherings may play host to hollow religious performance. Strong doctrinal positions may disguise ongoing moral compromises. Sin, doubt, and despair affect today's church as much as they hurt ancient Israel. This passage urges us to redirect our hearts toward God to receive his heartfelt welcome.

RESTORATION THROUGH REPENTANCE (1:1–6)

LITERARY STRUCTURE AND THEMES (1:1–6)

In this unit, Zechariah opened with an encouragement for the Jewish people in Jerusalem to repent and not be rebellious like their forefathers. His message opens with an introduction (v. 1) and concludes with a call for the people to repent (vv. 2–6).

The key themes in this unit are that God was angry with sinful people, so his people need to repent and forsake their evil ways.

- *An Urgent Message (1:1)*
- *Sin Requires Repentance (1:2–6)*

EXPOSITION

Before Judah's exile to Babylon, God sent prophets to call his people to turn to him and repent of their sins. For example, Jeremiah encouraged the people in Jerusalem to turn from their evil ways and listen to (and obey) God's instructions in the Torah. Jeremiah said this would involve "returning" (שׁוּב) to God, acknowledging their guilt and rebellious sinfulness by confessing it to God, rejecting their past sinful ways, and trusting in God's guidance and blessing (Jer. 3:11–14). Their fathers failed to repent, and thus many were killed and others were taken into exile.

After the return from exile, this failure to repent was still a major concern for both Haggai and Zechariah. Although the people responded positively to Haggai's preaching and had begun to build the temple three months earlier (Hag. 1), the people were not holy just because they were working on the temple building (Hag. 2:10–19). If the people wanted to receive God's full blessing, they needed to do more than this. Zechariah called for repentance and warned God's people to not follow the path of their forefathers, for God was angry with that generation because they did not repent. However, if the present generation would learn from these mistakes and "turn" (שׁוּב) to God, he would turn to them and not bring judgment on them.

An Urgent Message (1:1)

God communicated his thoughts to his people through a prophet at just the right time.

1:1. The superscription to the messages of Zechariah identified the historical setting as the time when the Persian Empire (539–332 B.C.)[1] controlled large sections of the civilized world and about eighteen years after Cyrus originally declared (in 538 B.C.; Ezra 1:1–4) that all exiled people in Babylon could return to their homelands and rebuild their temples (*ANET*, 315–16 in the Cyrus Cylinder).

Ezra interpreted this decree (Ezra 1:1–3) as God's act of "stirring up" (עוּר) the heart of Cyrus to let the people from Judah living in Babylonian exile return to their homeland, just as the prophet Jeremiah had prophesied (Jer. 25:11–12). Shortly after arriving at Jerusalem the people built an altar to restore sacrificial worship, and a year later they laid the foundation for the temple (Ezra 3:8–10). But rebuilding the temple was halted during the rest of the reigns of Cyrus and Cambyses (for sixteen years until

---

1   Curtis (2006, 93–109) presents an extensive study of the date formulas used in Haggai and Zechariah (and a few other books). He compares these formulas to the date formulas used in Babylonian documents and does not view them as editorial additions by a later editor. He concludes that they were put in this text before 515 B.C.

CHRONOLOGY OF THE PERSIAN PERIOD

Cyrus (559–530 B.C.)	Cambyses (530–522 B.C.)	Darius (522–486 B.C.)	Xerxes (486–465 B.C.)	Artaxerxes (465–424 B.C.)
Started building around 536 B.C. Zerubbabel/Joshua	No building for sixteen years	Temple completed in 516 B.C. Haggai/Zechariah	Haman's threats Esther/Mordecai	Reform/Wall rebuilt in 445 B.C. Ezra/Nehemiah/Malachi

520 B.C.) because of threats and opposition by the people living around Samaria (Ezra 4:1–5) and a change in Persian policies.

At this time Zerubbabel was the governor of the small territory of Judah (in Aramaic it was called Yehud), Joshua was the high priest (Zech. 3:1), and Haggai and Zechariah were the prophets God sent to encourage the people to rebuild the temple (Ezra 5:1–2). Zechariah came from the priestly family of Iddo (his grandfather; Neh. 12:16) and his father was Berechiah. It was possible that his father died young and that his grandfather raised him (Merrill, 2003, 88). Zechariah's prophecies came as the people started rebuilding the temple (Hag. 1) and about a month after they were encouraged to continue the project in Haggai 2:1–9. Zechariah called for the people to repent in November of 520 B.C., shortly before Haggai's message about holy living in Haggai 2:10–19.

Sin Requires Repentance (1:2–6)

God expected people who sin against him to repent so that he could forgive them.

1:2. Zechariah announced that the past sins of their forefathers caused God, the Lord of the armies of heaven, "to be angry" (קָצַף) with his people, and this led to their exile (2 Chron. 36) and the hard times the people were facing after the exile. Therefore, Zechariah exhorted

the people to "return, turn" (שׁוּב) to God in repentance in order to be forgiven. If they would do this, God would "return, turn" (שׁוּב) to them in forgiveness. The warning was clear and the choice was obvious, so it all came down to their willingness to turn from their sinful ways.

WORD ANALYSIS: The word שׁוּב can describe or refer to (a) a "change of motion, a turn" from one direction to another (in Gen. 15:16 the people would "return" from Egypt to Canaan); (b) a "change" of mind (in Judg. 11:35 Jephthah could not "change" his mind after he had made a vow); (c) how the prophets called the nation to "turn" from sin and repent (2 Kings 17:13; Jer. 3:11–12; Zech. 1:4); or (d) how God would "turn" from a position of judging people to graciously restoring them if they would "repent, turn" (2 Chron. 7:14; Jer. 18:5–10).

1:3–4. In order to strengthen his persuasive appeal for making this choice, the prophet reviewed what happened to past generations of God's people who did not repent. Earlier prophets warned them that they needed to "repent, turn" (שׁוּב) from their evil behavior (worshipping other gods and rejecting God's covenant instructions), which was contrary to their covenant agreement. This broken covenant relationship led to God's anger (2 Kings 17:18), the destruction of the nation, and their exile in Babylon.

132

1:5–6a. The prophet closed his message by asking three rhetorical questions. The implied answers to these questions were obvious. Zechariah asked, where are your fathers, where are the prophets who spoke to them, and did their prophecies of judgment come true? The answers were that their fathers were exiled and most were dead by now, their prophets had died, and God's warnings of covenant curses came true. Zechariah was encouraging his audience to learn from the past and not make the same mistakes again.

1:6b. Later some of these people admitted their sinfulness and responded positively ("they repented") to remove God's judgment (1:6b). Some commentators interpret this positive response as a reaction by Zechariah's audience in 520 B.C. (Petersen, 1984, 128; Boda, 2004, 179–80), but it is more likely that this repentance referred to the former generation that went into exile (Klein, 2008, 86; McComiskey, 1998, 1031; Baldwin, 1972, 91; Wolters, 2014, 39). Zechariah's audience also needed to repent before further judgment arrived.

THEOLOGICAL FOCUS

The exegetical idea (God was angry with former generations because they did not repent, so he judged them; but if the present generation would learn from these mistakes and turn to God, he would turn to them) leads to this theological focus: Sinful people who repent can restore their relationship with God.

The prophet made three important theological points. First, people who are sinners would be punished if they did not repent. God could not have a relationship with sinful people; in fact, he got angry when people sin (1:2) and he punished those who did not repent (1:4–5). The present generation should realize that when the past generation failed to follow God's instructions in the covenant, the curses of the covenant fell on them, revealing God's just anger. This happened because people did not maintain their holy relationship to God but turned away by following other gods. Second, people who sin were expected to repent, and it was the prophet's duty to call people to repent of their sins (1:4). Third, when people repent, they would restore their relationship with God. The only way to restore their relationship with God was for these sinful people to reject their sinful ways and "return, turn back" to follow God.

The practical message to learn from these experiences were, do not ignore God's word and rebel, do not ignore the warnings of God's judgment, do not delay repentance, and be assured that restoration is possible for everyone who repents.

PREACHING AND TEACHING STRATEGIES

Exegetical and Theological Synthesis

Zechariah 1:1–6 highlights the prophet's role in the temple rebuilding project. Like his fellow prophet Haggai, Zechariah inspired a people discouraged by political, socioeconomic, and religious conditions in Jerusalem. However, Zechariah made explicit what Haggai implied, namely, the need for God's people to change (i.e., repent). His initial message followed Haggai's by two months (1:1; cf. Hag. 1:1), proving how quickly God's people had wavered in their commitment. Returning to God offered them another new beginning.

Repentance is not a one-time decision but a way of life. The ebb and flow of human faithfulness suffers beneath the weight of daily duties, physical challenges, personal failures, external circumstances, and factors beyond our control. Zechariah's fourfold appeal in these verses to "your fathers" suggests the prodigal spirit is more normal than it is an anomaly. The prodigal spirit lives within each one of us, seeking self-protection, self-glory, or selfish gain rather than staying close to God. Thus, redirecting our focus from self toward God requires constant attention.

Fortunately, the call to change serves as a free pass home into God's warm embrace. Although our rebellion in its various forms (e.g., idolatry, social injustice, etc.) makes his nostrils flare, our willingness to admit wrongs opens the door to his mercy. Zechariah's fourfold use of "return/repent" envisions a restored relationship between God and his people, like the reunion between father and son envisioned in Hosea (Hos. 11; Jer. 3:14; cf. Luke 15:20).

Preaching Idea

Redirect your heart toward God to receive his heartfelt welcome.

Contemporary Connections

What does it mean?

What does it mean to redirect our hearts toward God? A right relationship with God—trusting, obeying, abiding, believing—requires focus and intention. Estrangement from God is as old as Eden (Gen. 3:23). And Zechariah's audience also illustrated the human tendency to drift from devotion to God. We'd rather seek comfort. We'd rather seek pleasure. We'd rather opt for idols we can control. Thus, our hearts must be guarded and constantly realigned (Prov. 4:23).

Does redirecting our hearts follow a strict formula? Certainly not! Formulaic religion constituted one of the recurring flaws in Israel's thinking (Isa. 29:13; 58:3–10; Amos 5:21–23; Hos. 6). Following a script for repentance can easily circumvent the heart's genuine sorrow. On the other hand, repentance will exemplify a few common features: recognition of sin as wrongdoing, admission of guilt, humble attitude, and commitment to return to living according to God's word (2 Chron. 7:14).

What does God's heartfelt welcome look and feel like? God's warm welcome stems from his role as a loving father (Exod. 4:22; Ps. 68:5; Isa. 9:6; Jer. 3:14; Hos. 11:1). Not only does he protect, provide for, and discipline those whom

he loves (Prov. 3:12), he also forgives his wayward children for wrongdoing (Isa. 1:18; Ps. 103). He gives them second (and third) chances to start fresh, choosing trust and obedience over idolatry and injustice (Deut. 30).

Is it true?

Is it true that God will give a heartfelt welcome to those who redirect their hearts toward him? Can we reach a point of no return? What if we don't feel the heartfelt welcome? These questions reflect honest wrestling with the Scriptures and personal experience. First, we must assert that repentance is not an emotion but a choice. Turning away from sin does not mean our desire to do wrong disappears; we must constantly fight the urge to choose our way over God's will. Honestly, many of us direct our heart to comfort, pleasure, and idols because they offer us instant relief and satisfaction. We are wise to acknowledge this fact as we redirect our hearts toward God. Furthermore, this act of redirection does not mean our hearts will be flooded with fuzzy feelings. Sometimes prolonged battles with deception, promiscuity, or addiction will leave us feeling more weary than relieved on our journey back to God. Feelings of freedom, forgiveness, and gracious welcome may come later.

Second, we must realize that God's mercy is great, but his offer of mercy may not last forever. He is slow to anger, which implies that his fuse eventually ends (Exod. 34:6). Perhaps the greatest obstacle to God's warm welcome is our stubborn hearts (Exod. 34:9; Deut. 9:6). He will not coerce us to return. God calls, beckons, woos, and longs for our return, but he does not force us. He may even allow adversity to grab our attention (Amos 4:6–13). If we die having never given our hearts to God, the door into his grace shuts forever. Fortunately, until our death or until history climaxes at the day of judgment, God will speak through prophets and preachers, personal suffering and Scripture, conscience and circumstances to draw us back to himself.

Now what?
How do we redirect our hearts to God? What must we say or do to receive a heartfelt welcome? As mentioned above, there is no formula for redirecting our hearts toward God. No boilerplate prayer or set of penitent postures exists to insure forgiveness, a fresh start, and healing. Rather, redirecting our hearts begins with our awareness of being lost, estranged, indifferent, or far from God's ideal. We add to that awareness a sense of grief, sadness, guilt, disappointment, or shame, which each person will express differently. Perhaps it helps to recognize that our misdirected hearts not only miss God's goal for our lives, but also limit our experience of his fatherly love. To abide with him is to enjoy his presence, peace, and protection; to venture out on our own sinful path is to expose ourselves to danger (Pss. 1; 23; cf. Lev. 26; Deut. 28).

Redirecting our hearts, then, moves from awareness to intention. We intend to seek God. We intend to obey his commands. We intend to finish the work he gives us. And we take the necessary steps to follow that intention to fulfillment. This may mean we step back when our anger begins to boil rather than letting it erupt. We might start asking God daily to seek our hearts and know our anxious thoughts (Ps. 139:23–24). We might decide to safeguard against pornography by installing a filter on our phone and seeking out accountability rather than giving into lust. Of course, anything we do to redirect our hearts toward God works in partnership with his promise to make our hearts new (Ps. 51:10; Jer. 31:33; Ezek. 36:26).

Creativity in Presentation
Our heart is like a compass, pointing toward our deepest longings (Smith, 2016, 13). If we want sleep, our hearts may point toward a bed. If we want sweets, our hearts may point toward a cake. If we want intimacy, our hearts may point toward a spouse, friend, or family member. Sadly, what our heart most desperately needs but does not always want is God. So

our hearts must be redirected toward him. Consider illustrating the heart's pull toward other desires (and the challenge of redirecting it) by setting up several items on the stage or projector screen that you feel pulled toward (e.g., cake, cell phone, couch). Use the ceiling as the directional designation for God. In your hands, hold a giant heart-shaped pillow or cardboard cutout. While pointing at the props, confess how your heart is pulled toward specific comforts, pleasures, and idols. Then, through great strain, show how you must redirect your heart toward God, pointing it at the ceiling.

A NT example is Jesus's prodigal son parable. It is a memorable story that captures the imagery of a warm welcome home. Moreover, it has inspired numerous pieces of artwork and music, from Philips, Craig, and Dean's moving song "When God Ran" to the Rolling Stone's bluesy "Prodigal Son" to Rembrandt's evocative painting *The Return of the Prodigal Son*. Showing this picture or playing one of these songs as part of the sermon may help people visualize a dramatic homecoming. The people who had returned from their Babylonian captivity were being given the opportunity to be God's prodigal son.

Hollywood often tugs the heartstrings as they depict heartfelt homecoming scenes. At the close of Pixar's charming story *Inside Out* (2015, directed by Pete Docter), eleven-year old Riley returns home after selfishly attempting to run away from her parents. Her recent move across the country had caused Riley emotional upheaval (depicted by five characters inside her head: Joy, Sadness, Anger, Fear, and Disgust). She does not make it far beyond the bus station before changing her mind, disembarking, and returning home to her parents' loving embrace. More recently, *The Greatest Showman* (2017, directed by Michael Gracey) closes with the powerful song "From Now On." Its refrain champions the idea of a fresh start: "And we will come back home / And we will come back home / Home again!" Ambitious showman and circus creator P. T. Barnum (played by Hugh Jackman) sings the lines as a confessional. He has deceived his wife and dodged an affair. Upon seeing his softened heart, his wife (played by Michelle Williams) welcomes him back. Playing one of these homecoming scenes may provide a moving example of God's heartfelt welcome.

Regardless of the creative elements you implement, be sure the message stresses the following: Sinful people who repent can restore their relationship with God. Therefore, we should redirect our hearts toward God to receive his heartfelt welcome.

- The word of God comes (1:1).

- The misdirected heart is an age-old problem (1:2–6a).

- The redirected heart is a better option (1:6b).

DISCUSSION QUESTIONS

1. What lessons do we need to learn from the past preaching of the prophets (Zech. 1:2–6) so that we do not make the same mistakes as our forefathers?

2. How would you define *repentance*? Who are some biblical role models for repentance?

3. What makes it hard to "redirect our hearts to God" (Zech. 1:2–6)?

4. Why is it important to avoid a formula for repentance?

5. How have you seen the "prodigal spirit" at play in your life and in the church?

Zechariah 1:7–17

EXEGETICAL IDEA

God knew what was happening in every nation, so he announced his anger with some nations, his compassion toward his own people, the building of the temple, and the filling of Jerusalem with joyful people.

THEOLOGICAL FOCUS

God's anger with sinful people does not overshadow his compassion for those who follow him.

PREACHING IDEA

God's not blind to our trials but brings healing on his timeline.

PREACHING POINTERS

Three months after sharing his first message, Zechariah recorded his first of eight visions. He saw a patrolling horseman and angelic messengers. To the original audience, the imagery would have brought assurance of God's watchfulness and power. While the specific details of the vision—different colored horses, myrtle trees, ravines, and various speakers—remain in question, the overall message is clear: God's plan to intervene on behalf of his people was a foregone conclusion. He would manifest his sovereign control in compassion for Jerusalem and rage against the nations.

The view of God in today's church must be challenged. For many believers, God appears as a distant despot or indifferent deity. God does not oversee our lives, answer our prayers, or heal our wounds. And on rare occasions of divine intervention, God's timing does not align with our wishes. We easily dismiss such a distant and indifferent God. Of course, God remains emotionally engaged with his people, working a plan for restoration in his timing. He maintains absolute control, shows tender compassion, and expresses justified fury. This passage rebuffs modern misunderstandings of God, offering assurance that he's not blind to our trials but brings healing in his timeline.

GOD'S COMPASSION BRINGS RESTORATION (1:7–17)

LITERARY STRUCTURE AND THEMES (1:7–17)

In this unit, Zechariah discussed the first of eight visions in his prophecy. He began his message by recalling the time when God spoke to him (v. 7). He then described a vision of patrolling horsemen (vv. 8–11). Zechariah closed with the news of God's anger with some oppressive nations and his passion to restore Jerusalem and the temple (vv. 12–17).[1]

The three major themes in this unit through this first vision are divine sovereignty, God's anger, and his compassion.

- *God's Visionary Message (1:7)*
- *The Vision (1:8–11)*
- *God's Anger Is Contrasted with His Compassion (1:12–17)*

EXPOSITION

The OT speaks often of God's great compassion. His compassion for Gentiles is evident in the book of Jonah. It was especially evident when God brought his people out of their backbreaking slavery conditions in Egypt, his stirring of Cyrus to let the Jews return to Jerusalem, and through king Darius's offer to pay the full cost of rebuilding the temple. God's zeal and compassion for his people insured the restoration of the temple.

God's Visionary Message (1:7)

God communicated his thoughts to his people through a prophet when it was needed.

1:7. Zechariah received his first message (1:1–6) sometime in October–November. Then three months later on the twenty-fourth day of the eleventh month in the second year of Darius, God spoke once again to the prophet Zechariah in a series of eight visions. Historians have found little information that indicates exactly what was happening in Jerusalem on this specific day. The mention of a lack of conflict among the nations would suggest that this vision happened after Darius put down the rebellion in Babylon (522–520 B.C.) and before Darius's military campaign in Egypt in 519–518 B.C. This vision indicates that God wanted his people to renew their commitment to work on rebuilding the temple. These words of encouragement by God through the prophet Zechariah came five months after they first began rebuilding the temple (Hag. 1:15), so the leaders and the people were being reassured by this vision that God was still watching over and strongly supporting the restoration of the temple.

The Vision (1:8–11)

God's angelic beings were involved with what happens around the world.

1:8. The word of the Lord that came to the prophet (1:7) was in the form of something "I saw" (רָאִיתִי) in the night (1:8). In this vision Zechariah heard several supernatural participants speak. Although some parts of this vision scene are left unexplained, initially the prophet identified a reddish chestnut horse and its rider standing in a valley among some myrtle trees. Following behind this "man"

---

1   Tiemeyer (2015, 58–59) notes that in Zechariah 1:8–11, the "visionary impressions dominate," and 1:12–17 contains oral communications within the vision.

TIMELINE OF EVENTS

Hag. 1:1	First day	Sixth month	August 29, 520 B.C.	Haggai spoke
1:15	Twenty-fourth day	Sixth month	September 21, 520 B.C.	Started building the temple
	Tenth day	Seventh month	October 7, 520 B.C.	Day of Atonement
	Fifteenth day	Seventh month	October 11, 530 B.C.	Sukkot festival started
2:1	Twenty-first day	Seventh month	October 17, 520 B.C.	Haggai spoke
Zech. 1:1		Eighth month	November, 520 B.C.	Zechariah prophesied
Hag. 2:10	Twenty-fourth day	Ninth month	December 18, 520 B.C.	Haggai spoke
Zech. 1:7	Twenty-fourth day	Eleventh month	February 15, 519 B.C.	Zechariah's eight visions

(1:10) were other horses (reddish, sorrel, and white) probably with riders (based on "they reported" in 1:11), but the riders were not mentioned and the total number of horses of each color was not recorded.[2] At that time, horses in the ancient Near East were primarily used for military purposes, so it is not surprising that the prophet would see them "going back and forth, patrolling" (a *hithpael* reflexive verb from הָלַךְ) the earth and exerting dominion over it. The activity of these horsemen communicated to Zechariah that God had sovereign knowledge of all events on the earth and had control over everything that happened (1:11). The significance of the color of the horses was left unexplained, so this factor did not figure into the meaning of the vision. Their location in a "low area" among myrtle trees/bushes may put these horses in a place in or near Jerusalem that Zechariah would have recognized, or some suggest that it may represent the paradise-like, tree-filled garden throne room of God where his angels report to him (Petersen, 1984, 144; Wolters, 2014, 45), but neither interpretation was clarified in the interpretation of the vision. The myrtle is a six to twelve foot tall evergreen bush/tree that gives off a pleasant fragrance.

1:9–11. The man riding the reddish chestnut horse was called "my lord," and he seems to be identical to "the angel of the Lord" in 1:11 (both were standing among the myrtle trees). In some other OT narratives, "the angel of the Lord" took on the form of a human being (Gen. 18:1–2, 17, 22; 32:24–30) and sometimes presented himself as identical to God, yet somehow distinct (Exod. 3:2; 23:20–23; 32:34). Although some conclude that there was only one angel in this vision—"the Angel of the Lord" (Baldwin, 1972, 93), it seems more likely that there were two main angels (cf. Boda, 2004, 196; Klein, 2008, 100; Merrill, 2003, 94; Petersen, 1984, 144).

> **The Role of the Angel of the Lord**
> 1. The Angel of the Lord functioned as a divine messenger (Zech. 1:11–12) in 1 Kings 19:5–7 when it encouraged Elijah to arise and eat, then again in 2 Kings 1:3 where the Angel gave Elijah a message for Ahaziah.
> 2. The Angel of the Lord brought God's judgment when the Angel destroyed 185,000 Assyrian troops in the army of Sennacherib (2 Kings 19:35; Isa. 37:36) and when the Angel killed 70,000 Israelites because of David's sin (2 Chron. 21:12–15).

---

2   If these horses were patrolling the whole earth, it would make sense to imagine that there were many horses of each color. As described by 2 Maccabees 5:2–4 and 10:29–30, the armies of heaven include a large cavalry of horses.

3. The Angel of the Lord tended to merge with the role of God in Genesis 16:10–13 when the Angel spoke to Hagar and she responded "You are a God who sees," and in Judges 2:1–4 where the Angel of the Lord claimed to be the one who brought them up from the land of Egypt.

The paragraph ends with the report that the horsemen who patrolled the earth found the nations of the earth at "peace and quiet" (1:11). This report meant that the rebellion in Babylon that started around 522 B.C. was over and the disturbance in Egypt had not started. This kind of news would usually have been interpreted as a good sign because no one was threatening to destabilize the empire and no one was threatening to attack the Jewish people in Jerusalem. But since the postexilic community was still subservient to Persian authority and did not control its own destiny, peace and quiet meant that there was no hope for changing their weak, subordinate status in the future.[3] They longed for God to shake up the nations, to deliver them from foreign domination, and to give them sovereignty over their own future.

TRANSLATION ANALYSIS: 1:11

NASB[95] "peaceful and quiet"

HCSB "calm and quiet"

NIV[84] "at rest and in peace"

NKJV "resting quietly"

NRSV "remains at peace"

All these variations communicate that the nations were not at war, so "peaceful" communicates a lack of fighting better than "quiet" or "calm."

God's Anger Is Contrasted with His Compassion (1:12–17)

God's plan was to have compassion on Jerusalem and allow his people to build the temple, but he would display his anger against the nations.

1:12. The second half of this visionary experience prophesied a dramatic change in the peaceful status of the nations and what would transpire at Jerusalem in the coming years. To our surprise the Angel of the Lord responded to the news of peace and quietness with a passionate intercessory lament (1:12) similar to laments in the Psalms (Pss. 13:1–2; 79:5; 80:4; 90:13). The "how long" question expressed a certain level of frustration and invited God to answer this lament. How long will God be angry (Zech. 1:12)? This lament has two parts: how much longer will God be angry, and how long will God not "show mercy" (רָחַם) to restore Judah and Jerusalem? Since God was known as one who was "compassionate and gracious" (Exod. 34:6) and the one who promised the establishment his kingdom (Isa. 2:2–5; 4:2–6; 9:1–7; 11:1–16; 60–61), the people longed to know when God would act to fulfill these promises. The reference to the seventy years of judgment was known from the prophecies of Jeremiah (Jer. 25:11–12; 29:10) and some postexilic books (2 Chron. 36:21; Dan. 9:2) where it referred to the seventy years of exile in Babylon (605–538 B.C.). Since the exile ended many years earlier in 538 B.C. and Zechariah was now speaking in 519 B.C., in this passage Zechariah must be referring to the seventy-year period between the destruction of the temple (587 B.C.) and the completion of the rebuilt temple in Jerusalem (516 B.C.; Ezra 6:15).

---

3   This report of peace among the nations must refer specifically to that period of time immediately after the revolt of Gaumata was put down and the end of the revolt in Egypt, because only a few years later political problems arose in Media, Elam, and Armenia. John Bright, *A History of Israel*, 4th ed., Westminster Aids to the Study of the Scriptures (Louisville: Westminster John Knox, 2000), 369.

WORD ANALYSIS: The noun from this root רָחַם, "show mercy," means "womb," but it can also refer to the tender "compassion" a mother has for the child from her womb. It was a word that described a strong emotional feeling; thus, it was a fitting word to describe God's "compassionate" grace to sinful people who repent. It was the opposite of being angry (Zech. 1:12) or uncaring.

1:13. God responded to these lamenting questions about his compassion toward Jerusalem with good and "comforting" (נָחַם) words (1:13). The words he spoke in this reply are recorded in 1:14–17.

1:14–15. The messenger angel gave Zechariah two proclamations to communicate to those in Jerusalem. The first proclamation contains two statements and the logical conclusion drawn from these statements. The first statement (1:14) expressed God's strong emotional "zeal, jealousy, passion" (קָנָא) toward his people and the place where the temple was built (Zion). This zeal was a strong desire to have worship at the rebuilt temple in Jerusalem. The second statement expressed God's strong anger with the nations who were at ease (1:15). The second half of 1:15 is somewhat unclear. It probably contrasted God's limited anger with his people (it lasted "a little while") with his severe unending anger with the nations that extended the misery of God's people for a long time.

1:16. The logical conclusion to these two factors was that God would mercifully turn to restore Jerusalem as the Angel in 1:12 requested, and that God's temple would be rebuilt. Proof of this was symbolized by the measuring line the builders would stretch out to mark off the walls of the city and the walls of the temple building (1:16b).

1:17. The second proclamation expanded God's promises to the cities outside Jerusalem. God would restore them and fill them with people

and good things ("prosperity"). These gracious acts would demonstrate to all that God had truly "comforted, had compassion on" (נָחַם) his people and that he had "chosen" (בָּחַר) Jerusalem. This would be a sign of God's commitment to maintain his covenant relationship with his people and the restoration of temple worship.

THEOLOGICAL FOCUS

The exegetical idea (God knew what was happening in every nation, so he announced his anger with some nations, his compassion toward his own people, the building of the temple, and the filling of Jerusalem with joyful people) leads to this theological focus: God's anger with sinful people does not overshadow his compassion for those who follow him.

This vision addresses the three theological themes of divine sovereignty, God's anger, and his compassion. The circumstances of life can sometimes cause one to question or become impatient with God's sovereign control of this world. When this happens, some will wonder if it will ever be possible for God to fulfill all his promises. During these days, people will long to experience God's compassionate grace in concrete ways. This vision demonstrates that God knew what is happening (he is omniscient) and was still in control of everything that happens (he is omnipotent). He would be angry with those who oppose him and would have great zeal to demonstrate his compassion for his own people (he is just). In this context, God promised to act against the surrounding nations and show strong compassion toward his people, Jerusalem, the temple, and the cities of Judah.

PREACHING AND TEACHING STRATEGIES

Exegetical and Theological Synthesis
Zechariah 1:6–17 provides a theologically rich portrait of God. He is sovereign, all-knowing, jealous, compassionate, angry, and conversant

with his people through angels, prophets, and visions. The first vision introduced the Angel of the Lord, a mysterious manlike representation of God, who referenced Jeremiah's prediction of an exile lasting seventy years (Jer. 25:11–12; 29:10). That both prophets spoke of seventy years hints at God's control of time.

The interchange between the Angel of the Lord and God underscored the emotional connection between the Creator and his creation. In verse twelve, the Angel of the Lord voiced his feelings of frustration. Not only did his lament open with a standard complaint ("How long?"), but the Angel of the Lord also accused God of a mercy deficit and anger surplus. Such raw dialogue leaves no room for conceiving of God as one-dimensional or his creation as emotionally disengaged.

In addition to emotional honesty, the passage highlights God's commitment to his covenant. Earlier God promised to scatter Israel if they rebelled (Deut. 28:64) and restore them if they repented (30:1–5). He kept both promises. Moreover, he promised a return of his presence, restoration of the temple, and a Davidic descendant seated on the throne (2 Sam. 7:8–17; Ezek. 43:7). These latter promises remained unfulfilled in Zechariah's day. While some people appeared cynical (Hag. 2:3), God reaffirmed his commitment to the covenant by stating his intention to indwell, bless, and prosper Jerusalem.

Preaching Idea

God's not blind to our trials but brings healing on his timeline.

Contemporary Connections

What does it mean?

What does it mean that God's not blind to our trials but brings healing on his timeline? And if he sees our trials, why doesn't he stop them? These questions address the complex topic of human suffering and God's sovereignty. Trials come in many forms, from financial loss to physical pain to relational brokenness to mental illness to spiritual warfare to communal tragedy. Some trials result from poor choices made by us or others. Sometimes God uses them to discipline his children (Prov. 3:12). Often trials simply reflect life in a fallen world. But trials never subvert the sovereignty of God. In a memorable conversation at the end of Job, the Lord spoke from the whirlwind and asserted his management of the world. He oversaw everything from weather patterns to Job's family fortune (Job 38–42). The subtext of Job implies that God controls everything, so don't question it.

But we do question God's control. The psalmists regularly asked God why they suffered, how long it would last, and why their enemies seemed to triumph (e.g., Pss. 4, 6, 13, 35, 62, 79, 80, 88, 89). Implied in their *asking* is the belief that God *does see* our pain. However, pain has the effect of blinding us to God's compassionate control, making him seem blind to our current plight. Most of these lament psalms resolve in a reaffirmation of trust, which means admitting our perspective on life is limited, whereas God's transcendent view is wise (Isa. 55:8–9).

Is it true?

Is it true that God's not blind to our trials but brings healing on his timeline? Yes! God sees the suffering of his people. He made that loud and clear to Moses when calling him from the burning bush (Exod. 3:7–9). Ironically, Moses's trials with Pharaoh began when he tried to free his people on *his* timeline, not God's, and murdered an Egyptian (2:11–15). God took four hundred years before working a plan of escape for the Hebrew people; and he let Moses pass forty years as a shepherd before restoring him to lead the exodus. We often confuse God's slowness with blindness. Fortunately, his slowness is often an act of grace (Exod. 34:6; Num. 14:18; Ps. 86:15; cf. 2 Peter 3:9).

In fact, God allows trials both to discipline his people and draw them toward himself. Joseph's trials led to growing dependence. A great deal of time lapsed before he saw God bring healing among his brothers who betrayed him (Gen. 50:20). The trials suffered by the wilderness generation resulted from their lack of faith (Num. 14). Zechariah's audience, having been disciplined through the Babylonian exile, now wanted God to draw near to Jerusalem (Zech. 1:12).

Nonetheless, trials can overwhelm us, turning our eyes from heaven to ourselves. They can make us feel isolated. A cancer diagnosis, divorce, or major house repair can consume us. A church conflict or family fight may make life feel bleak. We might give our best try at resolving our trials. But when they persist, we tend to question God's goodness or involvement in our suffering. Sadly, like Zechariah's audience, we settle into indifference while waiting on God. It takes tenacity to trust his timeline for healing.

Now what?

How should God's people respond to the fact that he's not blind to our trials but brings healing on his timeline? Does this remove from us any responsibility for healing? First, it bears repeating that we are severely limited in our understanding of God's ways. Perhaps, someday we will know God's hidden counsel (Isa. 48:6; Jer. 33:3; Dan. 2:22). So far that day has not come, so we face our trials with humility, repeating, "God, I don't understand, but I trust you."

Second, anyone who has walked with God for any length of time has learned that trials often resolve with positive gains. Thus, it helps to reflect on past healing with gratitude. "Give thanks to the Lord for he is good," the Psalms repeat, often recounting God's involvement in the psalmists' trials (Pss. 106, 107, 136). Gratitude means looking for the good in all circumstances, even if our feelings incline us to fixate on what's wrong. Amid divorce proceedings, we may remember God's unfailing love for us. Following the death of a loved one, we may recount the beautiful memories God allowed us to make and now fondly remember. Facing a job

termination, we may watch how God provides through friends, savings, or other employment opportunities. In these dark times, the all-seeing God stands by us (Ps. 23:4; Isa. 43:1–3).

Finally, healing often comes faster in healthy community. Because trials can drain our energy, steal our passion, and drive us to isolation we must leave space for others to help us. Sometimes we need a companion in misery, someone who will echo our pain and sympathize with us in our suffering. Sometimes we need a counselor who will listen to our trials, asking appropriate questions to help us maintain hope. Sometimes we need a prayerful community, people who bring our need to God when we've grown too tired to ask again for healing. And sometimes we need the presence of people who refuse to believe God is blind but speak freely of his compassion. God often uses his people as healing agents.

Creativity in Presentation

Most people know someone who has had a knee replacement. Not only is the pain acute prior to the procedure, but the rehab process is grueling. Doctors will predict a twelve-week timeline for healing, but some factors remain hard to account for: infection, flexibility, pain tolerance, and commitment to the process. Consider presenting a twelve-week timeline for a rehab process (these are available online). Explain how people would prefer that the healing last just one day, but that is not realistic. Let people know, "Rehab hurts. Healing has a timeline. But, generally, those most faithful to the process experience the greatest levels of healing." Then ask the congregation, "Did you know God has a timeline for your healing? There's only one problem: he doesn't tell you how long it'll take. He just asks you to trust him." Pictures of a knee surgery might graphically enhance your discussion.

Because the passage discusses God's sovereignty, you might consider working through the difference between our limited control and God's ultimate control. We all wrestle with the illusion of control. We select our marriage partners, choose our outfits, shape our career paths, customize our diets, pick our friends, and decide what TV shows to watch. Various symbols may represent this illusion of choice:

- a ring for marriage
- a shirt on a hanger for clothes
- a name badge for career
- a bag of chips for diet
- a printed Facebook logo for friends
- a remote control for TV

While we can make some choices in these areas, our control has severe limits. God, on the other hand, has complete control. Symbols of his control may include the following:

- a thermometer for weather
- a globe for the rotation of the world
- a baby doll for the reproductive process
- a cross for salvation

To nuance the contrast between our limited control and God's ultimate control, you might suggest ways we can wisely respond to his providence. Sunglasses or an umbrella symbolize our response to his control of weather. A global missions prayer guide symbolizes our response to God's governance of worldwide evangelism.

Finally, you might illustrate our faulty view of God with a bit of sanctified sarcasm. Instead of a God who sees everything, we picture him as selectively seeing or turning a blind eye. You might illustrate by saying, "Pretend I'm God. And I'm watching you." At this point scan the audience, slowly. Point your middle and pointer finger at your eyes and then the crowd. Then add, "But sometimes I get bored by you, so I look at other things." Pull out a cell phone and scroll. "Or I see you getting into trouble, and I don't want to shame you." Cover your eyes with your hands, but playfully peak through. "Or, even worse, I see you struggling, and I just can't handle the pain.

So, I tune it out." Pull a blindfold from your pocket and wrap it around your head. Once it's in place, say, "Ahh, that's better. Now I don't have to deal with your problems. Sure is nice to be God." Allow a pause for this imagery to settle in. Then ask, "Is this really what we think of God? That he's blind?"

Ultimately, communicate these key ideas: God's anger will cause him to judge the sinful nations, but he will have great compassion on his people. So he will intervene on their behalf and restore them. Or, simply, God's not blind to our trials but brings healing on his timeline.

- The word of God comes again (1:7).

- God's eyes roam everywhere (1:8–11).

- His timeline tests our emotional resolve (1:12–17).

DISCUSSION QUESTIONS

1. Who is the Angel of the Lord, and what was his role in Zechariah 1:7–13?

2. If God has zeal and compassion for the Jewish people, what should our attitude be toward Jewish people?

3. What aspects of your life feel like they have slipped out of God's control?

4. How has God used "trials" or "losses" to shape you, your family, and your church?

5. Why is God's slowness a good thing? How have you seen people confuse God's slowness with blindness?

6. What healing do you wish God would speed up in your life, family, and church?

Zechariah 1:18–2:13

EXEGETICAL IDEA
God's zeal for Jerusalem would result in stronger nations defeating the nations that scattered his people, but God's presence in Zion signaled the restoration of his people, and this would draw many Gentiles to worship him.

THEOLOGICAL FOCUS
God will judge the sinful people of this world and protect those who follow and worship him.

PREACHING IDEA
Old losses are fertile ground for new beginnings.

PREACHING POINTERS
God showed Zechariah two more visions meant to instill his hearers with hope. First, God would bring judgment (i.e., "four artisans/craftsmen") on the nations (i.e., "four horns") that scattered God's people from their land. Then he would set in motions a plan to expand Jerusalem and dwell within the city. This news would result in joyful songs and awed silence. While the visions lack specific names and set timelines, the imagery would have uplifted the original audience. God's loving affection and good intentions for his people overshadowed their painful losses in exile.

God's people suffer many losses today. In many countries around the world, following God leads to the loss of political freedom, job security, personal comfort, and one's own life. In the West, evangelicals are losing their majority voice in the public realm while the religiously nonaffiliated (e.g., Nones) and antagonistic (e.g., New Atheists) camps continue making gains. Political battles favoring secular values (e.g., same-sex marriage, transgender bathrooms, recreational drug use) over biblical values make God's people feel like they have lost their influence on the nation's conscience. Fortunately, losses in popularity, political persuasion, and personal comfort do not spell the end of Christian faith in the West or anywhere else. In fact, these losses often catalyze greater efforts to trust God and live according to his purposes. This passage challenges us to rethink old losses as fertile ground for God's new beginnings.

GOD'S JUDGMENT OF HIS ENEMIES AND RESTORATION OF WORSHIP (1:18–2:13)

LITERARY STRUCTURE AND THEMES (1:18–2:13)

In this unit, God revealed to Zechariah a vision of four horns that scattered Israel, Judah, and Jerusalem, plus four artisans/craftsmen that destroy these horns (1:18–21). God then revealed to his prophet another vision of a surveyor taking measurements, which anticipated the coming of many people to Jerusalem and the restoration of worship (2:1–13).

The major two themes in this unit through these second and third visions are that God plans to judge the nations, and God has a passionate zeal to restore, rebuild, multiply, and bless his people.

- ***The Destruction of the Enemies of God's People (1:18–21)***
- ***The Restoration of Worship (2:1–13)***

EXPOSITION

The first vision expresses God's anger with the nations that scattered God's people (1:15) but does not identify which nations would receive his judgment. Since the Persians had recently defeated Babylon, the nation that had scattered many former residents of Judah and Jerusalem into exile, most readers would see these events as a partial fulfillment of what the prophet was saying. The second vision predicts that God's people would come back to Jerusalem, and that was what had begun to happen when Cyrus let them return to Jerusalem (Ezra 1:1–6) in 539 B.C. Zechariah's vision also foresees a time in the future when multitudes of Jews

and Gentile would gather in Jerusalem. God would protect them from all harm, and they would joyfully worship God.

The Destruction of the Enemies of God's People (1:18–21)

God would orchestrate events so that the enemies of God's people would be destroyed.

1:18–19. On that same night, the prophet "saw" (רָאָה) a second of eight visions. This second vision contains four horns. Unfortunately, Zechariah never explained if these were four horns on two oxen (Baldwin, 1972, 104), the four horns of an Israelite altar for burnt offerings (Petersen, 1984, 165), or metal horns on a military helmet of a soldier (Meyers and Meyers, 1987, 135). The use of horns to represent the strength of a person/nation was common in the ancient Near East and the Bible. For example, Deuteronomy 33:17 refers to Joseph's horns as pushing other people around; Psalm 75:10 prophesies that God would cut off the horns of the wicked and lift up the horns of the righteous; and Psalm 18:2 describes God as a rock, fortress, deliverer, shield, and the "horn of my salvation." Daniel 7:8, 11, 20, 24; and 8:20 use horns to symbolize ten strong kings, and the Megiddo Ivory has someone wearing a four-horned helmet to symbolize their power. Zechariah understood what horns represented, but the angel did not say which nation these horns represented. So, he inquired about the meaning of the horns, and the messenger angel explained that these horns represent the nations that "scattered" (זֵרָה) the people of Judah, Israel, and Jerusalem (1:19), but he did not name any foreign nation or king. Some have taken these four horns as a symbol of all the persecutors of the Israelites (from the Canaanites to Babylonians; Merrill, 2003, 101), while others point to specific nations such as Assyria, Babylon, Persia, and Greece (Barker, 1983, 615). It is impossible to resolve this issue, but hypothetically, the horns could even represent two kings (two horns each) from two different nations (Assyria and Babylon).

1:20–21. The action in the vision continued with the appearance of four artisans/craftsmen who could work with wood, stone, or metal. These individuals came to terrify and overthrow the four horns that scattered God's people and kept them in bondage so severely that "no one could lift up his head" (1:21; cf. Judg. 8:28). These artisans or craftsmen were not identified by name, so the main point of the vision was not to give specific political or military details about the past or future wars, but to give assurances and hope that God was sovereignly in charge of the destiny of his people. This vision communicates that God's zeal was to have compassion on Jerusalem (1:14) and have anger against the nations (1:15). God did not give up on his covenant people but would sovereignly control their future and would "dehorn/uproot" (יָדָה) their oppressors.

The Restoration of Worship (2:1–13)

The unwalled city of Jerusalem would be inhabited by many people of Judah, so God would protect them with his presence, draw people from the nations to Jerusalem, and restore worship and his covenant relationship with his people.

2:1–2. Zechariah's third visionary message begins with Zechariah seeing a man with a "measuring cord" (חֶבֶל מִדָּה). This measuring cord was used by construction workers in the

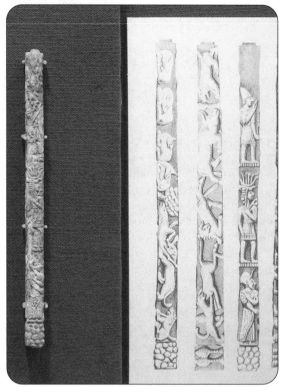

Megiddo ivory plaque depicting man wearing a horned helmet. Courtesy of Daderot.

process of laying out the parameters for the foundation of a wall, and it appears to be the same "line" (קָוֶה) stretched over Jerusalem in 1:16. After questioning, this man informed Zechariah that he was in the process of "measuring" (מָדַד) where to build the walls of the new city of Jerusalem. This means that Zechariah was now seeing the fulfillment of the prophecy in 1:16.

> **Subdivisions for**
> **"The Restoration of Worship" (2:1–13)**
> - God Will Protect His People (2:1–5)
> - The Restoration of God's People (2:6–9)
> - The Worship of God (2:10–13)

2:3. Suddenly the scene is interrupted by the angel who was speaking with Zechariah and another angel who was "emerging" (יֹצֵא) on the scene. One angel was instructed to run over to the young man measuring Jerusalem (2:4) in order to explain to him why his work of laying out the plans for the construction of the walls of Jerusalem was unnecessary. This young man was probably the man in 2:1 (Meyers and Meyers, 1987, 153–54) and not the prophet Zechariah as some suggest (Hill, 2008b, 540; Merrill, 2003, 104; Redditt, 1995, 58).

2:4. The angel's message to the young man was for him to stop "measuring" (מָדַד) where to build the walls of the new city of Jerusalem because Jerusalem would be an open village without walls due to the massive number of people and the large number of animals dwelling in the city. This sounded very similar to the eschatological promises of a vast population in Jerusalem mentioned in other prophetic books (Isa. 54:1; Ezek. 36:10–11).

2:5. A second reason why the young man should stop setting out these measuring lines was that the wall was not needed because the glory of God would dwell in Jerusalem (cf. Ezek. 43:1–9). He would be a wall of fire around the city, providing protection from any harm. This idea was reminiscent of God's protection of his people in the pillar of fire by night and the cloud by day during the exodus events when the Israelites were trapped between the Red Sea and the Egyptian army (Exod. 13:21; 14:19–20, 24–25).

This vision must have made some people wonder if God was giving instructions to Zechariah about not building the walls of Jerusalem in their postexilic times. Or did the overall context suggest to them that this vision was describing events in a later eschatological age? Since the postexilic people acted contrary to this vision and rebuilt the walls of Jerusalem under the leadership of Nehemiah,

there is no record of the glory of God's fiery presence resting in the postexilic temple in Jerusalem. Moreover, since this fiery wall of protection was not manifested at that time and later did not protect God's people in Jerusalem from the oppressive Greeks and Romans, this prophecy must be pointing to God's eschatological plans, not the postexilic context of the audience. Ultimately, God would protect his people by his presence, so there would be no need for a wall (vv. 1–5).

2:6–7. Zechariah opened the next part of his visionary explanation with an expression that was meant to grab attention: "hey you" (הֹוי). While it introduces a lamenting "woe" oracle in Amos 6:1, here the repeated exclamation "hey you" (הֹוי הֹוי; Zech. 2:6) marks the beginning of a challenge thus issued to other Jews who were not in Jerusalem to return home.

> *TRANSLATION ANALYSIS:* 2:6, הֹוי הֹוי
> NASB[95] "Ho there!"
> NIV[84] "Come, come"
> HCSB "Get up"
> NRSV "Up, up!"
> NKJV "Up, up!"
> As a word used to grab someone's attention, each culture will have its own idiom, so "Hey you!" or "Heads up!" or even "Wake up!" might be appropriate today.

Thus, "hey you" (הֹוי) was used to gain peoples' attention; it communicated the need to listen up (cf. Isa. 55:1). The Lord's instruction was that the remaining people living in Babylon and those dispersed to other countries ("to the four winds") should "flee" (נוס) and "escape" (מָלַט) to Zion. Two factors raise questions about the meaning of this part of Zechariah's message. First, at this date (520 B.C.) Babylon was defeated nineteen years earlier in 539 B.C. and many Jewish people had returned, so what future defeat of Babylon was the prophet referring to, or was Babylon just a symbol of any nation that might plunder God's people in the future? Second, if this applied to Zechariah's time, it would seem that Zechariah should have preached this message to people living in Babylon rather than to the people in Jerusalem. Thus, in view of these two factors it is more likely that this message was meant to assure people in Jerusalem about God's future plans.

2:8–9. The interpretation of Zechariah 2:8–9 is difficult because of three interpretive questions: (1) who was speaking these words, (2) who was the "me" who was sent by God to punish the nations, and (3) what does the word "glory" (כָּבוֹד) mean in this context? Since the Lord of Hosts spoke at the beginning of 2:8, it would appear that the "me" refers to God himself, but if this was the case, who was the one who sent God (he would not send himself)? Usually God was the one who would send someone else to do his will. In addition, 2:9 ends with the one speaking, saying that "the LORD of hosts has sent me," so the "me" would not then be the Lord of hosts. Most interpreters have resolved this problem by concluding that the prophet Zechariah was quoting what the Lord said. Thus, it is more likely that the phrases "he sent me" and "then you will know that the LORD of Hosts has sent me" referred to the prophet Zechariah (he is the "me"), who was quoting what God said to him. In this last phrase of 2:9, the prophet Zechariah claimed that God would establish the legitimacy of his prophetic words by fulfilling this prophecy (Petersen, 1984, 178; Baldwin, 1972, 109–10; Boda, 2004, 234; Hill, 2008b, 542–43). A second approach to this problem suggests that the "me" was the Angel of the Lord[1] (McComiskey, 1998, 1060; Unger, 1970, 49), who was sent by God to defeat the nations and fulfill this prophecy (2:9b).

TRANSLATION ANALYSIS: 2:8

NASB[95] "After glory He has sent Me against the nations."

HCSB "He has sent Me for His glory against the nations."

NIV[84] "After the Glorious One has sent me against the nations."

NKJV "He sent Me after glory, to the nations."

NRSV "(after his glory sent me) regarding the nations"

All translations here have the words correct, but the grammar is unclear and we are not sure who "one" and "me" refer to. So in this case, no one translation can be declared the most correct.

The final problem concerns the meaning of the difficult phrase "after glory he sent me" (2:8). Wolters (2014, 81–82) lists sixteen different ways interpreters have dealt with this phrase (including emending the text). Some reinterpret the preposition "after" (אַחַר) and translate it as "with" (as it is in 1:8, "with red"), while others have changed the text to "who, which" (אֲשֶׁר) or to "one, unique" (אֶחָד), but these emendations should be rejected. Others question the meaning of "glory" (כָּבוֹד) and have suggested the unlikely translation "after the Glorious One sent me" / "after (his) Glory sent me" (Meyers and Meyers, 1987, 155) or "after glory (a vision) he sent me" (Klein, 2008, 121) or "after he has honored me" (Boda, 2004, 236). The odd translation "with insistence he sent me" is favored by Baldwin (1972, 109). If the Hebrew text has suffered an error in transmission, it would be difficult to fix it to everyone's satisfaction. So the best approach would be to try to make sense of what we have and not emend this verse to change what it says. If "after" was used temporally, one might translate the phrase "after (showing) his glory he sent me." This might refer to the prophet seeing the glory of God when he was called to be a prophet (similar to Isaiah 6). Yet, the book of Zechariah does not include an

---

1   See earlier sidebar on the Angel of the Lord.

account of Zechariah's call experience, so it is impossible to verify this kind of interpretation. Thus, it is better to interpret the word "after" (אַחַר) as showing purpose, "to go after / in order to show his glory he sent me." This would not require any hypothetical call narrative in which the glory of God appeared to the prophet but would view the purpose for Zechariah's ministry to be the glorification of God.

The sending of the prophet against the nations would mean that Zechariah would give oracles and visions that would express God's condemnation of the foreign nations (cf. 1:15, 20–21; 2:9) much like the preaching of several other prophets (Isa. 13–23; Jer. 46–51; Ezek. 25–32; Amos 1–2). Part of the reason for God's judgment of these nations was that they were touching something very precious, the pupil of God's eye (lit., "the gate of his eye"). This metaphor explained how sensitive God was about anyone who would plunder his people and how protective he would be of his people. The eye is a very sensitive and extremely important part of any person's body, so if someone was trying to injure a person's eye, the victim being attacked would fight with all their might to prevent the loss of their eyesight. Since God's people were as precious as the pupil of his eye, he would do everything possible to protect them. In order to provide additional assurances, in 2:9, God emphatically promised that he would aggressively "shake" (נוּף) his "fist" (יָד, lit., my "hand"; cf. Job 31:21; Isa. 10:32) against the powerful nations that might try to plunder his people (cf. 1:15, 21). He would defeat them so severely that they would end up being plundered by the people who were their slaves (2:9), an interesting analogy of the reversal of fortunes that was comparable to the Israelites' plundering of the Egyptians at the time of the exodus (Exod. 12:35). In order to emphasize the truthfulness of this amazing prophecy, the prophet asserted that when these things

actually happened, everyone would understand that his prophetic words were valid, true, and the very words of God (2:9b).

TRANSLATION ANALYSIS: 2:9
NASB[95] "For behold, I will raise my hand over them."
HCSB "I will move against them with power."
NIV[84] "I will surely raise my hand against them."
NKJV "For surely I will shake my hand against them."
NRSV "See now I am going to raise my hand against them."
Both the literal "my hand" and "raise" make good sense as long as the pronoun "against" is used and the reader remembers that God is a Spirit and does not literally have a hand.

2:10. The final paragraph pictured a future time of great joy when many people would worship God in Jerusalem. When God would dwell again in Jerusalem, Jews and Gentiles would joyfully worship him. This did not refer to what would happen immediately in the difficult postexilic period of Haggai, Zechariah, Ezra, Nehemiah, and Malachi but pointed to the time when God would establish his future kingdom on earth.

2:11–13. The prophet's words describe what would happen in Jerusalem "in that day" (2:11, a phrase that often signaled events in a distant eschatological period. The Jewish people ("the daughters of Zion") and people from "many nations" (Gentiles), yes, "all people" (2:13) would be silent and worship God at that time. This prophecy was consistent with Isaiah's claim that "many nations" would stream to Jerusalem to hear God teach (Isa. 2:2–3) and that the nations would seek him (Isa. 11:10). Foreigners would join the people of Israel when they returned to their land (Isa. 14:1–2), and people from Egypt, Assyria, and Israel would worship God together (Isa. 19:20–25). Later, Isaiah prophesied that all nations would turn to God and be saved (Isa. 45:22) and that the suffering Servant would be a light to the nations (Isa. 49:6).

> ### The Suffering Servant
> Isaiah 40–55 refers to two servants: the people of Israel and a chosen Servant.
> 1. The people of Israel are pictured as God's chosen servant (Isa. 41:8–9; 44:1–2, 21), but they are characterized as blind and deaf (42:18; 43:8).
> 2. A chosen Servant who would bring forth justice (42:1–4) is pictured as one who would function as a light to the nations and a covenant to the peoples (42:6; 49:6) to open the eyes of the blind (42:7) so that God's salvation would reach to the ends of the earth (49:7). People would strike the second servant and humiliate him (50:6–7), reject, scourge, kill, and bury him (53:7–9) like a guilt offering of a sacrificial lamb. He would be wounded and give his life because of our transgressions (53:5) so that he could bear the guilt of our sins (53:12). God would be satisfied with his sacrifice, and this act would justify many (53:11), so in the end this servant would be exalted (52:13), see the wonderful fruit of his labor (53:10), and intercede on behalf of sinners (53:12).

At that time, people from many nations would come to Jerusalem to worship God when his glory would be dwelling in Jerusalem (Isa. 56:6–7; 60:1–16), for God would gather all nations to Zion to see his glory (Isa. 66:18–23). This news helps explain why the angel said that the city of Jerusalem would have so many people that it would be too big for a wall (Zech. 2:4). Zechariah and Isaiah both knew that at some future date God would dwell among his people (Zech. 2:10–11; Isa. 60:1–3) and that his glory would dwell in Zion (Zech. 2:5). This would be the time when God would bring his people back to dwell in the land of Israel (cf. Ezek. 40–48) and demonstrate by his fulfillment of past prophecies that he

had not given up on his "chosen" (בָּחַר) covenant people.

Those who would experience these marvelous events would express two emotional responses. First, they would respond with great joy, shouting, and singing (Zech. 2:10; cf. 3:14–15) because of God's grace and the thrill of being in his glorious presence. Second, these worshippers would respond with reverent silence (cf. Ps. 46:10) at the majestic sight of the awesome glory of their God who would dwell in his holy temple (Zech. 2:13; cf. Ezek. 43:1–8). By faith the people in Zechariah's day should believe God's promises and live with confidence knowing that Israel's holy transcendent God would one day dwell on earth with his people. His distant presence in heaven would no longer produce a vague feeling of hope, for he would be seen with their eyes, heard with their ears, and worshipped with thankful hearts.

THEOLOGICAL FOCUS
The exegetical idea (God's zeal for Jerusalem would result in stronger nations defeating the nations that scattered his people, but God's presence in Zion signaled the restoration of his people, and this would draw many Gentiles to worship him) leads to this theological focus: God will judge the sinful people of this world and protect those who follow and worship him.

There are two major theological principles in these two visions. First, God planned to judge those nations that scattered his people into distant lands (1:18–21; 2:8–9). The prophecy offers no timeframe for these divine acts, but God's just judgment would fall on these sinful nations. This prophecy was not about revenge but about holding people accountable for their actions. Second, any audience that reads or hears Zechariah's visions would understand something concrete and exciting about God's passionate zeal for his people (1:12–14). These new prophetic visions were not just pleasant words; they summarized what God would do in the coming years. God promised to protect his people from all harm and restore them to their land (2:1–7). The God who chose Israel as his covenant people long ago would pour out his covenant love to them and bring them back to Jerusalem, allowing many Gentile people to join them (2:11). God would dwell in their midst, and Jews and Gentiles would joyfully worship him, sometimes in silence and sometimes with joyful shouts (2:10–13). May that day come quickly!

PREACHING AND TEACHING STRATEGIES

Exegetical and Theological Synthesis

Zechariah 1:18–2:13 does not provide a precise timeline for the fulfillment of Zechariah's words. It does, however, highlight the details of his prophecy: Jerusalem without walls, the glorious advent of God, and the inclusion of Gentiles into Israel's worship. Although some events did not come to pass in Zechariah's day, the contemporary audience noted that God had launched the reversal of exile. And since God's people currently faced internal and external opposition in their temple rebuilding project, Zechariah's words of hope—immediate and future—inspired them.

What deserves greater development is Israel's responsibility for the exile. Her ongoing breach of the covenant—evident in idolatry, injustice, poor leadership, and anemic witness among the nations—sealed her fate (Ezek. 16:15–63). Before the people ever settled into the Promised Land, Moses warned the nation of dispersion if they disobeyed God (Deut. 28:64–68). And yet, the Lord did not cast out Israel quickly. The slow-to-anger God gave his people centuries of second chances before saying, "Enough is enough" (Exod. 34:6; Joel 2:13). What Moses depicted as eventual and opaque, Jeremiah made immediate and clear: seventy years of exile by the hands of Babylon will soon commence (Jer. 25:8–13).

Since Adam and Eve's rebellion in Eden, human sin effects divine consequences. Our first parents experienced exile from the garden and estrangement from God (Gen. 3:22–24). Generations later, human rebellion led to the flood, erasing all human life from the planet but Noah's family (Gen. 6:6–8). Divine judgment may spell the loss of life, land, physical capacity, or political freedom; however, the losses God's people suffer under his discipline may not last forever. Exile can be redemptive (Hos. 2:14–17). It can cleanse our palates to taste God's mercies anew (Lam. 3:22–23). It can sharpen our resolve to live as a witness to his glory (Isa. 55:4–5). The faithful few that learn from their errors are more likely to see God's work of restoration.

Preaching Idea

Old losses are fertile ground for new beginnings.

Contemporary Connections

What does it mean?

What does it mean that old losses are fertile ground for new beginnings? Does any loss apply? Not all losses are created equal. The kinds of losses envisioned by the passage result from God's people rejecting his authority. They were mired in sin, so God sent them into exile. As scattered people, they lost their temple, political freedoms, national leaders, and religious identity. What the people felt collectively, many people likely felt on an individual level: loss of security, stability, identity, control, and hope. When such losses compound for groups or individuals, the sum effect may feel overwhelming.

Sometimes God's people suffer loss immediately following their sin. Other losses come gradually. Adam and Eve lost their access to Eden after a single misstep (Gen. 3:22–24). Moses lost his royal position in a single day (Exod. 2:14–15). David lost his reputation gradually, as his reign stumbled to a dysfunctional end (2 Sam. 10–24). This pattern persists yet today. Some Christian families gradually lose their cohesiveness when they allow loose sexual boundaries. Some Christian business owners immediately lose their reputation following a scandal. Some churches gradually lose their evangelistic witness when their indifference to hurting people rises to the surface. Some Christian colleges immediately lose donors after evidence of discrimination.

It should be noted that each loss is an opportunity for introspection, a chance to ask: What did we do wrong? What could we have done differently? What can we change? What is God teaching us? What new beginning might God work from this loss? These final two questions move groups from gazing at their navels to peering at God's horizon. Hope always looks forward and outward. God can transform our guilt from sin into a glorious end. Ashes may become beauty; barren wombs may become full; arid deserts may become fertile valleys in God's restorative plan (Isa. 61).

Is it true?

Is it true that old losses are fertile ground for new beginnings? Yes, but this does not mean we always notice, appreciate, or take advantage of new beginnings. Haggai's audience gave more energy to lamenting the lost temple than building the renewed structure (Hag. 2:3). King Manasseh did not take advantage of the religious gains King Hezekiah made but reverted to their former idolatry (2 Kings 21). The book of Judges records repeated cycles of God's people falling back into sin shortly after God had granted them a new beginning.

God's people remain equally guilty today of neither owning nor learning from old losses. Due in part to arrogance, indifference, and bigotry, the evangelical church in America has not only lost political influence but also cultural relevance and younger adherents. Infighting, backstabbing, and disunity among Christians has led to a loss of credible witness. We should own these losses, not blame them on the rise of secularism. In fact, it is by confessing our power

grabbing, incivility, and lack of love that God's people open themselves to new beginnings. Perhaps, the church will learn to work together across denominational lines, avoid political platforms, and practice the humble art of listening.

The principle also applies at the personal level. The loss of a job for a breach of ethics may be fertile ground to explore more honest labor. The loss of a friendship due to malicious words may be fertile ground for new ways of speaking the truth in love. We must remember that God can redeem our errors. And though a lost job or broken friendship may not be restored, he may work in us so we are more honest and kinder in the future.

Now what?

What should we do with our losses to experience the fertile ground of new beginnings? First, we must resolve not to rush. Losses cause pain, which provokes a variety of emotional responses. Denial, anger, doubt, fear, anxiety, and depression mark our losses. Healing doesn't result from a short-circuited process but begins when we own our part in a loss. We cannot feign innocence. We should admit our culpability. In the case of a corporate loss, making space for corporate lament and confession—missing elements in most white Protestant worship gatherings—may powerfully bond God's people together.

Second, as we accept losses and work through the feelings they induce, we are wise to analyze the circumstances and causes. A group leader, including a parent, boss, pastor, or coach, may ask: What did we do to induce the loss? What could we have done differently? What does God want us to learn as we move forward? Collectively, we may debrief, dialogue, pray, and seek outside counsel both to grieve the loss and find the fertile ground. Personally, we may journal, pray, or talk with a trusted friend or counselor to grieve the loss and find the fertile ground. Again, patience is essential because answers to these questions are complex.

Finally, we must learn to look beyond losses to the hope of restoration (Zech. 2:10–12). God may not always work on our schedule, but he keeps his promises. He may not use means we prefer, but his ends are perfect (Isa. 46:10). In fact, many of the OT figures experienced more losses than new beginnings, but they kept their eyes fixed ahead on God's forgiveness (Heb. 11). Collectively and individually, we must learn to trust that God will provide full healing, fresh meaning, and new opportunities. It does little good to grovel in our sin.

Creativity in Presentation

People love restoration stories. Whether watching home remodeling shows or beauty makeovers on TV, we enjoy seeing something old or broken receive a face-lift. Consider showing a commercial or clip from one of the current total home makeover shows (e.g., *This Old House*, *Flip or Flop*, or *Love It or List It*). Chip and Jo-anna Gaines, from *Fixer Upper*, have used their celebrity platform to talk about marriage, family, and faith from a winsome Christian perspective in *The Magnolia Story* (2016). Chip's follow-up book, *Capital Gains: Smart Things I Learned Doing Stupid Stuff* (2017), details how some of his personal failures resulted in teachable moments from God. Perhaps someone in your congregation flips homes or renovated a portion of his house. A live or recorded interview with before-and-after images might help illustrate the beauty of a new beginning.

My wife and I (Tim) took up the eco-friendly act of composting a few years ago. We collect waste—banana peels, apple cores, coffee grounds, potato skins, eggshells, and other decomposing fare—and place it in a lidded container in the kitchen. Every few days we dump it in the designated pile in the backyard with dead leaves and grass clippings. The smell from the container repels me, but the soil at the bottom of the compost box is fertile ground. To reach it, we stab the top layer of waste with a pitchfork and turn it over. The waste we collect symbolizes our "losses," the indulgence and excess in our lives. Even though we amass losses, under the proper conditions, God can turn it into something useful. Having a small composting container and pot with fresh soil available might drive home the point.

Chuck Colson could have considered his life over following the Watergate Scandal that lead to Richard Nixon's resignation as the thirty-seventh president of the United States (in office: January 20, 1969–August 9, 1974). Colson's political career ended when he was sentenced to serve prison time. Amid these losses, Colson became a follower of Jesus. His life turned fertile for ministry. He began Prison Fellowship and authored numerous books, including autobiographical works, *Born Again* (1976) and *Life Sentence* (1979), and theological works, *Loving God* (1983), *Being the Body* (2003 [1992]), and *The Faith* (2008). Similarly, since 1986 Father Gregory Boyle has provided a new beginning for more than seven thousand ex-gang members through Homeboy Industries in Los Angeles. They offer career training, job opportunities, tattoo removal, and therapy to clients. Boyle describes new beginnings for gang members in his book *Tattoos on the Heart: The Power of Boundless Compassion* (2010).

As you work through the passage, be sure the sermon stresses the following: God will judge the sinful people of the world and protect those who follow him and worship him. Moreover, old losses are fertile ground for new beginnings.

- The groups harassing God's people won't last (1:18–21).
- New beginnings will come for God's people (2:1–5).
- The guilt hanging over God's people won't last (2:6–9).
- New beginnings will come for all peoples (2:10–13).

DISCUSSION QUESTIONS

1. What losses did Israel's breach of covenant (Deut. 28) inflict on the people? How did God bring about those losses?

2. What does the judgment of the "four horns" teach about God's character?

3. How do the "nations" fit into God's future plans?

4. What are some biblical examples of "eventual" losses that God inflicts? What are biblical examples of "immediate" losses he inflicts? How have you seen both eventual and immediate losses in your life?

5. How do you explain our reluctance to learn from old losses?

Zechariah 3:1–4:14

EXEGETICAL IDEA

After God's Adversary accused God's religious servant the high priest Joshua of sinfulness, God cleansed Joshua and restored him to serve in the temple; then God encouraged the political leader Zerubbabel with the promise that God's Spirit would enable them to complete the restoration of the temple.

THEOLOGICAL FOCUS

God's servant leaders should not be discouraged because of difficult circumstances, for God forgives sins and will empower them to do the work he has called them to do.

PREACHING IDEA

God can powerfully use imperfect leaders.

PREACHING POINTERS

The fourth and fifth visions narrow from a national to personal focus. Zechariah received heavenly insight concerning Jerusalem's earthly leaders: Joshua the high priest and Zerubbabel the governor. The original audience likely had a low view of its leaders. Persian rule, lackluster harvests, regional tensions, and a stuttering temple project had done little to impress anyone. But God assured Zechariah that these two leaders had his vote of confidence; they were called, cleansed, and empowered to undertake their tasks.

Leaders in today's church and parachurch organizations face tremendous pressure. Leadership books create an expectation for them to master time management, vision casting, self-analysis, motivation, delegation, innovation, and countless other abilities. Leaders live under a microscope: every accomplishment is analyzed; every failure, exposed. If they do not change their organizational culture or build the bottom line fast enough, they are questioned or replaced. We prefer effective leaders over faithful elders, dynamic speakers over dutiful shepherds. This section suggests that God's approval of a leader matters more than man's opinion. Indeed, God can powerfully use imperfect leaders.

RESTORATION OF GOD'S SERVANTS (3:1–4:14)

LITERARY STRUCTURE AND THEMES (3:1–4:14)

These two visions of Joshua the high priest followed by the golden lampstand and two olive trees communicate messages of assurances that (a) God chose, forgave, and cleansed Joshua so that he could serve as high priest and as a sign of the coming fulfillment of both near and distant prophecies (3:1–10); and (b) God's Spirit would enable Zerubbabel to finish constructing the temple (4:1–14).

The theme that permeates this unit through these fourth and fifth visions is that there was an Adversary that would try to disqualify God's servants; however, through the work of God's Spirit and his power, God's leaders would complete the task he had given them.

- *Restoration of the High Priest (3:1–5)*
- *Implication of the Courtroom Action (3:6–10)*
- *The Complete Restoration of the Temple (4:1–14)*

EXPOSITION

Many people in Judah were ill-informed about the instructions God gave in the Torah about the role of the priests and their responsibilities at the temple because the temple was not rebuilt and thus had not been functioning normally for the last seventy years. In addition, some leader at the temple and at the top of the government were failing to serve Yahweh and the people faithfully. As a result, there was a serious need for someone to challenge and encourage the failing leadership at the temple (the high priest Joshua) and at the head of their local government (the governor Zerubbabel). In order to resolve this problem, God removed Joshua's sin and challenged him to serve as a faithful priest (Zech. 3), then he empowered Zerubbabel with his Spirit to finish building the temple (Zech. 4). God's servant leaders should not give up hope because they had failed to live a pure life every second of every day, for God forgave their sins and would empower his servants to do the work he had called them to do.

Restoration of the High Priest (3:1–5)

The spiritual Adversary of the priests tried to condemn God's servant, but God forgave the high priest Joshua's sins and prepared him for service and to be a sign to others.

3:1–2. Chapter 3 opens in God's courtroom. Zechariah claimed that God "caused me to see" (וַיַּרְאֵנִי) a vision of the heavenly courtroom of the divine council with the Angel of the Lord on one side of the high priest Joshua, some additional angels in the background (3:4–5), and "the Adversary" (הַשָּׂטָן; or "Satan," NASB[95] NIV[84] HCSB NKJV NRSV) making accusations against Joshua. Usually a person's (human or supernatural) name is not preceded by the definite article "the" (e.g., "the Bob," or "the Abraham"). Thus, it appears that the term that is used to describe this accuser was not his name but a description of his role (i.e., "the Adversary"; Klein, 2008, 134–35). This indicates that the understanding of "the Adversary" in the OT was not as fully developed as the understanding of "Satan" in the NT (Baldwin, 1972, 113; Merrill, 2003, 120; McComiskey, 1998, 1069), so one cannot impose all one knows about Satan from the NT back onto this passage.

Although there is some ambiguity about who did what, this vision came from God (not the interpreting angel; Baldwin, 1972, 113), and

God functioned as the judge at this trial (Meyers and Meyers, 1987, 182) with the Angel of the Lord serving in the role of a defense attorney. The charge against the high priest Joshua was not spelled out in the vision, so it is impossible to guess what the accusations were. The discouraging implications of this accusation were that the spiritual leader Joshua could not function as high priest and would be unworthy of overseeing the reconstruction of the temple in Jerusalem. However, the decision of God in this trial was to give a strong "rebuke" (וְּגָעַר) to the Adversary (3:2) by countering what he said and rejecting the implications of these charges.

3:3. Since the filthy clothes of the high priest would be removed (3:4), implying the removal of something sinful, some part of the accusation against Joshua was true. The high priest was guilty of some sin that could disqualify him from serving as high priest at the altar to make atonement for sins if he did not confess this sin and receive God's forgiveness. God's rebuke of the Adversary (3:2) was partially based on the fact that God "chose" (בָּחַר) Jerusalem to be the place where the temple was to be built and the place where people and priests would come to pray and have their sins forgiven. In the first vision (1:7–17), God's zeal was to act compassionately toward Jerusalem and Zion with comforting words because out of his grace he "chose" (בָּחַר) Jerusalem as the place for his temple (cf. 1:16). Although some view Joshua as a symbol of the sinfulness of the whole nation of Israel (Klein, 2008, 132; Petersen, 1984, 195–96; Boda, 2004, 252; 1069; Smith, 1984, 199), this seems unlikely, for it is hard to understand how the whole nation would serve in the temple as priests (3:7) and how the whole nation was a symbol to others that God would bring the Branch/Sprout mentioned in 3:8.

Joshua's filthy clothes indicated that Joshua was guilty of some personal sin, but God opposed the conclusion that this sin permanently excluded Joshua from serving

in the temple (Merrill, 2003, 120) or that it prevented him from leading in the reconstruction of the temple. Thus, the temporary failures of this one important man Joshua would not derail the eternal plan of God for his people or eliminate his service as high priest on the national Day of Atonement (Lev. 16). A second reason (1:2b) why God's plan would not fail was that God purposely chose Joshua to be the high priest and delivered him from "the fire" of exile in Babylon and brought him back to Jerusalem to serve as high priest. Johnston (2012, 192) thinks this experience was "Joshua's investiture as high priest in a purification ritual," but the

The Garments of the High Priest. Courtesy of Internet Archive Book Images / Flickr (public domain).

event as described in the vision seems to take place at a heavenly court scene where Joshua was on trial; plus, there is no indication that this happened at the beginning of his priestly service. God metaphorically compared Joshua to a stick burning in a fire (the exile) with God graciously reaching down to remove that stick from the burning fire so that it would not be destroyed by the fire. God would not give up on Joshua because he chose him to have a significant leadership role as high priest.

3:4–5. God resolved this spiritual leadership problem by forgiving and taking away Joshua's sins. Joshua should be wearing the pure linen clothes of the holy high priest, but before that could happen. Someone had to remove the "filthy" (צֹאָה) clothes he was wearing as he stood by the Angel of the Lord.

Priestly Garments

The high priest wore a special garment of fine linen, which is described in detail in Exodus 28 and 39 and included a breastplate, an ephod inlaid with twelve stones, a special robe and tunic, a turban and a sash made of gold blue, and purple and scarlet cloth. On the hem of his garment were pomegranate-like objects of blue and golden bells. He wore a crown of pure gold with an inscription saying "Holy to the LORD" that was kept in place by a blue belt.

The priests who served in the temple were to be holy, set apart from sin and set apart to the work of God at the tabernacle/temple. At the beginning of their time of service a priest was consecrated for service as outlined in Exodus 29, Leviticus 8, and Numbers 8:5–25, but it seems that Joshua was already serving as high priest earlier when Haggai gave his prophecies. At this time, Joshua's clothes were stained with vile "excrement" (צֹאָה; cf. Deut. 23:14; Ezek. 4:12), symbolizing his sinfulness and unworthiness to serve as high priest.

Leviticus 22:6–7 spells out what a ceremonially unclean priest should do. After confessing his sins, he should bathe and change his priestly garments. But in this setting, the Angel of the Lord instructed other angels in the courtroom to remove Joshua's filthy garments. The removal of the filthy clothes symbolized the "removal" or "passing over" (עָבַר) of Joshua's guilt. After this, Joshua was clothed with fine clean clothing and a clean turban on his head to symbolize that the high priest was spiritually fit to give spiritual leadership to those who came to worship God at the altar and to direct those who were working on rebuilding the temple.

Implication of the Courtroom Action (3:6–10)

God's courtroom action of forgiving and cleansing Joshua, the one he had chosen to serve as high priest, implied that not only would this action pertain to the fulfillment of near prophecies but also to the coming fulfillment of far-off, messianic prophecies.

3:6–7. Zechariah now transitioned from a description of the action completed in 3:1–5 to a speech that challenged Joshua to think about his future role in the temple and the implications this would have on others. Would this sin cause God to remove him from leadership, or would God's forgiveness of this sin cause God to restore his leadership role over temple worship and his oversight of the reconstruction of the temple (3:6–7)? In clear, unmistakable words, God "witnessed, charged, testified" (עוּד) to Joshua the conditional promise that "if" (אִם) he would faithfully act in godly ways (his personal moral walk) and closely follow God's instructions in his priestly duties (his faithfulness to his responsibilities), then Joshua would be granted the privilege and responsibility of "judging," "governing," or "ruling" (דִּין) over the temple, as well as the freedom to be among those standing in God's heavenly courts through his prayers.

WORD ANALYSIS: The term דִּין is used in several different contexts. "Judging" might involve (a) the human responsibility of defending the rights of the poor (Ps. 72:2, 4; Prov. 31:9; Jer. 5:28; 22:16; 30:13); (b) the general action of "judging, evaluating" if people were following the law (Ezra 7:25); (c) the act of "quarreling, disputing, judging" what was right (2 Sam. 19:9; Eccl. 6:10); or (d) the act of "judging, controlling" the action of priests in the temple (Zech. 3:7).

The challenge to walk in God's ways and keep his statutes was a common requirement for all Israelites who desired to maintain their covenant relationship with God (e.g., Lev. 18:30; Deut. 8:6), but in this context the Lord was specifically concerned with the purity of Joshua's heart and his ability to faithfully carry out his priestly duties at the temple (Lev. 8:3). The ability to walk among those standing here (3:7b) must refer to the awesome privilege to communicate with and be in the midst of the members of God's heavenly court. This probably included his daily prayers for sinners who came to the temple to restore their relationship with God, his requests for guidance when advising or working with Judah's political leaders, insight in dealing with the priests who served under him, prayers for the sick, and intercession for wisdom in guiding workers as they completed the reconstruction of the temple.

3:8. The final verses outlined some near and distant implications (Smith, 1984, 20, takes 3:8–10 as eschatological) for the priests, the temple, and issues related to the fulfillment of future prophecies. This message was to Joshua the high priest and the regular priests that worked with him. These priests were a symbolic "sign" (מוֹפֵת) that God would do something special in the future, just like Ezekiel was a prophetic sign (מוֹפֵת) of what was about to happen in Jerusalem; that is, the people would soon go into exile (Ezek. 12:6, 11).[1]

TRANSLATION ANALYSIS: 3:8, "symbols" *(מוֹפֵת)*

NASB[95]	"they are men who are a symbol"
HCSB	"these men are a sign"
NIV[84]	"who are men symbolic"
NKJV	"they are a wondrous sign"
NRSV	"they are an omen"

Usually symbols represent something, but they are not prophetic signs of something to come.

Other signs like the rainbow were everlasting memorial signs to help people remember what God did in the past (the flood that killed all but eight people) and what God promised he would not do again (the rainbow in Gen. 9:8–17). Sometimes God offered signs to prove that he was God and to help motivate people of weak faith to trust him and follow his instructions (Judg. 6:36–40; Isa. 7:10–12). Zechariah prophesied that in the future, Joshua and the priests would be a sign that God would bring fourth "my Servant the Branch [צֶמַח]." This term would be better rendered "Sprout," which picks up the idea of the horn of David "springing up" in the messianic Psalm 132:17.

WORD ANALYSIS: The word צֶמַח can refer to (a) a physical "sprout" that grew out of the ground from a seed (Gen. 2:9; 19:25; Ezek. 16:7; 17:2) or (b) the "sprouting" of a person. Psalm 137:17 refers to the fulfillment of the Davidic covenant when God said, "I will cause the horn of David to sprout [צֶמַח], I will prepare a lamp for my anointed." There is a messianic ("horn of David" and "my anointed") connection with this concept in Jeremiah 33:15 (cf. 23:6), in which God

---

1   Isaiah and his sons were seen as a sign to their generation (Isa. 8:18). Lena-Sofia Tiemeyer suggests that these priests were a sign of the removal of guilt from the land in one day (Zech. 3:9). Lena-Sofia Tiemeyer, *Zechariah and His Visions: An Exegetical Study of Zechariah's Vision Reports*. Library of the Hebrew Bible / Old Testament Studies 605 (London: Bloomsbury T&T Clark, 2015), 137.

promises, "I will raise up for David a righteous Sprout/Branch [צֶמַח] and he will rule as king and succeed." Ezekiel 34:23–24 and 37:25 refer to an eschatological messianic leader as "my servant David" who would shepherd his people. Isaiah prophesied that "my Servant" would bring forth justice and be a light to the nations (Isa. 42:1–6; 49:6) and die for the sins of others (Isa. 52:13–53:12; cf. G. V. Smith, 2009, 159–74, 340–60, 378–87, 430–72). Second Temple literature also looked for a righteous "Branch" as a king based upon these OT texts of Scripture (4Q161; 4Q174; 4Q252; 4Q285; cf. Bateman, 2012, 276–88). The NT identified this person as Jesus (Bock, 2012, 331–403).

3:9. The second promise was more difficult to understand than the first in 3:7, but it was related to a stone set before Joshua that had seven eyes on it, an inscription engraved on it, and this stone had something to do with the removal of the nation's iniquity in one day. Attempts to identify the stone include the suggestion that this stone was the stones on the high priest's breastplate that were engraved with the names of the twelve tribes of Israel (Exod. 28:17–21) or the gold sign worn on the forehead of the high priest (Exod. 28:36–38; Wolters, 2014, 102; Redditt, 1995, 65; and Boda, 2004, 257–58). However, the stone might be a symbol of the Messiah (Barker, 1983, 626; Smith, 1984, 201; Merrill, 2003, 128), who elsewhere was referred to as a stone of stumbling (Isa. 8:14–15), the chief stone that the builders rejected (Ps. 118:22–23). Nevertheless, the most likely view is that this stone was the foundation cornerstone or the capstone (4:7) of the temple Joshua was building.

The meaning of the seven eyes seems fairly clear since Zechariah 4:10 identifies the seven eyes as the all-seeing eyes of God which oversee everything that was happening on earth. Thus, the seven eyes were not carved on the stone; instead, the seven eyes of God were focused on the stone and the completion of the temple. Since the words of the inscription on the stone

are not provided, it is impossible to know what this inscription said. One suggestion (Merrill, 2003, 128; Wolters, 2014, 107) is that God would engrave the very next words in this verse ("I will take away the guilt of this land in one day") on the stone. Those interpreting this as the gold sign on the high priest's turban (Petersen, 1984, 211) would point to words engraved on it ("Holy to the LORD" in Exod. 28:36), while those taking a messianic view suggest that this refers to the wounds engraved on the body of Christ when he was persecuted before and during his crucifixion. A preferable interpretation would suggest that this stone was either the foundation cornerstone or the top capstone (as in Zech. 4:7, 10) which had an inscription on it and that the laying of this stone would mark the completion of the temple reconstruction. This promise functioned as an encouragement to Joshua and his fellow priests who were working on the rebuilding of the temple because God was promising that it would be completed.

The final phrase of 3:9 promised the removal of the guilt of the land in one day. In Zechariah's day this would be true and descriptive of what happened on the Day of Atonement (cf. Lev. 16) when the high priest entered the Holy of Holies once a year to atone for the sins of the nation. Some view this verse typologically and interpret this clause prophetically to refer to the work of the messianic Sprout/Branch. Thus, this prophecy would refer to the future time when God's suffering Servant of Isaiah 52:13–53:12 would die and take away the sins of others in one day (Boda, 2004, 258). Later Second Temple literature picks up some of these themes (Bateman, 2012, 253–302) and it is advanced further in the NT (Bock, 2012, 331–441), but these go beyond what Zechariah understood.

3:10. The final verse refers to an ideal time in the future ("in that day") when there would be peace and prosperity with people enjoying the fruits of a good life with their neighbors (cf. Mic. 4:4), similar to the peace and prosperity the people enjoyed in the reign of King Solomon (cf. 1 Kings 4:25). This time of harmony and fellowship with others reflected the Israelite beliefs about the future blessing God's people would enjoy in the time of the Sprout/Branch (the Messiah). So, with both near and distant implications in view, Joshua could continue to be high priest and would be a sign of God's future plans.

The Complete Restoration of the Temple (4:1–14)

God's Spirit would empower Zerubbabel to finish building the temple.

4:1–2. The fifth vision was about the political leader Zerubbabel, the governor of Judah, who would complete the restoration of the temple. This vision was paired with the fourth vision about the spiritual leader Joshua, the high priest, who would oversee the construction of the temple and be in charge of what would happen in the temple once it was completed. In this vision the interpreting angel who spoke to Zechariah in the first and third visions (Zech. 1:9, 13–14; 2:3) "aroused, stirred" (עוּר) the prophet and asked him what he saw. Zechariah reported that he saw a lampstand, but there was no hint of any relationship between this lampstand and the pure gold lampstand that provided light in the holy place of the tabernacle (cf. Exod. 25:31–40) or one of the ten lampstands that gave light inside Solomon's temple in Jerusalem (1 Kings 7:49; 2 Chron. 4:7). Although some assume this lampstand was a temple lampstand, this was never stated, plus it is fairly certain that Zechariah had never seen any of the lampstands in Solomon's temple because he was born in Babylon during the exile. In addition, the second temple was still in the process of being rebuilt, so no lampstands were burning brightly in the temple when Zechariah received this vison.

For the lampstand in Zechariah's vision, one might expect something very similar to a seven-branch menorah candelabrum like the one engraved on Titus's arch in Rome, but archeologists have not found any of these fancy lampstands in excavations earlier that 100 b.c. (Baldwin, 1972, 119). Instead, earlier clay lampstands were designed having a round column pedestal with a receptacle area for oil at the top. The clay on the edge of this receptacle/bowl would be crimped several times along the edge of the bowl to make thin spout like places to put several wicks. Although it is hard to know exactly what Zechariah was describing in 4:2, it included a big receptacle "bowl" (גֻּלָּה) for storing oil above the base. Since most large and small lamps found by archeologists have a round bowl-like shape to hold the oil with spouts for the wicks, this part of the description would probably match existing patterns for lamps at that time.

The Lampstand in the Ruins of Dan
During the archeological excavation of the ruins of the city of Dan in northern Israel, a lampstand from the Iron Age was found with seven spouts (see the picture in Petersen, 1984, 220, 222), another in a tomb at Dothan, and a third at Taanach.

WORD ANALYSIS: The word גֻּלָּה was used to describe some aspect of (a) a pool of water in Joshua 15:19, (b) a round bowl-like shape at the top of the two pillars in front of Solomon's temple in 1 Kings 7:41, or (c) a golden bowl in Ecclesiastes 12:6. Thus the word referred to a round, curved bowl-like object.

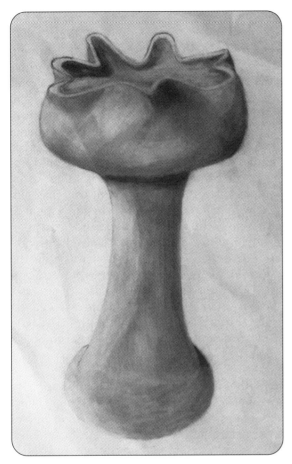

Illustration of the lampstand found in the ruins of Dan. Courtesy of Hannah Vander Lugt.

Hebrew will repeat numbers ("seven and seven") to give a distributive sense, this repetition means "seven spouts for each" of the seven lamps; thus, there were forty-nine wicks giving light (Baldwin, 1972, 120; Meyers and Meyers, 1987, 237).

WORD ANALYSIS: This word מוּצָקוֹת, *"narrow sprout," and the similar term* מוּצָקוֹת, *"pipes" derive from different roots. Some (Merrill, 2003, 132) have connected* מוּצָקוֹת *to the root* יָצַק, *"to pour," and thus derived the meaning "channels, pipes" that would transfer/pour the oil from the larger bowl into the smaller lamps. It seems better to follow Wolters (2014, 116), who connects this word to the root* צוק, *"to be narrow," in which case it referred to the "narrow spout" on the rim of the lamp where a wick would be placed.*

4:3–5. In addition to the lampstand, Zechariah saw two olive trees located on each side of the lampstand. There was no explanation of the role of the olive trees at this point, but one might assume that they would provide the olive oil that was needed to keep the lamps lit. Nevertheless, this was not explained and there was no explanation as to why it is not necessary to crush the olives in order to extract the oil. When asked, Zechariah had to admit that initially he did not know what this all meant. The messenger angel seemed surprised that Zechariah did not know what this vision implied, but the prophet humbly admitted that he needed help in understanding this vision. Ultimately, through the work of God's Spirit, God's people would complete the rebuilding of God's place of worship (4:6–7).

The lampstand in this vision had seven additional smaller bowls placed around the large receptacle for oil, and each of these seven individual bowl lamps had seven "spouts" (מוּצָקוֹת) or notches where wicks could be placed. Merrill (2003, 132) translates "spouts" as "pipes" (מוּצָקוֹת) that would carry the oil from the large receptacle at the top to the seven smaller lamps below. He believes there were fourteen pipes (seven on each side). One difficulty with this description is the author's use of the word "seven" three times in this clause (lit., "seven lamps upon it, seven and seven spouts for the lamps that were on the top of it"). Since

The Vision's Content: Some interpreters find a major disjunction between the content of the vision (4:1–6a, 10b–14) and the explanation in the oracle in 4:6b–10a; thus, they raise questions about the unity of this vision. But if the bright lights of the lampstand were symbolic of God's presence, one can understand that this part of the vision supported some ideas in 4:6b–10a. Both the presence and power of God's Spirit would be there to help Zerubbabel (4:6) as well as the seven omniscient eyes of God (4:10) that sovereignly controlled everything that was happening.

4:6. Some (Petersen, 1984, 238–42; Boda, 2004, 277) have compared this scene and the words spoken about the stone in 4:7 to what happened at a foundation ceremony when royal buildings were built in the ancient Near East. This event would include a royal figure (a king or governor) involved with the building and the ceremony. In terms of other elements of this comparison, the metal in 4:10 was similar to the metal tablet in Assyrian building deposits, the stone in 4:7 was similar to the Mesopotamian foundation stone, and the shouting of "blessing/grace" might be comparable to Mesopotamian ritual cheers.[2] In contrast, others discount these comparisons or accept only the first point (a royal figure was involved in the rebuilding process), which would be true of any major religious building project at that time (Wolters, 2014, 117–18).

The angel provided three words of encouragement concerning the rebuilding of the temple based on the vision in 4:1–5. This visionary picture of trees and a lampstand was a prophetic message from God about the weak Davidic governor of Judah named Zerubbabel. The initial part of this message in 4:6 was rather cryptic because the angel did not provide any verbs and did not relate the sentence to any event, project, or contemporary issue. Thus, 4:6 indicates that the governor will not succeed based on his own "military strength"

(חַיִל), nor by/though his own "human power, status, authority" (כֹּחַ), but he would have success by/through "my Spirit" (רוּחִי). Thus on the one hand, Zerubbabel would not resolve all his problems by using the small Jewish militia in Jerusalem to overthrow the armies of the Persian Empire or defeat the people from Samaria. On the other hand, this did not mean that Zerubbabel was to do nothing or that the human strength of many workers would not be needed to complete the rebuilding of the temple. Instead, the main point was that success would come because of the movement of God's powerful Spirit. This was the same powerful Spirit of God that was involved with creation (Gen. 1:2), the Spirit that was with the nation of Israel when they came out of Egypt and went through the Red Sea (Hag. 2:5). God's fulfillment of this promises would remind those in Jerusalem that nothing was too difficult or impossible for God to accomplish (Gen. 18:14; Jer. 32:17, 27).

4:7. The second part of this explanation to Zerubbabel compared his task to a "great mountain." The prophet said the "great mountain" before him would become a "plain, level field" (מִישׁוֹר). Some variously interpret this mountain as symbolizing the Persian Empire, the passivity of the people in Jerusalem, a human political opponent (Tattenai, the provincial governor), the pile of rubble around the temple building, the Samaritans, or the high priest Joshua (Wolters, 2014, 122; Tollington, 1993, 146–48). Yet, the solution must be related to putting the capstone on the temple building. The Persian Empire and the Samaritans were not defeated at this moment, and the high priest Joshua was not opposing or interrupting the work on the temple. Thus, the great mountain

---

2   For further information on foundation ceremonies in the ancient Near East, see A. Laato, "Zechariah 4,6a–10b and the Akkadian Royal Building Inscriptions," *Zeitschrift für altestestamenliche Wissenschaft* 106, no. 1 (1994): 53–69. For an extensive study of foundation deposits, see Richard S. Ellis, *Foundation Deposits in Ancient Mesopotamia*, Yale Near Eastern Researches 2 (New Haven: Yale University Press, 1968).

probably stood as a metaphor for all the factors that made the task of building the temple so difficult. The promise here is that the problems and difficulties involved with building the temple (this great mountain) would be resolved by God and removed.

This building process would conclude with Zerubbabel bringing forth the "first stone, head stone" (הָאֶבֶן הָרֹאשָׁה), which some interpret to be a stone from the former temple building (Petersen, 1985, 240; Boda, 2004, 277). Others take this stone to refer to "the primary stonework" of the foundation, not the foundation cornerstone because this building probably had a flat roof, but even with a flat roof there was a final stone that completed the construction of the walls (Wolters, 2014, 123). However, it seems better to view this stone as the final stone (the capstone) at the completion of the temple (Baldwin, 1972, 121; Merrill, 2003, 143; Klein, 2008, 161; Redditt, 1995, 69), for the very next verses refer to Zerubbabel finishing the temple (4:9). The final point was that the people would praise God for his help in restoring the temple. This praise would be generated from the people because Zerubbabel would one day place the capstone on the temple building to finish its construction (4:7). Later, Ezra 6:15–18 describes the completion of the temple building and its joyful dedication by the priests, Levites, and the rest of the people. This involved a great celebration, the offering of many sacrifices, and according to Zechariah 4:7 shouts of "grace, grace to it" (חֵן חֵן לָהּ). "Grace" here referred to God's undeserved favor or blessing on someone. Out of a joyful and thankful heart of praise, the people shouted out their desire for this holy building to be blessed by God.

4:8–9. Consistent with the claims of 4:7, the interpretation given here provides another promise concerning Zerubbabel's completion of the temple. God proclaimed that Zerubbabel, who began the work of "laying the foundation" (יָדַד) and building the walls of the temple to their present height, would finish building of the rest of the temple. This implied a completion of the temple in the near future within the lifetime of the governor Zerubbabel. Zechariah then concluded verse 9 with the reminder that when God's prophecy about the completion of the temple would come true in a few years, the people would know that Zechariah was a true prophet of God and that his words about the completion of the temple were based on a genuine revelation from God (Klein, 2008, 162).

4:10. The final interpretive message in this brief oracle provided one more word of encouragement and challenge about the completion of the temple. Apparently, some were pessimistic about ever getting the temple completed, and others "despised" (בַּז) how small the temple seemed to be when compared to the glories of Solomon's temple (cf. Hag. 2:3). Instead of despising and ridiculing the present temple building, the seven eyes of God would be glad when he would see the plumb line ("stone of tin," הָאֶבֶן הַבְּדִיל) in the hand of Zerubbabel. Since heavy lead would be a more likely metal to use in a plumb line, some (Baldwin, 1972, 122–23) interpret this as a "stone of separation" or "dividing." Thus, it symbolized the separated, holy nature of the Jewish community. Others think that this was a "tin tablet" (Petersen, 1984, 243; Boda, 2004, 277; Merrill, 2003, 145) similar to what was found in Mesopotamian building deposits. However, since there was no evidence of Hebrew buildings having foundation deposits, and the Hebrew word is "tablet" (לוּחַ) and not "stone" (אֶבֶן), this suggestion would seem to be unlikely. Consequently, there is no agreement on the explanation of this "stone of tin," but most treat it as a plumb line. Apparently, this stone of tin had something to do with the construction and was a positive sign that the building of the temple restoration was progressing. God's sovereign oversight and control of what was happening in Jerusalem and throughout the earth was pictured as the seven eyes of God, a concept somewhat parallel to the different horsemen in the first vision who roamed back and forth throughout the earth (Zech. 1:8–11). Ultimately, God's Spirit would enable Zerubbabel to complete the rebuilding of God's place of worship.

4:11–12. Zechariah requested an explanation of the meaning of the olive trees introduced in 4:3 and the "pipes" or "spout." Nothing the interpreting angel said in 4:6–10 explained the symbolism of the two trees in the vision. Consequently, once the spiritual explanation in 4:6–10 was completed, Zechariah still did not understand how the olive trees fit into the three points in 4:6–10. The first inquiry was about "a flowing stream" (שִׁבֹּלֶת; Judg. 12:6; Ps. 69:3; Isa. 27:12; Petersen, 1984, 236–37) or "an ear of grain" (Gen. 41:5–27; Ruth 2:2; Job 24:24; Isa. 17:5). In the context of an olive tree, this may refer to a group of olives (similar to an ear of grain) on a tree. The second factor questioned was the significance of the two golden "pipes, spouts, conduits" (צַנְתְּרוֹת) that transport the golden oil.

> **"Pipes, Spouts, Conduits"** (צַנְתְּרוֹת): The word צַנְתְּרוֹת was used only here in the Hebrew Bible so its meaning cannot be firmly established. If the word was related to צִנּוֹר "pipe," this would make sense, but there was no ת in this root as there was in צַנְתְּרוֹת. Wolters (2014, 144–46) translated this word as "pressers" since the olive had to be pressed to get the olive oil to flow out of the olive fruit and Tiemeyer (2015, 167) follows this interpretation.

4:13–14. The explanation provided in 4:14 ignored several parts of the question and only touched on the olive trees which were identified as the two anointed ones who were standing before the Lord. Since priests and kings were anointed when they entered service for God and because this vision was directed to Zerubbabel in 4:6, it was natural to conclude that these two olive trees represented the high priest Joshua and the Davidic governor Zerubbabel (Klein, 2008, 165; Baldwin, 1972, 124; McComiskey, 1998, 1093). Others have argued that the two anointed ones were the either the prophets Haggai and Zechariah (Boda, 2004, 275) or they are two divine beings (Tiemeyer, 2015, 162–64).

The limited amount of explanation of the various part of this vision left much to the imagination of interpreters, for even the lampstand was not clearly explained. It seems unlikely that the lampstand was a symbol of God (Klein, 2008, 167) or the Messiah (Unger, 1970, 82), for they did not need the help of others to keep their light shining. It is possible that the lampstand represented the future lampstand that would stand in the temple and shine as a witness to the Jewish community (Baldwin, 1972, 124). Although all the details of the vision were not fully explained, the main message of the vison was contained in the theological explanation in 4:6–10. Ultimately, the olive trees represented God's two servants (vv. 11–14).

THEOLOGICAL FOCUS

The exegetical idea (after God's Adversary accused God's religious servant the high priest Joshua of sinfulness, God cleansed Joshua and restored him to serve in the temple; then God encouraged the political leader Zerubbabel with the promise that God's Spirit would enable them to complete the restoration of the temple) leads to this theological focus: God's servant leaders should not be discouraged because of difficult circumstances, for God forgives sins and will empower them to do the work he has called them to do.

The two theological points in these visions relate the success of the two leaders of the community. First, the Adversary tried to disqualify God's servant, the sinful high priest Joshua, but God forgave him and gave him important responsibilities. Second, through the work of God's Spirit, God's servant Zerubbabel would complete the tasks God gave him.

The fourth vision emphasizes the importance of spiritual leaders being holy and responsible in their service to God. Spiritual leaders must confess their sins so that they are able to lead others in worship. Although the Adversary may try to discourage people by pointing to their sinfulness, God does not give up on his chosen servants just because of one failure. Instead, he forgives and challenges his chosen leaders to be responsible and accountable as leaders, to serve as godly people who can intercede on behalf of others in the throne room of God Almighty. A spiritual leader's testimony will be seen by others and his faith will cause others to have confidence in God's present plans for his people as well as his future eschatological plans to establish his kingdom.

The fifth vision taught those working on the temple that God's chosen leaders are important, but God's work will be completed only through the work of God's Spirit. Human work is needed to finish the job, but no work of God is ever accomplished simply though human effort. Zerubbabel would restore the temple because God was sovereignly in control of the situation. This was not the time for negative complaining about the beauty or small size of the building. The last stone would soon be put in place and the temple would soon be finished.

PREACHING AND TEACHING STRATEGIES

Exegetical and Theological Synthesis

Zechariah 3:1–4:14 introduces key spiritual personalities: the Satan and the Spirit. The former brought an unspecified accusation against Joshua. The latter empowered Zerubbabel as he finished rebuilding the temple. While much speculation could result from parsing the name and actions of the Adversary (i.e., Satan), the text focuses on God: his words and actions. He rebuked the Satan (twice for good measure), expressed his choice both of Jerusalem and Joshua, and ordered Joshua's cleansing.

The heavenly courtroom scene surfaced two interesting notes about the high priest. First, the accusation against him was accurate but not effective. If God did not speak as Joshua's advocate, the priest stood condemned. Accusations without an advocate are damning. Fortunately, God often stands ready to defend his people. He vouched for Job's righteousness (Job 1:8; 2:3). He stood beside Joseph when Potiphar's wife raised false accusations against him (Gen. 41:38). Through sign and wonder, he advocated for Moses in Israel's court of public opinion and Pharaoh's royal court (Exod. 3:11–12; 4:1–9; 8:19). And God stood as Daniel's defender, providing him wisdom to advise foreign kings (Dan. 4:9, 18; 5:11, 14) and rescuing him from certain death in the lions' den (6:21–22).

Second, God's advocacy (i.e., Joshua's "clean slate") did not give the high priest a perpetual pass on righteous living. God's vote of confidence came with conditions: he expected his people to live according to his law. Psalms 1 and 119 demonstrate the importance of God's law for right living. Of course, the vision about Zerubbabel added an important detail to carrying out our God-given duties: our success does not depend on us. The Spirit empowers God's people to live ethically and lead powerfully. Zechariah's predecessors predicted a time when God's Spirit would breathe new life into his people (Ezek. 37:1–10), branding their very hearts with God's law (Jer. 31:31–34).

Preaching Idea

God can powerfully use imperfect leaders.

Contemporary Connections

What does it mean?

What does it mean that God can powerfully use imperfect leaders? Simply this: God does not rely on the skill, ability, competency, or social networking of a leader in the church or parachurch organization in order to achieve great ends. Nor does he select morally flawless people to serve as leaders. He appoints imperfect men and women with diverse backgrounds to accomplish powerful feats—from building walls to fighting battles to planning feasts to shepherding people.

We commonly appoint leaders who pass the eyeball test. Israel selected King Saul as their premier king because of his stature and looks (1 Sam. 9:2). His appearance deceived in that he proved to be a disloyal king. David, the ruddy runt of Jesse's stock, became a powerful leader in God's program, for he was a man after God's heart (1 Sam. 16:6–13; cf. 13:14; Acts 13:22). We can allow family name, religious education, job training, and former experience to convince us someone will be a capable spiritual leader. Surely, many well-trained priests and well-groomed princes turned out to be poor leaders. God, on the other hand, chooses imperfect men and women who are humble of heart.

Is it true?

Does God really use imperfect leaders? Yes, God can use raw, inexperienced, untalented people to lead others. His Spirit turns many blank canvases into ministry masterpieces. He empowers stuttering speakers with occasional eloquence (e.g., Moses), timid judges with victory in battle (e.g., Gideon), and apprentices with experienced instructors (e.g., Elijah and Elisha). Nevertheless, God more often takes advantage of our gifts, talents, training, and personal experience. Moses's education aided him in writing Israel's early law and history. David's musical abilities allowed him to craft scores of psalms. In other words, God's vote of confidence is not limited to our defects but extends to our gifting.

Moreover, God can use morally imperfect people to lead. He used dishonest Abraham and deceptive Jacob to lead the emerging nation of Israel (Gen. 12:10–20; 27:1–40). God used murderous Moses to deliver Israel from Egypt (Exod.

2:11–12). God used promiscuous Rahab to lead her family from Jericho's overthrow (Josh. 6:17). God used generations of compromised judges to deliver Israel from foreign opponents. God used adulterous David to lead the united kingdom (2 Sam. 11–20). And he used the stained high priest Joshua to lead the postexilic community in worship (Zech. 3:6–10).

But does God's powerful work through imperfect leaders encourage moral compromise? Certainly not! For example, after cleansing Joshua, God clearly commanded him to continue walking in his ways (Zech. 3:7). Furthermore, he withdrew his Spirit from Saul for the king's rebellion (1 Sam. 15:22–31). God's use of imperfect leaders is not an endorsement for imperfect living. He does rebuke bad behavior (2 Sam. 12). Likewise, criminal acts and patterns of abuse should rightly disqualify church and Christian ministry leaders from their positions.

Now what?

What should we expect from the imperfect leaders God uses? Simply put, we should expect imperfection. Leadership expectations in the church deserve a healthy conversation. Long gone are the days when the pastor can simply preach and give care. In today's culture, we ask them to serve as vision-casters and culture-shapers, coaches and trainers, recruiters and assimilators. Spiritual leaders are imperfect people with limited resources; they cannot demonstrate perfect skill in all areas of ministry. They will make mistakes and need a margin of grace.

So how should we appoint, assess, and encourage our church leaders? When we appoint, assess, and encourage our leaders, we must stress the importance of character and competency. We want to see humility, discernment, integrity, and love more than selfishness, arrogance, and anger. Their consistency and maturity matter more than perfect performance. Furthermore, churches and Christian organizations should provide realistic job descriptions and timely reviews that assess leaders in their key tasks. Vague job descriptions leave room for speculative assessments. Finally, providing church leaders with teammates, staff, or partners who support them may keep them encouraged rather than feeling defeated.

For those in leadership positions, regularly listening to God goes a long way against feeling swayed by the crowd. Reading the Bible and reflecting on God's promise to empower his people can build a leader's confidence. Remembering moments where God provided a powerful word of advice, a powerful point of connection, or a powerful moment of healing can help the leader look beyond her imperfections. Finally, spiritual leaders should take time to pray, rest, praise, confess, play, seek counsel, and connect with people who encourage them. Accusing voices will come, but a leader may control the volume by faithfully observing such soul care measures.

Creativity in Presentation

God calls all sorts of imperfect leaders into service. Biblical characters head the list: Moses, Rahab, Gideon, David, Josiah, Mary, Peter, Paul, and James. Each of these figures could have been rendered unqualified to serve due to their stain or defect, but God still enlisted them. Consider playing "Name That Imperfect Leader" to foster participation.

> **Excursus. Name That Imperfect Leader**
> "I stole a man's wife and sent her husband to the front lines to be killed." **Who is King David?**
>
> "I was an uneducated, small business owner who wrote a few letters." **Who is Peter?**
>
> "I was an old, barren women who became the mother of many nations." **Who is Sarah?**
>
> "I was an undermanned, reluctant military leader whom God empowered." **Who is Gideon?**

> "I was a murderer and political refugee whom God sent to confront the king." **Who is Moses?**
>
> "I was a prostitute who risked my life by harboring foreigners." **Who is Rahab?**
>
> "I ran when God called me into service, but he hunted me down and called again." **Who is Jonah?**
>
> "I led reform for God's people even though I began my rule as an eight-year-old." **Who is Josiah?**

Films and literature convey the power of imperfect leaders. In the Harry Potter series, Dumbledore empowers his young and restless protégé Harry when many of the faculty favor smarter, richer, or more popular students. In Tolkien's *The Hobbit*, Gandalf choses Bilbo Baggins to join a band of traveling dwarves as their resident "burglar." Gandalf sees in Bilbo many unseen talents, making much use of the unassuming little Hobbit. Gandalf similarly empowers Bilbo's adopted "nephew" Frodo Baggins, who serves as unlikely ring-bearer in the Lord of the Rings trilogy. The Oscar-nominated film *Darkest Hour* (2017, directed by Joe Wright) beautifully captures how the stubborn, aloof, and contested Prime Minister, Winston Churchill (played by Gary Oldman), powerfully leads England in decisive action against Adolf Hitler. *The King's Speech* (2010, directed by Tom Hooper) takes place within the same time period, showcasing the profound leadership of the stuttering King Albert (played by Colin Firth) during World War II.

Using costumes and props may help the congregation visualize how God can powerfully use imperfect leaders like Joshua and Zerubbabel. Consider preaching a portion of the message in a dirty bath robe, tattered jeans, or stained shirt before exchanging it for a polished graduation gown. To illustrate Zerubbabel's limited skill set, display a simple toolbelt, equipped with a screwdriver, hammer, and small level. Then roll out an industrial toolkit and assortment of power tools. Saying something like, "God can powerfully use leaders who don't look the best or dress the best. God can powerfully use those with limitations."

Whatever creative elements you blend into the sermon, be sure to stress that God's servant leaders should not be discouraged because of difficult circumstances, for God forgives sins and will empower them to do the work God has called them to do. Therefore, God can powerfully use imperfect leaders.

- God can clean a leader with stains (3:1–5).

- Clean leaders should stay clean (3:6–10).

- Weak leaders should seek God's strength (4:1–5; 11–14).

- God can strengthen weak leaders (4:6–10).

DISCUSSION QUESTIONS

1. What was the solution to Joshua's problems in 3:1–8, and did this problem forever eliminate him from serving God? Would the same thing apply for people today?

2. What do we know about the Adversary who spoke against Joshua? How should we understand his role today?

3. What moral failures should discredit spiritual leaders? How should a spiritual leader handle his or her moral failures?

4. How do the three statements to Zerubbabel in 4:6–10 apply to situations today?

5. What does it look like to rely on the power of the Spirit rather than our own power?

Zechariah 5:1–11

EXEGETICAL IDEA
God's curse would fall on all sinners (those who steal and swear falsely), then God would remove the wickedness of idolatry from the land.

THEOLOGICAL FOCUS
Before there can be spiritual restoration with God, all forms of evil must end.

PREACHING IDEA
Evil has a divine expiration date.

PREACHING POINTERS
Zechariah observed God's intention to put an end to evil in two visions. First, the prophet saw a flying scroll whereby God cursed upon the people for theft and misuse of his name, and he called out their transgressions. Next, there appeared a covered basket containing a woman that symbolized idolatry; God would rid the land of her wickedness. For both visions an angel provided the prophet with an interpretation. The original audience would have understood the need for God to stamp evil with its expiration date. In fact, they would have welcomed it, knowing that the blessings of the covenant cannot coexist with human rebellion.

Evil lingers yet today. Endless news cycles harp on the misdeeds of sinful men and women, corrupt nations and institutions: child trafficking and sexual harassment, bullying and mass shootings, insider trading and corporate deceit, racial and sexual inequality. Much of the evil that plagues us today is the product of misguided human efforts. Our attempts to eradicate evil through education, politics, activism, finances, and religion may be well-intentioned but are often as unrealistic as Hollywood's endless line of superhero films. Until God puts an end to evil, we will experience its effects. Fortunately, this passage assures us that evil has a divine expiration date.

RESTORATION REQUIRES
THE REMOVAL OF EVIL (5:1–11)

LITERARY STRUCTURE AND THEMES (5:1–11)

God revealed to the prophet Zechariah two visions, a flying scroll and a woman in a basket, to indicate that the complete restoration of fallen humanity's relationship with God would be possible in the future. To make this possible the first thing that would happen was a curse on sin, which would purge the land of evil (vv. 1–4). The second was the complete removal of the worship of idols (vv. 5–11).

The resounding themes in this unit through these sixth and seventh visions are that all types of sinning would end, and all people who sin would be judged and removed.

- ***God Will Remove Sinful People (5:1–4)***
- ***The Removal of Idolatry (5:5–11)***

EXPOSITION

In the preceding messages, the chief problem was that sin interfered with the establishment of God's kingdom on earth. Zechariah knew that some Jews sinned and needed to repent (1:2–6), some evil nations were at ease even though they oppressed and scattered God's people (1:15, 19), some religious leaders sinned (3:4), and some people stole, swore falsely, and worshipped idols. In order to resolve the problem of sin, God said he would put his curse on "everyone who steals" (5:3a), "everyone who swears falsely in God's name" (5:4), and all idols in order to remove the main causes of sin from the earth. These sins represented all the sins that people commit, and a key part of God's plan for the future was to have a world without sin.

God Will Remove Sinful People (5:1–4)

God's warning was known to all: a curse would fall on all sinners.

5:1–2. The sixth vision started similar to other visions with the familiar phrase "I lifted up my eyes and I looked and behold" (cf. 1:18; 2:1; 6:1). The "angel who was speaking with me" (similar to 1:19; 2:3; 4:4, 11–14) entered this vision in 5:2 to ask Zechariah what he saw in this new vision. Zechariah described a huge flying scroll measuring thirty by fifteen feet (5:2), but it was unclear where it was flying from or where it was going to. Although Merrill (2003, 148) maintains that this enormous scroll was fifteen feet in diameter when the scroll was rolled up, it appears that this scroll as described in the vision was unrolled. This size of a scroll was very unusual because most scrolls (including the largest Dead Sea scroll, 1QIsaᵃ) were made of animal skins and were only about one foot wide, though some could be almost thirty feet long (when skins were sown together). The second unusual factor was that this scroll was flying up in the air, though there was no record of any angelic beings unfurling it or pulling it through the sky. Two questions immediately arise: why was the scroll flying, and what was the significance of the large size of this scroll? As in other visions, strange and unusual things happen in this vision, so the exaggerated size of the scroll was not that bizarre. One answer to these questions about the scroll is simply, we do not know. Another commonsense approach might explain the large size by pointing to the practical need for a large number of people to see the scroll, and for these people to be able to read the message required large letters written on a large scroll. Thus, in this approach there was no spiritual meaning to the large size. Meyers and Meyers (1987, 280–81) and Boda (2004, 292) have suggested a connection between the size of this scroll and the portico of Solomon's temple (1 Kings 6:3), the two cherubim in the holy place (1 Kings 6:23–26), the holy place in the tabernacle (Exod. 26:15–28), and the bronze altar at the temple (2 Chron. 4:2), but none of these suggestions are convincing because this vision makes no connection between the scroll and any part of the tabernacle/temple (Wolters, 2014, 158). The size of the scroll had a utilitarian purpose of making it possible for everyone to see what was written on the scroll. This made everyone accountable for responding appropriately to the message on the scroll.

5:3–4. The voice questioning Zechariah about what he saw was probably the interpreting angel (Tiemeyer, 2015, 186), for he asked similar questions in 4:2, 14. The importance of the scroll was based on the "oath" or "curse" (אָלָה) written on it (5:3). Although the term used throughout the covenant in Deuteronomy 27:15–26 and 28:16–19 was often "curse" (אָרַר) the word used here (אָלָה) can appears in the positive sense of a covenant "oath" (אָלָה) people took when entering into their covenant relationship with God (Deut. 29:12, 14]; cf. 1Q28 6:14–21) and in the negative sense of the fulfillment of a self-condemning "oath, curse" that would fall on anyone who broke their covenant commitment (Deut. 29:19–2). Thus when the children of Israel entered into their covenant relationship with God, they agreed to the blessings God would give to them for loving, fearing, serving, and worshipping God, as well as the self-condemning curses that

would fall on them if they did not keep their covenant obligations (Deut. 27–28). In this vision two specific curses were mentioned, one on each side of the large scroll. Contrary to Meyers and Meyers (1987, 284), who relate swearing falsely to perjury or lying under oath (i.e., the ninth commandment in Exod. 20:16), the sin of "the one who steals" (הַגֹּנֵב, Zech. 5:3b; cf. the eighth commandment in Exod. 20:15) probably represented all the commandments related to improper action toward one's neighbor. The offense of "the one who swears falsely" (הַנִּשְׁבָּע, Zech. 5:3c) in the name of God (cf. the third commandment in Exod. 20:7) represented all the commandments that govern a person's relationship to God.

The interpretation of the last part of Zechariah 5:3 is particularly difficult because two quite different approaches seem almost equally possible. Some have translated the final verb as a prophetic perfect describing what would happen in the future (see translation analysis) when the curse would fall on the land, while others (Baldwin, 1972, 127; Merrill, 2003, 150) argue that 5:3–4 should refer to what "will" happen to the guilty people, while still others prefer a past tense "have remained up till now unpunished" (Petersen, 1984, 245) or "has been cleared" (Boda, 2004, 294) or "has gone unpunished" (Wolters, 2014, 158). Since the curse of the scroll had already gone out in 5:3a, it seems best to conclude that the future effects of this curse would cause those sinful people "to be purged, cut off." This curse would also have an impact on the homes of the sinners, for this curse would "remain, lodge" (לוּן) in their houses until these homes ended up being destroyed (5:4). This indicated that God's plan for the nation involved both the restoration of people who confessed their sins (Zech. 1:1–6) as well as the destruction or removal of those who refused to repent (5:3–4). This theme is explained more in the next vision.

NASB[95] "everyone who steals will be purged away"
NIV[84] "every thief will be banished"
HCSB "every thief will be removed"
NRSV "everyone who steals shall be cut off"
The interpretation of this verse is complicated because the translation of the verb (נָקָה) could be "to acquit, leave unpunished" or "to purge, to cut off." It is possible to argue that נִקָּה is a *niphal* perfect or a *piel* perfect.

The Removal of Idolatry (5:5–11)
God would remove the evil of idolatry from his land.

5:5–6. Almost as a continuation of the sixth vision, the angel speaking to Zechariah appeared in the seventh vision and asked the prophet what he saw. The interpreting angel identified a moving object either "going out" or "coming forth, approaching, coming into view" in the vision (Petersen, 1984, 254). This ephah basket, which was probably made of palm branches, reeds, or cane, may refer to a certain type of container or specifically to the size of a container that would hold an ephah of grain. The amount of grain that would fill an ephah basket would be a little less than a bushel of grain, but in the imaginative world of a vision it may have been an oversized ephah basket (like the oversized scroll). The ephah container was commonly used to carry or store grain or flour (Ruth 2:17; Lev. 5:11). Zechariah asked what this meant, and the angel explained that this basket was "their eye" (עֵינָם) throughout the land. Some translations rendered this idea as "their appearance, resemblance," while others followed the Old Greek reading and emended the Hebrew text from "their eye" to "their iniquity" (עֲוֹנָם) based on the common confusion between the letters *vav* (ו) and *yod* (י). This slight change to "their iniquity" would agree with the designation of the woman in the basket as "wickedness" (הָרִשְׁעָה) in 5:8.

NASB[95] "This is their appearance in all the land."
HCSB "This is their iniquity in all the land."
NIV[84] "This is the iniquity of the people throughout the land."
NKJV "This is their resemblance throughout the earth."
NRSV "This is their iniquity in all the land."
"Their iniquity" seems to be a minor emendation that fits the context.

In Zechariah 1:4, God issued a call for people to turn from evil, which was similar to the call for the removal of the dirty clothes (the sins) of the high priest in 3:4, so the issue of the removal of iniquity was a common theme in several of Zechariah's messages. The word "wickedness" could refer generally to any kind of evil, so it could be used to describe serious moral or social sins, ritual impurities, pagan worship, or injustice in the legal system (cf. 5:3–4).

5:7–8. Some question if there was a real woman in this basket because its size was too small, so an interesting alternative is to conclude that this was a figurine or statue of a woman. If so, this woman would likely be a pagan statue of a goddess—maybe Ishtar or Asherah (Boda, 2004, 306; Redditt, 1995, 75; Smith, 1984, 210). In order to reveal what was in the ephah container, someone (possibly the angel) lifted up a heavy lead lid that was on top of this basket in order to look inside. This revealed "wickedness" (הָרִשְׁעָה) that was personified as a woman sitting inside this container. Possibly wickedness was represented by a woman simply because the word "wickedness" is a feminine word (Baldwin, 1972, 129), but she may represent a female goddess. It seems at this point that there was a danger that the woman might leave the confinement of the basket because someone threw her back down inside the container and slammed the heavy lead lid (lit., "stone") back on top of the basket to prevent her escape (5:8). This action represented

God's power over evil and his control over it. Although people may try to resist sin and ask God to forgive them, only God was able to remove the curse of idolatry from the land.

5:9. A second aspect of the vision involved two flying women (their nature and identity is not explained) approaching the basket. These women had powerful wings that looked something like the large wings of a stork. These large wings enabled them to lift up the heavy ephah container and carry it away (5:9), giving the impression that the land of Israel would be free from this wickedness in the future. This removal of evil idols was parallel to the theme of the removal of evil people in the preceding vision (5:1–4).

5:10–11. The angel then told Zechariah that the container was taken to Shinar, a term for the territory of Babylon, the land where the Tower of Babel was built (Gen. 11:1–9). Once out of Israel and resting in Babylon, someone would build a "house, temple" (בַּיִת) for it. Once this temple was completed, the woman idol of "wickedness" would be set on a pedestal base like any other idol (cf. Jer. 27:17), suggesting that it would be confined to this place and would not migrate to or exist in the land of Israel ever again. This implies that the evil that would be removed from the land was the sin of idolatry (Hill, 2008b, 553).

THEOLOGICAL FOCUS

The exegetical idea (God's curse would fall on all sinners [those who steal and swear falsely], then God would remove the wickedness of idolatry from the land) leads to this theological focus: Before there can be spiritual restoration with God, all forms of evil must end.

The two visions in Zechariah 5 addressed the problem of sin in the nation and how God would resolve this problem so that complete restoration might be possible. The first theological theme was that as long as sins against others (stealing, slander) and against God

(idolatry) continued to flourish, it was hard for God to bless his people and establish his rule on earth. The resolution proposed in these two visions raises the second theological principle. That is, God would cut off and purge the land of evil people by causing his covenant curses to fulfill their intended purpose on those who continued to break his covenant stipulation. Third, this vision assured the audience that God would root out the source of sinful disloyalty to God by removing the pagan female deities that plagued the land of Israel for so many years. The spiritual restoration of any people and the renewal of their covenant relationship to God is dependent on the removal of sin, which separates people from God (cf. Isa. 59:1–2).

PREACHING AND TEACHING STRATEGIES

Exegetical and Theological Synthesis
Zechariah 5:1–11 exposes the problem of evil. Wickedness, embodied in the form of small female statue (likely feminine due to the idolatry problem in Jerusalem or the etymology of the Hebrew word for wickedness), makes a memorable appearance in an airborne basket. But she is quickly whisked away by two winged women. In the prior vision, wickedness is spelled out in detail on a flying scroll. Theft and swearing falsely represent sins against God and neighbor. Together the two visions suggest God is neither stranger to nor paralyzed by evil. Rather, he is sovereign over it.

Sin and evil have a long history in the biblical narrative. The first reference to evil appears in the garden of Eden. God prohibited eating from the tree of the knowledge of good and evil (Gen. 2:17; cf. 3:22). The first reference to sin follows in the story of Cain and Abel (4:7). By Noah's day, the wickedness of man was so great, God had no choice but to destroy the earth and start fresh (6:5–8). Sin taints every successive story. The pride of Babel (11:1–9), perversion of Sodom and Gomorrah (13:13; 18:20), jealousy of Joseph's brothers (37:4), ingratitude of the wilderness generation (Num. 11), idolatry of the Israelites (Isa. 42:17; 44:9–20), greed of the wealthy (Amos 4), and hypocrisy of spiritual leaders (Mic. 3) embody various expressions of sin and evil.

More remarkable than the reality of evil is God's restraint in addressing it immediately. His long fuse and profound patience demonstrated his desire for repentance (Exod. 34:6; Num. 14:18; cf. 2 Peter 3:9). Furthermore, he often has turned human evil on its head, bringing some good from bad circumstances (Gen. 50:20; Ps. 23:4–5). In fact, he occasionally used wicked men as one of the weapons in his sovereign arsenal (Jer. 27:6; Hab. 1:6–11). Most notably, the fate of the suffering Servant showed God's ability to reap healing and secure forgiveness from crushing pain (Isa. 53). God, not evil, will have the final word.

Preaching Idea

Evil has a divine expiration date.

Contemporary Connections

What does it mean?

What does it mean that evil has a divine expiration date? Simply put, God will put an end to evil. It has a limited shelf life. God is not the author of evil, but he will be its executor as he brings history to a close (Isa. 65–66). In the meantime, God has intervened in history to condemn sin and exact punishment for human wickedness. Examples abound: God expelled Adam and Eve from Eden for their sin (Gen. 3:22), marked Cain for murder (4:9–16), and flooded the world for its wickedness (Gen. 6–9). He stopped the construction project in Babel (11:1–9), announced the punishment for the Amorites (Gen. 15:16), and drowned Pharaoh's army in the Red Sea (Exod. 14–15). God stalled various rebellions in the wilderness (Exod. 32; Num. 21), had Achan stoned for deception (Josh. 7:22–26), and used judges to put down evil opponents (Judg.

1:11–19). For the evil that persists in the present, God will someday put an end to it.

What kinds of evil have a divine expiration date? These are the same forms of evil experienced in Zechariah's day: personal, institutional, and natural. Hurricanes and floods, corporate greed and national apartheid, sexual perversion and self-harm, discrimination and senseless murder will end. God alone knows the expiration date of the various forms of evil, but we can be certain they will not endure after history's climax (Joel 2:11; 3:18; Zech. 13:2).

That God alone knows the expiration date, however, should not discourage us from purging as much evil as we can from our immediate surroundings. The Mosaic Law demanded the elimination of idolatry and injustice (Exod. 20:1–17; Lev. 19). Prophets echoed the call to eliminate these evils (Isa. 1:17; 58; Amos 5:24; Mic. 6:18; Hab. 2:15–20). Our fight against evil will not ultimately rid the world of its presence; that is God's prerogative, but we should not grow weary working to make the world right.

Is it true?

Is it true that evil has a divine expiration date? Indeed, but God does not always intervene to stop evil in its tracks. Bullies still get away with abuse. Corporations continue to mistreat their employees. Politicians still retain power through deceit. The prosperity of the wicked, as frustrating as it may be, is temporal.

Nor does God broadcast his expiration date for evil. OT prophets spoke of the day of the Lord when God would execute justice (e.g., Joel 1:15; 2:2, 11; Zeph. 1:9, 15–16; Zech. 14:1–8). This day spoke of the climax of history, when God would put an end to evil, fulfill his promises for shalom (i.e., peace), and establish his Messiah's reign (2 Sam. 7:8–16; Pss. 2:7; 110:1, 4; Dan. 7:13–14). Zechariah, like many figures in the OT, did not experience the fulfillment of God's promise in his day. An incomplete temple, absent king, Persian rule, and unjust society made it obvious the end had not yet come.

While the end date remains obscure, several notable passages provide a foretaste of a world without evil (Isa. 11:6–9; 65:17–25; Mal. 4:1–7; Zeph. 3:6–21; cf. Rev. 21:1–8; 22:1–5). Lions and lambs lie down together. Infant death no longer plagues families. The produce from our labor comes freely without the threat of thieves or locusts. Neighbors (both local and international) know one another as allies not enemies. The struggle and stigma of disability are gone. Righteousness and joy reign. And God dwells among his people.

Now what?

How should we respond to the divine expiration of evil? Simply put, we should remain realistic about our ability to end it on our own. Our best intentions to eradicate evil through criminal justice, nutrition, environmental improvements, politics, religion, education, or economics will inevitably lead to unintended harm. Energy-efficient vehicles may produce new forms of waste. Policies for workplace equality may shift injustice to others. Campaigns for tolerance may lead to deviant sexual practices. Innovative technologies to learn and connect with others may hijack brain chemistry and feed depression. Humans excel at accidentally advancing evil: personal, institutional, and natural.

Does this mean we abandon our efforts to reduce evil? Absolutely not! We must simply recognize setting expiration dates on evil is God's prerogative. In fact, our first response to the problem of evil is to acknowledge it within ourselves. According to Russian novelist Aleksandr Solzhenitsyn ([1974] 2007, 1:75) in *The Gulag Archipelago, 1918–1956*, this is "easier said than done" since "the line dividing good and evil cuts through the heart of every human being." Thus, addressing the wickedness in our own hearts should be the first response to evil. How do we add to greed, prejudice, violence, bitterness, idolatry, addiction, pride, selfishness, and other evils in the world?

Once we expose our evil hearts to God, then we begin to bring reform to our immediate surroundings. Justice and good news work in partnership (Isa. 40:8–10; 52:7; 63:1–3). As we tell the good news of God conquering evil, we live as good neighbors: finding ways to reduce bullying in our schools, poverty in our neighborhoods, idolatry of personal comfort, pollution in our cities, consumerism among our youth, corruption in our institutions, and suffering on our planet. Realistically, we cannot tackle all evils without doing some evil to ourselves (e.g., burnout, Messiah complex). Wisdom, then, prompts us to find one or two areas where our passions intersect with local evils.

Finally, we remain patient. Evil will persist today as it did in Zechariah's day. Our energy will vacillate. Others will not share our passion for social justice. Positive outcomes will surface slowly. The Psalms teach us to lament the prosperity of evil as an act of entrusting its expiration to God. The prophets teach us to live justly. In either case, we remain steadfast and immovable since our work in the Lord is not done in vain (1 Cor. 15:58). And some day God will execute evil for good.

Creativity in Presentation

People will relate to the expiration idea by showing several common items. Magazine subscriptions expire. Licenses expire. Leases expire. And milk expires. In each case, some authority figure holds the keys to deciding an expiration date. (Comedian Jerry Seinfeld quips that dairy cows determine the expiration date of their milk; they whisper the date to the farmer milking them.) While we can renew expired contracts, we cannot renew expired consumables. They go into the waste basket. Likewise, God will renew the world, but he will dump evil in the trash. To punctuate the imagery, consider collecting expired food from your refrigerator, pantry, or basement storage. Now and then my (Tim's) church's deacon pantry becomes a treasure trove of expired goods! Display the food on the stage and invite people to eat if they dare. For dramatic effect, pour chunky milk into a drinking glass and offer it to a congregation member.

When we face evil in the form of personal suffering or natural disasters, we often soothe ourselves with the line: "This too shall pass." I've heard people mutter this while caregiving for a spouse with dementia, slogging through an intense semester of college, paying off credit card bills, or wrestling with anxiety over a broken relationship. "This too shall pass" recognizes the evils that we experience have an expiration date, but we must amend the phrase to communicate God, not time, puts an end to evil. Consider describing various evils and asking the congregation to respond to each one by repeating, "God will end it."

Assure them that someone in authority probably knows the expiration date, but the rest of us watch and wait until we find it knocked to the ground. Assure the congregation God has stamped evil with a "Condemned" notice, but its destruction date remains in the future.

Be sure the creative elements reinforce the key idea: Before there can be spiritual restoration with God, all forms of evil must end. Evil has a divine expiration date.

- God won't let injustice last forever (5:1–4).

- God will send our idols packing for good (5:5–11).

> **Excursus: "God will end it."**
> PASTOR: "My arthritic fingers."
> CONGREGATION: "God will end it.'"
> PASTOR: "COVID-19."
> CONGREGATION: "God will end it."
> PASTOR: "My addiction to food."
> CONGREGATION: "God will end it."
> PASTOR: "My being underappreciated at work."
> CONGREGATION: "God will end it."
> PASTOR: "My battle with cancer."
> CONGREGATION: "God will end it."
> PASTOR: "Child slavery."
> CONGREGATION: "God will end it."
> PASTOR: "Spousal abuse."
> CONGREGATION: "God will end it."
> PASTOR: "Idolatry of personal security."
> CONGREGATION, "God will end it."

Condemned buildings can illustrate the uncertain timeline of God's judgement. Whether a residential home or commercial property, condemned structures often remain in their derelict condition for prolonged spans before any leveling takes place. Consider taking images of familiar properties that are condemned but not yet destroyed. Or find a YouTube video of an old sports stadium or skyscraper being imploded.

DISCUSSION QUESTIONS

1. What were the dominant forms of evil Zechariah addressed in 5:1–11?

2. What warning did God give his people about the effects of idolatry and injustice?

3. What would have compelled someone in Zechariah's day toward idol worship? What forms of idolatry are common today?

4. How does God expect his people to deal with evil today? How do our efforts to eradicate evil often end in futility?

5. What are some biblical examples where God has brought good ends from human evil? How have you seen this principle in your life?

Zechariah 6:1–8

EXEGETICAL IDEA
God's angelic forces were everywhere, doing his will and appeasing his wrath.

THEOLOGICAL FOCUS
God's sovereign presence everywhere enables him to carry out his desires everywhere.

PREACHING IDEA
God has every square inch of the earth under his watch.

PREACHING POINTERS
Despite the ever-expanding borders of the Persian Empire, secured by the efforts of King Darius, God's rule remained a reality. This is the meaning of Zechariah's eighth and final vision: horses marching in every direction, sent by God on patrol. Although the original audience lived under the umbrella of Persian rule, marked by instability and uncertainty, Zechariah assured them that they lived under God's watch. He was in control. He would prevail over the nations. The picture of patrolling chariots and horses assured them that the divine reign has no borders.

Today God's people doubt his control of local and global events. We doubt his power when our prayers remain answered. We doubt his sovereignty when tragedy strikes or suffering persists. The complex of global problems proves especially troublesome to our faith: the advance of Islam and secular humanism; widespread malnutrition and inequality for females; terrorism and mass shootings; drug abuse and overdose fatalities; kidnappings and human trafficking. People can cherry-pick evidence from across the planet that God is capricious or impotent. This passage curbs such fallacious thinking, affirming that God has every square inch of the earth under his watch.

RESTORATION OF GOD'S SOVEREIGN RULE OF THE EARTH (6:1–8)

LITERARY STRUCTURE AND THEMES (6:1–8)

This eighth vision opened with four patrolling chariots and horses coming from God (vv. 1–3). The four chariots were sent out to patrol to the north and south (vv. 4–6). The vision closed with chariots going to the north to appease God's wrath against the nations in that area (vv. 7–8).

The overwhelming theme of this unit with this eighth vision is that through God's universal presence and power, he has established universal control over all world powers.

- *God's Patrolling Presence (6:1–3)*
- *God's Patrol Appeases His Wrath (6:4–8)*

EXPOSITION

Records of the military conflicts in this period of Persian history describe enormous political changes with the Persians taking control of most of the surrounding countries. This included the defeat of Media (550 B.C.), Lydia (546 B.C.), Babylon (539 B.C.), Cyrus, Phoenicia, and Egypt (525 B.C.), Macedonia (512 B.C.), plus Anatolia, Armenia, Azerbaijan, Tajikistan, Bulgaria, and Pakistan. So it appeared that the Persian kings were sovereign over the whole world and that they determined the future for every people group. However, God revealed to Zechariah that he knew about and controlled all these past events, and through his Spirit he would carry out his will throughout all these nations to appease his wrath.

God's Patrolling Presence (6:1–3)

God sent his ministering spirits to various parts of the world to carry out his will.

6:1–3. The eighth vision started like several other visions (1:18; 2:1; 5:1, 9) with Zechariah lifting up his eyes and looking at what was before him. The prophet saw four chariots with different colored horses (6:2–3) similar to the four different colored horses in the first vision (1:8). The difference is that the horses in Zechariah 1 were coming back from a long patrolling mission to report their findings, but the chariots and horses in this vision seem to be leaving a meeting and going out from between two bronze mountains (6:1–3) to dispense God's wrath on the earth. These connections make vision one and eight something like bookends around the other visions (Merrill, 2003, 161). Like the horsemen, these chariots and horsemen expressed the idea that God knew everything that was happening throughout the whole globe and that he was able to exert military control (symbolized by the chariots) over all nations in all directions. Later in 6:5, the four chariots were identified with the four winds of heaven, implying they were going out to the four points of the compass. No interpretation of the colors of the horses was given in 1:7–17 or here in 6:1–8, so speculation on this point should be avoided. Although this vision was limited to only a few chariots, Psalm 68:17 indicates that "the chariots of God are ten thousand." Their movement of "going out" (יָצָא, used seven times in this vision) from between the two mountains would suggest that they were on a mission to carry out God's will from heaven. The two bronze mountains are somewhat mysterious, though the place where God dwelt was sometimes connected to Mount Sinai (Exod. 19–20), Mount Zion (Ps. 48:1–3), or Mount Zaphon in the north (Ps. 48:2). Some ancient Near Eastern texts picture gods living on a mountain, and some (Barker, 1983, 636) identify this as God's abode between Mount Zion and the Mount of Olives in Jerusalem. Nevertheless, these mountains were never identified in this vision. If the chariots were going out throughout the earth, patrolling and carrying out God's will, then it seems logical that God was located in this vision somewhere on the other side of the two mountains (Smith, 1984, 213). The reference to bronze may refer to the color of the mountain at dawn when the sun was first rising (Boda, 2004, 319) or the ore within the mountain (Wolters, 2014, 173).

God's Patrol Appeases His Wrath (6:4–8)

God's chariots would carry out God's punishment of nations.

6:4–5. The visionary explanation initially appeared to have the four chariots going out in four different directions (the "four spirits" in 6:5), but the later, more detailed explanation in 6:6 did not indicate that each chariot would patrol in a different area. Zechariah 6:6 begins in an unusual fashion (starting with "which") and only refers to chariots going to the north and south. These difficulties have caused some to add a clause at the beginning of 6:6 about the horses and chariots going to the east (Petersen, 1984, 263–64; Meyer and Meyer, 1987, 326), but there is no evidence in the Hebrew to support this reading.

6:6. A second problem was raised when the text has the white horses in 6:6 going "after them" (אַחֲרֵיהֶם), meaning they would follow the black horses going north. But why were two chariots going in the same direction? Since there was no reference to any horses going west, a solution to this problem would be to argue that "after

them" (אַחֲרֵיהֶם) was "after the sea" (אַחֲרֵי־הַיָּם), meaning the white horses were going west toward the Mediterranean Sea (Petersen, 1984, 263–64; Barker, 1983, 638). Nevertheless, it is possible that only the north and south were mentioned because Israel's main enemies lived to the north and south.

6:7–8. Up to this point there was no reference to the ones driving these chariots. It is possible that the strong ones, powerful ones" (הָאֲמֻצִּים) in 6:7a could refer to angelic beings that drove these chariots. Arguing against this conclusion would be the use of this same term to describe the horses in 6:3. The horses and chariots role was to patrol the earth and accomplish God's sovereign will in the lands where they patrolled (6:7b). Although no specific divine command was recorded up to this point about destroying God's enemies, it is evident in 6:8 that God instructed these horses and chariots going to the north land to not only patrol, but also execute God's plan against some nation. The concept that "they have given my spirit rest" could have a positive meaning of having God's Spirit resting on someone for their good (Kline, 2001, 214–15), but in this context it appears to refer to the resting of God's Spirit after some punishment satisfied God's just anger against some nation. Thus, one might hypothesize that the passage referred to God's past judgment on Babylon in 539 B.C. through the Persian king Cyrus (Merrill, 2003, 168). Since this happened eighteen years earlier than Zechariah's prophecy, it would be more likely that this prophecy may refer to the judgment against Babylonian when it revolted against the Persian king Darius (Wolters, 2014, 179) at the beginning of his reign (522–520 B.C.).[1] The fulfillment of this action would indicate that the judgment of the nations in Zechariah's

---

1   For an article by an interpreter holding this view, see Mark J. Boda, "Terrifying the Horns: Persia and Babylon in Zechariah 1:7–6:15," *Catholic Biblical Quarterly* 67, no. 1 (2005): 22–41.

first and second visions had already happened. It is unlikely that 6:8 refers to action against the Persians, for the Persians graciously let the Jews return to their land (Ezra 1:1–5) and financed the rebuilding of the temple (Ezra 6:8).

TRANSLATION ANALYSIS: 6:8b, הֵנִיחוּ אֶת־רוּחִי
NASB[95] "have appeased My wrath"
HCSB "have pacified My Spirit"
NIV[84] "have given my Spirit rest'
NKJV "have given rest to My Spirit"
NRSV "have set my spirit at rest"
The idea of giving rest to my Spirit means that God would no longer be angry, since the evil people in the north would soon be punished.

THEOLOGICAL FOCUS

The exegetical idea (God's angelic forces were everywhere, doing his will and appeasing his wrath) leads to this theological focus: God's sovereign presence everywhere enables him to carry out his desires everywhere.

The theological message is twofold. First, God is omnipresent; that is, he is present everywhere; and second, God is omnipotent and has the power to accomplish his will at any time or place he desires. This message of hope communicated through this vision was that God was, is, and would be sovereignly in control of everything that would happen throughout the world. He knew what was happening though his patrolling spirits, and he would be able to accomplish his will against anyone who might oppose his plans. No nation in the past or in the future would be able to resist the fulfillment of God's prophetic predictions or his judgment.

PREACHING AND TEACHING STRATEGIES

Exegetical and Theological Synthesis

Zechariah 6:1–8 notes the continuity between the first and final visions, namely, God's control. Both scenes require angelic interpretation

and include horses of four different colors. In either visionary instance, the horses appeared on mission, as described in their "going out" at God's request. Finally, in each case, God sent the horses on a global patrol. Yet, the final vision provided more directional clarity, listing north, south, and eastbound travel routes.

What the eighth vision adds to the discussion is the depiction of God as divine warrior (Zeph. 3:17). The theme reaches back to the exodus, when God led his people out of Egypt and through the Red Sea to conqueror Pharaoh's army. Moses inscribed divine-warrior language in his victory song (Exod. 15). Throughout their wilderness wanderings and conquest of the land, God won battle after battle for his people (Deut. 1:21; 2:21, 33; 3:3; 7:17–24). He empowered Joshua, Gideon, David, Elijah, Jeremiah, and Daniel. He was their dread champion (Jer. 20:11).

Not only do numerous psalms underscore God's might (Pss. 2, 68, 94, 105, 110), but they also describe him as refuge and defender (Pss. 18, 63, 121), sometimes in the stark language of imprecatory prayers (Pss. 58, 59, 137). While battle imagery may appeal to our baser impulses for revenge and bloodshed, the image of an avenging God builds our confidence in his power and justice. All territory lies under his jurisdiction; enemies beware.

Preaching Idea

God has every square inch of the earth under his watch.

Contemporary Connections

What does it mean?
What does it mean that God has every square inch of the earth under his watch? In theological terms, God is all-knowing and always present. But according to Psalm 139, God's constant watch is personal and a cause for praise. God predicts words before they proceed from our lips (vv. 1–2). His presence shadows our

every move (vv. 7–8). His intimate knowledge of us even predates our birth (vv. 15–16). This constant watch over human life should not only produce wonder (Ps. 8), but also trust in God's ability to provide help in distress (Pss. 33; 139:19–22).

God's expansive watch extends beyond individuals; he oversees the activities of all nations. OT prophets often predict ruin or reward for Israel's neighbors (Isa. 14–23; 60–66; Jer. 46–51; Ezek. 25–32; 38–39; Amos 1:1–2:3; Jonah 3:1–4; Obad. 1–14; Nah. 1:12–14; 3:1–19; Zeph. 3:20; Zech. 14:16–19). God controls the hearts of kings (Prov. 21:1), including foreign kings, who rule under his sovereign watch (Ps. 2; Isa. 40:23; 45:1; Dan. 2:41). Even creation benefits from God's watch: he names every star, sees every flower, and keeps chaotic weather under control (Pss. 104:5–9; 147:4; Prov. 8:29; Isa. 40:7–8, 26).

How God's all-seeing eye translates into action is a different question. No sin escapes his notice. And the heavenly Father rewards secret acts of obedience (Matt. 6:1, 4, 6, 18). However, punishment and reward are not always immediate. God's constant attention to human affairs does not equate to quick intervention in our activities. Final judgment may be the moment when his watch translates into our reward or ruin (Zech. 1:18–2:13; cf. 1 Cor. 3:14–15; 2 Cor. 5:10; Rev. 20:11–15). So, his people must patiently, sometimes painfully, await his ultimate justice with great resolve.

Is it true?
Is it true that God has every square inch of the earth under his watch? Yes! God sees everything. His knowledge has no boundaries. He discerns our secret thoughts (Ps. 44:21). He knows the beginning from the end in all human affairs (Isa. 46:8–11). He never rests his eyes but keeps constant watch over his people (Ps. 121:4).

Ironically, God's ever-watchful eye may cause equal measures of horror and hope for individuals. Horrified, Adam and Eve tried to hide from God after taking from the Tree of Knowledge of Good and Evil (Gen. 3:8). Terrified, Jonah sought to escape God's presence on a westbound boat for Tarshish (Jonah 1:3). Those who realize they have rejected God's command often become painfully aware of his watchful eye. For some, like David, it sparks confession (Ps. 32); and for others like Manasseh (2 Chron. 33:10–13; cf. Prayer of Manasseh), God's watchful eye leads to anger, denial, guilt, and shame.

On the other hand, those experiencing suffering often experience the warmth of his watchful eye. Hagar learned that God saw her pain of rejection (Gen. 16). Hannah knew God saw her pain of barrenness (1 Sam. 1). Likewise, Zechariah's vision instills hope in God's oversight of international affairs. A healthy awareness of God's watch is critical for his people when they read negative headlines about persecution of Christians, global slavery, and the rise of atheism. Those who trust God amid suffering are more likely to turn despair into action: fighting social injustice, sharing good news, overcoming addictions, or restoring broken relationships.

Now what?
How should we respond to the notion that God has every square inch of the earth under his watch? God's perfect knowledge and enduring presence should provoke three responses. First, awe appropriately describes the way we should feel about God's nearness and knowing. After encountering God's breathtaking oversight of the cosmos, Job modeled the proper response: humble awe (Job 40:3–5; 42:1–6). We might echo the sentiment.

Second, when David reflected on God's watch over the intimate details of his life, he invited God to inspect him. "Search . . . know . . . test . . . see me," David prayed (Ps. 139:23–24). He laid bare his anxieties and offenses before God. God knows our struggles and weaknesses without our requesting a spiritual audit, but the act of seeking his feedback opens us to change.

Finally, God's ubiquitous eye can ease our anxieties. Our daily tasks alone can drain us. When we add to our own problems the ills of the world, we can feel perpetually weighed down. The weight increases when we consider, for better or worse, global suffering. Watching the news or engaging with social media tends to feed our worries. Entertaining ourselves only provides temporary relief. But when we remember God is watching every news cycle, live broadcast, and square inch of the earth, we can trust him to supervise the planet.

Creativity in Presentation

The idea of a watchful eye plays a part in several films. Consider playing a clip or trailer from one of them. *The Eye in the Sky* (2015, directed by Gavin Hood) plots a likely future where government surveillance sees all. A similar future is created in *The Circle* (2017, directed by James Ponsoldt), where tech giant Eamon Baily (played by Tom Hanks) encourages complete transparency by placing micro-cameras on every square inch of the earth, including our bodies. Finally, in the theatrical version of Tolkien's Lord of the Rings trilogy (directed by Peter Jackson), the menacing Eye of Sauron keeps a constant watch over all Middle Earth. When first introduced in *The Fellowship of the Ring* (2001), Saruman (played by Christopher Lee), a good wizard turned bad, describes the Eye of Sauron to Gandalf (played by Ian McKellan): "His gaze pierces cloud, shadow, earth, and flesh. You know of what I speak, Gandalf . . . a great Eye, lidless, wreathed in flame." Images of the darting, burning, amber eye dance across the screen as Saruman talks. Note that these movies portray watchfulness negatively (as do most films dealing with surveillance), as something to escape. God's watch is inescapable but need not be scary for those who know him.

Another way to illustrate the watchful eye of God, if you have the technical capacity, is to set up cameras around the sanctuary during the sermon. Recruit extra camera workers and video technicians to manage the equipment. At a certain point (or points) in the sermon, cue the video crew to project images of people sitting in different areas. Use cross-fades and varied angles to cover the whole seating area. Consider flying a drone around the parking lot, or using prerecorded images from the hallways, offices, nursery, and attic to stress that God's eye covers every inch. Perhaps a camera shot of the bathroom door might provide comic relief.

The United States Navy uses the term "watch" to capture the duty of its officer on deck to keep others safe. The solider holds a post on the bridge of the ship for several hours, keeping an eye out for threats. During the change of the guard, the serving officer announces his relief, and the incoming officer claims his role as watchman. Seventeen primary duties of the "watch" are spelled in detail on the "Officer of the deck" Wikipedia article. Furthermore, "Fair winds and following seas. Sir, we have the watch," is a popular slogan recited at naval funerals (e.g., U.S. Senator John McCain in 2018).

The Earth as seen from Apollo 17. Courtesy of NASA/JPL-Caltech (public domain).

Finally, if you can locate a few different sized globes or maps, you might be able to visualize the way the world looks from God's perspective. Starting with our limited perception, you can describe how we can see only the four walls around us. Or, if outside, we cannot see beyond the horizon. But when we unfold a map, use Google Earth, or look at a globe, a bigger picture comes into view. While holding up a map or globe, make the comment: "Because our presence is limited, so it our perception. Because God's presence is unlimited, so is his perception. To him, all of life is like an unfolded map or globe. Every inch is under his watch." (You might even comment how God's unlimited intelligence means he could figure out how to fold up the map in a single attempt!)

Whatever creative approach you develop, be sure to punctuate the key truth: God's sovereign presence everywhere enables him to carry out his desires everywhere. Or, simply, God has every square inch of the earth under his watch.

- God shows up even if we don't know it (6:1–3).

- God goes to places we cannot even see (6:4–6).

- God makes right what we cannot remedy ourselves (6:7–8).

DISCUSSION QUESTIONS

1. How would Zechariah's audience have understood God's sovereignty in light of the expanding Persian Empire?

2. What was the importance of the directional details of the four patrolling chariots and horses?

3. What recent historical situations make God's people question his sovereignty?

4. What are the different responses people have to the idea of God's ever-watchful eye? What provokes the different responses?

5. How does Psalm 139 model a healthy, personal response to God's sovereignty?

Zechariah 6:9–15

EXEGETICAL IDEA

The placing of a crown on the head of Joshua the high priest elevated his status, encouraged people to return to Jerusalem, and was a sign that in the future God would raise up a messianic Branch/Sprout who would serve as both priest and king.

THEOLOGICAL FOCUS

God's promise of a future Davidic King reinforces and underscores God's plans for his people now and in the future.

PREACHING IDEA

Only God can give an absolute guarantee.

PREACHING POINTERS

God returned his focus to the restoration of the temple and role of the high priest. In a previous vision, Joshua received God's vote of confidence; now Joshua received an ornate crown. Fashioned from the offerings of three men returning from exile, the decorative headpiece signaled God's favor. More importantly, God bestowed on Joshua a symbolic name: Branch. The crown and title assured the original audience of God's current support of the temple restoration and his future installment of a royal-priestly leader. Such assurance intended to inspire their faithful work.

In an age of uncertainty, people crave guarantees. We look for guarantees as we face a major surgery, purchase a new car, or invest for retirement. We want guarantees that our marriage will last, ministry programs will impact lives, and medication will relieve chronic pain. Sadly, many guarantees cannot hold weight, leading us to disappointment, doubt, and cynicism. We can project this on God. It is not enough that he has promised to remain present in our lives; we want constant reassurance that his word proves true. We want writing on the wall, lucid dreams, prophetic words, or symbols in our soup to reaffirm his promises. This passage reminds us that only God can give an absolute guarantee.

GOD'S RESTORATION OF THE BRANCH/SPROUT AND THE TEMPLE (6:9–15)

LITERARY STRUCTURE AND THEMES (6:9–15)

Zechariah 1:1–6:15 begins in 1:1–6 with a narrative exhortation to repent, and now it ends in 6:9–15 with narrative material that does not have the usual visionary introduction ("I lifted up my eyes again and looked, and behold") that is found in the eight visions revealed in 1:7–6:8. Instead, the "word of the LORD" was the source of Zechariah's information and there was no visionary experience (6:9). So this preaching unit opens with men bringing silver and gold to make crowns for Joshua (vv. 9–11) and then moves to Joshua's completion of the temple as a sign of the coming priestly messianic King (vv. 12–13). The unit ends with Joshua's crowns placed in the temple, and a statement that many would come to help finish the temple (vv. 14–15).

The encouraging theme of this unit is that God makes promises and fulfills promises, which should cause many to turn to God, repent of their sins, live consistent with their covenant stipulations, and look forward to the coming of the future messianic King.

- *Honoring the Current Leader (6:9–11)*
- *Honoring a Future King-Priest (6:12–13)*
- *The Crown: A Prophetic Sign (6:14–15)*

EXPOSITION

Because of the Babylonian conquest of Judah in 587 B.C. and the dominant role of royal Persian kings, there was little realistic hope among those living in Jerusalem at that time for the possibility of a resurgence of an independent and powerful Israelite nation led by a strong messianic figure. Judah was too small, too weak, and too devoid of strong leaders who could resist the Persian influences or limit its political control. Nevertheless, the godly prophet Zechariah still had hopes and a messianic ideal that he did not want the people to forget.

The surprising placing of a crown on the head of Joshua the high priest rather than the Davidic heir Zerubbabel introduced a significant twist from earlier royal hopes, and this elevation in Joshua's status must have confused some but encouraged others to return to Jerusalem in order to participate in this new era when God would raise up a messianic Branch/Sprout who would serve as both priest and king.

Honoring the Current Leader (6:9–11)

As a means of honoring the high priest's authority, a crown was made and placed on the head of Joshua as a sign of things to come.

6:9–10. God's words instructed the prophet to go to the home of Josiah, take the silver and gold the three new arrivals (Heldai, Tobijah, and Jedaiah) brought with them from the exilic community in Babylon, and make it into royal "crowns" (עֲטָרוֹת) (6:11). This plural noun probably meant that two crowns were made from this precious metal (some thought these were for Joshua and Zerubbabel (Merrill, 2003, 173; Meyers and Meyers, 1987, 350–51; Smith, 1984, 218).

6:11. The instructions in this sign act, however, point to putting a crown only on Joshua the high priest, so there was only one ornate crown[1] made of two (one of gold and one of silver) interlocking crowns (Wolters, 2014, 184; Hill, 2008b, 556). Since it was not normal for a high priest to have a royal crown, some interpreters drop the name Joshua and replaced it with the Davidic governor Zerubbabel (Redditt, 1995, 79; Mitchell, 1912, 185–86) or hypothesize that a second crown was placed on Zerubbabel (Meyers and Meyers, 1987, 350, 355). Neither of these alternatives should be followed because 6:11 only refers to placing a crown on the head of the high priest.

Honoring a Future King-Priest (6:12–13)
Joshua was honored with the title the "Branch" (or Sprout"), for he would help finish building the holy temple and he would be in charge or rule (like a king-priest) over the construction and the later operation of the temple, plus he would symbolically foreshadow the coming of the future messianic Branch/Sprout.

6:12. Since Joshua had already served as high priest for many years, this was not an act of conferring on him the authority of a high priest for the first time; rather, it was an act that conferred on him the power and responsibility of a ruler, and this symbolically pointed to the future (6:11) when the messianic figure known as the "Branch/Sprout" (צֶמַח) would sprout forth and function both as high priest and royal king (6:12–13).

WORD ANALYSIS: This word צֶמַח is used 33 times as a verb and 14 times as a noun in the OT. The verb can refer (a) literally to the "springing" up of a plant or the budding of a leaf on a tree (Gen. 2:5; Exod. 10:5), or the "growing" of hair or a beard (2 Sam. 10:5; Ezek. 16:7); (b) metaphorically to the growth or "springing up" of God's word (Isa. 55:10–11), righteousness and praise (Isa. 61:11), or salvation (2 Sam. 23:5); or (c) as

a reference to the messianic "Branch/Sprouts" of the Lord from the seed of David (Isa. 4:2; Jer. 23:5–6; 33:15; Zech. 3:8; 6:12) who will reign as a royal priestly king.

Johnson (2012, 198–200) sees the relationship between Joshua and the future messianic Branch as an example of an "already/but not yet" situation in which Joshua was the "functional equivalent" to the Branch and typologically and symbolically representative of what would happen in the future when the messianic Branch appeared. But he sees Joshua sitting on the throne of David only in a metaphorical sense but functioning as a ruler in the absence of a Davidic heir. This approach to the role of Joshua may undermine the role and authority of the governors (Zerubbabel and Nehemiah), who seemed to remain as the political leaders of the community, and overestimate the high priest's authority outside the temple complex.

This "Branch" (or Sprout") title was bestowed on Joshua, and this title should be connected with the eschatological messianic "Branch" (or Sprout") in Zechariah 3:8, Jeremiah 23:5–6, and the root from the line of Jesse in Isaiah 11:1. Already in Isaiah 4:2–4 there was a general association of the coming of the "Branch" (or Sprout") with the washing away of sin, but in Zechariah the "Branch" (or Sprout") has two roles: (a) this Branch/Sprout will in some ways be similar to the reign of a king, and (b) he will carry out the duties of the high priest. It was only a small step for the divine revelation about the high priest in Zechariah 3:8 to view the priest Joshua as symbolic of "my Servant" the Branch/Sprout in 6:12–13. The Servant in Isaiah 42:1–13 had the royal responsibility of bringing justice to all nations, and then he became a sacrifice to bear the sins of many (Isa. 53:1–12). After predicting the coming of the righteous Davidic Branch/Sprout in Jeremiah 23:5–6 and 33:15, God promised in Jeremiah 33:17–18 that David and the Levitical

---

1   This term was used in some cases outside the reference to a king (Isa. 28:3; Ezek. 16:12; Prov. 4:9).

priests would never lack a man to fulfill these roles. Ezekiel 34:23–24 and 37:24–28 connected "my Servant" to the Davidic ruler who would rule in a time of peace and great multiplication, when there would be a new everlasting covenant between God and his people, and when God would dwell in the midst of his people in his sanctuary. No person living at the time of Joshua fully fulfilled these two roles (Hill, 2008b, 558), and one should not interpret Zechariah to be referring to two different people (Boda, 2004, 339–40) or follow some of the later interpreters in the Second Temple period at Qumran (CD; 1Q28; 1Q28ᵃ) who tried to deal with this problem by hypothesizing a Davidic Messiah and a Levitical Messiah.

Qumran: Qumran is the name of the ruins on the northwest corner of the Dead Sea which is often connected to the Essenes community and the Dead Sea Scrolls. It is likely that many of these scrolls were copied in the scriptorium and then hidden in nearby caves to protect them from destruction by outsiders. The occupants were dissatisfied with the corrupt priest in Jerusalem, so they withdrew to the desert to prepare the way for the coming of the Lord (Isa. 40:3). Their "pesher" hermeneutical method of interpreting prophecy enabled them to take some distinctive views on prophetic fulfillment (a Levitical and a Davidic Messiah), and their pesher commentaries on different books of the OT provided an application that fit their situation.

6:13. One of the responsibilities of Joshua, this priest-king figure would be to build the "royal palace temple" (הֵיכַל) of the Lord (6:12–13). Those who think the future "Branch" or "Sprout" was symbolically referring to Zerubbabel in that historical context, naturally think that Zerubbabel would be the one who would build the temple, since this agrees with the prophecy in Zechariah 4:6–9 (Petersen, 1984, 276–77). But some hold that this referred to the temple of the future Davidic Royal, which would be an eschatological temple (Meyers and Meyers, 1987, 356). The royal honor and majesty of this messianic figure who would sit on the throne would be great (6:13), and there would be peace and no discord or problems between the role of being both king and priest.

TRANSLATION ANALYSIS: 6:13b
NASB[95] "and the counsel of peace will be between the two offices."
HCSB "and there will be peaceful counsel between the two of them."
NIV[84] "And there will be harmony between the two."
NKJV "And the counsel of peace shall be between them both."
NRSV "with peaceful understanding between the two of them."
Conflicting interests might create tension between the roles of a priest and the king, but since both offices would be filled by one person, these conflicts would disappear.

The Crown: A Prophetic Sign (6:14–15)
The crown would serve as a prophetic sign of what God would do concerning a future Davidic King and prompt people in Babylon to come to help build the temple in Jerusalem.

6:14. Once this symbolic act was performed, the crown was not regularly worn by Joshua. Instead, it was placed in the earthly temple that was in Jerusalem as a reminder of the sacrificial giving of these men. The crown would serve as a prophetic sign to those who came to the temple to worship. The priests would explain to worshippers that the crown signified a future joining of the priestly and kingly role when the messianic priestly Branch/Sprout would appear. Many felt that knowledge of this sign and its promises would attract people to return from the exile in Babylon.

6:15. Since the text did not limit those coming to help rebuild the temple to only those who were living in exile, some (Klein, 2008, 205; Baldwin, 1972, 137) suggest that this also refers to the coming of the foreign nations, a theme found in Zechariah 2:11 and 8:22, and in prophets such as Isaiah (Isa. 2:2–4; 19:18–25; 60:1–9; 66:18–22).

This chapter ends with two reminders about the future. First, Zechariah told the audience that when all these things happened, readers would understand that the words Zechariah spoke were true and from God (6:15b). Second, Zechariah reminded his listeners of the covenant stipulations in Deuteronomy 28:1 where the blessings and curses of the Sinai covenant were introduced. The fulfillment of these prophetic announcements would come true when the people of God listened to and obeyed what God said. Thus the various aspects of restoration mentioned in Zechariah 1:1–6:15 announced that the people of Judah would repent and turn back to God (1:1–6), exiles would return to the land and worship God (2:7–13), their leaders Joshua and Zerubbabel would renew their commitment to serve God (4:1–5:1), sin would be removed from the land (5:1–11), and people would trust in God's sovereign control of their situation (6:1–8). Faithful acceptance of God's instructions in past revelation would be a sign of the restoration of the hearts of these people, and this kind of heartfelt obedience would be characteristic of the messianic age of the Branch/Sprout.

THEOLOGICAL FOCUS

The exegetical idea (the placing of a crown on the head of Joshua the high priest elevated his status, encouraged people to return to Jerusalem, and was a sign that in the future God would raise up a messianic Branch/Sprout who would serve as both priest and king) leads to this theological focus: God's promise of a future Davidic King reinforces and underscores God's plans for his people now and in the future.

There are two theological themes in this message. First, when God makes promises, he fulfills them, some now and some in the future. Although life was difficult for many Jews in the postexilic period, and the temple rebuilding was not completed as quickly as some would have expected, God's plans were secure, unchangeable, and trustworthy. These promises of God should cause many to turn to God, repent of their sins, live consistent with the covenant stipulations, and look forward to the coming of the future messianic Branch/Sprout.

Second, God's promise of a future Davidic King was reinforced by his present dealings with the high priest Joshua in the time of Zechariah. God did not leave his people without hope but helped them comprehend his plans by the use of symbols and signs that people could understand. In this situation God used the generous gold and silver gifts of exiles to reassure Joshua about his role as well as the future role of the Davidic messianic Branch who would come to earth to fulfill God's plan of restoring his kingdom. In both eras God's kingdom strategy would involve the peaceful joining of the priestly and royal roles in one person who would serve as their ruler and restorer of worship.

PREACHING AND TEACHING STRATEGIES

Exegetical and Theological Synthesis

Zechariah 6:9–15 details the role of the Branch/Sprout in Israel's future. A brief word analysis traces the Branch/Sprout imagery to the seed of David (Isa. 4:2; Jer. 23:5–6; 33:15), previously mentioned in conversation with Joshua (Zech. 3:8). In this passage the discussion develops, picturing the two "hats" (i.e., crowns) the Branch/Sprout would wear: royal and priestly. Interestingly, while Zechariah focused on Joshua's royal role, his contemporary, Haggai, spoke of Zerubbabel's rule and symbolic ring (Hag. 2:20–23). Nonetheless, Zechariah paved the way for a future Messiah serving as royal-priest (cf. Isa. 42:1–13; 53:1–12; Jer. 33:17–18).

Additionally, the exegetical section ties this final word (not vision) of God to the opening call to repentance (Zech. 1:1–6). In that first scene, God ("the LORD who rules over all") appealed to Israel's faithless ancestors. He bemoaned their history of doubting his promises and disobeying his word. Doubt and disobedience seem to be partners in a ruined life. Adam and Eve doubted and disobeyed God in Eden before being expelled (Gen. 3). The wilderness generation doubted and disobeyed God before losing in battle to the Amalekites (Num. 14–15). Saul doubted and disobeyed God before getting removed from his throne (1 Sam. 15). Israel's national doubt and disobedience caused their exile to foreign lands (Deut. 28:58–68; Jer. 7).

On the other hand, God rewards lives marked by trust and obedience. Abraham trusted and obeyed God's call to leave his father's land, bear the sign of circumcision, and offer up his son. Jeremiah trusted and obeyed God's call to preach judgment and promise to his people. Nehemiah trusted and obeyed God's urging to rebuild Jerusalem's walls. Similar narratives of trust and obedience brighten the landscape of Israel's history. The guarantee that God keeps his promises often inspired trust and obedience (Deut. 7:12; 29:13; 30:20; 2 Sam. 22:31).

Preaching Idea

Only God can give an absolute guarantee.

Contemporary Connections

What does it mean?

What does it mean that only God can give an absolute guarantee? What kinds of guarantees does he make? Throughout the OT, God made specific promises to select people. To Abram, he guaranteed a famous name, a seed and son, and land to inherit (Gen. 12:1–3; 17:4–8; 22:15–18). To Moses, he guaranteed success in delivering Israel from bondage (Exod. 3–4). To Israel, he guaranteed blessings for obedience and curses for breaking their part in the covenant (Lev. 26; Deut. 28). For David, he guaranteed a son to sit on the throne (2 Sam. 7:8–16). Through several prophets, he guaranteed a new heart for his people (Jer. 31:31–33; Ezek. 11:19). And to Zechariah's audience, he guaranteed success for the high priest in rebuilding the temple (Zech. 6:9–15).

In addition to the specific promises, God makes many general guarantees to his people. He guarantees his love and forgiveness, provision and presence, mercy and protection, comfort and discipline as they walk with him through the challenges of life (e.g., Pss. 16; 18; 68; 103; Isa. 40:29–31; 41:10; 54:5; Hos. 11). In fact, his holy character guarantees his care (Exod. 34:6; Num. 23:19; cf. Titus 1:2). While fulfillment of specific promises reinforces God's faithfulness, the general guarantees he grants to all his people provide daily assurance (Lam. 3:22–23).

Is it true?

Is it true that only God can give an absolute guarantee? How we discern his absolute guarantees from wishful thinking? People can and will make promises. We keep some; we break others. Many marriages dissolve. Companies often do not honor their warranties. Renters break their leases. Parents prolong their promise of a family vacation for yet another year. In other words, no human guarantee is absolute.

With God, however, guarantees are absolute. He fulfills specific promises—Abraham, Moses, David—and honors general guarantees—love, forgiveness, presence. Unfortunately, we want God's guarantees on our timeline. As Zechariah made clear in 1:18–2:13, God keeps his promises on his schedule, which may include far-off future dates. Fortunately, along the way he may give signs, like Joshua's crown (Zech. 6:9–15) or Noah's rainbow (Gen. 9:8–17), ensuring his faithfulness.

God's Miraculous Signs

God often used miraculous signs as a reminder of his power, provision, and presence. The Exodus story brims with signs of God breaking into history to save his people: pillars of fire and cloud, deadly plagues and parted seas (Exod. 7:3; Deut. 4:34; 6:22; 26:8). On the first Passover, God's people stained their doorposts with blood as a sign of God's protection (Exod. 12:13). Later, he instructed his people to wear special wristbands and headbands as a memorial sign of his deliverance (Deut. 6:8). Memorial stones signified to God's people how he keeps his promises to provide, deliver, and remain with them (Gen. 35:1; Josh. 4:7). Ultimately, the entire tabernacle (and temple) system—from beautiful craftmanship to items with the ark of the covenant to priestly garments to liturgical calendar—served as a sign of God's holy presence (Exod. 25:8).

Finally, we must avoid the mistake of attributing to God absolute guarantees that he never actually made. This is wishful thinking. God did not absolutely guarantee health, wealth, fame, and success for his people. He did not absolutely guarantee thriving local churches, fully functional families, or immediate answers to every prayer. He did, however, absolutely guarantee his provision and presence in trying circumstances for those who walk with him (Isa. 43:1–2).

Now what?

How should we respond to God's absolute guarantees? Moreover, how do we keep from claiming specific promises as general guarantees? First, we may mine history for examples of God keeping his promises. We see him keep his promise to Abraham in providing Isaac, to Moses in delivering his people from bondage, to Joshua in claiming the Promised Land, to David in maintaining his royal line, to Hezekiah in adding fifteen years to his life, to Jerusalem in her limited exile, and to Zechariah in Joshua's service as high priest. Reflecting on these promises establishes an impressive case for God's trustworthiness.

Second, we must not absolutize every promise in Scripture. Not every guarantee applies to all people at all times. God's promise to Noah not to destroy the world again by flood is a universal promise (Gen. 9:8–11). God's promise to deliver Israel out of Egypt is a national promise (Exod. 3–4). The promise of future prosperity is directed to God's people on the verge of exile (Jer. 29:11–13). We must avoid naively claiming God's promises that have a specific, historic referent or person in mind; however, we can thoughtfully draw from these promises the conclusion that God regularly provides, delivers, and empowers his people.

Third, we must curb our enthusiasm for personalized signs. God may use circumstances in our past, encouragement from our friends, a sense of discontent, or a timely song on the radio. But he typically speaks through time-tested signs of Scripture, creation, conscience, and other people. Often, we do not need signs or revelation as much as reminders of his faithfulness.

Finally, we should pay attention to the people, objects, or circumstances in which we place too much trust. Career, relationships, prosperity, technology, popularity, and religion cannot offer absolute guarantees. Companies will not always honor their warranties. Parents will not always keep their promises. Church leaders will not always follow through with their plans. Without becoming jaded, we should not expect the guarantees of others to be absolute.

Creativity in Presentation

The engagement ring is perhaps the most iconic symbol of a guarantee. It signifies love, fidelity, and the promise of marriage. Women love sharing their proposal stories, especially if the groom-to-be made elaborate plans, spoke meaningful words, or expressed himself romantically. Consider telling an engagement story as a way of illustrating our guarantees of fidelity. Remind them that God is our faithful husband (Isa. 54:5). While even our engagement and marital vows are not absolute, God faithfully keeps his promises.

A variation on the illustration above is to discuss various forms of down payments or collateral people use as a guarantee. A set amount of money and signature may serve as a guarantee of full payment on a new vehicle or home. Presenting a driver's license and credit card at a hotel reception desk might serve as a guarantee to return rented towels, games, or sports equipment. I (Tim) once gave my hat to an usher at the movie theater, guaranteeing to come back after using the restroom. I was a teenager without a ticket, and he suspected I was trying to sneak into a film without paying. You want to make the connection that God's guarantees are strengthened by symbols, down payments, and collateral, to assure us he keeps his promises.

ALDI, a growing discount grocery chain, promises low prices by outsourcing bagging of groceries and returning carts to its customers. ALDI also sells store brand foods, stamped with its "Twice as Nice Guarantee." The company website explains, "We believe we have the best quality products around. We've designed and tested our brands to meet or exceed the national brands in taste and quality. We're so confident in our products that every item in our stores is backed by our unbeatable Twice as Nice Guarantee." Unsatisfied customers may replace an item and receive their money back. As "nice" as this guarantee sounds, have the congregation compare it to God's "Infinitely Absolute Guarantee." To make the key idea stick, a display of numerous ALDI products and enlarged version of the "Twice as Nice" logo might prove effective.

No matter how you illustrate the sermon, be sure to communicate this: God's promise of a future Davidic King reinforces and underscores his plan for his people now and in the future. More simply, only God can give an absolute guarantee.

- God may use a significant sign to reinforce his guarantees to us (6:9–11).

- God may use a significant leader to reinforce his guarantees to us (6:12–13).

- God may take a long time to make good on his guarantee to us (6:14–15).

DISCUSSION QUESTIONS

1. What were some OT signs or symbols given by God to assure his people that he keeps his promises?

2. What is the significance of the two "hats" (i.e., crowns) given to Joshua?

3. What might happen if we rely too heavily on signs?

4. How is the role of the Sprout/Branch developed in the OT and Second Temple period?

5. How do we distinguish between specific and general promises made by God? What are some common promises mistakenly claimed by people today?

FOR FURTHER READING

Boda, M. J. 2004. *Haggai, Zechariah*. NIV Application Commentary. Grand Rapids: Zondervan.

Klein, G. L. 2008. *Zechariah*. New American Commentary 21B. Nashville: B&H.

Smith, J. K. A. 2016. *You Are What You Love: The Spiritual Power of Habit*. Grand Rapids: Brazos.

Tiemeyer, L-S. 2015. *Zechariah and His Visions: An Exegetical Study of Zechariah's Vision Reports*. Library of the Hebrew Bible / Old Testament Studies 605. London: Bloomsbury T&T Clark.

GOD'S RESTORATION OF JUSTICE AND BLESSINGS, NOT FASTING (7:1–8:23)

Many people of Judah were keeping the fasts by mourning on the day that commemorated the defeat of Jerusalem, but others questioned if this was still necessary. So Zechariah encouraged these people to instead pay more attention to what would please God (be justice, kind, and compassionate) and encouraged them not to forget God's eschatological promises, for in some future day they would enjoy a joyful feast instead of spending their time fasting and lamenting.

Zechariah 7:1–8:23 can be divided into two preaching units: (1) Questions about Worship and Fasting (7:1–14), and (2) God Plans to Bless His People, So Feast Instead of Fast (8:1–23). At the very end of this section is a list of books and articles for further reading that may helpful in understanding these preaching units.

Zechariah 7:1–14

EXEGETICAL IDEA

Some people wondered if they still needed to keep the fasts that commemorated the defeat of Jerusalem, but Zechariah exhorted the audience to focus on what God wanted them to do (execute justice, show kindness, and show compassion) and to remember God's eschatological promises, for in the future they would feast and not fast over their past failures.

THEOLOGICAL FOCUS

God does not accept worship from insincere people who refuse to follow his ethical standards.

PREACHING IDEA

Real remorse provokes positive change.

PREACHING POINTERS

Two years had passed since Zechariah's first vision, but the people remained reluctant to declare God's victory. A group of folks living outside Jerusalem came to the priests to inquire about the need to continue their memorial fasts. Rather than answer their questions, God raised a few of his own through Zechariah to expose their false remorse and insincere worship. Then he stressed the need for acts of love—justice, mercy, and compassion—rather than acts of penance. For the original audience this was not a new message but an echo of Moses and other prophets. The encounter reiterated their need to dispense with their solemn rituals and return to showing justice.

It's embarrassing when God's people today prefer showing a gloomy face to doing good deeds. Evangelicals lament their loss of political influence, legal protections, and opportunities to speak freely about their faith in public. We bemoan today's loose sexual ethic, consumer impulse, and vulgarity. We groan about diminishing loyalties to church activities and flighty tendencies of younger generations. Sadly, our remorse neither accepts personal responsibility nor motivates positive change. Inauthentic remorse looks inward and acts pathetic. Real remorse looks outward and acts positive. This passage reminds us that real remorse provokes positive change.

QUESTIONS ABOUT WORSHIP
AND FASTING (7:1–14)

LITERARY STRUCTURE
AND THEMES (7:1–14)

Zechariah 7:1–14 addresses a concern of the people. They asked if they needed to continue fasting, so the prophet inquired about their motives for fasting (vv. 1–7). Zechariah then instructed them to focus more on treating others justly, showing kindness, and caring for the poor (vv. 8–10). Zechariah concluded with an expectation that they should avoid making the same mistakes that the former inhabitants of Jerusalem and Judah made that caused God to scatter them abroad and desolate their land (vv. 11–14). The themes of worship, ethical behavior, and having compassion on the weak are treated in Zechariah 7:1–14.

- *Questions about Worship and Fasting (7:1–7)*
- *Instructions about Ethical Behavior (7:8–14)*

EXPOSITION

Don't worry about fasting, focus on doing justice to avoid God's wrath. Their parents failed to act justly, and God's wrath brought his covenant curses on the nation (Lev 27: Deut. 27–28). God's wrath brought death to thousands, the destruction of Jerusalem and the temple, plus life in Babylonian exile. Surely Zechariah's audience did not want to repeat that cycle again.

Some people wondered if they still needed to keep the fasts that commemo-rated the defeat of Jerusalem, but Zechariah exhorted the audience to focus on what God wanted them to do (execute justice, show kindness, and show compassion) and to re-member God's eschatological promises, for in the future they would feast and not fast over their past failures.

Questions about Worship and Fasting (7:1–7)

People wanted to know if they should continue fasting, so Zechariah countered their question with a question about their sincerity and moti-vation for fasting.

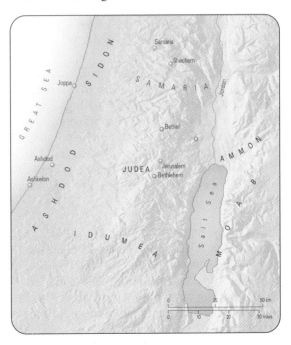

The Location of Bethel (Beit El), Samaria, and Jerusalem

7:1–2. Although Bethel is only twelve miles north of Jerusalem, its past relationship to the temple holding the golden calf (1 Kings 12:29) and its proximity to the people from Samaria who opposed the Jewish attempt to rebuild the temple (Ezra 5:1–5) might raise questions in the mind of the prophet about its people's orthodoxy and their motivations. But Ezra 2:28 indicates that 223 Jews who returned from exile settled in Bethel, so if these men were from that group of returnees, Zechariah would have no reason to condemn this delegation for unorthodox beliefs or question their motivations. It appears that these men were not associated with the people in Samaria who opposed the rebuilding of the temple because that issue did not come up. But it is not completely clear if the "they sent" refers to the leaders named in this verse who sent someone, meaning Sharezer and Regem-melech sent men (in which case these two men are the subjects of the verb), or if "they sent" refers to the people of Bethel who sent these men to Jerusalem (in which case these two men are the object of the verb). What we do know is that some men came to Jerusalem with pure intentions to seek God's will concerning the issue of fasting. Their desire to "entreat the face of the LORD" (Exod. 32:11; 1 Kings 13:6; Jer. 26:19; Dan. 9:13) might involve prayers and sacrifices at the temple to win God's help in regard to their question about their need to fast. Often a person would contact a priest or prophet to receive a specific answer from God about a very serious issue.

7:3. The question this delegation asked was whether the Jewish people should continue to fast on the seventh day of the fifth month to remember the disastrous day when the royal palace and the temple were destroyed with fire by the Babylonian captain of the guard Nebuzaradan in 587 B.C. (2 Kings 25:8–9; Jer. 52:12–16). Although there was never any command from God to institute this day as a day of fasting, it was natural for the people to remember the tragedy of this destruction. It was natural for the people to want to fast to remember their

failures, to ask God for mercy, to plead with God to change their world, and to restore the nation to greatness. But since the temple was now halfway completed, it seemed like they had mourned and fasted long enough. The answer to this question will be given in the final paragraph (8:18–20).

7:4–5. Zechariah's initial response "to the people of the land" (7:5, meaning the Jews living in Judah, as in Hag. 2:4) and the priests in 7:4–14 was not a direct answer to the question raised (see 8:18–20 for that answer). Zechariah initially asked three probing questions (7:4–6) that inquired about the motivations of the people who faithfully mourned and fasted for the past seventy years (Jer. 25:11–12; 29:10). The seventy years of exile in Jeremiah 29:10 probably referred to the time the first exiles were taken in 605 B.C. and extended past Cyrus's initial decree to allow the Jews to return to their land (539 B.C.) until the time the exiles actually arrived back in Jerusalem around 537/536 B.C. Since this chapter was dated to 518 B.C. (almost twenty years after the first group returned from exile), this reference to the seventy years could refer to the time from the destruction of the temple in 587 B.C. until 516 B.C. when the rebuilding was finished, similar to the understanding in Zechariah 1:12.

The first question asked about the sincerity of their fasting (7:5). Did their fasting involve a spiritual searching of their hearts, an examination of their action, and a tearful acknowledgement of their sins against God and others? Did they have a determination to turn from their sinful ways and a strong commitment to faithfully love and serve God in the future? Were these fasts (in the fifth and seventh months) all about getting closer to God (7:5) and deepening their piety, or were these times of fasting more of a ritual experience (Merrill, 2003, 184) and self-pity because of all the difficulties they were facing (Barker, 1983, 644)? It seemed that one might be able to imply that the second explanation more accurately described their fasting.

7:6. The second rhetorical question asked about their eating and drinking. Did they not eat and drink to satisfy themselves and their natural needs (7:6) rather than focusing on God as the one who provided them with the food and water they needed to survive (Mc-Comiskey, 1998, 1127)?

7:7. In the third question, Zechariah asked the audience if his "words" (הַדְּבָרִים) were basically the same as the well-known teaching of earlier prophets before the exile when the land was peaceful and fully occupied (in the southern Negev area as well as in the fertile foothills of the Shephelah). This comparison would demonstrate that Zechariah would not be responding to their questions with some new theological teaching that was different from earlier prophets such as Isaiah (see Isa. 58). Although some (Boda, 2004, 359; Meyers and Meyers, 1987, 395; Smith, 1984, 224) connect Zechariah 7:7 with what follows, the next word from the Lord begins in 7:8, so it would make more sense to view 7:7 as the conclusion to 7:4–6. Nevertheless, the brief reference to the former prophet in 7:7 does help orient the reader to the answer in 7:8–14.

Instructions about Ethical Behavior (7:8–14)
Past generations failed to follow the ethical demands of the Torah or listen to the prophets, so God exiled them from their land.

7:8–9. A word from God caused Zechariah to remind the audience about the internal attitudes and external behavior that God requires of his people. Although there was nothing wrong with fasting, if the nation exhibited positive moral characteristics, God would have never judged the nation. They would have never needed to mourn and fast over the destruction of Judah and Jerusalem. The prophet repeated

instruction about the way God wanted his people to treat one another in three exhortations (7:9) and two prohibitions (7:10).

First, the judges and those who took people to court were to treat others with true "justice" (מִשְׁפָּט) when they had legal disputes. They were not to pervert justice by bribing judges or giving false testimony at a trial (7:9a; cf. Isa. 56:1). This would require the judges to know the instructions for just judgment in Exodus 18:18–23 and 20:1–23:33, to seek God's wisdom in order to decide the case fairly, and to make the penalties appropriate to the situation (not too harsh and not to soft). Second, people must relate to each other with "lovingkindness" (חֶסֶד) or an attitude of steadfast covenant love toward other people who were part of covenant family of Israel (7:9b). Since God treated his covenant people with steadfast covenant love (Exod. 34:6), the people of Israel were expected to exhibit this same characteristic in their relationships with others (see Hos. 6:6; 12:6; Mic. 6:8) and not be mean or vindictive. Third, God's people were to have "deep compassion" (רַחֲמִים) toward others, like the strong emotional compassion a mother has for her own children (cf. 1 Kings 3:26). This would require patience, forgiveness, and a deep love for others, rather than a selfish attitude of getting even or taking advantage of others.

7:10. The two prohibitions in 7:10 condemned aggressive oppression of the weak and powerless members of society (the widow, orphan, the poor, and the alien living in the land)[1] and warned people not to plan evil deeds against one another (cf. 8:17; Mic. 2:1–4) or dream up false accusations against another person. The things that the people from Bethel should be focused on were having pure motives, kind actions, and honesty in relationships. These things were far more important than fasting over the failures of a past generation. If the earlier generations had

---

[1] The Torah and the prophets repeatedly criticized these abuses (Deut. 10:18; 24:14; Isa. 10:2; Jer. 7:6; Amos 3:6–8; 4:1; 8:4–6; Ezek. 22:7) and warned the people not to oppress the weak and vulnerable who could not defend themselves.

paid attention to these principles, the destruction of Jerusalem would have never happened and there would be no need to mourn and fast.

7:11. Instead of listening to God's instructions in the laws of Moses and his admonitions in the preaching of the prophets, the people of Judah hardened their hearts, stubbornly turned their "shoulder/back" on God, rebelled, and refused to hear or respond positively to God's direction.

7:12–14. Since the people obstinately refused to soften their hearts, they were not able to internalize the ethical standards of conduct found in the Mosaic Law, which were repeated again and again when the Spirit of God inspired the prophets with the similar messages. This rejection of God's ways caused God to pour out his wrath on Judah (7:12b) and send his people into exile in Babylon. Since they refused to listen to God, God refused to listen to them when they cried out in desperation as the enemy was destroying Jerusalem (7:13; cf. Isa. 59:1–2). Consequently, these people were scattered in other nations where Israel's God was not worshipped. Although the Assyrians did bring some foreign people back into Israel after it was defeated in 722 B.C. (2 Kings 17:24), there is no record of a similar repopulation of Judah and Jerusalem after the Babylonians destroyed Jerusalem in 587 B.C. Thus, the deportation of people left some farming areas and most of the cities of Judah with a much smaller population for about seventy years (7:14).

THEOLOGICAL FOCUS

The exegetical idea (some people wondered if they still needed to keep the fasts that commemorated the defeat of Jerusalem, but Zechariah exhorted the audience to focus on what God wanted them to do [execute justice, show kindness, and show compassion] and to remember God's eschatological promises, for in the future they would feast and not fast over their past failures) leads to this theological focus: God does

not accept worship from insincere people who refuse to follow his ethical standards.

The themes of worship, ethical behavior, and having compassion on the weak intersect with one another in this prophecy. When people came to worship, it was important for them to have the right attitude, for insincere actions or words motivated by self-pity would not be pleasing to God. If the people of Judah exhibited attitudes and actions that portrayed a life of love, justice, humility, and compassion for others, and if they refused to oppress the weak and defenseless, God would accept their worship. Thus, far more important than observing multiple fasts was the need to transform their lives by sincerely serving God and by paying attention to God's instructions about their responsibility to practice social justice. If people wished to avoid the wrath of God, they would obey God's law, help the oppressed, have compassion on the orphan and widow, and display a sincere attitude of love for one another. Fasting was not the key to pleasing God.

PREACHING AND TEACHING STRATEGIES

Exegetical and Theological Synthesis

Zechariah 7:1–14 highlights God's ability to see through religious charades. While a direct answer to the question about fasting ("Did you really fast for me?") will come in the following chapter (8:18–20), God's indirect response underscored his ability to detect human motives. With three questions he exposed Israel's insincerity, self-satisfaction, and neglect for his word. In previous visions and oracles, God had already called out their impurity and idolatry (3:4; 5:7), and their injustice and deception (5:3). Indeed, their rebellion landed them in exile. But their sin did not keep God from mercifully extending them an invitation to return to him (1:3, 6, 16; 3:4).

Zechariah joined other prophets who chided God's people for their religious duplicity. Amos condemned the songs and festivals

Israel observed, calling them a mockery (Amos 5:21–23). Their countdown to the end of Sabbath, so they could return to the marketplace, did not escape his notice (8:5). Isaiah cried foul on Israel's parade of sacrifices and prayers (Isa. 1:11–14). He criticized their fasting as a mask for self-indulgence (58:1–5). Following each of these rebukes, God reminded his people of their need to change, becoming merciful, humble, and just (Mic. 6:8).

The OT recorded numerous stories of real remorse and positive change. In the Joseph novella, older brother Judah changed from betrayer, runaway, and liar early on to a responsible kin (Gen. 37–38, 43–44). In his penitent psalms, David captured the shame he felt for his sin (Pss. 32, 51). In his repentant prayer, the wicked king Manasseh changed his tune when captured by the Assyrians, a prayer which God honored (2 Chron. 33:10–13). Not all positive change lasted, however, as is evident in Jonah's quick turn from penitent prophet to self-loathing loser (Jonah 4:1, 9).

Peaching Idea
Real remorse provokes positive change.

Contemporary Connections

What does it mean?
What does it mean that real remorse provokes positive change? What does real remorse look like? Real remorse shows up in a variety of expressions: publicly or secretly, individually or collectively, verbally or tearfully. David fasted, prayed, and prostrated himself before God in real remorse when confronted for wronging Uriah. Psalms 51 and 32 express his remorse and desire for positive change. Ezra tore hair from his beard and head when confessing the marital infidelity rampant among his people (Ezra 9:3–4). The whole congregation echoed his prayer, provoking them to dissolve foreign marriages and commit to purity (10:1–7). Nehemiah's corporate confession provoked praise

and a reaffirmation of the covenant (Neh. 9–10). In each case, the genuineness of the remorse is proven by the positive change that follows. Contrarily, false remorse sounds like a pity party; it provokes no change, only self-loathing.

What kind of positive change does God have in mind? Positive changes include acts of love: a kind word, a listening ear, quality time, an act of service, or a gentle touch. They also envision works of justice: care for the poor and widow, comfort for the hurting, protection for the weak. Zechariah called out his people for overlooking the needs of their vulnerable neighbors while indulging their own appetites. Often the first step in positive change is a simple shift in focus from self to others. Compassion toward others marks the changed heart.

Is it true?
Is it true that real remorse provokes positive change? Yes, but positive change may not come immediately. Real remorse blends a mixture of complicated emotions: denial, guilt, regret, anger, shame, and grief. God is familiar with our wide range of emotional expression. In fact, he has recorded our deep sorrow, fiery anger, grave confusion, firm trust, and titillating joy in Scripture (Pss. 16, 22, 88, 137, 146). What is more important than our emotional expression is its direction. Most lament (i.e., grieving) or imprecatory (i.e., angry) psalms conclude with declarations of praise, trust, or thanksgiving. In other words, real remorse prompts a positive change of outlook.

Lest we limit positive change to a simple shift in perspective, we must remember that Zechariah called for positive change in behavior among one's neighbors. False remorse provokes lip service but little enduring care for hurting, broken, and marginalized people. Real remorse, on the other hand, lifts us from the sorrow of our sin to engage compassionately with those around us. Those who are truly saddened by their greed may increase their generosity to organizations fighting poverty. Those who are honestly disgusted by abortion may volunteer at a pregnancy center or serve as a foster parent. Those who feel sincere grief over discrimination may find ways to advocate for the needs of minorities and immigrants. And we must remember Zechariah's call for positive change did not merely apply to individuals. He envisioned the entire community moved by real remorse. Powerful change comes from communities driven by compassion and real remorse.

Now what?

How do we express real remorse? How do we begin to make positive changes? The first step toward real remorse is to admit our pitiful state. Real remorse may stem from moral failures, personal losses, unfair situations, or conflicts we have contributed to. As mentioned above, some sorrow in suffering, whether self-inflicted or merely the consequence of living in a fallen world, is permissible. But God wants us to bring our laments to him, so he can replace them with joy (Jer. 31:12–13; Lam. 3:19–24; Neh. 10:1–5). If remorse results from our rebellion, we must honestly confess our errors to move toward positive change (Ezra 10; Pss. 32, 51).

A second step toward positive change is to shift our gaze outward. A focus on others— family and friend, neighbor and enemy—provides opportunities to show compassion. And as we look outward, we will acknowledge the depth of suffering around us. We daily interact with victims of poverty, abuse, and neglect. We can lament the injustice that surrounds us, but it does little good to commiserate forever. Positive change for others begins by praying, "God, show me where to act compassionately today." Churches can pray, "Show us where to show your care." Then we act. The more frequently we show compassion, the more naturally mercy integrates into our everyday lives.

Because our capacity to love deeply comes directly from God, we must sustain our outward focus with an upward one. Looking to God—as Lord of Hosts, revealer of truth, forgiver of sins, covenant-maker, promise-keeper, and savior— lifts our eyes beyond the world's woes. We experience compassion fatigue when we work from our own resources. When we look to God for strength, he infuses our acts of justice with joy.

Creativity in Presentation

I (Tim) have an unfortunate reputation for being a "sore loser." As much as I might push back with claims of becoming a "better sport," I have earned the title. Every loss stirs up mock remorse. I bellow and moan the following remarks: "This game is rigged." "I wasn't ready." "It's not fair." "You cheated." "Everybody teamed up against me." "I'm never playing again." Such sentiments likely have a ring of familiarity because you may have said them yourself. A few contests with a "sore loser" can discourage anyone from further competition with him. His self-loathing steals the joy from the game. Consider sharing a personal "sore loser" story and the remorse you expressed as a result. Feel free to reenact it and ham up the details. People tend to appreciate when a pastor owns his foibles! Ask the audience: "Is this what we look like to God in the game of life? Are we really sorry if we never change?"

The typical pity party (as depicted in TV, literature, and movies) captures the essence of false remorse—it is self-focused, indulgent, and leads nowhere. A pity party often includes several of the following elements: gallons of ice cream; sad music; romantic movie marathon; sentimental items destroyed by fire, scissors, or darts; excessive sighing; sweatpants; and venting to a friend. Consider collecting these items (and wearing sweatpants) while you act out a pity party. (You might note how our pity parties are far more indulgent than Israel's three fasts.) In the opening scene of *Bridget Jones's Diary* (2001, directed by Sharon Maguire), Bridget (played by Renée Zellweger) throws a quintessential pity party: sitting alone on a couch, watching Frasier, wearing pajamas, drinking wine, and singing "All by Myself." The clip lasts nearly two minutes. After showing the clip, you might say, "I worry this is how we sometimes look to God, throwing pity parties that don't lead to positive change but only reinforce our grief."

Real-life examples of positive change might stir your congregation to action. In 2007, Atlanta Falcons's quarterback, Michael Vick, was indicted for dogfighting and cruelty to animals. After being publicly humiliated and sent to prison, Vick released a statement of remorse. While many questioned the authenticity of his statement, proof of his remorse came with positive changes: admitting his wrongs, repaying his debts, and advocating for the humane treatment of animals. Bill W. experienced positive change, moving from the lonely fight with alcoholism to cofounding Alcoholics Anonymous. (Addicts realize the change process requires more than expressing remorse; rehab requires vigilance, sacrifice, counseling, and accountability.) John Newton, author of the hymn "Amazing Grace," met God on the raging seas. A near-death experience lead to real remorse, positively changing the trajectory of Newton's life. Several years after his conversion, Newton abandoned the seas and entered the clergy. Real remorse eventually gripped Newton as he reflected on his time as a slave trader. He began to speak against slavery, positively influencing William Wilberforce, England's iconic abolitionist. Newton's beloved song, "Amazing Grace," remains one of the most recognized tunes in history.

All the creative elements should point toward the key truth: Following God's instruction is far more important than mourning the severe punishment that came from past failures. Real remorse provokes positive change.

- God can see through our religious fakery (7:1–7).

- God calls us to live compassionately (7:8–10).

- Lack of compassion may have lasting consequences (7:11–14).

DISCUSSION QUESTIONS

1. What historical moments motivated Zechariah's audience to fast?

2. What are appropriate times and motivations for fasting?

3. How did other OT prophets reinforce Zechariah's complaint about false piety and injustice?

4. What are the marks of real remorse? Which biblical figures model this?

5. What acts of compassion and justice does your church participate in?

Zechariah 8:1–23

EXEGETICAL IDEA
God's great zeal for his covenant people would result in God saving them, returning them to their land, giving them peace, and blessing them, so God's people should practice justice in all their relationships and turn their fasting days into days of feasting and rejoicing.

THEOLOGICAL FOCUS
In the future, God's people will be restored and transformed, so they will celebrate rather than mourn.

PREACHING IDEA
"Save the date" for an upcoming party with God.

PREACHING POINTERS
God had something great in store for his people. He had planned a series of feasts with his restored people and their neighbors. Zechariah shared this news in his answer to the question of fasting raised in the previous chapter. The exile had ended. Rebuilding had begun. Renewal was on the horizon. To the original audience, this news was meant to breathe fresh hope into their labors and curb any defeatist (or nationalistic) leanings. The Lord of Hosts had scheduled a feast (several, actually) and invited all who obey him to indulge.

The church today could benefit from a second glance at God's festive side. The Lord Almighty has infused his creation with wonders galore: teeming animals, rushing waters, succulent greenery, savory flavors, and glorious image-bearers. Too many people settle for a gloomy God bent on enforcing rules and inflicting punishments. While we cannot whitewash his jealousy, anger, and wrath, neither should we minimize his joy. The present abounds with a million little gifts from the Father of lights. The future will abound with parties and peoples beyond counting. This passage instructs us to "Save the date" for an upcoming party with God.

GOD PLANS TO BLESS HIS PEOPLE, SO FEAST INSTEAD OF FAST (8:1–23)

LITERARY STRUCTURE AND THEMES (8:1–23)

Zechariah opened this unit with God assuring the people that his zeal for the remnant would result in the restoration of the nation (vv. 1–8). Then he reported that God would end all wars, bring fertility to their crops, and bestow his blessings (vv. 9–13). He reminded them that they needed to treat others with compassion and justice and assured them that God would have compassion on them (vv. 14–17). Zechariah ended this message with the promise that God would turn their fasting into joyous feasting, and this would attract many to join God's people (vv. 18–23).

Two major themes in this unit are the restoration of Jerusalem and the nation's past ethical failures to treat others with justice and compassion. God's people needed to love their neighbors and maintain the highest standards of honesty.

- *God Will Gather and Restore a Remnant (8:1–8)*
- *God's Blessing Will Bring Peace and Fertility (8:9–13)*
- *Do as God Does: Treat Others with Compassion (8:14–17)*
- *People Should Feast, Not Fast (8:18–23)*

EXPOSITION

The terror of the Babylonian military defeat of Judah and Jerusalem left a deep scar on the psyche of the Judeans. This traumatic experience of losing everything they owned, losing their freedom, losing many family members, and losing hope that God would deliver them was not easy to overcome. They had nowhere to turn and they could do nothing to save themselves. However, it was cathartic to remember those who were killed in the invasion and to remember how horrible it was. They expressed their grief in a lament and commemorated it all with a fast. Maybe God would see their present suffering and, in his mercy, would reach out and help them. Of course, by the fourth year of Darius (7:1a; 518 b.c.) they had already observed these fasts for more than seventy years, and by this time about half of the new temple was already standing. So some thought this might be time to reevaluate these fasts. Was it still necessary to keep these fasts?

God Will Gather and Restore a Remnant (8:1–8)

With great zeal God would restore a transformed and faithful remnant of God's covenant people from all over the world to Jerusalem where God would dwell in their midst.

8:1–2. This new word from God, the Commander of the Armies of Heaven, struck a note of optimism about the future. Drawing on themes in the first night vision (Zech. 1:14), Zechariah reminded his audience that God was exceeding "zealous/jealous/passionate" (קִנֵּא) about Zion (8:2). This concept referred to God's passionate emotional protective feelings toward his people, the covenant nation of Israel. The covenant required exclusive love for God and the rejection of all other gods, so in the past when Israel turned her back on God and refused to listen to him, the people soon started worshipping other gods. This aroused the strong emotional desire (God's zeal/jealousy) to restore his relationship with his people (cf. Zech. 1:14) as well as his anger about their sinful rejection of him. Meyers and Meyers (1987, 411) and Boda (2004, 380) believe God's great anger was directed toward the foreign nations based on 1:14–15, but the text indicates that God's great anger was initially "toward her" (לָהּ); that is, Zion. Wolters (2014, 231–32) argues that God was angry with Zion for her unfaithfulness, but at the same time he was zealous in his deep love to restore that relationship. It seems better not to view the last line of 8:2 as referring to God's "zealous" or "jealous" (קִנְאָה) "wrath" (חֵמָה) toward his people, but instead attribute his action to the "burning passion" Zechariah described, because this was not a time when his wrath would punish them.

TRANSLATION ANALYSIS: 8:2, "burning passion; zeal" (קִנְאָ)
NASB[95]: "with great wrath I am jealous for her"
HCSB: "I am jealous for her with great wrath."
NIV[84]: "I am burning with jealousy for her."
NKJV: "With great fervor I am zealous for her."
NRSV: "I am jealous for her with great wrath."
God's deep love for his people caused his "burning" (חֵמָה) "zeal" (קִנְאָ) to be aroused.

8:3. Because of his deep emotional connection to his people, God repeated the promise he made back in Zechariah 1:16 and 2:10 that he would return to Jerusalem and dwell in the midst of his people (8:3). His presence would transform Jerusalem into a "City of Truth," and Mount Zion would be a "Holy Mountain" set apart to God. Ezekiel 43:1–5 predicts that in the future, God would return to dwell in his temple in Zion. This would suggest that God's permanent residence would be in Jerusalem with his people. Isaiah 1:26 claims that the future city of Jerusalem would be called a "Faithful, Truthful City" (Zech. 8:3), and Isaiah 52:1 plus Joel 3:17

refer to a future day when Jerusalem would be a Holy City.

TRANSLATION ANALYSIS: 8:3, "city of truth" (עִיר־הָאֱמֶת)
NASB[95]: "Then Jerusalem will be called the City of Truth."
HCSB: "Jerusalem will be called the Faithful City."
NIV[84]: "Jerusalem will be called the Faithful City."
NKJV: "Jerusalem shall be called the City of Truth."
NRSV: "Jerusalem shall be called the faithful city."

In this new setting, the people in the city of Jerusalem would be so thoroughly transformed that they would demonstrate two of the key characteristics of God's action (his faithfulness and holiness). After God defeated the enemies that would attack Jerusalem (as in 14:16–21), he would come to earth, establish his kingdom, and everything would be holy. This adjective "holy" modifying the city of Jerusalem was derived from God's holy presence. From that time on, the people would faithfully keep their covenant commitment to love God with all their heart, and they would reject the sinful ways of their past and be "set apart, holy" (קֹדֶשׁ) to God.

8:4–5. At that future time, Jerusalem would be alive and filled with an older generation as well as the many young people (cf. Jer. 30:18–21) enjoying the pleasures of life in the open squares around the city.

8:6. This picture may have seemed like an impossibility to the small remnant of people listening to the prophet in the postexilic era, but it was true. Some may have wondered if things would actually be that wonderful or if it would be possible for God to accomplish this transformation (8:6), but God would be able to do miraculous things (פָּלֵא). Years earlier, while the Angel of the Lord was visiting Abraham and Sarah, he told them that they would have a baby in their old age because nothing was too "impossible" or "miraculous" (פֶּלֶא) for God (Gen. 18:14). Just before the destruction of Jerusalem, Jeremiah foretold of a future day when Jerusalem would be filled with people buying and selling homes because nothing was too "miraculous" or "impossible" (פֶּלֶא) for God to do (Jer. 32:17, 27).

> *TRANSLATION ANALYSIS: 8:6, "marvelously impossible" (פֶּלֶא)*
> NASB[95]: "If it is too difficult in the sight of the remnant"
> HCSB: "Though it may seem incredible to the remnant"
> NIV[84]: "It may seem marvelous to the remnant"
> NKJV: "If it is marvelous in the eyes of the remnant"
> NRSV: "Even though it seems impossible to the remnant"
> God has the ability to do what is marvelously impossible for human beings to imagine as possible, thus most would call these incredible acts miracles.

8:7–8. Zechariah agreed with this theological approach and knew it was not impossible for God to save his people in the far corners of the world and bring them back to Jerusalem. When this would happen, God would restore his covenant with them, he would be their God, and they would be his covenant people (8:8b). This idea sounded like the prophecy of the new covenant in Jeremiah 31:33, which says, "I will be their God and they will be my people." Since nothing comparable to this ever happened in the postexilic era, this must be referring to God's plan to restore the nation in the eschatological age.

God's Blessing Will Bring Peace and Fertility (8:9–13)

The problem of the past would end, and God would bring about a time of peace and remove his curse on his people.

8:9–10. Zechariah now left his description of the blessing of the eschatological kingdom in order to talk about what would happen in the next few years. The political, economic, and spiritual setting of the nation would be dramatically different from the depressing situation that characterized Jerusalem just a couple years ago.[1] Two years before this prophecy, Haggai spoke to the people in 520 B.C. about the goal of restoring the temple (1:1–15). In response, the people began to work on the temple by rebuilding the foundation (Hag. 2:18). The admonitions to "be strong" (חָזַק) at the beginning (Zech. 8:9) and at the end of this paragraph (8:13) are reminiscent of Haggai's threefold charge (Hag. 2:4) for the governor Zerubbabel, the high priest Joshua, and the people to "be strong" (חָזַק) and not give up on building the temple. Although this new temple did not seem to be as grand as Solomon's huge temple (2:3), it would end up being much more glorious than Solomon's temple (2:9).

8:11–13. Zechariah reminded his audience of the trials of the past few years in order to contrast those difficult days with the changes that God would bring about in the present era. Before they started work on restoring the temple foundation in 520 B.C. (Hag. 2:15–18), the economy was terrible because God sent a drought on the land around Jerusalem (Hag. 1:6, 10–11). Thus, it was very difficult to get paid a decent wage or to make a living by farming (Zech. 8:10a), and there was no peace (Zech. 8:10b). Wolters (2014, 239) suggests that the reference to wages not being available for human labor or for renting an animal may reflect the situation around 519–518 B.C. when the Persian king Darius marched through Judah in order to put down a revolt in Egypt. The descriptive clause "everyone was against his neighbor" at the end of Zechariah 8:10 may reflect the conflicting priorities among the Judeans (some pro- and some anti-Persian)

---

1   This earlier period that was mentioned was not the period right after 538 B.C. when the Jews first returned to Jerusalem (Ezra 1–3) but refers to a period a couple years earlier in 520 B.C. (Hag. 1–2; Ezra 5).

as well and a lack of good leadership that would channel the nation's energy toward the accomplishment of the nation's highest priority of rebuilding the temple.

In contrast to these problems in the past, God was "now" (Zech. 8:11a) committed to dealing with his people in a different way. God would give the small group of people in Jerusalem crops that would produce abundant grain (cf. Hag. 2:18–19). Vines would yield much fruit because the heavens would give enough moisture (the dew) for the things the people would grow (Zech. 8:12). In contrast to the economic collapse of the past, in Haggai 1:6, 10–11, God would turn the earlier curse into a blessing of salvation, so there would be no need to fear about the future (Zech. 8:13). How the Jewish people would become a blessing was left unexplained, but this idea was likely drawn from texts such as Genesis 12:1–3. At that time, God promised Abram that he would make Abram into a great nation, and through this nation God would bring a blessing on all the families of the earth. This opportunity to function as God's blessing on others should motivate the people of Judah to move forward in faith. They should worship God faithfully, live just and holy lives, complete the rebuilding of the temple, and witness to others about God's love.

Do as God Does: Treat Others with Compassion (8:14–17)
God's past judgment had ended, the time of blessing had arrived, so the people should aim to please the Lord in the way they interact with others.

8:14–15. Zechariah now admonished the people concerning God's purposes (זָמַם) that he planned for his people. These purposes were a part of God's determined design for his people and this plan included both God's judgment of various nations and the salvation of a remnant of his people. For example, when the children of Israel sinned by worshipping the golden calf and at

Baal-Peor, it was God's plan to punish them severely, but God did not destroy them completely. Much later the nation was destroyed by Babylon and spent seventy years of exile in Babylon (Jer. 29:10a), but God's plan was to give them hope and to return them to their land (Jer. 29:10b–14). Zechariah repeatedly described various aspects of God's "plan, purpose" (זָמַם) for his people in his visions in Zechariah 1–6. For example, Zechariah 1:14–16 explains God's decision to deal positively with his people by defeating their enemies and by having compassion on them. Isaiah 14:24–27 outlines God's plan (עֵצָה) for the mighty nation of Assyria, and Isaiah assured his audience that no one could stop God's plans because no one can overcome the power of God's stretched-out hand. Zechariah 8:15b records God's plan to do good things for his people; thus, they should not worry about the future.

8:16–17. As long as the people faithfully did what God instructed them to do (cf. Zech. 7:9–11), treated others justly, spoke the truth, and let justice rule in the courts, it would be possible for God to bless them. If they hated what God hates, refused to devise plots against others, and rejected the temptation to be a false witness at court (8:17), God's purposes could be worked out through them. This indicated that their failure to practice ethical behavior in the past (Zech. 7:9–11) led to their downfall, so a restoration of ethical behavior consistent with God's holy character must be demonstrated in the future when God would pour out his blessings on them.

People Should Feast, nNot Fast (8:18–23)
Fasting would cease, but joy, truth, and peace would characterize future feasts; then many people from around the world would join them in worshipping God.

8:18–19. A new word from God came to conclude this message on fasting. At this point God instructed Zechariah to provide an answer to the initial question about fasting raised in 7:3. A quick and easy answer to the question of fasting might have included only one verse, but the prophet wanted to teach a bigger lesson, not just give a simple answer to the initial question. Zechariah wanted to remind his audience that their many years of fasting arose because of their sinful failure to keep the covenant stipulations and their unwillingness to listen to God's warnings of coming judgment through the prophets (7:4–14). These failures led to the defeat of Judah and Jerusalem, seventy years of exile, and many years of endless fasting on the (a) fourth; (b) fifth; (c) seventh; and (d) eleventh month (8:19). All these fasts involved the people of Judah lamenting and fasting over their past failures as well as feeling sorry for themselves (7:5–6). By emphasizing the terrible consequences for their failures, the prophet was able to contrast the negative results of their sinfulness with the alternative possibility of what could happen if the people would repent of their ethical failures, follow the ethical instructions God gave them, and respond positively to the message the Spirit gave to earlier prophets.

Although the past history of the nation was bleak, the people needed to remember that God still had a future hope for national revival and divine blessings (8:1–8). God had good plans for the nation (8:15), for he knew that these past days of fasting would end and the people would one day joyfully feast and rejoice in everything God would do for them (8:19; cf. Isa. 51:3). This was the sign of a restored relationship with God and a deep love for truth and peace. These people would not accept lies or deceptive teaching but would love to hear the true teachings of God.

8:20–23. At that time, many people from many nations would observe how the blessings of God would be poured out on his people, and they would want to experience a similar blessing from God. These people would come to seek God and request his favorable response to their petitions. Many people would join the returning Jews because they would know that God would be in their midst. This was consistent with the predictions of the prophet Isaiah who saw many nations gathering in Jerusalem in the last days to hear God teach (Isa. 4:2–3). People from Egypt and Assyria would worship God (Isa. 19:18–25; 11:16), and others as well from Pathros, Cush, Elam, Hamath, and the islands of the sea (Isa. 11:11). Isaiah 60:1–7 describes the coming of people from Midian, Ephah, Sheba, Kedar, and Nebaioth, while Isaiah 66:18–21 refers to people coming from all nations to see the glory of God, including people from Tubal, Javan, Tarshish, Put, and Lud.

THEOLOGICAL FOCUS
The exegetical idea (God's great zeal for his covenant people would result in God saving them, returning them to their land, giving them peace, and blessing them, so God's people should practice justice in all their relationships and turn their fasting days into days of feasting and rejoicing) leads to this theological focus: In the future, God's people will be restored and transformed, so they will celebrate rather than mourn.

Time of Fasting	Reason for Fasting	References
Fourth month	Fall of Jerusalem	2 Kings 25:3–7; Jeremiah 39:2–3
Fifth month	Burning of temple	2 Kings 25:8–9; Jeremiah 52:12–14
Seventh month	Death of Gedaliah	Jeremiah 41:1–3
Tenth month	Start of war on Jerusalem	2 Kings 25:1; Jeremiah 52:4

There are two major theological themes in this chapter. First, there is the theme of God's determined zeal to see the faithful city of Jerusalem restored so that God could dwell among his people. At that time, he would miraculously restore many people to Jerusalem, renew his covenant, and pour out his blessings on them. Although 7:1–8:23 begins and ends with questions about fasting, the prophet turned much of the discussion away from the ritual of fasting to the more fundamental questions about why they were fasting. Fasting can turn into self-pity, something filled with pessimism and hopelessness, and a religious ritual that does not admit the failures of the past. While fasting the people should recognize their failures and determine not to repeat that behavior, look optimistically to the future promises of God's blessings, and feast with joy because others would want to be a part of their joyous feasts.

Second, there is the theme of the nation's past ethical failures to treat others with justice, kindness, and compassion. Instead of loving their neighbor as themselves and maintaining the highest standards of honesty, some people oppressed the weakest members of society and took what little they had. Fasting was good, but it needed to be accompanied by a commitment to social justice and care for others, for this was an essential way that they demonstrated their faith in action.

PREACHING AND TEACHING STRATEGIES

Exegetical and Theological Synthesis

Zechariah 8:1–23 explains God's passionate desire for his people, evident in his jealousy for, defense of, and dwelling with them. But it also explains why the news of restoration and blessing was too good for some to believe. First, Zechariah's timeline looked far into the future. Second, Israel's recent memory recalled more struggle—draught, poverty, and battle—than triumph. Nevertheless, the prophet delivered the admonition to be strong, treat others ethically, and celebrate.

This tension between past trials and future hope colors much of the Scriptures. Many heroes of the faith overlooked loss, loneliness, failure, and oppression to gaze at a future hope. Abraham awaited a son (Gen. 17:9–22). Moses envisioned a capable successor (Num. 27:12–23). Naomi anticipated a kinsman redeemer (Ruth 3). David bided his time before becoming king (1 Sam. 18–31). And Jeremiah counted seventy years before exile would end (Jer. 25). Each of these figures suffered. Each of these figures endured through hope.

Furthermore, hope plays a prominent role in Israel's collective memory and imagination. Sabbath, annual feasts, and the year of Jubilee provided opportunities for Israel to eat, drink, and celebrate freedom as they reflected on God's past faithfulness (Lev. 25; Deut. 15–16). The Jewish people feasted (i.e., Purim) after their escape from Haman's evil plan to have them executed (Est. 8:15–17). Providing powerful imagery of a future banquet, the prophet Isaiah described God's people dining with neighbors, indulging on fine wine and succulent meat (Isa. 25:6–9). Zechariah and Zephaniah also foresaw a future where celebration would replace mourning (Zech. 8:1–23; Zeph. 3:14–20).

Preaching Idea

"Save the date" for an upcoming party with God.

Contemporary Connections

What does it mean?

What does it mean to "save the date" for an upcoming party with God? When will the party take place? What kind of party is it? Who is invited? As stated above, the party described will come in the far-off future. Moreover, it will be an inclusive event, the first wave of invitations extended to Israel, but God will reserve plenty of space for all peoples. God's enduring desire to bless all nations will come to fruition (Gen. 12:1–3; Ps. 67; Isa. 2:2; 49:6; 51:4; Zech. 14:16).

To "save the date" means accepting God's invitation into a life of future blessing. This requires trust and obedience. Certainly, a host of OT figures—Abraham, Joseph, Moses, Rahab, Joshua, Ruth, David, Abigail, Elijah, Josiah—modeled lives receptive to God's invitation, especially considering that many of them did not experience the fullness of God's promised blessings (Heb. 11). Their trust and obedience, though imperfect, is remarkable.

The same cannot be said generally for God's people. The prophets regularly questioned the genuineness of Israel's trust and obedience. Their persistent idolatry and rampant injustice told an alternative story. Zechariah railed against the people for both evils (Zech. 5:1–11; 7:8–10). Impatience with God's timing often drives us to live on our own terms. Because we want quick fixes and instant gratification, we buy on credit, feed our sexual impulses, and tell white lies to smooth over conflict. Ignoring biblical wisdom is an invitation to trouble. When we heed God's Word in daily matters, we prepare ourselves for the party to come.

Is it true?

Is it true we should "save the date" for an upcoming party with God? By all means! Most people have anticipated a birthday party, wedding ceremony, or Christmas celebration. We mark the calendar, prepare a side dish, and pick out a fancy outfit. We know the joy of looking forward to festive gatherings with loved ones. Thus, an eternal party overflowing with joy should appeal to all. But God knows not everyone will accept his invitation. Repeated references to a "remnant" imply an exclusive guest list—not an inclusive welcome—at God's upcoming party (2 Kings 19:30–31; Ezra 9:8; Isa. 10:20–22; Jer. 23:3; 31:7; Mic. 2:12; Zeph. 3:12; Zech. 8:6, 11, 12). Only those whose trust and obedience verify their invitation will join God's celebration.

Is the upcoming party exclusive for God's people? The peoples streaming to Jerusalem in Zechariah's prophecy would come from all directions to "seek the Lord's favor" (8:20–22). They acknowledged that he dwelt with his people (8:23). Their desire to meet with God and join the party gave evidence of their faith. Ruth is a prime example of an individual who accepted God's invitation even though she had no Jewish heritage (Ruth 1:16). God does not close his borders to people who trust and obey him. But not all peoples will place their faith in God. Plenty of people, from every tribe and tongue, will deny him and stand outside the party. Only people who evidence true faith will enter the party.

Now what?

Assuming we have received a "save the date" for God's upcoming party, how should we prepare? What do we do while we wait? How shall we keep our anticipation stoked? First, we must admit that waiting is difficult. Any child waiting to open Christmas presents, bride awaiting her wedding day, or couple counting down days for a planned vacation will testify to the pains of waiting. Some people grow numb and lose hope while they wait for God. Others increase their resolve, especially as they know their end date draws near. Unfortunately, we do not know when God's party begins.

Second, while we wait for God's party, he calls us to live like worthy guests. He exhorts us to live ethically, adorned in justice, love, courage, and honesty (Zech. 8:16–17). The current life functions as a dress rehearsal for life in the kingdom-to-come. In the Sermon on the Mount (Matt. 5–7), Jesus expanded upon Zechariah's brief exhortation. He commended righteousness, reconciliation, purity, fidelity, honesty, mercy, love, secret piety, trust, and selflessness. This list of virtues can feel overwhelming. But just like we put on one article of clothing at a time, it makes sense to identify a single virtue we can practice until we gain some mastery.

Finally, to keep our anticipation stoked, it is critical to remember God's past activities, his present work, and future promises. Reading his Word keeps our memory fresh. Praying gives us perspective for the day. Praise transports us from the here and now to the heavenly realm. In addition to practicing these spiritual disciplines—Scripture reading, prayer, and praise—we remain eager for the upcoming party with God when we extend the invitation to those who do not yet know him. Evangelism lets others know there is a God who offers them a "save the date" for a party more glorious than they could imagine.

Creativity in Presentation

As a pastor, I (Tim) receive many invitations to birthday parties, graduations, and weddings. They come in the mail with fancy stationary, ornate handwriting, lovely pictures, and a bold imperative at the top: "Save the Date." These mailings command our attention, build our anticipation, and beckon some response before the actual party. Consider describing the excitement you feel when you receive a "save the date" from a couple you long to see married. Project a recent "save the date" card from a couple (or several) in the church to make it relevant to your audience. Articulate the specific responses required by a "save the date": marking the calendar, sending an RSVP, making hotel reservations, buying a gift, or selecting a dress.

Other events you mark on the calendar with childlike anticipation can illustrate the point: family vacation, camping trip, movie premier, graduation, or birthday or retirement party. On the release date for the seventh and final Harry Potter book, *The Deathly Hallows* (2007), my wife and I traveled forty-five minutes to a Borders Bookstore (may it rest in peace) for a Harry Potter Party. Patrons dressed like their favorite characters. A protracted line snaked through the store. Live music boomed, interrupted by a worker announcing the time and awarding prizes. It was festive. People respond with similar fanfare to major sporting events, *Star Wars* premiers, and holiday parties. Whatever event has made you giddy, describe it in vivid detail before making the parallel to the God's upcoming party.

Perhaps the best way to illustrate the upcoming party with God and all peoples is to throw a party in conjunction with your message. Plan a potluck, carry-in, picnic, outdoor service, or feast to align with the message. Weeks in advance, send out "save the date" invitations to people in the congregation. Empower your best party planners to undertake the details: invitations, decorations, food, dessert, music, and dancing. Having the party at the church may be more manageable, but throwing it in a local park opens the door for inclusiveness. Who knows, perhaps a stranger with a gloomy view of God may stumble into the celebration, hear God's people enjoying good company, and decide to "save the date" to the everlasting, abounding, inclusive party with God. Case in point, Tony Campolo (1990, 3–9) shares a touching story of a public birthday party he organized for a prostitute. Its result: several outcasts put their trust in Jesus, becoming insiders at God's upcoming party.

Ultimately, the sermon should emphasize the following: In the future, all God's people will be restored, so they will celebrate rather than mourn. We should "save the date" for an upcoming party with God.

- "Save the date" because God wants us at his upcoming party (8:1–8).

- "Save the date" because God's party will be better than you can imagine (8:9–13).

- "Save the date" because God's party will have a great vibe (8:14–17).

- "Save the date" because God's party will have global variety (8:18–23).

DISCUSSION QUESTIONS

1. How does Zechariah 8:1–23 speak to God's national plan of redemption? How does it address his global plan of redemption?

2. What do Israel's annual feasts and weekly sabbaths suggest about God's character?

3. What are the ethical expectations for those who will enjoy God's blessed future?

4. What are effective ways to keep our anticipation of God's blessed future stoked?

5. Is it possible for God's people to be more inclusive without compromising our core beliefs? Explain.

FOR FURTHER READING

Campolo, T. 1990. *The Kingdom of God Is a Party: God's Radical Plan for His Family*. Dallas: Word.

GOD WILL DEFEAT JUDAH'S ENEMIES AND RESTORE THE NATION, BUT THE PEOPLE WILL REJECT THEIR SHEPHERD (9:1–11:17)

These chapters discuss God's restoration of his people, the defeat of their enemies, the rejection of their shepherd leader, and some initial steps to establishing the kingdom of God among his people. These themes are present in three preaching units, which were a great encouragement to the prophet's audience in Jerusalem. Although they faced many problems and had enemies that wanted to destroy them, God's message through Zechariah was intended to challenge them to trust God because God was promising to remove Judah's enemies and install a messianic King (9:1–17). They could trust God to provide strong shepherd leaders for the nation, to strengthen and empower his people to defend themselves against their enemies, and to restore the nation (10:1–11:3). But they should know that many would reject the good shepherd leader who would bring unity and grace that God could provide. Instead, they would follow the evil shepherd who would destroy God's flock (11:4–17). Now that the prophet had explained some problems they would face and the choices before them, it was imperative for the people to choose wisely, to follow the right leader, and to trust God and reject idolatry, for the consequences of these choices were very different. At the center of these promises was the hope of a righteous King who would bring salvation and peace (9:9–10).

Zechariah 9:1–11:17 can be divided into three preaching units: (1) God Will Remove Judah's Enemies and Install a Messianic King (9:1–17); (2) Trust God for Strong Leaders, Restoration, and the Defeat of Your Enemies (10:1–11:3); and (3) The Shepherds and the Sheep (11:4–17).

Zechariah 9:1–17

EXEGETICAL IDEA
After God had consumed the nations on the northern (Syria and Phoenicia) and western (Philistia) borders, he would raise up a righteous and humble messianic Savior-King who would restore a time of peace, joy, and freedom from foreign domination.

THEOLOGICAL FOCUS
God will restore his people by eliminating his enemies, installing a humble King, and defending his people.

PREACHING IDEA
God has a grand plan for lasting peace.

PREACHING POINTERS
While the first eight chapters of Zechariah centered around visions, the closing five chapters recounted God's words verbalized (i.e., oracles) by the prophet. Each oracle cycled through key themes of God's protection, justice, mercy, and Messiah. They looked beyond immediate circumstances to far-off realities. The first of these speeches predicted an era of peace, following the defeat of local and distant opponents. Zechariah spoke of deliverance and peace coming through a divinely appointed King to inspire his original audience to maintain their trust in God.

We do not live in peaceful times. Unrest defines Western politics, the global arms race, civil rights, economic inequality, climate change, gun violence, and the spread of disease. Two minutes of nightly news and social media may quicken our pulse and cloud our willingness to think critically. Our growing anxiety has led to myriad attempts to foster inner peace. Yoga, meditation, mindfulness, massage, daily affirmations, salt caves, and kombucha teas head the list. As effective as these interventions might feel in the short term, they cannot secure long-term peace. Global and spiritual unrest require divine intervention. This passage teaches us that God has a grand plan for lasting peace.

GOD WILL REMOVE JUDAH'S ENEMIES AND INSTALL A MESSIANIC KING (9:1–17)

LITERARY STRUCTURE AND THEMES (9:1–17)

In this unit, Zechariah opened his message with God defeating the surrounding nations (vv. 1–8). Once God defeated his enemies, a humble King would appear to reign in peace (vv. 9–10), and God's King would defend his people (vv. 11–17).

The major themes in this unit are the restoration of God's people and the coming of their promised messianic King.

- *God Will Defeat the Surrounding Nations (9:1–8)*
- *God Will Send a Humble King in a Time of Peace (9:9–10)*
- *God's Restoration and His Defense of His People (9:11–17)*

EXPOSITION

Although the prophet did not predict the date when these events would happen, and he did not name the king of the kingdom who would defeat some of the nations surrounding Judah, the following centuries brought about a decline in Persian power and a rise in the power of Greece, which is mentioned as a rising threat in 9:13. God would overpower the surrounding nations, protect his people, and send his humble King.

After God had consumed the nations on the northern (Syria and Phoenicia) and western (Philistia) borders, he would raise up a righteous and humble messianic Savior-King who would restore a time of peace, joy, and freedom from foreign domination.

God Will Defeat the Surrounding Nations (9:1–8)

God would defend his people by removing Judah's enemies.

9:1. Zechariah's "burdensome oracle" (מַשָּׂא) contains the difficult words of God shared throughout Zechariah 9–11 (Meyers and Meyers, 1993, 90) and not just the first paragraph (McComiskey, 1998, 1159). Although verbs need to be supplied in 9:1, it seems best to insert a future orientation indicating that God's word "will be" against the city called Hadrach (located south of Aleppo), and his resting place "will be" in Damascus, two important cities in Syria. Hadrach and Damascus are two important cities that were just outside of the northern borders of the former kingdom of Israel.[1] These sovereign acts of God would be so significant that they would attract the attention of all the tribes of Israel as well as all mankind.

9:2–4. When these events happened, many people from the nations would observe how God had gained control over the bordering cities of Hamath in northern Lebanon and the two important Phoenician coastal cities of Tyre and Sidon (9:2). These would be significant military events because the island fortification of Tyre seemed almost impregnable to attacks, and it was unusually rich because of Tyre's trade with other nations around the Mediterranean Sea (9:3,

---

1   The reader can locate Damascus on a map. Hadrach was probably located somewhere north and west of Damascus. Tyre is located on the Mediterranean coast.

cf. Ezek. 27–28). Wolters (2014, 265) thinks that this prophecy about the destruction of Tyre's "army" (9:4, חַיִל) and the loss of her wealth was fulfilled when Alexander the Great defeated Tyre in 332 B.C. (cf. Redditt, 1994, 110). Yet others reject this conclusion (Smith, 1984, 252) or favor an eschatological interpretation (Baldwin, 1972, 158; Merrill, 2003, 218). In this war context, the former argument makes sense for the order of events to be the historical defeat of Tyre's army, the removal of the people, the destruction of the city and its walls, and the burning of what remains (9:3–4) by Alexander's army. One could argue (as Baldwin, 1972, 160) that "wealth" would be an appropriate translation of חַיִל in light of the reference to gold and silver in 9:3, but it would be unlikely that the victorious army would throw Tyre's wealth of gold into the sea. Instead, they would collect all of Tyre's riches and take them for themselves as booty at the end of this war. When an army would defeat a city, it would often destroy parts of the walls of the city. Since this city was on an island, the most natural place to throw the stones from the walls of the city would be the sea. This would make it very difficult for any survivors to come back and rebuild this fortress.

WORD ANALYSIS: The term חַיִל can refer to (a) the "army" of a nation; (b) the "wealth, status" of a nation or person; or (c) the "power, strength of character" of someone. The related term חֵיל refers to the "ramparts, fortifications" of a city.

9:5–7a. The next verses describe God's judgment against several Philistine cities (Ashkelon, Gaza, Ekron, Gaza, and Ashkelon arranged in a chiastic order). In the time of Zechariah, some of these cities were already in ruins (Ekron was destroyed in the sixth century), though it is likely that people lived in and around these Philistine cites. The Philistine people in the vicinity of these cities would see what God's wrath would do to other cities to the north, and this would cause them great fear and agony because these people knew the same thing could happen to them. Consequently, their hope of escaping from a similar shameful destiny would wither away (9:5) (הוֹבִישׁ). This defeat was communicated by pointing to the loss of their king and citizens (9:5b), a sign of the exile of many Philistine people. Foreign people from another place would settle in their cities, ending all hope for reviving the proud Philistine nation (9:6). This defeat would enable God to bring an end to the loathsome religious practices of eating meat from unclean animals with blood still in it (9:7, cf. Isa. 65:4; 66:3; Ezek. 33:25–28). These divine judgments proved that human wisdom, excellent defenses, great wealth, and military strength would not prevent God from destroying his enemies. The biblical perspective was that one should not trust in military forces (Deut. 17:16; Ps. 20:7), riches (Deut. 17:17; Ps. 49:6; Jer. 9:23–24), or human leaders (Ps. 146:3). Instead, the future of every nation depended on their trust in God (Pss. 20:7b; 146:5; Prov. 3:4–5; Isa. 7:1–9).

WORD ANALYSIS: This word הוֹבִישׁ could derive from (a) בּוֹשׁ, "to put to shame, be ashamed," which would indicate that their hopes would turn to shame; or (b) יָבֵשׁ, "to wither," which would indicate that their hopes would dry up. Both interpretations indicate that the Philistines had no hope.

9:7b–8. Suddenly in the midst of these words of military victory over various enemies, Zechariah pointed to a future time when a remnant of the defeated Philistines would join and become a part of the religious community of Judah (cf. Zech. 2:11; 8:23), just like a remnant of the Jebusites (they founded the city of Jerusalem; Gen. 10:16; Judg. 1:21) who stayed in Jerusalem after David conquered it many centuries ago (2 Sam. 5:6–9). Zechariah recognized that there remained a remnant. Then God promised to dwell in Jerusalem and protect the temple and his people from domination by foreign armies that might pass through the land (9:8). This exclusive prediction that no oppressor would ever pass thorough the land means that all warfare had ended, so this promise must have eschatological significance (Klein, 2008, 269), for many oppressors attacked Jerusalem after 520 B.C.

Some suggest that the last clause in 9:8 could refer to what the prophet has seen (he is the "I") and now understood through this divine revelation (Larkin, 1994, 66; Wolters, 2014, 277), while others believe it could be an expression of assurance by God himself (he is the "I") that all these things would happen because God foreordained them, and his eyes would be watching over these predictions until all were fulfilled (Merrill, 2003, 217; McComiskey, 1998, 1163; Redditt, 1995, 114).

God Will Send a Humble King in a Time of Peace (9:9–10)

God's people would rejoice when they saw their righteous, humble, and victorious King.

9:9. In addition to the developments promised in 9:1–7, the prophet excitedly called on everyone in Zion to rejoice and shout exaltations because their long-expected messianic King would arrive in Zion (cf. Isa. 9:1–7; 52:7–10; Zeph. 3:14–15; Zech. 2:10). This announcement of a coming King would have been viewed as a reference to the earlier promise that God would raise up a Ruler from the line of Judah who would hold the king's scepter and crush his enemies (Gen. 49:10; Num. 24:17). This would be the Son in the Davidic covenant who would reign on the throne of David forever (2 Sam. 7:13–16; 1 Chron. 17:12–14). This King would rule in Zion and over all the nations on earth (Pss. 2:6–9; 72:1–11), and he would be the Wonderful Counselor, Mighty God, Eternal Father, and Prince of Peace who would reign on the throne of David forever (Isa. 9:5–7). He would be the righteous Davidic King (the "Branch") who would rule wisely, justly, and

with righteousness (Jer. 23:5–6), and the Davidic Servant who would reign as prince forever (Ezek. 37:24–25). Zechariah 9:9b characterizes this messianic King's reign as a time of justice and saving action (cf. Isa. 45:21), but this King would not present himself like the traditional, proud and victorious ancient Near Eastern warrior king. Instead, he would be a humble man (like the Servant in Isa. 52:13–53:12) and ride on a donkey, an image of a peaceful ruler. He would not follow the behavior patterns of a proud military hero by riding on a strong war horse.

Image of a Peaceful Ruler: There was a biblical tradition of some biblical rulers or their sons riding on a donkey. For example, the thirty sons of Jair (Judg. 10:4) and the seventy sons of Abdon (Judg. 12:14) rode on donkeys, plus David rode out of Jerusalem on a donkey (2 Sam. 16:2). Military commanders rode strong and fast horses, not slow and stubborn donkeys.

9:10. To further emphasize this Ruler's peaceful intentions, the prophet reported that when this King would reign, the instruments of war (the horse, chariot, and bow) would be eliminated from the nations (cf. Isa. 2:4; Mic. 5:10–11) because warfare would be a thing of the past. Once war was eliminated, nations would talk about peace because God would judge between the nations and would settle all disputes between them (Isa. 2:4). This new era of God's rule in his kingdom would impact all nations in all locations, even to the far ends of the earth. This implied the universal sovereignty of God's kingdom over the political situation of his own people (9:8b) as well as all the people of the whole earth ("to the ends of the earth"; 9:10b; cf. Pss. 2:8–9; 72:8–11). The international impact of the peaceful reign of the Messiah would remove oppression (9:8b), end all wars (9:10a), and insure peace (9:10b). The promises in 9:10 described eschatological times that would be fulfilled sometime in the future, not in the postexilic era.

God's Restoration and His Defense of His People (9:11–17)

Through God's sovereign power, the righteous and humble messianic Savior-King would defeat Judah's enemies.

9:11–12. Some have interpreted the divine promise to set the prisoners free, to cause them to come home to Jerusalem to their stronghold, and to give them a double blessing (9:11–12) to function as a call for the remaining Jewish exiles still in Babylon to come home to Jerusalem (Petersen, 1995, 61; Meyers and Meyers, 1993, 140; Boda, 2004, 419; Klein, 2008, 278). But Wolters (2014, 282) rightly objects to this conclusion because the Jewish people were never in prison while in Babylonian exile, and Cyrus's decree allowed any one of them to return home more than twenty years earlier (in 538 B.C.), so those still remaining in exile had nothing restraining them from returning to Zion. Thus because of God's previous covenant relationship and promises, sealed by blood (cf. Exod. 24:1–8), God would be faithful to his covenant and would deliver his people in Zion from whatever imprisoned or prevented their full spiritual restoration. Although the cistern without water is reminiscent of the Joseph story (Gen. 37:24), the interpretation of the imagery of Zechariah 9:11–12 should focus on the fact that the people had no hope, rather than on the specific illustration used to describe their hopelessness. The stronghold they would return to was Zion because that would be where God would "encamp, dwell" (9:8, חָנָה) and where the messianic King would come (9:10). Those who respond to this call would enjoy great blessings from God.

9:13. Judah and Ephraim (the northern tribes) are pictured here as God's arrow, bow, or sword, the instruments that God would use to bring about the defeat of his enemies, the Greeks (9:13). The Greeks were involved in Syro-Palestine life as early as 738 B.C. when a Greek official wrote to the Assyrian king Tiglath-pileser III. Some conclude that the Greeks were well known, for "from the seventh century B.C.E. on, Greek mercenaries, traders, and even tourists became significant in eastern Mediterranean life." (Hayes and Mandell, 1998, 20). During the time of Zechariah (by 516 B.C.), the Persian king Darius had already defeated the Greeks in Samos and the Hellespont, but he would later lose several battles (at Marathon and Salamis) against the Greeks. Thus, this reference to the defeat of the Greeks was not historically out of place in the time of Zechariah, so there was no need to view this verse as a later addition reflecting the Maccabean revolt against either the Greek Hellenization policies or the abominable religious practices of Antiochus IV Epiphanes. Wolters (2014, 289) views this as a prophecy about the future Maccabean Revolt in 164–167 B.C., but Merrill (2003, 229) understands this language as eschatological and as such would refer to God's defeat of whatever foreign power might oppose God's people in the future.

Maccabean Revolt: From 198–163 B.C. a series of Seleucids kings ruled over Judea. One of the most notorious of these kings was Antiochus IV Epiphanes who came to power in 175 B.C. To unify his kingdom Antiochus IV promoted a vigorous Hellenization program including the worship of himself in the form of the Olympian Zeus. The high priest Meneleus bribed the king so that he could be appointed to that position, then he and Antiochus plundered the temple of its treasures and ordered all Jewish worship to stop. This meant no Sabbath worship, no circumcision, plus he destroyed some Torah scrolls, and forced people to offer pigs on pagan altars and the main altar of burnt offerings at the temple. At that point, Jewish priest Mattathias defied the king's command, and he and his five sons and many other followers fled to the mountains to organize a revolt against these policies. Judas Maccabeus was put in charge of the forces of the resistance, and they defeated several military attempts to stop their revolt. Soon the Maccabees were able to restore normal Jewish worship, remove the altar of Zeus, and gain some freedom from outside control on December 14, 163 B.C.

9:14. At some point during these battles, God would reveal himself in all his glory in a theophany. The use of lightening as a symbol for God's arrow may represent the brightness, power, or swiftness of the destructive force of his attack.

Theophany: Judges 5:4–5, Psalm 68, and Habakkuk 3:3–4 each depict a theophany where God came from the south to do battle with his enemies, although the vision in Zechariah 6:1 pictures God's location between two mountains, which some locate in the north (Mount Zaphon). On many occasions God hurled his lightening (sometimes compared to arrows) on the earth (Pss. 18:13–14; 144:5; Hab. 3:4), plus lightening was sometimes connected to a theophany appearance (Exod. 19:16–20; Ps. 18:7–15). God was the Divine Warrior who would control all that happened on the battlefield. Using traditional holy war imagery (the sword, arrow, and trumpet), the prophet described how God would direct the outcome of the battle to gain victory over his enemies.

9:15–17. The results of these battles would be determined by God's action of shielding his people just like he protected his people in battles in the past. Twice God defeated the Philistines for David (1 Chron. 14:8–12; 14:13–17), and God protected Asa and defeated Zerah the Ethiopian (2 Chron. 14:9–14). In the time of Hezekiah, God defended Jerusalem from the much larger Assyrian army (more than 185,000 troops) under Sennacherib by sending an angel to kill most of the Assyrian army (Isa. 37:35–36). In the future victorious battle mentioned here, the defeat of the enemy is pictured as God's work, though the people would play a role in subduing the enemy troops and

destroying their instruments of war (slingshots in 9:15a). After the battle, the victorious troops would celebrate loudly in a victory banquet (9:15b; Baldwin, 1972, 170) that has so much wine that it would fill one of the large basins used to catch the blood of an animal brought for sacrificing. But make no mistake, these human troops would not win the battle; it would be the Lord who would save them in that eschatological battle (9:16). Why would God save them in this battle? Because these people were God's sheep; God viewed them as precious to him as the large and expensive sparkling jewels in a king's crown. God would value them as good and beautiful (9:17).

THEOLOGICAL FOCUS

The exegetical idea (after God had consumed the nations on the northern [Syria and Phoenicia] and western [Philistia] borders, he would raise up a righteous and humble messianic Savior-King who would restore a time of peace, joy, and freedom from foreign domination) leads to this theological focus: God will restore his people by eliminating his enemies, installing a humble King, and defending his people.

The restoration of God's people in Zion would be accomplished because of God's sovereign plan to remove some of the nations who lived on Israel's territory. Some nations would lose their land, but other people would join and be a part of the restored remnant of God's people. In God's own time, he would restore a just and humble messianic King in Jerusalem, and this would eventually lead to a time of peace and belonging to a king. These gracious and powerful promises became the basis for future generation to confidently put their trust in God.

PREACHING AND TEACHING STRATEGIES

Exegetical and Theological Synthesis
Zechariah 9:1–17 provides a geographical tour of Israel's enemies. Locally, he would

overthrow Tyre and three Philistine cities. Abroad, he would overpower the Greeks. None could withstand God's force. God's mode of war included three elements: his might, his king, and his people. He would outmuscle his enemies and surround Israel (9:4–8), send his conquering king (9:9–10), and use his people as an instrument of war (9:13) as he marched on foreign opponents (9:14). Reminiscent of Joshua's conquest of Canaan or David's defeat of Goliath, the battle belonged to the Lord, even if his people played a small part in the fight.

This idea of instrumentality—whether going to war or giving witness—describes God's work through human agents since the dawn of time. He designed humans to bear his image: ruling, subduing, tending, and caring for creation (Gen. 1:26–28; 2:7). He sent Abram to serve as a blessing to the nations (Gen. 12:1–3). He called Israel to represent him as a royal priesthood (Exod. 19:5–6). Israel's commission to live as a "light to the nations" (Isa. 42:6; 49:6; 60:3) would see fulfillment in the last days' feasts described in Zechariah (Zech. 8:13, 20, 22–23; 14:16–18).

God's people today function as his divine instrument. We are meant to bear witness to his presence by holy, honest, compassionate interaction with our neighbors (Exod. 19:5–6; cf. 1 Peter 2:9). We are empowered by his Spirit to use the gifts he has distributed to each member (Joel 2:28–29; cf. 1 Cor. 12). We are beacons of hope through whom the good news of deliverance shines (Isa. 42:6; 49:6; cf. Matt. 5:14–16). We are ministers of reconciliation and ambassadors of the divine King, bringing the message of peace with God to all peoples (Isa. 52:7; Nah. 1:15). Victory, glory, and praise belong to God, but as his instruments, we help him achieve his ends.

Preaching Idea
God has a grand plan for lasting peace.

Contemporary Connections

What does it mean?
What does it mean that God has a grand plan for lasting peace? What is lasting peace? In the immediate context of the speech, lasting peace envisions the elimination of enemies both near and far. A day will come when God's people will live without rivals or oppressors. God will overthrow them. His people will experience rest. More broadly, the idea of lasting peace includes full lives, rich harvests, harmony with neighbors, productive labor, and intimacy with God (e.g., Isa. 11:1–9). In other words, lasting peace is holistic.

Furthermore, lasting peace should also touch our relationships and inner lives, nurturing in God's people good theology, rising confidence, diminishing anxiety, and resolve in spiritual warfare. When we recognize God as a peacemaker, we strive to live at peace with others whenever possible (Rom. 12:18). When we remember that God's serves as our defender, we trust him to uphold our reputation when falsely accused. When we recall God's role as judge, we resist the urge to publicize our condemnation of others, leaving it to God to give the verdict.

And what does God's grand plan entail? Zechariah mentioned a royal figure integral to establishing lasting peace (Zech. 9:9–10). For his audience, the humble king aligned with other images of a promised leader for Israel: Lion of Judah (Gen. 49:9–10), Star of Jacob (Num. 24:17), the Son of David (2 Sam. 7:8–16), and suffering Servant (Isa. 52:13–53:12). This messianic figure claimed global authority (Pss. 2:8–9; 72:8–11) and special kinship with God (Pss. 2:6–7; 110:1; Isa. 9:5–7), but according to Zechariah's description, he would lead with humility rather than a strong fist. In the NT, Jesus embodied these roles, including his iconic entrance into Jerusalem, acting out Zechariah's prophetic speech by his unassuming transport on a donkey. Although angels shouted, "Peace on earth" (Luke 2:14) at his birth, Jesus admitted that peace, in a civic sense, was not the goal of his first advent (Matt. 10:34).

Is it true?

Is it true that God has a grand plan for lasting peace? He certainly does. However, the grand plan will not be fully realized until God's humble king comes at the climax of history. National strife, social injustice, and physical ailments will remain until God makes all things new (Isa. 65:17–25; Mic. 4:1–5). As long as sinful people inhabit a fallen world, conflict will ensue.

But can we experience lasting peace today? We can experience glimpses of lasting peace today. Sadly, our experience of peace—internal and external—often feels fleeting. Peace treaties among warring nations may provide temporary peace, but wars often resume (e.g., World War II). Marital counseling may provide temporary peace for conflicted couples, but their fights often resurface. Accountability groups may provide temporary peace for the alcoholic, but relapses are common. Sadly, human attempts at lasting peace—from mediation to medication to meditation—do not last.

Fortunately, lasting peace with God is available. He is a promise-keeping, peace-making, merciful, and loving defender of his people. We can apprehend a lasting sense of peace by knowing that God rules the world (Exod. 15:16; 1 Chron. 16:31; Isa. 52:7; 66:1–2; Pss. 93:1; 97:1; 99:1), forgives our sin (Num. 6:24–26; Pss. 51; 103; Isa. 1:18; Ezek. 37:25–27; Mic. 7:18–20), and provides guidance for establishing peaceful community (Exod. 20:8–17; Ps. 133; Jer. 29:7). Lasting peace with God is a grand reality whether a person feels it or not.

Now what?

How do we respond to the short-term nature of peace today? Initially, we imitate the humble king of Zechariah's speech. Peacemaking is one of the distinguishing virtues of God's people (Gal. 5:22). Making peace means extending mercy toward people who have offended us, forgiveness toward those who ask, and working to see others thrive. Like Aaron, we can pray for others to experience God's peace (Num. 6:24–26). Like Jeremiah's exhortation, we can "seek the peace of the city" (Jer. 29:7). While we may not be able to secure peace in every interpersonal or national conflict, God's people should, as much as possible, live at peace (Rom. 12:18).

Ultimately, we await the fulfillment of God's grand plan. He works on a different timeline than we do. Our earthly trials will someday end. Our interpersonal conflicts will someday resolve. Our personal suffering will someday abate. Fixating on our current woes and inability to solve them wearies us. In our pursuit of short-term peace, we must remember its fullness commences when the messiah comes at the climax of history. In the meantime, we may enjoy a foretaste of mercy, forgiveness, reconciliation, and healing. We may enjoy peace with God. And this enjoyment climaxes in public proclamation: "God's humble king is coming! The humble king reigns! The humble king will bring lasting peace!" This is good news (Isa. 52:7).

Creativity in Presentation
Military conflict often sparks both strong, anti-war sentiments and profound pleas for peace. Some of the loudest opponents to the Vietnam War came through musicians protesting bloodshed and championing peace. John Lennon's "Give Peace a Chance" heads the lists of memorable tunes decrying war in the name of peace. Consider playing this song in the message to surface the emotions wrapped around war and peace. During the war in Iraq, Andrew White, an Anglican priest in Bagdad, did not abandoned his parish but worked for reconciliation among rival Islamic groups. He earned the moniker "Vicar of Bagdad" for his commitment

to peace. A three-part series by the same title is posted on YouTube by VICE Media.[2] Without getting too political, you might emphasize the profound desire for peace without glossing over the costliness of peace.

In *Kung Fu Panda 2* (2011, directed by Jennifer Yuh Nelson), bad dreams haunt the main character, Po (voiced by Jack Black). His nightmares replay a childhood tragedy where he was separated from his birthparents. As Po wrestles internally to make sense of his past, an old enemy, Lord Shen (voiced by Gary Oldman), arises with new weaponry (canons) to put China under his thumb. In a climactic scene (approximately three minutes long), Po settles the score with Lord Shen and his past by finding "inner peace." This peace helps him stop a foe and silence his doubts. Consider playing this clip (2:43 on YouTube), followed by the comment: "But Po's peace is short-lived. How do I know? There's a *Kung Fu Panda 3* (and more to come) with new enemies and new doubts. Self-directed inner peace can only take us so far."

A story of interpersonal conflict may help people from the church resonate with their need for lasting peace. While you might guard the details to preserve some dignity, most families provide a wealth of materials to draw from. I (Tim) have recently faced unrest and brokenness in my extended family. A death and remarriage situation stirred up discord. It came to a head at a recent vacation where we raised our voices, pointed fingers, and aired unfiltered feelings. The fallout has been months of separation and some family counseling. We are a group of eight, God-fearing adults who are licking our wounds and grasping for peace. Although we are learning communication skills for short-term peace, we may not experience full restoration until the humble king comes at the climax of history. We need God to fulfill his grand plan

to experience full healing. You might share your own conflict-resolution story to highlight the challenge of peacemaking.

Creative elements aside, the sermon should emphasize this: God will restore his people by eliminating his enemies, installing a humble King, and defending his people. God has a grand plan for lasting peace.

- In God's grand plan, our conflict with others won't last (9:1–8).

- In God's grand plan, a humble King ensures lasting peace (9:9–10).

- In God's grand plan, our security is his priority (9:11–17).

---

2   VICE Staff, "The Vicar of Baghdad," *VICE* (blog), July 1, 2014, https://www.vice.com/en_us/article/znwqw4/the-vicar-of-baghdad-part-1-484. For the first of this three-part series on YouTube, see *The Vicar of Baghdad*, VICE Special (VICE Media, 2014), https://www.youtube.com/watch?v=YnLzdakPXYY.

DISCUSSION QUESTIONS

1. Who were the enemies of God's people in Zechariah's day? What surprises you about the list of named opponents in 9:1–18?

2. How did God deal with his enemies in the OT? What role did Israel play in warfare?

3. What does the prophecy of Zechariah 9:9–10 refer to? What evidence is there that this prophecy was not fulfilled completely at Jesus's first coming?

4. How is "inner peace" different than God's lasting peace? How does our culture train us to grasp for "inner peace"? Be specific.

5. What are ways we currently experience God's peace?

Zechariah 10:1–11:3

EXEGETICAL IDEA

Although problems abound all around, God's people must depend on him (not false gods or godless leaders), follow God's leader, and believe God's promises to restore his people and defeat their enemies.

THEOLOGICAL FOCUS

Trust God in difficult times, for he will strengthen his people as he has promised.

PREACHING IDEA

It's best to bank on God in bad circumstances.

PREACHING POINTERS

Circumstances did not look promising in Zechariah's day. Lack of rain led to poor vegetation. Lack of leadership led to religious confusion, vulnerability to enemies, and geographical displacement. But in the this passage, God helped Zechariah look beyond bad circumstances. The prophet spoke of God—mighty and compassionate, jealous and angry—gathering his people and empowering them against their enemies. Neither dead idols nor empty rituals could guarantee them victory; God would win their battles. This message was meant to restore the joy and confidence of Zechariah's original audience.

Bad circumstances plague God's people today. Messages about global poverty, political strife, untreatable diseases, unhealthy foods, economic disparity, and racial tensions abound. Personal struggles with mental illness, high blood pressure, career disappointment, theological confusion, and family dysfunction disrupt our lives. And churches are hindered by untrustworthy leaders, biblical illiteracy, laws affecting religious freedom, and rising tides of disaffecting believers. Rather than trusting God to remedy bad circumstances, we have learned to bank on common sense, slick marketing, church programs, technical savvy, political strategy, social networks, and personal abilities. In other words, we trust our flawed systems and limited resources to turn our bad circumstances into bright outcomes. This passage reminds us that it's best to bank on God in bad circumstances.

TRUST GOD FOR STRONG LEADERS, RESTORATION, AND THE DEFEAT OF YOUR ENEMIES (10:1–11:3)

LITERARY STRUCTURE AND THEMES (10:1–11:3)

Zechariah 10:1–11:3 opens with God's rejection of Judah's evil leaders (10:1–3a). After removing Judah's evil leaders, he would provide strong leaders (10:3b–7) and then gather his people from the nations (10:8–12). Zechariah closed with the defeated nations lamenting their ruined condition (11:1–3). The major theme is that God's people should have confidence in God's plans and the leader he would provide, for any other path would disappoint and bring sorrow.

- *God Rejects Judah's Evil Leaders and Will Give Them a New Leader (10:1–7)*
- *God Will Gather His People from the Nations (10:8–12)*
- *The Defeated Nations Will Lament (11:1–3)*

EXPOSITION

The leaders in the Persian capital, in the province Beyond the River, in Samaria, and in Jerusalem were not always ready to resolve the challenges they faced. Some Persian officials were helpful and cooperative (Cyrus initially in Ezra 1, but not in Ezra 4:4–5). Darius supported the building of the temple in Ezra 6, but Tattenai the government official remained neutral (Ezra 5). Even Joshua the high priest was not perfect and Zerubbabel needed encouragement from time to time (Zech. 3–4). Since we do not know the exact date of the message in Zechariah 9–14, it is impossible to pinpoint the identity of all the problematic leaders Zechariah described. Some of them trusted in diviners and had idols (Zech. 10:2), some were Assyrians and Egyptians (Zech. 10:11), and some of them were rulers. It is tempting to point to the bad leader that arose during the intertestamental period, but the prophet was more concerning with warning people about certain types of people rather than naming names and predicting an exact date. To counter the leaders that were leading his people astray, God would provide his people with capable godly leaders and lay low the powerful nations and their proud leaders.

God Rejects Judah's Evil Leaders and Will Give Them a New Leader (10:1–7)

The evil leaders that followed idolatrous ways did not protect God's people, so God would remove them and restore the strength of the nation.

10:1. The prophet Zechariah addressed the practical questions about who to trust as a leader. Since some political and spiritual leaders would lead people away from God, it was important to distinguish between the godly and ungodly leaders. From their past history, the audience knew that all they needed to do was to ask God in faith and he would identify who was to be anointed as their next king. Another example of this trust in God was important for farmers. If the people would pray for God to send the spring rain (sometimes called the later rain; Deut. 11:13–15) that usually came in March and April, he would send them rain showers that would cause their crops to grow.

The Early and Later Rain: Little to no rain falls in Israel from May to September, but there are two seasons of rain between October to April. Usually the "former rain" comes sporadically in mid-October or early November, and this is the time when farmers plough and plant seeds (wheat and barley) in the ground. Later in February and April, the heavier "later rains" fall to help the crops mature before harvest. Merrill (2003, 236) notes that the term "latter rain" is used in Joel 2:21–25 to describe an eschatological time when God would give much rain and increase the fertility of the land. The reference in Zechariah 10:1–2 must refer to an evil time when people were not asking rain from God. Instead, they were depending on pagan sources and practices for spiritual advice and their material needs.

Praying for rain was worthwhile because God had the power to control the storm clouds as well as the lightning and thunder (Job 28:26; 37:6, 11–12), but his granting of moisture was connected to the faith and faithfulness of his people (1 Kings 17:1; 18:41–45; Amos 4:7–8). Long ago, Moses told the nation that if the people would love God, follow his instructions, and faithfully serve him, God would send them the rain they needed for their grain fields, vineyards, and grass for their cattle (Deut. 11:13–14). Some chapters later in the covenant blessings, God promised to give his faithful people rain (28:11–12), but if they did not obey God, the curse of no rain would fall on the nation (28:23–24). Hundreds of years later, the prophet Jeremiah understood that God would bless his people with rain (Jer. 5:24), and he taught the people that Judah's harlotry would cause God to withhold the spring rain (3:2–3). He argued that idols were not able to send rain (14:22). Only God sends the rain. This biblical teaching was in direct contradiction to the pagan claims that Baal was the god of the thunderstorm who provided rain and fertility to the land (cf. 1 Kings 18), so the people had to choose which god/God they would follow. The stories in Kings

and Chronicles show that the nations of Judah and Israel frequently followed Baalism (in the reign of Ahab and Jezebel, Ahaz, Athaliah, and Manasseh) rather than the God of Israel. These failures lead to the exile of the nations.

10:2. Instead of asking something from God, some people of Judah would consult spiritual leaders from pagan cults for spiritual advice. These pagan practices included relying on the "teraphim" for wisdom about a decision they needed to make. The meaning of "teraphim" (תְּרָפִים) is uncertain. Commentators have suggested four different roots for teraphim: "old rags," "interpreters" that were used to understand dreams, "demon spirits," and "healer, protectors" (Hamilton, 1995, 294), but none of these provide much help in understanding the teraphim. These images were considered to be "gods" by Laban (Gen. 19:30) and were used for divination concerning future events in Judges 17:5 and 18:5, but a Nuzi document portrayed these idols as objects that determined inheritance rights. Some believe that the teraphim "were figurines representing a family's dead ancestors, and were used in necromancy to convey messages from the realm of the dead" (Meyers and Meyers, 1993, 186–87; Wolters, 2014, 310).

Nuzi Tablets: The ancient city of Nuzi, located not far off the Tigris River in Babylon, was excavated beginning in 1925. Archaeologists found about five thousand tablets, mostly about legal and business issues (*ANET*, 219–20), but there are some that illustrate social customs during the patriarchal period. In the OT, the teraphim appear to be small images of a god in human shape (in Genesis 31:19, Rachel hid them by sitting on them), though the one in 1 Samuel 19:13 must have been quite large, for one was about the size of a man. Rachel's stealing of the teraphim has suggested that these objects may have had something to do with inheritance rights, and a document from Nuzi (*ANET*, 219–20) has been used to support this theory, but this support is of limited value because the Nuzi material is from a different culture and hundreds of years earlier than Zechariah.

Such competing evidence could suggest that teraphim had different uses in different cultures and that their use probably changed over time. There are competing opinions about the size, shape, status, and significance of the teraphim. It would appear from Genesis 31:19–35 that Rachel's ability to hide the teraphim from her father by sitting on them required that these were small images. While this small size may be required in Rachel's case, David's wife Michal must have put a much larger teraphim in her bed to represent David in 1 Samuel 19:11–17. The act of consulting these objects by the king of Babylon in Ezekiel 21:21 was in a setting where the king needed to decide between two paths. So, he used divination, the examination of the liver of an animal, and information from the teraphim to help him decide what to do. This account did not explain exactly how the teraphim were used or manipulated to provide the information needed to make this decision.

TRANSLATION ANALYSIS: 10:2, "teraphim" (תְּרָפִים)

NASB[95]: "For the teraphim speak iniquity, and the diviners see lying visions."

NIV[84]: "The idols speak deceitfully; diviners see visions that lie."

HCSB: "For the idols speak falsehood, and the diviners see illusions."

NKJV: "For the idols speak delusion; the diviners envision lies."

NRSV: "For the teraphim utter nonsense, and the diviners see lies."

Those that do not translate or interpret "teraphim" do not help the modern reader understand the ancient culture in which this term was used or what the author was trying to communicate.

In addition to using the teraphim, people used other types of divination that produced a deceitful or false view of reality. This divination might include the examination of some part of the entrails of an animal. If the heart was normal, that would imply one answer (yes); but if there was some abnormality, then that would communicate the opposite answer (no). Similar answers could be communicated by an astrologer based on his interpretation of the relationship between the moon and a planet, or a necromancer might communicate with the dead (cf. King Saul and the witch at Endor in 1 Samuel 28). These common methods of communicating with the divine in various pagan religions were forbidden in the Pentateuch (Lev. 19:26; Deut. 18:10–14), and Jeremiah strongly condemned the diviners and false prophets in his day, for they did not communicate what God said but deceived people into believing lies (cf. Jer. 23:9–40).

Zechariah admonished people to think about the value of the predictions gained from these pagan methods of communicating with supernatural powers. The results of such pagan inquiries were absolutely worthless because they produced deceitful advice, gave false information, and offered useless and baseless comfort to those who heard them. Such statements delegitimized these practices and warned people that it would be foolish to believe anything these methods produced. Since many people did use these pagan methods of finding the will of the gods, the people ended up aimlessly walking around like sheep that were "terrified" (עָנָה) because they had no reliable shepherd (10:2b). The term "shepherd" likely functions as a metaphor for a royal figure (Ezek. 34). So, the evil practices described in 10:2 had a negative effect on God's sheep because many shepherd kings (especially in the northern ten tribes of Israel) did not root out these evil practices, and some like Ahab in Israel, plus Ahaz, and Manasseh in Judah, actually promoted these pagan practice (Klein, 2008, 290).

10:3a. God's anger was particularly against the shepherds, the godless kings, who promoted these practices in Judah and Israel. The prophet Jeremiah complained about the same problem of evil shepherds (referring to Jehoiakim, Coniah, and Zedekiah in Jeremiah 22:18, 24; 23:1–2) not taking care of the flock. Ezekiel 34 and Zechariah 11 also castigate the evil shepherds for not leading the flock of God's people in an acceptable manner. The negative leadership of these kings and their officials was explained by comparing the officials to male goats who led the sheep / the nation astray. God's plan was to destroy these shepherd leaders because they acted like aggressive and proud male goats that did not take care of God's flock.

10:3b. At this point the prophet turned from condemnation of past worthless leaders to a message of hope for the future because God would give them good leaders to strengthen Judah (10:3b–6) and Ephraim (10:7). In the place of these shepherd kings, male goats, diviners, and pagan religious leaders, God would provide new leadership for Judah. Then his people would symbolically function as a majestic horse fit for battle (10:3b). This represented an amazing transformation of the people of Judah from weak sheep to becoming a metaphorical strong war horse. This is somewhat similar to the war imagery used in Zechariah 9:13 where Judah and Ephraim are pictured as a bow and arrow. In both cases, God would use his people to accomplish the military defeat of his enemies.

10:4. Additional metaphors in 10:4 describe Judah as a "corner, cornerstone" (פִּנָּה), a reference to a solid corner foundation for a building, but also a leader who provided a solid foundation for his people. Another metaphorical description of Judah is a "tent peg" (יָתֵר), which was a post that was pounded into the ground to keep a tent from blowing over (Isa. 54:2), or it could refer to a peg that was driven into a wall so that objects could be hung on it (Isa. 22:23,

25). This figure of speech was used in Isaiah as a symbol of a leader, so it fits with the first metaphor of a cornerstone. This peg symbolized something solid that others could depend on (Baldwin, 1972, 174). Another metaphor for Judah was a bow used in battle (10:4c), which was already mentioned in Zechariah 9:13, but here this word described what this leader would do with this weapon. Finally, he announced that the people would go out (probably to war) together with their trustworthy "commander" or "ruler" (נוֹגֵשׂ).

WORD ANALYSIS: This word פִּנָּה can refer to (a) the "corner" of an object (a water cart in 1 Kings 7:34, an altar in Exodus 27:2, a roof in Proverbs 7:12, or a house in Job 1:19), or something at the "corner" of a wall (Zeph. 1:16) or street (2 Chron. 28:24); (b) a foundation "corner" stone of a building (Ps. 118:22; Jer. 51:26) or the earth (Job 38:9); or (c) a symbol/metaphor of a leader (or the Messiah) who functions like a solid "corner" stone for society (Judg. 20:2; 1 Sam. 14:38; Isa. 19:13; Zech. 10:4).

Taken together with 10:3b (the mighty war horse) and the battle imagery of the following verse (10:5), Zechariah 10:4 refers to God giving the nation of Judah a leader who would lead them in this battle. Many commentators (e.g., the Aramaic Targum, Klein, 2008, 293–94; Merrill, 2003, 239–40; Curtis, 2006, 191; Smith, 1984, 265) find in these images a messianic reference based on the fact that this leader would come from Judah, which fits the promise in Genesis 49:10 that the future ruler would come from the tribe of Judah. The references to the people rejecting the cornerstone in Psalm 118:22 and Isaiah 28:16 were interpreted in the NT to be prophetic references to Jesus (Matt. 21:42; Mark 12:10–11; Luke 20:17; Acts 4:11; 1 Peter 2:6–7; cf. Bock, 2012, 331–458). Finally, Zechariah 9:9–10 portrays the Messiah fighting in battle just like 10:4–7. Although these metaphors were not the typical messianic images used in messianic prophecies throughout the prophets, they do fit the ideas in Zechariah 9:10a and the eschatological focus of the rest of this chapter (but Redditt [2012, 63] rejects the messianic interpretation). The rest of the chapter will deal more with what God (not the Messiah) would do for and through his people to establish his kingdom on earth.

10:5. Earlier in 10:3b, God promised to make the people of Judah like "mighty men" (גִּבּוֹר), and this is repeated again in 10:5a and 7a. This victory over their enemy was graphically described as an act of "treading" or "trampling" (בּוּס) their enemies into the mud (cf. Mic. 7:10b) as the army moved forward to fight additional troops. They would be successful in the battle because God would be with them, just as Zechariah 9:14–15 promised. This victory by God's people would overpower the foot soldiers as well as the fast-moving cavalry, producing a complete and shameful defeat of this future enemy. This would happen because God would give "great strength, a warrior's strength" (גֶּבֶר) to the people from Judah and even save people from the northern ten tribes (symbolized by Joseph).

10:6–7. This restoration of the whole nation would not be something they deserve, but it would be totally dependent on the compassionate grace of God (10:6). They deserved rejection, destruction, and exile and that was what they got, but in this new day God would treat them as his children (their past rejection would be forgotten) and bring them back to their land. At that time, they would ask God for things (10:1), and he would compassionately answer them with his blessings (10:6b). In order to further emphasize the amazing things that would happen at that time of restoration, Zechariah reaffirmed that the northern nation of Ephraim would be a "mighty warrior" (גִּבּוֹר), and the people would rejoice in the Lord because he would restore the nation (10:7). Although this great victory was not compared in 10:7 to God's

earlier defeat of the mighty Egyptians army in Exodus 14–15, in both cases God's presence and power were the factors that determined who would be victorious.

God Will Gather His People from the Nations (10:8–12)
Earlier God exiled the nation, but now he would bring them back to their land.

10:8–9. God's restoration of his people would involve a gathering (10:8, 10) of thousands of them from the nations where they were scattered (lit., "sown" זֶרַע) when a stronger nation (Assyria) defeated Israel in 722 B.C. (10:9a). At just the right time, God would signal to them (lit., "whistle"; cf. Judg. 5:16). This would be an act of divine redemption (10:8) when God would cause his people to remember his past redemption from Egypt and yearn for him (10:9). Hill (2008b, 579) notes that whistling has a negative tone elsewhere, but here it is used in a positive way. When a shepherd whistled for his sheep to come, it was not negative (Judg. 5:16).

10:10. In response, God would gather his people from Ephraim back into their former land (to places like Gilead and Lebanon), specifically he would gather those still living in Egypt and Assyria. Lebanon was considered part of the Promised Land in Deuteronomy 3:25, "the land beyond the Jordan, the hill country, and Lebanon" (cf. Deut. 11:24; 1 Kings 9:19). The last phrase in 10:10 could be translated "he will not find them," but most have translated this something like "and there will not be room enough for them." The idea of "room" (lit., "enough," מָצָא) is implied in the latter translation based on the context of many new people coming into the land. Since the population of Judah was quite limited after the exile (Ezra 2:64–67) and only a few were from Ephraim, this prophecy must be referring to a much greater eschatological multiplication of the people in their land.

10:11–12. In order to accomplish this restoration of the people back into their land, God would go before his people as they attempt to return. Using imagery of the first exodus experience, God would strike the sea to make a path (as in Exodus 14) for his people or dry up the river (as in Joshua 3), or humiliate the proud Assyrians (as God did when an angel killed 185,000 Assyrian troops in Isaiah 37:36). The power of God would strengthen his people as they returned home proudly, identifying themselves with the name of their powerful and compassionate God.

The Defeated Nations Will Lament (11:1–3)
The military defeat of the foreign nations would bring great mourning.

11:1. In 11:1–3, the mood changes from the promises of hope, being gathered back to the land, God's redemption of the people, and his strengthening (10:8–12) to a setting in which there is hopelessness and lamenting by the leaders of various nations. On the literal level, the prophet pictured a disastrous fire, fallen trees, destruction, wailing, and a ruined pastureland. These factors, along with the imperative exhortation to "wail" demonstrate that 11:1–3 is a call to lament, which would be consistent with the announcement of the end of the "glory" or "pride" (גָּאוֹן) of Assyria and the removal of the ruler in Egypt (10:11). A key to understanding and interpreting these images would be to look at the use of similar symbolic language in other prophetic books. For example, in Ezekiel 31 Assyria was called a cedar from Lebanon (31:3–9) that became greater than all the other trees (nations) in the forest, but its pride caused God to have other nations cut down this tree (Ezek. 31:11–17). In Isaiah 10:33–34, the prophet described God's judgment of Assyria as the cutting down of a great forest, and he ended the oracle referring to this event as "Lebanon will fall" (G. V. Smith, 2007, 266). Although Merrill (2003, 250) concludes that both the trees and the

shepherds were symbols that pointed to kings (cf. Dan. 4:20–23), most other prophets used trees as a symbol for a nation, and a shepherd as a metaphor for a king (in Nahum 3:18, the leaders of Assyria are called shepherds). Thus, Zechariah was assuring his Jewish audience of God's commitment to destroy the surrounding nations (Egypt and Assyria in 10:11) with this call for the nations and their kings to lament the approaching destruction. Zechariah 10:11 informs the reader that this would be an act of God, but the focus of 11:1–3 is on the devastating effects of this destruction.

11:2–3. These nations would wail and lament because all the glorious things in Egypt and Assyria (10:11) would be destroyed. Even their powerful king (the shepherds of 11:3) would wail in despair because the glory of their palaces, temples, monuments, and walled cities, which brought them great pride, would lie in ruins. It is possible that the thoughts in 11:3 were influenced by the similar statements in Jeremiah 25:34–36, for both passages assert God's sovereign authority over the nation and his ability to destroy the kings of other nations.

THEOLOGICAL FOCUS
The exegetical idea (although problems abound all around, God's people must depend on him [not false gods or godless leaders], follow God's leader, and believe God's promises to restore his people and defeat their enemies) leads to this theological focus: Trust God in difficult times, for he will strengthen his people as he has promised.

Zechariah's message offered both a challenge as well as words of hope that would give his audience confidence in God's plans for the future. The first challenge was to trust God for what they needed and not let themselves be deceived by false or deceptive information from sources that did not depend on God. Second, they needed to trust God to remove the useless kings and deceptive officials and strengthen the nation by providing a solid godly leader they could depend on. Third, these changes would result in the transformation of the nation into a mighty war machine that God would use to destroy their enemies. Fourth, at that time God would redeem his people, but the nations would lament when they were defeated. The audience must trust God to accomplish his plans.

PREACHING AND TEACHING STRATEGIES

Exegetical and Theological Synthesis
Zechariah 10:1–11:3 reiterates the power, compassion, and faithfulness of God in his plan to restore his people. He heard prayers, controlled weather, kept covenant, empowered the nation, and overthrew its enemies. While God's timeline did not always mesh with his people's expectations—he often spoke of eschatological events, not immanent ones—he revealed his far-off purposes to instill hope. Additionally, his use of symbolism (e.g., shepherds, cornerstone, fallen trees) and exodus imagery (e.g., Egypt, pass through the sea) wove Israel's past and future into a single story of redemption.

As the nation's history unfolded, Israel's constant stumbling blocks were syncretism and idolatry. Often spurred by the intermingling with pagan neighbors, God's people set up altars, Asherah poles, and shrines; they consulted mediums—all deplorable practices in God's eyes (Exod. 20:4–6; Deut. 12:3; 1 Kings 14:15). Good kings rid the land of these practices (e.g., Josiah; 2 Chron. 34:3). Bad kings left them or allowed them to multiply (e.g. Manasseh; 2 Chron. 33:3). Like sheep, the people followed the lead of their kings, underscoring the need for a righteous ruler (Ps. 72).

But even God-fearing kings posed a problem, for God's people quickly substituted the human representative for the divine king. We easily put our confidence in human leaders, horse-driven chariots, and imposing towers rather than the Lord of Hosts to protect us (Ps.

20:7; Isa. 31:1). We bank on religious laurels, superstitions, and signs for guidance rather than God-with-us (Zech. 10:2). Sadly, misplaced faith and pride are perennial problems. The remedy is forsaking idols and focusing on God (Jer. 9:23–24).

Preaching Idea
It's best to bank on God in bad circumstances.

Contemporary Connections

What does it mean?
What does it mean that it's best to bank on God in bad circumstances? To bank on God is to trust him to protect, empower, keep his promises, and abide with his people. We accept no substitutes. And we face myriad bad circumstances today: physical ailments and emotional trauma, financial turmoil and relational challenges, cultural pressures and environmental issues. Life is a series of misfortunes. Job expressed his trust in God despite his personal losses (Job 13:15). David chronicled his trust in God despite threats on his life (Pss. 3, 16, 23, 62). Hezekiah trusted God despite taunts from Assyria (2 Kings 18:15; Isa. 37–38). These men demonstrated the value of banking on God, who heard their prayers and upheld them.

Does banking on God mean human agents and institutions are incapable of helping us? Not exactly. God typically works through human agency. He calls individuals—Abram (Gen. 12:1–3), Moses (Exod. 3), Gideon (Judg. 6), Samuel (1 Sam. 3), Isaiah (Isa. 6)—into service. He enlists institutions—the nation of Israel and, today, the church—to represent him. He places governing authorities in their seats to uphold justice (Dan. 2:21, cf.; Rom. 13:1). Thus, politics, medicine, money, career, relationships, religion, and health can provide provisional help in bad circumstances. God uses them as an aspect of his common grace. Our mistake is to confuse gifts of common grace with God himself. Politics, medicine, money, career, relationships, religion, and health cannot bear the weight of our trust. We turn them into idols by banking on them instead of God. Only God is ultimately reliable.

Is it true?

Is it true that we should bank on God in bad circumstances? Yes! We must reaffirm our belief that God guarantees total triumph for his people in the future (Ps. 2; Joel 3; Zeph. 3:6–20; Zech. 14:1–11). This includes victory over rebellious nations, godless people, demonic forces, personal suffering, and death (Gen. 3:15; Isa. 11:1–9; Pss. 2:6–12; 16:10–11). In fact, the biblical narrative records several inspiring accounts of those who banked on God in bad circumstances. When death appeared certain, Shadrach, Meshach, and Abednego banked on God to deliver them from the fiery furnace (Dan. 3:17–18). Similarly, Daniel banked on God to vindicate him when persecuted for praying to God contrary to King Darius's edict (6:20–21). Ironically, even the king who put Daniel in a bad circumstance banked on God after the faithful prophet emerged from the lions' den unscathed (6:25–27).

Does this mean God always gets us out of bad circumstances? No. Sometimes God uses bad circumstances for punitive reasons. An entire generation perished in the wilderness for their rebellion against God (Num. 11:14–35). Samson died as a Philistine captive for betraying his Nazarite vow (Judg. 16:23–31). King Uzziah ended his reign in obscurity, afflicted with a skin disease, for his royal pride (2 Chron. 26:16–21). God's discipline is a mark of paternal love (Prov. 3:11–12). When our selfishness, unwise decisions, and cruel treatment of others result in bad circumstances, rather than expecting God to bail us out, our first response should be repentance.

Other times God allows bad circumstances to linger to instill trust in his people (Rom. 5:1–5). Bad circumstances remind us of the limits of our control. We cannot always convince others to reconcile with us, but we can bank on God to give us patience. We cannot always find the right treatment for disease, but we can bank on God to supply us strength. We cannot manage the mix of hormones wreaking havoc on our emotional life, but we can bank on God to encourage us through friends, family, and the Bible. Moreover, bad circumstances fix our minds on God's promised better days ahead (Isa. 66:17–25; Mic. 4:1–5). Even amid the bad circumstances in Zechariah's day, God admonished his people: "Bank on me! I will defeat your enemies. I will bring justice. I will restore you and make you whole again."

Now what?

How do we bank on God in bad circumstances? First, we must admit the gravity of our bad circumstances. Additionally, we should consider and confess our part in making life hard. Not always, but often, bad circumstances are self-inflicted, as evident in the exile of God's people (Deut. 28:58–68). This pattern also translates to personal circumstances. We may suffer from bad financial circumstances because of uncontrolled spending. Bad health circumstances may result from poor eating and exercise habits. Bad work circumstances may stem from unethical practices. Then again, many bad circumstances are beyond our control, like those inherited at birth (e.g., generational poverty or genetic disorder) or experienced by "accident" (e.g., tornado or car crash).

Second, we approach banking on God much like we manage our personal finances. We make deposits both in small, steady increments and well as large, lump sums. Small, steady investments of trust may comprise of talking with God about our daily schedules, marking his daily provision, heeding his daily promptings, and enjoying his daily presence. Large, lump sums of trust follow our receiving an unexpected financial gift, a long-awaited answer to prayer, delivery of a healthy baby, or surprising peace in the face of a loved one's death.

Finally, banking on God goes beyond learning from personal experience. We must study God's faithfulness to his people throughout time. He sustains creation. He gave Abraham a beloved son. He saved Israel from Egypt. He allowed Solomon to build a temple. He sent the Messiah to conquer sin and death. He has empowered his people to bear witness to him among the nations, even in the face of persecution. We know countless stories of God's leadership, guidance, and provision in the lives of our friends and family. Each tale of God's faithfulness amid bad circumstances adds to the trust account, giving us greater reason to bank on God.

Creativity in Presentation

The piggy bank is an iconic image. Both young and old people understand the power of placing small deposits into the slot for later access. Consider setting a piggy bank on the stage—better yet, get a five-foot model made from cardboard—to illustrate the importance of regular deposits. Hold up enlarged replicas of various coins. Make sure "In God We Trust" stands out. As you place each coin in the piggy bank, specify an attribute or activity of God that makes him worth banking on. You might say, "This represents the time God helped me battle anxiety about my career, so I'm banking on him." Or, "This represents the time God helped me during a hard season of parenting (or marriage), so I'm banking on him." If you cannot craft a giant piggy bank or find a small one, a picture projected on the screen will suffice.

Exposing how we trust people, products, and services for health, happiness, and security might prove convicting. Pay attention to the way marketers sell trust. CNN claims to be the most trusted name in news. Captial One claims to be the best credit card for your wallet. Every lawyer billboard claims to defend your case with utmost care. Every insurance company claims quick, affordable, personal, reliable protection. In fact, the whole concept of "brand loyalty" preys on the misplaced trust we blindly give to people, products, and services. Consider compiling an array of trustworthy people, products, and services you use each day and demonstrate how you unconsciously bank on them.

> **How Brand Loyalty Affects My Day**
> - I roll out of bed and bank on Folgers to wake me up. It's the best part of waking up.
> - I pour a bowl of Wheaties, so I can feel like a champ. And the milk does my body good.
> - I brush my teeth and bank on Crest to whiten my smile and freshen my breath.
> - I drive my Ford to the office and bank on its ability to Go Further (or at least go far enough).
> - I do, however, stop for gasoline at the Marathon station and bank on those thirteen gallons to be the best in the long run.

Toward the end of the Civil War film *Glory* (1989, directed by Edward Zwick), soldiers from the 54th Massachusetts gather around a fire to sing and talk with God. Theirs was among the first military units of Black soldiers to fight for the North, and they mustered their courage in a gripping scene of raw, honest worship. They clap and chant the refrain, "O my Lord, Lord, Lord, Lord." Then a different member of the battalion prays. The cycle repeats: chorus, prayer, chorus, prayer. The following day the men are scheduled to march on Fort Wagner, most of them to their death, but they bolster their resolve to fight knowing that God goes with them. While dated, this scene remains moving and may give a picture of what banking on God sounds like.

Ultimately, the sermon should convey these truths: God's people can trust God in difficult times, for he will strengthen them as he has promised. Thus, it's best to bank on God in bad circumstances.

- We can bank on God to get rid of bad leaders (10:1–3a).

- We can bank on God to send us better leaders (10:3b–7).

- We can bank on God to save us from bad circumstances (10:8–12).

- We can bank on God to get rid of bad people (11:1–3).

DISCUSSION QUESTIONS

1. What were the characteristics the bad leaders Zechariah mentioned?

2. How did the theology of Zechariah's speech challenge the idols of his day? What idols are common in our day?

3. In what ways do we allow circumstances to taint our view of God? What bad circumstances have we caused in our lives? What bad circumstances result from living in a fallen world?

4. What OT heroes banked on God despite bad circumstances?

5. What are some "small and steady" and "large, lump sums" of trust you've placed in God?

Zechariah 11:4–17

EXEGETICAL IDEA

Evil shepherds would be removed and a good shepherd would restore God's covenant between Judah and Israel, but the people would reject this good shepherd, so unity and delight would be lost and a foolish shepherd would come and destroy the flock.

THEOLOGICAL FOCUS

The rejection of the good leaders will lead to destruction, for many will follow worthless leaders.

PREACHING IDEA

Let's cut loose from bad leaders.

PREACHING POINTERS

God gave Zechariah a new role in this section of the text. The prophet was to act like a shepherd to God's people. As the narrative unfolds, Zechariah gripped a staff in each hand and sent uncaring leaders packing. Sadly, the people showed preference for their godless figureheads, resulting in a series of prophetic signs—two broken staffs, thirty shekels tossed aside—capped off by an oracle of woe. Shepherding imagery struck a familiar note with Zechariah's original audience, for they had known both God and Israel's kings as their shepherds. The intense language and evocative gestures intended to fill his hearers with dread if they remained in the shadow of uncaring shepherds.

Bad leaders in any context threaten the well-being of people under their care. This is true today. An arrogant pastor can belittle his congregation. A stubborn coach can sabotage his team's chance of victory. Distant parents can undermine the security of their children. An ambitious CEO can create a culture of restlessness and fear in the workplace. Leaders set the tone and standard in which their followers rise and fall. Unfortunately, we allow careless leaders to remain in their post because we are more comfortable with the status quo. Instead, as the passage suggests, we should cut loose from bad leaders.

THE SHEPHERDS AND THE SHEEP (11:4–17)

LITERARY STRUCTURE AND THEMES (11:4–17)

This message included a sign act in which (a) the good shepherd removing some bad shepherds who were destroying the flock, and then he tried to bring unity and delight to the nation, but the people rejected him as their shepherd (11:4–14); so then (b) the people turned to follow the destructive, foolish shepherd (11:15–17).

The theme(s) in this unit are that God will use the good shepherd to remove evil shepherds, the good shepherd will care for God's flock but be rejected by the people, so this will bring an end to unity, and a preference to follow an evil shepherd.

- ***The Good Shepherd's Service Is Rejected (11:4–12)***
- ***Rejection of the Good Shepherd and Unity (11:13–14)***
- ***The Worthless Shepherd (11:15–17)***

EXPOSITION

Many people in Israel made their living by tending sheep, so they had no difficulty understanding the analogy of the ideal leader of the nation being compared to the leader of sheep. A good king and a good shepherd love their sheep, protect them from predators, and take pity on them when they are sick or injured. Kings and shepherds should not mistreat their sheep or allow others to slaughter them but love them and protect them from unscrupulous shepherds. This metaphorical way of speaking had a shocking ending in which the sheep rejected the good shepherd who cared about the unity and protection of the sheep. Instead, the sheep followed a destructive, foolish shepherd.

The Good Shepherd's Service Is Rejected (11:4–12)

In this sign act, Zechariah played the role of the good shepherd who defended the flock by removing destructive shepherds and by pasturing the flock of Israel to bring unity, but they rejected him.

11:4. Zechariah was told to "shepherd the flock destined for slaughter" (11:4; cf. Jer. 12:3), though this was more of a drama, sign act, or role playing in symbolic action rather than the prophet actually assuming the political responsibility of a shepherd king.[1] Although the purpose of raising sheep was to sell their wool and sell their meat for a profit, the impression in this drama was that this slaughtering of sheep was an evil act outside the norms of a caring shepherd who loved his sheep (e.g., Ps. 23; Ezek. 34). This sign act would involve Zechariah taking on the role of a shepherd/king and wisely caring for the people (the sheep) in Judah, though no specific instructions were provided on how he should go about fulfilling this role of shepherding this doomed flock. He would have to fight off those who would try to kill his sheep, remove any bad shepherds, and lovingly encourage the people to transform their lives.

---

1   In Israel and other countries, it was common to use the metaphor of shepherd to characterize the leadership role of a good king. Ezekiel 34 used this metaphor to describe God's leadership role, and this figure is picked up and used similarly in the NT.

11:5–6. God explained to Zechariah the terrible situation of the flock, his precious people. God showed him that at some point, the shepherds (kings/rulers) abused God's flock by selling them to a buyer who would slaughter them, so neither the kings selling the sheep nor the other kings buying the sheep were interested in protecting and caring for the sheep. The callousness of the buyers who slaughtered these sheep was shameful, for they seemed to have no sense of guilt about their failures to care for the sheep and no fear of being punished for their evil acts. The sin of the sellers was evident in their pious, hypocritical claim that the Lord had blessed them and made them rich through these abusive acts (11:5). Although no evil king (the shepherd) was identified by name, it is possibly that this story was intended to encapsulate the abusive kings of Judah (= shepherds) in the coming days (11:5b) and oppressive foreign kings. When the good shepherd cared for the sheep, he removed them from the hands of the bad shepherds. But eventually, God would not intervene compassionately to stop these oppressive neighbors (רֵעֵהוּ), the evil kings, for God's plan was to strike the land and not deliver his people out of the hands of their enemies. Although some (Barker, 1983, 676) assert that this referred to the future persecution of the Jews during the Roman era, there

is no biblical identification of these kings and no hint about the date when this judgment would fall on them.

11:7a. The next part of the sign act describes how Zechariah (11:7–12) acted out some typical or symbolic shepherding activities to demonstrate that he was shepherding the oppressed and afflicted flock of God that was destined for slaughter. Merrill (2003, 257) identifies this afflicted group as "the oppressed remnant within Israel that had maintained its covenant faith," while Boda (2004, 463) thinks this negative description was consistent with the historical evidence of life in the early Persian period. Both commentators provide hypothetical conclusions that are not expressly described in this passage.

> *TEXTUAL ANALYSIS:* The text has "afflicted, oppressed, needy" (עֲנִיֵּי), which is widely accepted (CSB, NKJV, NASB[95], McComiskey, 1998, 1194; Klein, 2008, 327; Larkin, 1994, 110), but others emended the text to read "Canaanites" or "the sheep merchants" (NRSV, ESV; Baldwin, 1972, 180; Smith, 1984, 268).

11:7b. In an attempt to faithfully shepherd the flock, Zechariah chose two rods/staffs and named one "delight, pleasantness" (נֹעַם), which likely referred to the "delight" (Wolters, 2014, 370–71 prefers the "graciousness" of God) that God would have in the restoration of the covenant relationship with his people. The second rod was called "union, unity," which referred to the solidarity or close bond that joined Judah and Israel together as one people. The prophet's actions appear to be fairly similar to God's instructions that Ezekiel should take two sticks, write Judah on one and Israel on the other, and then join them together (Ezek. 37:15–28). Although it is impossible to know if the audience of Zechariah knew what Ezekiel wrote, at least it provided some orientation to those who were aware of it. Having heard God's instructions, the prophet was now

Shepherds Taking Their Sheep to the Pasture. Courtesy of Matanya.

prepared for the responsibility of leading the flock of God's people. Zechariah 11:7 reported that the prophet acted out his role as best he could as he tried to lead this difficult flock, but Curtis (2006, 217) thinks that Yahweh was the good shepherd in 11:4–16.

WORD ANALYSIS: This word נֹעַם can refer to (a) the "pleasant" appeal of an object or person to one of the five sense of an observer; for example, the ear can hear "pleasing, delightful" words in Psalm 141:6, and the tongue can identify "pleasant" food (Ps. 141:4); or (b) the wonderful emotional feeling of "delight" in another person (David for Johnathan in 2 Sam. 1:26), the "delight" the female found in the handsome male (Song 1:16), or God's "delight" in others (Ps. 90:17).

11:8. Without warning, this shepherd removed three kings (shepherd) in one month. Of course, Zechariah did not actually take a knife and literally kill anyone; this was a sign act in which he announced these deaths in order to communicate God's will to others. Commentators have produced all kinds of guesses about the identity of these three shepherds, but this prophecy was about the future, and the names of these kings were not known to Zechariah, and they are still unknown to us. Although Zechariah was the one who removed these rulers, there is no description of how his audience responded to the removal of these leaders. If three kings would be forcibly removed in one month (some see this as indicating a short time period rather than a literal thirty days), it would point to a time of great political unrest and instability that would come on the nation. Wolters (2014, 374) correctly views the impatience in 11:8b as coming after 11:8a; thus, the source of Zechariah's impatience was with the people / the sheep. One might guess that the reason for the sheep being exasperated with Zechariah was that some of the

people liked the three kings/shepherds that were removed from office.

Who Are the Three Shepherds?

Several suggestions have been offered for identifying the three shepherds. They include (a) Moses, Aaron, and Miriam; (b) Cyrus, Cambyses, and Darius; (c) kings, priest, and prophets; or (d) Pharisees, Sadducees, and Essenes. Moreover, Merrill (2003, 258) suggests the three shepherds were the final three kings of Judah. Redditt (2012, 83) concludes *"that the shepherds symbolized the indigenous religious leadership of fifth-century Judah, who were themselves controlled by governors serving the interest of the Persians"* (emphasis in original). He defines these leaders as Levites/priests here in chapter 11 but expands the leaders in 12:10–13:6 to Davidites, Levites, and false prophets. This definition puts a dark cloud over the high priest Joshua, but there is little that justifies this except Zechariah 3, but that chapter ends with Joshua's sins forgiven.

TRANSLATION ANALYSIS: 11:8

NASB[95] "My soul was impatient with them, and their soul was weary of me."

NIV[84] "The flock detested me, and I grew weary of them."

HCSB "I became impatient with them, and they also detested me."

NKJV "My soul loathed them, and their soul also abhorred me."

NRSV "I had become impatient with them, and they also detested me."

Impatience with someone can lead to detesting them.

11:9–11. Consequently, because the people rejected Zechariah's leadership, he told the audience that he would no longer shepherd (lead) the sheep (people) but would let them die and slaughter each other. Thus, Zechariah would not have pity on them, just like God would have no pity on them (11:6). Then Zechariah broke the rod called "delight, pleasantness" (11:10) to symbolize the end of God's delight in the covenant agreement he made with the whole nation (Judah and Israel; 11:7). This symbolic act presumably would be understood by some in the audience as a sign that the unity between the nations of Judah and Israel was over and that he took no delight in them. Since this covenant relationship was over, God would have no obligation to protect these people from neighboring nations that might attack and destroy them in the future. Although this would be a hard truth to swallow, when the weak, afflicted sheep/people saw what Zechariah did, they certainly would understand the meaning of the symbolism of breaking this first rod (11:11).

11:12. Then in a somewhat odd twist, the shepherd Zechariah asked an unknown group defined as "them" to pay him his wages for caring for the sheep. Although it is unclear who he was speaking to, at first it might appear that Zechariah was asking the oppressed sheep to pay for his services. However, Boda (2004, 464) identifies the "them" at the beginning of 11:12 as the nations/peoples mentioned at the end of 11:10. Others (Curtis, 2006, 199; Baldwin, 1972, 184; Petersen, 1995, 96; Merrill, 2003, 199) thinks that the "them" referred to the "sheep-merchant" who bought and sold the sheep (11:5, 11). Yet, McComiskey (1998, 1200) proposes the more general idea that "they" were "the leaders of the community."

The price that was paid for Zechariah's services to the sheep was thirty pieces of silver (Zech. 3:12), an amount that was equal to the compensation due to an owner of a slave that was killed by an ox (Exod. 21:32) in the time of Moses, some nine hundred years before the time of Zechariah. This was a significant increase (50%) over the twenty

shekels the Midianites paid for the young slave boy Joseph in Genesis 28:28. But Leviticus 27:3–4 valued a man from twenty to sixty years old at fifty shekels and a woman at thirty shekels. Since these costs were present in a culture far removed from Zechariah, they provide little help in estimating the price of a slave hundreds of years later in the Persian era. Many view the thirty shekels in Zechariah 11:12 as an insulting low amount (Hill, 2008b, 583; Klein, 2008, 337–80) because the phrase was understood to be a Semitic expression or idiomatic way of saying that the shepherd's work was not worth a lead nickel (the nonliteral, sarcastic meaning of thirty shekels). Wolters (2014, 380) referred to the use of thirty shekels in Sumerian and in an Akkadian passage in the Amarna letters where the expression is used as an idiomatic way of saying "almost nothing"; that is, the person worth thirty shekels was viewed with contempt and as having little value.

Two other factors need to be considered in interpreting this passage: (1) Was there any indication that the shepherd Zechariah was being sold as a slave? Or (2) was he merely being paid for his work over a brief period of time, and if so, was the pay connected to his value as a person or the number of days of service caring for the sheep? Unfortunately, there is no exact information about how long the shepherd Zechariah took care of the sheep in this sign act (but according to 11:8, it was a least one month). So if we do not know the full length of his service, it is impossible to determine if this payment was generous, normal, or miserly. Wolters (2014, 380–81) contends that this was in fact a high wage for working only a month because a Babylonian account from the Persian period[2] indicates that a laborers wage would be one

---

2   Al Wolters corroborates these conclusions based on the Persepolis Foundation 263 Tablets and the Persepolis Treasury Tablets, which refer to 3 BAN a month, which equals one shekel. Al Wolters, *Zechariah*, Historical Commentary on the Old Testament 19 (Leuven: Peeters, 2014), 381.

shekel per month. Others viewed this as a miserly amount to pay Zechariah (Boda, 2004, 465; McComiskey, 1998, 1200; Klein, 2008, 337), but this largely depends on whether one interprets a "magnificent price" (11:13) as an honest assessment of the thirty pieces of silver (Redditt, 2012, 86; Hill, 2008b, 584; Meyers and Meyers, 1993, 279) or as a sarcastic remark (Merrill, 2003, 261; Larkin, 1994, 130). In spite of the many questions about the interpretation of the details of this sign act, one must not lose sight of the larger symbolic meaning. The prophetic shepherd was so exasperated by the stubborn sheep that he gave up on leading the sheep. This would leave an ominous sign about the future that every reader would understand.

Rejection of the Good Shepherd and Unity (11:13–14)

The work of the shepherd to unify the two nations of Judah and Israel was a failure.

11:13. The people did not seem to object to the shepherd's plan to end his work with the sheep, object to paying him some wages, or argue about the end of God's delight and the unity of the nations. Their lack of response demonstrated their minimal desire to follow God and his servant the shepherd.

Once the silver was received, God instructed Zechariah, who acted in the role of the good shepherd, to "throw it" to the "potter" or "former" (יֹוצֵר) who was in the Lord's house (11:13).

What Is a Potter or a Fashioner?

If this word is translated "potter," it refers to a person who sold pottery at the temple, or it might refer to a fashioner of metals. Potters were used in the temple to make plates, bowls, and pitchers for those eating in the temple area as well as for water containers to clean up the bloody mess after an animal was killed, skinned, and cut up into pieces for a sacrifice. In addition, God was a "fashioner" of the things on earth (Isa. 45:9), and Wolters (2014, 384–85) thinks this term could also refer to God who fashioned the world.

There was no explanation of the significance of this action and no information about what the "potter, fashioner" might do with this silver. In addition, some commentators follow the Syriac translation, which has אוֹצָר "treasury" (Meyers and Meyers, 1993, 277–78; Petersen, 1995, 87; see the "treasury" of the temple, as a more likely place to deposit money), but Baldwin (1972, 185) and Merrill (2003, 262) support the reading "potter." It is difficult to interpret the meaning of all this unexplained symbolic action. One might suggest that the giving of the thirty shekels to the temple demonstrated the sacrificial giving of this shepherd and his willingness to follow whatever God commanded him to do, but the deeper meaning of this action was never interpreted in this narrative.

11:14. In the last verse of this paragraph, the destruction of the staff "union" indicated that at some later point, the covenantal solidarity between these two people groups (Judah and Israel) would end, and they would no longer act as brothers.

The picture created by this sign act pointed toward a future time, but no specific time frame was included in the drama. Limited information about the evil or good leaders (shepherds) was provided, so it would be difficult to connect these individuals in other prophetic texts or historical eras. Thus, about all that can be said is that this sign act pointed to a future time of unbelief and a refusal to follow the shepherd/king that God sent them. It is possible that some readers would connect the removed evil shepherds with the shepherds that scattered the sheep in Jeremiah 23:1–2 or Ezekiel 34. In response, God said that he would raise up good shepherds and eventually the Davidic King (= Branch) who would shepherd his people with justice and righteousness (Jer. 25:5–6; Ezek. 34:23–24; Zech. 9:9–10). One difficulty with this connection is that the shepherd in Zechariah 11 would not be successful, but the Davidic Shepherd in Jeremiah 25, Ezekiel 34, and Zechariah 9 would be successful. Zechariah 12–13 refers to a time when the Davidic Shepherd was pierced (12:10) when someone would strike the Shepherd (13:7), but that imagery is not found in this paragraph. These piercing passages remind one of the suffering of the Servant in Isaiah 50:3–13 and 52:13–52:12.

The Worthless Shepherd (11:15–17)

Zechariah lamented the coming foolish shepherd who would devour God's flock.

11:15–16. This extended symbolic sign act ended with Zechariah taking on the role of a "foolish, worthless" (אֱלִיל) shepherd (11:17) in order to contrast the character of the good shepherd and the worthless shepherd, and contrast the results of the leadership of each shepherd. This evil, foolish shepherd would not take care of the sheep by rescuing the lost, would refuse to treat and bandage those with diseases or broken legs, and would not even feed the sheep. Instead, he would senselessly injure, kill, devour, and destroy the flock (11:16). Although there was no description of what Zechariah actually did to illustrate the role of the foolish shepherd, one would assume that he acted out what God instructed him to do with sufficient clarity that his audience understood the contrast between the good shepherd and the worthless shepherd. The text included no hint concerning the identity of this worthless shepherd, but Klein (2008, 345–46) points to evil people living in Zechariah's own time, while Merrill (2003, 266) views this shepherd figure

as the "the whole collective leadership in Israel from Zechariah's time forward, culminating at last in the last epitome of godless despotism, the individual identified in the New Testament as the Antichrist (1 John 2:18; 4:3; 2 John 7)." Since the prophecy does not point to any specific fulfillment, one should be careful not to insert names but to pay attention to the theology, practical goals, and methods of an evil leader/shepherd, for following this worthless leader would surely have disastrous results.

WORD ANALYSIS: This word אֱלִיל can refer to (a) the "non-existence, nothingness, worthlessness" of an idol god (Lev. 19:4; Ps. 97:5; Isa. 2:8; Hab. 2:18); (b) the "worthless, futile" vision of a false prophet (Jer. 14:14); or (c) a "worthless" doctor (Job 13:4) or "worthless" shepherd (Zech. 11:17).

11:17. The final woe oracle was a lament that Zechariah gave to end this sign act about the foolish/worthless shepherd.[3] No doubt dressed in sackcloth and ashes, Zechariah lamented the fact that this shepherd would abandon the flock, demonstrating his worthlessness. Because of this, a sword would cut off his arm and blind his right eye so that this shepherd would not have the physical ability to see or to lift up and carry an injured sheep that needs help. These acts of maiming and blinding this shepherd point to the end of his rule over God's sheep (Meyers and Meyers, 1993, 291–92). If this passage was read and understood in conjunction with Ezekiel 34, God's future plans for his sheep would become clearer, and the contrasting role of "the one shepherd, my servant David" (Ezek. 34:23–24) would become more evident.

THEOLOGICAL FOCUS

The exegetical idea (evil shepherds would be removed and a good shepherd would restore

---

3   Zechariah's condemnation of the worthless shepherds is similar to some of the accusation against the shepherds in Ezekiel 34. Both prophets condemned these evil shepherds and announced God's judgment on them.

God's covenant between Judah and Israel, but the people would reject this good shepherd, so unity and delight would be lost and a foolish shepherd would come and destroy the flock) leads to this theological focus: The rejection of the good leaders will lead to destruction, for many will follow worthless leaders.

The sign act in 11:4–17 involved the prophet acting out the role of the good and evil leader (shepherd) in order to communicate more clearly what would happen to God's people (sheep) and their leaders (the shepherds) in the future. This dramatic presentation effectively communicated to those watching that God was greatly concerned about his covenant people, determined to remove evil and worthless leaders because they were destroying his flock, and planned to send a good leader (shepherd) to care for his people. These insights should assist any group of people (sheep) in evaluating various leaders so that they can understand which leaders truly serve God and faithfully care for his people (sheep). By analyzing the behavior of various shepherd leaders, anyone should be able to judge a shepherd as good or foolish. Anyone striving to take on a leadership role today would be wise to pay attention to what God expects of good leaders (shepherds).

PREACHING AND TEACHING STRATEGIES

Exegetical and Theological Synthesis
Zechariah 11:4–17 details the prophet's sign acts and their effects. For his performance, Zechariah chose two staffs and symbolically named them before breaking them. Their destruction demonstrated God's displeasure at Israel's disobedience and the disunity of his people. Between his shattering of the two staffs, Zechariah collected dues for his leadership duties, only to launch his thirty-shekel earnings into the potter's field.[4]

Sign acts are common stock among Israel's prophets. For three years Isaiah tramped naked through his land as a sign of what was coming—Assyrian exile (Isa. 20). Jeremiah bought, buried, and unearthed a filthy waistband as a sign of coming judgment on Judah (Jer. 13:1–11). Ezekiel lay on his side for 390 days, turned, and endured another forty days of stillness as a sign of impending exile (Ezek. 4:4–8). Hosea married a harlot as a sign of God's commitment to his unfaithful people (Hos. 3). These sign acts reinforced the prophets' spoken words.

Furthermore, the shepherding imagery is applied both to God and those who lead his people. The shepherd paints a picture of protection, care, and guidance. God is the ideal shepherd (Ps. 23). Moses, David, and Amos served as shepherds prior to (and in preparation for) their appointed leadership roles (Exod. 3:1; 1 Sam. 16:11; Amos 1:1). On the other hand, prophets often rebuked bad leaders of their day for abusive and selfish oversight of their constituents (Jer. 23:1–2; Ezek. 34:1–10; Zech. 10:3).

Preaching Idea
Let's cut loose from bad leaders.

Contemporary Connections

What does it mean?
What does it mean to cut loose from bad leaders? Bad leaders are not unique to Zechariah's context; history has an unlimited number of tyrants and those who cut loose from them. Judas Maccabeus, a Jewish revolutionary, cut loose from Antiochus IV, who was an oppressive, godless opponent of the Jewish people (167–164 b.c.). Dietrich Bonhoeffer, a German pastor, cut loose from Adolf Hitler, who was an abusive, manipulative, and self-serving leader.

---

4   Gospel writers remembered the event, citing it in their description of the "blood money" Judas received for betraying Jesus (Matt. 27:1–8; cf. Acts 1:18–19). See earlier related note on 11:14.

But bad leaders trickle down to everyday life. They come in many forms: abusive and oppressive, manipulative and passive-aggressive, bitter and emotionally unstable, religiously motivated and secular. Cutting loose from them means separating oneself, creating space from, or standing against their influence.

We may set boundaries that keep us outside the immediate reach of a bad leader. A wife may seek temporary separation from an oppressive husband rather than suffer his abuse. An employee may request to report to a director rather than to a self-serving, ladder-climbing supervisor. An adult child may limit interactions with a manipulative parent—only on holidays or by phone—to protect herself from emotional harm. To stand in the path of repeated oppression, abuse, selfishness, or manipulation only enables bad leaders.

While all leaders may be prone to uncaring moments or seasons of misguided passion, what sets a bad leader apart is the consistency and intensity of his behavior. Bad leaders show a pattern of oppression, abuse, selfishness, and manipulation. They create a culture of fear, suspicion, and mistrust rather than joy, innovation, and connection. Their criticism tears down rather than uplifts. Their words open wounds rather than heal. Whether male or female, bad leaders make preserving the ego their mission.

Is it true?

Is it true that we should cut loose from bad leaders? Yes, but cutting loose is complex. Separating from bad leaders looks different depending on the context. Sometimes we need to cut loose from bad leaders completely. We may need to change jobs or request a transfer, quit a team or leave a church. When bad leaders steal our joy, corrupt our attitudes, manipulate us to live unethically, or push us to the point of despair, cutting loose is advised.

Other times cutting loose requires a certain level of due process, diplomacy, or discernment. Leaders, by definition, have authority—ascribed

or assumed—making them hard to separate from. In some cases, bad leaders can displace blame, ruin others' reputations, or inflict further pain. Citizens cannot cut loose from their political leaders without due process. Employees cannot oust their bosses without certain appeals. Wives cannot divorce their husbands without legal counsel. Sadly, cutting loose may not always result in a clean break.

Now what?

How do we cut loose from bad leaders? First, we must realize that cutting loose may neither be quick nor straightforward. Depending on the nature of the relationship—familial, social, recreational, volunteer, or vocational—different rules of separation apply. Furthermore, our cutting loose will affect others, so we should be cognizant of the ripple effect of our departure. In some churches, the exit of one family launches a mass exodus. The resignation of an influential staff person may inspire others to quit. Thus, from the outset we must consider the following questions: What is the nature of our relationship with the bad leader? Whom will our departure affect? Whose counsel can we seek to sort through this complex issue? What damage would be done if we didn't cut loose from this bad leader?

Second, we must make an exit plan. Do we depart dramatically or slip away quietly in the night? Do we speak our mind to the bad leader before leaving? Do we invite a mediator into that conversation? Do we share our grievances with others? Do we leave the door open for future restitution, or do we never look back? These questions tie into the initial step. How we exit depends on the nature of the relationship and ensuing ripple effect.

Third, we must maintain our integrity by avoiding slander. Not all bad leaders are criminals, heretics, or evil people. Some are simply immature and selfish. Launching a crusade against bad leaders is typically not needed. God will not give them the last laugh; he will expose

The United States Declaration of Independence. Original courtesy of the Second Continental Congress; 1823 facsimile reproduction courtesy of William Stone (public domain).

them. In time, their followers will scatter, and their influence will dissolve, as in the case of Hitler, Antiochus IV, and other bad leaders.

Creativity in Presentation

To illustrate cutting loose, secure a large pair of scissors, rope, and two people willing to have their arms or legs tied together. Identify one of the participants as the "leader" and the other as the "follower." After tethering their arms or legs together (with plenty of slack between the two), ask the leader to guide his follower through various scenarios, saying: "Leader, drag your follower through the mud." [Encourage them to act out crawling through mud.] "Leader, take your follower over a cliff." [Encourage them to jump off the stage.] "Leader, pull your follower down." [Encourage them to both fall to the ground.] "Leader, go to the bathroom (or dentist)." [Encourage the follower to cut loose—quickly!—with the scissors you provided. Test in advance that the scissors can sever the rope.]

In American's "coming of age" story, the people chose to cut loose from Great Britain. Rebelling against "taxation without representation," the Founding Fathers declared independence from their birthparents. Consider reading (and projecting) the opening two paragraphs from the famous United States Declaration of Independence, highlighting "the Right of the People to alter or abolish it, and to institute a new Government." Also note the driving aim to preserve "unalienable Rights" given by God for "Life, Liberty and the pursuit of Happiness." Having an exceptional reader from your congregation, live or filmed, will add to this illustration's dramatic effect. Wikipedia provides a helpful overview of the historical background, text, meaning, and impact of the document.

As a pastor, I (Tim) frequently hear emotional stories of people cutting loose from bad leaders at home, church, and work. A wife cut loose from an uncaring husband after twenty-plus years of emotional neglect. A family cut loose from a former church after the father's repeated attempts to discuss shady financial practices of the elders were ignored. A young man cut loose from his employer after his boss continued to overschedule, underpay, and disrespect his time off the clock. None of these people cut loose without emotional pain. Before using their stories, get permission and guard some details to protect their privacy. An interview with someone who has cut loose would be even more compelling. If you prefer historical examples, consider retelling how Bonhoeffer or Judas Maccabeus cut loose from bad leaders in their day.

Whatever way you choose to make the message stick, be sure to communicate this: The rejection of the good leaders will lead to destruction, for many will follow worthless leaders. So let's cut loose from bad leaders.

- We have a better future when we follow good leaders (11:4–7).

- We have a bad habit of rejecting good leaders (11:8–14)

- We have a worse habit of accepting bad leaders (11:15–17).

DISCUSSION QUESTIONS

1. What made the shepherding imagery so impactful for Zechariah's audience?

2. What makes trying to name the three bad shepherds misguided? What is the main purpose of Zechariah's imagery and sign acts?

3. Who were some good leaders from the OT? What distinguished their leadership?

4. What makes cutting loose from bad leaders complicated?

5. What are some helpful approaches to dealing with bad leaders in life?

FUTURE RESTORATION OF GOD'S PEOPLE AND THEIR SHEPHERD (12:1–14:21)

In the second half of Zechariah 9–14, God provided additional prophesies about his future plans for his people, which includes God saving his people from their enemies, the gift of a spirit of mourning for the one they had pierced, the end of all idolatry, the defense of his people at the final battle for Jerusalem, and the establishment of the kingdom of God where God would reign as King.

These chapters begin with an introduction to the whole section in 12:1 (similar to 9:1). In this context, the "burdensome oracle" (מַשָּׂא) that came from God to the prophet Zechariah was concerning military attacks on Israel. These three chapters (12:1–14:21) are frequently marked with the phrase "in that day" (12:4, 6, 8, 9, 12; 13:1, 2, 4; 14:1, 4, 6, 9, 13, 20, 21) indicating that these verses predict what would happen in an eschatological setting in the distant future. The opening section (12:1–9) and the closing prophecy (14:1–21) tell about a major war when all the nations of the earth would attack Judah and Jerusalem, but God would miraculously save his people from destruction.

Zechariah 12:1–14:21 can be divided into three preaching units: (1) God's Strength Will Defeat the Nations That Attack Judah (12:1–9), (2) God's Grace and Cleansing Will Transform All Israel and Judah (12:10–13:9), and (3) After Defeating His Enemies, God Will Reign as King (14:1–21). At the very end of this section is a list of books and articles for further reading that may helpful in understanding these preaching units.

Zechariah 12:1–9

EXEGETICAL IDEA
In the future, the nations would gather together against Jerusalem, but God would watch over his people, save the people of Jerusalem, and pour out his grace on them.

THEOLOGICAL FOCUS
God's people know that God will watch over and rescue them from their enemies.

PREACHING IDEA
God's strength is our secret weapon.

PREACHING POINTERS
Zechariah's preaching remained focused on what would happen in days ahead. He delivered another speech from God predicting future battles and firm victory for his people. The Lord would come to Jerusalem's defense. He would empower his people to fight, transforming the weakest of men into warriors. Vivid imagery—a colossal stone and fiery pot—and allusions to Israel's past—exodus, covenant, David and Goliath—grab the listener's ear. For the original audience, "that day" Zechariah spoke of could not come too soon. While they may not have looked forward to facing enemies, they certainly longed to see God's strength at full force.

God's people need to remember the greatness of his strength yet today. The Western world has trained us to be radically self-reliant. We have learned to harness science and technology, consult data and research, amass wealth and weapons, and practice medicine and mindfulness techniques to increase human potency. At our fingertips, we have more power than any people before us. Our glowing screens are a "portkey" to global knowledge and networks. Who needs God's wisdom when Google gives us our information? Who needs a community of faith when Facebook provides us unlimited social connectivity? But no amount of human progress can rival God's power. This passage reminds us that God's strength is our secret weapon.

GOD'S STRENGTH WILL DEFEAT THE NATIONS THAT ATTACK JUDAH (12:1–9)

LITERARY STRUCTURE AND THEMES (12:1–9)

Zechariah opened this unit with a prophesy predicting that people would recognize that God was defending Judah and Jerusalem when the nations were attacking them (vv. 1–5). He closed the paragraph with a description of how God will save and magnify Judah, Jerusalem, and the house of David (vv. 6–9).

Three themes in this unit are that God defends, gives hope, and assures his people.

- *Be Assured, God Will Save Judah and Jerusalem (12:1–6)*
- *God Will Save and Magnify Judah, Jerusalem, and the House of David (12:6–9)*

EXPOSITION

During the Persian era, Judah was a small nation with little to no military strength to defend itself against invading armies. If the Persians, Greeks, Parthians, or Romans would attack Judah with large armies, they would easily defeat them. This left the people feeling vulnerable and in need of God's providential hands of protection. Zechariah announced the good news that when future attacks would come, the people could depend on God for protection. When Jerusalem would stagger from a massive attack by its enemies, God would confuse the enemy, defeat them, and defend his people.

The prophet acknowledged that sooner or later, some nations would gather together against Jerusalem and attack it. But in such situations, they did not need to fear, for God had promised to watch over his people and pour out his grace on them. Then the eyes of God's people would be opened, and they would bitterly mourn for the one they had pierced.

Be Assured, God Will Save Judah and Jerusalem (12:1–6)

Many nations would attack Judah and Jerusalem, but God would defend his people.

12:1. In addition to the identification of the topic ("concerning Israel" in 12:1a), this introductory verse has an expanded reminder concerning some of the powerful creative acts of God (12:1b). In a style similar to a hymn (cf. Amos 4:13; Ps. 104:2–6), Zechariah reminded his Jewish audience in Jerusalem that God's power extended universally to all the heavens and the earth. He was the one who set the foundations of the earth in place, he stretched out the heavens across the skies, and shortly after that he created man and gave him a spirit (Gen. 1; Job 38:4; Ps. 24:2; 102:26; 104:5; Prov. 3:19; Isa. 45:18; 51:16). These amazing accomplishments highlight the power and authority of the God who would make numerous redemptive promises about the future in the next few chapters. These divine acts provided assurances to those reading these words that God had the power to do what he promised.

12:2a. At some unknown date, all the nations would gather to fight against Jerusalem (12:3b; cf. 14:1), but God's plan was to make Jerusalem a "cup" (סַף) of staggering that would cause the attacking nations to stumble when they drink from it. Jerusalem may appear to be as desirable as a cup of good wine, but when the nations drink from that cup, it would have a kick that would knock them off their feet. This imagery was somewhat similar to ideas in Isaiah 51:17–23 and Jeremiah 25:15–29, so some would be familiar with these metaphors. These earlier prophets described how Judah would drink the cup of God's wrath, which would lead to the drunkenness and devastation of God's people (Isa. 51:17–20; Jer. 25:18), and then Judah's enemies would drink from this cup of God's wrath in order to bring about their staggering and destruction (Isa. 51:21–23; Jer. 25:19–29). Zechariah used this imagery to communicate to his audience that there would be an eschatological event (like Zech. 14) when there would be widespread opposition to Jerusalem by many nations, but God assured the people of Judah that this enemy would not defeat Jerusalem.

12:2b. The last part of 12:2 has caused much confusion, for some (RSV; Wolters, 2014, 405; Baldwin, 1972, 189) translate this part of the verse "it will also be necessary for Judah [to join] the siege of Jerusalem," but why would Judah join in the destruction of fellow inhabitants in Jerusalem? Merrill (2003, 274) resolves this problem by suggesting that Judah along with Jerusalem would be attacked and both would cause the nations to reel and be devastated. Since 12:4 describes God watching over Judah, surely Judah would not join the enemies attacking Jerusalem in 12:2b. So it is best to conclude that the nations would attack both Judah and Jerusalem (Klein, 2008, 353; McComiskey, 1998, 1209).

12:3. Zechariah used another unusual metaphor to describe Jerusalem on that eschatological day ("in that day") when the nations would attack it. He compared Jerusalem to a heavy, unmovable stone that would cause injury to anyone who tried to move it. Commentators have suggested several possible backgrounds for the imagery of this unmovable rock. It could be drawn from a group of porters who worked together to move a large stone to its proper location along a wall and then struggled to lift the stone to the top of the wall where it belonged (Baldwin, 1972, 189). Boda (2004, 483) pictures this as a heavy stone carried by a pack animal that would produce a "bloody gash," not a muscle strain. Merrill (2003, 274) thinks Zechariah was picturing all the spoils from war as so heavy that they could not lift it up to carry it away. Others connect this stone to the "top stone" in Zechariah 4:7, 10 (Meyers and Meyers, 1993, 317), or to the stones that ancient men lifted to test their strength (Wolters, 2014, 407). Even though the cultural background of the imagery could possibly fit any of these situations, the main point was to create an imaginary situation of something that was impossible to lift. They would not be able to lift the stone; that is, they would not be able to defeat the city without experiencing significant personal injures because God would fight against the nations that attack Jerusalem.

12:4. One of the ways that God would undermine those sieging Judah and Jerusalem would be to disorient, throw into panic, and confuse the horses (cf. Exod. 15:1) of the enemy (probably horses in the cavalry) by striking them with blindness (12:4a, 4b). This judgment was included among the curses that would fall on Israel for disobeying God's instructions in Deuteronomy 28:28–29, but in this instance, this curse would fall on Israel's enemies. In addition, the riders of these horses would go mad (though the reason for this madness was not explained), but God would carefully watch over each of his people and preserve them (12:4b).

12:5. This divine deliverance would be so miraculous that the various "clans" (NASB[95]; NRSV; NIV[84]) or "governors, leaders" (NKJV; HCSB) of Israel would respond to God with the heartfelt conviction that Jerusalem survived because their powerful God was strengthening and defending them (12:5).

TRANSLATION ANALYSIS: 12:5

NASB[95] "A strong support for us are the inhabitants of Jerusalem through the Lord of hosts."

NIV[84] "The people of Jerusalem are strong, because the Lord Almighty is their God."

HCSB "The residents of Jerusalem are my strength through the Lord of Hosts."

NKJV "The inhabitants of Jerusalem are my strength in the Lord of hosts."

NRSV "The inhabitants of Jerusalem have strength through the Lord of hosts."

All these translations say the same thing, even when the "inhabitants of Jerusalem" are made the subject or the object of the sentence.

God Will Save and Magnify Judah, Jerusalem, and the House of David (12:6–9)

People could be confident that God would empower his people, save them, and destroy the attacking nations.

12:6. The prophetic description of this great battle employed additional metaphors to describe what would happen "in that day" (12:6, 8, 9). Judah's destructive power over its enemies was compared to a firepot, a bronze container that one could use to carry live coals from one place to another (Exod. 27:3; 1 Kings 7:50) or a pot for cooking food (1 Sam. 2:14) or a container for carrying water (1 Kings 7:30). If one would put this hot firepot (Judah) next to or under a pile of wood (the nations), the flames from the firepot would cause the wood to burn up. A similar result would happen if a flaming torch (Judah) was placed next to or under sheaves of grain (the nations). All the attacking nations would suffer defeat, but the people living in Jerusalem would remain safe and continue to dwell in Jerusalem.

12:7. Why would this happen? All credit would go to God who would save the people of Judah, Jerusalem, and those from the house of David (12:7). Giving priority to Judah over Jerusalem may seem surprising at first, but this probably meant temporal priority in delivering the countryside of Judah first and then later defeating the rest of the enemy army stationed around Jerusalem. God was making the point that everyone was important and no group should raise itself up as more important than the other. Judah, Jerusalem, and the royal house of David were all important to God. Even though the royal line of David would be the source of the nation's hope for a messianic king (cf. Isa. 9:1–7; Jer. 23:5–6; Zech. 9:9–10), this did not mean that God was only concerned about the royal house of David. Johnston (2012, 206) argues that this passage indicates that "God would elevate the common folk to the same social status as the Jerusalemites and Davidites."

12:8–9. This divine defense of Judah and Jerusalem at that eschatological time/day would include God's protection and strengthening of his people to face the challenges before them. God's salvation would involve both his defensive acts of delivering the people from the coming attack, but also the empowerment of his people. The transformative power of God would impact many. Even the weak who often stubble and fall would be as strong as the powerful warriors from the house of David (12:8a). This claim was similar to the promises of Isaiah 40:30–31. Sometimes the young men faint and get tired in battle and the youths stumble and fall, but those who put their hope in the Lord would gain new strength from God. In these statements the prophet may have been thinking of the weak having the strength comparable to God's strength that manifested itself in David when he defeated the Philistine giant Goliath (1 Sam. 17), or God's empowerment of a later Davidic king Asa who defeated a million Egyptian troops under Zerah (2 Chron. 14:9–15). To make this future strengthening even more astonishing and radical, Zechariah compared the future strength of the royal house of David to God's strength or to the supernatural power of the Angel of the Lord (11:8). This could be a reference to the power of the messianic King (Zech. 9:9–10), who would reign and rule over the whole world and end all wars (Isa. 2:2–4). The comment about being like the Angel of the Lord who goes before them would have reminded the audience of the exodus events when the Angel of the Lord went before the people to show them where to go and then went behind them to protect them from the oncoming Egyptian army (Exod. 14:19). Such promises gave strong assurance that God's people would be victorious in this final battle, and these promises prepared the people to put the more detailed description of this battle in 14:1–11 into the broader perspective of 12:1–9.

THEOLOGICAL FOCUS

The exegetical idea (in the future, the nations would gather together against Jerusalem, but God would watch over his people, save the people of Jerusalem, and pour out his grace on them) leads to this theological focus: God's people know that God will watch over and rescue them from their enemies.

Three key theological points are embedded in this prophecy. First, God would be ready, able, and strong enough to defend his people from those nations that would attempt to annihilate them. The nations would be gathered together for the purpose of defeating Jerusalem, but God would strengthen his people for the fight and defend them, for God would confuse the enemies and save his people. Second, although this future battle would be difficult, hope of restoration was possible because the victory would be secure. God, the one in charge of the battle would defeat his enemies and save his people. Third,

God's promises would give the audience listening to the prophet assurances that they could trust God during these difficult days because he had proven that he was able to fulfill his promises.

PREACHING AND TEACHING STRATEGIES

Exegetical and Theological Synthesis

Zechariah 12:1–9 underscores God's power in creation and deliverance. Zechariah continued to beat the drum of the Lord's sovereign might and covenant faithfulness. The God who formed the world would fight for his people. The God who empowered David would empower his people in battle. The God who led the exodus would lead the inhabitants of Jerusalem. The God who sustained the faint of heart would multiply his strength to secure the glory of his people.

What is less clear in this section is the timing of "that day"—the climax of history—in which God would vindicate his people. References to future enemies, battles, heroes, and outcomes pick up steam at this point in the book. Because the tolerant Persians were an unlikely enemy, many in Zechariah's day may have speculated a future, unknown enemy (e.g., Greeks or Romans).

Finally, in addition to the prophet's focus on God's power, Zechariah also depicted God as a promise-keeper. He made several references to the future of the Davidic dynasty, alluding to God's promise to retain a son on David's throne (Zech. 12:8–12; 2 Sam. 7:8–16). In a previous oracle, Zechariah referenced a coming king (9:9–10) in alignment with other prophets' prediction of the Messiah (Isa. 9:1–7; Jer. 23:5–6; Mic. 5:2). By keeping his promise to David, God intended to benefit all people through a royal son (Pss. 2:6–12; 72; 110).

Preaching Idea

God's strength is our secret weapon.

Contemporary Connections

What does it mean?

What does it mean that God's strength is our secret weapon? OT miracles of deliverance certainly displayed God's strength. He drowned Pharaoh's army in the sea after a series of supernatural plagues (e.g., the exodus). He toppled the city of Jericho with a marching band (e.g., Joshua). He overthrew enemy Syrian forces with fiery chariots (e.g., Elisha) and Midian opponents with flaming pots (e.g. Gideon). But these examples of strength are not normative. Even in the NT, God limited his display of power through miraculous signs.

So how does God manifest his strength today? God manifests his strength by giving us inner fortitude and supportive community to face everyday battles. His powerful Spirit empowers his people (Zech. 4:6; cf. Eph. 1:19–20). We do not war against local enemies or oppressive kings but unseen spiritual forces (Dan. 10:13; cf. Eph. 6:12). Today's battles comprise physical, emotional, spiritual, mental, and relational warfare, as Satan aims to upset, accuse, and destroy God's people (Zech. 3:1; cf. John 10:10; Rev. 12:9–12). As we fight depression, physical injury, or damage to our reputation, God's strength sustains our hope that we will not be overcome (Isa. 43:1–7; 54:17; Ps. 91; cf. Rom. 8:31–39). As we suffer slander, abuse, oppression, and persecution from without, or wrestle with doubt, insecurity, addiction, and guilt from within, God's strength upholds us.

Is it true?

Is it true that God's strength is our secret weapon? Yes! His strength has profound effect on our lives. It sustains creation, fortifies our faith, and empowers his people to accomplish great feats (Eph. 3:20–21). Does his strength have to be a secret? No. We are not required to keep his strength a secret. His strength is absolute (Exod. 15:18; Pss. 93:1; 97:1; Dan. 4:34); earthly power is derivative (Ps. 2; Prov. 21:1; Isa. 45:1; Dan. 4:28–37; cf. John 19:8–12). Zechariah painted a picture of God easily overturning global forces by empowering his people for battle (12:2–9). Psalmists and prophets praised God's mighty power (Pss. 21:1; 33:13–17; 71:7; Isa. 28:2; Zeph. 3:17).

On the other hand, God's people must avoid a triumphal spirit. Joseph and Daniel modeled this principle well. Each resolutely served a foreign king, knowing God's strength had undergirded their success. They provided wise counsel when asked, undertook the political work on their plate, and summoned God's strength in the face of false accusations. Contrarily, Israel often suffered for assuming that God's strength would secure for her easy victory (Num. 14:39–45; Josh. 7; 1 Sam. 4). His strength is not weaponry we can manipulate.

Nor does God's strength guarantee our success in all the battles of life. He will provide inner fortitude and supportive community to help us escape some trials, defeat some addiction, silence some accusers, and overcome some fears. But other times, God's strength will elude us. We will feel defeated by a tough diagnosis, workplace conflict, or sexual temptation. None of these temporary losses nullifies Zechariah's affirmation of God's strength. It simply means his ultimate victory is yet to come.

Now what?

How do we draw upon God's strength? First, we must remember that we battle on multiple fronts: physical, emotional, spiritual, mental, and relational. These battles are an ongoing reality. For those in the secular West, seeing the battle requires a new set of lenses (Boa, 2017, 133–53). Beneath our simmering anger, nagging doubt, and lingering depression, we realize there may be spiritual dynamics at play. Beyond our physical battles, we recognize that God will sustain our bodies (Ps. 16:10–11). Amid our relational battles, we recall how God gives us supportive community who will stand beside us (e.g., 1 Sam. 18:1). We must not ignore our battles but respect their complexity.

Second, we must realize our true source of strength. God both protects and empowers us. He fights for us and through us. We apply his strength by memorizing Scripture. It guards us against straying from his path, surrendering to enemies, or sinning against him (Ps. 119). Moreover, we can add to our arsenal various psalms that celebrate God's might in battle (Pss. 18, 31, 46, 59, 62, 68). Singing songs (e.g., Chris Tomlin's "Whom Shall I Fear [God of Angel Armies]") and hymns (e.g., Martin Luther's "A Mighty Fortress") with a similar theme can also bolster our application of his strength (Exod. 15).

Finally, we must endure. The surest fruit of God's strength is our ability endure in our battles (Ps. 46; Isa. 26:3; cf. Rom. 5:1–5). Joshua serves as an ideal example. Not only did he heed the call to "be strong" as he led Israel's conquest of the Promised Land (Josh. 1:6, 9), but he stayed faithful to God until death (24:15). God's strength is our secret weapon from the start of a battle until its final punch. And because Zechariah did not specify an end date, endurance is essential.

Creativity in Presentation

During my (Tim's) childhood, I enjoyed playing the hand game "rock paper scissors." Most people in the congregation will be familiar with the simple game. One of the unwritten rules (or, really, a way to cheat) is the use of a fourth weapon. (A secret weapon. In my day, it was a gun or a bomb, but it would likely be more appropriate to strike a Superman pose and claim "invincibility.") Any player using a secret weapon would not reveal it immediately but would wait until the opportune time, late in a match or to finish off a "Best of Five" series. Consider engaging your congregation in a "Best of Five: Rock Paper Scissors Battle." Have them pair up with someone beside them. After a minute, invite a challenger to the stage. Play up the fact that you can ensure victory. You have a secret weapon. After a normal round or two, strike the Superman pose (legs spread shoulder width apart, hands on hips,

back arched, head tilted to the side). Let the congregation know how confident you felt with "invincibility" at your disposal. Ask them how they would feel having a secret weapon, not just for a silly game, but for spiritual battle.

Rules for Rock Paper Scissors

Two people face off; left arm extended, hand face up; right arm extended, hand in a fist. Both players chant, "Rock, Paper, Scissors, Shoot," knocking their fist into the open palm three times before contorting the right hand (on "Shoot") into one of three shapes:

- Rock (fist),
- Paper (flat hand, palm down), or
- Scissors (pointer and middle fingers extended in V-shape).

Rock beats scissors (crushes them), but loses to paper (which covers it).

Scissors beats paper (cuts it), but loses to rock (gets crushed).

Paper beats rock (covers it), but loses to scissors (gets cut).

If both players show the same shape, the match results in a tie. Often a "best of" (3, 5, 7) series determines the winner.

A recurring theme in superhero films is the possession or production of a secret weapon. No matter if the weapon is a superhuman serum (e.g., *Hulk*, 2003; *Captain America*, 2011), deadly poison (e.g., *Wonder Woman*, 2017), or military technology (*Iron Man*, 2008; *Ant Man*, 2015; *Spider-Man: Homecoming*, 2017), the quest to secure it typically backfires. These movies teach that we should not confuse brute force with God's strength. Pose the question to your congregation: What's our obsession with secret weapons? Why don't they ever work?

Other famous "secret weapons" from Hollywood include *Star Wars*'s Death Star and *Indiana Jones*'s Lost Ark. The last is especially relevant, since the Nazis misconstrue the biblical ark of the covenant as a divinely powered weapon for world domination in *Raiders of the Lost Ark* (1981, directed by Steven Spielberg). Of course, their plan backfires, sealing the Nazis' fate. You might show a clip of Indiana Jones (played by Harrison Ford) and Sallah (played by John Rhys-Davies) uncovering the ark, and then describe the aftermath of it being opened: Nazi faces begin to melt. You might state: "Perhaps, some secret weapons are worth keeping a secret!"

Finally, personal testimonies can illustrate the power of God's strength in life's battles. My former neighbor suffered a miscarriage two weeks before her daughter's due date. The loss was crushing to her and her husband, but God's strength carried them. He showed up in the prayers of friends, meals from church, presence of family, and certainty of their faith. I've seen others battle cancer, overcome broken marriages, and face job uncertainty with patient resolve and helpful support. My wife suffered years of self-hatred and self-harm before God's strength delivered her. His powerful love won her heart. She freely shares her testimony with women who face similar struggles. "The war is won," she says, "but skirmishes remain." She daily relies on God's strength. Similar stories can make the message personal, giving hope to your congregation.

The creative elements should all point to the key idea: God's people know that God will watch over and rescue them from their enemies. Or, God's strength is our secret weapon.

- The mighty Creator wants to speak to us (12:1).

- The mighty Lord will defend us against our accusers (12:2–5).

- The mighty Lord will strengthen us in our battles (12:6–9).

DISCUSSION QUESTIONS

1. What did Zechariah mean by his repeated reference to "that day"? How would his original audience have understood the phrase?

2. How does God's strength show through creation?

3. What specific stories of deliverance in the OT testify to God's power?

4. How might we understand God's strength as our secret weapon? How do we guard against a triumphalist spirit while knowing that God is on our side?

5. How do you explain the times God chooses not to intervene on behalf of his people? What is our responsibility as we wait on his deliverance?

Zechariah 12:10–13:9

EXEGETICAL IDEA
In the distant future when God's grace and compassion would be poured out on the families of Israel, they would weep bitterly for the one they had pierced, be cleansed of their sins, reject false teachings, and renew their covenant with God.

THEOLOGICAL FOCUS
God's grace brings mourning for past sins, purification from sin, an end to false prophecy, and the restoration of the covenant with God.

PREACHING IDEA
Fresh starts often leave deep scars.

PREACHING POINTERS
Renewal for God's people came at a cost. Starting fresh, like many of life's battles, required some casualties. In Zechariah's day, God issued a death sentence for idols, false prophets, his Messiah, and many of God's people. While reminders of God's grace were intended to encourage the original audience, the prophet also exposed their grievous sin. Grace was costly. Zechariah's message evoked a longing for a fresh start, even if the path appeared painful.

Those desperate for a fresh start in our day must beware of quick, pain-free fixes. Changing our thinking, actions, and relationships requires both human intention and divine intervention to habituate. A perfectly clean slate will not happen this side of heaven. Sadly, the world peddles self-improvement as a cheap imposter to starting fresh. We're compelled to improve everything—from our sleeping habits and sex life to our reading speed and waistline—in a few simple steps. Take a nap. Swallow a pill. Scan first sentences. Avoid carbs. Meanwhile, new rules for self-improvement will replace old ones, and we remain in a state of spiritual decay. This passage offers a helpful corrective, assuring us that fresh starts often leave deep scars.

GOD'S GRACE AND CLEANSING WILL TRANSFORM ALL ISRAEL AND JUDAH (12:10–13:9)

LITERARY STRUCTURE AND THEMES (12:10–13:9)

This message described how God's grace would cause his people to mourn for the one they had pierced (12:10–13:1); then God would remove all false sources of hope (13:2–6), and finally the shepherd would be struck and the sheep would be purified in order to renew their covenant with God (13:7–9).

Three themes in this unit are grace, cleansing, and a new covenant relationship with God that would overwhelm God's people so that they would mourn over their past mistakes of piercing the one for whom they then mourned, practicing idolatry, and believing false prophecies.

- *God's Grace Will Cause Israel to Mourn for the One They Pierced (12:10–13:1)*
- *God Will Put an End to Idolatry (13:2–6)*
- *Striking the Shepherd Will Cause Scattering, Refinement, and Then Covenant Renewal (13:7–9)*

EXPOSITION

The history of Israel is full of dark clouds and failure because the people did not recognize and follow the good leaders and prophets God gave them. In the early period, they rebelled against Moses and God when they worshipped a golden calf (Exod. 32), and in the time of the judges they accepted Baalism (Judg. 2–3). In the postexilic era, they married pagan women (Ezra 9–10) and did not put glorifying God first, so they worked on their own homes instead of building God's temple (Hag 1). Isaiah even referred to a day in the future when they would kill God's chosen servant who was supposed to be a light to all mankind (Isa. 49:6), establish justice for all people (Isa. 42:1–4), and die to pay for the sins of many (Isa. 53). However, few understood God's plans; few faithfully followed him.

These failures continued year after year until God intervened and brought a time of judgment that led to repentance. At that time, people would recognize the error of their ways, and God would graciously forgive them. The prophet Zechariah announced a future day when God's grace would bring about another transformational change in the thinking of his people. Then they would weep and plead for mercy, and they would mourn for the one they had pierced. Consequently, God would transform their hearts, cleanse them, remove all idols and the temptation to worship them, and end all deceptive false prophecy. This would lead to a time when the people would go through a period of great refinement and sorrow for their past mistakes.

God's Grace Will Cause Israel to Mourn for the One They Pierced (12:10–13:1)

Because of God's grace, every person from every Jewish family would bitterly mourn the death of the person they had pierced.

It appeared that the victory over Judah's enemies in 12:1–9 would happen before the mourning in 12:10–13:9 "in that day," but it is possible to understand the mourning and cleansing in 12:10–13:1 as a prerequisite to God's saving action in 12:1–9 (Klein, 2008,

362). Or it is possible to view God acting out of pure grace (12:1–9), which would result in the opening of the heart to a new understanding, great mourning (12:10–13:1), and a cleansing from impure things (13:2–6). It is impossible to know if these messages were put in chronological order or if they happened at the same time, though some might claim that it is logical first to remove Israel's enemies (12:1–9), then to restore Israel itself through mourning and cleansing (12:10–13:1), and finally to have God remove all false teachings (13:2–6).

12:10a. Initially, God promised to pour out a spirit of "grace" (חֵן) and "supplications, a desire to seek for God's blessings" (תַּחֲנוּנִים) on the royal house of David, the people Jerusalem, and the people of Judah. Elsewhere, God promised to pour out his Spirit on all mankind so that people would be able to prophecy and see visions (Joel 2:28–29) and to bring the dead to life (Ezek. 37:14). Through the gift of the Spirit, God would pour out his blessings on his people (Isa. 44:3), on the Messiah (Isa. 11:2), on his Servant who would establish justice in all the earth (Isa. 42:1), and on the land to bring back its fertility (Isa. 32:15). Zechariah also referred to the Spirit enabling Zerubbabel to finish building the temple in Jerusalem (Zech. 4:6), and the Spirit speaking to the nation through prophets (Zech. 7:12). Consequently, some view Zechariah 12:10 to be describing God's divine Spirit (Barker, 1983, 683; Boda, 2004, 485) granting grace on the royal Davidic house and the people in Jerusalem. Although this thought is true of God's work in other passages, this verse only refers to God influencing the "spirit" of the people. In this context, the "spirit" seemed to refer to a change in the human spirit (the attitude) of the leaders. The people of Jerusalem would be infused with a desire to be gracious and a willingness to be awakened with a new desire to seek God in prayer and repentance (McComiskey, 1998, 1214; Merrill, 2003, 279; Klein, 2008, 364). This would require a major transformation of

the thinking and behavior of these people (cf. Ezek. 36:26), a change that would reverse the stubbornness of the past and introduce an attitude of repentance, graciousness, seeking God's favor, mourning for the mistakes of the past, and prayer for God to forgive them.

One of the purposes of granting this special gift of grace was so that "they would look on me whom they have pierced" and mourn, a clause that has several difficulties. The "they" must refer to the leaders in the royal house of David as well as the Jewish people living in Jerusalem and Judah. A straightforward reading would suggest that they "pierced" (דָּקָר) God in some way and would at that time weep bitterly over what they have done. But the very next phrase expanded on this action by saying "and they will mourn for him," rather than mourn for "me." Some resolve this inconsistency by emending the earlier pronoun "me" to "him" to alleviate the problem (Meyers and Meyers, 1993, 336; Petersen, 1995, 106, 108; Redditt, 1995, 132; NRSV), but there is no textual basis for this solution. Others view God as being symbolically pierced (disregarded or abandoned) when his ways were rejected or one of God's servants was martyred or one of the prophets was killed (Hill, 2008b, 590). Since 13:6 has a similar picture of someone striking a shepherd with a sword, it is likely that 12:10 referred to this same good shepherd of 11:4–14 (McComiskey, 1998, 1214). It is possible that the literal understanding of the death of this person was connected to the death of the suffering Servant of Isaiah 53, but in Zechariah there is no explicit statement that the one pierced was dying to provide atonement for many. But Klein (2008, 368) connects the cleansing of a fountain in 13:1 with the work of the suffering Servant of Isaiah 52:13–53:12. The Babylonian Talmud cites Zechariah 12:10 as referring to the Messiah (b. Sukkah 52a), and the NT author of John 19:34, 37 saw this verse fulfilled when the soldiers pierced Jesus just before he was taken down from the cross.

TRANSLATION ANALYSIS: 12:10

NASB[95] "so that they will look on Me whom they have pierced"

NIV[84] "They will look on me, the one they have pierced."

HCSB "and they will look at Me whom they pierced"

NKJV "Then they will look on Me whom they pierced."

NRSV "when they look on the one whom they have pierced"

The Hebrew has אֵלַי, "on/unto me," which is a more accurate than "the one."

12:10b–13. The prophet gave an unusual amount of attention (four and a half verses) to the large number of families that would "mourn" (סָפַד) for this one who was pierced. Public mourning and weeping were very open and expressive in that culture, being accompanied with sackcloth and ashes. These people would not hesitate to express their deep emotional feelings and would publicly declare the bitterness of losing someone as precious as a dear family member. These families would feel deep grief for what they had done to the one they had pierced. Their mourning would be gut-wrenching, and their weeping would be as loud as parents mourning after the death of an only child or a firstborn son (12:10).

In order to strengthen the audience's appreciation of this mourning in Jerusalem, the prophet Zechariah compared it to the weeping of Hadad-rimmon in the plain of Megiddo. Unfortunately, there is no clear record in the biblical accounts about what happened in relationship to Hadad-rimmon. This could be the name of a person, maybe the person who killed the Israelite king Ahab at Megiddo (1 Kings 22:34; Baldwin, 1972, 193), but the biblical text made no mention of great weeping for the evil king Ahab, so this would seem unlikely. Another possibility would be to connect the mourning for Hadad-rimmon to the mourning for the Canaanite storm god

Hadad, who was probably the same as the Assyrian storm god Raminu or the Aramean god Ramman. But it would be odd and inappropriate to compare the gross pagan cultic weeping for a pagan god to the good weeping for the one pierced (Merrill, 2003, 283). So it is more likely that Hadad-rimmon was the name of the place near Megiddo where the righteous king Josiah was killed by the Egyptian king Neco (2 Kings 23:28–30; 2 Chron. 35:21–25). This tragic event did produce a period of great morning for the nation of Judah (Merrill, 2003, 277; Klein, 2008, 371). The mourning in Zechariah 12:10–13 would impact the land of Judah and the individual lives of every family member in Judah, from the royal family of David to the family of the prophet Nathan (12:12), from the family members in the priestly tribe of Levi to the wise man Shimei (12:13; cf. 1 Kings 1:8; 4:18). God would graciously work in the hearts of the leaders and the people, so they would understand their mistake of killing the pierced one and confess their sins.

13:1. The prophet announced that in that eschatological time, a "fountain" (מָקוֹר, an artesian well) would be opened (a passive verb, so it was probably opened by God) so that the royal tribe of David and the people of Jerusalem could receive cleansing from sin and any impurities. This would suggest that there would be a great revival and that the political leaders of the nation at that time would be able to lead the people in godly paths. In the early Levitical law, washing with water was seen as a symbol of cleansing (Lev. 14:4–9, 48–53; Num. 19:7–9, 13, 17–21; 31:23). This spring of water probably referred to the same water source for the living waters mentioned in Zechariah 14:8, and it could coincide with the water flowing out from under the threshold of Ezekiel's new temple (Ezek. 47:1–12; cf. Joel 3:18). In Ezekiel 36:25, God announced that "I will sprinkle clean water on you, and you will be clean; I will cleanse you from all your iniquities and from your idols." This imagery would indicate that those mourning their sin of piercing the person mentioned in Zechariah 12:10 would repent and have their sins forgiven.

WORD ANALYSIS: The noun מָקוֹר can refer to (a) a "spring, a water fountain" (Prov. 25:26; Jer. 2:13); (b) God as a "source" of life if used metaphorically (Jer. 2:13; 17:13); (c) a "source" of life (Ps 36:9; Prov. 10:11; 16:22; 18:4; Jer. 51:26); or (d) a "source" of blood (Lev. 12:7; 20:18). This word points to the place of origin or source of a flowing liquid.

God Will Put an End to Idolatry (13:2–6)
All forms of false worship will cease.

13:2a. The second paragraph outlines further steps in the transformation of God's people in that eschatological age. Two major changes are mentioned: the end of idol worship (13:2a) and the end of false prophesy (13:2b–6). A major problem throughout Israel's history was the existence of foreigners and Israelites who worshipped pagan idols, particularly the idols connected to the worship of the Canaanite fertility god Baal and the goddess Asherah. From the beginning of the covenant community, God forbade the making and worship of other gods, as outlined in the first and second commandments (Exod. 20:3–5); yet the people at Sinai built a golden calf (Exod. 32). In the time of the judges, the people repeatedly rejected God and his covenant stipulations and served this god Baal (Judg. 2:11–13; 3:7; 6:25; 10:6; 18:17–18). This continued in the northern tribes of Israel, especially during the time of Ahab and Jezebel (1 Kings 16:29–33), and in the southern tribes in the reign of Athaliah, Ahaz, and Manasseh (2 Chron. 22:10–23:15; 33:1–25). In several sermons, the prophet Isaiah warned of the uselessness of idols because they can do nothing and were a deceptive illusion (Isa. 41:21–29; 43:9–13; 44:9–20; G. V. Smith, 2009, 141–52, 200–204, 228–40). Earlier in the vision of the woman in the basket in Zechariah 5:5–11, there was the prophecy about the removal of idolatry from the land of Israel, and 13:2a predicts a future era when the idols and even the names of the idols would be banished, forgotten, and removed from the memory of God's people.

13:2b. Although God's removal of idols would help the people maintain their covenant relationship to God, this was not all that God would banish from the earth. God would also remove the false prophets and all impurity from the land (13:2b). Deuteronomy 13:1–5 warned the nation not to trust a prophet or dreamer who might encourage people to follow another god. Israel's God condemned those who practiced the false religious practices, including witches, sorcerers, mediums, spiritists, and those who spoke to the dead (Deut. 18:10–11; Lev. 19:26, 31; 20:6). The prophet Jeremiah repeatedly confronted the deceptive false prophets who said there would be peace (Jer. 5:11–13; 6:13–15; 8:11–12; 14:13; 23:17), spoke falsehoods, used divinations, had futile dreams, and gave deceptive prophecies in the name of Israel's God (Jer. 14:14; 23:16). Some prophesied through Baal (Jer. 23:13) and were not called by God, nor did they stand in the council of God to hear what God was saying (Jer. 23:22). Ezekiel condemned the false prophets who misled the people saying that there would be peace (Ezek. 13:1–17). There was even some evidence of some false prophecy in the time of Nehemiah (Neh. 6:12–14). In addition, God would remove all ritual impurities (13:2c; Lev. 7:20–21; Num. 19:13), including the impurity involved with idolatry (Ezek. 36:17). The "unclean spirit" that would be cut off was a supernatural force similar to the lying spirit that deceived Ahab and caused him to go into battle even though God revealed to Micaiah that Ahab would die (1 Kings 22:19–23) or the evil spirit that controlled king Saul when he tried to kill David (1 Sam. 16:14; 16:23). This evil spirit was probably the one deceiving the false prophets to speak lies in the name of God (Merrill, 2003, 289). These verses point to the sinless circumstances that would exist when God establishes his eschatological kingdom.

13:3. It seems odd to read in 13:3–6 that there would be some people who would still want to prophesy after God had just said in 13:2 that all false prophets would be cut off. Baldwin (1972, 196) suggests that "the persistence of false prophecy to his own time leads Zechariah to envisage its possible recurrence, even after the Lord has dealt with it." Nevertheless, it would make more logical sense to see 13:3–6 as a description of what was prophesied before the stopping of false prophecies in 13:2b; that is, 13:3–6 describes the difficult human interactions that took place in the process of ending all false prophecy (13:3). This opposition to prophets would not just be a mild verbal rebuke, but the parents of someone who wanted to be a prophet would take matters into their own hands and in obedience to the commands to kill a false prophet in Deuteronomy 13, they would "pierce" (דָּקַר)[1] their child in order to kill him.

13:4. Seeing God and society's determination to eliminate false prophecy from his future kingdom, the existing prophets would become ashamed of their false prophecies in the past (cf. Jer. 22:22; Mic. 3:7), and they would reject their prophetic role and remove the usual clothing worn by a prophet (13:4). Although the false prophet would wear pious clothing to look the part of a real prophet, their real purpose was to deceive people into thinking they were the real thing.

13:5–6. In the future, these prophets would disassociate themselves with anything characteristic of being a prophet and even swear that they had nothing to do with being a prophet (13:5). Instead, these prophetic figures would claim to be farmers, much like Amos (Amos 7:10–15). Amos was telling the truth about his role, while these false prophets would be lying about their occupation. The final claim of these false prophets would be that they were not prophets but were indentured workers on the land since their youth (McComiskey, 1998, 1221). They would make deceptive comments about their earlier life in order to hide the evidence of their past association with false prophecy (13:6c). The excuse that the marks on the prophet's body were due to an accident or a brawl in the house of "my friend" (מְאַהֲבָי) was likely a lie to cover up the fact that he had participated in pagan cultic practices in which prophets cut themselves (cf. 2 Kings 18:28), which was forbidden in the law of Moses (Lev. 19:28).[2] The translation "my friend" could be rendered "my lover" (Merrill, 2003, 292; Petersen, 1995, 127; Wolters, 2014, 437) and refer to pagan cultic prostitution, or "my lover" could refer to his love for a pagan god.

---

1   This is the same term used for the killing of the one whom people would mourn for in 12:10. Thus, in 12:10, the people opposed the one doing God's work and pierced him, but now they would oppose people who rejected God's work and pierce them—even if they were one of their own children.

2   The reason why these prophets cut themselves is never explicitly explained, but in the Mount Carmel contest between the prophets of Baal and the prophet Elijah, it seemed that this was to awaken the god Baal, to show the seriousness of their plea for Baal to act on their behalf in this contest between Baal and Yahweh, or to demonstrate the depth of their devotion and love for Baal.

TRANSLATION ANALYSIS: 13:5b

NASB[95]   "for a man sold me as a slave in my youth"

NIV[84]   "the land has been my livelihood since my youth"

HCSB   "for a man purchased me as a servant since my youth"

NKJV   "for a man taught me to keep cattle from my youth"

NRSV   "for the land has been my possession since my youth"

The false prophet claimed that he was a slave who worked the soil since his youth.

Striking the Shepherd Will Cause Scattering, Refinement, and Then Covenant Renewal (13:7–9)

A sword would kill the shepherd, the sheep would scatter, and many would die, but then those remaining would seek the Lord to recommit themselves to their covenant relationship with God.

The short final poetic ending of this section picks up three common themes. First, the shepherd was disrespected (cf. 11:9–12) and someone was pierced (cf. 12:10). These ideas may be connected to the striking of "my shepherd" in 13:7. Second, the wars against Judah and Jerusalem (12:2–3, 9; 14:2–5) may be connected to the scattering of sheep and the death of many people in 13:8. Third, a future renewal of God's covenant relationship with his people in 13:9 would be a natural outflow of the people walking in the name of the Lord (10:12) and their purification (13:1). It is also important to notice the differences between these passages, for 13:7–9 speaks of the eschatological future day (like 12:10), but the story about the good and useless shepherd in 11:4–17 is not prefixed by the "in that day" phrase.

13:7. God, who is sovereign over everything that would happen, would instruct a sword, an instrument of war and death, to strike "my shepherd" who was "my associate" (13:7).[3] There was a close relationship between God and his friend or associate who was "my shepherd," but no explanation was provided to identify the shepherd or comprehend why God commanded this to happen. Since the word "shepherd" was often used in the OT to symbolically refer to a king (or of God, the shepherd King; Ezek. 34) and the context of Zechariah 9–14 refers to several shepherd kings, this shepherd may refer to one of them. Although one might connect this shepherd to the punishment of the worthless shepherd who was attacked with a sword in 11:17, that person would hardly be an associate/companion/friend of God. Merrill (2003, 293–95) thinks this person was punished by God for unfaithfulness, but this would seem to read too much into the text. Redditt (2012, 121) argues that the shepherds in 11:4–16 were local priests and the worthless shepherd in 11:17 and 13:7 was the high priest, but the identification of these roles was not stated in this text. Based on Ezekiel 34 and 37, Boda (2004, 513) identifies the evil shepherds as non-Davidic leaders in postexilic Yehud. Klein (2008, 387) connects the shepherd who was pierced in 12:10 with this shepherd in 13:7 because in the NT, Jesus quoted Zechariah 13:7 and applied this verse to himself (Matt. 26:31; Mark 14:27). Curtis (2006, 218) argues that the prophecy about the killing of the shepherd in 12:10 and 13:7 was influence by the death of the Servant in Isaiah 53.

Once someone killed the leader of the people, it would be natural for the sheep to scatter (13:7b). The fact that God would "turn my hand against" the sheep was left

---

3   The phrase גֶּבֶר עֲמִיתִי means "a man, my associate," and it appears mainly in Leviticus used of a "companion, fellow priest, neighbor, friend" (Lev. 5:21 [Eng. 6:2]; 18:20; 19:15, 17; 24:19; 25:14, 15, 17).

unexplained, but it may be due to their rejection of the good leader (shepherd). This was not a phrase that provided assurance that God would turn his hand toward his people to protect the flock (McComiskey, 1998, 1224). This prophecy specifically referred to God's judgment on the "little ones," a symbol that points to the suffering of the powerless, weak, and helpless people who would not be able to defend themselves in a military context. Baldwin (1972, 198) suggests that this pointed to the scattering of Jesus's disciples after the crucifixion as well as the future persecution of the church (Mark 13:19, 24; Rev. 11).

13:8. The eventual results (marked by "it will come about") of this persecution of believers would be the death of two-thirds of the sheep, with the remaining one-third surviving a time of severe persecution and refining. Klein (2014, 390) makes a case for this prophecy being fulfilled in the Roman era of the first century A.D. when there was severe persecution of Jews and Christians, but persecution existed against believers many years before and after the first century.

13:9. Those who emerge from this time of testing would be a purified remnant that trusts God (13:9a; cf. 13:1), and they would be willing to renew their commitment to a faithful covenant relationship with God (13:9b). At that time, those refined believers would seek God's face, pray for his mercy, and commit themselves to be his faithful followers. God would hear their sincere prayers, respond to their requests, and restore his covenant relationship with them (13:9b). Since this prophecy was referring to eschatological events in the future, this probably described the establishment of God's new and eternal covenant of peace with his people in the future (Isa. 55:3–5; Jer. 31:31–34; Ezek. 34:25; 37:24–26; Hos. 1:10; 2:18–20; 3:5).

THEOLOGICAL FOCUS

The exegetical idea (In the distant future when God's grace and compassion would be poured out on the families of Israel, they would weep bitterly for the one they had pierced, be cleansed of their sins, reject false teachings, and renew their covenant with God) leads to this theological focus: God's grace brings mourning for past sins, purification from sin, an end to false prophecy, and the restoration of the covenant with God.

The theological focus of 12:10–13:9 is centered around four key themes explained as follows but not necessarily in chronological order. First, someone would strike (or pierce) a shepherd (12:10; 13:7) and scatter the sheep (13:7), resulting in the death of two-thirds of the people (13:8). Second, this would lead to a difficult time of divine refinement and testing (13:9). Third, at this time, God would completely eradicate things that might tempt the people to stray from their commitment to faithfully serve God. This would include the removal of idols and every unclean thing associated with the worship of the worthless man-made objects of wood. In addition, all false prophets would cease to give their deceptive messages because any false teaching would be met with the threat of death (13:2–6). Fourth, after a time of great testing and purification, the righteous remnant would restore their covenant relationship with God (13:9b).

Thus, in a brief review of the end times events, the prophet foresaw that there would be both persecution, scattering, and refining, leaving only those who trust God and desire to live in covenant commitment to God. These warnings spoke about the future, but they were instructive to people living in any period of history because they revealed what God wanted his people to do (13:9b) and what they should avoid (13:2–6), and they warn of the difficult life for which they should prepare (13:8–9).

PREACHING AND TEACHING STRATEGIES

Exegetical and Theological Synthesis

Zechariah 12:10–13:9 demonstrates that purging, cleansing, and refining are God's priority, marks of a gracious new beginning for his people. This spirit of grace is the focus of the passage, which appears to differ with previous texts that mention the divine Spirit (4:6; 7:12). Here, God was concerned with the inner disposition of the people who are mourning (12:10). A fresh start begins from the inside out.

Their fresh start moved forward with the removal of idols and false prophets. Idols and false prophets plagued Israel for centuries, and the nation was unable to fully realize its holy calling when held in their grip (e.g., Exod. 32; Mic. 3:5–7). Handcrafted idols served as substitute gods, diverting worship from Israel's Creator to his creation (Exod. 20:3–5; cf. Rom. 1:21–22). So God interceded, using true prophets to mock idols for their inability to communicate, control weather, or even move (1 Kings 18:20–40; Isa. 41:21–29; 44:9–20; Hab. 2:18–20).

God's grace, however, did not leave his people unaccountable. The postexilic prophets and leaders continued to motivate God's people toward faithfulness. Haggai rebuked people for abandoning the temple reconstruction to work on home improvement projects (Hag. 1:4–5). Malachi contended with his audience for shoddy sacrifices, rampant divorce, and social injustices (Mal. 1:6–3:5). Nehemiah and Ezra used corporate confession and contracts to hold God's people accountable in their period of renewal (Ezra 9–10; Neh. 9–13). A fresh start was not a free pass for God's people to live as they pleased.

Preaching Idea

Fresh starts often leave deep scars.

Contemporary Connections

What does it mean?

What does it mean that fresh starts often leave deep scars? Historically, nations and people bear deep scars even after a fresh start. Though changed since the days of Hitler, Germany still bears deep scars of their violent past. America still lives with deep scars of slavery tainting its history. Recovering addicts and alcoholics have deep physical and emotional scars. Abusers and sex offenders have inflicted deep scars on others and will carry scars on their record. While a fresh start may move us beyond the reach of certain evils, their imprint on our past will remain.

Because we all struggle with different vices, abuses, learned behaviors, and relational styles, every path to a fresh start will look different. Some will fight sexual addiction; others will suffer constant discontentment. Some will withdraw from people in self-protection; others will act codependent. Some will benefit from extensive silence and solitude; others will experience growth in corporate worship. As diverse as each path to renewal may appear, they all ultimately lead us to purer love of God and others (Deut. 6:4–5; Lev. 19:18).

What kinds of scars accompany a fresh start? The scars we earn along the path to renewal are tied God's grace. As Zechariah intimates, by grace God cleanses, refines, and purifies his people (12:10; 13:1–2, 9). He may use personal crisis, family tragedy, or natural catastrophe to purge, cleanse, and refine us. He may prune our social circle, finances, or physical capacities to purge, cleanse, and refine us. We, too, may opt for a fresh start, electing to end a toxic friendship, alter reckless spending habits, or end our social media addiction. These changes may leave deep scars—emotionally, socially, physically—but the fresh start is worth it.

Is it true?

Is it true that fresh starts often leave deep scars? Yes. Poll any group of believers, and they will share stories of God's grace amidst their most difficult periods of suffering. It is axiomatic that hard things happen to us in a broken world. And yet, God does not abandon his people as they walk through "the valley of the shadow of death" (Ps. 23:4). Like Joseph, God may stand beside us when we are wrongly accused. Like Naomi, God may send loving companions when our lives look bankrupt. Like Daniel, God may protect us in the face of violence. Life may inflict God's people with deep scars, but out of the pain he gives fresh starts.

The suffering Zechariah's audience experienced stemmed from generations of idolatry, prophetic deception, and disobedience to God's law. Exile etched a deep scar on their collective memory. Similarly, many of our scars stem from our sinful choices. Drunkenness and deception leave deep scars. Slander and theft leave deep scars. Adultery and abuse leave deep scars. These choices may result in loss of job, friendship, marriage, or reputation. However, they may also provide an opportunity for contrition, repentance, humility, and mercy.

Can we experience a fresh start without the deep scars? Surely not all positive change or renewal requires deep scars. However, the old exercise adage "No pain, no gain" holds some relevance. A muscle must suffer microscopic tears that damage it during a workout to increase its bulk and strength. Likewise, we experience spiritual renewal when our we suffer some stress, strain, or tearing. We lose some sleep to offset our lack of prayer. We sponsor a starving child to counteract our selfishness with money. We upset the comfortable family rhythms to spend more time serving in our community. We cancel our Netflix, Hulu, Amazon Prime, and many other possible subscriptions to dethrone our idolatry of entertainment. Each of these decisions may come with a certain amount of sting, if not scarring, which is a good indication of renewal.

Now what?

How do we start fresh? First, we must realize that change is complicated. Our lives have inertia that is hard to redirect. They have patterns that are difficult to reroute. They have situations beyond our control. We cannot simply declare a "fresh start" and expect our families, careers, spending habits, exercise routines, prejudices, and biology to change. Fresh starts are fraught with complication.

Second, we must recognize that a fresh start requires God's grace. Zechariah recognized God's grace in strengthening the people's inner disposition (12:10). Likewise, God allows trials in our lives to purge, cleanse, and refine us from selfishness and idolatry. Interpreting our hardships through the lens of God's discipline (Prov. 3:11–12; cf. Heb. 12:4–11) teaches us to rely on his provision and presence rather than to run from our pain to an idolatrous panacea. An idol constitutes any replacement for God, something we set as our first joy, primary escape, or deepest source of meaning. It is often a good thing—marriage, work, health, technology—but we treat it as an ultimate thing. God's gracious work of renewal will ask us to do the hard work of dethroning idols of any form and denying self. Dethroning our idols keeps God at the center of our lives and allows us to receive his goods as gifts. It may also mean accepting singleness, setting limits on work hours and screen time, or embracing a low metabolism.

Finally, we must keep a long-term view of growth. Although fresh starts often follow landmark events (both good and bad), most of our development happens slowly. Peterson (2000) calls this "a long obedience in the same direction." In a world of "religious tourists," more eager for spiritual thrills than growth, it is not uncommon to find believers stunted when the boredom and bruises of life pile up. End times imagery, like Zechariah's, compels us to keep looking ahead to the ultimate fresh start when God arrives. Until then, the deep scars we bear can remind us of better days ahead.

Creativity in Presentation

My (Tim's) wife delivered our second child through a cesarean section birth. She bears the scar just above her waistline. Her labor lasted nearly thirty hours. We tried every trick in the natural birth book, but progress stalled. Her contractions were not moving and the baby had begun to bruise her insides. The emergency C-section likely spared her and our daughter from fatal complications. The scar serves as a daily reminder of near-death and new life. While my wife despised the pain, we both love the outcome. Our daughter delights us. Most people in your congregation have scars from critical surgeries—removing an appendix, extracting a tumor, repairing a knee—that have given them a new lease on life or renewed sense of comfort. Consider showing some scars and sharing their stories to illustrate their role in renewal. Remember that some scars stem from poor choices (e.g., drunk driving) and others from the corrupted state of our world (e.g., C-section surgery).

The movie *Return to Me* (2000, directed by Bonnie Hunt) is a "heartfelt" romance about Bob Reuland's (played by David Duchovny) decision to donate his wife's heart after she suffers an unexpected death. The recipient of the transplant, Grace Briggs (played by Minnie Driver), later becomes his fated love interest. Before Grace's heart surgery, her friend Megan Dayton (played by Bonnie Hunt) calms her anxiety by celebrating the renewal she will feel after the surgery: her newfound ability to ride a bike, travel to Italy, and date handsome men. After the surgery, Grace acts self-conscious about her scar, so her grandpa (played by Carroll O'Conner) counsels, "Tell everyone you're the luckiest girl in the world." While the "scar" reflected suffering for both Bob and Grace, it also sparked a new chapter of life for the couple. A clip from the movie might reinforce the sermon's preaching idea.

A final illustration comes from C. S. Lewis's Narnia series. In Lewis's ([1954] 1970) *The Horse and His Boy*, the boy Shasta is riding a horse alone in the pitch dark through the cold mist and icy wind of a mountain pass. Unable to see anything ahead and feeling quite lost, as well as being very tired and hungry, he laments his most "unfortunate" life, when the breathing of an unseen, giant presence emerges at his side. The Thing (or Person) listens as Shasta recounts his orphaned childhood, cruel guardian, perilous escape from the city of Tashbaan, and haunted travels, among tombs and deserts, where lions chased him. Then the Large Voice replies, "I do not call you unfortunate." The voice of Aslan speaks and explains that he was the lion who, unbeknownst to the boy, intervened for Shasta at critical points to preserve his life. When Shasta asks the lion why he wounded his traveling companion Aravis, the daughter of the Tisroc, the Voice replies, "Child . . . I am telling you your story, not hers. I tell no one any story but his own" (Lewis, [1954] 1970, 158–59). While we may not know why God writes scars into another person's story, he often shows us the meaning of our misfortunes given enough time.

No matter how you choose to make the message stick, be sure to emphasize that God's grace brings mourning for past sins, purification from sin, an end of false prophecy, and the restoration of the covenant with God. Or, simply, fresh starts often leave deep scars.

- We should grieve our errors before getting a fresh start (12:10–13:1).

- We should purge our idols to prompt a fresh start (13:2–6).

- We may have to endure deep scars to experience a fresh start (13:7–9).

DISCUSSION QUESTIONS

1. How are Zechariah 12:1–9 and 12:10–13:1 related?

2. In what ways did false prophets in the OT abuse their religious influence?

3. What great changes were predicted in Israel in Zechariah 13:1–6?

4. What does a fresh start reveal about God's character? What does it require of us?

5. What scars do you have to remind you of a fresh start in life?

Zechariah 14:1–21

EXEGETICAL IDEA

At the climax of history, the nations would attack Jerusalem, but God would deliver the city, bring major changes in nature, and reign as king; then all nations would pay homage to him.

THEOLOGICAL FOCUS

In the distant future, God will rescue his people, reign as King, and restore his kingdom.

PREACHING IDEA

Get in God's corner: he's the undisputed, everlasting King of the world.

PREACHING POINTERS

Talk of end times continued as Zechariah painted a conclusive picture of days ahead. God would defeat his enemies and renew creation. Jerusalem would become an international hub of praise. Holiness would spread to all peoples. While Zechariah's original audience realized these climatic events may not occur soon, the message still intended to lift their spirits. None of their enemies—from Egypt to Babylon to unforeseen opponents—would prevail. God's justice, nearness, and holiness would win out. The assurance of his reign instilled trust and inspired celebration.

God's reign often goes unnoticed in our day. We bow our hearts to cheaper versions of ascendency: sports trophies, academic honors, business achievements, and celebrity awards. Moreover, the rise of social media has expanded the spotlight, giving the illusion that anyone can achieve fifteen minutes of fame with enough followers, likes, retweets, and activity from a given post. Gluttons for attention abound in our modern age. People build their platforms and careers like personal empires. Our tiny kingdoms and temporary fame will not endure. This passage redirects our focus; we celebrate because God's the undisputed, everlasting King of the world.

AFTER DEFEATING HIS ENEMIES, GOD WILL REIGN AS KING (14:1–21)

LITERARY STRUCTURE AND THEMES (14:1–21)

Zechariah's final message predicted that the nations would attack Jerusalem and partially defeat it, but God would miraculously intervene and rescue a remnant (vv. 1–5). When he comes to earth, God would defeat the nations and transform the world (vv. 6–11). Then all nations would worship the King at his temple (vv. 16–21).

The two themes of defeat and victory in this unit are dramatically contrasted based on the contrasting evil works of the nations that hate God's people and the work of God to defeat his enemies, which would completely rid the world of the forces of evil and rescue his people. One more time, God would come to earth in power to transform the world by defeating those who oppose him and by bringing major transformations in people and in nature in order to create a new era of universal worship of God the King.

- *God Will Rescue Jerusalem (14:1–5)*
- *God Will Transform the World and Jerusalem (14:6–11)*
- *God Will Defeat His Enemies (14:12–15)*
- *All People Will Worship the King at His Temple (14:16–21)*

EXPOSITION

The prophets divided world events into three major segments. The first segment of time referred to past events to draw lessons from past experiences and past instructions. For example, this could include a reference to the life of Noah, Abram, slavery in Egypt, the exodus, the wilderness journey, as well as many references to what God instructed them to do in the covenant stipulations of the Torah. The second segment of history was the present. This included all the historical events that were presently happening, both the good times and the bad. The instructions from God in this segment came when God spoke to various prophets to call the people to repentance and to warn them about the approaching fulfillment of the curses outlined in the covenant documents (Lev. 26; Deut. 27–28). These prophecies frequently referred to near-term events that were sometimes called "the day of the Lord," because at that time God would dramatically end an era of history for some nation (Amos 5:18–20 for Israel; Isa. 13 for Babylon). In light of later use of this kind of terminology, one might conceive of these events as the intermediate day of the Lord, which were precursors of that final day. The third segment of time was the ultimate and universal day of the Lord at the end of time when God would defeat the forces of evil and set up his kingdom. At the climax of this era God would come in power to rescue a remnant of his people from the onslaught of the attacking nations. Then God would recreate a new world where he would reign as King, and all mankind would worship him. This is the era Zechariah referred to in chapter 14.

God Will Rescue Jerusalem (14:1–5)

When the nations attacked Jerusalem, some would die, but God would fight for his people and make a way for many to escape.

14:1–2. The final events in human history would be determined by the earthly arrival of God himself who "is coming" (בָּא is a participle) to put an end to the evil men and nations that oppose God's work on earth. At that time God would gather many nations to Jerusalem for this great battle,[1] and he would initially allow parts of Jerusalem to be captured and plundered by these enemy nations (14:2). Half of the city would be captured, suffer greatly, and many end up being removed from the city. This oppression against Jerusalem could be similar to the refinement process mentioned in 13:9, though its reference to two-thirds of the people being cut off (13:8b) must refer either to a different attack or additional people outside the city of Jerusalem.

14:3–5. Once this work of refinement and testing was accomplished, God the great Warrior would fight for his people (as he did in Exodus 15) and rescue the other half of the city of Jerusalem (14:3). He would do this by coming to the Mount of Olives, the tall hill just east of the city of Jerusalem. He would cause this mountain to split in the middle (similar to the dividing of the Red Sea in Exodus 14) so that people could escape to the east through the valley created by an enormous earthquake (14:4). An earthquake this large would be another record-setting one, so the prophet Zechariah compared it to an earlier large earthquake in the time of King Uzziah. This was the major earthquake that the prophet Amos predicted (Amos 1:1; 8:8; 9:5) around 760 B.C. (Smith, 1998, 48).

The description of this battle has some similarities to Zechariah 12:1–9 and to Joel 3:9–17. Joel spoke about a final battle when all the nations would gather together in the Valley of Jehoshaphat against Israel. At that time God would judge the nations, roar from Zion, be a refuge for his people, dwell among his people

in the holy city of Jerusalem, and pour out his blessing on his people (Joel 3:18, 20). This may be related to the battle mentioned in Ezekiel 38–39 where the nations, led by Gog, would attack God's people, but in the end, they would be defeated by God. Then God would make his glory known among the nations, restore his blessings on his people, and pour out his Spirit on them (Ezek. 39:21–29). The details in these prophecies differ significantly based on the different purposes of each prophecy, thus some question if these prophesies all refer to the same event (Merrill, 2003, 300) even though they have numerous common features. If a prophecy did not mention some details like the partial capture of Jerusalem, that does not mean that the prophecy denied that point, it only means that it omitted the discussion of certain issues in order to focus on other more important points that the audience needed to hear.

Many translations state that when God comes to earth, he would come with the "holy ones with him" (14:5b). Although the term "holy ones" was used from time to time to refer to humans (Lev. 21:7–8), here it could refer to an angelic army (cf. Ps. 89:6–8; Job 5:1) that would assist in defeating God's enemies and delivering his people from death (Redditt, 2012, 131; Hill, 2008b, 600; Merrill, 2003, 306). Others (Wolters, 2014, 459; Boda, 2004, 524–25) believe the "holy ones" refer to the people who would be delivered in these circumstance because the "with you" (in a few manuscripts) at the end of verse 5 most likely refers to the "you," which is Jerusalem in 14:1. Thus 14:5b was promising God's presence with his people as they escape from Jerusalem through a great valley created by this enormous earthquake that split the Mount of Olives. This would be similar to God's presence being with the Israelites as they walked through the waters of the Red Sea (Exod. 14–15).

---

1   Baldwin views this as an "ideological conflict to remove a non-co-operative element that blocked the way to an international world order," but an ideological conflict usually will not be resolved by a massive earthquake. Baldwin, *Haggai, Zechariah, Malachi*, 200.

God Will Transform the World and Jerusalem (14:6–11)

When God comes, part of the present world order would be changed. For example, there would be light all day long (i.e., no darkness), fresh water would flow from Jerusalem, the topography of the land would change, and the curse would not exist.

14:6–7. God's personal appearance on earth at this time would not only impact the outcome of the battle for Jerusalem, but also some aspects of nature. First, Zechariah mentioned the changes in the sky that would affect the source of light on earth. When the prophet said that there would be no light, he was not predicting a time of complete darkness on the earth. There would be light from the glory of God's presence (cf. Isa. 60:1–3), for verse 7b claims that there would be light on the earth all the time. Zechariah's description of that eschatological era was consistent with Isaiah 60:19–20, which says that the sun and moon would not be the source of light on the earth; instead, "the LORD will be your everlasting light." Thus, the normal light and darkness cycle of each day would be ended, and it would be light all the time. It is more difficult to say what would happen to the sun and moon. Interpreters translate the last phrase in 14:6 in quite different ways depending on whether the translators follow the Greek LXX interpretation "cold and frost" or if they try to make sense of the Hebrew "the glorious ones will congeal/thicken." If the sun and moon are the "glorious ones," this phrase may refer to some sort of transformation that would cause their light to be diminished or darkened. Merrill (2003, 307) views this as a reversal of creation, but Isaiah 65–66 refers to a coming new creation. It seems that God's new creation would not involve a return to a pre-creation world; rather, it would be a completely different world, for the very first distinction between day and night (Gen. 1:3–5) would not exist in this new world because of God's presence.

TRANSLATION ANALYSIS: 14:6

NASB[95] "there will be no light; the luminaries will dwindle"

NIV[84] "there will be neither sunlight nor cold, frosty darkness"

HCSB "there will be no light; the sunlight and moonlight will diminish"

NKJV "there will be no light; the lights will diminish"

NRSV "there shall not be either cold or frost"

Since there will be no need for light from heaven because of the brightness of God's glory on earth, it will appear that the sun, moon, and stars have dimmed and lost their brightness.

14:8. The second change in nature would be the outpouring of fresh water from Jerusalem. Although the City of David had a limited source of water from the Gihon Spring (2 Kings 20:20), it was not sufficient to supply drinking water for a large city. So, God would supply a much greater source that would transform the agricultural production of the land. This gushing spring would be the source of a great stream of water all year long with some of the water flowing to the east toward the Dead Sea and some flowing to the west toward the Mediterranean Sea. This was described in terms similar to Ezekiel's description of the waters flowing out from under the threshold of the temple in Jerusalem toward the east (Ezek. 47:1). His description included a great river that would turn the Dead Sea into a place where fish would live, with trees and marshes around the shoreline (Ezek. 47:7–12). Other prophets also viewed the eschatological era as a time of God's rich blessings of water and the great fertility of the land (Isa. 4:2; 30:23–26; 35:1, 6; 41:17–19; Jer. 31:9, 12; Ezek. 34:26; Hos. 2:21–22; Joel 3:18; Amos 9:13). This imagery presents the theological concept that God would be the source of all life and all the blessings from creation.

14:9. The third change would be the inauguration of God's rule on earth and the full realization of the glorious hope shouted in the enthronement psalms (Pss. 93:1; 97:1; 99:1): "The LORD reigns." This would no longer be just a confession of faith. It would be a reality that everyone would experience because God would be there in full control of everything. Although other gods in the surrounding ancient Near Eastern countries were viewed as a king of some part of nature (the rain, the grain, the mountains, the moon), they had to fight for authority and sometimes lost their control and were killed (e.g. Tiamat and Baal).[2] In contrast, the God of Israel was the one and only God who had all power over every part of nature, every person, every nation, and even the heavens. He was the "Lord, Master" of the whole earth (Josh. 3:11; Ps. 97:5; Mic. 4:13), the God of gods and Lord of lords (Deut. 10:17; Dan. 10:47), the King that Isaiah saw sitting on his throne (Isa. 6:1; cf. Ps. 47:2, 8), and he was worshipped as "my God and my King" (Ps. 68:24; 84:3; 145:1). The Lord was the one who would sit as King forever (Ps. 29:10), his throne was established from long ago (Ps. 93:2), and he did and would rule over all nations (Ps. 22:28; 47:7–8), who were nothing in his eyes (Isa. 40:15, 17). In former days, he ruled over this sinful world from his throne in heaven, but Zechariah 14:9 understood that a new phase of his rule on earth would commence "in that day." When he appeared on earth in all his glory and miraculously delivered Jerusalem with the power of an earthquake, all flesh would see him and recognize that there was only one God and King.

14:10–11. The final change in nature would involve a change in the topography of the land. A literal reading of this promise might picture a leveling of the land around Jerusalem to the depth of the Arabah lowland where the Jordan River flows, plus the raising of the elevation of the city of Jerusalem above the surrounding mountains. It is not clear why these changes extend only from Geba (1 Sam. 13:3), a city in the tribe of Benjamin about six miles north of Jerusalem, or only to Rimmon, a village that may be identical to Ein Rimmon, which was south of Jerusalem (Neh. 11:29). The second half of Zechariah 14:10 describes the future dimensions of Jerusalem based on a number of gates. Meyers and Meyers (1993, 445) identify the Benjamin Gate with the more well-known eastern Sheep Gate that was located just north of the temple courtyard. Some place the "First Gate" (apparently it did not exist at this time) on the western side of the city and identify it with the Old City Gate (Neh. 3:1) or the Mishneh Gate (Hill, 2008b, 601), while Meyers and Meyers (1993, 446) locate it on the eastern wall. The Corner Gate was on the west (Jer. 31:38; 2 Kings 14:13; 2 Chron. 26:9), but the exact location of the Tower of Hananel (Neh. 3:1; Jer. 31:38) is unknown, though Wolters (2014, 465) places it on the northern wall. Although Zechariah's audience probably knew the location of each of these important places, the main point that was being made was that the city would still exist after this terrible war and many people would live in it. With God being present there in all his glory, the city would be "secure" (בֶּטַח), and it would never again be cursed by God or be forced to suffer the destruction of a "holy war" (חֵרֶם) of judgment.

God Will Defeat His Enemies (14:12–15)
God would strike with a plague the armies that attack Jerusalem.

14:12–13. Although God would rescue the people in Jerusalem from the attacking nations

---

2 For an article that surveys the use of kingship terminology for the gods in Mesopotamia, Ugarit, Egypt, and among the Hittites, and that also notes similarities and differences between the OT God-King and the ANE gods, see Gary V. Smith, "The Concept of God / The Gods as King in the Ancient Near East and the Bible," *Trinity Journal* 3 (1982): 18–31.

in 14:2–5, it appeared that not everyone in these nations would be completely eliminated. In order to insure security (14:11b), most of these enemies would be punished and destroyed. This would be accomplished by a divine "plague" (מַגֵּפָה) that would cause the flesh, eyes, and tongues of the enemy soldiers to rot (14:12). Merrill (2003, 314) suggests that there might be hyperbole in these statements, while Klein (2008, 417) identifies this plague as "a wasting disease, pictured in figurative language." Whatever the exact nature of the plague,[3] it would completely devastate Israel's enemies and leave them and their animals helpless (14:15). This disaster from God would naturally strike great fear, confusion, and panic into the hearts of many (14:13), for these people would soon become blind, unable to eat, and have no one to help or heal them. Total chaos would be the result, and these enemy soldiers would soon turn against each other, just like the Midianites killed each other in the time of Gideon (Judg. 7:22) or the soldiers from Moab, Ammon, and Edom killed each other in the time of Jehoshaphat (2 Chron. 20:23).

14:14–15. Other soldiers from outside Jerusalem would join in the destruction of these enemy troops, and the enemy would be defeated. There would be an enormous amount of booty left behind (14:14), and God's terrible plague would also fall on the enemy's horses that they needed to ride and the cattle they needed for food.

All People Will Worship the King at His Temple (14:16–21)

After this victory, all the nations would come to Jerusalem to worship God at the Feast of Booths, and God's plague would fall on anyone who may try to skip this event.

14:16. In closing, the prophet reported what would happen after the battle over Jerusalem had ended and the city was secure. Many people from many nations who were not killed in the war over Jerusalem would come to Jerusalem to worship God (14:16), somewhat similar to Zechariah's prophecies in Zechariah 2:10–13 and 8:1–23. Isaiah's prophesies in Isaiah 4:2–4, 11:10–11, 19:18–25, 45:22–23, 60:1–14, and 66:18–21 predicted the future coming of many people from many nations to Jerusalem to worship God. The specific worship event described in this message was the annual pilgrimage to Jerusalem on the Feast of Booths (also called Tabernacles).

> **Feast of Booths**
>
> This feast was celebrated in Israel from the fifteenth day of the seventh month to the twenty-second day (Lev. 23:33). This feast was a time to thank God for his abundant grace in giving a good harvest (Exod. 23:16; Lev. 23:39; Deut. 16:15) and for rescuing the nation from Egypt and providing for the Israelites when they were in the Sinai wilderness for forty years living in tents (Lev. 23:42–43).

God's sovereign role in protecting and providing for the Israelites in the Sinai wilderness and for defeating the enemies of Jerusalem in the great final battle in Zechariah 14:1–15 justified the worship of God as the King over everyone and as their almighty Commander of the Armies of Heaven (the Lord of Hosts; 14:16). The Feast of Booths traditionally included Gentiles (Deut. 16:14), so that may be the reason why this feast was highlighted. The reading of the Law of Moses was an important feature of the Feast of Booths from the time of Moses (Deut. 31:9–13) to the postexilic celebration of the Feast of Booths

---

3 **Digital Extra**: "the plague" Hill (2008b, 602) reports that some view this wasting and rotting flesh as the results of a massive amount of radiation on troops involved in a nuclear war. But we don't really know.

(Ezra 3:4; Neh. 8:14–18). This celebration likely ended with some sort of recommitment to the covenant (Neh. 8:13–18; Baldwin, 1972, 206; Klein, 2008, 423). At minimum, the purpose for reading the Law was so that the people would hear it and learn to fear the Lord, plus follow the positive instructions in the Law (Deut. 31:12–13).

14:17–19. The author warned of the hypothetical possibility that some people from various parts of the earth might decide not to come to Jerusalem some year to celebrate the Feast of Booths and honor God as their King (14:17). If this should happen, then God would withhold his blessing of rain. Thus, they would have no crops for which to be thankful. This response was consistent with the covenant curse in Leviticus 26:4 and Deuteronomy 28:22–24, and with what God did when his own people failed to honor and worship him (1 Kings 17–18; Amos 4:7–8). Having laid down this principle, Zechariah 14:18–19 applies this principle to a hypothetical rebellion ("if") that might arise in Egypt (or any other nation—14:19), but the Hebrew text of 14:18 is difficult, so many translations read the withholding of rain from 14:17 into the first part of 14:18 (see translation analysis). Redditt (2012, 139) connects this

NASB[95] "If the family of Egypt does not go up and enter, then no rain will fall on them."

NIV[84] "If the Egyptian people do not go up and take part, they will have no rain."

HCSB "If the people of Egypt will not go up and enter, then rain will not fall on them."

NKJV "If the family of Egypt will not come up and enter in, they shall have no rain."

NRSV "And if the family of Egypt do not go up and present themselves, then on them shall come the plague."

The word "plague" occurs in the second half of the sentence in 14:18b, so the prediction of no rain in the first part of the sentence in 14:18a seems to be inferred from 14:17 or implied from the latter part of 14:18 or both.

Egyptian rebellion with the building of a Jewish temple in Elephantine Egypt around 525 b.c., but Zechariah was referring to eschatological events in the distant future, not any sinful worship in the time of Zechariah. In light of Isaiah 19:18–25, it would seem unlikely that Egypt would rebel, but if that hypothetically did happen, Egypt would once again face a serious plague sent by God.

Ancient Egypt and Elephantine Island in the Nile.

14:20–21. The final "on that day" prophecy was centered on the theme of holiness. In the past, the title "Holy to the LORD" was the gold sign placed on the turban of the high priest (Exod. 28:32) to remind the high priest and all who interacted with him of his high moral calling to consecrate himself as one set apart to God. But holiness was not limited to the high priest, for the whole covenant nation was to be "a kingdom of priests and a holy nation" (Exod. 19:6). They were not to be like the foreign nations but were to be "a holy people to the LORD" (Deut. 14:2,

21), for God was holy, and his people should be holy (Lev. 19:2). Since there was security and peace on earth, even the unclean war horses would be set aside from their usual roles of fighting wars and consecrated to God as holy horses (Zech. 14:19). The small bells on the harness probably each had one letter on them (Wolters, 2014, 471), but together they spelled out the message of holiness for all to see. Similarly, the holy cooking pots at the temple would be used to boil the meat for the priest (Lev. 7:32–34), and the holy pots would be set aside for the worshippers to cook the meat of the peace offering (Lev. 7:15–18). This was normal in the past, but in the future every pot in Jerusalem would be holy (Zech. 14:21). These two examples were probably meant as representative examples of the spread of holiness from only a few people and objects connected to the temple, to the widespread consecration of every object, animal, and person, for everything would be holy and consecrated to the Lord. The Canaanite worshippers of Baal would not exist in God's kingdom, for everyone would be holy (14:21b).

THEOLOGICAL FOCUS

The exegetical idea (At the climax of history, the nations would attack Jerusalem, but God would deliver the city, bring major changes in nature, and reign as king; then all nations would pay homage to him) leads to this theological focus: In the distant future, God will rescue his people, reign as King, and restore his kingdom.

When God will miraculously rescue his people from their enemies and reign as King on the earth, everything will change. The outcome of the battle for Jerusalem belongs to the Lord, so he will be victorious over his enemies and reign on earth as King forever. The theological situation will dramatically change because everyone and everything will be set apart to God as holy. At this time a

new world will arise, Jerusalem will gain new importance, God's glory will shine over the earth, springs of water will flow to nourish the earth, and all the people on earth will be holy and part of a holy worshipping community that glorifies God.

PREACHING AND TEACHING STRATEGIES

Exegetical and Theological Synthesis

Zechariah 14:1–21 describes several features to expect at the climax of history, including God's preservation of a remnant in Jerusalem, renewal of creation, welcome of nations to the Feast of Tabernacles, and sanctification of the worshipping masses. The passage cycles through theological themes recurrent in previous chapters, emphasizing God's sovereignty, might, justice, and holiness.

Of equal importance is Zechariah's global vision, which appears earlier in the book. When the prophet encountered a man headed to Jerusalem with a measuring line, he spoke of nations joining God's people in worship (2:10–13). Later, when Zechariah called God's people to end their fasting, he predicted a day with people from all nations who would beg to feast with them (8:20–23). This international emphasis aligns with that of Isaiah and Ezekiel, who envisioned all peoples bowing to God as a restored people, temple, and city shined as a light to the nations (Isa. 45:22–23; 49:6; 60:1–14; 66:18–21; Ezek. 39:21–29).

In fact, the global vision of God reaches back to Eden, where God appointed Adam and Eve to represent him, bearing his image and ruling over all creation (Gen. 1:26–28). Echoes of this commission ring in God's covenant with Noah (9:1–6). God reiterated his desire for all nations to know him and flourish under his reign in his covenants with Abram (12:1–3) and Moses (19:5–6). His heart for the nations to pay him homage is threaded throughout various psalms (e.g., Pss. 67, 96) and prayers (1 Kings 8), as well as his inclusion of foreigners, such as Rahab and Ruth, into his company of adoring people (Josh. 6:25; Ruth 2:11–12; cf. Deut. 23:3–8).

Preaching Idea

Get in God's corner: he's the undisputed, everlasting King of the world.

Contemporary Connections

What does it mean?

What does it mean that God is the undisputed, everlasting King of the world? God's sovereignty is asserted throughout the Scriptures in his acts of creation and deliverance, provision and protection, judgment and wrath. The Lord communicates his universal reign through Isaiah, saying, "Heaven is my throne, and the earth is my footstool" (Isa. 66:1). A series of psalms declare praise for his reign (Pss. 93:1; 95:3; 96:10; 97:1; 99:1). To be in his corner is to respect his authority, praise his power, and show loyalty to him as King of the world.

Unfortunately, not everyone stands in God's corner. Nations rage and individuals foolishly deny his authority (Pss. 2:1; 14:1). Goliath taunted Israel's army, tacitly undermining God's reign (1 Sam. 17:8–11). The chief advisor of the king of Assyria mocked God and considered him powerless against the king's aegis (Isa. 36:4–10; 37:10–13). Israel rejected God as ruler in her infamous request for a king (1 Sam. 8:4–9). And today people live by their own set of rules or impulses, defiant of the true King of the world.

Of course, disrespect and refusal to honor God's reign will not persist. Isaiah predicted a day when every knee will bow to God and every tongue will declare his power (45:23, cf. Phil. 2:9–11). Surely some will bow out of humble compulsion more than reverent praise. And yet, the scene envisions a universal proclamation of God's undisputed, everlasting reign. To deny God as King of the world is futile (Mic. 6:1–8). At history's climax, awe for God will replace opposition, and his reign will endure the test of time.

Is it true?

Is it true that God is the undisputed, everlasting King of the world? Yes. God's sovereignty transcends the short shelf life of human rule. Human leaders in every realm have risen to power, expanded their influence, and eventually faded into memory. Infamous leaders like Nero (Roman emperor, r. A.D. 54–68), Genghis Khan (Mongolian emperor, r. 1206–27), and Pol Pot (Cambodian leader of Khmer Rouge, 1975–79) headed kingdoms that no longer exist. Even fame, a cultural form of influence, does not last long. Former childhood celebrities (e.g., Mary-Kate and Ashley Olsen from *Full House*) drifted from stardom to gossip columns. Once-dominant athletes (e.g., Tom Brady) cede their influence to younger stars (e.g., Patrick Mahomes). Contrarily, God neither grows old nor gets dethroned.

Although God's fame as Creator and King is not universally acknowledged today (nor was it in Zechariah's day), we can get in his corner by respecting his title as undisputed, everlasting King of the world. He welcomes those who pay homage to him. In fact, the Scriptures set a precedent for celebrating God's sovereignty. They are full of narratives (Judg. 8:22–23; 1 Sam. 8:4–9) and poetic reflections of his undisputed, everlasting reign (Exod. 15:1; Pss. 93; 95; 97; 99). Moreover, Jewish feasts and weekly sabbaths still publicly proclaim God's undisputed, everlasting reign. The current flood of worship music, concerts, and conferences testifies to God's undisputed, everlasting reign. And in quiet, subversive ways, the regular gathering of God's persecuted people—from ancient Babylon to modern Bangladesh—speaks to his undisputed, everlasting reign. According to

Zechariah, these declarations of God's undisputed, everlasting reign will someday become a global chorus.

Now what?

How should we get in God's corner? What's our role in proclaiming his undisputed, everlasting reign? Getting into God's corner comprises several steps: submission, allegiance, and praise demonstrate our commitment to the undisputed, everlasting King of the world. Submission surrenders our tendency for autonomy (Gen. 3:5) and heeds God's way of living. We each operate a miniature kingdom of me (Willard, 1997, 21), full of self-will, ego, and small dreams. Submission may sound similar to Isaiah's famous line: "Here I am, send me" (Isa. 6:8).

After submission follows allegiance. The life of faith is not cognitive assent to a set of principles; it is a life of faithfulness to a sovereign person (Hab. 2:4; Rom. 1:16–17). Bates (2017, 77–100) makes a compelling case for reading the NT word "faith" as "allegiance." Citizens of the United States of America likely connect allegiance terminology to their elementary school days, beginning each morning by pledging to the flag. The gesture, of course, reflects one's commitment to live as a good, respectful citizen. Eagle Scouts likewise pledge loyalty to their troop, military members to their unit, and sorority members to their sisters. A pledge is a promise to embody the governing values of the group. Similarly, allegiance to God implies our living as citizens of his kingdom, committing our lives to his just ethic and global mission to draw people to himself (Exod. 19:5–6).

Allegiance peaks in the honor and praise we lavish on God. While our obedience at times feels like duty, it is sweetest when marked by praise. We might share the vision that the "whole earth is full of his glory" (Isa. 6:3). We might bang drums, strum guitars, and raise our voices to "praise of the LORD" (Pss. 146–50). We might tell stories to strangers, friends, and upcoming generations of God's goodness, deliverance, and power (Pss. 79:13; 145:4). We might gather for corporate worship, community service, or communion to remember God's faithfulness. However we pay homage to the undisputed, everlasting King of the world today is a mere rehearsal for the eternal song of praise (Rev. 7:9–12).

Creativity in Presentation

Queen's song "We Are the Champions" (1977) would make an effective bumper at the beginning of this sermon. Consider playing the tune as you march to the stage. Come out at the chorus with fists pumping, head bobbing, raising a trophy or medal in the air. The whole song lasts three minutes, so a thirty second clip would probably suffice. After the music dims, ask the congregation: "Do you feel like a champion or loser most of the time? A champion or loser at work? A champion or loser at home? A champion or loser with your finances, friendships, and faith?" Then add: "Guess what? Everyone in God's corner becomes a champion. We are the champions . . . of the world. Those loyal to the King of the world are on the winning team. Forever. So let's keep on fighting 'til the end."

During my (Tim's) childhood, Mike Tyson reigned as heavyweight champion of the boxing world. I remember watching him decimate opponents in the first round, after landing a few deadly jabs to their head. The opening ceremony always struck me as lavish. Tyson's contender danced around in a silk robe, throwing punches at a phantom fighter while an announcer read his name, nickname, and record (e.g., Michael "Jinx" Spinks; thirty-one wins; zero losses; twenty-one by knock out). Meanwhile, Tyson, the titleholder, strutted down the aisle to his theme song (also beating the air), while the baritone voice of the media person cried, "And in this corner, 'Iron'

Mike Tyson. The undisputed, heavyweight champion of the world!" Remind people, as unstoppable as Mike Tyson (or Muhammad Ali, incumbent politician, or some reigning sports team) seemed at his peak, he lost his title. All sports champions do. Only God's reign remains eternally undisputed.

Mike Tyson's Boxing Career Highlights

Tyson emerged on the boxing scene in 1985, earning his first heavyweight title a year later, the youngest ever "undisputed" champion. He won fifty of fifty-eight fights, more than ten in the first round by knockout. The latter half of his career was marked by an unlikely loss to James "Buster" Douglas (1990), biting Evander Holyfield's ear in a match, criminal charges, and prison time. He remains an iconic and controversial figure in American sports history.[4]

Artist Andy Warhol famously quipped that "In the future, everyone will be world-famous for fifteen minutes." Reality TV and internet videos have given credence to his claim. Dr. Seuss (1990, 35, 37) likewise captures the idea in his classic *Oh, the Places You'll Go*, where the main character enjoys short-lived fame:

> *Fame!* You'll be as famous as famous can be, with the whole wide world watching you win on TV.

> Except when they don't
> Because, sometimes, they won't.

Consider projecting Seuss's four-page spread (pp. 34–37) and reading the text to the congregation. Explain the short-lived nature of our fame. Some examples from pop culture can reiterate the point. Then be sure to contrast these examples with God's everlasting fame as King of the world.

Examples of Long-forgotten or Short-lived Fame

- "Who was Alex Michel?" The first bachelor from the TV show by the same name (2002).
- "Who was Justin Morneau?" Minnesota Twins baseball player who won the 2008 Homerun Derby.
- "Who was Robert Matthew Van Winkle?" One-hit wonder who rapped "Ice Ice Baby" (1990) and was known professionally as Vanilla Ice.
- "Who was Katherine G. Johnson?" Mathematician and one of the first African American women to work as a NASA scientist; she calculated trajectories for NASA missions and was recently depicted in the film *Hidden Figures* (2016)
- "Who was Selma Lagerlöf?" Swedish writer and teacher who was the first woman to win the Nobel Prize in Literature (1909).
- "Who was Nadya Suleman?" Woman known as Octomom for birthing eight babies in 2009.

Whatever creative details you adopt or amend, make sure to stress the main idea: In the distant future, God will rescue his people, reign as King, and restore his kingdom. So we should get in God's corner: he's the undisputed, everlasting King of the world.

- God will fight for his people (14:1–5).

- God will transform our world (14:6–11).

- God will defeat our enemies (14:12–15).

- God will welcome us into his corner (14:16–21).

---

4   "Mike Tyson," International Boxing Hall of Fame, accessed March 31, 2020, http://www.ibhof.com/pages/about/inductees/modern/tyson.html.

DISCUSSION QUESTIONS

1. What will happen on the final great Day of the Lord, according to Zechariah 14:1–5?

2. What are the three segments of time God's prophets referred to? How did they speak differently about each segment of time?

3. According to Zechariah 14:6–21, what transformations will happen to the earth and its people when God comes to dwell with humanity?

4. What are ways to proclaim our loyalty to the King of the world today?

5. Who will not be included in the everlasting worship of the divine King?

FOR FURTHER READING

Boa, K. 2017. *Life in the Presence of God: Practices for Living in Light of Eternity.* Downers Grove, IL: IVP Books.

Boda, M. J. 2004. *Haggai, Zechariah.* NIV Application Commentary. Grand Rapids: Zondervan.

Motyer, J. A. 1998a. "Haggai." In *Zephaniah, Haggai, Zechariah, and Malachi,* 963–1002. Vol. 3 of *The Minor Prophets: An Exegetical and Expositional Commentary,* edited by T. E. McComiskey. Grand Rapids: Baker.

Tiemeyer, L.-S. 2015. *Zechariah and His Visions: An Exegetical Study of Zechariah's Vision Reports.* Library of the Hebrew Bible / Old Testament Studies 605. London: Bloomsbury T&T Clark.

INTRODUCTION TO MALACHI

OVERVIEW OF INTRODUCTORY ISSUES

Author: Malachi

Place: Jerusalem

Date: 420–400 B.C.

Readers: Priest and people in Judah.

Historical Setting: During the reign of Darius II (423–404 B.C.) and after Nehemiah's governorship (445–430 B.C.).

Occasion for Writing: Malachi confronted religious secularization, no fear of God, skepticism, and a failure to follow biblical teachings, which were undermining the identity of the Jewish people.

Genre: Prophecy

Theological Emphasis: People must honor God and follow his instructions in the Torah.

AUTHORSHIP OF MALACHI

These prophecies are attributed to a man named "Malachi" (1:1) in the Hebrew text, but the Greek LXX translates this word as a noun ("his messenger"), implying an anonymous author? Other Greek translators (Symmachus and Theodotian) understood the Hebrew word (מַלְאָכִי) to be the name of the prophet "Malachi." Some modern commentators contend that this word ("my messenger") comes from the prophecy in Malachi 3:1 where God promised to "send my messenger and he will clear the way before me." But it would be rather presumptuous for this prophet to claim that he was that future messenger, plus this would contradict the NT claim that John the Baptist was this messenger (Matt. 11:10–11; Mark 1:2). In addition, the structure of this superscription is similar to the superscriptions in other prophetic books, and the word "Malachi" fills the slot where most prophetic books place the name of the author. The phrase "by the hand of/through" was a common Hebrew way to identify the agent that accomplished something (cf. Exod. 9:39; 34:29; 2 Sam. 28:17).

"Burden of the Word"

The phrase "the burden of the word of the LORD to Israel through Malachi" (1:1) is constructed as the name of the author similar to the superscription in Hosea 1:1 ("The word of the LORD that came through Hosea"), Joel 1:1 ("The word of the LORD that came to Joel"), Jonah 1:1 ("The word of the LORD to Jonah"), Micah 1:1 ("The word of the LORD that came to Micah"), and Zephaniah 1:1 ("The word of the LORD that came to Zephaniah").

This book reveals few specifics about the life of the prophet (for example, it does not claim that he was a Levite), but his writings indicate that he was a bold person who confronted the sins of the Jews living around Jerusalem. He stood up against the unfaithful priests who did not honor God (1:6; 2:2) and called people to repentance (3:7). Malachi understood the deep love of God for his people (1:2), that his justice would bring punishment on those who did not fear God (2:17–3:5), and that God would oppose people who mistreated others (2:10–16; 3:5).

PLACE OF WRITING

There is no statement identifying the place where this book was written or when it was included in the Hebrew canon. However, these prophecies confront the failures of the priests at the Jerusalem temple (2:1–9), the people who brought unacceptable sacrifices to offer at the Jerusalem temple (1:6–14), and those who did not give their tithe at the temple (3:6–12). Thus, these written oracles apply to Jewish people living in and around Jerusalem.

DATE OF WRITING

The setting of the book of Malachi is in the postexilic era when the Persians were a world power. Since the temple was in use (1:6–14), the prophet spoke these words sometime after Haggai and Zechariah (520–516 B.C.) encouraged the people in Jerusalem to rebuild the temple during the reign of the Persian King Darius I (Hag. 1:1). Since Malachi did not give the names of any Jewish governors or foreign rulers and did not refer to any datable international events, there is no consensus on the date when Malachi spoke these oral messages or when these prophecies were written down on a scroll.[1] One historical event mentioned was the destruction of Edom (1:3–4), but Malachi did not indicate how many years ago that happened. One can only say that Malachi spoke sometime after the Babylonian king Nabonidus defeated Edom in 552 B.C.

Many date Malachi close to the time of Ezra/Nehemiah because (a) Ezra 9–10; Nehemiah 10:30; 13:23–29; and Malachi 2:10–16 refer to the problem of intermarriage with foreigners, and Ezra and Nehemiah encourage people to divorce foreign unbelievers; (b) Malachi 1:6–2:9 and Nehemiah 13:4–9, 29–30 refer to problems with the priests; (c) social injustice was condemned in Malachi 3:5 and Nehemiah 5:1–13; and (d) tithing was a concern in Malachi 3:8–12 and Nehemiah 10:32–39; 13:10–13.

CHRONOLOGY OF PERSIAN KINGS AND INFLUENCES ON JEWISH PEOPLE

Cyrus (559–530 B.C.)	Cambyses (530–522 B.C.)	Darius (522–486 B.C.)	Xerxes (486–465 B.C.)	Artaxerxes (465–424 B.C.)	Darius (423–404 B.C.)
Started building Zerubbabel/Joshua	no building	temple completed Haggai/Zechariah	Haman's threats Esther/Mordecai	Reform/Wall rebuilt Ezra/Nehemiah	Malachi

---

1   Although Malachi 1:3–4 refers to the defeat of the Edomites, the enemy that defeated them was not mentioned. It could hypothetically refer to the Babylonian or to a later Nabatean defeat.

GENERAL CHRONOLOGY OF THE PROPHETS				
Prophet	Estimated Ministry	Period	Audience	
Amos	767–753	Pre-exile	Northern Israel	A S S Y R I A 900 B.C. to 612 B.C.
Hosea	755–715	Pre-exile	Northern Israel	
Micah	735–701	Israel in exile Pre-exile Judah	Judah	
Isaiah	739–685	Pre-exile	Judah	
Nahum	663–612	Israel in exile Pre-exile Judah	Nineveh / Assyria	
Zephaniah	632–628	Israel in exile Pre-exile Judah	Judah	B A B Y L O N 612 B.C. to 539 B.C.
Habakkuk	626–609	Israel in exile Pre-exile Judah	Judah	
Jeremiah	605–586	Israel in exile Pre-exile Judah	Judah	
Daniel	605–535	Judah in exile	Judah	
Ezekiel	597–571	Judah in exile	Judah	
Obadiah	After 586	Judah in exile	Edom	
Jonah	??	Judah in exile	(about) Nineveh	
Haggai	520–520	Post-exile	Returned Jews	P E R S I A
Zechariah	520–480	Post-exile	Returned Jews	
Joel	515	Post-exile	Judah	
Malachi	**450**	**Post-exile**	**Returned Jews**	
Chart created by Herbert W. Bateman IV, *Isaiah: How to Read, Interpret and Understand the Prophet* (Leesburg, IN: Cyber-Center for Biblical Studies, 2016). Reprinted by permission of Herbert W. Bateman IV.				

Three possible dates are proposed: (a) Malachi spoke and wrote his prophesies before the arrival of Ezra and Nehemiah in Jerusalem (from 500 to 460 B.C.), during the reign of Darius I or Xerxes. (b) Since the issues in Malachi are so similar to those in Nehemiah 13, others date Malachi to 433–430 B.C. in the reign of Artaxerxes I, when Nehemiah was absent from Jerusalem for a few years (Neh. 13:6). (c) Still others propose a slightly later date (420–400 B.C.) after Nehemiah's time in Jerusalem because Ezra and Nehemiah pushed Jews to divorce their pagan wives (Ezra 9; Neh. 10:30; 13:23–27) in order to preserve a holy seed (Ezra 9:2; 10:1–44), but in contrast Malachi opposed those who divorced their Jewish wives (Mal. 2:10–16). It would seem logical that too much divorce would arise in the years only after Ezra and Nehemiah liberalized this practice. At that time divorce became acceptable, but some men inappropriately divorced even their Jewish wives. Thus, the date of writing for this prophecy would likely be somewhere between 420–400 B.C.

HISTORICAL SETTING

Although Malachi said little about political events, if his ministry was around 420–400 B.C., and the place of writing was in Jerusalem, it is possible to identify some of the things happening in the Persian Empire in that general time period. Some year earlier, Artaxerxes I (465–424 B.C.) fought several battles against the Egyptians and Greeks, but eventually Artaxerxes was able to establish many years of peace due to a treaty known as the Peace of Callias. When Artaxerxes died, his son Xerxes II became king, but he was assassinated by the satrap of Hyrcania who took on the name Darius II Nothus (424–404 B.C.). Nothing is known about his policies toward Judah, though an Aramaic Elephantine Papyri letter (dated to 419 B.C.) indicates that he was supportive of the Jews who lived at a fortress in Upper Egypt, so one would expect a positive relationship with those who lived in and around Jerusalem. Because of the peaceful conditions Artaxerxes established, it is not surprising that Malachi said nothing negative about the political situation in Judah. During these years, Joiada (433–410 B.C.) and then Johanan (410–370 B.C.) served as the high priest in Jerusalem, Arsames was satrap over the province of Egypt, Sanballat and then his sons were governors over Samaria, and Bagoas was the governor of Judah. Since Malachi addressed internal religious problems, the political events in the outside world had minimal impact on his messages.

OCCASION FOR WRITING

Judah's economy was heavily dependent on agriculture, so earlier droughts (Hag. 1:10–11) and various agricultural plagues (Mal. 3:9–11) made it difficult to survive and pay the heavy Persian taxes (Neh. 5:4–5). The increase in marriages to foreigners and divorce caused social insecurity in the family and had negative implications on the theological education of children (Neh. 13:23–25; Mal. 2:15) if a man married an unbeliever. The topics Malachi addressed suggest that many in his audience were not well-founded in the faith of their forefathers, so Malachi corrected errors in the people's thinking (some thought God did not love them) to counteract the secular culture that was undermining the faith and distinctive practices of the Jewish people.

ORIGINAL READERS

The prophecies of Malachi were addressed and applied originally to the Jewish people living around Jerusalem who doubted God's love for them (Mal. 1:1–5), questioned if God dealt justly with people (Mal. 2:17–3:5), and doubted that it actually paid to serve God (Mal. 3:13–4:3). Malachi portrayed this as a time of rampant secularization when the Jewish people were questioning their faith, were unaware of the biblical basis that supported a traditional understanding of God's love for his people, and were giving up on some of their distinctive ethical traditions.[2] These theological problems were partially caused by priests who did not fear God or teach the people to follow God's instruction (2:1–9). Consequently, there was a need for a prophet like Malachi to address these questions in order to reestablish Mosaic traditional practices, a biblical ethic, and a true faith based on their covenant with God.

---

2   C. R. Wells, "The Subtle Crisis of Secularism: Preaching the Burden of Israel," *CTR* 2 (1987): 39–52 or Gary V. Smith, *An Introduction to the Hebrew Prophets; The Prophets as Preachers* (Nashville: Broadman and Homan, 1994), 328.

THEOLOGICAL EMPHASIS OF MALACHI

Malachi treated numerous theological issues in his preaching, but the central theme was the need for people to fear and honor God. This generation of Jews was not honoring God by faithfully maintaining their covenant relationship with him. They forgot about God's great love for them when he delivered them from Egyptian bondage (Exod. 14–15) and his gracious act of choosing them as his covenant people (Deut. 7:6–7). The people did not recognize the hand of God in blessing them, in judging wicked nations (Mal. 1:4; 2:17), or in determining the fruitfulness of their crops. Secular humanistic thinking began to cloud their understanding, so some did not even believe God was in control of the future or would bless the righteous and judge the wicked (Mal. 3:13–14). Consequently, Malachi taught the people that they needed to fear God and honor him by recognizing that he was a divine King (Mal. 1:11, 14). God would have compassion on those who fear and serve him (Mal. 3:17–18) but bring destruction on the arrogant who do not fear God (Mal. 2:1–4; 4:1).

If a person questions God's love (1:1–5), his justice (2:17), and doubts that it pays to serve God (3:14), this would make a difference in how one practices his faith day by day. If these things are true, why should a person worry about bringing a pure offering to the temple (1:8), divorcing a Jewish wife and marrying an unbeliever (2:10–16), or feel it was necessary to tithe (3:8). If there is no inner fear of God and no burning desire to honor him, then the basis of all beliefs about God become confused and the ethical principle in God's word becomes compromised. People would start acting like most other secular people who do not follow God's instruction. Malachi confronted these problems head on and called people to repent (1:1–6; 3:7), for the priest to honor God (2:1–9), for everyone to reject the secular way of life and thinking, and instead follow the ethical teachings of Moses and the prophets. Since the secularization of culture has increased in our modern era, some people wonder about these same questions today.

OUTLINE OF MALACHI

The prophecies of Malachi were organized around a series of similar rhetorical oracles that argue for theological positions that were not supported by many in Judah. Achtemeier (1986, 172) thinks these oracles were "court cases, tried before the priest in the temple with the prophet playing the role of the priest in his imagination."[3] But most view these questions and answers as "disputation speeches." The structure of a typical disputation speech includes:

- a claim or theological statement by the prophet,
- a rejection or questioning of the prophet's statement by the audience,
- a prophetic argument that supports the original theological claim, and
- a concluding statement (negative or positive).

In contrast, Clendenen (2004, 223) finds only three chiastic units, each containing words of motivation, situation, command, situation, and motivation, but Hill (1998, 29) has critiqued a few of the shortcomings of this approach. The following outline displays several variations in the six disputation speeches of Malachi, but freedom of expression within the framework of this general form critical category should be expected, for variation is evident in most other literary genres as well. An epilogue provides a final unit. Thus Malachi can be divided into seven preaching units.

---

3   J. O'Brien, *Priests and Levites in Malachi* (SBLDS 121; Atlanta: Scholars Press, 1990), 63 suggests that the whole book was a series of accusations in a covenant lawsuit, but Hill (1998, 31–33) rejects this hypothesis.

1. God Loves His People Israel (1:1–5)

2. The Priests Do Not Fear God (1:6–2:9)

3. Unfaithfulness in Covenant Relationships (2:10–16)

4. God Is Just (2:17–3:5)

5. Return to God and Give Your Tithe (3:6–12)

6. Does It Pay to Serve God? (3:13–4:3)

7. Epilogue: Obey God's Instructions (4:4–6)

FOR FURTHER READING

Clendenen, E. Ray and R.A. Taylor. 2004. *Haggai, Malachi*. New American Commentary. Nashville: Broadman and Holman.

Hill, Andrew E. *Malachi*. 1998. Anchor Bible. New York: Doubleday.

Ross, Allen P. 2016. *Malachi: Then and Now*. Wooster, OH: Weaver.

Verhoef, Pieter. 1987. *The Books of Haggai and Malachi*. New International Commentary on the Old Testament. Grand Rapids: Eerdmans.

Malachi 1:1–5

EXEGETICAL IDEA

God demonstrated through his action that he chose to love the Israelites, the children of Jacob, rather than the Edomites, the children of Esau.

THEOLOGICAL FOCUS

God loves his people despite the way his people feel about it.

PREACHING IDEA

God's deep love should stir our dull senses.

PREACHING POINTERS

Malachi opened with a bold declaration of God's love to Israel. Sadly, the Jewish audience disputed the claim and asked for proof of God's commitment. Recent history had caused them to question God's affection: the destruction of the temple, exile, foreign rule, and their return to a ruined country. Malachi countered their argument with evidence of God's covenant fidelity, namely, the selection and preservation of Jacob (i.e., Israel) rather than Esau (i.e., Edom). The dispute caused his original audience to give God's deep love a second look.

Even today, to question God's love is human. During life's tragedies, unanswered prayer, or lonely moments, we doubt the quality of God's love. We equate love with feelings; we conflate it with warm affections, giddy emotions, happy thoughts, and perpetual smiles. By contrast, the love of God centers on his choice, commitment, acts of sacrifice, and selfless care. His love is an undeniable, historical fact. The passage affirms that God's deep love should stir our dull senses.

GOD LOVES HIS PEOPLE ISRAEL (1:1–5)

LITERARY STRUCTURE AND THEMES

After the superscription, this first dispute includes God's claim to love the people of Israel (v. 2a), but they rejected this claim (v. 2b). So the prophet provided a justification for this truth (vv. 2c–4) and described the impact his love would have in the future (1:5).

This unit's central theological theme is that God loves Israel.

- *A Timely Message (1:1)*
- *God Loves Israel (1:2a)*
- *An Objection (1:2b)*
- *The Justification of the Claim (1:2c–4)*
- *Love for God in the Future (1:5)*

EXPOSITION

Late in the Persian era, the Jews lived in a time when life was not easy because of poor harvests, secular thinking that was undermining traditional religious beliefs, and (3:11) and the lack of any influence on world events that were happening all around them. Since the priests were not teaching the Torah well or practicing much of what it said, the people became somewhat unaware of God's past dealings with Israel and his covenant requirements. So the Jewish people were somewhat resistant to accepting the theological and practical implications of being God's chosen people who were restricted by the Torah. Malachi presented a logical defense of several key components of their faith in order to reorient their thinking to the worldview of the Torah and its perspective on the relationship they had with God.

A Timely Message (1:1)

The word of God came at a specific time to the people of Judah to confront those who needed to listen to what God had to say.

1:1. Most prophetic books begin with a superscription[1] that identifies some information about the context, the audience, the author, and the source of the message. This brief superscription classifies this prophecy as a "burdensome oracle" (מַשָּׂא) that contains the "word of the LORD." This identifies the source of the prophet's information and inspiration, though the term "burdensome oracle" (מַשָּׂא) indicates that this is a difficult or weighty prophecy. God used the personal involvement of the prophet Malachi to deliver this message, for it came "by/through, by the hand of" "By the hand of" בְּיַד indicates the personal involvement of the one communicating this message to the audience Malachi. The audience that heard this message was the people of Israel living around Jerusalem.

God Loves Israel (1:2a)

Based on God's words to his people (see Deut. 7:7) and his actions (God's choice), one could be sure that God loved Israel.

1:2a. The prophet's first claim was a statement of reassurance that God loved (אָהַב) his people Israel. These words were a reminder that Israel's past, present, and future history were defined by God's acts of love (e.g. Exod.14–15). God's love toward Israel came out of a heart of deep personal affection for Israel, for they were his

---

1 The term "superscription" classifies this verse as a prefix to a written source. A superscription communicates the literary nature of the writing and usually identifies the author, general date, and audience.

chosen covenant people (Deut. 7:6–7).[2] They were his prized possession, set apart from all the other families on the earth (Exod. 19:4–6).

WORD ANALYSIS: אָהֵב
This word "love" described the following meanings in different contexts: (a) in an interpersonal context, the deep emotional feelings of affection a man has for his wife (Gen. 24:67—Isaac loved Rebekah), or a father has for a son (Gen. 22:2—Abraham's loved Isaac); (b) in a political context, love can describe the loyal affection people have for their ruler (1 Sam. 18:16—the people loved David); (c) in wisdom texts, unwise selfish people love or greatly enjoy being with the rich (Prov. 14:20), while the wise person loved reproof (Prov. 27:5); or (d) in a relational context, God's love for Israel caused him to choose them to be his covenant people (Deut. 7:6–8; 10:15; 23:6). So God's great love (אָהֵב) preceded the covenant obligations, but his "steadfast covenant love" (חֶסֶד) was the term to describe a partner's relationship in a covenant relationship. Jeremiah 31:3 called God's love for Israel an everlasting love.

An Objection (1:2b)
Life's difficulties made people question God's love for them. In the light of the many problems the people of Israel were facing in this secular age, the claims about God's love seemed somewhat hollow to some people in Malachi's audience, so they questioned what the prophet was saying.

1:2b. In response to the prophet's claim, the people had the audacity to question if God really loved them. This question indicates that they interpreted historical events of the past in a secular way, assuming that such events were determined only by the decisions of powerful men, not God. Possibly some Israelites were thinking that the destruction of Jerusalem in 587 B.C. and their seventy years of exile were concrete evidence that God did not love them. They were not thinking about God's great love toward them when he chose them to be his special people or his deliverance of them from exile in Babylon.

The Justification of the Claim (1:2c–4)
The contrast between God's treatment of Israel and Edom provided evidence for God's great love for the people of Israel.

1:2c–4. Malachi responded to the people's ungrateful attitude with historical evidence that demonstrated God's deep love for his people. He pointed to God's decision to choose one (he loved Jacob) of the sons of Isaac and Rebekah (Gen. 25:21–26) and not to choose the other (he hated/did not choose Esau). God's choice of Jacob was revealed to Rebekah before the two boys were born (Gen. 25:22–23), so Jacob did nothing to earn or deserve God's love. God's gracious choice was evidence of his love. When God did not choose Esau, he did not shower his "love, preference" on Esau, so Esau received the opposite of love ("no preference, hatred"). Hating (שָׂנֵא) or not loving was a negative emotional response to what was rejected.

> **God's Love**
> There is nothing that Jacob did to deserve God's love, and it may appear to humans who do not know God that his love is extended in a rather arbitrary manner. In actuality there is a plan and a purpose for each of God's choices, so they are not just arbitrary but part of God's plan. Sometimes God's choices (like his choice of Israel to be his covenant people) did not work out very

---

2 Clendenen (2004, 230) connected 1:1–2:9 in one large chiastic section, but there was little verbal connections between 1:1–5 and 1:6–2:9 other than the final statements that God would be magnified among the nations in 1:5; 2:11,14. Malachi 1:1–5 was about God's love while 2:1–2:9 was about the priests who failed to honor God, two different themes.

well, and those who were chosen did not want to serve as God's servants. When Israel strayed from God, he chose to discipline the one he chose out of love in order to cause his people to turn back to him. These acts of discipline were not arbitrary but based on the covenant blessings and curses. On the individual level, Saul was chosen to be the king, but twice he refused to follow God's direction (he offered a sacrifice after not waiting for Samuel to arrive in 1 Samuel 13 and he did not kill the Amalekites in 1 Samuel 15), so God rejected him from being king over his people. These examples demonstrate that rejecting God's love has serious consequences.

WORD ANALYSIS: שָׂנֵא

The word "hate" can refer to (a) the "lack of preference; less love" for one wife (Leah) compared to a "preference, strong love" for another wife (Rachel) in Genesis 29:30–31; (b) a helpful ally such as Hiram of Tyre, who could be called "loved, a dear friend" of David (1 Kings 5:1), but the Ammonites became a "despised, hated, an odious" enemy (2 Sam. 10:6); and (c) when God "despised, hated" abominable things including foreign gods (Deut. 12:31), Israel's sinful feasts (Amos 5:21), Israel's pride in her grand castles (Amos 6:8), and those who worshipped idols (Ps. 31:6).

Another historical choice provided a second contrast between the families of Jacob and Esau (1:3b). Both Edom (552 B.C.) and Israel were destroyed by Babylon (587 B.C.), but the audience knew that these two nations had quite different histories after their defeat. When Cyrus defeated Babylon in 539 B.C., God caused Cyrus to allow the Jewish exiles to return to Judah and build the temple (Ezra 1:1–5). But the Edomites' land remained in ruins in spite of strong attempts to rebuild and reoccupy it (Mal. 1:4). The Nabateans took over the land of Edom around 312 B.C. and drove the remaining Edomites into the Sinai, so the Edomites were not able to restore their land (R. Smith, 1984, 306; Glazier-McDonald, 1987, 37–40) because God was angry with them (1:4). One reason for God's anger was that the Edomites did not come to defend their brothers in Jerusalem (Obad. 11) but rejoiced over the misfortune of Jerusalem when the Babylonians attacked (Obad. 12; Ezek. 35:12–15). Then they took part of Judah's land for themselves (Ezek. 35:10; 36:5).

Love for God in the Future (1:5)

In later days, even foreigners would glorify God.

1:5. The conclusion of the first disputation includes a prophecy of what would happen sometime in the future. Even though some Israelites did not appreciate God's love at the time, in the future they would see God's majestic greatness in the way he would deal with nations beyond Judah's borders. This prophecy was consistent with other predictions that some Gentiles would worship God (Isa. 2:2–4; 11:10–16; 19:18–25; 42:6; 45:22–25; 60:1–14; 66:18–23).[3]

THEOLOGICAL FOCUS

The exegetical idea (God demonstrated through his action that he chose to love the Israelites, the children of Jacob, rather than the Edomites, the children of Esau) leads to this theological focus: God loves his people despite the way his people feel about it.

There are two theological themes in this initial disputation. First, God has chosen to love some people and intervened on their behalf. An example of this is God's loves for Israel and his choice of them to be his people (Deut. 7:6–7; Mal. 1:2). The history of God's

---

3   Ross (2016, 43–44) thought this referred to the time when God will be sovereign over all nations; thus, it refers to a time when the Gentiles will come to know the Lord.

preferential treatment of this nation demonstrates his love, particularly the exodus from Egypt in Exodus 14–15 and God's defeat of the Assyrian army that was surrounding Jerusalem in Isaiah 36–37. Another proof of God's love would be evident in God's dealing with other nations in positive ways (other nations would praise God in 1:5).

Second, God did not choose others (for example the Edomites) and did not give them preferential treatment. This second theme provides a complimentary focus. Neither the people who were not chosen nor the people who were chosen earned their status or deserved to be chosen. God's love was freely given and was available to both Israelites and Gentiles. The appropriate way to response to God's was to love God with all your heart, soul, and strength (Deut. 6:5).

PREACHING AND TEACHING STRATEGIES

Exegetical and Theological Synthesis

Malachi 1:1–5 explains key words and the historical context framing the initial dispute between God and his people. Malachi spoke to a postexilic audience inhabiting Jerusalem. Israel's fortunes, evident in the blessing to resettle and rebuild, contrasts with their distant relative (i.e., descendant of Esau) and neighbor, Edom. God thwarted the Edomites' attempts to reestablish home in their land. Moreover, God recalled his ancient choice of Jacob over Esau (Gen. 25:21–26).

At the core of God's love is his predisposition to choose on behalf of his people. His choice does not hinge on Israel's massive size or innate goodness, but rather reflects God's covenant faithfulness to his people (Deut. 7:6–8). He demonstrates his love both through acts of deliverance (Ps. 136) and pardon from sin (Ps. 103; Mic. 7:18–20).

Finally, God's love is not without emotional engagement. Although he is "gracious and compassionate, slow to anger, and abounding in love" (Exod. 34:6; Ps. 145:8; Joel 2:13; Jonah 4:2), God also grieves over his wayward children (Hos. 11). Their practice of idolatry tests his love for them (Exod. 32:7–14). Their false religion stirs his hate (Amos 5:21). Nonetheless, God affirms that nothing can thwart his surpassing love for his people (Isa. 54:10).

Preaching Idea

God's deep love should stir our dull senses.

Contemporary Connections

What does it mean?

What does it mean that God's deep love should stir our dull senses? How deep is God's love? How does he manifest it? God's deep love flows from his divine nature (Exod. 34:6; Isa. 54:10). It is eternal and unconditional. Furthermore, God's deep love is personal. In Malachi, love reflects God's deliberate choice of Jacob over Esau, Israel over Edom. Elsewhere, the OT showcases God's love with personal metaphors describing God's relationship to his people. He loves deeply, in word and deed, as a patient father (Hos. 11), gracious husband (Isa. 54:5), faithful shepherd (Ps. 100:3–5), and attentive vinedresser (Isa. 5:1–7).

God manifests his deep love by active involvement in the history of his people. In Psalm 136, the psalmist chronicled a series of events in Israel's history—from creation to conquest—each one punctuated with the chorus: "His love endures forever." Moreover, OT history is laced with answered prayers (e.g., Hannah gave birth to Samuel), miraculous deliverances (e.g., Israel escaped from Egypt), and military interventions (e.g., David defeated Goliath), each demonstrating God's deep love.

Unfortunately, *knowing* God's deep love is eternal, unconditional, personal, and active does not always mean we *feel* his deep love. No, his love often remains in the fact, not feeling, category. Whereas a mother might hug her child or a husband might treat his wife to a generous date, God's deep love does not directly touch our senses (e.g., sight, taste, smell). Thus, like Malachi's audience, we become desensitized to God's deep love, treating it as a platitude.

Is it true?

Is it true that God's deep love should stir our dull senses? Absolutely. But for various reasons our senses remain dull to his deep love. An unhealthy, romantic understanding of love dulls our senses. Hallmark and Hollywood condition us to reduce love to sentiment or sensuality. While God verbally reiterated his love through Malachi, he pointed beyond the words to his covenant faithfulness toward the people. Love expresses itself in many tangible ways. The OT recounts generations of God's provision, protection, pardon, and keeping promises for his people who constantly failed to keep their side of the covenant. The very fact that he did not altogether abandon his prodigal people testifies to his persistent affection for them (Hos. 11; cf. Luke 15:11–32).

Furthermore, our senses may be dulled to God's deep love because trying circumstances cloud our vision. The OT narrative is no stranger to this fog: Israel suffered bondage in Egypt, Job lost his livelihood, David lamented throughout the psalms, Jeremiah wept over Jerusalem, and Habakkuk complained about international threats. And yet, even these stories and psalms of despair reiterate God's enduring love and abiding presence. "I am with you" is the divine refrain (Gen. 15:1; 26:24; Exod. 3:12; Josh. 1:5; Isa. 41:10; 43:5; Jer. 42:11; 46:28).

Finally, sometimes God's deep love comes in the form of discipline. Love and discipline are not mutually exclusive but may reinforce one another. Any parent knows that healthy correction is a necessary means to redirect stubborn, selfish kids from harming themselves and others. Proverbs affirms God's discipline as a sign of his love (Prov. 3:11–12). The discipline Malachi's forefathers faced was an act of divine discipline driven by deep love (Deut. 28; 30).

Now what?

How do we live in the reality of God's deep love? What can we do to stir our dull senses? Whether we have walked with God for decades or joined his family in recent weeks, doubts concerning his love creep in. We may have experienced dark nights, deep valleys, or desperate circumstances that suggest God has abandoned us. We may feel lonely, depressed, distant, forgotten, or scorned by God. While the feelings are real, they also mislead us. We should acknowledge our negative feelings without being held captive by them. If we regularly feel overlooked or unwanted by God, we might even probe that feeling, identifying its triggers, frequency, and strength. Perhaps the feeling surfaces most readily after scanning social media, attending worship services, late at night, or interacting with certain family members or friends. If this is the case, our doubts concerning God's love may be mere projection. We cannot let misleading feelings override the stated fact of God's love.

After acknowledging misleading feelings, we are responsible to replace them with truth. But it is not enough to glibly proclaim, "God loves me." Most of God's people can verbally acknowledge his love, quoting verses and singing songs that mention it. Trusting in God's love is another matter, which involves deep, careful reflection on passages of Scripture and personal stories that affirm his care for us. Our reflection on truth may bridge into singing or journaling, but it often begins with five to ten minutes of reading (and rereading) select portions of Scripture that describe God's active, personal, and enduring love. This gap between knowing God's deep love and experiencing it deeply explains the purpose of Paul's powerful prayer (Eph. 3:18–19).

Passages Describing God's Love
Exodus 34:6–7; Deuteronomy 7:7–9; Psalm 103, 136; 145; Proverbs 3:11–12; Isaiah 54:10; Hosea 11:1–11; Micah 7:18–20; cf. Romans 8:35–39; 1 John 3:1–13; 4:7–19

Creativity in Presentation

To capture the element of God's choice (election) of Israel, share a personal story about selecting a spouse, friend, business partner, or friend. I (Tim) recall my stuttering, first attempt to "define the relationship" with my wife-to-be. We stood beneath a curtain of rain in an empty parking lot as I revealed my feelings for her. She was not impressed. She needed more than "lip service" for assurance. Aptly, she replied, "What does that mean? I'm interested in commitment." So I committed! Many years later, my wife and I adopted a son from Ethiopia. We found his profile on a Waiting Children list. After spending weeks praying and deliberating, we chose to pursue the adoption. Adoptive children often have trouble giving and receiving love, but this did not deter us from enfolding him into our family and showering him with affection. (I suspect something similar happens when we join the family of God. The "Does he love me?" question reflects our broken past more than his quality of love.)

Imagine, if you could, love without words. Gary Chapman (2015) describes a handful of ways to do this in his book *Five Love Languages*, most of which surpass lip service: Physical Touch, Receiving Gifts, Acts of Service, Quality Time, and Words of Affirmation. Ask people to assess nonverbal ways they express love throughout the day. Perhaps giving specific examples of each love language would help them. Then turn the conversation toward God, reflecting on nonverbal ways he shows love.

A subtle but powerful way to convey how God's deep love might stir our dull senses is to play the track or instrumentation to a well-known praise song (e.g., David Crowder Band's rendition of "How He Loves" or Stuart Townend's "How Deep the Father's Love for Us") without having singers or projected words. Instead, consider recruiting people who excel at interpretive dance or sign language. Invite them to the stage to embody God's love with choreography or sign. If neither of these options would fit your church's culture, consider involving youth in a pantomime. (Note: This will require several weeks of preparation and practice. Search YouTube for a trove of pantomime examples.) Ultimately, you want the sermon to communicate the following: God loved his people Israel. His deep love should stir our dull senses.

- Listen up: God declares his deep love for us (1:1–2a).

- Admit it: We are desensitized to God's deep love (1:2b).

- Wake up: God demonstrates his deep love for us (1:2c–5).

DISCUSSION QUESTIONS

1. Malachi gave two examples that proved God loved Israel (1:1–5). What additional evidence in the Pentateuch supports this point?

2. How do you understand the idea of God's hate? What made Esau so odious to God?

3. What causes *you* to question God's love? What causes *others* to question God's love?

4. How has God demonstrated his love to his people throughout history? What metaphors in Scripture convey his love? How do Gary Chapman's "love languages" help expand your notion of love?

5. How can you help stir people to experience God's love?

Malachi 1:6–2:9

EXEGETICAL IDEA
Israel's priests did not honor God when they conducted sacrificial worship at the temple (1:6–10), did not keep the Levitical covenant with God (2:8), and did not instruct the people faithfully (2:6–8). God would disqualify these priests from temple service and send a curse on them (2:1–3:9), but God would be honored among the nations (1:11, 14).

THEOLOGICAL FOCUS
All worship leaders and worshippers need to fear God, faithfully teach the Torah, and honor God in their worship.

PREACHING IDEA
Shortcuts in worship can come back to bite us.

PREACHING POINTERS
Although sacrificial worship had resumed in Jerusalem after the exile, a necessary sense of reverence was missing. This provoked God's second dispute with his people, which Malachi voiced to his original audience. God, through his prophet, called out the priests for cutting corners and cheating the sacrificial system. Their acts would fool neither parent nor local politician; they certainly could not fool their divine King. Malachi exposed how their errant thinking devolved into egregious worship. Fortunately, the original audience heard God's rebuke and took steps to improve their relationship with him.

Our furious pace of life today spurs a similar temptation for taking shortcuts. We prefer SparkNotes to unabridged literature. We listen to audio books at an accelerated pace. We watch YouTube channels for video game hints and tricks to amass extra lives and resources to win more quickly. Skimping on taxes, rolling through stop signs, and taking credit for others' work is epidemic. When so many areas of life tolerate cheating, it's no surprise to catch God's people cutting corners as we honor him. We lowball our tithes and offerings, give better energy to sports and business than weekly church gatherings, and treat evangelism as an add-on to life rather than an essential component. Malachi's message reminds us that shortcuts in worship come back to bite us.

THE PRIESTS DO NOT FEAR GOD (1:6–2:9)

LITERARY STRUCTURE AND THEMES

This second dispute includes two claims that the priests did not honor God when sacrificing at the temple (1:6a, 7a), but the priests object to both claims (1:6b, 7b), so Malachi illustrated their failures (1:8–10, 12–14a). This dispute ends with two positive conclusions about the nations that would honor God (1:11, 14b); plus two negative conclusions about the future ministry of the priests who did not honor God (2:1–9).

This unit's theological theme is the necessity of properly fearing and honoring God, which presents every person with the choice they must make. One can honor God and be blessed, or dishonor him and suffer rejection and a curse.

- *The Absence of Honor for God in Worship (1:6a, 7a)*
- *A Denial of the Charges (1:6b, 7b)*
- *They Offer Dishonorable Sacrifices (1:8–10, 12–14a)*
- *God's Name Will Be Great among the Nations (1:11, 14b)*
- *God's Curse on His Servants (2:1–9)*

EXPOSITION

Malachi introduced his second message with a series of questions that required the priests to reflect on the nature of their relationship with God. This rhetorical approach functioned as a way for them to discover their beliefs about God, identify any misunderstanding of their roles as priests, and to challenge them to honor God in everything they did. Many priests and many people did not honor God in their worship but were simply going through the motions without any real commitment to honor him. So God was sending a curse on the priests and rejecting their service at the temple, for they were leading many people astray rather than instructing them in the ways of the Lord from the Torah.

The Absence of Honor for God in Worship (1:6a, 7a)

Although people were going through the motions, God their Father and Master was not being honored during their worship.

1:6a. In this second dispute, God through his prophet confronts the priests in charge of temple worship. The prophet Malachi began with two everyday analogies that his audience would accept. Everyone would affirm that a son should honor his father (Exod. 20:12; Deut. 5:16) and that a servant should have a relationship of respect/honor/fear to his master. Since God was a Father and Ruler over his people (Exod. 4:22; Hos. 11:1; Jer. 3:4; Mal. 2:10), this analogy was not difficult to understand. It was essential that the priests "honor/glorify" (כָּבוֹד) God and help worshippers praise/glorify God at the temple. The priests probably assumed they were "honoring/glorifying" God through their service at the temple, but Malachi claimed that they despised God's name by the way they conducted worship (1:6a).

WORD ANALYSIS: כָּבוֹד
This word can refer to (a) something "weighty, heavy" (in the priest Eli was heavy 1 Sam. 4:18, or Moses's hands grew heavy in Exod. 17:2). A figurative use pictured God's yoke as "heavy, burdensome" (Isa. 47:6) or his hand as "heavy, strongly against" someone (Job 23:2). Another context described certain sins as "heavy, serious" (Sodom's sin in Gen. 18:20) or a hailstorm as "heavy, severe" (the plague in Exod. 9:18). (b) When Pharaoh

rejected God, he had a "heavy, hardened, unresponsive" heart that would not repent (Exod. 7:14; 8:15). (c) An "honorable, valued" person or place of importance was "honored" (Tyre was honored for its wealth in Ezek. 27:25). People "honored, glorified" God by giving him praise, pure sacrifices, and by treating him as holy.

1:7a. The second claim clarified the first claim by saying that the priest "despised" (בָּזָה) God's "name/reputation" (שֵׁם) by treating him with disrespect. The priests defiled (the opposite of keeping something holy) the altar of God by presenting defiled offerings on the table of the Lord / the altar of burnt offerings.[1] The priests were ignoring some central principles in Leviticus about worship at the temple (Ezek. 40:39–43; 41:42). For example, if a priest sinned, he was to offer a sin offering, a bull that had no defects (Lev. 4:2, 14). But if a common person sinned, he was to bring a female goat without defect (Lev. 4:28). Each case was different and each included instructions about the confession of sins, the use of the blood, and what to do with the fat of the animal, but the priests did not follow God's instructions.

The altar at the temple in Arad in southern Judah.
Courtesy of Hanay.

A Denial of the Charges (1:6b, 7b)

The priests were astonished and in denial of the charge that they defiled sacrificial worship at the temple.

1:6b, 7b. The priests responded negatively to the accusations by Malachi. They questioned, "How have we despised your name?" (1:6b). The response to Malachi's second accusation was a similar question: "How have we defiled you?" (1:7b). This self-defense either showed a lack of knowledge of Moses's instructions, the priests' decision to liberalize the sacrificial rules and make them easier for the people to accept, or just a lack of concern about honoring God. Possibly they were excusing these actions with the rationalization ("you say, think") that it is better to have them sacrificing some animal at the temple (even if it was unqualified) than to have them not come to the temple at all because they could not afford to give the correct sacrifice. The priests were probably pleasing the people by not strictly enforcing the Levitical rules concerning sacrifices. Malachi 1:8 and 13–14a list some of the unqualified animals that the priests allowed the people to sacrifice.

They Offer Dishonorable Sacrifices (1:8–10, 12–14a)

They sacrificed disqualified animals, defiling the altar and defaming God's name.

1:8–10. In order to counter the priests' rebuttal, the prophet substantiated his claims with specific charges. The first justification for claiming that the priests defamed the name of God was to point out how many people brought unqualified animals to offer as a sacrifice. Instead of rejecting these offerings, the priests ignored what God said and sacrificed blind, lame, and sick animals. Leviticus 22:19–25 laid out criteria that would identify an unacceptable

---

1   Clendenen (2004, 268), Hill (1998, 178), and Snyman (2015, 62) interpret the "table of the Lord" not as a reference to the Table of Showbread (Exod. 25:30), but to the altar of burnt offerings.

sacrifice (if it had defects, was blind, had fractures, was maimed, had open sores, scabs, deformities, had bruises, or places crushed, torn, or cut; cf. Deut. 15:21). It was the responsibility of the priests to evaluate each sacrificial animal to make sure it met these high standards (Lev. 27:11–12), but the priests largely ignored these rules. This showed ignorance or disrespect for God himself and his instructions in the law and disrespect for their duty to assist in restoring the sinner's relationship to God through the confession of sins and the offering of a pure sacrifice (Snyman, 2015, 62). Malachi rhetorically asked his audience if this was evil.[2] In a sarcastic challenge, Malachi asked if his audience would dare to give these animals to a political official, the "governor" (פֶּחָה), in order to pay their taxes (1:8b)? Would he be pleased with them? If a human governor (a minor authority on earth) would not accept defective animals, why would they expect God (a much greater authority in heaven) to graciously respond to these dishonorable offerings (1:9)? In fact, God would prefer[3] that the priests would close the doors of the temple complex (cf. 1 Sam. 3:13; 2 Chron. 29:3) in order to prevent the killing of useless sacrifices (Mal. 1:10). Earlier prophets (Hos. 6:6; Amos 5:21–22; Micah 6:6–8; Isa. 1:10–15) also criticized unacceptable worship at the temple.

1:12–14a. The second justification of the claim supplemented the accusations in 1:8–10 by adding additional details. Malachi repeated his claim that they "profaned, defiled" (חָלַל) God's name (cf. 1:6b), but in addition to this was the charge that the priests found their repetitious work of offering sacrifices at the altar day after day a "wearisome/tiring" (לָאָה) task. They were bored and "disgusted" (נָפַח, lit., "you sniff at it"). Their joy was gone; they were "impatient" or tired and did not value their special role as spiritual guides. The priests' lax attitude about what

animals to sacrifice meant that they sacrificed "stolen" (גָּזוּל), lame, and every other type of illegitimate sacrifice. So what would God do? God pronounced a curse on anyone who vowed to give him a valuable, sacrificial male animal (the most prized animal) but later "deceitfully" (נָכַל) decided to give God a less valuable, blemished animal (1:14a).

WORD ANALYSIS: לָאָה
The semantic range of meanings included (a) being "tired, worn out" (in Jer. 9:4, people were "worn out/exhausted" with sinning; in Job 16:7, God "wore out, exhausted" Job); (b) being "tired" of something (in Job 4:2, Job was "impatient?"; in Mic. 6:3, God asked if Judah was "tired" of him?); or (c) "to be unable" to do something (in Exod. 7:18, the Egyptians were "unable" to drink the water; in Jer. 20:9, Jeremiah was "unable" to stop speaking God's words).

God's Name Will Be Great among the Nations (1:11, 14b)

In spite of the failures to honor God in Israel, someday God's name would be feared by the non-Jewish nations all over the world.

Ahura-mazda

Ahura-mazda (*Ahura* means: "lord," *mazda* means "wisdom") was the highest spirit worshipped in Zoroastrianism by the Medes and Persians beginning around 500 B.C. He was a creator god in heaven, uncreated, changeless, and without equal, upholder of justice and truth. He was revealed to Zoroaster in a vision when he was fifteen years old, and thus Zoroastrianism became a major religion in Persia, and Ahura-mazda was a supporter of the Persian kings (particularly Darius I; 522–486 B.C.). At first these people made idols of this god, but later images were forbidden.

---

2   Baker (2006, 228) stated that, "These priests are not simply 'cheap,' they are being wicked."
3   The introductory word מִי indicated that this phrase was God's wish ("Oh that . . . one would").

1:11, 14b. Two conclusions point to the worldwide ("from the rising to the setting of the sun"[4]) recognition of God's greatness all over the world (cf. Ps. 113:3). But it is not as clear if Malachi meant that God's name "is" or "will be" great in every place incense "is" or "will be" offered in his name. If this is read as present tense, this would imply that it was possible to make offerings outside the temple in Jerusalem, so some hypothesize that it was possible that God would accept the sacrifices of heathens to idols.[5] Verhoef (1987, 226) rejects this interpretation as well as the suggestion that the monotheistic tendencies of the Persian worship of the god Ahura-mazda made their worship acceptable to God. A second approach suggests that this statement referred to sacrifices by proselytes from Gentile nations, but Snyman (2015, 71) rejects this interpretation because there was little evidence of any massive conversion of Gentiles at that time. A third interpretation identifies these people as Jews who lived among the Gentiles (e.g., at Elephantine in Egypt), but the worship at Elephantine was syncretistic and included other gods (Verhoef, 1987, 229).

TRANSLATION ANALYSIS: 1:11

NASB[95]	"My name will be great among the nations."
NKJV	"My name shall be great among the Gentiles."
NRSV	"For my name is great among the nations."
HCSB/ NIV	"My name will be great among the nations."

The Kingly Rule of God

A survey of the use of kingship terminology for the gods in Mesopotamia, Ugarit, Egypt, and among the Hittites draws out both the similarities and differences between the concept of God / the gods as king in the ANE and the Bible.

A fourth hypothesis essentially eliminates the problem of offering sacrifices in other places by interpreting offering sacrifices to mean "praying" to God, and a fifth analysis argues that "in every place" is a hyperbole (Snyman, 2015, 75–76); and finally a large group of commentators thinks this statement referred to what would happen in a later eschatological era (Baldwin, 1972, 230; Clendenen, 2004, 278; Merrill, 2003, 347; Ross, 2016, 64, Stuart, 1998, 1306), which makes the most sense. This vision of God's kingdom included people from many nations coming to Jerusalem to hear God teach his laws (Isa. 2:2–4), and for people from the ends of the earth to turn to God and be saved (Isa. 45:22). The nations would come to the glorious light of the Lord (Isa. 60:1–3) to declare God's glory among the nations (Isa. 66:19–23; Zech. 14:16–21). In contrast to the failures of the Jewish people of Malachi's day, these foreign believers would honor God by glorifying his name. They would recognize that God is the King (1:14) who sovereignly rules over everyone and everything. The kingly rule of God was one of the fundamental characteristics of the Hebrew (and the ANE) conception of God. He was called "the King of glory" (Ps. 24:7–10), "a great King over all the earth" (Ps. 47:2, 6–7), the "Lord who reigns" on his everlasting throne (Pss. 93:1–3; 96:10; 97:1; 98:6; 99:1), and a great King above all gods" (Ps. 95:3). Isaiah saw him as a King on his throne (Isa. 6:1, 5), a King, Judge, and Savior (Isa. 32:22), the Holy One, Creator, and King (Isa. 43:15).

---

4   This phrase is a *merismus*, a figure of speech in which the whole is represented by naming certain parts. By naming east (the rising of the sun) and west (the setting of the sun) the author has emphasized that all parts of the earth will honor God.

5   Snyman (2015, 70–71) rejects this approach because these pagan sacrifices were not "in my name" as 1:11 required. No other OT passage suggests that God will accept the sacrifices of pagans.

The Hebrew God	Ancient Near Eastern gods
Similarities	
Called King with ultimate power	Called king with power over one area
Has roles of a king: ruler, lawgiver, judge	Has some roles of a king
Differences	
Only one God	Many gods
No fighting for power; cannot be defeated	Must fight other gods for power; can be defeated
Has absolute authority over everything	Limited authority over one area
Has a covenant relationship with his people	No covenant relationship
Not represented by a part of nature	Connected to a part of nature
Chart Created by Gary V. Smith, "The Concept of God / The Gods as King in the Ancient Near East and the Bible," *Trinity Journal* 3 (1982): 18–31. Reprinted by permission of Gary V. Smith.	

God's Curse on His Servants (2:1–9)

Since the priests did not fear God or keep the Levitical covenant, God's curse would fall on them, and the people would despise them.

2:1–2. This final section began with "and now" (וְעַתָּה) which marks a turning point in the prophecy. The preceding verses tell what would happen to those who honor God (1:11, 14), but now the prophet dealt with what would happen to the priests who did not reverence God.

The Lord sternly rebuked the priests (2:1) with an initial "command, admonition, warning" (מִצְוָה) about what would happen to them due to their failure to function as godly priests who honored God. If the priests refused to take "this command, warning" seriously (lit., "take it to heart") and did not give "glory/honor" (כָּבוֹד) to God's name (cf. 1:6), then God would send "the curse" (הַמְּאֵרָה, from אָרַר)[6] on the priests and remove their blessings. The text does not explain what these blessings were, so some interpreters focus on the priests' future loss of material blessings (Snyman, 2015, 83; Redditt, 1995, 167), while others focus on the loss of their ability to speak blessings on the people (Lev. 6:16–18; Num. 6:23–26). Rather than focus on just one area, a more comprehensive curse would involve both (Baker, 2006, 241; Petersen, 1995, 188; Stuart, 1998, 1311–12; Clendenen, 2004, 289), so their loss of God's blessings meant a loss of "an enrichment—physical, spiritual, and/or material . . . that comes with a certain amount of empowerment or enablement" (Ross 2016, 84).

2:3. Two additional steps in God's judgment of the priests will follow. First, God will rebuke[7] their "seed" (זֶרַע). Although "seed"

---

6   H. C. Brichto, *The Problem of the 'Curse' in the Hebrew Bible* (Philadelphia: SBL, 1963) saw the curse as a ban on progress, movement, or capabilities, thus nothing would go right and success in all areas of life would be a thing of the past.

7   Hill (1998, 200) called this verb a future instantaneous participle that would describe what was happening now; thus, the translation "I am going/I am about to rebuke."

could refer to the seed of their crops (Glazier-McDonald, 1987, 67; Kaiser, 1984, 57) or to the "children, offspring" of the priest (Verhoef, 1987, 241; Baker, 2006, 242) or to both (Baldwin, 1972, 233), in this context the rebuke seems to refer to a curse on their children. However, it is unclear if this meant they would have fewer children or that their children would suffer under God's judgment. A second judgment was that the priests would be defiled by God figuratively spreading the putrid contents of the stomach and the feces from the intestines of sacrificial animals on the faces of the priests (2:3b). According to the Levitical instructions the internal organs and intestines were considered unclean and were burned outside the camp (Exod. 29:14; Lev. 4:11; 16:27). Having this foul intestinal matter spread on a person's face would be humiliating and extremely repulsive, but the main point was to symbolize that these priests were unclean and unable to serve God at the temple. Like the dung and intestinal organs that were discarded, these unclean priests would be thrown out with them.

2:4. Another problem with the priests was their failure to keep the covenant with Levi. When these humiliating things happened, these priests "will realize, understand" (יָדַע) two things. First, they would understand that God was the one who sent this "commandment, admonition, warning" (מִצְוָה) to them (2:4a). Second, they would realize that God's purpose (the word לִהְיוֹת, "in order that," expresses purpose) for sending this warning was because he wanted to preserve his covenant with the Levites (2:4b). When the priests failed to honor the terms of this covenant, this meant that their relationship with God was threatened. In this case God would try to preserve this covenant by correcting the priests' inappropriate behavior.

One complication with understanding this statement was that there is no passage in Scripture where God made a covenant with Jacob's son Levi; in fact, when Jacob came to bless his twelve sons, his words about the tribe of Levi sound more like a curse (Gen. 49:5–7). This curse was changed into a blessing at Mount Sinai when the tribe of Levi sided with Moses against those who worshipped the golden calf (Exod. 32:26–29). Then God instructed Moses concerning the establishment of the priesthood through Aaron, the son of Levi (Deut. 10:8–9), and added details about sacrifices (Lev. 1–7) and the process of dedicating the Levites (Exod. 29; Num. 8; 18). This may imply that God entered into a covenant with the Levites (see Deut. 33:8–11),[8] but no covenant with the Levites was mentioned until the high priest Phinehas stopped the Baal worship at Baal-Peor (Num. 25).

2:5–7. These verses indicate what God would do for and what he expected of those who served him as priests. First, God's covenant commitment was to give the priests "life and peace" (2:5a) instead of death and hopelessness, as implied in the curse of Jacob in Genesis 49:5–7. This life is described as a life with "peace, well-being" (שָׁלוֹם), which implied a long life that would be favored with the blessings of God. God's covenant with the high priest Phinehas is called "a covenant of peace" (Num. 25:12), but in order to have peace with God, one has to follow God's instructions. The basic obligation of the priests was to treat God with reverence and awe by glorifying his name. The priests were to approach their all-powerful holy God with an attitude of "fear, respect, awe" (יָרֵא). This was sacred space, and as Aaron's sons Nadab and Abihu found out (Lev. 10:1–3) a failure to treat God as holy could lead to death, or rejection as in the case

---

8   Jeremiah 33:20–21 confirms that there was a "covenant with Levi," but it offered no information about the original establishment of that covenant.

of Eli and his sons (1 Sam. 2:12–34). In earlier days, the priests feared God and carried out their sacrificial and teaching responsibilities with an attitude of reverence (Mal. 2:5b). But the priests in Malachi's day "despised my name" (1:6b) and "profaned it" (1:12a).

Second, the priests were to teach the Israelites all of God's instructions in the law of Moses (Lev. 10:10–11; Deut. 33:10). Initially the priests provided "truthful instruction," including oral exposition as well as a trustworthy practical application to the people (Snyman, 2015, 88). They did not misinterpret statutes that were unpopular or twist commandments to make them less stringent. This meant that "nothing opposite of the truth, nothing false, deceitful, or unreliable" (עַוְלָה) came out of their mouths (2:6b).

TRANSLATION ANALYSIS: 2:6, עַוְלָה
NASB[95] "unrighteousness was not found on his lips"
NKJV "injustice was not found on his lips"
NRSV "no wrong was found on his lips"
HCSB "nothing wrong was found on his lips"
NIV "nothing false was found on his lips"
All these options emphasize that the priest told the unperverted truth.

A third characteristic of these faithful priests was that they walked with God, a trait of the righteous lives of Enoch (Gen. 5:22, 24) and Noah (Gen 6:9), plus Abraham and Isaac (Gen. 48:15). The former priests were characterized by their peaceful behavior toward others.

A fourth positive point was that their teaching, their prayers, and their counseling with people enabled them to lead many people to repent of their sins and turn away from the evil path they were following (2:6b). Their teaching of the law of Moses persuaded some people not to sin (Verhoef, 1987, 249). The statements in 2:7 affirmed (כִּי) that the early priests communicated trustworthy instructions.

TEXTUAL NOTE: The translation of כִּי
"For" NASB[95], NIV, NRSV, NKJV, HCSB
"Verily; Indeed" Verhoef (1987, 249) and Hill (1998, 211)[9]

The priests "kept, preserved" (שָׁמַר) knowledge about God and what he required of them. Consequently, righteous people went to the godly priests to receive God's instruction from one who served as a faithful messenger of God (2:7b). From time to time God revealed his will through the prophets, but on a daily basis the priests would teach or proclaim what God had revealed to Moses and the prophets (R. Smith, 1984, 318), so their roles were somewhat similar but not the same (cf. Hos. 4:4–6).

2:8–9. This disputation ended by directing attention to "you," the exilic priests in the time of Malachi. Their character, behavior, and beliefs were set in contrast to the ideal priests described in 2:5–7. These priests failed to teach the wisdom found in the laws of God, so their teachings "have turned people from the way" (2:8a) that God set forth in the law. The exilic priests failed to teach what God said in the Torah, and they caused many to stumble (2:8b). Based on problems that Malachi confronted in other disputations, it seems that the priests failed to instruct the people on many issues (divorce, intermarriage with pagans, tithing, and divine justice). On account of these failures, the exilic priests "violated/corrupted/ruined" (שָׁחַת) the covenant with Levi (2:8c), which the earlier priests carefully preserved (2:4).

Having explained the reason for God's action against the unfaithful exilic priests, it was time to announce their punishment (2:9). Since they "despised" (בָּזָה) God and his altar (1:7, 12), now God would reverse the situation and cause them to be "despised" (בָּזָה) by the Israelite people (2:9). The basic reason for this action was because "you have not kept my ways," with the term "ways" (דֶּרֶךְ) being an ancient way of summarizing the lifestyle and beliefs that God wanted his people to follow (Deut. 9:12, 16; 11:28; 31:29; Pss. 1:5; 25:4; 119:14). A second accusation was that "you are partial" in your dealings with people. Thus the priests were granting special favors to one group, and in the process they "were causing people to stumble by their instructions" (2:8). Verhoef (1987, 253) interprets this to mean that they were motivated by material gain and were open to bribery from members of the upper class. Ross (2016, 89) thought this meant that these priests applied biblical teaching to different people in different ways, being more lenient on the rich and powerful and allowing them to present unacceptable animals for sacrifice.

THEOLOGICAL FOCUS

The exegetical idea (Israel's priests did not honor God when they conducted sacrificial worship at the temple [1:6–10], did not keep the Levitical covenant with God [2:8], or instruct the people faithfully [2:6–8], so God would disqualify these priests from temple service and send a curse on them [2:1–3:9], but God would be honored among the nations [1:11, 14]) leads to this theological focus: All worship leaders and worshippers need to fear God, faithfully teach the Torah, and honor God in their worship.

There are several practical lessons to learn from this disputation based on the theological principles or themes set out in these verses. First, it was important for both the worshipper and worship leader to make honoring God their chief focus in all of life and especially during worship time. Second, some of the responsibilities of worship leaders should include setting a positive example of service, being a peaceful person, speaking the truth, expressing awe at the privilege of worshipping God, living a righteous life, pointing out error in order to turn people to the truth, and not showing partiality or favoritism toward some

over others. Third, worship leaders who did not fear God, fulfill their responsibilities, and teach God law could not expect God to bless them. Rather they should expect God's curse and for God to remove them from a leadership role (2:2–3:9). Fourth, people should give God their best gifts, not what is left over or defective. Fifth, in spite of these failures on the part of some, one day people from all over the world would honor and glorify God as the great King who rules over all people and all nations (1:11, 14).

PREACHING AND TEACHING STRATEGIES

Exegetical and Theological Synthesis

Malachi 1:6–2:9 keys in on the role of the priest in Israel's worship of God. As the mediator between God and his people, the priest inspected and approved animal sacrifices. Apparently, priests in Malachi's day seemed more eager to please their human clients than God. Ironically, their shortcuts only made life more miserable for the people they sought to impress. God threatened to lock the gates to the temple altogether (1:10), cutting off the people from the altar and his presence.

This second dispute highlights a key truth about leadership. Leaders affect their constituents; good, bad, or indifferent, their choices force consequences on their followers. Not only do these priests appear spineless in their reluctance to reject blemished sacrifices, but they also look lazy in their disdain for daily duties (1:13). They had deemed the quality control aspect of their job to be arbitrary (e.g., Lev. 4; 22:19–25). Attending sacrifices was not busy work but holy work because they were called into service by the Lord of Hosts (Exod. 29; Deut. 10:8–9; Lev. 1–7). Their cheating the sacrificial system exposed their irreverence for God (Mal. 1:6–9, 14; 2:1).

Finally, the exegetical section provides a corrective to disastrous theology. God was not an uncaring, local despot. Various metaphors depict him as father (1:6), king (1:14), and covenant-sustainer (2:4). Moreover, God's redemptive concern extended beyond Israel; he sought glory from all nations (1:11, 14). This global vision transcended Malachi's day, pointing toward an eschatological future forecast by other prophets (cf. Isa. 66; Zech. 14). To give glory to God—to honor and revere him in word and deed for his indescribable worth—was the greatest service of any person at any time or place.

Preaching Idea
Shortcuts in worship can come back to bite us.

Contemporary Connections

What does it mean?
What does it mean that shortcuts in worship come back to bite us? What is worship? Worship is our way of expressing to God our loyalty, love, and gratitude for his greatness (Pss. 95; 145–150). Furthermore, worship includes obeying his law, giving him praise, offering him a variety of sacrifices, or serving others in his name. Both attitude and action, word and deed, and posture and practice matter in worship. Malachi's address to the priests focused on a specific, cultic form of sacrificial worship. The priests' poor sacrifices betrayed their irreverent posture.

What kinds of shortcuts do people take in worship? God's people are notorious for taking shortcuts. Instead of waiting for God's revelation from Sinai, they made a golden calf (Exod. 32). Instead of practicing justice, they pretended to honor God with sacrifices (Amos 5:21–25). Instead of pouring their hearts out in true confession, they put on an insincere show (Isa. 29:13). Instead of restoring the temple to its former glory, they returned to their comfortable homes (Hag. 1:1–6). Shortcuts in worship may include anything from skimping on financial giving, haphazard community service, last-minute preparations for a Sunday school class, choosing athletics over corporate gatherings, or giving our leftover energy to seeking God in prayer.

And if we broaden worship to mean honoring God in every aspect of life—attitude and action, word and deed, posture and practice—then we must beware of taking shortcuts in our relationships, work, health, finances, leisure, and community service. God invites his people to present all of life to him as an act of worship (Deut. 6:4–5; Mic. 6:8; cf. 1 Cor. 10:31; Col. 3:17).

Is it true?
Is it true that shortcuts in worship can come back to bite us? Yes, and a few biblical examples stand out. Nadab and Abihu, sons of Aaron, took a shortcut in their incense offering, and God consumed them with fire for it (Lev. 10:1–4). King Saul took a shortcut by not waiting for Samuel to sacrifice sheep, and God dethroned him for it (1 Sam. 15). King Jeroboam took a shortcut in building a rival temple in Samaria, and God prophesied the end of his royal line (1 Kings 13:1–3). And the shortcuts of the priesthood in Malachi's day did not escape God's notice.

But the principle proves true more broadly: shortcuts in any relationship or context can come back to bite us. Husbands who take shortcuts in planning dates for their wives may cause resentment. Students who shortcut their research by plagiarizing others may face expulsion. Builders who shortcut their construction efforts may lose clients and face lawsuits. Patients who shortcut the rehab process may not regain full capacity of their repaired knee. And pastors who shortcut their sermon preparation by preaching another person's sermon may lose their reputation and ministry post. Because worship can apply to all areas of life, a believer who takes shortcuts in his work and relationships ultimately robs God of the honor due him in daily life.

Finally, we should realize that God values the long road. When we refuse to take shortcuts, we create space for character formation.

Facing hardship helps us learn endurance, increase trust, and cling to hope (Pss. 16; 42). Maturity follows protracted trials, not shortened trails. God does not usually call us to unnecessary suffering—taking on a second mortgage to increase our tithe or refusing sleep to intercede for the persecuted church—but he does want us to live sacrificially. When we take shortcuts in honoring him with our whole life, we fail to become the people he envisions (Exod. 19:5–6; Isa. 42:6; 49:6).

Now what?
How do we avoid shortcuts in worship? What is the process in moving from hasty, sloppy, selfish service to slow, careful, honoring service? First, we are wise to invoke the occasional slowdown or stop (e.g., Sabbath rest) in our busy lives to assess our hearts. Our flurry of spiritual activity may look good and reap impressive outcomes, but our inner lives may suffer anxiety, anger, burnout, or bitterness as a result. Such unrest inevitably leads to shortcuts because the drive to be productive exceeds the joy in being present. A vacation may recharge a recent decline of energy at work. A monthly recess from playing on the worship band may allow for renewed appreciation to serve. A daily coffee break from studies may bring a wandering mind back into focus.

Second, we should view God with fresh eyes. When we are harassed by the demands of work, burdened by the hardships of life, or hardened by the deceitfulness of others, our conception of God suffers. We may ignore him or consider him a taskmaster. Shortcuts stem from errant theology. Consequently, our singing, giving, teaching, and serving can lose their earnestness, lack integrity, and become an empty ritual (Isa. 29:13). But when we remember the God who inspired the prophets—keeping covenant, ruling nations, offering forgiveness, seeking glory, and loving like a father—our lives should reflect greater earnestness and integrity.

Finally, we should give careful attention to areas where we most often take shortcuts.

We may take shortcuts in family worship by relegating prayer to a one-sentence blessing before dinner. We may take shortcuts in friendships by reducing the relationship to a string of text messages or social media likes. We may take shortcuts in our local church involvement by occasional attendance, sporadic service, and rare giving. We may take shortcuts at work by arriving late, leaving early, and doing just enough to get the job done. We may take shortcuts in our personal worship to God by limiting our devotion to a three-minute reading at the end of the day. Exposing our shortcuts allows us to reclaim our whole life as an act of worship (Rom. 12:1).

Creativity in Presentation
I (Tim) competed in cross-country during college. Our races covered eight kilometers, roughly five miles. Before each race, we received maps and course instructions, telling us where to turn and how to follow the flags marking the route. The course referee often said, "Runners, stick to the integrity of the line." During a high-stakes invitational, I recall the athletes out front strayed from the line, cutting a few corners and extending their lead; however, after crossing the finish line, they were disqualified. Their shortcut came back to bite them. Let the congregation know that "Life will present many shortcuts, but God wants us to be people with integrity. Those who stick to the integrity of the line view all of life as an act of worship."

History has shown that shortcuts can come back to bite us. Consider the banks outed for bogus loans during the housing crisis that began in 2007, Wells Fargo bankers creating false accounts to reach quotas, or athletes using performance-enhancing drugs to shortcut their recovery (e.g., Major League Baseball's "steroid era" in the late 1990s and early 2000s). These well-known shortcuts resulted in public shame and serve as an analogy to the dispute God had with Israel's priests.

A Few Notorious Shortcuts

A Few Notorious Shortcuts
- Major League Baseball player Mark McGwire cut corners by taking steroids.
- NCAA basketball coach Rick Pitino cut corners in recruiting college athletes.
- Enron executive Jeffery Skilling cut corners by insider trading.
- US president Richard Nixon cut corners by concealing details of Watergate.
- Elite cyclist Lance Armstrong cut corners by doping during Tour de France races.
- MIT Blackjack Team cut corners by counting cards in casinos.
- Dozens of Russian athletes cut corners by drug use in the 2014 Olympics.
- Mark Driscoll, former Mars Hill pastor, cut corners by bloating his book sales.

Children are experts at cutting corners. As a child, I (Tim) cut across lawns to get to my friends' homes, but not without hearing the wrath of my neighbors. I can recall attempts to cut corners in cleaning my bedroom. At first glance, my mother showed her approval; but when she checked beneath my bed and found piles of clothes, toys, books, and food scraps, her mood changed. In a similar vein, I cut corners in finishing my dinner, hiding piles of food under a napkin; my father was not tricked.

Adults also cut corners, as a friend of mine discovered during a recent home renovation project. The previous owner cut corners on electrical wiring, creating a fire hazard and doubling my friend's time and cost on the project. Our shortcuts sometimes come back to bite others as well. Draw from personal stories where cutting corners—on diet and exercise, home improvement and car repairs, homework assignments and work projects—resulted in more labor, cost, or other negative consequences.

Finally, if you feel adventurous, considering admitting from the beginning of the sermon that you did not have time during the week to study, prepare, and create your message. You took a shortcut instead and printed off a sermon from a preaching website. Assure them that you read it through once to confirm the content is biblical, sound, and relevant. Then confess, "If this goes well, I might start taking more shortcuts on my sermons." Give the line several seconds to settle before clearing the air. You did not take a shortcut in your act of worship.

Be sure the creative elements sync with the focus of the passage: All worship leaders and worshippers need to fear God and honor him in their worship. Indeed, shortcuts in worship can come back to bite us.

- Withholding our best from God is a shortcut (1:6–10; 12–14a).

- God wants respect from all peoples (1:11; 14b).

- Worship leaders be warned: God wants more from you (2:1–9).

DISCUSSION QUESTIONS

1. What other OT passages indicate that God's name will be honored by non-Jewish nations (1:5, 11, 14)?

2. What were ancient examples of useless worship? What are modern examples? What should be done in places where useless worship happens (1:10)?

3. What will be some of the criteria by which God evaluates religious leaders (2:1–9)?

4. What compels people to take shortcuts? How can you tame these impulses?

5. How do shortcuts affect our character, relationships, and life with God?

6. What are some biblical and modern examples of people who refused to take shortcuts?

Malachi 2:10–16

EXEGETICAL IDEA

Israel was a nation that worshipped one God, so people should not be unfaithful to that God or unfaithful to one another in marriage.

THEOLOGICAL FOCUS

Unfaithful treachery toward God and a marriage partner does not please God.

PREACHING IDEA

Let's cherish marriage and make it great again.

PREACHING POINTERS

God's case against Israel continued in a third dispute. Malachi addressed the people's infidelity to God and the miserable state of marriage in the land of Judah. The original audience was living in a time when both Ezra and Nehemiah encouraged men to divorce their pagan wives to maintain the spiritual purity of the nation. Sadly, many turned this exception for divorcing a foreign bride into a general rule that permitted them to divorce any wife. The twisted result of this process led some to think that it was permissible even to divorce a Jewish wife and then marry a foreign bride. The ugly situation resulted in a polluted temple, rejected worship, unhappy marriages, and the future progeny imperiled by these unholy mixed marriages—a far cry from God's intended design and deviation from the divorce imperative in Ezra and Nehemiah. Thus, Malachi begged his original audience to resurrect God's design for marriage.

In today's world, marriage does not always reflect God's ideal. Politicians have redefined marriage as a social contract, not a spiritual covenant. No-fault divorce laws have softened the sting of marital dissolution. The oft-cited fifty-percent statistic reveals that half of marriages end in divorce; Christian marriages are not immune. Moreover, cohabitation, polyamory, pornography, and domestic partnerships continue to gain mainstream approval. The solution is not for God's people to campaign just for a return to old-fashioned values, but to resurrect God's ideal. A good marriage is a gift and social good. This passage exhorts us to cherish marriage and make it great again.

UNFAITHFULNESS IN COVENANT RELATIONSHIPS
(2:10–16)

LITERARY STRUCTURE AND THEMES

This third dispute includes the claim that treacherous unfaithfulness was undermining the theological and family unity of the nation (2:10). The basis of this claim was that the people's treacherous unfaithfulness[1] in marriage profaned their worship (v. 11), so an initial conclusion was to cut off the unfaithful worshipper (2:12). A second justification of the claim was that these people were treacherous and weeping during worship (v. 13), and a third justification was the claim that their treacherous unfaithfulness in marriage led to divorce (vv. 14–16a). All these problems led to the concluding admonition to stop being unfaithful (v. 16b).

This unit's central theological theme is that many people were unfaithful to God in their marriages, and this was leading to unfaithfulness in their worship of God.

- *Unfaithfulness Undermines the Unity of the Faith and Family (2:10a)*
- *Unfaithfulness in Marriage Profanes Worship (2:10b–11)*
- *God Will Cut Off the Unfaithful (2:12)*
- *Unfaithfulness in Worship (2:13)*
- *An Objection (2:14a)*
- *Family Unfaithfulness in Marriage (2:14b–16a)*
- *Stop Being Unfaithful (2:16b)*

EXPOSITION

God opposed and rejected the worship of those who were unfaithful in marriage. Even though divorce was permitted earlier in Ezra 9–10 when it involved the removal of foreign wives who worshiped other gods, this was never meant to imply that God approved all divorces. He did not approve of divorce, especially when it involved violence or when a man divorced a Jewish wife in order to marry a foreign woman who worshiped other gods. Such marriages threatened national unity, spiritual unity, and the theological education of godly children.

Unfaithfulness Undermines the Unity of the Faith and Family (2:10a)

Hebrew faith and family ethics were based on Israel's belief in one God.

2:10a. The fundamental theological underpinning of Malachi's argument in this disputation was that the Jewish people were one unified ethnic and religious group because they had one father.[2] Since no father was mentioned by name, one might assume the father was Abraham (cf. Isa. 51:2) or Jacob (cf. Mal. 3:6; Baldwin, 1972, 237). Since "one God" was parallel to "one Father" and God was called a "father" in Malachi 1:6, many identify God as the father mentioned in the

---

1   Clendenen (2004, 326) prefers the HCSB translation "breaking faith," but it is not as strong as "treacherous unfaithfulness." E. Wendland, "Linear and Concentric Patterns in Malachi," *BT* 36 (1985): 116 outlined 2:10–16 into a modified chiasm, but several of the supposedly parallel sections of the chiastic were not really that parallel.

2   The question assumed that everyone would naturally give a yes answer. Verhoef (1987, 263) hypothesized that the occasion for this prophecy was the feast of penance (Zech. 7:5; 8:19), but this is just a guess.

first line (Kaiser, 1987, 75). God was seldom called father (see Deut. 32:6; Isa. 63:13; 64:8) in the OT, though it fits in with the second point (2:10a) that "one God created us." This creative act did not refer to God's creation of the world in Genesis but to the creation of the nation of Israel as a covenant people completely dedicated to God (Deut. 32:6; Isa. 43:1; 63:16; 64:8).

Unfaithfulness in Marriage Profanes Worship (2:10b–11)

God considered worshipping at the temple with an unbelieving spouse as an abomination that is contrary to the people's covenant obligations.

2:10b–11. In light of the theological unity stated in 2:10a, the question was, why were the people being "treacherously unfaithful" (בָּגַד) with other Jewish people in this covenant community?

> *WORD ANALYSIS:* בָּגַד
> This word can refer to (a) the deceitful way a master might deal unfaithfully with a female slave by selling her instead of making her a wife or concubine. Such action was a willful betrayal (Exod. 21:1–11). (b) In wisdom literature, this word described the treacherous unfaithfulness of Job's so-called comforters who turned against him in his time of suffering (Job 6:14–15). (c) In Jeremiah 12:1, this word described the unjust leaders who used treachery and deceit to get ahead in life. They deceptively spoke about God, appearing to be pious, but God was far from their thinking, and he did not guide their unfaithful behavior.

This act of deceptive unfaithfulness broke the covenant so seriously that Malachi concluded that they were "profaning, defiling" (חָלַל) the covenant their fathers agreed to keep at Mount Sinai (Exod. 19:1–6). Some seemed to forget about the special covenant relationship that the family of Israel had with God and the stipulations that were part of this arrangement.

The first act of treacherous unfaithfulness involved "detestable, abominable" (תּוֹעֵבָה) acts that profaned the holy temple of God. According to the Mosaic law, it was wrong for Israelite men to marry foreigners who worshipped other gods (Deut. 7:1–4), but it was worst for them to bring their pagan wives into God's holy temple area. Since God dwelt in this holy place, it was unacceptable for any pagan practices, foreign objects of worship, or even an unrepentant pagan person to be at the temple (cf. Deut. 7:25; 13:144–15; 17:4; 20:18). This would defile the place that God loved so dearly. Verhoef (1987, 268–69) and Stuart (1998, 1330–31) follow the Aramaic Targum and conclude that the nation that God chose was profaned by these acts. However, the context seems to indicate that the holy sanctuary of God was profaned (Clendenen, 2004, 332–33; Glazier-McDonald, 1987, 70; R. Smith, 1984, 319). There was a conflict between being set apart as the holy covenant people of God when worshipping at the temple and having pagan women who worshipped other gods at the temple. These women made it impossible for Judah to be one holy unified covenant people.

> ### "Detestable/Abominable" Acts
> Sins that were classified as "detestable, abominable" (תּוֹעֵבָה) were things like homosexuality, witchcraft, prostitution, child sacrifice, idolatry. These were serious sins that God loathed and hated. Another example of such sins is Ezekiel 44:7, which outlaws the bringing of spiritually uncircumcised foreigners into God's holy place.

God Will Cut Off the Unfaithful (2:12)

The consequence of profaning the temple was exclusion from the assembly of Israel.

2:12. God's judgment of the men of Judah was sharp and complete. No exceptions were offered for the guilty; they would be cut off from the family of Israel. Although there is some confusion about the interpretation of the phrase מֵעִיר וְעֹנֶה, "the one who awakes and responds," everyone agrees that this figure of speech denotes "everyone." This initial conclusion sounds somewhat similar to Ezra's campaign to stop the unholy marriages between Jewish men and foreign women who worshipped other gods (Ezra 9:1–10:44) and also similar to Nehemiah's attack on the Jewish men who married women from Ashdod, Ammon, and Moab (Neh. 13:23–29). But this plan of action was not the same as Ezra's or Nehemiah's, for Malachi promoted no plan for divorcing these pagan wives similar to Ezra (Ezra 9–10) or Nehemiah (Neh. 13). Instead, he spoke a prayer (Baldwin, 1972, 239; Ross, 2015, 117) that God himself would act against these sinful people. He warned them that they would be "cut off" (כָּרַת) from the tents of Jacob (Exod. 12:15, 19; Lev. 7:20–21, 27), but there were no details about how or when God would do this. Clendenen (2004, 342) views being "cut off" as "a divine sentence of condemnation that would eventually result in the cessation of one's name from the family of Israel."

TRANSLATION ANALYSIS: 2:12
NASB⁹⁵ "everyone who awakes and answers"
NKJV "the man who does this being awake and aware"
HCSB "to the man who does this"
NRSV "anyone who does this—any to witness and answer"
NIV "to the man who does this, whoever he may be"

Since this seems to be an idiom, an idiomatic "whoever, everyone" (without the literal "awakes and answers") would communicate the essence of what the prophet said.

Unfaithfulness in Worship (2:13)
God rejected the sacrifices of unfaithful and unrepentant people.

2:13. The second accusation was against people who were weeping and groaning at the temple altar when they offered a sacrifice at the temple. The exact reason for this weeping is not stated, but the result of this improper worship was that God rejected their sacrifices. Several suggestions are proposed: (a) Petersen (1995, 201–2) notes that the prophet Ezekiel condemned the people who were weeping for the Babylonian god Tammuz (Ezek. 8:14–15), so he concludes that the people in Malachi's day were weeping at the Israelite temple for the Canaanite god Baal to bring fertility back to the land (cf. Smith, 1984, 322; Glazier-Mc-Donald,1987, 99). (b) Stuart (1998, 1334) believes the people were following pagan practices that attempted to influence the gods / God by loud displays of emotions, but he says that it was the priests who were actually weeping at the altar because the lay person could not approach the altar. (c) Baldwin (1972, 239) accepts the inference of the Aramaic Targum that those weeping at the altar were the divorced wives mentioned in Malachi 2:14. (d) Snyman (2015, 111) argues that since weeping could be a sign of confession and sincere sorrow for sins, this behavior could be similar to the weeping exhibited when Ezra confronted the people about their sin of marrying pagan wives (cf. Ezra: 10:1). But in this case, it appears that the people were weeping "because" (מֵאֵין) God did not accept their offering or answer their prayers. But how would these people instantly know that God did not accept their offerings while they were still standing near the altar? One answer might be that Malachi was now informing them of God's displeasure with their sacrifices. But it is possible to translate מֵאֵין as "so that there is no" (rather than "because"), which would introduce a result clause (Ross, 2016, 108; Snyman, 2015, 111). This would mean that the last part of the verse would be: "and there will be no acceptance of your offering, or pleasure in accepting it from your hand." If this was the intended meaning, then this communicated that the offerings were brought, but the results were that God did not accept their worship.

An Objection (2:14a)
Unfaithful people find it difficult to accept God's criticism and warnings.

2:14a. The people responded with a brief request for the prophet to support his claim with some proof or rationale, for they could not accept what he was saying. Although this was not the traditional rejection of the prophet's opening statement as in Malachi 1:2, 6–7; 2:17; 3:8, 13, the question "why, for what reason" implied that the audience was not buying Malachi's claim in 2:13.

Family Unfaithfulness in Marriage (2:14b–16a)
A Spirit-led person would reject all forms of unfaithfulness in marriage because it would impact others, especially the children.

2:14b. One of the reasons for God rejecting the sacrifices in 2:13 was connected to the way Jewish men were being unfaithful to their marriage covenant. When the young Jewish couple was married, God witnessed the covenantal commitment each partner swore to the other person (cf. Ezek. 16:8; Prov. 2:17). God would be the one who would be called to bless this relationship with children and happiness (Gen. 1:28; Ruth 4:11; Prov. 5:18–19). But now some years later, these men were unfaithful to their original covenant companions (their wives). They were called "companions" because they were close friends who were joined together by a common way of thinking and a united purpose. But the marriage relationship was supposed to be characterized by a strong commitment and lasting unity. Malachi did not explain why a man might break his marriage covenant with his Jewish wife, though some speculate that a man might not be able to afford two wives so he had

to divorce one, or the original wife was getting old and was not very attractive, or a man might want to gain some economic advantage though marriage to a foreign wife. There probably were a host of different motivations.

2:15a. The final comments about this issue have several textual and interpretive problems that make it difficult to understand what Malachi said. Some say it is impossible (Verhoef, 1987, 275; Baldwin, 1972, 240). Yet, Malachi 2:15 seems to communicate the general truth that a spiritual man who wanted to raise up godly children would not deal deceptively with his Jewish wife and divorce her, but commentators and translations have proposed quite different ways of understanding the words in this verse. For example: (a) Who did the "one" at the beginning of the verse refer to, a person, a married couple who were one, or was the One actually God? (b) Was the "one" the subject or object of the verb? (c) Was the first part of 2:15 a question or a statement? (d) Did "spirit" refer to the Spirit of God, the human spirit, or sound spiritual judgment? There are no easy answers to these questions, so every conclusion must be presented with humility as a possible way of understanding the prophet. Some (Kaiser, 1984, 71; Ross, 2016, 122) with minor variations interpret this to be asking if God did not make Adam and Eve one flesh (Gen. 2:24), while others (Verhoef, 1987, 262, 277; Snyman, 2015, 114–15) conclude that Malachi was saying that "no one with a residue of spirit would act that way" and divorce his wife. Merrill's (2003, 364) unsatisfactory hypothesis is that the "one" was Abraham (cf. Isa. 51:2) who was seeking a godly offspring through Sarah and Hagar. Since Malachi 2:14 ends with a condemnation of the treacherous unfaithfulness of these men, it would seem natural for 2:15 to continue that same theme; thus, the "one" (the subject of the verb) would seem to refer to what any godly Jewish man (not God) would do. Since there was no sign that this was an interrogative sentence, it would appear that it is a statement and not a question. Malachi was admonishing his audience that a person who still had a remnant of the "spiritual bond / Spirit" (רוּחַ) in him would not divorce his Jewish wife.

TRANSLATION ANALYSIS: 2:15a

NASB[95] "But not one has done so who has a remnant of the Spirit."

NRSV "Did not one God make her? Both flesh and spirit are his."

NKJV "But did He not make them one, having a remnant of the Spirit?"

HCSB "Didn't the one God make us with a remnant of His life-breath?"

NIV "Has not the one God made you? You belong to him in body and spirit."

2:15b. The second half of the verse asks a rhetorical question and ends with a warning. The answer is to the question, what should a man ("the one") do who is seeking to have godly children? The answer implied in 2:11 is that he should not marry a pagan woman, and now we learn that he should not be treacherously unfaithful with his Jewish wife by divorcing her.

2:16a. This point in 2:15b is further emphasized in 2:16a, for God viewed divorce as an act of violence against the wife. Although some translations say "I hate divorce" (שָׂנֵא שַׁלַּח lit., שַׁלַּח is "sending away"), the verbal form is a third masculine singular "he hates," not a first person singular "I hate." Thus in 2:16, God was giving a reason why someone should not divorce his wife. If one hates and divorces his wife, he has covered himself (lit., "his garments") with violence. There was no explanation of what violence this referred to, but a despising hatred that was so strong that it caused the end of a marriage could have involved violent verbal as well as physical conflict. In addition, divorce could

lead to abuse and misuse of a woman by other men because she would be outside the protective covering of her former husband.

TRANSLATION ANALYSIS: 2:16a

NASB[95] "For I hate divorce"

NKJV "He hates divorce."

NRSV "For I hate divorce"

HCSB "For if he hates and divorces his wife"

NIV "The man who hates and divorces his wife"

The verb is masculine, third person singular, meaning "he hates."

Stop Being Unfaithful (2:16b)

Unfaithfulness should not be a characteristic of godly people.

2:16b. The solution was for men to stop being unfaithful (2:15b, 16b) in their worship and in their marriages. Marriage was a blessing to all who were faithful to one another, but deceptive treachery and unfaithfulness killed the joy, trust, and spiritual unity of even the strongest marriage.

THEOLOGICAL FOCUS

The exegetical idea (Israel was a nation that worshipped one God, so people should not be unfaithful to that God or unfaithful to one another in marriage) leads to this theological focus: Unfaithful treachery toward God and a marriage partner does not please God.

Such unfaithfulness makes worship unacceptable, marriage unsuccessful, and childrearing unbiblical. The theological basis behind Malachi's message in this disputation is as follows: First, there was only one God, so family formation should be between two people who come from families of faith in the one true God. Second, believers should avoid the conflict that could lead to marriage problems, including the act of divorcing a believing spouse, and instead be faithful to the person they marry. Third, God considered the act of marrying an unbeliever to be a serious act of treacherous unfaithfulness, so God rejected the worship of the family made up of a believer and an unbeliever. Fourth, if a believer wanted to have godly children and have God accept their worship, a man should not marry a pagan woman who worships other gods. God condemns any unfaithful acts that undermine the unity of the faith and the unity of the family.

PREACHING AND TEACHING STRATEGIES

Exegetical and Theological Synthesis

Malachi 2:10–16 exposes the depth of Israel's transgression. Malachi uses strong language ("treacherously unfaithful," "profaning," and "abominable" acts) in God's third dispute with his people. Israel's love affair with foreigners makes them vulnerable to idolatry and polluting the temple. A holy God makes no allowances for tainted worship; rather, he condemns the unfaithful.

That God can cut off people from fellowship is his divine prerogative. He alone stands over all people as a perfect and impartial judge (Gen. 19; Ps. 7:11; Eccl. 3:17; Ezek. 18:30). Surely, the Lord will show mercy on some, but ethnicity and birthright does not guarantee their good standing (Exod. 33:19; Amos 2; cf. Rom. 9:14). The Assyrian and Babylonian exiles stand as a testimony to his unwillingness to spare his own people. Fortunately, God removes the curse of disobedience and grants life to those who choose to walk in his ways (Deut. 30:15–20).

To understand God's vehement opposition to divorce (Mal. 2:16), we must recall two attributes of his reflected in marriage: goodness and love. Marriage was an essential part of his original design. God made male and female in his image to fill the earth together, care for creation together, obey God together, and enjoy companionship (Gen. 1:26–31; 2:18–25). And marriage was very good. The fall did not spoil its goodness.

To preserve this original goodness, God inscribed laws protecting marriage against adultery, abuse, and divorce (Exod. 20:14, 17; 21:7–11; 22:16–17; Deut. 24:1–5). Wisdom literature exalts marriage for its gift of sexual union (Prov. 5; Song of Songs). Furthermore, the marriage relationship signifies God's commitment to Israel (Hos. 1–3; Ezek. 16; Isa. 54:5). Human marriages serve as a signpost of God's love. A careless approach to marriage corrupts the imagery of God's goodness and love.

Preaching Idea

Let's cherish marriage and make it great again.

Contemporary Connections

What does it mean?

What does it mean to cherish marriage and make it great again? While Scripture does not double as a marriage manual, it does convey the greatness of marriage from its opening pages. Marriage is the primal human relationship. In the beginning, God gifted Adam with a bride to serve as his partner, lover, and equal in work, rest, and worship. God designed marriage to be great. A great marriage instills confidence, security, laughter, affection, and love between husband and wife. A great marriage models fidelity, sacrifice, and care to rising generations.

Sadly, all marriages struggle to reach the divine ideal. No couple lives in perfect union. Marriages that began as an intimate friendship may drift into a distant relationship as the pressures of family, work, and home life increase. Troubled marriages experience rivalry, rifts, suspicion, and contempt. And when abuse, adultery, or acute differences enter a marriage, divorce often follows. Most people who enter a marriage covenant do not intend to divorce, but many relationships end in dissolution.

While the shrinking (or delayed) marriage rate in the West may look like a historic anomaly, the presence of divorce has a long track record. Although God provided allowances for divorce in the Mosaic law (Deut. 24:1–5), the few exceptions test the rule: God wants couples to stay together. The biblical rule is that marriage is a great gift from God. Husband and wife should cherish marriage by upholding their commitment to a life of mutual love, care, and service.

Is it true?

Is it true that we should cherish marriage and make it great again? Absolutely, and we must begin by remembering that God intended marriage between one male and one female as a great gift (Gen. 1:26–31; 2:18–25). It is the beautiful design of marriage that makes its many corruptions—polygamy, adultery, abuse, rape—so treacherous. We shake our heads at Jacob's partial treatment of Leah, Shechem's rape of Dinah, Judah's maltreatment of Tamar, David's affair with Bathsheba, and Solomon's harem of women. The perversions reaffirm the rule.

Meanwhile, the OT records several stories of great marriages. Abraham protected Sarah and they faced decades of barrenness together. Boaz looked beyond Ruth's outsider status and accepted her as a bride. David wedded the widowed Abigail whose timely words spared him from violent rage. Great marriages may stand in the background of the OT, but their great virtue shines an occasional light.

We prove that we cherish our marriages by small sacrifices, acts of service, spiritual prompts, tender touches, and words of affirmation husband and wife share. A great marriage means a lifetime of supporting one another as image bearers. But we must also realize marriage is not a divine birthright. Some people will be called to singleness (Matt. 19:10–12; 1 Cor. 7:32–35). While much activity in church life revolves around married couples and family units, this reflects ministry philosophy more than biblical mandate. In other words, both healthy singleness and happy marriages are worth cherishing.

Now what?

How do we cherish marriage and make it great again? Is marriage for everyone? Is divorce an option? Can a happily married couple ever coast? These are important questions. First, we must remember that marriage is a gift from God but not a given for all people. Furthermore, not all marriages will live a "happily ever after" story. Interpersonal relationships are complex. The more intimate the relationship, the greater the complexity. Like no other relationship, marriage exposes our selfish tendencies and shadow side. Thus, married couples will always face conflict. To cherish marriage is to accept the gift and face the conflict.

Second, we must work the commitment. Making marriage great requires years of hard work. Quick and easy steps do not exist; we arrive through communication, patience, love, sacrifice, and bearing with one another. Prayer and counseling, date nights and marriage retreats, honest conversations and good listening will likely aid the hard work of marriage. Life circumstances will change during a marriage—finances, free time, family dynamics—but a consistent commitment to one another shows how much we cherish the relationships.

Third, we should focus more on the biblical ideal for marriage rather than the few exceptions for divorce. Human nature tends to exploit inches of grace for miles of autonomy. People in Malachi's day appropriated the divorce decree given to Ezra and Nehemiah. Essentially, they said, "If they could do it, why can't we?" The same logic applies today: divorce and domestic partnerships appear to be so normal that examples of great marriages get lost. We must honor and celebrate the great marriages in our society as a reflection of God's good design.

Fourth, we should acknowledge that marriage is not a necessity. Today people can flourish in society as singles. The sexual pressures may be great, but economic and social forces do not inhibit healthy singleness. In Malachi's day, singleness came at a greater cost.

Finally, we should caution believers considering interfaith marriages. "Missionary marriages" often struggle because each partner disagrees on core convictions. Couples will either coexist spiritually, or they will contend with one another. Neither outcome approaches God's design for union. Sadly, interfaith marriages may result in the unbeliever wandering off or the believer wandering from the faith. King Solomon serves as the classic example of a heart corrupted by foreign brides (1 Kings 11:1–8; cf. 2 Cor. 6:4).

Creativity in Presentation

I (Tim) am coming to the end of an intense season of premarital counseling. Four couples sought my advice in preparing for married life. I also helped plan four different wedding ceremonies. Although each couple was different, I gave similar counsel: "Don't let wedding planning get in the way of preparing for marriage." Sadly, the stress of mailing invitations, booking venues, setting menus, ordering tuxes, buying dresses, and staying conversant with the bridal party takes over. People lose their minds in wedding plans. Describe an elaborate wedding you have officiated, attended, or watched on TV. Share some wedding facts culled from the Internet.

Fast Facts about US Weddings and Marriages (2016)
- $35,000 = average cost of a wedding
- $78,000 = average cost of a wedding in Manhattan, New York (most expensive place)
- 340,000 = number of destination weddings
- $582 = average cost for a cake
- $278 = average payment to officiant
- 141 = average number of guests
- 5 = average number of bridesmaids
- 5 = average number of groomsmen
- 29 = the average age of bride
- 31 = average age of groom
- 64 = percentage of couples who created a hashtag for their wedding
- 40 = percentage of weddings in the fall
- 12 = percentage of weddings on a farm, in a barn, or at a ranch

NOTE: There is no national average cost recorded for premarital counseling!

In May of 2018, Prince Harry of England and Meghan Markle of America tied the knot in an internationally televised event. Seven years earlier, a similar telecast captured the wedding of Prince William and Kate Middleton. These royal ceremonies each boasted more than 29 million and 23 million viewers, respectively, tuning in to enjoy extravagant sights and sounds. People love a royal wedding, even if they know nothing of the quality of the couple. Consider playing a one-minute summary of a royal wedding. Ask your congregation if they watched or read about the event. Ask them if a great wedding ceremony is certain to lead to a great marriage? Ask them if royalty does marriage better than the rest of us?

Most congregations reflect a mix of single and divorced individuals, struggling and flourishing couples. Any spotlight on marriage requires sensitivity to the range of experiences. Nonetheless, we honor God and his ideal by championing healthy marriages: couples who reflect mutual care and sacrifice, tenderness and understanding, honesty and compromise, teamwork and love. Identify a few great (i.e., healthy) marriages in your congregation who display these characteristics. Interview them for the sermon (live or recorded), asking them to share two or three secrets that have made marriage great. I learned from one seasoned husband the key to keeping his wife happy: he starts her morning by delivering a mug of coffee to her bedside table. Fifty years later, she is warmed by his commitment. Another wife may be equally happy by her husband staying out of the kitchen!

In the end, the sermon should revolve around these exhortations: Unfaithful treachery toward God and a marriage partner do not please God. So, let's cherish marriage and make it great again.

- Let's admit we have commitment problems with God (2:10–12).

- Let's admit that our commitment problems sound awful (2:13).

- Let's admit that we have commitment problems in marriage (2:14–16).

DISCUSSION QUESTIONS

1. What does Malachi 2:10–16 warn against if one wants to raise godly children?

2. What made interfaith marriage so damaging for Israel? Is this true today? How would you counsel a believer considering an interfaith marriage?

3. How might we turn marriage into an idol? What does the Bible teach about singleness?

4. How has Western society undercut the greatness of marriage? What are some of the far-reaching social effects?

5. What are signs you cherish marriage?

Malachi 2:17–3:5

EXEGETICAL IDEA
Although some questioned God's justice, a messenger would prepare the way for God's coming to his temple, and then the Messenger of the Covenant would refine the wicked and present the righteous to God.

THEOLOGICAL FOCUS
God is just, and the Messenger of the Covenant will establish justice through refinement.

PREACHING IDEA
Someday God will scrub out the stains of social injustice.

PREACHING POINTERS
God voiced his fourth dispute against the people of Israel over their persistent moaning about injustice. They had accused God of being slow and soft in his treatment of wrongdoing. He responded by giving a preview of his future arrival, his plans to establish justice at that time, and the special message bearer leading the charge. God's coming would refine the world, judging obstinate people for breaking the covenant and purifying priests for holy service. Malachi's message exposed his original audience's doubt, intending to replace it with trust in God's justice.

The existence of evil, suffering, and social injustice serve as obstacles to belief for many people today. They cannot imagine a good and powerful God allowing injustice to persist. The fast-paced, nonstop, one-click ethos of the Internet Age has generated an inability to wait. We are conditioned for speed not slowness, efficiency not patience. The hurried nature of life affects our view of God. He does not act quickly enough to stop terror, eradicate disease, and end inequality. His justice lags, while we grow restless with social injustice. We fuss. We complain. We may even take matters into our own hands. This passage calls us to pause, take a breath, and remember: someday God will scrub out the stains of social injustice.

GOD IS JUST (2:17–3:5)

LITERARY STRUCTURE AND THEMES

This fourth dispute includes a claim that the people had wearied God with their complaints (v. 17a), but the audience objected (v. 17b). So Malachi explained how they had questioned God's justice (v. 17c). The prophet concluded with the promise that God's Messenger of the Covenant would establish justice (3:1–5).

In spite of the injustice in this world, God is just as well as patient with those who act unjustly, Eventually, all will be held accountable before God for their actions when God purifies and refines those who act unjustly.

- *The People Weary God (2:17a)*
- *An Objection (2:17b)*
- *Some Question God's Justice (2:17c)*
- *The Messenger of the Covenant Will Establish Justice (3:1–5)*

EXPOSITION

Although bad things happen to good people and the wicked are not punished immediately, God's justice would be seen when he and the Messenger of the Covenant come to judge and refine the world.

The People Weary God (2:17a)

Endless complaining was wearying to God.

2:17a. The next prophetic statement introduced a new area of dispute concerning people (3:5) who were wearying God with their words, but the prophet did not initially explain what words the people were saying. Weariness (יָגַע) can be defined as an emotional and physical tiredness created by extended attention to a difficult task that requires a great deal of effort. Weariness can cause physical and emotional exhaustion because of the amount of energy required to deal with the problem over a long period of time. When the prophet described the all-powerful God as being wearied, he was anthropomorphically describing God's frustration with the people's attitude and his disappointment over the endless complaining of his people.

An Objection (2:17b)

There is a human tendency to not admit failures or face the reality of one's shortcomings.

2:17b. As in the previous disputations, the prophet's audience objected to the charge and asked for an explanation of this charge. They did not see themselves as people who had frustrated or wearied God. They saw their unhappiness with their difficult situation in life as a completely legitimate complaint that they had a right to voice. Their dissatisfaction was likely not just with their own lot in life, but probably reflected their feeling that others had not received God's judgment as they should have.

Some Question God's Justice (2:17c)

The people seemed to be blaming God for not judging the wicked immediately, so they questioned his justice.

2:17c. God responded by quoting the words that caused him so much weariness. He was tired of people constantly complaining and opposing the way he was justly dealing with them and their opponents. Many (Baldwin, 1972, 24; Verhoef, 1987, 284; Kaiser, 1984, 76) suggest that the people were complaining that God was not just because the prophecies in Isaiah through

Zechariah were not fulfilled and the Messiah had not yet come. But Malachi 2:17c indicates that people were complaining about the injustice that every evil person (a hyperbole) on earth was not being judged by God. It seemed to them that God treated these evil people far too patiently. Thus, this was the problem of theodicy (Petersen, 1995, 207), an issue that Malachi would address again in 3:13–18. These people did not believe God was acting like a just God (cf. Exod. 34:6–7; Job 8:3; 40:8; Zech. 7:9; 8:16). This complaint was also raised in others biblical books (Habakkuk, Job, Ecclesiastes, Ps. 73). Redditt (1995, 176) thinks the people in Judah were complaining about the financial success of "certain members of the elite and of people who collaborated with the Persians for gain," but nothing in this paragraph would narrow the problem to this specific issue.

The Messenger of the Covenant Will Establish Justice (3:1–5)

God would send a messenger to warn of his coming and then send the Messenger of the Covenant to judge some and refine others so that there would be acceptable worship at the temple.

3:1. God responded that someday when he would come to earth, he would establish justice in several steps. First, God's coming would be preceded by the appearance of "my messenger" (3:1; מַלְאָכִי), a term that did not refer to the prophet Malachi as some suggest (Snyman, 2015, 130) but may be an angel, the Messiah, or Elijah (Mal. 4:5–6; Verhoef (1987, 287–88). This messenger would be the same person mentioned in Isaiah 40:3 (cf. Isa. 57:14; 62:10) who would "clear the way for the LORD in the wilderness," a role the NT assigned to John the Baptist (Matt. 3:1–3; Mark 1:2–4; Luke 3:2–4).[1] The responsibility of "clearing a way" referred to the ancient Near Eastern practice of villagers repairing the road a king would use to enter the

village by eliminating the boulders, smoothing the path, and making the road straight (cf. Stewart, 1998, 350, who points to Exod. 23:20). When this idea was applied to the coming of God to his temple, this imagery referred to the spiritual preparation of the hearts of the people for God's coming. After this time of preparation, the second step was that God would suddenly come in his glory (cf. Isa. 60:1–3) to dwell in his temple (as in Ezek. 43:2–4). Though it is impossible to quantify the time between each step, the third step would be the coming of the "Messenger of the Covenant." Many conclude that the coming "Lord" (אָדוֹן) was Yahweh (as in Mal. 1:6, 12, 14), but it was unclear who was the "Messenger of the Covenant." R. Smith (1984, 328) suggests that the angel of the Lord was the Messenger of the Covenant, while Petersen (1995, 210) thinks that "my messenger," the Messenger of the Covenant, and Elijah of Malachi 4:5 were all the same person. The NT evidence argues for a messianic interpretation; thus, Jesus was the Messenger of the New Covenant (Ross, 2016, 135; Clendenen, 2004, 385; Kaiser, 1984, 82–83; Snyman, 2015, 135).

3:2–4. Although one might assume that the coming of these three figures would result in a time of blessing, 3:2–3 describes this as a time of just judgment. The prophet pointed to the future "coming day" (3:2) as a time of refinement and purification that would be hard to endure. When a pure and holy God would come, who on earth would be able to stand before him? The fire of God's refinement would impact everyone, not just the enemies of Israel. God's refinement would be intense like the fire in a smelter that refines gold (3:3; cf. Isa. 1:25; 48:10; Zech. 13:9), and through this process God would purify the priests, the sons of Levi. This would resolve the problem of sinful priests offering unacceptable sacrifices (Mal. 1:6–2:9). Then the righteous people

---

1   Glazier-McDonald, 1987, 128–35 identified the Messenger of the Covenant as the Lord.

of Judah would present themselves and their gifts to God as pure and honorable sacrifices that would please God (3:3b–4).

3:5. The final verse catalogs the sinners God would swiftly judge when he would come to refine his people. First, God would judge the sinful sorcerer, a person who practiced various types of divination and witchcraft by examining the heart or liver of an animal in order to determine the will of the gods.

Forms of Divination

Other religious priests tried to divine the will of the gods by (a) studying the movement of the stars, planets, and moon; (b) studying the normal or abnormal conditions of the internal organs of an animal; (c) interpreting the way oil would form patterns on the surface of the water; or (d) watching how smoke would rise into the air. In *Prophecy and Society in Ancient Israel*, Robert R. Wilson (1980, 89–134) describes these divination methods used in the ANE.

Through these practices, the sorcerer would attempt to control the future by repeating magical incantations and various rituals. Such activity was forbidden in Exodus 22:18, Leviticus 19:31, 20:6, Deuteronomy 18:12, and 1 Samuel 28, but some sinful people were involved with these activities.

Second, God promised to bring justice to adulterers, all those who failed to control themselves and engaged in sexual activity outside of marriage. This sin was forbidden in the Ten Commandments (Exod. 20:14; Deut. 5:18), in Levitical laws (Lev. 18; 20:10–21), and in wisdom literature (Job 31:11–12; Prov. 5:3–20; 6:20–35; 7:1–27). The third sin of swearing falsely or committing perjury in court was also forbidden in the Ten Commandments (Exod. 20:16; Deut. 5:20), in Levitical laws (Lev. 5:22, 24), and in the prophets (Jer. 5:2; 7:9; Zech. 5:4). Since oaths were sworn in the name of the Lord (Lev.

19:12; Num. 30:2; Deut. 10:20), a lie violated the truth and profaned the name of the Lord. The fourth sin involved not paying a laborer his wages, or shamefully oppressing the powerless widow, orphan, and alien. In each case, a weaker member of society was defrauded or oppressed and not treated fairly. Deuteronomy 24:14–15 warns that one should not oppress a hired servant by not giving him his wages at the end of the day. The law (Exod. 22:21–24; Deut. 24:17–22; 27:19) and the prophets (Isa. 1:17; 10:2; Jer. 7:6; Mic. 2:9; Zech. 7:9) exhorted people to care for the vulnerable widows, orphans, and aliens because God would judge those who take advantage of these people. The last group of sinners included the refinement of anyone who did not fear God (Mal. 1:6–7; 2:5; 3:16; 4:2). An essential requirement of the covenant relationship with God was that the Israelites should love God with all their hearts (Deut. 6:5; 11:1, 13, 22; 30:6, 16, 20) and that they should fear and honor him (Deut. 6:13, 24; 10:12, 20). Fearing God was a requirement for the wise (Prov. 15:33; Eccl. 12:13) and a key theme in the prophets (Isa. 11:2–3; 33:6; 59:19; Jer. 5:24; 10:7; 26:19; 32:39–40; 33:9; Jonah 1:9; Hab. 3:2).

THEOLOGICAL FOCUS

The exegetical idea (although some questioned God's justice, a messenger would prepare the way for God's coming to his temple, and then the Messenger of the Covenant would refine the wicked and present the righteous to God) leads to this theological focus: God is just, and the Messenger of the Covenant will establish justice through refinement.

If that was true, then God's treatment of people must be just. Although people sometimes question the justice of God because negative things may happen to a righteous person or because nothing negative immediately happens to a wicked person, this disputation teaches that God would reestablish justice in the last days. Consequently, people must prepare for that day when God would even the score and refine those people who murder, oppress the weak, swear false statements, and refuse to fear God. Although a person might not see immediate blessing fall on the righteous or the immediate judgment of the wicked, everyone should be assured that justice would happen in due time. Everyone would be held accountable for their actions.

PREACHING AND TEACHING STRATEGIES

Exegetical and Theological Synthesis

Malachi 2:17–3:5 discusses Israel's faulty theology and God's corrective. God's people thought his justice lacked speed and showed partiality; their tiresome complaining belabored the theme. Ironically, they feigned innocence when God corrected their poor attitude. Humans have proven historically adept at identifying others' sin, while overlooking their own. We think of evil as an "out there" problem, rather than a stain "within."

Of course, God did not turn a blind eye to evil. His delay was deliberate but not indifferent. That he is slow to anger and abounding in love is central to OT theology (Exod. 34:6; Num. 14:18; Pss. 103:8; 145:8). Delayed judgment gives more people an opportunity to turn back their hearts to him (Amos 4).

God's judgment may be slow, but it is also purifying. The Lord Almighty presents himself as a launderer and metalworker (Mal. 3:2 cf. Isa. 1:25; Zech. 13:9). He aims to clean and refine what belongs to him (Ps. 51:10; Zech. 3:5). While God cannot look gladly upon sin-stained people, he can happily put them through the spin cycle of repentance and forgiveness to make them white as snow (Isa. 1:16–18).

Preaching Idea

Someday God will scrub out the stains of social injustice.

Contemporary Connections

What does it mean?

What does it mean that God will someday scrub out the stains of social injustice? What is social injustice? Social injustice comprises an array of wrongs suffered by people who are vulnerable for various reasons: orphans, widows, racial minorities, immigrants, homeless, and poor. Social injustice takes place at individual and corporate levels; it may be systematic (e.g., racism) or situational (e.g., spousal abuse).

God's prophets cried out against social injustice, especially when under the guise of religious practice (Isa. 1:16–18; Amos 5:21–24). They campaigned instead for humble acts of mercy toward others (Mic. 6:8). The prophets harkened back to the Mosaic law, which demanded justice for women (Exod. 22:16–17), slaves (22:2–10), unborn children (21:22–25), property owners (22:1–15), and the poor (Lev. 23:22). The weekly sabbath (Exod. 20:8–11) and Year of Jubilee wove justice and freedom into the fabric the Hebrew calendar (Lev. 25). Care for widows and orphans was paramount (Deut. 10:18; 14:28–29), as beautifully chronicled in the story of Ruth, Naomi, and Boaz.

Is it true?

Is it true that someday God will scrub out the stains of social injustice? When and how will this happen? We must recognize that divine judgement rolls out in unpredictable stages. Sometimes God immediately quells social injustice. Sometimes he defers justice. He sent the flood after centuries of human corruption (Gen. 6–8), but quickly turned Sodom and Gomorrah to ashes (Gen. 19; cf. 2 Peter 2:6). The northern and southern kingdoms experienced exile more than 150 years apart; Uzziah contracted leprosy for an act of pride (2 Chron. 26:16–21). Whether instant or eventual, God's justice prevails.

God uses a variety of means to scrub out the stains of social injustice. He employs both legal systems (e.g., Mosaic Law) and loving people (e.g., Boaz) who insist on justice. He enlisted armies to oust oppressive foes from the Promised Land (e.g., Joshua, Judges), and he used exile to scrub out the stains of injustice from his very own people (Jer. 25 cf. Deut. 30:1–10). Like Habakkuk, not everyone appreciates God's cleansing process (1:2–4 cf. Ps. 4), but someday his scrubbing will be complete (Isa. 65:17–25).

In the meantime, God expects his people to live justly (Mic. 6:8). Historic efforts to abolish slavery (e.g., William Wilberforce), expose abuse (e.g., #MeToo), end poverty (e.g., drilling wells), halt racism (e.g., civil rights movement), and stop tyranny (e.g., Bonhoeffer's stand against Hitler) are examples of God's people overturning social injustice. We have made marginal gains for the flourishing of women, minorities, orphans, the oppressed, and the poor in our world, but such gains reveal the deeply rooted nature of social injustice. As revealed in the prophets, God does not limit social justice to political heads but envisions justice irrupting at the grassroots level (Amos 5:24).

Now what?
What are believers to do until God scrubs out the stains of social injustice? Our best response is to be part of the solution, not a contributor to the problem.

First, God wants us to be conscious of social injustice immediately before us. Before we call out injustices in society, we should diagnose injustice in our churches. How do we protect children and women from abuse? How do we embrace people from broken marriages, lower socioeconomic classes, different ethnic backgrounds? How do we honor our elders, provide for widows, and guard against exploiting unpaid volunteers? These questions treat social justice as a personal crisis before we campaign as our nation's conscience.

Second, God wants us to live as just people. We own our mistakes, prejudices, and wrongdoing. We admit them to God, ask for forgiveness, and commit to change into people who live

justly, love mercy, and walk humbly (Mic. 6:8). As repentant people seeking social justice, we pay attention to local and global issues we can engage in. Some will seek justice through mentoring at-risk youth. Some will seek justice through fostering neglected children. Some will seek justice through petitioning for political change on gun laws. Some will seek justice through developing friendships with minorities and hearing their pain. Some will seek justice through financial contributions to relief or development organizations aimed at eradicating hunger.

Finally, God's people must reaffirm their trust in his ultimate justice. Our best efforts for social justice may only make a small impact. Instead of growing weary doing good, we should continue to do good while wait eagerly for God's eschatological renewal of society (Isa. 65:17–25). God will get the last word. His justice will reign. Trusting him for ultimate justice means we live justly in anticipation of his justice. Someday he will scrub out every stain of injustice from the fabric of society. Until then, we can focus our energies on a few local stains.

Creativity in Presentation
Take a cue from detergent commercials and demonstrate the power of God's stain removal. Compared to lesser brands (e.g., religious activity, social justice, good works, politics), God works wonders. Find a light-colored shirt you're willing to mark with several dark, red spots. Set up a table on the stage or platform area displaying various laundry products: stain removal sprays and sticks, bleaches, and detergents. Apply the products to the different marks. Dip the treated garment in a large bowl of warm water. As you carry out the illustration, talk about difficult stains to remove—blood, grass, coffee, oil—and strategies for removal. Compare such stains to the social and moral stains of cyclical poverty, greed of Wall Street, criminalization of black males, marginalization of the elderly, and horrors of child trafficking. Assure

them that God will remove these stains, starting with our efforts.

Crime shows shed light on the hidden stains at a crime scene. Detectives roam through the room shining special UV (ultraviolet) or blue light over carpet, walls, or furniture to detect saliva, semen, blood, urine, or other would-be clues. These exposed stains may point toward a perpetrator, moving the CSI agent in the direction of justice. Consider showing a brief clip of a CSI unit using UV light to reveal stains at a crime scene. Afterwards ask your congregation what evidence God might discover if he trolled through their homes, neighborhoods, workplaces, or churches with his forensic light. Ask them what stains linger even after our best attempts to conceal them.

Historical examples of incremental justice efforts can illustrate the role God's people play in society. Christian colleges and universities have been rethinking their treatment of students with same-sex attractions, adopting safe places and more inclusive policies for homosexual believers committed to celibacy but in need of community.[2] The election of President Obama followed decades of social justice for black people, reaching back from the emancipation of slaves (1863), to the right to vote (Fifteenth Amendment, 1869), to the integration of blacks and whites into public schools (Brown vs. Board of Education, 1954), to the Civil Rights Act (1964), to affirmative action efforts to level the playing field in education and employment for blacks to the ongoing outcry concerning police brutality against black males. While many in the church remained distant in the battle for racial equality (and many still do), many leaders in the movement, such as Martin Luther King Jr., John Perkins, and Eric Mason, have been galvanized by their faith.

Eric Mason is pastor, author, professor, and speaker who lives in inner-city Philadelphia. He leads Epiphany Fellowship and Thriving, an urban training center for Christian leaders committed to serving in urban contexts. He has authored numerous books.

John M. Perkins is a minister, writer, speaker, and leading Christian voice in civil rights. He has spent time both in the White House and in prison for his work as an activist. His foundation, dedicated to racial reconciliation and healing, takes a holistic approach to community development, including education, health, business, church, leadership training, and housing.

Consider research on other incremental, social justice gains by the believers that might best connect with your congregation. These might include drilling wells in developing countries, expanding education opportunities for at-risk youth, care for orphans through adoption, or combating sex trafficking. Parachurch organizations dedicated to different social justice topics can provide relevant data and ways to practice social justice.

A Short List of Parachurch Organizations Dedicated to Social Justice

Water for Good: Drills wells in Central African Republic. www.waterforgood.org

Show Hope: Provides adoption support, grants, and services to families pursuing adoption; runs

---

2 See Tyler Streckert, "What It's Like to Be Gay at Wheaton," *Christianity Today* (May 21, 2016), accessed online, https://www.christianitytoday.com/ct/2016/june/what-its-like-to-be-gay-at-wheaton-college.html (accessed 10/29/2018). Corey (2016, 53–74) and Kinnaman and Lyons (2016, 167–180) also provide helpful insight on this conversation. Preston Sprinkle offers some of the best theological reflection in the area at The Center for Faith, Gender, and Sexuality www.centerforfaith.com).

an orphan care center in China. www.show-hope.org

Samaritan's Purse: Provides international relief following national tragedies and runs Operation Christmas Child to provide gifts to impoverished children. www.samaritanspurse.org

Compassion International: Dedicated to holistic care for poor children in developing countries through sponsorships. www.compassion.com

Habitat for Humanity: Partners with businesses, churches, and communities to provide affordable and sustainable housing to people in need. www.habitat.org

Feed My Starving Children: Partners with other NGOs to supply packed food for needy kids. www.fmsc.org.

International Justice Mission: A global organization seeking to eliminate slavery and human trafficking. www.ijm.org

Note: Many denominations have launched their own relief, development, and justice ministries. Moreover, communities have local, unaffiliated ministries dedicated to social justice issues.

- We moan: Does God sees our messy world? (2:17).

- Rest assured: God sees it and will someday come (3:1).

- Be prepared: God has a lot of cleaning to do (3:2–5).

Ultimately, make sure to emphasize the central truth: God is just, and the Messenger of the Covenant will establish justice through refinement. Or simply, someday God will scrub out the stains of social injustice.

DISCUSSION QUESTIONS

1. What might be some ways people weary God today (cf. Mal. 2:17)?

2. How did the Mosaic Law prescribe a just society? How did the prophets reinforce this?

3. How do modern issues of injustice compare to those in the Old Testament?

4. In what ways does God's ultimate justice inform our current beliefs and practices?

5. How should God's people engage issues of social injustice today? What may happen if God's people neglect social justice issues?

6. Who are some historic champions of social justice causes?

Malachi 3:6–12

EXEGETICAL IDEA
God was faithful and didn't change his character, so if people repented of their sins, turned to God, and showed their trust by tithing, then he would remove the curse on their crops and provide his blessings.

THEOLOGICAL FOCUS
If people change and quit robbing God, then he will prosper his people with all their physical needs.

PREACHING IDEA
Ante up and give God his due.

PREACHING POINTERS
The reality of judgment in the fifth dispute resulted in a call to return to living God's way. The Lord brought a new charge against his people: they had skimped on their tithing. The Law demanded a percentage of produce and livestock set aside for God to support the priesthood. The people's failure to give God his due had resulted in lackluster harvests—a covenant curse. In this dispute, the prophet Malachi drew attention to his original audience's self-deception, which only hurt them. God's words were a reality check. He had better in store for the whole nation than the storehouses currently contained. He wanted Israel to return to him and receive his blessings.

People struggle to give God his due today. The Western world promotes greed and consumption rather than generosity and stewardship. We are taught to pay ourselves first so we can retire in style. We learn to spend in advance—credit cards, college loans, and financing options—accruing debt and adding interest. Greed says to buy more than we need, often on a whim. This lack of financial restraint often leads to thin margins, spotty giving, and general anxiety. And when we do give, it may be to assuage guilt as much as aid others in need. Failure to view our financial resources from God's perspective results in our robbing God. This passage implores us to rethink our relationship to money: to ante up and give God his due.

RETURN TO GOD AND GIVE YOUR TITHE (3:6–12)

LITERARY STRUCTURE AND THEMES

This fifth dispute includes a claim that God had not changed; instead, the people turned against God (vv. 6–7a) and needed to return to God (v. 7b). After an initial objection in 3:7c, Malachi explained that the people had robbed God and were cursed because they did not give their tithes to God (3:8–10). However, if they gave their tithe, abundant blessings would come (3:10c–11), and others would call them blessed (3:12).[1]

This unit includes the theological themes of blessing and withholding blessing, which were developed based on a person's willingness to return to God and follow his instructions.

- *God Does Not Change (3:6–7a)*
- *Turn/Return to Me (3:7b)*
- *An Objection (3:7c)*
- *You Robbed God (3:8a)*
- *An Objection (3:8b)*
- *Tithing Will Remove the Curse (3:8c–11)*
- *Blessing and a Great Reputation (3:12)*

EXPOSITION

Many people were having a difficult financial time because God did not provide a large harvest. Instead, he sent something that devoured their harvest of grains, grapes, and other fruits (3:11) because many people were not tithing from the abundant blessings he provided the previous year. Malachi reminded his audience that if people rob God by not giving their tithe, God could not bless them, but if they turned back to God and

honored him with their tithe, then he would abundantly bless them.

God Does Not Change (3:6–7a)

God was consistent in his treatment of his people, but his people were not always consistent in their relationship to God.

3:6–7a. Some recognize a strong interconnection between the idea that God does not "change" (שָׁנָה) and the preceding and following disputations (Baldwin, 1972, 245; Baker, 2006, 281–82).

> WORD ANALYSIS: שָׁנָה
> This root was used in several different contexts: (a) Psalm 89:34 repeats God's commitment to the Davidic covenant (Ps. 89:28–29); God will not "change, alter" what he promised. Malachi 3:6 portrays God as faithfully keeping his promises and not "changing" his commitment. (b) In Job 14:20, Job charged that God overpowered him, "changing, altering" his life and destroying his hope. (c) In Jeremiah 2:36, Judah was a nation that "changed" its political leanings back and forth between Egypt and Assyria.

God's just dealings with his people assured them that he did not change the way he dealt with sinners or with those who repent (1 Sam. 15:29; Jer. 4:28; 15:6; 20:16; Ezek. 24:14; Hos. 13:14; and Zech. 8:14). God announced that he was Yahweh, the God who would not change his commitment or his love for his people (cf. 1:1–5), the instructions he gave concerning giving pure

---

1   Merrill (2003, 376) found that E. Wendland's, "Linear and Concentric Patterns in Malachi," *BT* 36 (1985): 108–21 analysis of a chiastic structure was helpful, but some parts of the chiasm do not match very closely.

sacrifices (cf. 1:6–2:9), his promises to justly deal with sinners (cf. 2:17–3:5), nor his demand that people should tithe (3:6–12).[2] God's stipulations in the covenant with their forefathers promised blessing on those who followed his instructions (Lev. 26–27) but a curse on those who ignored God instructions (cf. Deut. 30:6–20). So if the people wanted to continue their covenant relationship with God, they needed to make some changes in their lives. God did not vacillate concerning the principles that governed his relationship with Israel but was faithfully committed to graciously and justly deal with his people.

Turn/Return to Me (3:7b)
God promised to return to and be present with those who returned to him and followed his instructions.

3:7b. Although this dispute seemed very serious, it was possible to resolve these problems if the people of Judah would humble themselves, make some changes in their thinking and actions, and "turn, repent" (שׁוּב) of their sin. God desired a restored relationship; he patiently called his people to come back to himself. This offer for a restored relationship came with the promise that God would "turn" (שׁוּב) to them with grace and favor; thus, he indicated that he was willing to forgive and was committed to the restoration of their covenant relationship. The history of Israel was dotted with various calls for the people to repent in the historical (1 Kings 8:33; 2 Chron. 6:38; 30:6–9) and prophetic books (Amos 4:6–13; Jer. 3:10–12; 15:19; 24:7; Zeph. 2:1–3; Zech. 1:3).

An Objection (3:7c)
People often do not see their own faults but blame others or God for their problems.

3:7c. Although one would expect someone to repent or change their mind at this point in the discussion, Merrill (2003, 376) maintains that the people resisted God's call because of "a perverse self-deception and inverted sense of righteousness . . . and flagrant self-centeredness." So the people defiantly questioned God: What do we need to do to return to God? It seemed that some were not aware of any problems in their relationship to God. This would suggest that the secular worldview of the people was more influential in their thinking than the theological perspective of the Torah. They did not think of themselves as sinners who needed to repent of their sins.

You Robbed God (3:8a)
Not giving God want he deserved was tantamount to robbing God.

3:8a. Malachi gave an example of one of the problems areas where repentance was needed. The people "robbed, seized, defrauded" (קָבַע) God. This happened when people circumvented God's instructions to give a tenth to God and instead took something that belonged to God (Snyman, 2015, 150). An earlier example of this appeared in Malachi 1:14 where an individual vowed to give God an expensive male animal but later ended up bringing an unacceptable inferior substitute as a sacrifice. Part of the reason why this was happening (this robbing of God) was that the priests failed to properly instruct the people, so they thereby caused many to sin (2:8–9). In 3:10, the example of robbing God is the failure to bring the full tithe to the temple as God instructed them (Lev. 27:32).

An Objection (3:8b)
Even when told, some people refused to admit their guilt.

---

2   Clendenen (2004, 404–408) has a long excursus about the immutability of God and discusses different views about God's ability to change.

3:8b. As in 3:7c, the people questioned this accusation, harden their hearts, and expressed doubts about this charge. It is hard to know if these people were (a) not aware of what was required in the Mosaic instructions (Lev. 27:30), (b) uninformed about the tithing example of their forefathers (Abram in Gen. 14:20 and Jacob in Gen. 28:22), (c) thought they could get away with only giving a small portion of their tithe, or (d) just rebelled against what they knew they were supposed to do.

Tithing Will Remove the Curse (3:8c–11)
The people were cursed for not giving their tithes, but the agricultural curse would be removed if they turned from their old ways and gladly gave God a tenth of their income.

3:8c. The people were not faithfully giving 10 percent of their income to God at the temple, so in a real sense they were robbing God. Leviticus 27:30–33 states that a "tenth" (מַעֲשֵׂר) of everything (crops and animals) was holy and belonged to God, so they robbed God by keeping what was supposed to be given to God. These temple tithes provided for the physical needs of the priests and Levites, who did not receive any inheritance of land like the other tribes (Num. 18:21–32; Deut. 14:21–27). Similar problems existed a few years earlier in the time of Nehemiah (around 445 B.C.) when people ignored their responsibilities or refused to give their full tithe. At that time, many Levites and singers at the temple left Jerusalem in order to go to work in the fields so that they could feed their families (Neh. 13:10–11). Nehemiah reprimanded the people for not bringing their tithes, so they repented and brought their tithes and first fruits to the temple (Neh. 10:34–39). Now a few years later during the ministry of Malachi, this problem existed once again, but at this time there was no evidence that the Levites abandoned the temple and went to work in the fields like they did in the time when Nehemiah was the governor of the land.

3:9. God's warning was that he had cursed the people because they robbed God's temple of tithes and offerings. Thus one of the justifications for repenting and tithing was to remove God's curse. The exact nature and the extent of this curse was not explained in 3:9, but the plague that devoured their crops in 3:11 was the result of this curse. The irony was that the people were not giving a tithe because they had poor crops, but the reality was that they had poor crops because they were not giving their tithe to God's temple. By not giving the tithe that belonged to God, the people were not trusting God to supply their needs in the future.

3:10. The second part of this justification provided a motivation for repentance and tithing. If they would do this, God would miraculously open the windows of heaven and give them abundant blessings. If they responded to his call to action, God said that "there will be food in my house" (3:10, וִיהִי טֶרֶף בְּבֵיתִי), meaning that their obedience would provide food for the Levites to eat. God's requirement was to bring the "full tithe, all the tithe" (אֶת־כָּל־הַמַּעֲשֵׂר, Mal. 3:10; Lev. 27:30) according to the Mosaic instruction, not 7 percent or 9 percent, but a full 10 percent. This outward act of bringing their full tithe would be visible proof that an inward change of heart had happened; that is, they had returned to God. God challenged them to "test" (בְּחַן) him in this promise and see if he would not be reliable and true to his word. The blessing God promised was connected to the "floodgates, windows" of heaven, but here they seem to refer to a broader blessing than just rain (cf. Gen. 7:11; 8:2), though abundant rain could be included as part of these rich blessings. God's work of pouring out a blessing was not pictured as a minor or a small token amount of divine grace. This blessing was pictured as a large work of God ("emptying heaven") that would allow the people to produce more than sufficient for their needs. This promise of divine blessing on those who tithe was a covenant promise in Deuteronomy 14:28–29 and in the detailed account in Deuteronomy 26:12–15.

WORD ANALYSIS: בָּחַן

This word can mean (a) to try or test a metal to authenticate the purity of the gold (Job 23:10); (b) to authenticate or judge the reliability of a claim someone makes; thus, Joseph tested the reliability of the claims made by his brothers who came to Egypt to buy grain (Gen. 42:15–16), and both Job (Job 12:11) and Elihu (Job 34:3) claimed to be able to test or judge the reliability of the words others spoke; (c) the Israelites sinned when they failed to trust God and tested God's patience by questioning his promises and complaining while they were going through the wilderness (Ps. 95:9); (d) in this rare case in Malachi 3:10, God invited people to "test, evaluate" him in order to authenticate the reliability of his promises; and (e) God himself "tested, examined" the faithfulness and true character of his people (1 Chron. 29:17; Prov. 17:23; Jer. 11:20; 12:3; 17:10; 20:12).[3]

3:11. The third justification that should motivate the audience to change (i.e., "to repent") and begin to tithe was the promise that God would end the curse (3:9). He would rebuke what was eating their crops (possibly locust) and causing fruit to wither and drop to the ground (possibly a lack of moisture). God the Creator and the controller of nature had the sovereign power to give abundant blessings as well as crushing curses (cf. Lev. 26; Deut. 28) because the land belonged to God (Lev. 25:23).

Blessing and a Great Reputation (3:12)

All nations would call the people of Israel favored by God (3:12).

3:12. The results of God's work would have a positive international impact, similar to the conclusions already announced in 1:5, 11, 14. Once the nations saw the abundant provision that God would give to his people, these nations would realize that God's agricultural riches had transformed the Hebrew nation into a "delightful land" (Isa. 62:4), the new earth (Isa. 65:17–19; 66:22). God would multiply the produce of all plants (Ezek. 36:29–30) so much that wine would run down the hills, and the plowman would overtake the harvester because of the enormous size of the harvest (Amos 9:13).

THEOLOGICAL FOCUS

The exegetical idea (God was faithful and didn't change his character, so if people repented of their sins, turned to God, and showed their trust by tithing, then he would remove the curse on their crops and provide his blessings) leads to this theological focus: If people change and quit robbing God, then he will prosper his people with all their physical needs.

There are four theological themes in this fifth disputation. First, when people strayed from God's instruction, someone needed be brave enough to call them to change, to return to God, and to repent of their sins. Second, God's ways of blessing the righteous and cursing sinners were well known, and they had not changed, so people should not expect a blessing if they do not honor God. Third, those who love and trust God knew that God would provide for their needs in the future, so they gladly gave a tithe to God. Fourth, those who refused to trust God and failed to tithe would not experience God's blessing until they repented.

---

3   Hill (1998, 311–13) in an excursus on Divine Testing noted that God tested people to evaluate their faith and obedience, while people test God when they doubt his faithfulness and disobey. Only on rare occasions (as in Mal. 3:10) did God invite people to test him so that he could prove his faithfulness.

PREACHING AND TEACHING STRATEGIES

Exegetical and Theological Synthesis

Malachi 3:6–12 explores an important piece of theology proper: God is immutable. He does not change. People and culture certainly change, but God does not. His holiness, love, justice, and covenant faithfulness will remain. Likewise, his mercy endures, leaving an open invitation for his wandering people to repent, turn from their errors, make amends, and come home to him.

A second unchangeable reality is the sinfulness of all human beings. God's people excuse their disobedience, shift blame, and play dumb. "How have we robbed you?" is yet another denial in Malachi's series of disputes. Being the second challenge to their miserable worship practices (cf. 1:6–2:9), Israel could not claim ignorance. Furthermore, God pointed back to Israel's roots ("from the days of your fathers") to indicate the historic pattern of selfish stewardship. Cain selfishly gave God a partial offering (Gen. 4:2–5, cf. Jude 11). Achan selfishly hoarded plundered riches from Jericho (Josh. 7:20–21). Solomon selfishly built a palace for himself, taking twice as long to complete it as the temple (1 Kings 7:1).

Financial misconduct comes in many forms. Greed, hoarding, coveting, using unjust scales, and earning interest on others' debts comprise a short list of sins (e.g., Exod. 20:17; 22:25; Lev. 25:36–27; Deut. 23:19; 5:13–16). The Mosaic Law does not condemn wealth but views it as a means to love your neighbor (e.g., gleaning laws). Amos and Isaiah attacked the disparity of wealth and suffering of the poor in their day (see Amos 4–6; Isa. 58). Wisdom literature champions industrious work and monetary gain (e.g., Prov. 6:6–11). And these themes permeate the Old Testament.

Gleaning Laws

One of God's legal means to curb greed and care for the poor was the gleaning law (Lev. 19:9–10; 23:22). This mandate required land owners to leave the edges of their fields unharvested so that poor people (e.g., widows, foreigners) could pluck the remaining produce for their sustenance. The story of Ruth provides an example of gleaning laws in action. Ruth, a widowed foreigner, received permission to reap from the edges of Boaz's field. Moved with compassion, Boaz, an upright and wealthy landowner, showed extended generosity toward Ruth and her mother-in-law, Naomi (Ruth 2:1–17).

Preaching Idea

Ante up and give God his due.

Contemporary Connections

What does it mean?

What does it mean to ante up and give God his due? What do we owe God? In short, we owe God everything. All our goods—our biweekly paycheck and daily bread, our old cars and new clothes, our smart phones and book collections—come from God. His blessings are manifold but not guaranteed (Lev. 26). In a painful series of losses, Job learned that God may both give and take away our prosperity (Job 1:21).

The question is whether the prescribed giving in the Levitical law applies to our giving today. Does the command to give to the temple of God translate into a demand to give to the church? Interestingly, the answer is both yes and no. In Jesus's limited references to tithing, he never rebuked the general populace for inconsistent and self-serving charity, only the Pharisees (Matt. 23:23; Luke 11:42; 18:12). In contrast, he praised a poor widow for her exceptional offering at the temple (Luke 21:1–4). God uses generous gifts and faithful offerings to maintain various religious institutions—churches, parachurch ministry, faith-based non-profit organizations—by providing for their personnel, programming, administrative, and maintenance costs. The apostle Paul expected the church to set aside monies regularly to pay its leaders and provide for the poor, giving not out of compulsion but in glad and growing measure (1 Cor. 16:1–3; 2 Cor. 9; Phil. 4:14–18; 1 Tim. 5:17–18). If anything, ten percent may serve as a baseline for giving.

Nevertheless, God does not restrict generous gifts and faithful generosity just to religious institutions. Giving God his due also includes caring for the poor and marginalized in society. Some charities make better use of gifts, giving all monies toward the mission. St. Jude's Children's Research Hospital and the Ronald McDonald House Charities respectively turn more than 80 percent of their gifts into medical care and research to defeat childhood cancer and other life-threatening diseases as well as short- or longer-term housing for families with children who are seriously ill or injured. Other charities, such as March of Dimes, absorb most of their giving in overhead costs for the organization. Certainly, giving God his due means first doing some homework and choosing an honorable cause that stewards the monies well.

Is it true?

Is it true we should ante and give God our due? Yes, but our heavenly Father is less interested in a compulsory gift than a grateful offering. C. S. Lewis ([1943] 1996, 127) captures this beautifully in his picture of a child asking his father for sixpence to buy the father a present. The gift does not enrich God (nor does it rob him) but does bring him pleasure if we give well. Giving should come from a grateful heart, seeing ourselves as stewards of God's goods. Giving should come from a discerning mind, wanting to make the best use of our resources to further God's mission. Finally, giving should come from a steady hand, making a habit of loosening our grip on every dollar that comes into our possession.

But how does God "get his due"? Must it come through the offering plate and receive a year-end receipt to gain God's notice? Certainly not. Giving to God comes in many forms. We can give financially to food banks, disaster relief, missionary support, adoption, Bible translation, scholarship funds, pregnancy centers, social justice organizations, school fundraisers, and local churches. We can give volunteer time to mentoring elementary school students, adult literacy programs, nursing homes, Scout programs, political canvasing, homeless shelters, community cleanup projects, and local church ministries. And though the forms of giving abound, the attitude of the giver is best when cheerful (2 Cor. 9:7).

Now what?

How do we ante up and give God his due? To "ante up" means to give first. (The term comes from the poker table, where a player puts in his "ante" before receiving his cards.) We start by having a financial plan. Determine to set aside a portion for God whenever money comes in. Set aside a reasonable amount (or percentage) from each paycheck to direct toward God and his priorities.

Next, identifying where we can faithfully contribute is crucial. We can give God his due inside and outside the walls of the church. Admittedly, the breadth and number of giving opportunities for local churches, parachurch organizations, short-term ministry trips, crisis relief efforts, cancer research, elderly care, and neighborly needs often feels paralyzing. Moreover, some agencies steward the monies better than others, giving a majority if not 100 percent to the cause rather than large amounts to overhead costs. Whether we provide a one-time donation for crisis relief, monthly sponsorship for an orphan, or weekly electronic fund transfer to the local church, we should practice discernment and discipline in our giving. In any case, faithful giving guards us from robbing God.

Finally, we should remain open to increasing our giving as new income streams or needs arise. When God provides us more money, time, and opportunity to steward, the demand for wise stewardship rises. God will happily receive a greater return on his investment. But if we settle into mechanical patterns of giving, we may not see new opportunities to give. Fortunately, increased giving often leads to increase joy, as we see God's blessings spread beyond us.

Creativity in Presentation

The idea of "anteing up" conjures up images of the poker table. While playing cards, especially with bluffing and betting, may cause controversy in some churches, the imagery remains useful. Recently a couple from my (Tim's) church hosted a Texas hold 'em night to raise funds for a school in Uganda. Twelve men, many novices at cards, had to learn the ins and outs of the game. The only real money exchanged was the "ante" given for the school in Uganda. In other words, God received his due while our men's group enjoyed some harmless betting and bluffing.

Find a clip from *21* (2008), *Casino Royale* (2006), *Ocean's Eleven* (2001), *Rounders* (1998), *Casino* (1995), or *Maverick* (1994). These films, which revolve around the poker table, demonstrate the need to ante, bluff, and show one's hand. In such films, "the House" often exacts brutal force when they think they're getting swindled; they will get their due. Perhaps the safest example takes place in *Maverick* (directed by Richard Donner). A great interchange happens after Bret Maverick (played Mel Gibson) catches Annabelle (played by Jodie Foster) bluffing. She can't believe it, but her "tell" betrays her. The whole table, including the dealer, notices her holding her breath. Likewise, God easily spies our "tells," bluffs, and cheating ways.

Consider this humorous illustration: At the beginning of the sermon, mention the recent shortfall in offerings. State the weekly need (e.g., $4,600) and provide a lower number of received monies (e.g., $1,725). Warn the congregation how "God is not happy when he does not get his due." Let them know you will collect a special offering before you preach. Call it the "ante" and say: "No giving, no preaching." Let the line settle for a moment before cutting the tension. However, as you move into the message, give your people fair warning you will not pull many punches on the topic of cheating God.

Finally, research giving trends in your local church. The following questions can be repurposed as a survey (using paper copies, Google Forms, or SurveyMonkey) to see if your church "antes up." Compare your church to figures listed in the annual "State of the Plate" report.

What organizations or causes do individuals from your church give to?

What charities, nonprofits, and projects does your church collectively give to?

How do people in your church decide what causes or organizations to give to?

How many solicitations do your people receive on a weekly basis to give charitably?

What percentage of their income have your church people decided to donate?

How does this percentage compare to the non-Christian world?

Are people's giving percentages rising or falling?

What are other ways people in your church give?

You want to be careful neither to manipulate people into increased giving nor overwhelm people with unlimited giving opportunities; rather, shed light on the potential for God to work wonders through an uptick in sacrificial giving.

Fast Facts on Church Giving (from 2016)[4]

- 59 = percentage of churches who experienced annual decline in giving

- 49 = percentage of people who want a phone app for giving

- 41 = percentage of churchgoers who give consistently to their church

- 14 = percentage of people who want envelopes in pews/chairs

- 0 = dollar amount from those who miss church and have no digital giving option

DISCUSSION QUESTIONS

1. How can tithing serve as an important barometer of a person's love for God (Mal. 3:10)?

2. What was the purpose of the OT tithe? How is the idea adapted in the NT?

3. When did you last "rob" God? How do you nurture "cheerful" giving?

4. What makes talking about money in church services potentially awkward?

5. What are specific ways we can give to God's purposes? What might be reasons or causes not to give to and why?

In the end, let the message remind people that if they change and quit robbing God, then he will prosper them with all their physical needs. Therefore, we should ante up and give God his due.

- Giving God his due begins with a return to his ways (3:6–7).

- Giving God his due requires that we stop withholding our pay (3:8–10).

- Giving God his due results in more riches to give away (3:11–12).

---

4 https://get.tithe.ly/state-of-the-plate-2016-report-infographic accessed 7/7/2018.

Malachi 3:13–4:3

EXEGETICAL IDEA
Although some questioned if it paid to serve God, when God would come to judge the world he would distinguish between the righteous and the wicked, between those who feared and served God (his "prized possessions") and those who refused to fear and serve him.

THEOLOGICAL FOCUS
God will spare those who fear and serve him but destroy the arrogant who refuse to honor him.

PREACHING IDEA
God is inclined to stick a pin in our pride.

PREACHING POINTERS
The prophet Malachi spoke on God's behalf in a sixth and final dispute with his people. He redressed his original audience's cynicism about serving God, which to them apparently paid less than self-service. The argument echoed an earlier complaint that God's justice was lacking. In the current section, the prophet reassured them that God remembered and rewarded the righteous, humble, and God-fearing, but he despised the arrogant. Those who revered the Almighty would help God as he uprooted those who refused to honor him in a climatic, coming day. This glimpse into the future aimed to inspire Malachi's original audience towards humble service.

Pride is prime currency in our age. We tend to exalt big-headed athletes, celebrities, and CEOs for their bravado and bold accomplishments. We often ignore the elderly, disabled, less educated, or ethnic outsider. We teach young people to prize self-esteem above integrity. Even the church is seduced by self-importance, as evident in the numerous church campuses that look like shopping malls, leadership conferences that promise to catalyze growth, and programming that claims to be the best hour of the week. When excellent performance becomes the measuring stick for a worship service, arrogance overtakes God as the focus. Such religious pomp will not last. This passage reminds us how God's inclined to stick a pin in our pride.

DOES IT PAY TO SERVE GOD?
(3:13–4:3)

LITERARY STRUCTURE AND THEMES

This sixth and final dispute includes the claim that people had been saying harsh things about God (v. 13a), but some objected (v. 13b); so it was necessary for the prophet to justify this claim. Although some of these arrogant people questioned if it paid to serve God (vv. 14–15), the righteous feared God (v. 16), for they knew that God would spare those who feared him, but not the wicked (3:17–4:3).[1]

It is arrogant to think that it does not pay to serve God. God keeps records of all we do, so there will be a day of accountability when God will spare those who fear and serve him and severely judge those who do not.

- *The People Said Harsh Things (3:13a)*
- *An Objection (3:13b)*
- *There Is No Benefit in Serving God (3:14–15)*
- *A Positive Response by the Righteous (3:16)*
- *God Protects His Own Possessions but Will Destroy the Wicked (3:17–4:3)*

EXPOSITION

When times were tough and things didn't work out as smoothly as one might have expected, some would wonder where God was and why he had not intervened to prevent those difficult days. Although God never promised to make this life on earth easy with no problems, God did promise that he would spare those who feared and served him, but not the arrogant who refused to serve God.

The People Said Harsh Things (3:13a)
Some people criticized the way God ran the world because it appeared that God did not reward those who feared him.

3:13a. The initial charge was that some people spoke "harsh, strong, difficult" (חָזַק) words against God. Apparently in a posture of superiority, they arrogantly criticized or blamed God for what was happening. This seems be a variation or continuation of the accusation in 2:17 that God was not just.

An Objection (3:13b)
Some critics did not accept responsibility for what they said.

3:13b. Following the script in other disputations, the audience denied the prophet's charge and pleaded their innocence. Either they did not remember what they said or they felt that their perspective was justified and was not really harsh, just a statement of the facts.

There Is No Benefit in Serving God (3:14–15)
Some critics thought that God would never reward the righteous.

3:14. At this point the prophet reminded these cynical people of what they had previously said.

---

1   Ross (2016, 164) and Clendenen (2004, 230) put 3:13–4:6 all in one unit, but 4:4–6 functioned more like an epilogue to Malachi's message, and possibly to the book of the twelve minor prophets.

First, they had the audacity to claim that it was "ineffective, useless" (שָׁוְא) to serve God because nothing was gained by it.

WORD ANALYSIS: שָׁוְא
This word can refer to (a) "false, useless" visions or prophecies (Ezek. 12:24) or "false, worthless" testimony (Deut. 5:20); (b) "useless, worthless" idols (Ps. 31:6; Jer. 18:15); (c) "ineffective, useless" punishment (Jer. 2:30), or (d) "useless" service to God (Mal. 3:14).

Usually a religious person would expect some sort of reward from God, but these people did not see God doing anything good for them. Apparently, they thought that the success they achieved was based solely on their own efforts. These people thought that the basis for experiencing God's favor was (a) faithful service, (b) following the law, and (c) exhibiting mourning characteristic of repentance. So they perfected the external behavior patterns one would expect of a pious saint, but from God's perspective these acts lacked spiritual validity. They paraded their righteousness and had a gloomy face, but it was all a show and an attempt to manipulate God and others. Yet "mere works without faith are insufficient" (Stuart, 1998, 1378). Since their fake piety was not rewarded by God, their response was, why bother trying to please God if he doesn't reward you?

3:15. Even worse, these people actively undermined the biblical teaching that God would punish the wicked. Based on examples of delays in justice, these people described the arrogant people as blessed and built up by God. It was not clear who they were describing as arrogant. Maybe they thought this applied to their Persian rulers, other heathen people, or a specific group like the Edomites (Mal. 1:4). But Verhoef (1987, 318) and Ross (2016, 164) reject these options and argue that the arrogant were the evil Jewish people mentioned later in 4:1. The perspective that the wicked are

blessed (cf. Ps. 73:1–14) was just the opposite of traditional biblical ethics that God would justly punish the wicked (Mal. 3:10; Ps. 1:1–5). These people also claimed that some people sinfully "tested" (בָּחַן) God's patience and were never punished for testing God. This would be just the opposite of the biblical norm that the righteous (not the wicked) would escape God's judgment (Prov. 11:21). These real-life examples made them question the value of maintaining a rigorous righteous life of devotion to God and caused them to doubt if there was any benefit for those who served God and followed his instructions. These were harsh words that were destructive and promoted a false understanding of God ways.

Although it was normal for there to be some delay between the committing of an evil act and God's just response because God normally left some time for a person to repent. Nevertheless, the biblical narratives, prophetic discourse, and legal texts all affirm that God would eventually bring a just reward to the righteous and a punishment to the wicked.

A Positive Response by the Righteous (3:16)
Godly people knew that God would remember the righteous person who fears him.

3:16. Having quoted what the pious hypocrites said, Malachi briefly described what the righteous minority did and said. They "feared, revered" (יָרֵא) God and consequently had a theological perspective on God's justice that was quite different from the cynics in 3:14–15. The righteous looked to other faithful believers for mutual support. They recognized that God did pay attention to the faithful; he was not ignorant of what people were doing as the cynics thought. Some interpret God's "book of remembrance" (cf. Exod. 32:32; Pss. 69:29; 87:6; Dan. 12:1) as a list of names written by the faithful on a scroll on earth (like Ezra 10; Stuart, 1998, 1382), but it would appear that this was actually written on a scroll in heaven (Merrill, 2003, 383; Hill, 1998, 360; Redditt, 1995, 183; Clendenen, 2004, 443). The existence of this book would be a great source of encouragement for the righteous minority who faithfully honored God. They knew that nothing was forgotten.

God Protects His Own Possessions but Will Destroy the Wicked (3:17–4:3)

God would spare those who feared him, but not the wicked.

3:17–18. In order to bring this dispute to a close, Malachi responded to the righteous with assurances that it would be worthwhile to fear and serve God because he would justly reward them. This meant that he would distinguish between the destiny of the righteous and the wicked (3:18). God's justice would determine what rewards would come to the righteous and what punishment would fall on the wicked on the eschatological day of the Lord (3:17; 4:1, 3; cf. 3:2). God told the righteous (not the whole nation) that they belonged to him; they were his "prized possession" (סְגֻלָּה), a term that referred to the precious royal gems of a king. This terminology was used in Exodus 19:1–6 (Deut. 7:6; 14:2; 26:18) when God first made a covenant with Israel at Mount Sinai. At that time, God promised that if Israel maintained their covenant relationship with him, they would become his "prized possession," a holy nation, and a kingdom of priests. Now Malachi reminds his listeners that those who fear and serve God would be his prized possession. In the eschatological era, the righteous would be distinguished from the wicked cynics who questioned God's justice (3:18) and doubted that anyone would be rewarded for righteous behavior. In first person declarations, God promised, "I will spare these righteous people from any judgment because I love them dearly, like a father loves his son." The stand the righteous have taken would be vindicated by God's action.

4:1. Then Malachi turned his attention to explain what would happen to the arrogant evildoers on the day of the Lord (4:1). That day was metaphorically compared to a time of intense burning, like what would happen in a furnace or oven. The wicked were symbolically compared to a plant that produced grain. No mention was made of any good grain, only the stubble part of the plant and the roots. These evildoers were compared to the worthless stubble, which had little value and would burn up quickly in a hot furnace (cf. Ps. 83:13–15; Isa. 5:24). Their destruction was metaphorically pictured as a complete removal of everything that might have life, including the roots and branches. No detailed interpretation of this plant metaphor was provided, but one could assume that if the roots were destroyed, this plant would never grow from the roots, implying an end of the genealogical line of these evildoers.

4:2. Those who feared the name of God were described with a very different metaphor. The heat of the sun presented a positive picture of warmth and the stimulus that would cause plants to grow. Added to this positive idea was the concept of the "sun of righteousness" that had healing in its wings. This symbol of a winged sun disk was common in Mesopotamia as well as Egypt (cf. Keel, 1978, 27–28). Not everyone agrees on the interpretation of the image of a winged sun disk. For example, Petersen (1995, 225) thinks the "disk surely symbolizes the sun, and the wings signify the heavenly vault or sky, or possibly the rays of the sun." Petersen points out that Shamesh, the sun god of Mesopotamia, was a god of justice and law, which would fit the issues of justice in this dispute. In the OT itself, the coming of God's glory to the earth was pictured as a great light that would remove all darkness (Isa. 60:1–3), for the Lord would provide all the light that would be needed (Isa. 60:19–20; 24:23). The coming messianic figure in Isaiah 9:2–9 was also pictured as a great light, and the glorious eschatological promises included God providing healing and safety for those under his wings (Isa. 30:26; 53:5; 58:8). Verhoef (1987, 328) thinks this was a messianic symbol that communicated the belief that "on the day of the Lord righteousness will become apparent just like the shining of the sun in all its brightness and blessedness."

The results of the coming of this great light and his healing would bring a new sense of joy and excitement (4:2b). Malachi expressed this extraordinary joy by comparing it to the joy and excitement young cattle feel when they are let out of the confinement of a small barn and given complete freedom to run and jump in the open field.[2]

4:3. The final comment at the end of this conclusion was that righteous would trample on the ashes of the wicked who were burned like the stubble. The fire of God's justice would destroy the wicked on the day of his judgment (4:1). So when the righteous who feared God walked on their ashes, this would serve as a symbol of their victory over the evildoer and as a vindication of the stand the righteous took in fearing and serving God (3:17–18).

THEOLOGICAL FOCUS

The exegetical idea (although some questioned if it paid to serve God, when God would come to judge the world he would distinguish between the righteous and the wicked, between those who feared and served God [his "prized possessions"] and those who refused to fear and serve him) leads to this theological focus: God will spare those who fear and serve him but destroy the arrogant who refuse to honor him.

This disputation characterizes the life and theological destiny of those who fear God and those who do not fear God. The unbeliever who did not fear God needed to realize that people

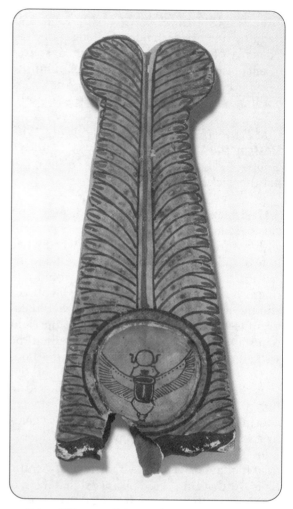

Painted Plume with Sun Disk Containing Winged Kheper Beetle. Courtesy of Los Angeles County Museum of Art / Public domain.

could be quite cynical because they seldom observed an immediate positive or negative reward for their behavior. Nevertheless, this did not mean that they could establish a theological principle that God would never distinguish between the righteous and the wicked. The lesson to learn is that if there is no reward now, there

---

2 Growing up on a dairy farm in Iowa I witnessed this phenomenon every spring when we released our cows from the confinement of the barnyard into the fresh green grass of the pasture.

surely will be a reward on the final day of God's judgment. The main principle to remember is that God will spare the righteous and heal them on that day, but his fiery judgment will bring complete decimation of the wicked. Thus it does pay to serve God.

PREACHING AND TEACHING STRATEGIES

Exegetical and Theological Synthesis
Malachi 3:13–4:3 resurfaces questions of God's justice and timing. In an earlier dispute (2:17–3:5), the people "wearied" God with their words. In the present dispute, they had spoken "harsh" words against God. Consistent with the rest of the book, the people shook their heads at God's argument. The all-knowing, never-changing Lord Almighty exposed the mixed motives and impure affections his people continued to deny.

God's superior knowledge applies to time, as well (Ps. 90). Whereas humans want justice exacted immediately, God judges eventually (Hab. 1–2). His patience leaves room for repentance and restoration (Joel 2:12–13; cf. 2 Peter 3:9). Ironically, if God brought the hammer of justice down as soon as we committed a sin, none of us would stand (Pss. 14:1–3; 103:3; Eccl. 7:10; Isa. 64:8). Those who lament the long gap between rebellious deed and guilty verdict are themselves benefactors. We are all blind to our own arrogance in claiming innocence!

Eschatological judgment surely provokes fear in many people. Some fear, in fact, is healthy if it stirs awe of God who mercifully writes the names of the faithful in his book of life (Exod. 32:32; Dan. 12:2; Mal. 3:16). But the neurotic fear of end times often results from a misreading of prophetic and apocalyptic literature. Even today these graphic symbols and visions remain difficult to interpret and inspire speculative fiction such as *The Late Great Planet Earth* (1970) and Left Behind series (1995–2007). God gave glimpses into the future to assure us, not

alarm us. We should remember that God will return and make things right ("Surely the day is coming . . ." [4:1]) and release our need to know when he will arrive.

Preaching Idea
God's inclined to stick a pin in our pride.

Contemporary Connections

What does it mean?
What does it mean that God's inclined to stick a pin in our pride? What is pride, and how does it contrast from healthy self-confidence? Pastors and theologians often identify pride as the original sin and root of all human rebellion. This is an accurate assessment. Both in the garden of Eden and at the Tower of Babel, humans betrayed their desire to shake off human limits and become like God (Gen. 3:5; 11:4–6). Willful disregard of God's law betrays our human preference for autonomy (i.e., self-rule). Pride says, "My way is better than God's way."

Wisdom writers and prophets likewise speak harshly against pride—haughty eyes, stubborn hearts, and inflated egos (Prov. 6:17; Jer. 9:23; 13:10; Hos. 7:10). God hates arrogance and promises to knock down proud people (Prov. 8:13; 16:5; Zeph. 3:11). His repulsion for arrogance applies to all people, but he gives special attention to Israel's leaders and foreign kings. Nathan rebuked King David for his crimes against Uriah and contempt for God's law (2 Sam. 12:7–12). The priests confronted King Uzziah for his illicit incense offering (2 Chron. 26:16–21). Ezekiel condemned the self-exalting king of Tyre (Ezek. 28:1). Daniel recorded the plight of the proud king of Babylon (Dan. 4).

Proper self-confidence, on the other hand, comes from knowing God. It takes him seriously without taking oneself too seriously. Self-confident people trust that God understands them, loves them, and intends to use them for his purposes (Exod. 19:5–6; Isa. 49:6). For example,

Jeremiah modeled self-confidence. He embraced God's calling to speak difficult words of judgment (1:4–10). When the people opposed his ministry, Jeremiah persevered rather than raged, which was a sign of his humility (Jer. 37:11–21). Perhaps Jeremiah learned self-confidence from one of his own exhortations: let's not boast in our wisdom, strength, or riches but in that we understand and know God (9:23–24). Ultimately, self-confidence stems from firmly rooted trust in God (17:7–8).

Is it true?

Is it true that God's inclined to stick a pin in our pride? If so, what does this process look like? God does not follow a singular path to deflate our egos, but he does humble us. God allows hardship and suffering, ridicule and mockery, rises and falls, celebrity and infamy. The story of Joseph captures God's providential hand in squeezing from the arrogant youth his sense of self-importance. He plummeted from his father's favorite dreamer to his brothers' latest victim; from Potiphar's right-hand man to his wife's scapegoat; from prisoner number three to Pharaoh's second-in-command. By the end of the narrative, Joseph had matured from boastful brother to kindly kin.

Stories of God Sticking a Pin in Pride

- God stuck a pin in proud King David, who considered himself above the law with Uriah (2 Sam. 12).
- God stuck a pin in proud King Uzziah, who thought Levitical privilege applied to him (2 Chron. 26).
- God stuck a pin in proud Haman, who thought his political maneuvering would win him favor (Esther 7).
- God stuck a pin in the proud kings of Babylon and Tyre, who viewed themselves as God's equals (Isa. 14, Ezek. 28; Dan. 4–5).
- God stuck a pin in the proud city Jerusalem, which practiced idolatry and disobeyed God's law (Jer. 13).
- God stuck a pin in the proud Edomites, who delighted in Jerusalem's demise and bragged about their fortified location (Obadiah).
- God stuck a pin in the proud, wealthy class that put their trust in riches and exploited the weak (Amos 4:1–3).
- God stuck a pin in proud religious leaders who claimed innocence while exploiting God's people (Mic. 3).

Not only do the Scriptures comprise numerous stories of God sticking a pin in human pride, but they also explicitly state God's intention to knock down self-exalting people. In fact, the word "humility" connotes living at ground level. Whether God dethroned a king, exiled a nation, sent a plague, withheld the rains or issued a curse, he intended to remind his people of their low standing in the presence of their sovereign Creator.

Inversely, God consistently raises up, honors, or exalts those who are humble (Job 5:11, cf. James 4:10). After losing his seat of power in Egypt, God appointed Moses to deliver his people and lead them in their exodus to the Promised Land. God turned the lowly shepherd David into an exalted king. He sent his Servant to suffer and serve as a praised vehicle of salvation for his people (Isa. 53). Even today God honors humble people, using their pain for good purposes. The racial oppression Rosa Parks faced, the persecution Richard Wurmbrand endured, the imprisonment of Desmond Tutu suffered, and the physical disability Joni Eareckson Tada has managed have given these humbled people platforms to testify to their trust in God.

Now what?

How should we respond to human pride evident all around us? How should we tame our own egos? It is important to begin with the latter question. Because we live in a society that encourages self-promotion (ascending the corporate ladder, sitting at the head of the class, or expanding our spheres of influence) and self-expression (through dress, social media, consumer purchases, and sexual exploration) we should beware of its effects on us. Our historical moment cannot help but make us feel some degree of self-importance. Nor can our historic roots: pride reaches back to Eden. We start taming our pride by admitting its persistence.

Second, as we analyze our ego, we should realize we often have blind spots (Prov. 12:15). Malachi envisioned God-fearing people speaking to and hearing from one another. One service we may provide for a fellow believer is an honest assessment of his character weaknesses (i.e., growth areas). But this requires a safe place of authentic, trust-filled relationships. One ministry specializing in creating and cultivating a culture of high trust in the church, the family, and the workplace is Trueface.org. Small groups, accountability partners, and mentoring relationships can also provide a safe context to let the air of out our egos. If, however, someone does not seek honest feedback, it is not prudent to provide it (Prov. 23:9).

Finally, God does not task us with pointing out the pride often found in business leaders, church leaders, athletes, politicians, and parents of gifted-and-talented children. God will typically deal them their blow—through hardship, suffering, or trying circumstances—without recruiting us to prick their hubris. He alone is the world's judge (Pss. 7:11; 50; 58).

Creativity in Presentation

A visual illustration may drive home the preaching idea. Purchase a bag of large, multicolored balloons. Prior to the message, inflate several and write on them the word "PRIDE" in large, bold print. As you talk about factors that feed pride—academic success, professional achievements, birth of children and grandchildren, hours of community service, completed home improvement projects, sporting victories—blow into the balloon. As you depict the increase in self-importance, the word "PRIDE"

will expand. Eventually, you'll talk about how God may stick a pin in our pride through the loss of a job, strained friendship, serious injury, house fire, or bankruptcy. Consider saying something like this: "When it comes to pride, God does not discriminate. He may stick a pin in the proud father. [Pop a balloon.] A proud banker. [Pop a balloon.] A proud student. [Pop a balloon.] A proud athlete. [Pop a balloon.] A proud student-athlete. [Pop a balloon.] A proud pastor. [Pop a balloon.] A proud volunteer. [Pop a balloon.] It's pretty loud and clear that God does not care for our pride."

People love to watch the mighty fall. Every year, millions of people fill out brackets to predict game winners for March Madness, the NCAA basketball tournament. Every year millions of people cheer for underdogs known as "Cinderella" teams (e.g., Davidson, Loyola-Chicago), who upset powerhouses (e.g., Duke, Kentucky) and gain brief fame. The love for "underdogs" cuts across athletics, including the "Miracle on Ice" U.S. hockey win over the Soviet Union in the 1980 Olympics or every NFL team to defeat the New England Patriots since 2001. While sporting analogies miss a swath of the congregation, the illustration may be more relevant if the timing of the message aligns with any national championship.

> **Great Sporting Underdogs**
> - Billie Jean King's defeat of Bobbie Riggs in Battle of the Sexes (1973)
> - Arizona Diamondbacks' defeat of the New York Yankees in seven-game World Series (2001)
> - Milan's defeat of Muncie Central in the Indiana State Championship (1954) depicted in *Hoosiers* (1986, directed by David Anspaugh)
> - Buster Douglas's defeat of undefeated boxing champion Mike Tyson (1990)
> - The fifth-seeded New York Giants' defeat of first-ranked New England Patriots in Super Bowl XLII (2008)

- James Braddock's defeat of defending boxing champion Max Baer (1935) depicted in *Cinderella Man* (2005, directed by Ron Howard)

Cinderella stories, of course, get their name from the land of fairy tales, where proud step-parents and evil tyrants always come tumbling down. Consider repurposing a well-known fairy tale to celebrate the deflated ego of Maleficent from *Sleeping Beauty*, the Wicked Queen from *Snow White*, Jafar from *Aladdin*, or Gaston from *Beauty and the Beast*. Any one of these films would have an accompanying clip to help illustrate what it looks like to have a pin stuck in one's pride. Or, if fairy tales will not resonate with your audience, Pixar's first installment of *Cars* (2006, directed by John Lasseter) warmly portrays the deflation (both ego and tires!) of Lightening McQueen (voiced by Owen Wilson). By the end of the film, McQueen learns the value of teammates and life out of the spotlight, but first his pride had to suffer a major blow.

No matter what creative elements you adopt and adapt for the message, highlight the core truth: God will spare those who fear him but destroy the arrogant who refuse to honor him. God's inclined to stick a pin in our pride.

- Proud people are self-serving (3:13–15).

- Humble people are God-fearing (3:16–17).

- Proud people are doomed (3:18–4:3).

DISCUSSION QUESTIONS

1. How would you respond to a friend who claims, "It doesn't pay to serve God" (Mal. 3:14)?

2. How will God distinguish between those who do and do not serve him (Mal. 3:17–18)?

3. What is the fear of God? What will happen to those who do not fear him (Mal. 4:1)?

4. What are clear marks of pride? What are more subtle signs of pride?

5. When have you experienced God sticking a pin in your pride? Be specific.

Malachi 4:4–6

EXEGETICAL IDEA
The people should read and obey the Mosaic laws and remember that God would send another Elijah before the day of the Lord to bring restoration to many.

THEOLOGICAL FOCUS
People who read and heed the Bible can expect a revival before the coming of God's glorious kingdom.

PREACHING IDEA
Until God finishes his work, we must rely on the Bible.

PREACHING POINTERS
The final few verses of Malachi rehearsed earlier themes: obedience to God's law, future judgment, and an invitation to change. Moses represented a voice from Israel's past; Elijah represented a forthcoming word from God. In this closing utterance, the original audience heard one last plea to observe God's word in order to escape judgment and experience a better future.

The Bible remains relevant for following God today. It is his primary communication tool. Sadly, biblical literacy is plummeting despite mass printing, distribution, and digitation of Bible translations. Furthermore, some people consider the Good Book old-fashioned, outdated, and oppressive. Secular scholars have deconstructed the Bible. Pragmatic preachers have reduced the text into a self-help manual. Religious hypocrites have turned the Scriptures into soapboxes. The authority and life-shaping power of God's Word is long-forgotten on many. Malachi's epilogue teaches us that until God finishes his work, we must rely on the Bible.

EPILOGUE: OBEY GOD'S INSTRUCTIONS
(4:4–6)

Remember, Elijah Will Come before the Day of the Lord

LITERARY STRUCTURE AND THEMES
The prophet Malachi had finished serving as an intermediary in six disputes between God and his people. The epilogue includes an exhortation to observe God's instructions through Moses in 4:4; it also includes a prophecy about Elijah's coming (4:5) to bring restoration and revival rather than a curse (4:6).

This unit's theological theme encourages people to read God's word in order to understand what God wants us to do to maintain our relationship to him. It is important for people to allow God's work of spiritual and family restoration to change their world, for before long the terrible day of divine judgment will fall on the earth.

- *Follow the Law of Moses (4:4)*
- *Elijah Will Bring Restoration (4:5–6)*

EXPOSITION

As a final warning and admonition, Malachi or the final arranger of the scroll of the Minor Prophets predicted that the day of the Lord would happen after Elijah would come. So the reader was encouraged to be prepared for this day by following what God had told them, for then they would escape God's terrible judgment.

Follow the Law of Moses (4:4)
God's people should read and obey what was written in the Torah.

4:4. The book of Malachi closes with what some call an appendix (some find two appendixes) or an epilogue whose content is closely tied to other themes in Malachi. For example, the idea that the people should follow God's instructions (4:4) is present in earlier disputations (1:6–2:9; 3:6–12), the day of the Lord theme is used in 2:17–3:5 and 4:1–3, and the idea of "turning, returning" (4:6) is found in 2:6, 2:8, and 3:7. Since these verses are not part of the final disputation, it would be appropriate to view them as a concluding exhortation.

The first challenge (4:4) was to "remember" (זְכָר) and not forget what God revealed about godly living in the covenant documents known as the Law of Moses (the Pentateuch). Malachi's preaching was a call to remember God's great love for his covenant people that was described in Genesis through Deuteronomy (Mal. 1:1–5), to pay attention to the sacrificial laws in Leviticus (Mal. 1:6–14), and to tithe as Moses instructed them in order to support the work of the Levites at the temple (Mal. 3:6–12). The priests in Malachi's day had failed to instruct the nation about the Pentateuch (Mal. 2:1–9), consequently many did not know what they were supposed to do.

Elijah Will Bring Restoration (4:5–6)
God would restore people to himself and restore broken families.

4:5–6. The exhortation in 4:5 was followed by a prophetic promise that God was planning on sending another great Elijah figure before the day of the Lord. This pointed back to Malachi's earlier comment about sending "my messenger" who would clear the way for the coming of the Lord (Mal. 3:1; cf. Isa. 40:3) as well as to the many prophetic references to the day of the Lord as a day of judgment for the unrighteous (Amos 5:18–20; Joel 1:15–20; 2:1–11; 3:9–17; Zeph. 1:14–18; Zech. 14:1–4, 12–15) and a day of salvation for the godly (Isa. 4:2–5; 10:10–16; 14:1–3; 19:19–25; 24:1–23; Jer. 30:8–131; Hos. 2:16–23; Joel 3:18–21; Zeph. 3:12–20; Zech. 14:5–11). If "my messenger" in Malachi 3:1 was identified with "Elijah" in 4:5, then we know a couple things about this Elijah's role. In Malachi 3:1, the messenger would prepare the spiritual way for the coming of God, and in 4:6 the Elijah figure will be involved with the restoration of family relationships. Since this restoration of the family seems to result in people not experiencing the terrible curse of God on the earth, this "restoration/turning" must refer to something much greater than just the settling of private family disagreement. This work of restoration could apply to the covenant people who were a tribal family, or Malachi may be thinking about the family of God and the restoration of his wayward Israelite children to the Father (God himself in 1:6; 2:10).

Elijah

Later in the NT (Matt. 17:1–13; Luke 9:28–36), Jesus appeared in his glory in the transfiguration narrative with Moses and Elijah. There Jesus seemed to identify Elijah with the coming of John the Baptist (Matt. 17:12–13; cf. Matt. 11:14), but some (Merrill, 2003, 392; Ross, 2016, 182) hold that there will be an eschatological Elijah who will appear before the second coming of the Messiah.[1]

Those who would listen to God's message through this Elijah figure should turn to God so that they would not have to endure the terror of God's final curse that would fall on all who reject God's grace.

THEOLOGICAL FOCUS

The exegetical idea (The people should read and obey the Mosaic laws and remember that God would send another Elijah before the day of the Lord to bring restoration to many) leads to this theological focus: People who read and heed the Bible can expect a revival before the coming of God's glorious kingdom.

The theological themes or lessons Malachi wanted his audience to learn in this unit were as follows: First, instructions on how God wants people to live can be derived from reading Scripture, especially the first five books of the Bible. Second, God's plan was to use men like Moses to record his thoughts and to instruct the nation so that they would know how to please God. In addition, God sent prophets like Elijah and Malachi to reinforce the need for people to repent and follow God's instructions. Third, in the future another Elijah figure would come and continue this restoration process to heal the broken relationships people have with one another and with God.

PREACHING AND TEACHING STRATEGIES

Exegetical and Theological Synthesis

Malachi 4:4–6 makes one thing clear: God speaks. When he spoke to Moses on Mount

---

1   W. Kaiser, "The Promise of the Arrival of Elijah in Malachi and the Gospels," *GTJ* 3 (1982): 221–33 or his "Witnessing and Expecting the Arrival of Elijah—Malachi 4:4–5," in *The Use of the OT in the New* (Chicago: Moody, 1985), 77–88 discusses these issues and concludes that this refers to both John the Baptist as well as an eschatological Elijah.

Sinai, what people heard as mere rumblings, Moses recorded as God's actual words. It is this spoken and written word that shaped successive generations of Israelites (Deut. 6). These same words inspired poems (Pss. 1; 119), prayers (Dan. 7), and revivals (2 Kings 23; Neh. 8).

It is God's written word that influenced the prophets, who followed in the footsteps of Moses (Deut. 18:15–22). God sent them to rebuke kings (1 Sam. 12; 1 Kings 17), call for repentance (Jonah 3; Amos 5), warn of exile (Jer. 25; Ezek. 7), and hint at future hope (Isa. 60–66; Jer. 30–33; Ezek. 38; Mic. 4; Zech. 14). Prophets were God's mouthpiece, decrying present sin and declaring coming judgment. Fulfillment of their speeches authenticated their truthfulness.

God even left a door open for future revelation. Malachi made this explicit in promising Elijah's return. More than four hundred years elapsed before Jesus identified John the Baptizer as Elijah (Matt. 11:14). These reapplied words from God in Malachi did not discredit his past utterances but expanded on them. God does not change (Mal. 3:6). Knowing all of God's Word is one of the best ways of relating to him and others.

Preaching Idea

Until God finishes his work, we must rely on the Bible.

Contemporary Connections

What does it mean?

What does it mean that until God finishes his work, we must rely on the Bible? God spoke through human authors in specific times and places. The writings of Moses, David, Jeremiah, Isaiah, and many other prophets underwent some process of compilation, editing, and arranging. When Malachi wrote, nearly all the Hebrew Scriptures were well recognized. Within a few centuries, the Hebrew Bible was verified by translation (e.g., the LXX), interpreted by various Jewish sects (e.g., a segment of the Essenes at Qumran), and used in worship (e.g., Luke 4:16–21). Eventually, the twenty-seven books of the Christian Scriptures were accepted, verified by translations, cited by early church fathers, and used in corporate worship together with the preceding thirty-nine books of the Jewish Scriptures. We call this combined work of the old covenant and new covenant Scriptures in sixty-six books the Bible.

Today opportunities to read (and listen to) the Bible are endless by virtue of digital technology and translation efforts. Moreover, a wealth of Bible study tools, preaching podcasts, and Christian literature provide helps for understanding God's Word. Although biblical understanding does not automatically translate to obedience, we can to know that God has revealed through his Word truth about himself, our world, sin, salvation, and the human condition.

Relying on his Word means letting the Bible shape our beliefs and behaviors. The Bible corrects misunderstandings of God (e.g., he is mean) with truth (e.g., he is merciful), so we give him due honor. The Bible curbs our wrong expectations (e.g., judgment) with eschatological hope (e.g., resurrection and rewards), so we remain patient. And the Bible charts a course for loving relationships with him and others, so we live with integrity and compassion. Until God brings history to its climax (i.e., the day of the Lord), we must rely on his Word as our guide to the blessed life.

Is it true?

Is it true that until God finishes his work, we must rely on the Bible? Yes, it is in our best interest to heed the Bible. Moses instructed parents to raise their children to rely on God's law in order to cultivate lasting fidelity (Deut. 6:4–9). King Josiah resurrected national reliance on God's Word after rediscovering the Hebrew Scriptures (2 Kings 23). Ezra called the postexilic community to rely on God's Word by reading them large portions at a worship service

(Neh. 8). When God's people failed to rely on the Bible, they often faced dire consequences.

Relying on God's Word remains critical today as we inch ever closer to the climax of history. Unfortunately, it is easy to dismiss the Bible as outdated or accept other voices as more reliable on various matters. Churches may rely more on business principles than biblical principles to spur growth. Parents may rely more on parenting trends than biblical teaching to discipline their children. Students may rely more on social networks than biblical counsel for their sexual ethic. And all of us may rely more on self than Scripture to make daily plans, career decisions, or ethical codes.

God, of course, can speak through parents, peers, teachers, conscience, life situations, and myriad other sources. But we must take caution against relying on them for ultimate truth. Those who rely on God's Word will take their big questions about God, his world, sin, salvation, and the human condition to the Bible. They will filter cultural information through the Bible. They will come to God's Word expecting that through it, God still speaks today (Heb. 4:12). Thus reliance is a posture that invites God's Word to speak first and last into the questions and direction of our lives.

Now what?

How do we rely on the Bible? Is there a best way to read the Bible to build reliance? Each person's Bible reading habits will look different. Some people love the prophets; others crave the psalms. Some people meditate on Paul's letters; others gravitate to the Gospels. Some people read (and reread) a book until it's in their bones; others skip around the text like a hopscotch game. While certain reading strategies may prove more helpful for understanding, not every bit of biblical data translates into reliance. Thus, reliance begins with the expectation we bring to our time in the Bible. We should come with open ears and eager hearts, asking God to speak.

Furthermore, healthy Bible reading habits help form reliance on God. When we have patterns for hearing and applying God's Word, it remains hidden in our hearts, keeping our memory of God's faithfulness fresh, love for him pure, and treatment of others just (Ps. 119). Habits begin with small choices pointed in the same direction. Choosing a time, place, and Bible reading plan will provide a promising start to good changes. Of course, devotional writings (e.g., *My Utmost for His Highest, Our Daily Bread, New Morning Mercies*, YouVersion's The Bible App, and others) and sermons also offer biblical reflections that foster reliance.

Finally, we should look for ways God's Word can spill into our relationships. Talking about what God teaches us not only sharpens our thinking and grows our convictions, but it also helps create accountability with other believers. If, after reading Malachi 3:6–12, we admit to a friend our need to live more generously, we've given that person permission to follow up weeks later. Family dinners, small groups, and discipleship clusters provide a healthy context to build reliance on God's Word together.

Creativity in Presentation

To spark the need to know the Bible better so you can better rely on it, consider providing a "Pop Quiz" at the beginning of the message. Introduce the quiz by sharing your concern that people know less of the Bible today than in recent generations. Let them know this pop quiz may reveal our need to change (or restart) some of our Bible reading habits.

Sample Questions for Pop Quiz or Interview

- What are two of five books Moses wrote?
- What is a psalm? Who wrote most of the psalms?
- How many of the twelve minor prophets can you name?

- What is Jonah famous for? Why did it happen?
- Who were the four guys who wrote about Jesus? (Hint: Their books are called Gospels.)
- Name at least five of Jesus's miracles?
- What is the Golden Rule?
- How many disputes did God raise with his people in Malachi? (Bonus: What were they?)

The pop quiz should not shame people for ignorance or a faulty memory but reveal their need for better Bible reading habits. You might do an oral exam, distribute written quizzes, project the questions on a screen, or create an online, interactive quiz using Poll Everywhere or Kahoot!.[2]

A variation on this illustration is to prerecord brief interviews with people in the community. Ask them questions about the Bible and capture their responses. Chances are most folks could not name the four gospels or would give God credit for saying such things as "he helps those who help themselves" or "cleanliness is next to godliness." Surely some responses would be humorous, but the whole video would get people in your church wondering if their answers would have been more precise. A three-minute clip on YouTube of comedian Michael Jr. asking random shoppers to finish well-known Bible verses would produce a similar effect.

Finally, consider critiquing the way we describe the Bible. Let people know that no metaphor does God's Word justice. Is the Bible a blueprint? Is it a holy book? Is it a game plan for life? Is it God's love letter to us? Is it an epic story? Each analogy misses something. Then assure people when we talk of the Bible as revelation, we capture something of its communicative nature. Project images of various devices that speak: e.g., alarm clock, car dashboard, cell phone, and voice-controlled smart speaker. Project images from nature that speak: e.g., tree, river, animals, and storm cloud. Project images of people that speak: e.g., baby, spouse, celebrity, and political figure. Then point to your stomach or a sore joint and describe how it speaks. Summarize by saying, "All around us the world is speaking. Our screens, pets, and people in our house. God speaks too. We need to learn to listen. We need to learn to rely on the Bible. We look to it first. (Hold up one finger.) We let it speak last. (Use the same finger to gesture a terminal "period" in the air.) The Bible is more than a blueprint or holy book, it is the living and reliable Word of God."

Throughout the sermon, be certain to emphasize this summons: Read and heed God's Word and expect a preacher to preach revival. Or simply this: Until God finishes his work, we must rely on the Bible.

- We all need a fresh hearing of God's Word (4:4).

- We all hope God will finish his work (4:5–6).

---

2 Both Kahoot! and Poll Everywhere are online services used to foster real-time interaction in training events, community gatherings, business meetings, and classrooms. They use trivia questions, polls, and word maps to help groups visualize their collective thinking. Many of their services are free, but some features cannot be used without paying. These are but two of numerous online services.

DISCUSSION QUESTIONS

1. What future role did Malachi envision for Elijah to play?

2. What role was the Law of Moses to play for Malachi's original audience?

3. What is the relationship between the OT and NT?

4. How do you seek a fresh hearing of God's Word? How do you promote Bible literacy?

5. How do our metaphors for God's Word affect the way we hear and heed it?

FOR FURTHER READING

Chapman, Gary. 2015. *Five Love Languages: The Secret to Love That Lasts*. Chicago: Northfield.

Clendenen, E. Ray and R. A. Taylor. 2004. *Haggai, Malachi*. New American Commentary. Nashville: Broadman and Holman.

Corey, Barry. 2016. *Love, Kindness: Discover the Power of a Forgotten Christian Virtue*. Carol Stream, IL: Tyndale.

Hill, Andrew E. *Malachi*. 1998. Anchor Bible. New York: Doubleday.

Kinnaman, David and Gabe Lyons. 2016. *Good Faith: Being a Christian When Society Thinks You're Irrelevant and Extreme*. Grand Rapids: Baker.

Lewis, C. S. 1995. *Mere Christianity*. New York: Touchstone.

Ross, A. P. 2016. *Malachi: Then and Now*. Wooster, OH: Weaver.

Snyman, S. D. 2015. *Malachi*. Historical Commentary on the Old Testament. Leuven: Peeters.

Verhoef, Pieter. 1987. *The Books of Haggai and Malachi*. New International Commentary on the Old Testament. Grand Rapids: Eerdmans.

REFERENCES

Achtemeier, E. 1986. *Nahum–Malachi*. Interpretation: A Bible Commentary for Teaching and Preaching. Atlanta: John Knox.

Allen, D. 2001. *Getting Things Done: The Art of Stress-Free Something*. New York: Penguin Books.

Arrian. *Arrian: Anabasis of Alexander; Indica*. Translated by P. A. Brunt. Rev. text and translation. 2 vols. Loeb Classical Library 236, 269. Cambridge: Harvard University Press, 1983–89. Originally published 1929–33. All citations are to the 1983–89 edition.

Baldwin, J. G. 1972. *Haggai, Zechariah, Malachi*. Tyndale Old Testament Commentary. Downers Grove, IL: InterVarsity Press.

Ben Zvi, Ehud. 1991. *A Historical-Critical Study of the Book of Zephaniah*. Beihefte zur Zeitschrift für die alttestamentliche Wissenschaft 198. Berlin: De Gruyter.

Baker, D. W. 1988. *Nahum, Habakkuk, and Zephaniah*. Tyndale Old Testament Commentaries. Downers Grove, IL: InterVarsity Press.

———. 2006. *Joel, Obadiah, Malachi*. NIV Application Commentary. Grand Rapids: Zondervan.

Ball Jr., I. J. 1988. *A Rhetorical Study of Zephaniah*. Berkeley: BIBAL Press.

Barker. K. L. 1983. "Zechariah." In *Expositor's Bible Commentary*, edited by F. E. Gaebelein, 7:595–697. Grand Rapids: Zondervan.

Barker K. L., and W. Bailey. 1998. *Micah, Nahum, Habakkuk, Zephaniah*. New American Commentary. Nashville: Broadman & Holman.

Bateman IV, Herbert W. 2004. *History of the Second Temple Period: An Examination of Judaism During the Second Temple Period*. Rev. ed. Winona Lake, IN: n.p.

———. 2012. "Part 2: Expectations of a King" in *Jesus the Messiah: Tracing the Promises, Expectations, and Coming of Israel's King*, by H. W. Bateman IV, D. L. Bock, and G. H. Johnston, 211–330. Grand Rapids: Kregel.

———. 2016. *Isaiah: How to Read, Interpret and Understand the Prophet*. Leesburg, IN: Cyber-Center for Biblical Studies.

Bateman IV, H. W., D. L. Bock, and G. H. Johnston. 2012. *Jesus the Messiah: Tracing the Promises, Expectations, and Coming of Israel's King*. Grand Rapids: Kregel.

Bates, M. W. 2017. *Salvation by Allegiance Alone: Rethinking Faith, Words, and the Gospel of Jesus the King*. Grand Rapids: Baker Academic.

Beale, G. K. 2008. *We Become What We Worship: A Biblical Theology of Idolatry*. Downers Grove, IL: IVP Academic.

Berlin, A. 1994. *Zephaniah: A New Translation with Introduction and Commentary*. Anchor Bible. New York: Doubleday.

Boa, K. 2017. *Life in the Presence of God: Practices for Living in Light of Eternity*. Downers Grove, IL: IVP Books.

Bock, D. L. 2012. "Part 3: The Coming of a King." In *Jesus the Messiah: Tracing the Promises, Expectations, and Coming of Israel's King*, by H. W. Bateman IV, D. L. Bock, and G. H. Johnston, 331–458. Grand Rapids: Kregel.

Boda, M. J. 2003a. "From Fasts to Feasts: The Literary Function of Zechariah 7–8," *Catholic Biblical Quarterly* 65 (3):390–407.

———. 2003b. *Haggai and Zechariah Research: A Bibliographic Survey*. Tools for Biblical Study 5. Leiden: Deo.

_____. 2004. *Haggai, Zechariah*. NIV Application Commentary. Grand Rapids: Zondervan.

_____. 2005. "Terrifying the Horns: Persia and Babylon in Zechariah 1:7–6:15." *Catholic Biblical Quarterly* 67 (1):22–41.

Boyle, Gregory. 2010. *Tattoos on the Heart: The Power of Boundless Compassion*. New York: Free Press.

Briant, P. 2002. *From Cyrus to Alexander: A History of the Persian Empire*. Translated by P. T. Daniels. Winona Lake, IN: Eisenbrauns.

Bright, J. 2000, *A History of Israel*. 4th ed. Westminster Aids to the Study of the Scriptures. Louisville: Westminster John Knox.

Brooke, G., J. Collins, T. Elgvin, P. Flint, J. Greenfield, E. Larson, C. Newsom, É. Puech, L. H. Schiffman, M. Stone, and J. T. Barrera, in consultation with J. VanderKam. 1996. "252. 4QCommentary on Genesis A (Pls. XII–XIII)." In *Qumran Cave 4, XVII: Parabiblical Texts, Part 3*, 185–208. Discoveries in the Judaean Desert 22. Oxford: Clarendon Press.

Bruckner, J. 2004. *Jonah, Nahum, Habakkuk, Zephaniah*. NIV Application Commentary. Grand Rapids: Zondervan.

Campolo, T. 1992. *The Kingdom of God Is a Party: God's Radical Plan for His Family*. Dallas: Word.

Chisholm Jr., R. B. 1990. *Interpreting the Minor Prophets*. Grand Rapids: Zondervan.

Chisholm Jr., R. B., and Herbert W. Bateman IV. 2016. *Isaiah: Reading the Prophet with Understanding*. Leesburg, IN: Cyber-Center for Biblical Studies.

Clines, D. J. A. 1979. "Cyrus." *The International Standard Bible Encyclopedia*, edited by G. W. Bromiley 1:867–68. Grand Rapids: Eerdmans.

_____. 1979. "Darius." *The International Standard Bible Encyclopedia*, edited by G. W. Bromiley, 1:847–49. Grand Rapids: Eerdmans.

Clark, D. J. and H. A. Hatton. 2002. *A Handbook on Haggai, Zechariah, and Malachi*. UBS Handbook Series. New York: United Bible Society.

Collins, J. J. 2013. *Joel, Obadiah, Haggai, Zechariah, Malachi*. New Collegeville Bible Commentary 17. Collegeville, MN: Liturgical Press.

Colson, Charles W. 1976. *Born Again*. Old Tappan, NJ: Chosen Books.

_____. 1979. *Life Sentence*. Lincoln, VA: Chosen Books.

_____. 1983. *Loving God*. Grand Rapids: Zondervan.

Colson, Charles W., and Harold Fickett. 2008. *The Faith: What Christians Believe, Why They Believe It, and Why It Matters*. Grand Rapids: Zondervan.

Colson, Charles, and Ellen Santilli Vaughn. (1992) 2003. *Being the Body*. Nashville: W Publishing. First published 1992 under the title *The Body: Being Light in Darkness* (Dallas: Word).

Cowley, A. E. ed. 2005. *Aramaic Papyri of the Fifth Century B.C.* Ancient Texts and Translations. Eugene, OR: Wipf & Stock. Originally published 1923 by Clarendon Press (Oxford).

Curtis, B. G. 2006. *Up the Steep and Stony Road: The Book of Zechariah in Social-Location Trajectory Analysis*. Academia Biblica 25. Atlanta: Society of Biblical Literature.

Danamayev, M. A. 2006. "Neo-Babylonian and Achaemenid State Administration in Mesopotamia." In *Judah and the Judeans in the Persian Period*, edited by O. Lipschits and M. Oeming, 373–98. Winona Lake, IN: Eisenbrauns.

DeRouchie, J. S. 2018. "Zephaniah." In *ESV Expository Commentary*, edited by I. M. Duguid, J. M. Hamilton Jr., and J. Sklar, 7:561–604. 12 vols. Wheaton, IL: Crossway.

DeYoung, K. 2012. *A Hole in Our Holiness: Filling the Gap between Gospel Passion and the Pursuit of Godliness*. Wheaton, IL: Crossway.

Dostoyevsky, F. (1866) 2008. *Crime and Punishment*. Translated by J. Coulson. Oxford World's Classics. Oxford: Oxford University Press.

Ellis, R. S. 1968. *Foundation Deposits in Ancient Mesopotamia*. Yale Near Eastern Researches 2. New Haven, CT: Yale University Press.

Feinberg, C. L. 1965. *God Remembers: A Study of the Book of Zechariah*. Portland, OR: Multnomah.

Fischer, J. A. 1972. "Notes on the Literary Form and Message of Malachi." *Catholic Biblical Quarterly* 34 (3):315–20.

Floyd, M. H. 2000. *Minor Prophets: Part 2*. Forms of Old Testament Literature 22. Grand Rapids: Eerdmans.

———. 2003. "Deutero-Zechariah and Types of Intertextuality." In *Bringing out the Treasure: Inner Biblical Allusion in Zechariah 9–14*, edited by M. J. Boda and M. H. Floyd, with a major contribution by Rex Mason, 225–44. Journal for the Study of the Old Testament Supplement Series 370. London: Sheffield Academic.

Frankel, R. 1999. *Wine and Oil Production in Antiquity in Israel and Other Mediterranean Countries*. JSOT/ASOR Monograph Series 10. Sheffield: Sheffield Academic.

Freedman, D. N. 1990. "The Flying Scroll in Zechariah 5:1–4." In *Studies in near Eastern Culture and History: In Memory of Ernest T. Abdel-Massih*, edited by J. A. Bellamy, 42–48. Michigan Series on the Middle East 2. Ann Arbor, MI: Center for Near Eastern and North African Studies, The University of Michigan.

Gaines, Chip. 2017. *Capital Gaines: Smart Things I Learned Doing Stupid Stuff*. Nashville: W Publishing.

Gaines, Chip, and Joanna Gaines, with Mark Dagostino. 2016. *The Magnolia Story*. Nashville: W Publishing.

García Martínez, F., and E. J. C. Tigchelaar, eds. 1997. *1Q1–4Q273*. Vol. 1 of *The Dead Sea Scrolls Study Edition*. 2 vols. Leiden: Brill.

Glazier-McDonald, B. 1987. *Malachi the Divine Messenger*. Dissertation Series / Society of Biblical Literature 98. Atlanta: Scholars Press.

Good, R. M. 1982. "Zechariah's Second Night Vision (Zech. 2,1–4)." *Biblica* 63 (1):56–59.

Green, P. 1991. *Alexander of Macedon, 356–323 B.C.: A Historical Biography*. Hellenistic Culture and Society 11. Berkeley: University of California Press. Originally published under the title *Alexander the Great* (London: Weidenfeld & Nicolson, 1970). All citations are to the 1991 edition.

Guthrie, D., and J. A. Motyer, eds. 1970. *The New Bible Commentary, Revised*. 3rd ed. Grand Rapids: Eerdmans.

Hamilton, V. P. 1995. *The Book of Genesis: Chapters 18–50*. New International Commentary on the Old Testament. Grand Rapids: Eerdmans.

Hanson, P. D. 1975. *The Dawn of Apocalyptic: The Historical and Sociological Roots of Jewish Apocalyptic Eschatology*. Philadelphia: Fortress.

Harrison, R. K. 1969. *Introduction to the Old Testament: With Comprehensive Review of Old Testament Studies and Special Supplement on the Apocrypha*. Grand Rapids: Eerdmans.

Hasel, G. F. 1972. *The Remnant: The History and Theology of the Remnant Idea from Genesis to Isaiah*. Andrews University Monographs 5. Berrien Springs, MI: Andrews University Press.

Hayes, J. H., and S. R. Mandell. 1998. *The Jewish People in Classical Antiquity: From Alexander to Bar Kochba*. Louisville: Westminster John Knox.

Heath, C., and D. Heath 2011. *Switch: How to Change When Change Is Hard*. New York: Random House.

Herodotus. 1920–25. *The Persian Wars*. [*The Histories*.] Books 1–9. Translated by A. D. Godley. 4 vols. Loeb Classical Library 117–20. Cambridge: Harvard University Press.

Hill, A. E. 1998. *Malachi: A New Translation with Introduction and Commentary*. Anchor Bible 25D. New York: Doubleday.

———. 2008a. "Haggai." In *Minor Prophets: Hosea–Malachi*, by R. D. Patterson and A. E. Hill, 491–518. Cornerstone Biblical Commentary 10. Carol Stream, IL: Tyndale House.

———. 2008b. "Zechariah." In *Minor Prophets: Hosea–Malachi*, by R. D. Patterson and A. E. Hill, 519–608. Cornerstone Biblical Commentary 10. Carol Stream, IL: Tyndale House.

Hillers, D. R. 1964. *Treaty-Curses and the Old Testament Prophets*. Biblica et Orientalia 16. Rome: Pontifical Biblical Institute.

House, P. R. 1988. *Zephaniah: A Prophetic Drama*. Journal for the Study of Old Testament Supplement Series 69. Sheffield: Almond Press.

Johnston, G. H. 2012. "Part 3: Promises of a King." In *Jesus the Messiah: Tracing the Promises, Expectations, and Coming of Israel's King*, by H. W. Bateman IV, D. L. Bock, and G. H. Johnston, 37–209. Grand Rapids: Kregel.

Kaiser, W. C. 1984. *Malachi: God's Unchanging Love*. Grand Rapids: Baker.

———. 1987. "Divorce in Malachi 2:10–16," Criswell Theological Review, 2: 73–84.

———. 1992. *Micah, Nahum, Habakkuk, Zephaniah, Haggai, Zechariah, Malachi*. Communication Commentary 21. Dallas: Word.

Kapelrud, A. S. 1975. *The Message of the Prophet Zephaniah: Morphology and Ideas*. Oslo: Universitetsforlaget.

Kessler, J. A. 1987. "The Shaking of the Nations: An Eschatological View." *Journal of the Evangelical Theological Society* 30:159–66. https://www.etsjets.org/files/JETS-PDFs/30/30-2/30-2-pp159-166_JETS.pdf.

King, L. W., and R. C. Thompson, ed. 1907. *The Sculptures and Inscription of Darius the Great on the Rock of Behistûn in Persia: A New Collation of the Persian, Susian, and Babylonian Texts, with English Translations*. London: Longmans. https://archive.org/details/sculpturesinscri00brituoft/page/iii/mode/2up.

Klein, G. L. 2008. *Zechariah*. New American Commentary 21B. Nashville: B&H.

Kline, M. G. 2001. *Glory in Our Midst: A Biblical-Theological Reading of Zechariah's Night Visions*. Eugene, OR: Wipf and Stock.

Koole, J. L. 1967. *Haggai*. Historical Commentary on the Old Testament. Kampen: Kok.

Laato, A 1994. "Zechariah 4,6a–10b and the Akkadian Royal Building Inscriptions." *Zeitschrift für altestestamenliche Wissenschaft* 106 (1):53–69.

Larkin, K. J. A. 1994. *The Eschatology of Second Zechariah: A Study of the Formation of a Mantological Wisdom Anthology*. Contributions to Biblical Exegesis and Theology 6. Kampen: Kok Pharos.

Leupold, H. C. 1965. *Exposition of Zechariah*. Grand Rapids: Baker.

Lewis, C. S. (1954) 1970. *The Horse and His Boy*. The Chronicles of Narnia. New York: Collier Books.

Lobel, A. 1979. *Days with Frog and Toad*. I Can Read Book. New York: Harper & Row.

Luckenbill, D. D. 1926–27. *Ancient Records of Assyria and Babylonia*. 2 vols. Ancient Records, 1st Series. Chicago: University of Chicago Press.

Malamat, A. 1953. "The Historical Background of the Assassination of Amon, King of Judah." *Israel Exploration Journal* 3 (1):26–29.

Marenof, S. 1932. "Note Concerning the Meaning of the Word 'Ephah,' Zechariah 5:5–11." *American Journal of Semitic Languages and Literatures* 48 (4):264–67.

Mason, R. A. 1977. "The Purpose of the 'Editorial Framework' of the Book of Haggai." *Vetus Testamentum* 27 (4):413–21.

McComiskey, T. E. 1998. "Zechariah." In *Zephaniah, Haggai, Zechariah, and Malachi*, 1003–1244. Vol. 3 of *The Minor Prophets: An Exegetical and Expositional Commentary*, edited by T. E. McComiskey. Grand Rapids: Baker.

Merrill, E. H. 1994. *Haggai, Zechariah and Malachi: An Exegetical Commentary*. Chicago: Moody.

———. 2003. *Haggai, Zechariah, Malachi: An Exegetical Commentary*. Richardson, TX: Biblical Studies Press.

Mettinger., T. N. D. 1988. *In Search of God: The Meaning and Message of the Everlasting Names*. Translated by F. H. Cryer. Philadelphia: Fortress.

Meyers, C. L., and E. M. Meyers. 1987. *Haggai, Zechariah 1–8: A New Translation with Introduction and Commentary*. Anchor Bible. Garden City, NY: Doubleday.

———. 1993. *Zechariah 9–14: A New Translation with Introduction and Commentary*. Anchor Bible. Garden City, NY: Doubleday.

Mitchell. H. G. 1912. *Commentary on Haggai and Zechariah*. International Critical Commentary. Edinburgh: T&T Clark.

Motyer, J. A. 1998a. "Haggai." In *Zephaniah, Haggai, Zechariah, and Malachi*, 963–1002. Vol. 3 of *The Minor Prophets: An Exegetical and Expositional Commentary*, edited by T. E. McComiskey. Grand Rapids: Baker.

———. 1998b. "Zephaniah." In *Zephaniah, Haggai, Zechariah, and Malachi*, 897–962. Vol. 3 of *The Minor Prophets: An Exegetical and Expositional Commentary*, edited by T. E. McComiskey. Grand Rapids: Baker.

Nicholson, E. W. 1965. "The Meaning of the Expression אז in the Old Testament." *Journal of Semitic Studies* 10 (1):59–66. https://doi.org/10.1093/jss/10.1.59.

Oegema, G. S. 1998. "Tradition-Historical Studies on 4Q252." In *Qumran-Messianism: Studies on the Messianic Expectations in the Dead Sea Scrolls*, edited by J. H. Charlesworth, H. Lichtenberger, and G. S. Oegema, 154–74. Tübingen: Mohr Siebeck.

Patterson, R. D. 1991. *Nahum, Habakkuk, Zephaniah*. Wycliffe Exegetical Commentary. Chicago: Moody Press.

———. 2008. "Zephaniah." In *Minor Prophets: Hosea–Malachi*, by R. D. Patterson and A. E. Hill, 445–90. Cornerstone Biblical Commentary 10. Carol Stream, IL: Tyndale House.

Petersen, D. L. 1984. *Haggai and Zechariah 1–8: A Commentary*. Old Testament Library. Philadelphia: Westminster.

———. 1995. *Zechariah 9–14 and Malachi: A Commentary*. Old Testament Library. Louisville: Westminster John Knox.

Peterson, E. H. 2000. *A Long Obedience in the Same Direction: Discipleship in an Instant Society*. 2nd ed. Downers Grove, IL: InterVarsity Press.

Pressfield, S. 2012. *War of Art: Break Through the Blocks and Win Your Inner Creative Battle*. New York: Black Irish Entertainment.

Pritchard, J., ed. 1969. *Ancient Near Eastern Texts*. 3rd ed. Princeton, NJ: Princeton University Press. Originally published 1950.

Purvis, K. B., D. R. Cross, and W. L. Sunshine. 2007. *The Connected Child: Bring Hope and Healing to Your Adoptive Family*. New York: McGraw-Hill.

Ragozin, Z. 2017. *The Rise and Fall of the Assyrian Empire*. n.p., Jovian Press.

Redditt, P. L. 1994. "Nehemiah's First Mission and the Date of Zechariah 9–14." *Catholic Biblical Quarterly* 56 (4):664–78.

———. 1995. *Haggai, Zechariah, Malachi*. New Century Bible Commentary. Grand Rapids: Eerdmans.

———. 2012. *Zechariah 9–14*. International Exegetical Commentary on the Old Testament. Stuttgart: Kohlhammer.

Reeves, M. 2012. *Delighting in the Trinity: An Introduction to the Christian Faith*. Downers Grove, IL: IVP Academic.

Roberts, J. J. M. 1991. *Nahum, Habakkuk, and Zephaniah: A Commentary*. Old Testament Library. Louisville: Westminster John Knox.

Robertson, O. P. 1990. *The Books of Nahum, Habakkuk, and Zephaniah*. New International Commentary on the Old Testament. Grand Rapids: Eerdmans.

Ross, A. P. 2016. *Malachi Then and Now: An Expository Commentary Based on Detailed Exegetical Analysis*. Wooster, OH: Weaver Book Publishing.

Rowling, J. K. 2007. *Harry Potter and the Deathly Hallows*. New York: Arthur A. Levine / Scholastic.

Seuss, Dr. 1990. *Oh, the Places You'll Go!* New York: Random House.

Smith, C., with P. Snell. 2009. *Souls in Transition: The Religious and Spiritual Lives of Emerging Adults*. London: Oxford University Press.

Smith, G. V. 1982. "The Concept of God / The Gods as King in the Ancient Near East and the Bible," *Trinity Journal* 3:18–38.

———. 1994. "Malachi: Whom Do You Honor?" In *An Introduction to the Hebrew Prophets: The Prophets as Preachers*, 325–38. Nashville: B&H.

———. 1998. *Amos: A Commentary*. Grand Rapids: Regency Reference Library / Zondervan.

———. 2007. *Isaiah 1–39*. New American Commentary 15A. Nashville: B&H.

———. 2009. *Isaiah 40–66*. New American Commentary 15B. Nashville: B&H.

Smith, J. K. A. 2016. *You Are What You Love: The Spiritual Power of Habit*. Grand Rapids: Brazos.

Smith, J. M. P. 1912. *A Critical and Exegetical Commentary on the Book of Malachi*. International Critical Commentary. Edinburgh: T&T Clark.

Smith, R. L. 1984. *Micah–Malachi*. Word Bible Commentary 32. Waco, TX: Word Books.

Snyman, S. D. 2015. *Malachi*. Historical Commentary on the Old Testament. Leuven: Peeters.

Solzhenitsyn, A. I. (1974) 2007. *The Gulag Archipelago, 1918–1956: An Experiment in Literary Investigation*. Translated by T. P. Whitney. Vol. 1. 3 vols. HarperPerennial Modern Classics. New York: HarperCollins.

Stiebing, W. H., and S. Helft. 2018. *Ancient Near Eastern History and Culture*. 3rd ed. New York: Routledge.

Strange, J. F. 1982. "Greece." *The International Standard Bible Encyclopedia*, edited by G. W. Bromiley, 2:557–67. Grand Rapids: Eerdmans.

Stuart, D. 1998. "Malachi." In *Zephaniah, Haggai, Zechariah, and Malachi*, 897–962. Vol. 3 of *The Minor Prophets: An Exegetical and Expositional Commentary*, edited by T. E. McComiskey. Grand Rapids: Baker.

Stokes. R. E. 2014. "Satan, YHWH's Executioner." *Journal of Biblical Literature* 133 (2):251–70.

Sweeney, M. A. 2003. *Zephaniah: A Commentary*. Edited by P. D. Hanson. Hermeneia. Minneapolis: Fortress.

Taylor, R. A., and E. R. Clendenen. 2004. *Haggai, Malachi*. New American Commentary 21A. Nashville: B&H.

Tebow, T., and A. J. Jacobs. 2018. *Shaken: Discovering Your True Identity in the Midst of Life's Storms*. New York: Waterbrook.

Tiemeyer, L. S. 2015. *Zechariah and His Visions: An Exegetical Study of Zechariah's Vision Reports*. Library of the Hebrew Bible / Old Testament Studies 605. London: Bloomsbury T&T Clark.

Tollington, J. E. 1993. *Tradition and Innovation in Haggai and Zechariah 1–8*. Journal for the Study of Old Testament Supplement Series 150. Sheffield: JSOT Press.

Thompson, R. C. *The Prisms of Esarhaddon and Ashurbanipal, Found at Nineveh, 1927–8*. London: British Museum, 1931.

Unger, M. F. 1970. *Zechariah: Prophet of Messiah's Glory*. Grand Rapids: Zondervan.

Van De Mieroop, M. 2016. *A History of the Ancient Near East, ca. 3000–323 B.C.* 3rd ed. Blackwell History of the Ancient World. Chichester, UK: Wiley Blackwell.

VanderKam, J. C. 2004. *From Joshua to Caiaphas: High Priests After the Exile*. Minneapolis: Fortress.

Verhoef, P. A. 1987. *The Books of Haggai and Malachi*. New International Commentary on the Old Testament. Grand Rapids: Eerdmans.

Vlaardingerbroek, J. 1999. *Zephaniah*. Historical Commentary on the Old Testament. Leuven: Peeters.

von Rad, Gerhard. *Old Testament Theology*. Translated by D. M. G. Stalker. 2 vols. New York: Harper & Row, 1962–65.

Walker, L. 1985. "Zephaniah." In *Daniel and the Minor Prophets*, edited by F. E. Gaebelein, 7:537–68. *Expositor's Bible Commentary*. 12 vols. Grand Rapids: Zondervan.

Wendland, E. 1985. "Linear and Concentric Patterns in Malachi." *Bible Translator* 36 (1):108–21.

Whitcomb, J. C. 1979. "Cambyses." *The International Standard Bible Encyclopedia*, edited by G. W. Bromiley, 1:582–83. Grand Rapids: Eerdmans.

Willard, D. 1997. *The Divine Conspiracy: Rediscovering Our Hidden Life with God*. San Francisco: HarperSanFrancisco.

Wilson, R. *Prophecy and Society in Ancient Israel*. Philadelphia: Fortress, 1980.

Wise, M., M. G. Abegg Jr., and E. M. Cook, trans. 1996. *The Dead Sea Scrolls: A New Translation*. San Francisco: HarperSanFrancisco.

Wolters, A. 2014. *Zechariah*. Historical Commentary on the Old Testament 19. Leuven: Peeters.

Yamauchi, E. M. 1990. *Persia and the Bible*. Grand Rapids: Baker.